W9-CKF-680

Communications for the School of Health & Wellness

Compiled by:
Nancy Rishor and Fred Wood
Sir Sandford Fleming College

THOMSON
TM
CUSTOM PUBLISHING

ISBN-13: 978-0-17-646847-7
ISBN-10: 0-17-646847-1

Consists of:

Essay Essentials with Readings, Fourth Edition
Norton/Green
ISBN 0-17-640704-9, © 2006

Communication at Work, Fourth Edition
Finlay/Frank
ISBN 0-17-640703-0, © 2007

Handle with Care, Third Edition
Lucy Valentino
ISBN 0-17-641560-2, © 2004

Brief

Table of Contents

Essay Essentials

Student Exemplars

Journal/Newspaper Articles

Communication at Work

Handle With Care

Student Exemplar

Student Brochure

Detailed

Table of Contents

Student Exemplars

Journal/Newspaper Articles

Communication at Work

Handle With Care

Student Exemplar

Student Brochure

ESSAY ESSENTIALS

Introduction: Why, What, and How to Learn to Write

Few people enjoy writing; after all, it's hard work. Writing is a complex process, a learned skill that requires patience, concentration, and persistence. Unlike most of the skills you acquire in a career program, however, writing is not job-specific. **The skills you learn from this book will be useful to you in all your college courses** and **in every job you hold throughout your working life.** If you have graduated from college or university, your prospective employer will assume that you are able to communicate in writing frequently, correctly, and in a manner that will do credit to the company. The higher you climb on the organizational ladder, the more you will write and the more complex your writing tasks will become. Furthermore, evaluations of your performance in any job will be based at least in part on your communication skills.

Essay Essentials will teach you to write essays of various kinds. The word "essay" comes from the French *essayer*, to try or attempt. **An essay is an attempt to communicate information, opinion, or emotion.** In the context of a college or university, an essay is an exercise that gives students an opportunity to explore and explain their own and others' thoughts about a subject. In the larger world, essays appear in newspapers and magazines as editorials, reviews, opinion pieces, and commentaries on news and public affairs.

If at times the essay form seems artificial or unrelated to the kinds of writing you expect to do in your profession, remember that thinking, organizing, and researching are basic to all practical writing tasks. **In this book, you will learn how to find and organize thoughts, to develop ideas in coherent paragraphs, and to express yourself clearly, correctly, and concisely.** Once you've mastered these basics, you can develop any job-specific writing styles that may be required of you. If you can write well-organized, convincing, and error-free essays of five or more paragraphs, you will have no difficulty adapting your skills to business or technical reports, instructions, proposals, memoranda, sales presentations, commercial scripts, or legal briefs.

The fact that literacy is in decline does not make the ability to write less important; rather, it means that those who can write competently are in high demand. **You can learn to write well if you are willing to work at it.** We have designed this text to enable you to master the theory of good writing and to practise it successfully. Because it is more fun and more efficient to learn with others than it is to struggle alone, we have included many group-based exercises. To make the process less onerous, we have also introduced a few humorous essays, and, in Part 6, as many entertaining exercises as we could think of. If you follow the guidelines in this book, you will produce effective essays in college and creditable communications in your career.

THE WEBSITE

In addition to the material in this book, you will find useful information and helpful exercises on our website. Go to http://www.essayessentials4e. nelson.com and click on "Student Resources" to find the menu of options available to you. Under "More Information" you will find helpful supplements to the book, and under "More Practice" you will find additional exercises for the chapters in Part 6. The answers to these exercises are marked automatically, so you will know instantly whether or not you have understood the material.

Also on the website are practice tests, reference links, and an "Ask the Authors" button that enables you to send us any questions you have about *Essay Essentials* or about your writing. We take your questions seriously and will answer as soon as we get your message. Purchase of this book also entitles you to free access to InfoTrac®, an easy-to-use online library of source materials you can use for your research in this and other courses. You will learn more about InfoTrac® and other databases in Chapter 18.

WHAT THE SYMBOLS MEAN

This symbol in the margin beside an exercise means the exercise is designed to be done by two or more students working together. Carefully read the directions that introduce the exercise to find out how many students should participate and what task is to be performed. Often you are instructed to begin work in a pair or group, then to work individually on a writing task, and finally to regroup and review your writing with your partner(s).

This symbol means "note this." We've used it to highlight writing tips, helpful hints, hard-to-remember points, and information that you should apply whenever you write, not just when you are dealing with the specific principle covered in the paragraph marked by the icon.

This icon attached to an exercise means that the exercise is a mastery test designed to check your understanding of the chapter you have just completed. The answers to these exercises are not in the back of the book; your instructor will provide them.

GO TO WEB

EXERCISE

This symbol means that the *Essay Essentials* website has information or exercises to supplement the chapter you are working on. Log on to the website, click on the "More Practice" button, and then click on "Web Exercises." The information and exercises are arranged by chapter, so to get to the exercises for the apostrophe, for example, click on Chapter 38, and do the numbered exercises listed below the icon.

THE PROCESS OF WRITING

Writing is a three-step process consisting of
1. planning or prewriting
2. drafting
3. revising and editing

This book explains and illustrates two approaches to the process of writing: top-down and bottom-up. The **top-down approach** assumes that you know what you have to say before you begin to write. You identify your subject and main points, draft your thesis statement (the statement that orients your readers to the content of the paper), and plan your topic sentences (those sentences that identify the content of each paragraph). Research papers, business reports, and essay questions on exams are examples of writing that require a "top-down" approach.

The **bottom-up approach** is useful when you do not know ahead of time what you want to say. You discover your meaning through the act of writing. With this approach, you rely on prewriting strategies such as brainstorming and freewriting to get into the process of writing.

You will probably need to use both approaches. Sometimes you will discover your subject through writing; at other times, using "top-down" strategies will help you to express clearly what you already know. You should experiment with both approaches so that you can comfortably use whichever is more appropriate for a particular writing task.

WHAT YOUR READERS EXPECT

Whichever approach you use, your goal is to make your finished essay easy for your readers to read and understand. To achieve that goal, you must meet your readers' expectations.

Readers have five unconscious expectations when they begin to read a piece of extended prose. They expect to find

- paragraphs
- a sentence (usually the first) in each paragraph that identifies the topic
- unified paragraphs, each of which explores a single topic
- connections (transitions) within and between paragraphs
- a preview (in the introduction) of the content and organization of the paper

Keep in mind that readers want to obtain information quickly and easily, without backtracking. They rely on the writer—you—to make efficient reading possible.

Your readers will read more easily and remember more of what they read if you include a thesis statement to introduce them to the content and organization of the piece, and if you begin each paragraph with a topic sentence. If you do not organize and develop your paper and its paragraphs in a clearly identifiable way, readers will impose their own organization on the paper. The result will be longer reading time, or difficulty in understanding and remembering the content, or, worse, the assumption that a paragraph or even the whole paper has a meaning other than the one you intended. You can help your readers to read efficiently if you follow the old adage: "Tell them what you're going to tell them; tell them; then tell them what you've told them."

HOW TO BEGIN

Having a conversation with someone who never seems to get to the point is a tiresome and frustrating experience. Similarly, an essay—or any other form of written communication—that has no point and that rambles on will turn readers off.

How can you avoid boring, confusing, or annoying your readers? To begin with, you need to have something to say and a reason for saying it. Very few people can write an essay straight through from start to finish without spending a considerable amount of time thinking and planning. Some prewriting will help you to develop the structure more easily; freewriting and brainstorming (Chapter 3 will explain these) stimulate thinking.

Once you've determined what it is you want to say, you need to arrange your main points in the most effective order possible. If you organize your ideas carefully, you won't ramble. Writing an essay is like building a house. If you have a clear plan or blueprint, you can construct the house without the frustration of having to double back or even to start all over again from the beginning. A good plan saves time.

As a general rule, the more time you spend on prewriting and planning, the less time you'll need to spend on drafting and revising. Careful planning will enable you to produce papers that your readers will find clear and understandable.

THE PARTS OF AN ESSAY

An essay has a beginning, a middle, and an end. The most basic form is the five-paragraph essay, which teaches you everything you need to know about writing nonfiction prose. Think of this highly structured form of prose not as a straitjacket that stifles your creativity, but rather as a pattern to follow while you develop the skills and abilities you need to build other, more complex prose structures.

The beginning, or **introduction**, tells your reader the point, the purpose, and the scope of your essay. If your introduction is well crafted, its **thesis statement** will identify the main points you will discuss in the paragraphs that follow.

The middle, or **body**, of an essay consists of paragraphs that discuss in detail the points that have been identified in the introduction. In a short essay, each paragraph develops a separate main point. Each paragraph should contain three essential components:

- a **topic sentence**, which identifies the point of the paragraph
- development, or **support**, of the topic sentence. Supporting sentences provide the detailed information the reader needs in order to understand the point.
- a **concluding sentence** that either brings the discussion of the topic to a close or provides a transition to the next paragraph

The end, or **conclusion**, is a brief final paragraph. Unless your essay is very short, you summarize the main points to reinforce them for the reader, then say goodbye with a statement that will give your readers something to think about after they have finished reading your essay.

Bertrand Russell's "What I Have Lived For" is a good example of a well-structured essay. The introduction contains a clear thesis statement. Each paragraph of the body consists of a clearly identifiable topic sentence, development sufficient to explain it, and a concluding sentence. The conclusion is brief, pointed, and memorable.

WHAT I HAVE LIVED FOR
Bertrand Russell

INTRODUCTION
Thesis statement

Three passions, simple but overwhelmingly strong, have governed my life: the longing for love, the search for knowledge, and unbearable pity for the suffering of mankind. These passions, like great winds, have blown me hither and thither, in a wayward course, over a deep ocean of anguish, reaching to the very verge of despair.

BODY
Topic sentence

Support

Concluding sentence

I have sought love, first, because it brings ecstasy—ecstasy so great that I would often have sacrificed all the rest of life for a few hours of this joy. I have sought it, next, because it relieves loneliness—that terrible loneliness in which one shivering consciousness looks over the rim of the world into the cold unfathomable lifeless abyss. I have sought it, finally, because in the union of love I have seen, in a mystic miniature, the prefiguring vision of the heaven that saints and poets have imagined. This is what I sought, and though it might seem too good for human life, this is what—at last—I have found.

Topic sentence

Support

Concluding sentence

With equal passion I have sought knowledge. I have wished to understand the hearts of men. I have wished to know why the stars shine. And I have tried to apprehend the Pythagorean power by which number holds sway above the flux. A little of this, but not much, I have achieved.

Topic sentence

Support

Concluding sentence

CONCLUSION

Love and knowledge, so far as they were possible, led upward toward the heavens. But always pity brought me back to earth. Echoes of cries of pain reverberate in my heart. Children in famine, victims tortured by oppressors, helpless old people a hated burden to their sons, and the whole world of loneliness, poverty, and pain make a mockery of what human life should be. I long to alleviate the evil, but I cannot, and I too suffer.

This has been my life. I have found it worth living, and would gladly live it again if the chance were offered me.

Russell, Bertrand. "What I Have Lived For." Prologue. *The Autobiography of Bertrand Russell.* By Russell. Boston: Little, Brown, 1967. 3–4.

PART 1

Planning

1

Your Audience
and You

Before you begin to write anything—an essay, a report, an e-mail message, or a set of instructions—you must have something to write about (your subject) and someone to write for (your audience). Writing is communication, and for communication to take place, you (the writer) must be able to make your ideas or message clear to your readers.

Addressing Your Readers

As you plan, draft, and revise your paper, ask yourself the following questions:

- How old are your readers?
- What is their level of education?
- What do they do for a living?
- What is their income?
- What is their cultural background?
- Are they male or female?

While you must be careful to avoid generalizing or stereotyping, the answers to these questions do influence most people's views, and you would be wise to consider them before you begin to write.

Before you begin to plan an essay, write at the top of the page the specific audience for whom your message is intended.

Naturally, your instructor will be reading your early (and your late) assignments, but, for your first draft, you should write at the top of the page the name of someone other than your instructor whom you might expect to be interested in your subject. Be creative: your high-school principal, a recent immigrant, a union official, a member of the Liberal Party, a religious leader, the CEO of a polluting company, someone receiving social assistance income. Keeping this reader in mind will help you to plan, develop, and write your assignment in a tone and style appropriate to your message.

Spend a little time thinking about your subject in relation to your audience. Consider carefully the following three questions when you are deciding what to include in your essay.

1. What does my reader know about my subject?
2. What is my reader's attitude toward my subject?
3. What are my reader's needs in regard to my subject?

READERS' KNOWLEDGE

The first question will help you choose the kind and amount of information that should be included. Are you writing for someone who knows little about your subject, or for someone with fairly detailed knowledge? Do you have to cover all the basics, or can you take it for granted your audience is familiar with them? You don't want to bore your readers by telling them things they already know. On the other hand, if you fail to provide information they need in order to understand your message, you'll turn them off or lose them entirely.

READERS' ATTITUDES

The second question helps you decide how to approach your subject. Will your readers be sympathetic to what you have to say? If so, you will aim to reinforce their agreement. You will probably state your opinion up front, to show you're on their side. If, however, you think they may be hostile to what you have to say, you might lessen their resistance by providing reasons and support for your ideas before revealing your point of view. Gentle persuasion is usually more effective than confrontation in writing, as it is in life.

READERS' NEEDS

The third question helps you to decide whether to persuade or instruct, to compare or classify, to describe or analyze. Which approach will give your readers the information they need about your subject? The answers to this question will determine whether your remarks should be fairly general or quite specific. Do you intend to add to or reinforce your audience's general knowledge, or do you want your readers to apply your information only in specific situations?

Reflecting Yourself

Once you are clear about who your readers are, what they know, and what they need to know, you should spend a little time considering your role in the communication process. Any time you speak or write, you present yourself in a particular way to your audience. We all play a variety of roles. We choose a role, often unconsciously, that we hope will suit the expectations of the people we are communicating with. These roles are not false or hypocritical; they are simply facets of our personality that we try to match to the needs of each situation. Choosing and maintaining an appropriate role is essential in successful communication.

Each day, for example, you meet a variety of people. Some of them you know well—parents, siblings, friends, classmates, teachers, coworkers, supervisors. Others you know only casually—the cashier in the restaurant, the police officer at the radar trap, the enumerator for the upcoming election, the checkout person in the grocery store. With each of these people, whether the contact is casual or intense, you consciously or unconsciously adjust your language in order to communicate. If you speak to your spouse as you might to your dog, you'll be sleeping on the couch. If you speak to a salesperson as you would to a love interest, you'll get arrested.

Consider the following three questions when you are deciding what role would be most appropriate in a particular communication situation.

1. What is my purpose in writing?
2. What is my attitude toward my subject?
3. What are my readers' expectations of me in this communication?

YOUR PURPOSE

The most common purposes of writing are to inform, to persuade, and to entertain. Your purpose will depend largely on the needs and expectations of your readers. It will influence your choice of supporting details to develop your points and will affect your tone. How you say something often has more impact on your audience than what you say.

YOUR ATTITUDE

The second question requires you to clarify your attitude to the subject of your paper. This involves more than simply asking, "Am I for or against it?" You should consider how strongly you feel about the subject because your attitude will influence your tone as well as the kinds of evidence you present. You should also think about how personal you want to be in presenting your ideas, or how balanced and objective you wish (or are able) to be. In answering these questions, consider how closely your attitude toward the subject aligns with your audience's attitude. If your views coincide, then a fairly informal approach may be appropriate; if they differ, then an impersonal, objective approach is preferable.

YOUR ROLE

The third question requires you to think about what role your audience is likely to expect of you. If you write as an authority, will you be credible? If you write as a peer or friend, will you be effective? What are your readers likely to expect from someone in your position writing to them on this subject? Taking the time to think about your readers' expectations will help you to make appropriate choices with respect to the point of view you take, the examples and support you provide for your ideas, and the level of language you use.

Levels of Standard English Writing

Good writing involves more than the meaning of words and sentences. It also requires the choice of appropriate language. No one would submit a book review that began, "This is an awesome book with, like, ideas that sort of make you think, you know?" You know instantly that the language is inappropriate. Similarly, if you were discussing the book with friends over coffee and announced, "This book contains provocative and stimulating ideas that engage and challenge the reader," your language would be equally inappropriate.

Written English (e-mail notwithstanding) is usually more formal than spoken English. Because writers have time to consider what they want to say and how best to say it, they can choose their words carefully, arrange them in meaningful sentences, and organize ideas into logical paragraphs. An appropriate level of language is an essential part of effective writing.

Choose a level that suits both your topic and your reader. There will be times when you need to compromise; for example, when you send one message to several people. In such cases, the safe bet is to aim at the highest level of receiver and trust that the others will understand.

Sometimes it isn't clear what level you should be using. At such times, your reader's preference should determine your choice. Many colleges and universities expect students to write academic papers in formal English, which requires, among other things, third-person pronouns (*he, she, one, they*). Informal writing, with its first- and second-person pronouns (*I, me, you*), may not be acceptable. (See page 496 for an explanation of pronoun "person.") Ask your instructor about your school's policy and follow it.

Similarly, because employers tend to favour formal letters of application over casual ones, if you want to get the job, you will write a formal letter. For a talk you give to your class, an informal, conversational style may be appropriate. Most of what you read and write falls somewhere in the middle. Business documents, for example, are usually written in general-level Standard English.

There are no fixed divisions of language use; the three levels we've identified often overlap. To help you choose the most appropriate level for your message and audience, the table below outlines the basic features of informal, general, and formal written English.

	Informal	General	Formal
Vocabulary and Style	Casual, everyday; usually concrete; some slang, colloquial expressions, contractions. Written in 1st and 2nd persons.	The language of educated persons; nonspecialized; balance of abstract and concrete; readily understood. Can use 1st, 2nd, and 3rd persons.	Often abstract, technical, or specialized; no contractions or colloquialisms. Written in 3rd person.
Sentence and Paragraph Structure	Sentences short, simple; some sentence fragments; paragraphs short.	Complete sentences of varying length; paragraphs vary, but are often fairly short.	Complete sentences, usually long, complex; paragraphs fully developed, often at length.
Tone	Conversational, casual; sounds like ordinary speech.	Varies to suit message and purpose of writer.	Impersonal, serious, often instructional.
Typical Uses	Personal letters, some fiction, some newspapers, much advertising.	Most of what we read: newspapers, magazines, novels, business correspondence.	Academic writing, some textbooks, scientific reports, journal articles, legal documents.

No one level is "better" than another. Each has its place and function. Your message, your audience, and your purpose in writing are what should determine the level you choose.

Read the following selections and consider each writer's purpose, the audience for whom the message is intended, and why the writer's level of language is appropriate to the readers, the subject, and the purpose.

INFORMAL

Love him or hate him, Michael Moore has turned the world of documentary film on its ear. Documentaries are stuffy and boring, aren't they? They certainly aren't supposed to be wildly popular or turn their directors into media stars. But starting with *Roger and Me* back in 1989, Moore has almost single-handedly made the documentary fun, personal, and popular. Like most film students, I began thinking I wanted someday to make blockbuster Hollywood hits like the movies Canadians Norman Jewison and James Cameron are famous for, but now I'm a convert to documentaries and that other Canadian production star: the NFB.

Who is the intended audience? This paragraph is intended for general readers, not people who are looking for a scholarly discussion of film. The writer assumes some interest in and knowledge of Michael Moore and his films.

What is the writer's role? The writer wants to inform readers in a personal way about his point of view. He plays the role not of expert or teacher, but rather of a friend or acquaintance supplying the information for discussion in a casual way.

Why is the level of language appropriate? The use of contractions and colloquialisms ("the world . . . on its ear," "stuffy and boring") and especially the use of first and second persons in direct address clearly mark this as an informal and friendly communication. Short sentences and a conversational style add to the informal tone.

GENERAL

What is a documentary film? The so-called father of documentary film, John Grierson, called it "the creative treatment of reality," but that definition is uncomfortably broad. For example, is *Alexander* a documentary? What about *Troy* or *Amadeus* or *Lawrence of Arabia*? All are about real people and contain a version of historical events, but few would classify them as documentaries. The purpose of these films is to entertain (if you discount their real purpose: to make money), and perhaps purpose lies at the heart of the definition. The primary purpose of a documentary film is to inform.

Who is the intended audience? Readers of this paragraph will be knowledgeable enough about films to have seen at least one of the three major releases mentioned, and interested enough in film to want to know more about the documentary genre.

What is the writer's role? The writer is providing information from an expert point of view, but in a friendly way rather than as a lecture or formal instruction. The use of humour and casual language makes the information easy to absorb, and the direct address and use of questions add a friendly tone to the paragraph.

Why is the level of language appropriate? The vocabulary and writing style are easily understood by general readers. The use of second person ("if you discount their real purpose") adds to the personal nature of the language, as do the questions directed to the reader. This message is designed to appeal to the widest audience possible.

FORMAL

John Grierson, best known as "the father of documentary film" and the founder of the National Film Board of Canada, called documentary "the creative treatment of reality." Since its inception in 1939, the NFB has been presenting reality to Canadians and the rest of the world in creative ways. While it has earned recognition in other cinematic fields (notably animation), the NFB has achieved most of its international acclaim from more than 60 years of producing first-class documentary films, many of them Academy Award winners.

Who is the intended audience? The readers of this passage are literate and well read. They are people whose education and experience have enabled them to appreciate that good films can be informative as well as entertaining.

What is the writer's role? The writer's purpose is to highlight the achievements of the NFB to an audience of educated peers who share his aesthetic interests. The writer presents himself not as an expert addressing nonexperts, but rather as an enthusiast who wants to share knowledge with a receptive audience.

Why is the level of language appropriate? The vocabulary is fairly sophisticated, and the sentences are fairly long and complex. There are no contractions or colloquialisms, no first- or second-person pronouns. The writer addresses his audience as peers—fellow film enthusiasts—but not as close friends. The objective tone would be suitable for an article in a professional magazine.

Exercise 1.1*

Read the excerpts below and discuss the intended audience, the author's role, and the appropriateness of the language. Answers for this chapter begin on page 512.

1. One of the most frequent complaints about Wal-Mart, which employs 1.4 million people worldwide, is its failure to pay workers a living wage. Store employees are paid 20–30 percent less than the industry average, making many of them eligible for social assistance. It is estimated that American taxpayers fork out $2.5 billion a year in welfare payments to Wal-Mart employees (Head, 2004). Because the retailer hires hard-to-place workers, like recent immigrants, seniors, and single mothers, its employees are often afraid they will not find work elsewhere. The kind of work Wal-Mart does offer is gruelling: stores are intentionally understaffed—the strategy behind the company's legendary productivity gains—so that existing employees will work harder (Head, 2004). It is alleged that systemic discrimination against women within the corporation has denied the majority of Wal-Mart workers the chance at promotion, a charge that is now the subject of the largest civil-rights suit in US history.

Parmar, Deenu. "Labouring the Wal-Mart Way." 224.

Who is the intended audience? _____

_____

_____

_____

_____

What is the writer's role? _____

_____

_____

_____

_____

Why is the level of language appropriate? _____

_____

_____

_____

_____

2.   The "inletting" or "butt mortise" plane is designed to cut precise mortises for butt hinges, lock fronts, and strike plates, or to repair jambs, doors, furniture, and millwork, wherever the ability to do inletting is important. The plane has a completely open throat so that you can watch what you are doing. The 3/4" wide cutter is set at a 40 degree pitch for general work. This can be increased to 70 degrees (plus or minus) for difficult grain simply by inserting the blade bevel-up. For inletting, such as hinges, you set the blade extension at the hinge leaf thickness, score the outline and plane to depth, using overlapping strokes for a smooth bottom. The same technique would be used for a veneer repair on solid wood.

_____

Lee Valley Catalogue. Tenth Anniversary Issue, 1987–88. 23.

Who is the intended audience? _____

_____

_____

_____

_____

What is the writer's role? _____

_____

_____

_____

_____

Why is the level of language appropriate? _____

_____

_____

_____

_____

3.   Doing business with the Chinese is an enterprise fraught with peril for the unwary Western business person. While in the West most business is ultimately conducted face to face between the principals, negotiations seldom if ever achieve this intimacy in the Orient. It is common for gatherings of ten or more to take part in the early stages of agenda-setting and prioritizing, and the hapless Westerner who has not engaged the services of a Chinese guide will have to sort out the Party overseers from the ineffectual hangers-on and try to hone in on the power brokers who often remain in the background to assess and evaluate before making themselves known. Often the early stages of business relationships are conducted in the very formal atmosphere of banquets, with hierarchical seating arrangements and ritual toasts. Coping with the exotic atmosphere, the oblique method of negotiation, the recondite formality, and the unidentifiable food is a formidable challenge: one that should be undertaken without assistance by only the most intrepid and experienced of Western entrepreneurs.

Czereczovich, Katlin. "Business Abroad." *Canadian Women Entrepreneurs* Spring 2002: 91.

Who is the intended audience? _____

_____

_____

_____

_____

What is the writer's role? _____

_____

_____

_____

_____

Why is the level of language appropriate? _____

_____

_____

_____

_____

4.   A parent quickly learns that no matter how much money you have, you will never be able to buy your kids everything they want. You can take a second mortgage on your house and buy what you think is the entire

Snoopy line: Snoopy pajamas, Snoopy underpants, Snoopy linen, Snoopy shoelaces, Snoopy cologne, and Snoopy soap, but you will never have it all. And if Snoopy doesn't send you to the poorhouse, Calvin Klein will direct the trip. Calvin is the slick operator who sells your kids things for eighty-five dollars that cost seven at Sears. He has created millions of tiny snobs, children who look disdainfully at you and say, "Nothing from Sears." However, Dad-Can-I fought back: I got some Calvin Klein labels and sewed them into Sears undershorts for my high fashion junkies.

Cosby, Bill. *Fatherhood*. New York: Doubleday, 1994. 41–42.

Who is the intended audience? _____

_____

_____

_____

_____

What is the writer's role? _____

_____

_____

_____

_____

Why is the level of language appropriate? _____

_____

_____

_____

_____

5.   The conclusion of *Jane Eyre* has Jane and Rochester married at last. Jane no longer needs to compromise herself in order to be with him, and his first wife is not the only obstacle that has been removed. The man who insisted that she abandon her conscience to live in sin has changed significantly. Rochester now complements Jane as never before. His mutilation has been referred to as a "symbolic castration" by Richard Chase (qtd. in Gilbert and Gubar 368), but it is his spirit rather than his masculinity that seems to have been honed. Rochester has been humbled, and the taste of humility has taught him wisdom. He is able to admit to Jane, "I did wrong: I would have sullied my innocent flower—breathed guilt on its purity"

(Brönte 495; ch. 37). During their first engagement, Jane was unsure and often uncomfortable about her place in Rochester's life. In her description of their marriage, however, she says that "we are precisely suited in character—perfect concord is the result" (Brönte 500; ch. 38). Such a perfect fit is only made possible by Rochester's movement away from his earlier extreme. He has become a close match for Jane on every level, and therefore becomes her ideal mate.

Friedland, Jess. "The Evolution of Moral Balance in Charlotte Brönte's *Jane Eyre*." 322–23.

Who is the intended audience? _____

_____

_____

_____

_____

What is the writer's role? _____

_____

_____

_____

_____

Why is the level of language appropriate? _____

_____

_____

_____

_____

Exercise 1.2

As a class, select one of the five paragraphs found on pages 16–20. First, be sure you all agree on the intended audience and purpose of the paragraph. Your objective is to "translate" the paragraph for a different audience. The purpose of your revision will be the same as that of the original, but the language and tone will be adapted to suit the audience for whom the new message is intended.

Next, in groups of three, choose an audience for your revision from the following list. (Each group must select a different audience.)

elementary-school children	very hip, very cool grade 12 students
your family	your English instructor
a close friend	*Globe and Mail* readers
an elderly relative	your college newspaper

Once all groups have completed their translations, compare the results by reading the newly translated paragraphs aloud. Try to guess who each other's intended audience is. How do you know? How does the language work to meet the needs of the new audience?

The following exercise will give you practice in communicating effectively by adjusting your level of language to suit your purpose, your message, and your audience.

Exercise 1.3

Imagine, in each of the following situations, that you must deal with three different audiences face to face. Before you begin, analyze each audience in terms of knowledge, attitudes, and needs; then clarify the purpose of your message, your attitude toward your subject, and your audience's expectations of you.

1. You prepared your company's sales presentation in PowerPoint and stored it on the hard drive of your notebook computer. On your way to a meeting with clients in Detroit, your notebook was handled roughly by customs inspectors at the airport. When you got to the sales meeting, your computer would not open PowerPoint.

   You made the sales presentation as well as you could, but the clients were not impressed, and your company did not get the contract. Explain these circumstances to

   - your supervisor in the sales department
   - the U.S. Customs complaint bureau
   - a representative of the computer company, which claims its notebook computers are practically indestructible

2. At 8:30 this morning, your friend Jaron phones you from a police station. He has been arrested because, according to the arresting officer, he has 37 unpaid parking tickets outstanding. He claims he's innocent; he's never had a parking ticket. He has called to ask you to come down and bail him out. If you do so, you will be very late for work. Jaron refuses to call his parents for help. Tell this story to

- your parents
- your boss
- Jaron's parents

3. You recently bought a pair of silk pants from Bottom Drawers Pants Company. They ripped in the crotch the first time you bent over. You were dancing enthusiastically with a very attractive partner and were deeply embarrassed. Before you could recover your composure, the owner of the club asked you to leave immediately. Tell your story to

- Bottom Drawers
- the owner of the club
- your dancing partner

4. After only three weeks at your new job, you felt you had to tell someone that your fellow employees were routinely stealing office supplies, sales samples, and even tools and equipment. After speaking to your union steward and your manager, you were laid off without any explanation or warning, and as a probational employee you have no protection. Explain your situation to

- the president of your union
- a longtime employee of the company who doesn't know why you were let go
- an employment counsellor

5. You are short of money—so short you can't even buy gas for your car. If you can't get gas money, you will be late for work, and your boss is annoyed because you've been late twice this week already. Ask for money from

- your parents
- a friend
- someone who owes you money

6. Turn one of the 15 role-playing situations above into a written assignment.

Exercise 1.4

This exercise is designed to reinforce your understanding of the importance of knowing your reader. An effective communicator figures out ahead of time not only what his or her readers need to know, but also what they do not need to know. Some information is necessary and some is superfluous, with the mix varying widely from audience to audience. With this in mind, describe one of the following topics to three different audiences: choose one from each of the three groups listed below.

Topics: a favourite musician or group, a favourite standup comic or other performer

Group A: a grandparent, a teacher, an employer

Group B: a coworker, a classmate, an old friend you haven't seen in years

Group C: The president of your college or university or the Student Council Social Committee, whom you are trying to persuade to support a fundraising event featuring your topic.

2

Choosing the Right Words

In this chapter, we provide a brief introduction to language that is accurate and appropriate for your message and your audience. Our assumption is that you are writing for readers in academic and professional environments. Our goals are to help you convey your message clearly and in a way that will leave your readers with a positive impression of you and your ideas.

Before you get started, you need to equip yourself with a few essential resources and some basic knowledge of what kinds of language are inappropriate when you write.

The Writer's Toolkit

In addition to basic skills, all workers need tools. As a general rule, the better their tools, the better their work. Every writer comes equipped with a set of language skills acquired from birth. In most cases, however, these skills are not sufficiently developed to handle the complex task of producing clear, error-free prose in a professional style. Fortunately, tools are available to assist writers in bringing their language skills up to the standards required by professional environments. Collectively, we call these indispensable aids the Writer's Toolkit.

No one expects a writer to write without assistance. In fact, our first recommendation to beginning writers is to GET HELP! Every writer needs three basic tools and to know how to use them.

1. Buy and use a good dictionary.

A dictionary is a writer's best friend. You will need to use it every time you write, so if you don't already own a good dictionary, you need to buy one. For Canadian writers, a good dictionary is one that is Canadian, current, comprehensive (contains at least 75,000 entries), and reliable (published by an established, well-known firm).

A convenient reference is the *Gage Canadian Dictionary*, available in an inexpensive paperback edition. It is the dictionary on which we have based the examples and exercises in this chapter. Also recommended are the *ITP Nelson Canadian Dictionary of the English Language*, the *Canadian Oxford Dictionary* (2nd ed., 2004), and, for those whose native language is not English, the *Oxford Advanced Learner's Dictionary*. Unfortunately, no comprehensive Canadian dictionary is available on the Internet.

Begin by reading the "Guide to the Dictionary" in the front matter. The information in the Guide may not be very entertaining, but it is essential if you want to understand how to read your dictionary accurately. No two dictionaries are alike. In order to use your dictionary efficiently, you need to be familiar with its symbols, abbreviations, and the format of its entries.

Knowing what is in the dictionary guide will also save you time. For example, you may not need to memorize long lists of irregular plurals. Good dictionaries include irregular plurals in their entries. They also include irregular forms of verbs, adjectives, and adverbs. And if you've forgotten how regular plurals, verbs, adjectives, and adverbs are formed, you'll find that information in the guide as well.

2. Use spelling and grammar checkers responsibly.

Good spell-check programs can find typing errors and common spelling mistakes that distract your readers and make you look careless. They do have limitations, however. As we'll see, they can't tell if you meant to write "your" or "you're" and will not flag either word, even if it's used incorrectly. (You'll learn more about such words in Chapter 37, "Hazardous Homonyms.")

Also, since we use Canadian English, our spelling is frequently different from American spelling, which is the standard on which most word-processing programs are based. Set your program to Canadian spelling if the option exists. If it does not, be aware that words such as *colour, honour,* and *metre*—all correct Canadian spellings—will be flagged as errors.

Another useful tool is a hand-held spell checker. Conveniently pocket-sized and not expensive, these devices contain a large bank of words and can provide the correct spelling if the "guess" you type in is not too far off. Some checkers even pronounce the word for you. Ask your instructor if you can use this device (sound turned off, please) when you are writing in class and during exams.

The best advice we can give you about grammar checkers (they announce their presence by producing wavy green lines under words or sentences as you write on your word processor) is to use them with caution. So far, no grammar checker has been able to account for even most, let alone all, of the subtleties of English grammar. A grammar program is as likely to flag a perfectly good sentence, even to suggest a "fix" that is incorrect, as it is to ignore a sentence full of errors. "I done real good on my grammar test," for example, escapes the dreaded wavy green line.

3. Buy and use a good thesaurus.

If you repeat yourself, using the same words again and again, you won't communicate your thoughts interestingly, let alone memorably. Worse, you will bore your reader. A thesaurus is a dictionary of synonyms—words with similar meanings. For any word you need to use repeatedly in a document, a good thesaurus will provide a list of alternatives.

Synonyms are *not* identical in meaning. Your dictionary will help you decide which of the words listed in your thesaurus are suitable for your message and which are not. We do not recommend that you rely on the thesaurus in your word-processing program. For any given word, a word-processing thesaurus provides a list, in alphabetical order, of more-or-less synonyms, with no usage labels or examples. "More-or-less" is not good enough. At the very least, you need to know whether the synonyms offered are nouns or verbs and whether they are in general use or are informal, technical, derogatory, or even obsolete. For this information, buy a good book-form thesaurus and use it in conjunction with your dictionary. Two thesauruses are available in inexpensive paperback editions: the *Oxford Thesaurus of Current English* (2003) and *Roget's 21st Century Thesaurus in Dictionary Form* (3rd ed., 2005).

Use the information you find in a thesaurus with caution. Inexperienced writers sometimes assume that long, obscure words will impress their readers. In fact, most readers are irritated by unnecessarily "fancy" language. For more information on this topic, see the "Pretentious Language" section on pages 31–32.

NEVER use a word whose meaning you do not know. When you find a potential but unfamiliar synonym, look it up in your dictionary to be sure it's the word you need.

So far, we've introduced you to the tools you'll need as a writer and to the levels of language you can choose from when writing a message for a particular audience. Let's turn now to the writing errors you must not commit, no matter what message you're sending or the audience to which you're sending it: wordiness, slang and jargon, pretentious language, clichés, sexist language, offensive language, and "abusages."

The Seven Deadly Sins of Writing

1. WORDINESS

Wordiness—words and phrases that are not essential to the communication of your message—is annoying to readers, no matter what topic you are writing about. Good writing communicates a message as concisely as possible. Wordy messages take up your readers' time and try their patience. If you want to please your audience, be brief.

Sometimes wordiness results from a failure to revise carefully. In the editing stage of writing, you should be looking for the best words to express your meaning. Wordy expressions and awkward phrasing often pop into your mind when you are struggling to express an idea, and they often make their way into a first draft. There is no excuse for them to survive a careful edit and make their way into the second draft, however.

Here's an example of what can happen when a writer fails to prune his or her prose:

In my personal opinion, the government of this country of ours needs an additional amount of meaningful input from the people of Canada right now.

This wordy sentence could be nicely condensed into "In my opinion, our government needs to hear more from the people." The writer has chosen impressive-sounding phrases (*meaningful input, this country of ours*) and has slipped in unnecessary and meaningless words that should have been caught during editing (*personal opinion, an additional amount*). The result is a sentence that is so hard to read that it isn't worth the effort to decipher.

As you can see from the above example, one of the symptoms of wordiness is redundancy, or saying the same thing twice. Another is using several words where one or two would do.

The following list contains some of the worst offenders we've collected from student writing, corporate memoranda, form letters, and advertisements.

Wordy	Concise
a large number of	many

absolutely nothing/everything/
  complete/perfect
	nothing/everything/
	  complete/perfect

actual (*or* true) fact	fact
almost always	usually
at that point in time	then
at the present time	now
consensus of opinion	consensus
continue on	continue
could possibly (*or* may possibly, might possibly)	could (*or* may, might)
crisis (*or* emergency) situation	crisis (*or* emergency)
due to the fact that	because
end result	result
equally as good	as good
few and far between	rare
final conclusion	conclusion
for the reason that	because
free gift	gift
I myself (*or* you yourself, *etc.*)	I (*or* you, *etc.*)
I personally think/feel	I think/feel
in actual fact	in fact
in every instance	always
in my opinion, I think	I think
in the near future	soon
in today's society/in this day and age	now (*or* today)
is able to	can
many different kinds	many kinds
mutual agreement/cooperation	agreement/cooperation
my personal opinion	my opinion
no other alternative	no alternative
personal friend	friend
real, genuine leather (*or* real antique, *etc.*)	leather (*or* antique, *etc.*)
red in colour (*or* large in size, *etc.*)	red (*or* large, *etc.*)
repeat again	repeat
return back	return (*or* go back)
really, very	*These words add nothing to* *your meaning. Leave them out.*
8:00 a.m. in the morning	8:00 a.m.
such as, for example	such as

Wordy	Concise
take active steps	take steps
totally destroyed	destroyed
truly remarkable	remarkable
very (most, quite, almost, rather) unique	unique

Exercise 2.1*

Working with a partner, revise these sentences to make them as concise and clear as possible. Then compare your answers with our suggestions on page 513.

1. I myself personally feel that there is absolutely no basis in fact for the idea that UFOs exist.
2. Basically, I myself prefer modern contemporary furniture to old antiques.
3. I personally think Alison is faking her illness and pretending to be sick so she can stay at home and not have to go to work.
4. It has come to my attention that our competitor's products, though not equally as good as ours are, are nevertheless, at this point in time, selling better than those which we produce.
5. In my opinion, I believe that my essay is equally as good as Jill's and deserves equally as good a mark, which it would have got if it weren't for the fact that the professor hates me.
6. In my opinion, I doubt that this particular new innovation will succeed in winning much in the way of market share.
7. In my view, I feel that an English course that teaches the basic fundamentals is an essential prerequisite before a person can succeed in college, the business world, and the community at large.
8. "As a new beginning teacher," we told our English instructor, "you should try to understand the utter impossibility of gaining and holding the respect of us students so long as you are so completely and totally devoted to insisting that we follow grammar rules and regulations that totally inhibit the creativity in our writing."
9. I myself believe that, in all probability, this trend can be turned right around if we return back to basic fundamentals in our design process and introduce a few new innovations in our manufacturing process.
10. Due to the fact that the law, not to mention our company's policy, rules, and regulations, absolutely prohibits any mention of race, age, sex, religion, or marital status in official documents such as personnel documents, we have made sure that all such descriptors are entirely eliminated from our files, resulting in the fact that all our personnel documents are now almost virtually identical.

2. SLANG AND JARGON

Slang is "street talk": nonstandard words and phrases used by members of a group—people who share a culture, interest, or lifestyle. The group may be as large as a generation or as small as a high-school clique. Do you know what "amped," "badload," "busting," and "hodger" mean? Probably not. The whole point of slang is its exclusivity. It's a private language and thus not appropriate for a message aimed at a general reader.

Another characteristic of slang is that it changes quickly. Terms that were "in" last month are "out" today. Except for a few expressions that manage to sneak across the line that separates private language from mainstream English, most slang expressions are quickly outdated and sound silly. And finally, slang is an oral language. It is colloquial—that is, characteristic of casual speech—and not appropriate for use in professional or academic writing.

When you aren't sure if a word is appropriate for a written message, consult your print dictionary. The notation *sl.* or *slang* appears after words that are slang or have a slang meaning. (Some words, such as *house*, *cool*, and *bombed*, have both a general and a slang meaning.) If the word you're looking for isn't listed, chances are it's a recent slang term, and you should avoid using it in writing. Taking the time to choose words that are appropriate to written English increases your chances both of communicating clearly and of winning your readers' respect.

Exercise 2.2

- Working in groups of three or four, identify five current slang expressions.
- Now list five slang expressions that are no longer in use among your peers.
- Finally, define each current slang term in language appropriate to a general reader. (If you don't have a clear picture of a "general reader," write each definition in words your parents and teachers would understand.)

Jargon is similar to slang because it, too, is the private language of a subgroup; however, whereas the subgroups for slang are formed by culture or lifestyle, the subgroups who speak jargon are formed by profession or trade. The jargon of some professions is so highly technical and specialized it amounts almost to a private language.

Although jargon is useful, even necessary, in the context of some jobs, it is inappropriate in most writing because it does not communicate to a general reader. Our vocabulary and even the content of our writing are influenced by the contexts within which we work and live. In the following paragraph, D. E. Miller explains the extent to which our individual perceptions are influenced by our life experience.

A group of people witness a car accident. What each person sees, and how he or she describes it, is determined to a large extent by the language each one normally uses. A doctor or nurse would see and describe contusions, lacerations, and hemorrhages. A lawyer would think in terms of civil liabilities and criminal negligence. A mechanic would see crushed fenders, bent axles, and damaged chassis. A psychologist would be concerned about stress reactions, trauma, and guilt. You or I might see and describe the pain and injury caused by a driver's error in judgement or lapse of skill.

Miller, D. E. *The Book of Jargon.* New York: Collier, 1981. 26.

Jargon restricts your audience to those who share your specialized vocabulary and limits or destroys your ability to reach a wider audience. The cure for jargon is simple: unless your readers share your technical background, use nonspecialized language.

Exercise 2.3

Working in small groups, list as many examples of technical jargon as you can for each of the following occupations.

1. police officer (e.g., perpetrator, murder two)
2. nurse (e.g., bug, elopement risk)
3. car enthusiast (e.g., shift throw, stance)
4. financial analyst (e.g., beauty contest, fallen angel)
5. filmmaker (e.g., sync sound, M.O.S.)

Choose five technical terms from your own career field and write a general-level equivalent for each one.

3. PRETENTIOUS LANGUAGE

One of the challenges writers face when trying to adapt their style from the familiar to the formal level is a tendency to overcompensate. Many beginning writers try so hard to impress their readers that they forget that the purpose of writing is to communicate. Writing filled with abstract nouns, multi-syllable words, and long, complicated sentences is **pretentious**. All readers hate pretentious writing because they have to take the time to "translate" it into language they can understand. (Most teachers and supervisors won't bother. They'll just return the piece to the student or employee for revision.)

Sometimes called "gobbledygook," pretentious language has sound but no meaning:

> Our aspirational consumer strategy must position the brand's appeal to women shoppers who are seeking emblematic brands that are positively identified with health-oriented and fitness-centred lifestyles, so they can align their personal images with those lifestyle indicators.

This sentence, part of a marketing presentation to senior management, was written by a middle manager for a major yogurt company. What the poor writer is trying to say is that the company's customers want to be seen as people interested in fitness and health, so the company should advertise its yogurt accordingly.[1]

One symptom of pretentious writing is "buzzwords." These are words and phrases that become popular because they reflect the latest academic or psychological fad. They are often nouns with *-ize* added to them to make them into verbs: *utilize, verbalize, conceptualize*. What's wrong with *use, say,* and *think*? Every teacher knows this annoying trick; so do most managers. Instead of impressing readers, pretentious writing makes readers impatient and causes them to lose respect for the writer. If you really want to get your message across, write plainly and clearly in language your readers can understand.

Exercise 2.4*

Rewrite the following sentences, expressing the ideas in a way that allows the reader to grasp your meaning clearly, easily, and quickly. Then compare your answers to our suggestions on page 513.

1. We were forced to utilize the moisture-removing apparatus in our motorized personal conveyance when precipitate liquid impacted our windshield.
2. The chronologically less advanced generation sometimes achieves a communication deficit with authority figures and parental units.
3. The witness was ethically disoriented truthwise when she claimed that her interface with the accused resulted in his verbalization of an admission of guilt.
4. The parameters of our study vis-à-vis the totality of research in the field demonstrate that surveywise our validity is on a par with that of other instruments.

---

[1] This anecdote is paraphrased from Doug Saunders, "Aspiration Nation: Life Is but a Brand-name Dream," *Globe and Mail* 3 Jul. 2004: F3.

5. The cancellation of IMF funds to the Pacific Rim countries could lead to negative distortion of mutual interrelationships between developed and developing nations.

---

4. CLICHÉS

Unless you're a career civil servant or a longtime bureaucrat, writing pretentious language is a time-consuming and tiring task. You have to look up practically every word in a thesaurus to find a polysyllabic equivalent. Clichés, on the other hand, are easy to produce: they represent language without thought.

A **cliché** is a phrase that has been used so often it has lost its ability to communicate a meaningful idea to a reader.

> In this day and age, it seems that anything goes in our private lives. But in our professional lives, the name of the game is what it has always been: the bottom line.

In this day and age, anything goes, the name of the game, and *the bottom line* are clichés. Readers know what these phrases are supposed to mean, but they have been used so often they no longer communicate effectively. Cliché-filled writing will not only bore readers, but also affect their reaction to your message: "There's nothing new here. It's all been said before."

Spoken English is full of clichés. In the rush to express an idea, we often take the easy way and use ready-made expressions to put our thoughts into words. There is less excuse to use clichés in writing. Writers have time to think through what they want to say. They also have the opportunity to revise and edit. Writers are expected to communicate with more care, more precision, and more originality than speakers.

Clichés are easy to recognize if you are a native speaker. When you can read the first few words of an expression and automatically fill in the rest, the phrase is a cliché: free as a _____; a pain in the _____; last but not_____; it goes without _____. It is difficult to get rid of *all* clichés in your writing, but you can be aware of them and use them as seldom as possible.

The solution to a cliché problem involves time and thought. Think carefully about what you want to say; then say it in your own words, not everyone else's.

As you read through Exercise 2.5, notice how hard it is to form a mental picture of what the sentences mean and how hard it is to remember what you've read—even when you've just read it!

Exercise 2.5

Working with a partner, rewrite these sentences, expressing the ideas in your own words. When you're finished, exchange papers with another team and compare your results.

1. The boardroom was so quiet you could hear a pin drop.
2. It was raining cats and dogs, but we slept like logs through the storm.
3. When you are playing poker, you should keep your cool; otherwise, you could lose your shirt.
4. The CEO could not find a way to stay afloat, so she threw in the towel.
5. I burned the midnight oil and managed to finish the assignment at the crack of dawn.
6. Is this concept a flash in the pan or an idea whose time has come?
7. If we can nip this problem in the bud, there will be light at the end of the tunnel!
8. She stopped dead in her tracks. Lying on the floor was her son, crying his eyes out.
9. Your proposal is as good as they come; however, until the deal is signed, sealed, and delivered, we had better not count our chickens.
10. Even though I sweated it out night after night and kept my nose to the grindstone, I didn't meet my sales quota. As a result, I am sadder but wiser.

5. SEXIST LANGUAGE

Any writing that distracts your readers from your meaning is weak writing. Whether the distraction is caused by grammatical errors, spelling mistakes, slang, or the use of sexist language, your readers' concentration on your message is broken, and communication fails. **Sexist** (or gender-biased) **language** includes the use of words that signify gender (e.g., *waitress, sculptress, actress*) and the use of the pronouns *he, his, him* to refer to singular antecedents such as *everybody, anyone, no one*. Some readers object to terms that draw attention to gender differences, such as *man and wife* or *host and hostess*, preferring instead gender-neutral, inclusive terms such as *married couple* and *hosts*.

It is easy to dismiss nonsexist writing as "politically correct," but the language we use is a powerful force that influences the way we think. If we consistently refer to a *chairman* or *businessman*, we are perpetuating the idea that only men qualify for these positions. Far from being a politically correct fad, the use of inclusive or neutral words is both accurate and evenhanded.

Here are three tips to help you steer clear of sexist writing.

- Avoid using the word *woman* as an adjective. There is an implied condescension to phrases such as *woman athlete* and *woman writer* and *woman engineer*.
- Be conscious of the dangers of stereotyping. Physical descriptions of women are appropriate only where you would offer a similar description if the subject were a man. Just as some men can be excellent cooks, some women can be ruthless, power-hungry executives. It is possible for men to be scatterbrained and gossipy, while women can be decisive, tough, even violent.
- When making pronouns agree with singular antecedents, be careful that your pronouns do not imply bias. For example, "A teacher who discovers plagiarism must report it to *his* supervisor." Either use masculine and feminine pronouns interchangeably, or switch to a plural noun and avoid the problem: "Teachers who discover plagiarism must report it to their supervisors."

Exercise 2.6*

Correct the use of sexist or gender-biased language in the following sentences. Exchange papers with a partner and compare revisions. Then turn to pages 513–14 and compare your answers with our suggestions.

1. The well-known female producer Elaine May often regrets that she cannot go out in public without attracting the attention of fans and photographers.
2. Amy King, an attractive, blonde mother of two, first joined the company as a saleswoman; 10 years later, she was promoted to president.
3. A businessman sitting in the first-class cabin rang for the stewardess, a friendly gal who quickly arrived to assist him.
4. The list of ingredients on food packages contains information that may be important to the housewife, especially if she is the mother of young children.
5. The typical working man with a wife and two children is often hard-pressed to find time for recreation with his bride and the kids.

6. OFFENSIVE LANGUAGE

The last thing you want to do when you write is to offend your reader, even if you are writing a complaint. As we've seen above, some words occasionally used in speech are always inappropriate in writing. Swear words, for example, are unacceptable in a written message. So are obscene words, even "mild" ones. Offensive language appears much stronger in print than in speech and can provoke, shock, or even outrage a reader. Racist language and blasphemy (the use of names or objects that are sacred to any religion) are deeply offensive and always unacceptable.

Many writers have experienced the acute embarrassment of having a message read by people for whom it was not intended. What might have seemed at the time of composition to be an innocent joke may prove hateful to the unintended audience and mortifying to the writer.

It is wise to avoid all questionable, let alone unacceptable, expressions in your writing. Language has power: as many linguists have observed, our language actually shapes as well as reflects our attitudes and values. Those who use racist, blasphemous, sexist, or profane terms not only reinforce the attitudes contained in those terms, but also project a profoundly negative image of themselves to their readers.

7. ABUSAGES

Some words and phrases, even ones we hear in everyday speech, are *always* incorrect in written English. Technically, they are also incorrect in speech, but most people tolerate them in informal conversation. If these expressions appear in your writing, your reader will assume you are uneducated, ignorant, or worse. Even in some conversations, particularly in academic and professional environments, these expressions make a poor impression on your listeners.

Carefully read through the following list and highlight any words or phrases that sound all right to you. These are the ones you need to find and fix when you revise.

allready	A common misspelling of *already.*
alot	There is no such word. Use *much* or *many.* (*A lot* is acceptable in informal usage.)
anyways (anywheres)	There is no *s* in these words.
between you and I	The correct expression is *between you and me.*
can't hardly **couldn't hardly**	Use *can hardly* or *could hardly.*
could of (would of, **should of)**	The helping verb needed is *have,* not *of.* Write *could have, would have, should have.*

didn't do nothing	All double negatives ("couldn't see nothing," "couldn't get nowhere," "wouldn't talk to nobody") are wrong. Write *didn't do anything, couldn't see anything, couldn't get anywhere, wouldn't talk to anyone.*
for free	Use *free* or *at no cost.* (Also "free gift." Is there any other kind of gift?)
in regards to	Use *in* (or *with*) regard to.
irregardless	There is no such word. Use *regardless.*
media **used as singular**	The word *media* is plural. The singular is *medium.* Newspapers and television are mass *media.* Radio is an electronic *medium.*
most all	Use *most* or *almost all.*
off of	Use *off* alone: "I fell *off* the wagon."
prejudice **used as an adjective**	It is wrong to write "She is *prejudice* against blondes." Use *prejudiced.*
prejudism	There is no such word. Use *prejudice.* "A judge should show no *prejudice* to either side."
real **used as an adverb**	"Real good," "real bad," and "real nice" are wrong. You could use *really* or *very*, but such filler words add nothing to your meaning.
reason is because	Use *the reason is that*: "The reason is that my printer blew up."
suppose to	This expression, like *use to*, is nonstandard. Use *supposed to* and *used to.*
themself	Also "theirself," "ourselfs," "yourselfs," and "themselfs." These are all nonstandard words. The plural of *self* is *selves: themselves, ourselves,* and so on. Don't use "theirselves"; it's another nonstandard word.
try and	Use *try to.*
youse	There is no such word. *You* is the singular and plural form of the pronoun.

Exercise 2.7*

Correct the following sentences where necessary. Suggested answers are on page 514.

1. Irregardless of what you think, the problem between her and I has nothing to do with you.
2. If you want to be in the office pool, I need $5.00 off of you today because there will be no spots left by tomorrow.
3. Because they didn't finish the job theirself the way they should of, we will have to work real late to get it done.
4. I didn't feel like seeing nobody, so I went home, turned on the TV, and didn't do nothing for the rest of the night.
5. This use to be a real good place to work, but now we are suppose to work a full shift every day, or a penalty is deducted off of our pay.
6. Alot of young people today fight against prejudism not only in society but also within themselfs.
7. I'm suppose to ask youse if the reason for the delay is because there has been another bomb threat.
8. It's unresponsible of us to blame television or any other media for causing violence.
9. Television is partly responsible, however, for the fact that alot of ungrammatical expressions sound alright to us.
10. Between you and I, the reason I didn't speak to no one about Elmo's cheating is because he would of broke my arm.

3

Selecting a Subject

Approximately one-third of the time you devote to an essay should be spent on the planning stage (and the remainder to drafting and revising.) If you take the time to analyze your audience, find a good subject, and identify interesting main points to make about that subject, you will find that the mechanics of writing will fall into place much more easily than if you try to sweat your way through the paper the night before it's due. After you have considered your readers' background, needs, and expectations, the next step is to choose a satisfactory subject to write about.

Even when you are assigned a topic for an essay, you need to examine it, focus it, and consider different ways of approaching it. Depending on your knowledge of the topic and the readers you are writing for, the range of specific subjects for any broad topic is almost endless. For example, given the broad topic "Research sources," here are some of the approaches from which you might choose.

Can you trust Internet sources?
Interviewing to develop original source material
Books: still the best "random access device"
Journal indexes: an underused source of mountains of material
How to do an effective Internet search

Your first task, then, is to choose a satisfactory subject, one that satisfies the basic principles of the **4-S test**:

A satisfactory subject is significant, single, specific, and supportable.

If it passes the 4-S test, your subject is the basis of a good essay.

MAKE YOUR SUBJECT SIGNIFICANT

Your subject must be worthy of the time and attention you expect your readers to give to your paper. Can you imagine an essay on "How to buy movie tickets" or "Why I hate pants with button flies," for example, as being meaningful to your readers?

Exercise 3.1*

From the list below, choose those subjects that would be significant to a typical reader. Revise the others to make them significant, if possible. If not, suggest another, related subject that is significant. When you have finished this exercise, compare your answers with those provided on page 514.

1. Tips for travelling with small children
2. Using the reference library
3. Page-turning techniques
4. The perfect vacation spot
5. How to use the number pad on a calculator
6. Television is a threat to Canadian independence
7. Why you should write on one side of the page only

MAKE YOUR SUBJECT SINGLE

Don't try to crowd too much into one paper. Be careful that your subject is not actually two or three related subjects masquerading as one. If you attempt to write about a multiple subject, your readers will get a superficial and possibly confusing overview instead of the interesting and satisfying detail they expect to find in a well-planned paper. A subject such as "The problem of league expansion in basketball and other sports" is too broad to be dealt with satisfactorily in one essay. More manageable alternatives are "The problems of league expansion in the NBA" or "Why Montreal can't get an NBA franchise."

Exercise 3.2*

From the following list, choose the subjects that are single and could be satisfactorily explored in a short essay. Revise the others to make them single.

1. Causes of unemployment among college students and new graduates
2. Pub night at different colleges
3. How to change a tire and adjust the timing
4. The importance of accuracy in newspaper and television reporting
5. Methods of preventing the spread of STDs

6. Causes of injury in industry and professional sports
7. Nursing and engineering: rewarding careers

MAKE YOUR SUBJECT SPECIFIC

Given a choice between a broad, general topic and a narrow, specific one, always choose the specific one. Most readers find concrete, specific details more interesting than broad generalizations. It would be difficult to say anything very detailed about a huge subject such as "The roles of women in history," for example. But with some research, you could write an interesting paper on "The roles of 19th-century prairie women" or "Famous female pilots."

You can narrow a broad subject and make it more specific by applying one or more *limiting factors* to it. Try thinking of your subject in terms of a specific *kind, time, place, number,* or *person* associated with it. By applying this technique to the last potential subject above, you might come up with "Amelia Earhart's last flight."

Exercise 3.3*

In the list below, identify the subjects that are specific and could be explained satisfactorily in a short essay. Revise the others to make them specific by applying one or more of the limiting factors to each one.

1. Summer employment opportunities in my home town
2. Modern heroes
3. How to enjoy winter weather
4. The effects of government cutbacks on low-income families
5. The problems of urban living
6. How to repair your home appliances
7. Binge drinking among college women

MAKE YOUR SUBJECT SUPPORTABLE

You must know something about your subject (preferably more than your readers know), or you must be able to find out about it. Remember, your readers want information that is new, interesting, and thought provoking—not obvious observations familiar to everyone. You must be able to include *specific examples, facts, figures, quotations, anecdotes,* or other *supporting details.* Supporting information can be gathered from your own experience, from the experience of other people, or from both. If you don't know enough about your topic to write anything but the obvious, be prepared to do some research.

Exercise 3.4*

From the subjects given below, choose those that are clearly supportable in a short essay. Revise the others to make them supportable.

1. My career as a student
2. Movie review: *Star Wars: Episode III—Revenge of the Sith*
3. Crisis in the Canadian airline industry
4. The Chinese secret service
5. Space travel in the year 2100
6. Art through the ages
7. The hazards of working in a fast-food outlet

Exercise 3.5*

Together with a partner, discuss the acceptability of the potential subjects listed below. Indicate with check marks (✔) whether each subject below passes the 4-S test by being significant, single, specific, and supportable. Revise each unsatisfactory subject (fewer than four check marks) to make it a satisfactory subject for a short essay.

The 4-S Test

Subject	significant	single	specific	supportable	Revision
1. Computers	☐	☐	☐	☐	_____
2. Insomnia and other stress-related disorders	☐	☐	☐	☐	_____
3. The Arctic 200 years from now	☐	☐	☐	☐	_____
4. Dressing for an interview	☐	☐	☐	☐	_____
5. Architecture	☐	☐	☐	☐	_____

GO TO WEB

EXERCISE 3.1

Exercise 3.6

Write down three subjects that you think pass the 4-S test. When you've finished, exchange papers with another student and carefully check each other's work.

Once you have selected an appropriate subject, it's time to move on to the next stage: identifying solid main points to support that subject.

4

Managing the Main Points

While you were selecting subjects and testing them against the four principles presented in Chapter 3, you were thinking, consciously or unconsciously, about what you could say about them. **Main points** are the two or three or four most important things you have to say about your subject. Selecting them carefully is a vitally important part of the writing process.

Generating Main Points: The Bottom-Up Approach

If you are feeling intimidated by your task and unsure about how to present your subject, some prewriting activities can be helpful. Writers use several methods to stimulate thinking and prepare for a productive first draft. Two techniques are especially effective: freewriting and brainstorming. Either will get your creative juices flowing; we recommend that you try both to see which works best for you in particular situations.

Understand that you employ these techniques when you already have the necessary material in your head. Either you are writing from personal experience or you've done some research. (You'll learn about research in Part 5.) Freewriting and brainstorming are designed to get your ideas on the page in any order, shape, or form. Don't worry about making a mess. You can clean it up later.

FREEWRITING

Freewriting does what its name implies. It sets you free to write without worrying about any of the possible writing errors you might make that block the flow of your ideas. Forget about grammar, spelling, word choice, and so on, for a while, until you get some ideas down on the page. Here's how to go about freewriting:

1. Put your watch and a pad of paper on your desk. If you can type faster than you can write, open a new document on your computer. (Some writers find it helpful to turn the monitor off.) Write your subject at the top of the page or tape it to the top of your computer monitor. Ideally, your subject will have passed the 4-S test, but if you're really stuck, you can begin with just a word or a phrase.

2. Make a note of the time and start writing. Don't stop until you have written for three, five, or even ten minutes straight. Write anything that comes to mind, even if it seems boring or silly. If you get stuck for words, write your subject or even the last phrase you've written over and over until something new comes to mind. (Don't worry, it will!)

3. Write as quickly as you can. Don't pause to analyze or evaluate your ideas, and don't scratch out or delete anything. This technique is designed to get thoughts into words as quickly as possible without self-consciousness.

4. When the time is up, stop and stretch. Then read over what you've written. Underline anything that is related to your subject. Much of your freewriting will be irrelevant nonsense that you can delete. But what you have underlined will be useful in the next step: identifying the main points you will focus on to explain your subject.

5. Turn the phrases, fragments, and sentences you have underlined into clear, understandable points. If you don't end up with at least 10 points, continue freewriting for another few minutes and see what new ideas you can discover.

6. On a separate piece of paper, list the points you have identified. Study the possible relationships among these points and cluster them under two or three headings. These are your main points. Now you can move on to the next step: testing each main point to be sure it is satisfactory for your essay.

Here is an example of the freewriting technique. The assigned topic, for a course in law enforcement fundamentals, was "Crime and Punishment." Victor Chen was interested in the difference between crime as it is portrayed in the media and the reality of Canada's justice system. After doing some research and finding statistics that he thought might be useful, he drafted the following on his computer in 15 minutes.

What's really happening in our system in terms of crime and punishment is really different from what we see in the media. Look at TV crime shows. It used to be that all the courtroom shows were about defence lawyers trying to prove their clients' innocence. The prosecutors were the bad guys doing everything they could to put the defence attorney's client in jail or worse. There has been a big shift in the last five years or so and now we seem to have developed a taste for law and order. Now it's the prosecutors who are the good guys and the defence attorneys are trying to prevent their sleazy clients from escaping justice. The sad thing is that we form opinions about what goes on in real courtrooms based on stories like these. Almost all of the courtroom dramas on TV are American, and what goes on in American courtrooms is different from Canada's court procedures, so we are definitely not very aware of how our justice system really works.

To prove this, look at the study that was done by Roberts and Doob. They took a group of people and gave them the newspaper articles about a trial. When they had read the stories, they were asked about the trial. Most of them thought the criminal had gotten a sentence that was too light and only 15 percent thought the sentence was too tough. Then they took another group and gave them the court documents and transcripts of what actually went on in the trial. This group was reversed, more than half of them thought the sentence was too tough. Less than 20 percent agreed with the majority in the other group that the criminal should have got a longer sentence. This shows that we are getting a distorted impression of reality when we read about violent crime in the papers or on TV. It's like we're living in two worlds, the imaginary media one and the real one we don't know about. Also the news distorts violence. Reading the papers or watching TV, you'd think there was an epidemic of crime and that our streets are unsafe and murder was a common occurrence. This is so they can sell more papers and attract more viewers. In fact crime rates are falling. About half the crime reported in the news is violent while violent crime is actually less than 12 percent of cases that are reported. Murders are less than 1 percent of violent crimes but they are 25 percent of crime stories. If all you did was read the papers and watch TV you'd think that violence and murder were very common but actually they are quite rare. It's easy to see how we get the idea that violence in our society is a real problem. So it's really important that the people who make the laws don't rely on the media, because it is very distorted information.

After completing this freewriting exercise, Victor underlined all the points that he considered significant, supportable, and related to the subject. He quickly realized that the paper would be too long, and that one of his points was based on personal observation rather than provable facts. He crossed out everything related to television shows and then rearranged the other information into a rough outline of an essay with two main points.

Intro: the reality of the justice system and the media accounts of it are two different things. Take two examples: violence and court proceedings.

1. Crime
   • murders in reality vs. murders in the media
   • violent crime in reality vs. violent crime in the media
2. Courts—the Roberts and Doob study
   • opinions of group that read newspaper accounts of a trial
   • opinions of group that read court documents of a trial

Conclusion: lawmakers need to base decisions on reality and not on the media or public opinion.

Working from this rough outline, Victor developed a first draft. In reading it over, he noted where he needed to add more support to make the contrast clearer and more emphatic. After two more revisions and a careful edit, he submitted "Justice and Journalism," which you will find on pages 209–10.

Exercise 4.1

Choose a subject, or work with an assigned subject. Follow the six steps outlined on page 45 to see what main points you can come up with. Don't worry if your work is messy. Freewriting is a record of your thoughts, and thinking is messy.

BRAINSTORMING

In **brainstorming**, you write down a list of every idea you can think of about a specific subject. You can brainstorm alone, with a partner, or—best of all—in a group. If you run out of ideas too quickly, then try the age-old journalist's technique: ask the questions *who, what, why, when, where,* and *how* about your subject. Here's how to proceed. (The first three steps below assume you are working with a partner or in a small group. You can also do them by yourself, but you'll have less fun.)

1. Write your topic at the top of the page. Again, you will save time if you've checked your subject against the 4-S test. Decide how much time you will spend on this exercise: three, five, or more minutes. As in freewriting, working against the clock can bring surprising results.
2. Write down in short form—words or phrases—every idea you can think of that is even vaguely related to your subject. Choose the fastest writer in your group to be the recorder. Work quickly. Don't slow yourselves down by worrying about grammar or repetition.

3. When the time is up, relax for a minute, then go over the list carefully. Underline the points that seem most clearly related to your subject and scratch out any duplicates or any ideas that are vague, trivial, or irrelevant. If you don't end up with at least three or four points that are meaningful to you, brainstorm again for a few minutes, using the six journalist's questions to generate more ideas.

4. Working alone now, take your three or four most significant points and rephrase them in clear sentences on a new sheet of paper. Now you're ready to move on to the next step: testing your main points to ensure that they are suitable for use in your essay.

The following example demonstrates how brainstorming can be used to overcome the most frustrating inertia. The subject was "Your college English course." As you might expect, the class groaned when the subject was assigned, but one group's quick brainstorming produced some unique and interesting approaches to the topic. The time limit given for this exercise was four minutes. After brainstorming, at least one student was convinced that her career opportunities would improve if she learned how to communicate better.

Your College English Course

- have to take it
- should like it but I don't
- writing is important
- speaking's easier than writing
- bosses will hire you if you can write
- you can get a job
- letter of application
- have to write on the job
- have to write to the boss, other departments
- have to write to customers
- embarrassed about my writing
- people don't respect a poor writer
- writing helps you think
- writing helps you read better
- have to write reports
- need to know how to write a good report
- have to prepare slides for presentations
- need to write to get promoted

This list contains several significant points along with some irrelevant and trivial ones, which the group deleted. Then they talked about possible relationships among the remaining items on the list.

At this point, each student began working alone. After one student had underlined the points she felt were most important, she noticed that these points could be divided into two related ideas: what college English teaches and why it is useful. She then combined these two ideas into a thesis (a point of view about a subject). Here is her list of revised points.

College English is useful because
- it improves writing and thinking skills
- you will communicate better on the job
- you will get promoted

Exercise 4.2

In groups of four or five, brainstorm as many topics as you can in five minutes. Do not censor or cut any ideas. You should end up with at least 20 topics. Then exchange papers with another group, and edit that group's topics, crossing out any that are too broad or too narrow. Switch papers again, with a different group, and choose four topics that pass the 4-S test. Finally, select the best of the four topics and present it to the rest of the class, explaining why it's a good choice for an essay.

Exercise 4.3

Choose one of the two prewriting techniques presented in this chapter: freewriting or brainstorming. Generate as much information as you can in five minutes about one of the topics presented to the class in Exercise 4.2. Then narrow your information down to three main points, decide how to present them, and write a brief outline (no longer than the example given at the top of this page) for a short essay.

Generating Main Points:
The Top-Down Approach

Another way to find out what you have to say about a subject is to ask specific questions of it. Questioning lets you "walk around" your subject, looking at it from different angles, taking it apart and putting it back together again. Each question is a probe that enables you to dig below the surface and find out what you know. The top-down approach is more structured than the strategies we have discussed so far, but it has the advantage of producing clear main points with few or no off-topic responses. It also identifies for you the kinds of development you can use in your essay.

Questioning your subject works best if you know it well or have done some research but are not sure how to approach it. Any subject can be approached in a number of ways. The needs of your audience and your purpose in writing should determine the approach you choose.

Here's how to use the questioning technique to generate ideas:

1. Begin by writing your proposed subject at the top of the page, or tape it to your monitor.
2. Now apply the 12 questions listed below, one at a time, to your subject to see which ones "fit" best. That is, find the questions that call up in your mind answers that could be used as points to develop your subject. As you go down the list, you will probably find more than one question for which you can think up answers. Do not stop with the first question that produces answers. The purpose of this idea-generating technique is to discover the *best* approach for your target audience and writing purpose.
3. Go through the entire list and record your answers to any questions that apply to your subject. Ignore the questions that make no sense in relation to the subject.
4. Finally, study the questions that produced answers and choose the one that generated the ideas that are closest to what your reader needs to know and what you want to say.

The questions listed in the left-hand column lead to the kinds of essay development listed in the column on the right. Don't worry about these now. We'll discuss them in detail in Part 4.

The Answers to This Question	Produce This Kind of Paper
1. What does your subject *look, feel, sound, smell*, and/or *taste* like?	*Description*
2. How did your subject *happen*?	*Narration*
3. How is your subject *made* or *done*?	*Process*
4. How does your subject work?	
5. What are the main *kinds* of your subject?	*Classification/ Division*
6. What are the component *parts* of your subject?	
7. What are the significant *features, characteristics*, or *functions* of your subject?	
8. What are the *causes* of your subject?	*Cause/Effect*
9. What are the *effects* or *consequences* of your subject?	
10. What are the *similarities* and/or *differences* between your subject and *X*?	*Comparison/ Contrast*
11. What are the main *advantages/disadvantages* of your subject?	*Argument/ Persuasion*
12. What are the reasons *in favour of/against* your subject?	

Here is an example of how the process works. Alice Tam, a recent college graduate, has decided to write about her first job as a management trainee. Her target audience is general readers, not experts in her field. The subject passes the 4-S test: it is significant, single, specific, and supportable.

1. What does my job feel like?
   At first glance, this question doesn't make much sense. A *job* can't feel; the *employee* does. However, by interpreting the question loosely, Alice could describe her nervousness, her desire to do well, the pressures she felt, and the rewards of the job.

2. How did my job happen?
   This question doesn't sound promising. How Alice landed her job would be of interest to her family and friends, but probably would not appeal to a broader audience unless her experience was highly unusual or could be instructive to others.

3. How is my job done?
   The answer to this question is basically a job description, which would be of little interest to anyone other than Alice's close friends, her supervisor, or the person hired to replace her. Let's move on.

4. How does my first job work?
   All jobs are different; this question doesn't take us anywhere.

5. What are the main kinds of first jobs?
   This question might lead to an acceptable topic for a research paper on the kinds of entry-level jobs graduates from specific programs can expect to get, but the answers won't produce the sort of personal experience essay Alice wants to write.

6. What are the component parts (i.e., main requirements) of my job?
   Our writer might use this question as a starting point for a discussion of her main job functions, but this information would be of interest only to those in her career field, not to a broad, general audience.

7. What are the significant features of my job?
   This question has possibilities. Alice could tell her readers about those aspects of her job that apply to all first-time employees, perhaps limiting her focus to the aspects of the working world that she hadn't expected, that in fact surprised her.

8. What were the causes of my first job?
   This question doesn't produce useful answers. Most people work because they have to support themselves. The answer is self-evident.

9. What are the effects of my first job?
   This question raises some interesting answers. What effect has full-time employment had on Alice's life? She might discuss the self-esteem that

replaced her earlier insecurity and fear of the job search; she might discuss her new independence, both financial and social.

10. What are the similarities (or differences) between my first job and . . . what? A second or third job?
Our writer is still on her first job and so can't really comment on this question.

11. What are the main advantages (or disadvantages) of my first job?
This question produces answers that are easy to explain—and that's the problem with it. Unless Alice has a very unusual first job, the answers to this question are predictable and therefore of little interest to a broad audience.

12. What are the reasons in favour of (or against) my first job?
This question leads to answers that overlap with those produced by question 11. It would lead to an average essay, but not to anything outstanding or memorable.

After patiently going through the list, our writer found two questions, 7 and 9, that produced answers she felt she could work with. She especially liked the possibilities suggested by question 7. As Alice focused her thoughts, she realized that what she wanted to write about was the unexpected challenges she confronted when she joined the world of work. So she refined the question to capture what she wanted to write about ("What are the most significant challenges I faced in my first job?") and came up with three solid answers: the expectations of my boss, my coworkers, and myself. The essay that resulted from this process, "On-the-Job Training," appears on pages 188–89.

Generating main points is a time-consuming but worthwhile process. The more time you spend at this stage, the less time it will take you to draft your essay. To sharpen your skills, study the examples given below. Each consists of a 4-S test–approved subject, a question about that subject, and some answers the question produces that would form solid main points to support, explain, or prove the subject of the essay.

Subject	Selected Question	Main Points
Hockey violence	What are the reasons in favour of violence in hockey?	• releases aggression • keeps players alert • attracts fans
Law enforcement officers	What are the main functions of law enforcement officers?	• preventing crime • apprehending criminals • enforcing the law • acting as role models

Subject	Selected Question	Main Points
Job interviews	How do you make a negative impression in a job interview?	• be late • be inappropriately dressed • be ignorant about the company • complain about former employers
Essay topics	What are the characteristics of a satisfactory essay topic?	• single • significant • specific • supportable

Exercise 4.4

Working in pairs, apply the questions on pages 51–52 to each of the subjects listed below. Select the question that produces the answers you both like best, and list three or four of these answers as main points.

Subject	Selected Question	Main Points
1. Procrastination		• • • •
2. E-mail		• • • •
3. SUVs		• • • •

4. Business dress
codes

•

•

•

•

5. Ice cream

•

•

•

•

Exercise 4.5

In pairs, choose two subjects that you think would be suitable for short essays. Be sure all are significant, single, specific, and supportable. For each subject, list at least three strong main points. Use the questions on pages 51–52 to help you identify main points. When you've finished, exchange your ideas with another team, critique each other's main points, and make suggestions.

Subject   _____

Selected Question   _____

Main Points   •

    •

    •

Subject   _____

Selected Question   _____

Main Points   •

    •

    •

Testing Your Main Points

Now that you've practised identifying main points using freewriting, brainstorming, and the questioning approach, the next step is to examine the points you've come up with to make sure each is going to work as a major component in your essay. Some may be too minor to bother with; some may overlap in meaning; some may even be unrelated to your subject. Here's how to test your main points to be sure they are satisfactory. Whether you've arrived at your main points through freewriting, brainstorming, or questioning, the test is the same.

> Main points must be significant, distinct, and relevant.

ARE YOUR MAIN POINTS SIGNIFICANT?

Each main point should be worth writing and reading about. If you can't write at least one interesting and informative paragraph about a point, it is probably not significant enough to bother with. Don't waste your readers' time with trivial matters. In the following example, one of the main points does not have the same importance as the others; it should be eliminated or replaced. Which one would you discard?

Reasons for attending college
- to learn career skills
- to improve one's general knowledge of the world
- to enjoy the social life
- to participate in student government

ARE YOUR MAIN POINTS DISTINCT?

Each of the main points you choose must be different from all the others; there must be no overlap in meaning. Check to be sure you haven't given two different labels to what is really only one aspect of your subject. Eliminate or replace any main points that duplicate other points or that can easily be covered under another point. Here's an example of a list that contains a redundant main point. Which point would you eliminate?

Advantages of cycling

- improves fitness
- stimulates enjoyment of surroundings
- keeps one in shape
- doesn't damage the environment

ARE YOUR MAIN POINTS RELEVANT?

The main points you choose must be clearly and directly related to your subject. They all must be aspects of that subject and must add to the development of your readers' information on the subject. In this example, the third main point listed should be eliminated because it does not relate to the stated topic.

The miseries of winter

- numbing cold
- layers of uncomfortable clothes
- Christmas presents
- dangerous driving conditions

Exercise 4.6*

At least one main point in each item below is unsatisfactory. Identify each faulty point and explain why it should be deleted. When you have finished, compare your answers with those on page 515.

1. Business communication devices
   - telephone
   - e-mail
   - fax
   - mail
   - cell

2. Advantages of locating a business outside the city
   - cheaper cost of living
   - calmer pace
   - distance from suppliers and markets
   - government subsidies and tax benefits

3. Kinds of television commercials
   - boring
   - clever
   - misleading
   - puzzling
   - repetitive

4. Causes of college failure
- lack of preparation in high school
- procrastination
- poor study habits
- irregular attendance

5. How to choose a place to live
- determine your needs
- determine your budget
- find a reliable real-estate agent
- seek expert advice

6. Reasons for high staff turnover
- salary lower than industry standard
- no chance for advancement
- uncomfortable work environment
- competitors offer better pay

Organizing Your Main Points

After you've identified the main points for your essay and checked to make sure they are satisfactory, your final task in the planning process is to list them in order. (This list of points is sometimes called a plan of development or a path statement.) Main points are like menu items on a website: the more logically they are arranged, the easier it is to navigate your way through them.

There are four ways to order your main points: chronological, climactic, logical, and random.

CHRONOLOGICAL ORDER

When you present your points in order of time from first to last, you are using **chronological order**. You will find it most appropriate in process essays, but it can be used in other essays as well. Here are two examples.

Subject	Main Points
The process of writing a paper	• select an appropriate subject • list and edit the main points • write a thesis statement • write an outline for the paper • write a first draft • revise, edit, and proofread
The evolution of a relationship	• meeting • attraction • discovery • intimacy • disillusionment

CLIMACTIC ORDER

Persuasion most often uses a climactic arrangement, but climactic order is also common in papers based on examples, comparison or contrast, and classification or division. In **climactic order**, you save your strongest or most convincing point for last (the climax of your argument). You lead off your essay with your second-strongest point, and arrange your other points in between, as in this example.

Subject	Main Points
Advantages of a college education	• development of skills and knowledge • friendships and contacts with compatible people • potential for higher income • discovery of one's own potential

LOGICAL ORDER

Cause-and-effect essays, or any writing in which one point must be explained before the next point can be understood, are based on **logical order**. Your main points have a logical relationship, and you cannot take them out of order without confusing your readers. Consider the following sequence.

Subject	Main Points
Main causes of youth crime	• lack of opportunity or motivation for work • lack of recreational facilities • boredom • quest for "kicks"

The logical links here are clear: because of unemployment, recreational facilities are needed. Because of both unemployment and inadequate recreational facilities, boredom and the quest for "kicks" become problems. Readers must grasp each point before the next can be explained and understood.

RANDOM ORDER

On the rare occasions when your points can be explained in any order without affecting your readers' understanding, you can use **random order**. A random arrangement is possible only if all your main points are of equal significance and if they are not linked together logically or chronologically. In this example, all three points have equal weight.

Subject	Main Points
The garbage disposal crisis	• disposal sites are hard to find • cartage costs are high • new technologies are not yet fully developed

---

Exercise 4.7*

Choose the type of order—chronological, climactic, logical, or random—you think is most appropriate for each of the following subjects. Arrange the main points in that order by numbering them in the spaces provided.

Subject	Order	Main Points
1. How to impress a client	_____	_____ firm handshake _____ friendly closing _____ well-prepared sales presentation _____ knowledge of client's needs _____ appropriate business attire
2. How to handle tax preparation	_____	_____ do your own _____ don't bother to file a return _____ go to a franchise tax-preparation company _____ hire an accountant

3. Reasons for   _____   _____ it offers informative
listening to   programs
the CBC   _____ your taxes are paying for it
                                                      _____ it provides a sense of
                                                                Canadian unity

4. Methods of   _____   _____ nicotine patch
quitting smoking   _____ cold turkey
                                                       _____ gradual withdrawal

5. Causes of   _____   _____ incompetent or unfriendly
dissatisfaction   supervisor
with employment   _____ incompatible coworkers
                                                       _____ inappropriate pay for skills
                                                                and effort
                                                       _____ unfulfilling work
                                                                 assignments

GO TO WEB

EXERCISE 4.1

Exercise 4.8

Now go back to the subjects and main points that you developed in Exercise 4.5. First, reconsider your main points: are they all significant, distinct, and related to the subject? Next, put the main points in the order that is most appropriate for the subject to which they belong.

When you've finished this task, exchange papers with another student and check each other's work. Can your partner identify the order of points you have chosen? Does he or she agree with your choice?

In this chapter, you've learned how to identify main points, how to test them for suitability, and how to arrange them in the most appropriate order. You're ready now to go on to the next step: writing the thesis statement—probably the most important sentence in your paper.

5

Writing the Thesis Statement

The key to clear organization in any paper is a thesis statement near the beginning that announces the paper's subject and scope. The thesis statement not only helps a reader to see how you are going to approach the subject, but also serves to keep you, the writer, on track.

A **thesis statement** is one or more sentences that clearly and concisely indicate the subject of your paper, the main points you will discuss, and the order in which you will discuss them.

In business communication, technical writing, and some academic writing (e.g., research papers and dissertations) it is important to indicate the subject and scope of your paper at the outset. Readers expect this sort of preview.[1]

The number of sentences in a thesis statement depends on what the subject is, how best to phrase it, how many points there are, and how complex they are. A thesis statement in a short paper is usually a single sentence at the end of the first paragraph, but in a lengthy paper on complicated issues, it might be several sentences or even a paragraph long. Occasionally (in a technical description, for example), a writer will choose a short thesis and omit the main points from the thesis statement.

To write a thesis statement, you combine your subject and your main points. Here is a simple formula for constructing a thesis statement:

---

[1]In less formal writing, such as newspaper or magazine articles and informal essays—including some of the essays in this book—a thesis statement is unnecessary.

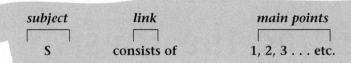

subject	*link*	*main points*
S	consists of	1, 2, 3 . . . etc.

These three elements can be combined in various ways. For example:

The most prolific producers of unnecessary jargon are politicians, sports writers, advertising copy writers, and educators. (Subject and main points are linked by *are*.)

Because the United States influences Canada's foreign policy, dominates its culture, and controls its economy, Canada is little more than an American satellite. (Main points precede subject and are linked to the subject by *because*.)

Fad diets are not the quick fix to weight problems that they may appear to be. On the contrary, they are often costly, ineffective, and even dangerous. (Subject is one sentence. Main points are in second sentence, linked to the first by *On the contrary*.)

Two cheers for democracy: one because it admits variety, and two because it permits criticism. (E. M. Forster) (Subject and main points are linked by a colon.)

Once you have mastered the basic formula, you can experiment with creative ways of expressing a thesis statement. Just be sure that it is appropriate in form, language, and tone to the kind of paper you are writing. The thesis statements in the exercise below range from short to long, formal to informal, and serious to flippant.

Exercise 5.1*

In each of the following thesis statements, underline the subject with a double line and the main points with a single line. When you have finished all seven, compare your answers with those on page 516.

1. Students who try to combine a full-time job with a full-time program face problems at school, at work, and at home.
2. To be successful in a broadcasting career, you must be talented, motivated, and hardworking.
3. The ideal notebook computer for business applications is reliable, lightweight, powerful, and flexible.
4. Establishing a local area network would increase efficiency and flexibility in the office.

5. The chairperson's job calls for a responsible and sensitive person, someone who is knowledgeable about company policy, sensitive to personnel issues, and a creative problem solver. It wouldn't hurt if he or she could also walk on water.

6. The business traveller can learn much from the turtle. Carry everything you need with you. Move slowly but with purpose and consistency. Keep your head down until you are sure you know what's going on.

7. Large energy producers and some provincial governments say we cannot afford to live up to the terms of the Kyoto Accord, which seeks to reduce the production of greenhouse gases. But can we afford not to comply with this international agreement? Can we afford to compromise the health of Canadians by continuing to pollute? Can we afford to risk the effects of global warming on our environment? Can we afford to fall behind the rest of the world in research and development leading to a solution to the problem of greenhouse gases?

Exercise 5.2

Each of the five introductions below contains a thesis statement. Working with a partner or in groups of three or four, identify the thesis statement in each paragraph.

1.   What does an interviewer look for in a new job applicant? Good credentials, good preparation, good grooming, and good communication skills are essential features for anyone who wants a job. No interviewer would seriously consider an applicant who comes to an interview without the required educational background and work experience, without information about the job and the company, without appropriate clothing, and without the ability to present ideas clearly in the interview.

2.   In the traditional manufacturing sectors, sales growth has stagnated in Canada over the past five years. Our products and services have secured as large a market share as we can expect, and we can anticipate further decline over the next 10 years as a result of increased competition. For these reasons, we have undertaken a study to determine where our best expansion opportunities lie. The following report outlines growth opportunities in the emerging markets of China and India.

3.   Suddenly a man steps into the road in front of me. He's wearing a uniform and he's waving his hand for me to pull over to the side. My heart pounds and my pores prickle with anxiety. I feel guilty, but I don't know what I've done wrong—maybe speeding 10 kilometres over the limit, but no more. Anyone who has been caught in a radar trap knows this momentary feeling of panic, guilt, and resentment. We fear that the police officer will be brusque and blaming, but we are often surprised. There are as many kinds of police officers as there are people. Four kinds, however, dominate the profession: the confident veteran, the arrogant authoritarian, the cocky

novice, and the friendly professional. As I roll down my window, I wonder which kind of police officer has stopped me.

4.   After a hard day's work, do you relax with two or three stiff drinks? Do you enjoy a few beers while watching a game on TV? Do you believe mixed drinks make a party more fun? Do you cool off with gin fizzes on a hot afternoon? If you answered "yes" to most of these questions, you are probably abusing alcohol. The line between excessive social drinking and a serious addictive habit is a blurry one. Most alcoholics don't know they are hooked until they try to stop drinking. What are the signs that a drinker is no longer drinking for pleasure only? If a person "needs" a drink, or drinks alone, or can fall asleep only after a few drinks, or can find enjoyment only when drinking, that person is probably in trouble.

5.   Ours is a transient society. Most of us travel more kilometres in a year than our grandparents travelled in a lifetime. We move from one city to another, one province to another, and one country to another. In the course of moving, we inhabit many homes. The family home of the past might have been inhabited by several generations, consecutively or concurrently. Today's average Canadians will probably have 10 or more addresses during their adult lives. Our restlessness is particularly hard on the children in our migrating families: they have to leave familiar surroundings and friends, and they must adjust to a new environment, new habits, and sometimes a new language. These children pay a heavy price for the mobility of modern impermanence.

Phrasing Your Statement of Subject

The first part of a thesis statement is the statement of subject. It identifies *your idea about* or *your approach to* your subject. It states a viewpoint that must be explained or proved. (The main points provide the explanation or proof.)

Your statement of subject should be as clear and concise as you can make it. It must not be boring, however.

Beginning writers often fall into the trap of stating the obvious: "In this paper, I am going to discuss . . ." or "The subject of this memo is . . ." Your readers *know* it's your paper; you needn't hit them over the head by pointing out the fact that the paper contains your ideas. Here are three examples of faulty subject statements and their revisions.

Poor	Better
In this essay, I am going to discuss violence in hockey. (What about it?)	Violence in hockey is misunderstood by the nonplaying public.

This paper is about Canada's
multiculturalism policy.
(What about it?)

Canada's multiculturalism policy is
neither practical nor desirable.

I am going to examine the
influence of Wal-Mart in Canada.
(What about it?)

With over 200 stores in Canada and
plans for expansion, Wal-Mart's effects
on labour are worth considering.

As soon as you write, "In this essay . . ." or "I am going to discuss (write about, explore) . . . ," you trap yourself into simply announcing your subject, not stating your idea or opinion about it. Avoid these traps. Always let your reader know *what it is about your subject* that your paper will explain or prove.

Phrasing the Main Points

When you combine your statement of subject with your main points to form your thesis statement, be sure that all your main points are phrased in the same way, in grammatically parallel form. If point 1 is a single word, then points 2, 3, and so on must also be single words. If point 1 is a phrase, then all the points following it must be phrases. If point 1 is a clause or a sentence, then the succeeding points must also be in clause or sentence form.

The following sentence contains a main point that is not parallel with the others.

Of the many qualities that combine to make a good nurse the three most important are strength, intelligence, and she must be compassionate.

Here is the sentence rewritten to be grammatically parallel:

Of the many qualities that combine to make a good nurse the three most important are strength, intelligence, and compassion.

Or, the sentence could be rewritten this way:

Of the many qualities that combine to make a good nurse the three most important are that she or he be strong, intelligent, and compassionate.

If you have trouble with grammatical parallelism, turn to Chapter 26 before you try the exercise below.

Exercise 5.3

In each of the following lists, one point is not parallel with the others. Rephrase the incorrect item so that all are in grammatically parallel form.

1. Our employees are
   a. motivated
   b. good training
   c. knowledgeable
2. Our doctor is
   a. full of compassion
   b. competent
   c. hard-working
3. I've noticed that my friends are increasingly
   a. concerned about smoking
   b. interested in fitness
   c. environmental awareness
4. To upgrade our educational system, we need
   a. more effective teacher training
   b. better liaison between levels of education
   c. students must be motivated to learn
5. An investment strategy must be
   a. based on current information
   b. appropriately diversified
   c. the client has to be tolerant of the degree of risk

Exercise 5.4

Work in pairs to develop two thesis statements for potential essays. Phrase the two thesis statements so that one has a poor statement of subject and the other lacks parallelism. Switch your creations with another team and identify each other's problems. Then correct the sentences. Exchange papers again. Did the other team identify and correct the problems you thought you'd created? If not, revise your own team's faulty sentences.

Exercise 5.5

Working with a partner, combine each of the following subjects with its main points to form a clear thesis statement that is expressed in grammatically parallel form.

1. Causes of stress
   - change of employment
   - financial problems
   - death of family member

Thesis statement: _____

_____

_____

_____

_____

2. Steps in finding a job
   - conduct an Internet job search
   - prepare a letter of application
   - perform well in the interview

Thesis statement: _____

_____

_____

_____

_____

3. How to save money
   - automatic payroll deductions
   - keep a record of expenditures
   - reduce impulse buying
   - establish and maintain a budget

Thesis statement: _____

_____

_____

_____

_____

4. Evolution of a recession
   - unemployment causes general economic slowdown
   - consumer buying decreases, resulting in inflation
   - inflation causes fear and further decrease in consumer demand

Thesis statement: _____

_____

_____

_____

_____

Exercise 5.6*

Working independently, combine each of the following subjects with its main points to form a grammatically parallel thesis statement. Then compare your answers to our suggestions on page 516.

1. Comparison between McDonald's and Wendy's (or any other two fast-food restaurants)
   - food
   - atmosphere
   - service
   - price

   Thesis statement: _____

   _____

   _____

   _____

   _____

2. Effects of urban overcrowding
   - traffic jams
   - too much air pollution
   - high rate of homelessness
   - violence on the streets

   Thesis statement: _____

   _____

   _____

   _____

   _____

3. Characteristics of a successful small business
   - adequate capital
   - marketable product
   - personnel that are dedicated
   - workable business plan

Thesis statement: _____

_____

_____

_____

_____

_____

Exercise 5.7

In groups of three or four, share the thesis statements you developed for Exercise 5.6 and discuss your decisions. As a group, revise each statement until you are all satisfied they meet the criteria for satisfactory thesis statements.

You have now covered all the steps leading to the construction of a good thesis statement. The exercises above have given you practice in the skills you need to phrase subjects and main points correctly and effectively.

Exercise 5.8 will walk you through the process of developing a thesis statement for a subject of your own choice. As you fill in the blanks in this exercise, you will be reviewing the first five chapters of this book and also testing your mastery of the writing skills they presented.

Exercise 5.8

1. Select a subject.

   _____

   _____

2. Test whether your subject is significant, single, specific, and supportable.

3. Using either a bottom-up or a top-down approach to generate ideas, identify three to five main points in support of your subject.

   _____

   _____

   _____

   _____

   _____

4. Test whether your main points are all significant, distinct, and clearly related to your subject.

5. Arrange your main points in the order that is most likely to guarantee your readers' understanding of your subject: chronological, climactic, logical, or random.

_____

_____

_____

_____

6. Rewrite your main points so that they are grammatically parallel: all single words, all phrases, or all clauses.

_____

_____

_____

_____

7. Combine your statement of subject with your main points to produce your thesis statement.

_____

_____

_____

_____

_____

The seven points listed in Exercise 5.8 summarize the steps to follow in planning an essay. Keep this outline handy and refer to it when you start your next paper or research report.

6

Preparing an Outline

Writing a paper is like building a house: you save much time and frustration if you start with a plan. For anything longer than about 250 words, writers need a plan or outline to guide them as they begin to build words into sentences, sentences into paragraphs, and paragraphs into the final product, whether it's a term paper, a research report, a business plan, or a market analysis.

Wise writers treat an outline as tentative, not something chiselled in stone. As you draft your paper, you may discover new ideas or a new structure that better suits your purpose. If so, change your thesis statement and outline to accommodate it. (It's a good idea to make these changes in pencil or in a new file because you may decide at the end of the draft that these new ideas weren't so great after all.)

If you have access to a word-processing program with an outline feature, try it out. These programs can be a great help to an inexperienced writer with little knowledge of how to plan a writing assignment.

As we have seen, all written messages consist of an introduction, a body, and a conclusion, but each of these may vary from one to several paragraphs in length, and from simple to sophisticated in style. The model format on the next page is a basic outline for a five-paragraph essay. Once you've mastered this basic structure, you can modify, expand, and develop it to suit any of the kinds of writing you'll be called upon to do.

Outline Format

Title _____

INTRODUCTION _____

Attention-getter* _____

_____

_____

Thesis statement <u>Subject consists of 1, 2, and 3.</u>

BODY <u>Topic sentence introducing main point 1 goes here.</u>

Support
for first
main point
_____
_____
_____
_____

<u>Concluding (or transition) sentence goes here.</u>
<u>(Transition or) Topic sentence introducing main point
2 goes here.</u>

Support
for second
main point
_____
_____
_____

<u>Concluding (or transition) sentence goes here.</u>
<u>(Transition or) Topic sentence introducing main point
3 goes here.</u>

Support
for third
main point
_____
_____
_____

<u>Concluding (or transition) sentence goes here.</u>

CONCLUSION _____

Summary
_____
_____

Memorable
statement*
_____
_____.

Note: Occasionally, a writer will begin a body paragraph with a transitional phrase or sentence. Variety adds interest to writing style. You will see examples of this technique in Part 4.

*Terms marked with an asterisk are explained and illustrated in Chapter 8.

The outline below follows the format on page 72. The final version of "Ready, Willing . . . and Employable" appears after the outline.

Ready, Willing . . . and Employable	*Essay title*
What are employers looking for today?	*Attention-getter*
Employers are looking for a new breed of employee: one who has knowledge, flexibility, and the right attitude.	*Thesis statement*
Knowledge is still first on the list.	*1. Topic sentence*
• colleges offer a broad range of programs to meet employers' needs • graduates must know current trends as well as theory • some employers test for knowledge • some rely on college's reputation plus recommendations of professors and recruiters	*Support for first main point*
Adaptability is essential for a prospective employee.	*2. Topic sentence*
• today's jobs require multitasking • flexible workers are more cost-effective and better problem solvers • flexible workers can adapt to change • students need to broaden their education and learn a variety of skills	*Support for second main point*
Employers complain about graduates' poor attitude.	*3. Topic sentence*
• graduates lack the ability to take direction, use team skills, communicate well, and motivate themselves • similar problems show up in class —chronic lateness —lack of cooperation —laziness • students need to correct these attitude problems on their own	*Support for third main point*
Students must be ready, able, and willing to work.	*Summary of main points*
With these skills, a good résumé, and professional contacts, graduates can enter the workforce with confidence.	*Memorable statement*

READY, WILLING . . . AND EMPLOYABLE

Attention-getter

What are employers looking for in today's job market? Several recent surveys point to a subtle shift in the requirements of businesses looking to hire college and university graduates. Only a few years ago, knowledge was the prerequisite to employment in most industries. Employers needed workers with the highly specialized skills of an emerging high-tech workplace. Now many of

Thesis statement

those skills are taken for granted, and other characteristics have become increasingly important. Employers are seeking a new breed of employee: one who has the knowledge required to do the job, the flexibility to adapt, and—most important—the attitude to succeed.

Topic sentence

Knowledge of how to do the job is, understandably, still first on the shopping list that employers bring to job fairs. Colleges across the country have responded to marketplace requirements with an array of programs designed to prepare students to meet the needs of industries from broadcasting to photonics, from microelectronics to winemaking. Graduates are expected to have

Support for first main point

up-to-the-minute information on current trends in their fields, as well as solid grounding in the theory and practice of their specialty. Some employers test applicants for this knowledge; others rely on the reputation of the institution, the recommendation of professors with whom they have professional connections, and the insights of recruiters. As valuable as knowledge is to the employer,

Concluding statement (transition)

however, an employee's flexibility is quickly becoming just as important.

Topic sentence

"Multitasking" is a buzz word often used to describe the ability to move quickly and easily between projects and work environments, bringing a wide range of skills to bear on a variety of situations. Adaptability is an essential characteristic of any prospective employee. Workers who can use their expertise simultaneously on several different tasks within a project are valuable not only because they are more cost-effective than several single-task specialists, but also because they tend to see projects holistically and are better problem solvers as

Support for second main point

a result. In addition, flexible workers are those who most quickly and easily adapt to changes in technology or work practice, and such changes are a way of life in today's work environment. Students must prepare themselves to be flexible workers by broadening their education and by learning as many skills as possible. Unlike their parents, workers in the current generation have little hope of finding a job that will require only one skill set over the course of a career. Adaptability is a critical skill, but even when combined with knowledge,

Concluding statement

it is not enough to ensure employability. Increasingly, attitude is the determining factor in who gets hired (and promoted!).

Transition

Employers continually complain to colleges and universities that students on placement and graduates in their first position fail to impress, not from lack of knowledge, skill, or preparation, but from a broad range of inadequacies best summed up as "poor attitude." Among the faults cited under this broad heading are inability to take direction, failure to work well with colleagues, inability to communicate effectively, and lack of enthusiasm and initiative. How can such problems be corrected before graduates reach the workplace? Colleges do not offer courses in attitude adjustment, but perhaps they should. Most of these problems have surfaced in classes long before graduation. Students who are chronically late, frequently uncooperative, constantly complaining, or visibly lazy are those who, with all the skills and ability in the world, will not succeed in any job worth having. Even highly motivated and ambitious graduates have sometimes had difficulty adjusting to entry-level positions when they find themselves working under the supervision of people they consider less talented or skilled. It is up to students themselves to correct their attitudinal deficiencies. They need to pay attention to the criticisms of teachers, classmates, even family members, and make an honest evaluation of consistently noticed faults. Only when such attitude faults have been identified and acknowledged can they be corrected, and only when they have been corrected will the student be an asset to an employer.

Topic sentence

Support for third main point

Concluding statement

As graduation draws near, most students view their coming transformation into workers with eagerness liberally mixed with anxiety. Statistics tell us that most college and university graduates find employment in their fields within a year of graduation. Armed with this encouraging information, together with a good résumé, professional contacts, and the knowledge, flexibility, and attitude to succeed, graduates can face employers and the workplace with confidence.

Summary and Memorable statement

Exercise 6.1

Read "Of Men and Machines in the 21st Century" (pages 189–91) and "Lightweight Lit." (pages 218–19). Identify in each essay the sentences that correspond to the major structural items in the outline formats that follow. If you're working through this textbook in order, you may not have studied some of the terms mentioned, but you should be able to make a good guess at identifying the attention-getter and the memorable statement. To make your task easier, the sentences in each essay have been numbered.

OF MEN AND MACHINES IN THE 21ST CENTURY

INTRODUCTION

Attention-getter   Sentence(s) _____

Thesis statement   Sentence(s) _____

BODY PARAGRAPH #1

Topic sentence   Sentence(s) _____

Support for first main point   Sentence(s) _____

Conclusion/Transition   Sentence(s) _____

BODY PARAGRAPH #2

Topic sentence   Sentence(s) _____

Support for second main point   Sentence(s) _____

Conclusion/Transition   Sentence(s) _____

BODY PARAGRAPH #3

Topic sentence   Sentence(s) _____

Support for third main point   Sentence(s) _____

Conclusion/Transition   Sentence(s) _____

CONCLUSION

Summary/Reinforcement   Sentence(s) _____

Memorable statement   Sentence(s) _____

LIGHTWEIGHT LIT.

INTRODUCTION

Attention-getter   Sentence(s) _____

Thesis statement   Sentence(s) _____

BODY PARAGRAPH #1

Topic sentence   Sentence(s) _____

Support for first main point   Sentence(s) _____

Conclusion/Transition   Sentence(s) _____

BODY PARAGRAPH #2

Topic sentence   Sentence(s) _____

Support for second main point Sentence(s) _____

Conclusion/Transition   Sentence(s) _____

BODY PARAGRAPH #3

Topic sentence   Sentence(s) _____

Support for third main point   Sentence(s) _____

Conclusion/Transition   Sentence(s) _____

CONCLUSION

Summary/Reinforcement   Sentence(s) _____

Memorable statement   Sentence(s) _____

Exercise 6.2

1. With a partner, choose either "The Train Ride" (pages 160–61), "A Slender Trap" (pages 221–23), or "A City for Students" (pages 242–43). Read the essay carefully and create an outline for it, following the format on page 72.

2. Compare outlines with another team that selected the same reading. Are there significant differences between the two outlines? If so, which outline best reflects the components of the introduction, body, and conclusion of the essay?

PART 2

Drafting

7

Understanding Paragraph Form and Function

What Does a Paragraph Look Like?

Essays are divided into paragraphs. **Paragraphs** are sentence groups that are separated from each other in their physical presentation and in their content. They usually have an indentation at the beginning (on a typed page, the first word begins five spaces in from the left margin) and some white space at the end (the last line is left blank following the paragraph's last word). Between the indentation and the final period comes the paragraph—a group of sentences that explains a single idea or topic.

If you were to draw a blueprint for a single paragraph, it would look like this:

A sentence that introduces the **topic** (or main idea) of the paragraph goes here.

Three or more sentences that specifically support or explain the topic go in here.

A sentence that concludes your explanation of the topic (or provides a transition to the next paragraph) goes here.

How Does a Paragraph Function?

Readers expect a paragraph to present a unit of thought or a single, developed idea. The white space at the beginning and end of each paragraph defines your thought units and also serves two other functions.

1. Paragraphs provide visual cues that make your writing "reader friendly." Imagine how intimidating the page you are now reading would be if were one continuous block of print: no headings, no indentations, no paragraphs.
2. Paragraphs divide your writing into linked but separate sections. Without paragraphs, ideas would blur and blend one into another. Readers would find it difficult to identify them, let alone follow the organization and development of the writer's thoughts.

In a typical essay, an introductory paragraph is followed by paragraphs that add details and depth to the ideas set out in the introduction. A concluding paragraph brings all the ideas together again and leaves the reader with a complete understanding of the writer's thinking.

Readers can tell a great deal about your thinking just by glancing at a page of your paper. A number of short paragraphs indicates a series of ideas, briefly (and perhaps superficially) explained. Long paragraphs—half a page or longer—suggest complex ideas that require explanation and details. They signal serious thought but are more difficult to read because they require close attention.

As a general rule, you explore one major idea or main point in each paragraph. When you have finished exploring one topic and wish to move on to another, you signal this shift to your readers by beginning a new paragraph.

How Long Should a Paragraph Be?

The answer to this question depends on the topic, your readers' familiarity with it, and your purpose in writing. If your topic is complex, your readers' knowledge is limited, and your purpose is to persuade readers who do not share your point of view, then you'll probably need a fairly long paragraph to accomplish your goal. On the other hand, if you're writing about a topic your readers are likely familiar with, and your purpose is simply to share with them your understanding of that topic, you may be able to accomplish your task in a few sentences.

Exercise 7.1

Work in groups of five or six. Each group will take one of the paragraphs below to read and analyze by answering the following questions. Share your analysis with the class.

- What is the topic of the paragraph, stated in a few words?
- How much knowledge of the topic does the writer assume the readers have?
- What is the writer's purpose in this paragraph?

1.   Violence as a way of achieving racial justice is both impractical and immoral. It is impractical because it is a descending spiral ending in destruction for all. The old law of an eye for an eye leaves everybody blind. It is immoral because it seeks to humiliate the opponent rather than win his understanding; it seeks to annihilate rather than to convert. Violence is immoral because it thrives on hatred rather than love. It destroys community and makes brotherhood impossible. It leaves society in monologue rather than dialogue. Violence ends by defeating itself. It creates bitterness in the survivors and brutality in the destroyers. A voice echoes through time saying to every potential Peter, "Put up your sword." History is cluttered with the wreckage of nations that failed to follow this command.

King, Martin Luther, Jr. "Three Types of Resistance to Oppression." *Stride Toward Freedom*. New York: Harper & Row, 1958. 215.

2.   Take William Lyon Mackenzie King, our prime minister through the war and, so it seemed, for all time until Pierre Trudeau came along and seemed to be prime minister for all time. King held power longer than any other Western politician in this century. How did such a pudgy, mundane little man do it? The truth is, he did it deliberately. He was shrewd and self-effacing, and he told his friends that he made every speech as boring as possible because then no one would ever remember what he said and hold it against him. Twenty-two years in power, droning on and on over the airwaves, and meanwhile, he was as crazy as a loon.

Callaghan, Barry. "Canadian Wry." *Canadian Content*. Ed. Sarah Norton and Nell Waldman. 2nd ed. Toronto: Harcourt, 1992. 92.

3.   *Vinaya* means humility; it is the complete surrendering of the self on the part of the *shishya* [the disciple] to the *guru*. The ideal disciple feels love, adoration, reverence, and even fear toward his *guru*, and he accepts equally praise or scoldings. Talent, sincerity, and the willingness to practise faithfully are essential qualities of the serious student. The *guru*, as the giver in this relationship, seems to be all-powerful. Often, he may be unreasonable, harsh, or haughty, though the ideal *guru* is none of these. Ideally, he should

respond to the efforts of the disciple and love him almost as his own child. In India, a Hindu child, from his earliest years, is taught to feel humble toward anyone older than he or superior in any way. From the simplest gesture of the *namaskar*, or greeting (putting the hands palm to palm in front of the forehead and bowing), or the *pranam* (a respectful greeting consisting of touching the greeted person's feet, then one's own eyes and forehead with the hands held palm to palm) to the practice of *vinaya* or humility tempered with a feeling of love and worship, the Hindu devotee's vanity and pretension are worn away.

Shankar, Ravi. "Studying Music in India." *My Music, My Life.* Delhi: Vikas Publications, 1968. 11–12.

4.   When I found [the snakeskin], it was whole and tied in a knot. Now there have been stories told, even by reputable scientists, of snakes that have deliberately tied themselves in a knot to prevent larger snakes from trying to swallow them—but I couldn't imagine any way that throwing itself into a half hitch would help a snake trying to escape its skin. Still, ever cautious, I figured that one of the neighborhood boys could possibly have tied it in a knot in the fall, for some whimsical boyish reason, and left it there, where it dried and gathered dust. So I carried the skin along thoughtlessly as I walked, snagging it sure enough on a low branch and ripping it in two. . . . I saw that thick ice still lay on the quarry pond and that the skunk cabbage was already out in the clearings, and then I came home and looked at the skin and its knot.

Dillard, Annie. *Pilgrim at Tinker Creek.* New York: Harper's Magazine Press, 1974. 73.

5.   [T]here needs to be a thorough revision of the maximum-penalty structure to remove the incongruities that riddle the current Criminal Code. Should forgery or certain kinds of fraud really have the same maximum penalty as sexual assault with a weapon? The maximum penalties are also much too high; most were created many decades ago, when our perceptions of the seriousness of various crimes differed from those today. The maximum penalty for breaking and entering is life imprisonment, for example, but in practice the average sentence is well under one year. This is called "bite and bark" sentencing; the system barks more loudly than it bites, and creates false expectations among the public.

Roberts, Julian V. "Three Steps to Make the Punishment Fit the Crime." *Globe and Mail* 7 Dec. 1993: A25.

Exercise 7.2

Write a short paragraph (five to seven sentences) that demonstrates your understanding of paragraph form and function. Choose any topic you like. When you have finished, exchange papers with another student and check each other's paragraph for

- Form: Is there a clear introduction to and conclusion of the topic?
- Function: Is the paragraph sufficiently developed for the reader to understand the topic clearly? The reader should have no questions left unanswered.

Crafting the Topic Sentence

The **topic sentence** in each paragraph is the sentence that clearly identifies what the paragraph is about—its main idea. The topic sentence focuses the paragraph, helps to unify it, and keeps you and your readers on track. In professional writing, the topic sentence is not always the first sentence of the paragraph. Sometimes it is more effective to announce the topic in the second, third, or even the last sentence. But professional writers, through years of practice, have earned the right to break the rules. Beginning writers should remember this: *most readers assume that the first sentence of a paragraph identifies the topic of that paragraph.* If your first sentence doesn't do this, then your readers may go through your paragraph assuming the topic is something other than what you intended. Miscommunication frustrates readers and wastes their time. To be absolutely clear, identify your topic up front.

A good topic sentence does three things:

1. It introduces the topic of the paragraph.
2. It makes a point about the topic.
3. It makes a statement that is neither too broad nor too narrow.

Readers appreciate writers who get to the point quickly, make the point clearly, and support or explain it adequately. They also appreciate writers who can make their points in an interesting way. Take the time to write topic sentences that are something more than straightforward, flat announcements of your main idea. Compare the following pairs of topic sentences.

Weak	Strong
I am going to explain why I love "trash."	I'm ashamed to confess my secret vice, but because we're friends, I can tell you: I love "trash."
This paragraph is about violence.	Violence as a way of achieving social justice is both impractical and immoral (Martin Luther King, Jr.).

A good way to introduce the topic so that it is both interesting and effective is to make a point about it. You save your readers' time and eliminate the risk of confusion if you make clear at the outset your idea about or your attitude toward your topic. Consider these examples.

Weak	Strong
Many people around the world enjoy music.	Nothing bridges gaps between cultures like music.
Canadians are different from Americans.	Canadians should be thankful for their differences from Americans.

Finally, the topic you choose must be "the right size"—neither so broad that you cannot support it adequately in a single paragraph, nor so narrow that it doesn't require support. The 4-S test that you used to determine whether a subject was suitable for a paper can also be applied to potential paragraph topics. If your topic is single, significant, specific, and supportable, it should form the basis for a solid paragraph. Take a look at these topic sentences.

Weak	Strong
The legal system in Canada discriminates against men. (too broad)	Single fathers who seek custody of their children are often treated unfairly in family court.
My children won't eat peas, broccoli, or spinach. (too narrow)	Getting young children to eat a balanced diet is not an easy task.
Cars should be banned from city streets. (too broad)	Cars should be banned from the downtown core from 7:00 a.m. to 7:00 p.m.

Exercise 7.3*

Read through each of the following paragraphs, then underline the topic sentence.

1.   The third consideration is perhaps the most important. Canada makes no economic sense. There may be excellent reasons for Canada's existence historically, socially, culturally, and even geographically, but the lines of trade and commerce flow north–south. If a government's chief concern is the economy, that government will naturally draw the country closer and closer to the United States, cinching in those belts of commerce that bind Canada to her southern partner. Only governments whose major goals are cultural or social will loosen the longitudinal ties and seek east–west bonds.

2.   Winston Churchill said, "Golf is a game whose aim it is to hit a very small ball into an even smaller hole with weapons singularly ill-designed for the purpose." It has been said that baseball is an activity where 14 men stand idly by while two play catch. In fact, all sports can be made ridiculous because the essence of sport is rules. If you really want to put a ball into a hole in the ground, it's very easy to do: pick it up, carry it to the hole, and drop it in. The fun in golf, as in all sports, is that the task is made challenging by very rigid and complex regulations. Reduced to its essential, sport is the attempt by one person or group to win dominance over another while encumbered by complicated rules. The rules in a game like hockey or baseball are enormously complex, while those in soccer or bowling are less so; however, the objective of all games is the same as the objective of war. Luckily, civilized humans have a love of rules and laws, and can take out their aggressions within the very rigid confines of the rule book.

3.   Seen by scanning electron microscope, our taste buds look as huge as volcanoes on Mars, while those of a shark are beautiful mounds of pastel-colored tissue paper—until we remember what they're used for. In reality, taste buds are exceedingly small. Adults have about 10,000, grouped by theme (salt, sour, sweet, bitter), at various sites in the mouth. Inside each one, about fifty taste cells busily relay information to a neuron, which will alert the brain. Not much tasting happens in the center of the tongue, but there are also incidental taste buds on the palate, pharynx, and tonsils, which cling like bats to the damp, slimy walls of a cave. Rabbits have 17,000 taste buds, parrots only about 400, and cows 25,000. What are they tasting? Maybe a cow needs that many to enjoy a relentless diet of grass.

Ackerman, Diane. *A Natural History of the Senses.* New York: Vintage-Random House, 1991. 138.

4.   Scholarly explanations of humor fall into three major categories. According to superiority theories, we laugh at the henpecked husband and the woman hit with a banana cream pie because the misfortunes of others make us feel better about our own lot. The 17th century philosopher Thomas Hobbes, for example, described laughter as a result of the "sudden glory" of increased self-esteem at the expense of others. Incongruity theories . . . stress the cognitive jolt of bringing together unrelated ideas. Thus the infant who chuckles when Mommy eats the baby food is savoring the incongruity of a grown woman making a fool of herself. Finally, tension-relief theories attribute our laughter to a sudden release from strain. Freud argued that our jokes, like our dreams, allow pent-up sexual and aggressive images to suddenly leap into consciousness, albeit in a disguised form.

"What's So Funny?" *Psychology Today* June 1978: 101.

5.   "Why do you want it?" This should be the first question a good computer salesperson asks a prospective customer. With the huge variety of computers now on the market, the determining factor in a purchase should be the job the machine will be expected to do. While a network card, premium audio system, and 21-inch VDT are great for watching movies, a user who wants a basic word processor would be throwing away money to buy them. Home users and small businesses often get carried away with the desire for gigantic memory capacity, lightning speed, and high resolution capability, but these are advertising gimmicks rather than useful purchases for most small users. On the other hand, it can be a costly error for a buyer to underestimate long-term computer needs and buy a machine that must be upgraded or replaced in a year.

Now compare your answers with ours on page 516.

GO TO WEB

EXERCISE 7.1

Exercise 7.4

Each of the following thesis statements contains a subject and main points. Working with a partner or in a small group, develop the main points of each thesis statement into effective topic sentences.

1. Volunteering is a valuable addition to a college education because it provides work experience, develops professional contacts, and enhances self-esteem.
2. Unemployment, poverty, and loneliness are factors that may lead to depression.
3. Canadians emigrate to other countries for three main reasons: a warmer climate, better job opportunities, and new cultural experiences.

Exercise 7.5

For each of the thesis statements below, develop the main points into effective topic sentences. Make sure each topic sentence you write introduces the topic clearly, makes a point about the topic, and is neither too broad nor too narrow.

1. The driver who caused your accident last weekend was probably one of four types: a road hog, a tailgater, a speed demon, or a Sunday driver.

2. There are three types of supervisor in this world: the good, the bad, and mine.

3. The thought of moving to the country is attractive to many city dwellers because of the slower pace, the healthier environment, and the closer-knit communities.

Developing the Topic

Once you've written your topic sentence, the next step is to develop it. An adequately developed paragraph gives enough supporting information to make the topic completely clear to the readers. Unless you are writing from a detailed outline listing all the supporting material you need, it's time to focus once again on your intended audience. Put yourself in your readers' place.

- How much information do your readers already have about your topic?
- Are they inclined to agree or disagree with you?
- What do your readers need to know to understand your point clearly?

There are seven ways to develop a topic. Not all will be appropriate in every case, and some will be more effective than others. Let your topic and your audience guide you in choosing the most appropriate kind(s) of development.

1. Tell a story. Everyone loves to read a story if it's relevant and well told. An anecdote can be an effective way to help your readers not only understand your idea but also remember it. Below are two examples that illustrate the use of narration to develop a topic.

I first experienced culture shock when I travelled to Egypt. I was walking down the main street on the day of my arrival when it suddenly struck me that the crowds on the street were stepping aside to make way for me. It was 1980, and my height, blond hair, and blue eyes were so unusual to the Egyptians that I was an object of intense curiosity. The staring and pointing followed me everywhere. Finally, unable to cope any longer with being constantly on display, I took refuge in the Canadian Embassy and spent a couple of hours quietly leafing through back issues of *Maclean's* magazine.

Imagine that two accountants do similar jobs for similar companies. One day they make the same discovery: with almost no chance of getting caught, they can embezzle a large sum from their employers. They can both use the money to pay off debts or buy a new car. The first accountant right away says to himself, "It's wrong to steal," and never considers the matter again. But the second accountant is torn. She, too, knows that stealing is wrong, but she's tempted and at first decides to go ahead. Then she decides she won't, and then that she will. Finally, after weeks of agonizing, she decides not to embezzle. Who is the morally better person?

Hurka, Thomas. "Should Morality Be a Struggle? Ancient vs. Modern Ideas about Ethics." *Principles: Short Essays about Ethics.* Toronto: Harcourt Brace, 1994. 83.

Exercise 7.6

Using a story to develop your topic, write a paragraph on one of following, or choose a topic of your own.

1. A road-rage experience
2. The day I became an adult
3. The customer is not always right
4. How not to treat employees
5. Defusing a tense situation

2. Define your topic. A definition paragraph explains and clarifies the meaning of a word or idea. Use the definition paragraph to explain a term that may be unfamiliar to your readers. (Write your own definition, please. Quoting from a dictionary is an overused and boring way to start a paragraph.) Below are definitions of two terms that the authors wanted to be sure their readers would understand from the *writers'* point of view.

Culture shock is the inability to understand or cope with experiences one has never encountered before. It commonly affects travellers who journey to lands whose climate, food, language, and customs are alien to the traveller. In addition to confusion and anxiety, culture shock may even produce physical symptoms: chills, fever, trembling, and faintness.

A hybrid is a cross between two established varieties of plant, animal, . . . or technology. The hybrid bicycle, for example, combines the features of a road bike with those of an off-road bike to produce a comfortable and efficient bicycle for short distance cycling. For most people, however, the word "hybrid" signifies a fuel-efficient, low-emission automobile. Hybrid car technology combines a gasoline or diesel internal combustion engine with a battery-powered electric motor. Its objective is to maximize the best properties of both the gas engine and the electric motor.

Howerth, Sara R. "The Gas-Electric Hybrid Demystified." 207.

You should include a definition, too, if you're using a familiar term in an unusual way. Here Martin Luther King defines what he means by "the length of life":

> Now let us notice first the length of life. I have said this is the dimension of life in which the individual is concerned with developing his inner powers. It is that dimension of life in which the individual pursues personal ends and ambitions. This is perhaps the selfish dimension of life, and there is such a thing as moral and rational self-interest. If one is not concerned about himself he cannot be totally concerned about other selves.

King, Martin Luther, Jr. "The Dimensions of a Complete Life." *The Measure of a Man*. 1959. Philadelphia: Pilgrim Press, 1969.

Exercise 7.7

Choose one of the following topics (or select one of your own) and write a paragraph in which you develop the topic by defining it.

1. Burnout
2. A good boss (employee, customer, colleague)
3. An extrovert (introvert)
4. A great artist (musician, actor, writer, etc.)
5. A bad habit

---

3. Use examples. Giving examples is probably the most common method of developing an idea and supporting a statement. Readers can become confused or suspicious when they read unsupported statements of "fact," opinion, or ideas. One of the best ways to support your topic is by providing clear, relevant examples.

Sometimes, as in the paragraph below, one extended example is enough to allow your readers to see clearly what you mean.

> Culture shock can affect anyone, even a person who never leaves home. My grandfather was perfectly content to be an accountant until he retired, and was confident that his company would need his services for the foreseeable future. Computers were "silly toys" and modern business practices just "jargon" and "a new fad." When he was laid off four years before his retirement, he went into shock. It wasn't just the layoff; it was the speed of change— the idea that he was stranded in a new and unfamiliar culture for which he was unprepared, and in which he had no useful role.

Sometimes a number of examples may be necessary to develop a point, as in this paragraph.

All sports may be reduced to a few basic skills, which, if learned properly at the outset and drilled until they are instinctive, lead to success. Tennis is no exception; however, few people seem willing to spend the time needed to master the basics. Having been shown the proper grip and swing for a forehand, backhand, and serve, my students seem to feel they can qualify for Wimbledon. The basics are not learned that easily. Many tennis schools are now using a system first developed in Spain that is very successful in establishing the correct stroke in new players: for the first month of lessons, they aren't allowed to use a tennis ball. For that first month, correct positioning, proper swing, footwork, and technique are drilled without any of the distractions of keeping score, winning or losing, or chasing errant balls. That's how important the basics are to winning tennis.

Green, Brian. "How to Play Winning Tennis." 173.

Exercise 7.8

Using examples to develop your topic, write a paragraph on one of following, or choose a topic of your own.

1. Parents and privacy
2. Computers: the biggest time-wasters of modern life
3. Childless by choice
4. Adjusting to life away from home
5. The incompetence (incomprehensibility) of men (women)

---

4. Use a quotation or paraphrase. Occasionally you will find that someone else—an expert in a particular field, a well-known author, or a respected public figure—has said what you want to say better than you could ever hope to say it. Relevant and authoritative quotations, as long as they are kept short and are not used too frequently, are useful in developing your topic. Two sources of quotations on practically any subject are *John Robert Colombo's Famous Lasting Words: Great Canadian Quotations* (Vancouver: Douglas & McIntyre, 2000) and *Bartlett's Familiar Quotations* (http://www.bartleby.com/101/). **Never forget to acknowledge the source of your quotation!** In the paragraph below, the writer introduces his topic with a thought-provoking quotation.

"Although one can experience real pain from culture shock, it is also an opportunity for redefining one's life objectives. Culture shock can make one develop a better understanding of oneself and stimulate personal creativity." As with any experience that forces us out of our comfort zone and shatters our complacency, culture shock can be an opportunity for growth and development, as this quotation from the College of Education at San Diego State University makes clear. The trick is to recognize this unpleasant experience as a starting point for personal change. Here's an opportunity to re-examine our preconceptions about our place in society, about our interactions with others, even about the path we have chosen to take in life: has it become a rut?

A **paraphrase** is a summary in your own words of someone else's idea. Remember to indicate whose idea you are paraphrasing, the way the author of "The Myth of Canadian Diversity" does in the following paragraph.

... [O]ur much-discussed ethnic differences are overstated. Although Canada is an immigrant nation and Canadians spring from a variety of backgrounds, a recent study from the C.D. Howe Institute says that the idea of a "Canadian mosaic"—as distinct from the American "melting pot"—is a fallacy. In *The Illusion of Difference*, University of Toronto sociologists Jeffrey Reitz and Raymond Breton show that immigrants to Canada assimilate as quickly into the mainstream society as immigrants to the United States do. In fact, Canadians are less likely than Americans to favour holding on to cultural differences based on ethnic background. If you don't believe Mr. Reitz and Mr. Breton, visit any big-city high school, where the speech and behaviour of immigrant students just a few years in Canada is indistinguishable from that of any fifth-generation classmate. (321–22)

Exercise 7.9

Choose one of the following topics (or select one of your own) and write a paragraph in which you develop the topic by using quotations and/or paraphrase.

1. The most inspiring (uninspiring) teacher you have known
2. Everything I know I learned from my mother (father, brother, etc.)
3. A favourite book (movie, website)
4. The wisdom of children
5. Father knows (does not know) best

5. Use a comparison. A comparison shows similarities between things; it shows how two different things are alike in a particular way or ways. If you

have a difficult or abstract topic to explain, try comparing it to something that is familiar to your readers, as this writer does.

Being left on your own in a foreign land is a bit like being forced to play a card game when you're the only one who doesn't know the rules. As the stakes get higher and the other players' excitement and enjoyment increase, you get correspondingly more frustrated and miserable. Finally, in desperation, you want to throw your cards on the table, absorb your losses, and go home.

In this next paragraph, the writer uses an **analogy**—an extended comparison—between a date and a car to make the point both clear and interesting.

The economy-model date features cramped conditions and a lack of power. The econo-date thinks that his personality can make up for the fact that you never go anywhere except for walks and never do anything that costs money. He tends to be shy, quiet, and about as much fun as an oil leak. It's not that he doesn't have money to spend; it's that he doesn't use any imagination or creativity to compensate for his lack of cash.

Exercise 7.10

Choose one of the following topics (or select one of your own) and write a paragraph in which you develop the topic by using comparison.

1. The modern workplace
2. E-mail
3. Two consumer products
4. Type A (Type B) personalities
5. Engineering (or computer science, arts, or nursing) students

6. **Explain steps or stages in a process.** Sometimes the most effective way to develop the main idea of your paragraph is by explaining how something occurs or is done—that is, by relating the series of steps involved. Make sure you break the process down into its component parts and detail the steps logically and precisely.

The first sign of culture shock is usually anxiety. The traveller feels uncomfortable and ill at ease; nothing looks, smells, sounds, or tastes familiar. Next, he may become resentful, even angry, and withdraw from his new surroundings, seeking isolation in safe, familiar territory—his room. Unfortunately, solitude reinforces anxiety and makes the situation worse. Over time, the victim of culture shock may begin to perceive the environment not as "strange but neutral" but as "strange and hostile." Friendly interaction with others and positive experiences in the new culture are the cure, but one is not likely to encounter either while cocooned in a small boarding house or hotel room. Fortunately, most travellers find that culture shock diminishes with rest. As anxiety lessens, curiosity grows, and they begin to venture out to participate in the life of the new country. In extreme cases, however, travellers suffering from culture shock can develop flu-like symptoms: fever, chills, sleeplessness, and a debilitating loss of energy. When these symptoms strike, it's time to call home for moral support and encouragement to get out and enjoy the sights and scenes one has travelled so far to experience.

In writing a process paragraph, you need to pay particular attention to transitions, which are discussed in the next chapter, or you'll leave your readers gasping in the dust as you gallop through your explanation. The paragraph below illustrates a simple yet effective use of transitions.

In 1983, a Harvard Medical School team led by Dr. Howard Green found a revolutionary way to repair burned skin. Here is how it is done. Doctors cut up a small patch of skin donated by a patient, treat it with enzymes, then spread it thinly onto a culture medium. After only ten days, colonies of skin cells begin linking up into sheets, which can then be chopped up and used to make further sheets. In twenty-four days, enough skin will be produced to cover an entire human body. About ten days later, the gauze is removed, and the skin soon grows into a surface much smoother and more natural-looking than the rough one a normal skin-graft usually leaves.

Ackerman, Diane. *A Natural History of the Senses.* New York: Vintage-Random House, 1990. 69–70.

Exercise 7.11

Choose one of the following topics (or select one of your own) and write a paragraph in which you develop the topic by describing the series of steps or stages involved in the process.

1. Career planning
2. Buying a used car
3. Understanding women (men)
4. Writing a business report
5. Getting out of debt

7. **Provide specific details.** Concrete, specific, descriptive details can be an effective way to develop your main idea. In the paragraph below, the writer uses specific detail to describe treatment for culture shock.

Culture shock can be alleviated by taking action to reduce the impact of the cause, and then treating each of the symptoms separately. Prevention is the best cure: introduce yourself gradually to a new environment. Explore in small stages, while keeping contact with safe and familiar surroundings. Don't plunge into the bazaar within an hour of your arrival in Marrakesh, but begin your exploration in the Western quarter and gradually expose yourself to the sights, sounds, and smells of areas that seem threateningly foreign. If you should come down with symptoms of shock, go to bed, stay warm, drink lots of bottled water, and sleep as much as you can. When you begin to feel better, take things slowly and avoid stressful situations where you have to make decisions or confront the unexpected. A guided bus tour of the city is a good way to begin familiarizing yourself with a new physical and cultural environment, and discovering what's available that you want to explore.

In some paragraphs, numerical facts or statistics can be used to support your point effectively. However, in keeping with Benjamin Disraeli's immortal comment ("There are three kinds of lies: lies, damned lies, and statistics"), critical readers tend to be suspicious of statistics. Be very sure that your facts are correct and that your statistics are current.

Canadians are great travellers. We not only travel around our own country, exploring every nook and cranny from Beaver Creek in the Yukon Territory to Bay Bulls in Newfoundland, but we also can be found touring around every other country on Earth. Statistics Canada reports that we take about 150 million overnight trips a year within our own borders. Abroad, we favour our next door neighbour by a wide margin above other destinations, averaging around 15 million overnight trips a year to the United States. The United Kingdom is our second favourite destination, with over 800,000 visits, followed by Mexico (over 600,000) and France (over 400,000). Of the Caribbean islands, Cuba is our favourite winter escape. Cuba ranks fifth overall, with 350,000 annual visits by Canadians. Of the Asian nations, Hong Kong, in tenth place, tops the list with 115,000 visits. Australia, in fourteenth place with about 90,000 visits, ranks just ahead of Japan. Rounding Canada's population off to about 30 million, we can use these figures to deduce that, on average, a Canadian travels within Canada five times every year and takes a trip abroad twice in three years.

Exercise 7.12

Using specific details to develop your topic, write a paragraph on one of following, or choose a topic of your own.

1. A web page
2. A migraine headache

3. The myth of the shorter work week
4. The best team in basketball (baseball, football, soccer, lacrosse)
5. Money can't buy happiness

In writing your own paragraphs, you will often need to use more than one method of development to explain your point. The seven methods described in this chapter can be used in any combination you choose.

How Do You End a Paragraph?

A good paragraph doesn't just end; like a door, it should close firmly, with a "click." Finish your paragraph with a statement that serves either as a **clincher**—an unmistakable and appropriate conclusion—or a **transition** to the new idea that will be developed in the next paragraph.

Exercise 7.13

Turn back to the paragraphs in Exercise 7.1 (pages 83–84). Reread each one and decide whether it ends with a clincher or a transition sentence.

Exercise 7.14

To stretch your imagination and improve your mastery of the kinds of support you can choose from to develop a topic, write a paragraph on one of the following topics, using two or more methods of development. Your target audience is your instructor and your classmates.

1. Getting along with coworkers
2. Performance appraisal
3. Training a new employee
4. Life is like a game of _____
5. Canadians don't appreciate how lucky they are

8

Keeping Your Readers with You

As you write, remember that it is your responsibility to make it as easy as possible for your readers to follow you through your essay. Unity, coherence, and tone can make the difference between a paper that confuses or annoys your readers and one that enlightens and pleases them.

Unity

Unity means "oneness." The contents of a paragraph must relate to a single main idea. All supporting sentences in the paragraph must clearly and directly relate to the topic sentence of that paragraph.

Achieving unity requires care. Your job is to develop the points that you have set out to make, not other points that may occur to you as you write. (The time to set down whatever happens to come to mind is in the prewriting stage, not the paragraph development stage.) Any material that does not clearly support the topic sentence should be deleted or moved to another paragraph in the essay—assuming, of course, that it is directly relevant there.

Take a look at the following paragraph. It contains several sentences that spoil the unity of the paragraph because they do not clearly relate to the topic.

(1) I knew I wanted to return to school, but did I want to be a full-time or a part-time student? (2) The major consideration was, not surprisingly, money. (3) If I chose to go to college full-time, then I would have to give up my full-time job. (4) The resulting loss of income would reduce my buying power to zero. (5) Even the tuition fees would be beyond my reach. (6) Also, my choice of program would be a difficult decision, because I still wasn't sure which career path to follow. (7) My other option was part-time education. (8) If I kept my full-time job,

I could at least pay for food, rent, and a modest amount of clothing. (9) Also, I could afford the tuition fees. (10) Going to school part-time costs less per year because the expenditure is spread over a longer period of time than it is in the full-time program. (11) Therefore, I chose to educate myself part-time, through continuing education courses. (12) While working, I could learn new skills in my spare time. (13) My career choice would still be in doubt, but I would have a longer time in which to make up my mind. (14) Money is scarce for a full-time, self-supporting student, but as a part-time student I could have the best of both worlds: a steady income and a college education.

Draw a line through the sentences that do not logically and directly support the topic of the paragraph: the writer's decision whether to be a full-time or part-time student.[1]

Exercise 8.1*

The paragraphs below contain some irrelevant sentences that disrupt unity. Read each paragraph and then, with a partner, find and cross out the sentences that don't belong. Answers for exercises in this chapter begin on page 517.

1.   (1) A good pizza consists of a combination of succulent ingredients. (2) First, you prepare the foundation, the crust, which may be thick or thin, depending on your preference. (3) I like my crusts thick and chewy. (4) The crust is spread with a layer of basil- and oregano-flavoured tomato sauce. (5) Next, a rich smorgasbord of toppings—pepperoni, mushrooms, green peppers, bacon, anchovies—should be scattered over the tomato sauce. (6) *Smorgasbord* is a Swedish word meaning a buffet meal; *pizza* is Italian in origin. (7) Last of all, a double-thick blanket of grated mozzarella cheese should be spread over all. (8) Pizza is simple to make—all you need is dough, tomato sauce, vegetables, sausage, herbs, and cheese—but the combination has an unbeatable taste.

2.   (1) Keeping a job is not easy in a tight market in which well-educated job-seekers are plentiful. (2) Here are a couple of hints you will find helpful in maintaining your "employed" status. (3) First, you should not only apply your specialized knowledge on the job every day, but also continually update it by taking seminars and evening courses to enhance your skills. (4) Doing your job effectively is difficult without becoming burned out. (5) Second, good communication—with the public, your fellow workers, and your supervisor—is perhaps the most important factor in keeping you on the payroll. (6) Upgrading your education and improving your communication skills are your best defences against the pink slip.

---

[1]The sentences that you should have crossed out because they do not belong in this paragraph and detract from its unity are 6, 12, and 13.

3.   (1) Comedies are my favourite way to relax. (2) Horror films terrify me, and adventures become tedious after the tenth chase, but comedies entertain and refresh me after a long shift at work. (3) Woody Allen pictures, especially the early farces, help me to take my mind off the stress of the day. (4) For example, *Bananas*, a satire about American politics in the 1960s, is more relaxing for me than a double martini. (5) It's also less fattening, and I've been trying to give up drinking. (6) *Sleeper*, a futuristic spoof, has me laughing, on average, twice a minute. (7) Perhaps my favourite, however, is *Annie Hall*. (8) After viewing it, I am so weak with laughter that I can go to sleep within minutes. (9) Now that all of Allen's comedies are available on DVD, I never need to feel tense and worn out for longer than it takes to insert a disc.

4.   (1) My department's job is to produce reports. (2) We research and prepare year-end reports, stockholders' reports, reports on the competition, on the customers, on the suppliers, and on just about everything else. (3) We think of ourselves as creative rather than technical writers because there is no future in our company for anyone who is critical or who dares to tell the truth if truth isn't what the senior managers want to hear. (4) Instead of fixing the problem, they punish the person who tells them what's wrong; that is, they "shoot the messenger." (5) I believe this saying originated in ancient days, long before there were guns, so presumably the original idea was "knife the messenger" or "behead the messenger." (6) If employees understand this management practice, however, they can protect themselves. (7) For example, our department has developed three rules to help us produce reports that are guaranteed a favourable reception. (8) First, teamwork is essential; without it, you have no one else to blame. (9) Second, when you don't know what you're doing, do it neatly. (10) Third, if at first you don't succeed, destroy all evidence that you ever tried. (11) With these rules to guide us, our department has survived three new managers in the past two and a half years.

5.   (1) The office manager who demands that all employees not only arrive on time but actually get in early to demonstrate their enthusiasm and drive is actually damaging productivity. (2) Such a manager is, of course, always in the office at least an hour early herself, and because she attributes her success to this habit, she demands it of others. (3) Not everyone is suited to an early start. (4) Individual biorhythms vary widely, and some employees may be better suited to demonstrating their keenness by staying late at night. (5) The old adage "The early bird gets the worm" is based on some truth, but there are many exceptions. (6) Besides, what office worker wants a worm, anyway? (7) For that matter, there are lots of other sayings and aphorisms that can apply just as readily to the situation. (8) If your manager cites this tired old phrase as her justification for demanding unreasonably early hours, you may want to point out that another saying is equally true: "The second mouse gets the cheese."

Coherence

Coherence means "sticking together." The sentences within each paragraph need to cohere, as do the paragraphs within an essay. If your sentences and paragraphs are not coherent, your reader will have great difficulty trying to fit together your bits of information to make sense of the whole. Sorting out sentences as if they were pieces of a puzzle is not the reader's job. It is the writer's responsibility to put the pieces together to form a complete and clear picture.

Coherence is achieved in two ways.

1. First, you need to arrange the sentences in each paragraph according to an organizational principle. Remember the options you chose from to arrange ideas in Chapter 4, "Managing the Main Points"? You should arrange your development within paragraphs in the same ways: chronological, climactic, logical, or, infrequently, random order. (Turn to pages 57–59 to review these.)
2. Second, you achieve coherence by providing **transitions**. Transitions are connections between one idea and the next within a paragraph, and between one paragraph and the next within an essay. Why are transitions needed? Read the paragraph below and you'll see clearly that something is missing. The paragraph has adequate development, but no transitions.

We were bored one day. We didn't know what to do. It was Friday. We thought about going to the library. No one really wanted to do schoolwork. We went to the mall. For a short time we window-shopped. We discussed what to do. It was agreed that we would drive to the American side of the border. We would do our shopping. It was a short drive. We went to a discount mall. The bargains were great. We spent much more money than we intended to. We went home. We discovered that with the American exchange, prices were better at home. We should have gone to the library.

Not very easy to read, is it? Readers are jerked abruptly from point to point until, battered and bruised, they finally reach the end. This kind of writing is unfair to readers. It makes them do too much of the work. The ideas may all be there, but the readers have to figure out for themselves how the ideas fit together. After a couple of paragraphs like the one above, even the most patient readers can become annoyed.

Now read the same paragraph, rewritten with transitions.

Last Friday we were so bored we didn't know what to do. We thought about going to the library, but no one really wanted to study, so we went to the mall and window-shopped for a while. After a long discussion about what to do next, we agreed to drive to the American side of the border for some serious shopping. A short drive later, we arrived at a discount mall, where the bargains were so great that we spent much more money than we had intended. Finally, we returned home, where we discovered that, with the American exchange, prices were better at home after all. We should have gone to the library.

In this paragraph, readers are gently guided from one point to the next. By the time they reach the conclusion, they know not only what ideas the writer had in mind, but also how the ideas fit together to form a unit. The transitions make the reader's job easy and rewarding.

You can choose from an array of strategies to improve the coherence of your writing. There are five techniques to master. Be sure to use a variety of these techniques every time you write. Nothing improves the polish of your prose more than the use of coherence strategies.

1. Repetition. Repetition focuses the reader's attention on an idea and creates a thread of meaning that runs through a paragraph or a paper, tying the whole thing together. Don't overdo it, though.

2. Synonyms. Frequent repetition of a key word can become monotonous after a while. You can keep the reader focused on the idea by using synonyms—different words that convey the same meaning.

3. Pronoun references. Another way of maintaining the focus but varying the wording is to use appropriate pronouns to refer to a key noun. (This technique involves pronoun–antecedent agreement, a topic covered in Chapter 32.)

4. Parallel structure. Phrasing your sentences in parallel form helps to maintain focus, reinforces the unity of your thoughts, and adds emphasis. Parallelism adds "punch" to your writing. (More punch is served in Chapter 26.)

5. Transitional words and phrases. Transitional words and phrases show the relationships between points in a paragraph as well as between paragraphs in an essay. They act like tape, sticking together the elements of a paragraph or a paper so your reader does not fall between the cracks. Use them the way you use turn signals on a car: to tell the person following you where you're going.

Here are some transitional phrases that will help make your writing read smoothly.

Transitional Function	Words/Phrases Used
1. To show a time relationship between points	• first, second, third • now, simultaneously, concurrently, at this point, while • before, to begin, previously • after, following this, then, later, next • finally, last, subsequently • during, meanwhile, presently, from time to time, sometimes
2. To add an idea or example to the previous point	• and, in addition, also, furthermore, besides, moreover, for the same reason • another, similarly, equally important, likewise • for example, for instance, in fact
3. To show contrast between points	• although, nevertheless, on the other hand, whereas, while • but, however, instead, nonetheless • in contrast, on the contrary, in spite of, despite
4. To show a cause-and-effect relationship between points	• since, because, thus, therefore, hence • as a result, consequently, accordingly
5. To emphasize or repeat a significant point	• in fact, indeed, certainly, undoubtedly • in other words, as I have said, that is to say
6. To summarize or conclude	• in brief, on the whole, in summary, in short • therefore, as a result, last, finally

The paragraph below illustrates the use of all five coherence strategies to achieve unity. As you read, pay particular attention to the writer's use of repetition and parallelism.

While the Internet can be a useful tool for some businesses, studies have shown that in most workplaces it is a time-wasting drain on resources. As a result of one such study, Deloitte and Touche have issued a report pointing out the "five G's": risks of allowing employees unsupervised Internet activity during business hours. A company risks Giving, handing trade or business secrets over to the competition or the general public. A company risks Gawking, time-wasting employee fascination with particular sites, including pornography. A company risks Gambling, an increasingly common and potentially addictive lure for surfers. A company risks Goofing off, the pointless surfing of sites that are unrelated to the task at hand. A company risks Grabbing, the downloading of virus-infected material and copyrighted software. To counter the five G's, Deloitte and Touche recommend that companies establish clear policy on Internet use.

Owner Manager Advisor newsletter. *Globe and Mail* 25 Jan. 1998: B15.

Exercise 8.2*

Working with a partner, identify the transitional words and phrases that create coherence in each of the sentence groups below.

1. The spruce budworm threatens B.C.'s forests, killing trees that have resisted all other predators. Therefore, governments at both the local and provincial levels have begun a controlled burn program.
2. The two women spent the whole day tramping from car dealer to car dealer. Finally, they found a used Toyota they could live with, but the price was higher than they had hoped to pay.
3. There are many jokes about cats. Unfortunately, however, in most of them the cat is either very unhappy or dead.
4. There are those who think Quebec would thrive as a separate state. On the other hand, some feel that its economic viability depends on a close relationship with the rest of Canada.
5. Although we fear the size and power of our big banks, we must admit that they serve us well when compared with the banking institutions of other countries. For example, Canadian banks are second only to Japanese banks, and ahead of those in the United States and Germany, in the number of ATMs per person they provide. In addition, they lead all three of these countries in the number of full-service branches per capita.

Exercise 8.3

In each of the following sentences, supply transitional words or phrases that help the meaning become clearer and make the sentence more coherent. When you've finished, exchange exercises with another student and check each other's answers. If you disagree with any of your partner's choices, explain why.

1. My first impression of my supervisor was that he was aloof and arrogant; _____, I discovered I was wrong. He was painfully shy.

2. Many bestsellers have become pathetic movies, now long forgotten. _____ many poor novels have been turned into movie classics, such as *Gone with the Wind*, that last forever.

3. Many sports were discovered by accident. _____, one day at Rugby school in the 1830s, an English schoolboy, during a game of rugby, threw the ball overhand down the field. Football (as we call it in North America) was born.

4. Architecture in the 20th century has become more streamlined, geometrical, and uniform. _____, it has become monotonous.

5. The Bush administration believes that an expensive and unproven missile defence system is needed to protect North American from a non-existent threat. _____, Canadians disagree.

Exercise 8.4*

Read the paragraphs below and identify the transitional strategies that contribute to coherence. Both paragraphs contain examples of all five techniques listed on page 102.

1. Finally, developing the proper attitude is the true key to winning tennis. I define winning tennis as playing the game to the best of your ability, hitting the ball as well as you know you can, and enjoying the feeling of practised expertise. Winning tennis has nothing to do with beating an opponent. Naturally, if you play winning tennis by learning the basics, practising sufficiently, and concentrating, you'll win many matches, but that is the reward of playing well, not the reason for playing well. People who swear and throw their racquets when they lose are very useful; they are the most satisfying players to trounce. But I don't understand why they play a game that causes them such pain. Tennis players who enjoy the feel of a well hit ball and the satisfaction of a long, skilfully played rally are winners, regardless of the score.

2. Travel abroad offers you the best education you can get. For one thing, travel is a course in communication skills. In order to function in a foreign language, you must practise every aspect of the communication process from body language to pronunciation. In fact, just making yourself understood is

a lesson in creativity, a seminar in sign language, and a lab in communication theory. Another educational aspect of travel is the history, geography, and culture that you learn about almost unconsciously. Everywhere you go, you encounter memorable evidence of historical events you may dimly recall from school, and you are continually confronted by the practical realities of geography as you try to find your way around. As for culture, no book or course of study could provide you with the understanding and appreciation of another society that living in it can. A third way in which travel educates is through teaching you about yourself. Your ability—or inability—to cope with unfamiliar customs, with language difficulties, and with the inevitable problems of finding transportation and accommodation will tell you more than you might want to know about yourself. Without the safety net of family and friends, perhaps without even the security of knowing where you'll spend the night, you develop self-reliance or you go home. Either way, you learn valuable lessons. While you may not get a diploma from Travel U., you'll learn more about the world, about people, and about yourself than you will in any classroom.

Now compare your answers to ours on pages 517–18.

Exercise 8.5

Now consider the ways coherence strategies can be used to promote the smooth flow of ideas throughout an essay. Identify the transitional techniques used in Bertrand Russell's "What I Have Lived For," on page 6.

Tone

As you write the paragraphs of your paper, be conscious of your **tone**. Your audience, purpose, and subject will all influence the tone you choose, which must be appropriate to all three. The words you use, the examples, quotations, and other supporting materials you choose to help explain your main points—all these contribute to your tone.

When you are trying to explain something to someone, particularly if it's something you feel strongly about, you may be tempted to be highly emotional in your discussion. If you allow yourself to get emotional, chances are you won't be convincing. What will be communicated is the strength of your feelings, not the depth of your understanding or the validity of your opinion. To be clear and credible, you need to restrain your enthusiasm or anger and present your points in a calm, reasonable way.

Here are a few suggestions to help you find and maintain the right tone:

- Be tactful. Avoid phrases such as "Any idiot can see," "No sane person could believe," and "It is obvious that...." What is obvious to you isn't necessarily obvious to someone who has a limited understanding of your subject or who disagrees with your opinion.

- Don't talk down to your readers as though they were children or hopelessly ignorant. Never use sarcasm, profanity, or slang.

- Don't apologize for your interpretation of your subject. Have confidence in yourself. You've thought long and hard about your subject, you've found good supporting material to help explain it, and you believe in its significance. Present your subject in a positive manner. If you hang back, using phrases such as "I may be wrong, but ... " or "I tend to feel that . . . ", your reader won't be inclined to give your points the consideration they deserve. Keep your reader in mind as you write, and your writing will be both clear and convincing.

The following paragraph is an example of inappropriate tone. The writer is enthusiastic about the topic, but the tone is arrogant, bossy, and tactless rather than persuasive.

It is time that governments at all levels did something completely out of character: take action. We need laws requiring the addition of 10 percent ethanol to gasoline. Ethanol burns cleaner than gas and also boosts octane, so it's completely obvious that the oil companies don't have to put so many poisonous additives in the gas to make our already too powerful cars go even faster. For another thing, anybody who has done any reading knows that ethanol is made out of corn, which is grown on farms and is a renewable resource. Growing it will make farmers happy, and drivers should also be cheerful because it can be produced for less than the outrageous prices we pay for straight gasoline. Adding 10 percent of the cheaper fuel should bring pump prices down, although I'm sure the oil companies will find a way to gouge the consumer. Obviously, the government is going to have to pass laws forcing the oil companies to add ethanol because there's no way these corporate creeps are going to do what is good for the environment and the economy at the expense of lining their own pockets. However, relying on government to do the right thing is just as precarious a proposition; I wouldn't hold my breath.

Now read the paragraph below, which argues the same point but in a courteous, tactful way.

Legislation requiring the addition of ethanol to gasoline is both sensible and overdue. The addition of 10 percent ethanol to the gasoline that is sold at the pump is sensible for two reasons. First, it makes the fuel that is burned in our cars and trucks cleaner. Ethanol burns hotter than gasoline and burns up more of the pollutants, rather than sending them out of the tailpipe. Because it provides a higher octane fuel, ethanol also eliminates the need for some of the toxic additives currently used to boost octane. Second, ethanol is a renewable source of energy that will provide jobs in rural Canada because it is made from corn. At current oil prices, ethanol is cheaper than gasoline, so its addition to our fuel will help to reduce costs for consumers. Why should governments have to legislate such a sensible course of action? The petroleum industry, from exploration to retail, is not about to voluntarily dilute its product—or, more important, its profits—by any amount, let alone 10 percent!

Exercise 8.6*

The following paragraph is a draft written for a general reader. The writer's purpose is to persuade her audience that city dwellers should be more aware of the labour that lies behind every packaged product we eat. Revise the paragraph to make it appropriate to its audience and purpose by deleting or rewording any lapses in tone. Then compare your answer with ours on page 518.

I'm from the city, so I may not know much about the subject, but it seems to me that we urbanites have lost touch with the food we eat. By this I mean, obviously, that we no longer appreciate the farmers and farm workers who supply the food that we enjoy every day. Anyone with half a brain should realize that most of the food we buy is prepackaged in Styrofoam, wrapped in plastic, or precooked and frozen by huge corporations whose goal is to make humongous profits by selling us the packaging, not the contents. Do any urban consumers understand that their ketchup is made from farm-grown tomatoes? Do any advertising-driven supermarket shoppers really think about the fact that those overpackaged frozen pork chops, so irresistible with their sprig of parsley, were once a pig, raised by a farmer? Not only are we ignorant, but also we could care less about the journey our food makes from farm to fridge. My guess is that if you asked most city kids where their food comes from, they'd say, "the food factory."

Revise the following paragraph, adding transitions and moderating its tone.

The armed forces of most nations are trained to be psychopaths. Canada's military personnel face a greater challenge: they need to be schizophrenics. The boot-camp training that recruits undergo, together with instruction in combat and weaponry, produces efficient and remorseless killers—psychopaths. The role of Canada's armed forces over the past 50 years has been to keep the peace. When the Nobel Peace Prize was awarded to the United Nations peacekeeping forces, Canada, as the only nation to have participated in every mission, considered the prize largely hers. Canada's elite forces played a traditional military role as hunters and killers in Afghanistan. Is Canada's military adequately trained for these two contradictory roles? Our country needs highly trained units of efficient psychopaths. The majority of armed forces personnel need training in mediation, conflict resolution, cultural sensitivity, basic medical treatment, and infrastructure repair. This is a hard concept for fans of the military to get through their thick skulls: soldiers trained to prevent violence. Peacekeeping is still the Canadian military's primary function. Canada's armed forces have two roles. Both must be prepared for.

9

Writing Introductions and Conclusions

All of the concepts you have studied so far can be applied to any paragraph. Two paragraphs, however—the first and the last—serve special purposes and need extra care. All too often, the introduction and the conclusion of a paper are dull or clumsy and detract from its effectiveness. But they needn't be dull or clumsy. Here's how to write good ones.

The Introductory Paragraph

The introduction is worth special attention because that's where your readers either sit up and take notice of your paper or sigh and pitch it into the wastebasket.

There are two parts to an introductory paragraph:
1. an attention-getter
2. a thesis statement

Getting and Holding Your Readers' Attention

Your readers must be attracted to your writing or there's no point in putting pen to paper or fingers to keyboard. The attention-getter must be appropriate to the content of your essay and to your intended readers. If your audience is known for a solemn approach to life and your topic is serious (environmental ethics, for instance, or equal opportunity policies in the workplace), then there is no point in leading off with a pun or joke, no matter how witty. Such an opening would be inappropriate and probably offensive to your readers.

Your attention-getter does not have to be a single sentence; in fact, good ones are often several sentences long. Your readers will be committing varying amounts of personal time to reading your writing. You owe it to them to make your opening sentences clear, interesting, and creative.

An effective attention-getter should be followed by an equally effective thesis statement, one that slides smoothly and easily into place. Your readers should be aware only of a unified paragraph, not of two separate parts in your introduction.

Below are eight different kinds of openings you can choose from to get your readers' attention and lead up to your thesis statement. In each of the example paragraphs, note how the attention-getter and the thesis statement are solidly linked to form a unified whole. To demonstrate that you can take many different approaches to a subject, depending on your purpose and your audience, we have used the same subject—physical fitness—in all of the introductions.

1. Spell out the significance of your subject. If your subject's significance can catch your readers' interest, they will want to know more about it, especially if it is a subject that affects them directly.

More and more young people are dying of heart disease. Despite the statistics that say most people in our society are living longer thanks to advances in medicine and surgery, the figures can be misleading. It is a fact that people in their thirties and forties are dying from coronary problems that once threatened people in their fifties and sixties. What has caused this change? Certainly, the increase in stress, the fatigue of overwork, the rise in obesity, and the decline in physical activity are all contributing factors. To combat the risk of cardiovascular disease, we need physical activity. Regular exercise can forestall the ravages of heart disease and promote longevity.

2. Begin with a well-phrased quotation. You might choose a famous statement, a popular slogan, or a common saying. Use a quotation when it sums up your point of view more succinctly and effectively than your own words could. As a rule, you should identify the source of the quotation.

"Who can be bothered?" "I'm much too busy." "I get all the exercise I need at the office." We've all heard excuses like these, excuses for avoiding regular exercise. Modern life, with its distractions and conveniences, tends to make people sedentary and lazy, but the human organism cannot tolerate inactivity and stress indefinitely. Eventually, it begins to break down. Those who want to keep in shape for the challenges of modern life should consider the benefits of working out a few times a week. Regular exercise can rejuvenate the body, refresh the mind, and improve self-confidence.

3. Use a startling statement. Sometimes a surprising remark (not an insult or a false exaggeration) is effective in getting readers' attention. A little-known or striking fact will have the same effect.

After the age of 30, the average North American puts on 10 to 20 kilograms of fat. Presumably, the cause for this startling increase in avoirdupois is a combination of metabolic changes, decreased physical activity, and hundreds of kilos of junk food ingested since childhood. It's difficult to stop the spread of middle-aged corpulence, but experts tell us we *can* resist the rise in flab by reducing our caloric intake and increasing our physical activity. Regular exercise can rejuvenate the body, refresh the mind, and improve self-confidence.

4. Ask a question or two. Questions are often an effective way to encourage interest because your readers will find themselves thinking of answers. Some questions are rhetorical; that is, they will not have specific answers. Others might be answered in your essay.

Have you been feeling sluggish and exhausted lately? Has your blood pressure increased along with your waistline in the past few years? Are you stalled in front of the television set every night with potato chips and a beer? If so, you are probably suffering from a common middle-aged ailment called *flabitis*. This malady strikes most people over 30: they put on weight, have trouble concentrating, tire easily, and prefer watching sports to participating in them. Fortunately, there is a cure for flabitis: a three-times-weekly dose of exercise. With regular exercise, you can rejuvenate your body, refresh your mind, and improve your self-confidence.

5. Begin with a generalization related to your subject. Generalizations can be useful for suggesting the context and scope of your subject. They must, however, be narrowed down carefully to a focused thesis statement.

Until the 20th century, physical exercise was part of the normal workday. Our ancestors were farmers, pioneers, sailors, and so on. Few of our parents, however, made their living by ploughing the land or chopping down trees. Since the early 1900s, the trend in work has been away from physical exertion and toward automation. Today's generation uses technology to reduce physical activity even further: they pick up the phone, ride the elevator, and take the car to the corner store. Modern inactivity has negative consequences that only physical exercise can counter. To sustain good health, sharpen your mental edge, and have fun, you should take up aerobics or sports and use your body in the way it was intended—actively.

6. Challenge a common opinion. Perhaps your readers have also doubted a popular belief. Your thesis statement can assert that an opinion is false, and the body of your paper can contain evidence to support your opposing view.

Physical activity is for kids. Adults don't have time to hit a baseball or run around a field chasing after one, or to do aerobics and lift weights in a gym. They have to earn a living, raise families, and save money for retirement. They can leave exercise to their children. I firmly believed this until one morning when, late for work, I ran after a bus. My heart pounded; my lungs gasped; my head swam. It had been some years since my last stint of exercise, and I realized I wouldn't be around to do my job, support my family, or enjoy retirement unless I got into the habit of doing something physical to maintain my health. Regular exercise can rejuvenate the body, refresh the mind, and broaden one's interests.

7. Begin with a definition. A definition is a good way to begin if you are introducing a key term that you suspect may be unfamiliar to your readers. If the subject of your essay depends on a personal meaning of a term that most people understand in a different way, a definition is essential.

Myocardial infarction: the very term is frightening. It occurs when a person's muscles slacken from disuse, the veins clog up with sticky fats, and the heart has to work too hard to sustain even minor exertion such as raking leaves or shovelling snow. The muscles of the heart become strained to exhaustion or balloon outward because the veins cannot pass blood quickly enough. In plain English, a myocardial infarction is a heart attack. If the victim is lucky enough to survive, physicians prescribe a regimen of less stress, low fat intake, and regular exercise.

8. Describe an interesting incident or tell an anecdote related to your subject. Readers like stories. Keep yours short and to the point by narrating only the highlights. The incident or anecdote you select might be a story from the media, an event involving family or friends, or a personal experience.

Last year, I got a free invitation in the mail to a fitness club. I responded, out of curiosity, but I needed to be convinced. After all, I was 35, had grown a little paunch, and was a bit short of breath on the stairs; 10 years had passed since I had last played sports. My first workout was a nightmare. My joints ached, my muscles throbbed, and my head spun. I was in worse shape than I thought. After a few weeks, those symptoms disappeared, and I began to enjoy myself. My paunch vanished and my muscles toned up. My capacity for concentration increased. Also, I met some new people who have become friends. Obviously, 10 years is too long between workouts, given that exercise not only rejuvenates the body and refreshes the mind but also improves one's social life.

Exercise 9.1

In small groups (four or five people), consider five movies you have all seen within the past year. How did each of these movies begin so that the audience was "locked in"? How do these movie "grabbers" relate to the kinds of attention-getters you have just read?

Exercise 9.2

Each of the following paragraphs is the introductory paragraph of an essay. Work in pairs and, using the strategy given in parentheses, write an appropriate attention-getter for each paragraph.

1. (significance of subject) _____

   _____

   TV commercials that portray unrealistic and unattainable lifestyles should be banned. Although I do not support censorship, I believe there is sufficient evidence of the damage done by these advertisements to justify eliminating them in the name of public interest. The objectionable commercials promote sexual stereotyping, set up unrealistic and dangerous expectations, and encourage irresponsible consumerism.

2. (quotation) _____

   _____

   Every sport has its strange expressions, just as every sport has its devoted fans, its famous teams, and its legendary heroes. A sport that gets very little attention in Canada but is very popular in many parts of the world, especially Commonwealth countries, is cricket. Like the sports that millions of Canadians follow enthusiastically, cricket is an exciting and fascinating game once you become familiar with its rules and style. In fact, it compares very favourably with baseball in skill, pace, and strategy.

3. (startling statement) _____

_____

Canadian roads are overrun by drivers who are a danger to themselves, their passengers, and others on the road. Inept drivers demonstrate their inadequacies in so many ways that it would be impossible to list them all in one short paper. Nevertheless, bad drivers can be broadly categorized as traumatized turtles, careening cowboys, and daydreaming dodos.

4. (question) _____

_____

Arranged marriages are a very important part of my culture. When my family moved to Canada, we left behind many of the traditions and customs that were as natural to us as breathing. However, my parents retained their right to choose a wife for me, even though they are aware that this custom is at odds with the Canadian way of life. Although their decision was at first difficult to accept, I believe there are good reasons that an arranged marriage may be best for me. The decision will be made by mature people in a thoughtful manner, uninfluenced by the enthusiasms of youth; the decision will be made by people who have at heart the best interests of our family, the bride's family, and me; and the decision will be made in accordance with a centuries-old tradition that has proven its success generation after generation.

5. (generalization) _____

_____

My first project manager was the sort of person that nightmares are made of. It's been a year since she was finally transferred to another department, but I still shudder when I recall our six months together. Denise was rude, bossy, and, worst of all, thoughtless.

6. (opinion you challenge) _____

_____

The evidence strongly suggests that overexposure to the sun can cause several forms of cancer at worst and premature aging at best. We can't completely avoid the sun's rays, but there are several measures we can take to prevent the damage that normal outdoor activity might cause. To enjoy the summer without fear, use an effective sun block, cover sensitive skin completely, and limit your time in the sun.

7. (definition) _____

_____

The choice of corrective lenses is an individual matter, but many people go through a tough decision-making process when confronting the issue. In deciding whether contact lenses or eyeglasses are more suitable, one should examine factors such as comfort, convenience, and appearance.

8. (anecdote or incident) _____

_____

Black flies are just one of the pests that make life less than comfortable in Canada during the spring, but they tend to be the most irritating. No method of combatting the pests is foolproof, but there are several methods that can be employed, either singly or together, to repel most of them. The campaign against the black fly begins with protective clothing, follows up with an effective repellent, and goes over the top with the secret weapon: garlic.

Exercise 9.3

With the class divided into four or five teams, consider the following essay topics. Each team will take one of the topics and develop the first sentence of an introductory paragraph for it. The sentence will then be passed in sequence to the next group, who will add a sentence to the paragraph. Continue this exercise until each paragraph contains both an attention-getter and a thesis statement. When each team gets back the paragraph it initiated, it will revise and polish the paragraph, identify the kind of attention-getter that has been developed, and underline the thesis statement. Share the results with the rest of the class. (Keep these paragraphs; you will need them later.)

1. Why I want to be a _____ (fill in your career choice)
2. Why I chose _____ (fill in your school)
3. How not to treat a coworker
4. My favourite TV show
5. The trouble with customers (parents, teachers, etc.)

The Concluding Paragraph

Like the introduction, the conclusion of your paper has a special form. Think of your favourite television sitcom. The last section of the show wraps up the plot, explains any details that might still be unresolved, and leaves you with a satisfying sense that all is well, at least until next week. A concluding paragraph works in a similar way.

The last paragraph of your paper has two functions.
1. It summarizes or reinforces the main points of your paper.
2. It ends with an appropriate memorable statement.

Your **summary statement** should be as concise as you can make it, and must be phrased in such a way that it does not repeat word for word the portion of your thesis statement that identifies the main points. (Note that a summary is not needed in a very short essay.)

A **memorable statement** is a sentence designed to leave your readers feeling satisfied with your essay and perhaps taking away with them something for further thought. Never end without a clincher. Don't just quit writing when your main points are covered, or you'll leave your readers hanging, wondering what to make of it all.

Six strategies you can choose from when you write a concluding paragraph are listed below. Each strategy is illustrated by an example paragraph. Identify the summary and the memorable statement in each conclusion.

1. End with a relevant or thought-provoking quotation. You can use this type of ending in two ways: repeat an earlier quotation but give it a new meaning, or place your subject in a larger context by supplying a new quotation from a recognized authority in the field.

Since I began lifting weights every second day, I have lowered my blood pressure, improved my productivity at work, and made some new friends at the fitness club. I will never be Arnold Schwarzenegger, but that isn't my goal. My muscles are pleasantly sore after a good workout, but as Arnold says, "No pain, no gain." As long as the pain is so little and the gain is so great, I will continue to enjoy my regular workouts.

2. Offer a solution to a problem discussed in your paper. You can plan an organization for your paper that will allow you to resolve a problem or neutralize negative consequences in your conclusion.

I've got the best intentions in the world. I know that exercise benefits me physically, mentally, and emotionally—but I still don't have the time. I didn't, that is, until last month, when I was home from work for a week because I sprained my ankle while walking the dog. That never would have happened if I had been in shape. Since then, I have forced myself to manage my time to allow for a fitness program. Four hours of exercise a week is not a very big investment of time compared with four days of lying on the couch with a painfully swollen foot.

3. End with one or more relevant or thought-provoking questions. The advantage of clinching with a question is that readers tend automatically to pause and consider it: questions stimulate thought. Before they know it, readers will begin to formulate answers to your question—and that activity will make them remember your points. Be sure your question relates directly to your subject.

My life has improved considerably since I took up jogging three times a week: I enjoy better health, less brain-fog, and more confidence. And I'm inspired to continue jogging by the fact that coronary disease runs in my family. My father and grandfather both suffered heart attacks in their fifties. If they had done regular exercise, could they have reduced their chances of coronaries? Would they still be alive today?

4. Point out the value or significance of your subject to your readers. If you emphasize your subject matter at the end of your paper, you can stamp its importance on your readers' memory.

Regular exercise is the best way to stay in shape, be sharp, and feel strong; it is the best way to reduce the risk of arthritis, arterial decay, and heart dysfunction. In a country where the most common cause of mortality is coronary collapse, everyone needs to consider the value of consistent exercise. It is a small daily inconvenience that pays large and long-term rewards.

5. Make a connection to a statement made in your introduction. This strategy provides your readers with a sense of closure. They will recall your earlier statement and feel satisfied that the loose ends have been tied up.

Having exercised now for six months, I can run for the bus without losing my breath, sweating profusely, or feeling dizzy. My body is in better trim; my endurance and confidence on the job have grown. After a lapse of 20 years, I have even taken up bicycling again: I go riding along local bike trails with friends. And now, when my children are playing baseball in the yard, I don't think, "Baseball is for kids." I'm first at the plate. Batter up!

6. End with a suggestion for change or a prediction about the future. Your suggestion for change will influence your readers if they have been persuaded by your arguments. Your predictions of events that might occur should not be misleading or exaggerated, or your readers will be skeptical. Make predictions that are possible and plausible.

If those of us who still prefer junk food, overwork, and television don't shape up, then the incidence of coronary disease will continue to rise. Moderate exercise will benefit body, mind, and spirit. If we follow common sense and change our habits of self-pollution and self-destruction, all of us can lead long, active, and healthy lives.

Exercise 9.4

Each of the following is the concluding paragraph of an essay. Working in pairs, underline the summary statement and write a memorable conclusion. See if you can use a different kind in each paragraph.

1. Both games are enjoyable for spectators and create real enthusiasm among fans. High schools that have chosen soccer have seen no reduction in school spirit or fan support. For educational institutions to make the switch from football is really a "no-lose" proposition because soccer provides dramatic advantages in reducing player injury, increasing player fitness, and shaving thousands of dollars from school expenses.

    _____

    _____

    _____

    _____

2. In retrospect, the NHL lockout was completely avoidable. It had been predicted and discussed for two years prior to the date of the lockout, yet neither side made a meaningful move to prevent it. Only when the 2004–05 season was on the edge of cancellation did the players and owners begin to make concessions that moved them closer to a settlement. Had these moves been made a year or even half a year earlier, the lockout need never have happened. But both sides engaged in brinksmanship in the hope that the other would cave in, and we are all living with the results.

    _____

    _____

    _____

    _____

3. Although the causes of dropout among first-year students are as individual as the students themselves, the effects are easier to categorize. Conflict with parents and others whose expectations have not been met

comes first, followed by a loss of self-esteem. The determination to succeed despite this unfair setback is common, but statistics show that low-paying, dead-end jobs are the norm for the college dropout. The situation is much worse, of course, for those who don't complete high school.

---

4. Employers who need to replace retiring workers with skilled young people must take into account the major differences between the generation of retiring boomers and the generation that is replacing them. Unlike their parents, who were raised to respect age and authority, members of Generation Y (broadly defined as anyone born after 1980), are used to calling their teachers and their parents' friends by their first names; they think of themselves as less experienced equals. They believe that their opinions count, that their feelings matter, and that they should be heard. While they lack the relentless career ambition and drive of their parents, they seek career satisfaction in enjoyable work, opportunities for growth, and more leisure time. They see "the good life" not as their parents did, as a matter of accumulating wealth, but as a satisfying balance between their professional and personal lives.

---

5. Drinking and driving must be stopped. To stop it will require substantial commitment from all levels of government, both in terms of money and in terms of political will. The penalties for driving while under the influence of alcohol must be increased, and more money must be spent for education and publicity. But, more than these measures, it will take the individual will of every Canadian to make the promise not to drive after drinking. Nothing will bring my sister back, but there are lots of other sisters out there—and brothers and mothers and fathers—who can be saved.

Exercise 9.5

With the class divided into the same teams as in Exercise 9.3, write concluding paragraphs to complement the introductions you developed. Here's how to proceed:

- Review the paragraph you developed for Exercise 9.3.
- Write the first sentence of a concluding paragraph for this same topic.
- Pass your sentence, together with your introductory paragraph, along to the next team, who will write a second sentence for the conclusion.
- Continue this process until the conclusion contains both a summary or reinforcement and a memorable statement.
- Return the paragraph to the team that initiated it for revising and polishing.
- Share the results with the rest of the class.

PART 3

Revising

10

The Three Steps
to Revision

No one can write in a single draft an essay that is perfectly organized and developed, let alone one that is free of errors. The purpose of the first draft is to get down on paper something you can work with until it meets your reader's needs and expectations. Planning and drafting should take about half the time you devote to writing a paper. The rest should be devoted to revision.

Revision is the process of refining your message until

- it says what you want it to say,
- your reader(s) will understand it, and
- your reader(s) will receive it favourably.

These three goals are the essentials of good communication. You can achieve them only if you keep your readers in mind as you revise. Because a first draft reflects the contents of the writer's mind, it often seems all right to the writer. But in order to transfer an idea as clearly as possible from the mind of the writer to the mind of the reader, revision is necessary. The idea needs to be honed and refined until it is as clear to your reader as it is to you. By revising from your reader's point of view, you can avoid misunderstandings before they happen.

What Is Revision?

Revision means "re-seeing." It does *not* mean recopying.

The aim of revision is to improve your writing's organization, accuracy, and style. Revising is a three-stage process. Each step requires that you read through your entire essay. The goal of your first reading is to ensure that your reader's information needs are met. In your second reading, you focus on paragraph and sentence structure. Your third reading concentrates on correctness. Here are the steps to follow in revising a paper:

1. Improve the whole paper by revising its content and organization.
2. Refine paragraph and sentence structure, and correct any errors in grammar.
3. Edit and proofread to catch errors in word choice, spelling, and punctuation.

Inexperienced writers often skip the first two stages and concentrate on the third, thinking they will save time. In fact, they waste time—both theirs and their readers'—because the result is writing that doesn't communicate clearly and won't make a positive impression.

The best way to begin revising is to let as much time as possible pass between completing your first draft and rereading it. Ten minutes, or even half a day, is not enough. The danger in rereading too soon is that you're likely to "read" what you think you've written—what exists only in your head, not on the paper.

If you haven't allowed enough time for this cooling-off period, there are two other things you can do to help you get some distance from your draft. If your first draft is handwritten, type it out. Reading your essay in a different form helps you to "re-see" its content. Alternatively, read your paper aloud and try to hear it from the point of view of your reader. Listen to how your explanation unfolds, and mark every place you find something unclear, irrelevant, inadequately developed, or out of order.

Step 1
Revise Content and Organization

As you reread your paper, keep in mind the three kinds of changes you can (and probably should) make at this stage:

1. You can rearrange information. This is the kind of revision that is most often needed but least often done. Consider the order in which you've arranged your paragraphs. From your reader's point of view, is this the most effective order in which to present your ideas?

2. You can add information. Adding new main ideas or more development is often necessary to make your message interesting and convincing as well as clear. It's a good idea to ask a friend to read your draft and identify what needs to be expanded or clarified. (Be sure to return the favour; you can learn a great deal by critiquing other people's writing.)

3. You can delete information. Now is the time to cut out anything that is repetitious, insignificant, or irrelevant to your subject and reader.

Your outline is the best place to begin checking the adequacy and organization of your information. Keep it beside you and change it as your revise your essay. In most cases, your paper will be improved by rearranging, adding, and subtracting ideas.

The thesis statement is your contract with your reader, so it should be the guiding principle of your paper. It should contain nothing that is not developed in the body of the essay, and there should be nothing in the essay that is not directly related to your thesis statement. When you find a mismatch between the thesis statement and the paper, change one or the other or both until the two agree. Using a word processor to move blocks of text around is as easy as shuffling a deck of cards.

If you are not already using a word-processing program, now is the time to begin. Before you start to revise, change the computer's settings to meet the format requirements of your paper: set the spacing, margins, font style and size, etc. (See Chapter 21 for instructions and examples.) Most people find it easier to revise from a paper copy, so print out your draft double- or triple-spaced. Read it through carefully, making notes for changes in the margins or in the spaces between the lines; then go back to the computer to make the changes.

Remember to save your work frequently. It takes only a split second to click on the Save icon, but that split second could save you hours—even days—in the event of a computer disaster. Learn to save your work in a systematic and easy-to-find filing system. Calling a paper "draft" or "essay" will cause frustration later when you want to reopen the file to revise it but can't remember the name of the file you were working on. Give each file a distinctive name (or name and number), and save each draft separately just in case you want to go back and use material from a previous version of your document.

Use the checklist that follows to guide you as you review your paper's form and content.

CONTENT AND ORGANIZATION CHECKLIST

ACCURACY

- Is your information consistent with your own experience and observations or with what you have discovered through research?
- Are all your facts and evidence up to date?

COMPLETENESS

Have you included enough main ideas and development to explain your subject and convince your reader? Remember that "enough" means from the reader's point of view, not the writer's.

SUBJECT

Is your subject

- significant? Does it avoid the trivial or the obvious?
- single? Does it avoid double or combined subjects?
- specific? Is it focused and precise?
- supportable? Have you provided enough evidence to make your meaning clear?

MAIN POINTS

Are your main points

- significant? Have you deleted any unimportant ones?
- distinct? Are they all different from one another, or is there an overlap in content?
- relevant? Do all points relate directly to your subject?
- arranged in the most appropriate order? Again, "appropriate" means from the reader's perspective. Choose chronological, climactic, logical, or random order, depending on which is most likely to help the reader make sense of your information.

INTRODUCTION

Does your introduction

- catch the reader's attention and make him or her want to read on?
- contain a clearly identifiable thesis statement?
- identify the main points that your paper will explain?

CONCLUSION

Does your conclusion

- contain a summary or reinforcement of your main points, rephrased to avoid word-for-word repetition?
- contain a statement that effectively clinches your argument and leaves the reader with something to think about?

Exercise 10.1*

Read the following draft outline for a short essay on how to write effective e-mail in a business environment. Working with a partner, rearrange the main points in chronological order, delete any unnecessary supporting points, and write a thesis statement to produce a working outline for the essay. Then compare your answer with our suggestion. Answers for exercises in this chapter begin on page 519.

E-Mail Excellence

Attention-getter: As the recipient of approximately 1,000 business-related e-mail messages every month, I am something of an expert on what is effective and what is not in e-mail correspondence.

Thesis statement: _____

_____

_____

_____

Main points:

I. Subject line

    A. always include one

    B. make sure it states clearly what the message is about

    C. never use vague subject lines such as "hello," or "message," or "are you there?"

    D. never leave the subject line blank

II. Attachments

    A. use sparingly

    B. may carry viruses

    C. take time to transfer and to open

    D. attach text-only files unless a graphic is absolutely necessary

    E. use only if necessary

III. Message

    A. Content

        1. be concise and to the point

        2. tell the reader what action is needed, by whom, and when

        3. don't be a novelist or a "Chatty Cathy"

        4. use plain English, not "cyberspeak"

        5. use an appropriate level of language in your message as well as in your salutation and signature

    B. Format

        1. use bullets to identify points you want to emphasize

        2. leave white space between points

        3. avoid sending your message in uppercase letters (shouting)

        4. avoid smilies and other "cute" computer shorthand symbols

Summary: If you follow my recommendations on these three points whenever you write an e-mail, you will make the recipient of your message very happy.

Memorable statement: Especially if you're writing to me.

Step 2
Revise Paragraphs and Sentences

Here, too, you should allow time—at least a couple of days—between your first revision and your second. Read your draft aloud, and use this list of questions to help you improve it.

PARAGRAPH AND SENTENCE CHECKLIST

PARAGRAPHS

Does each paragraph

- begin with a clear, identifiable topic sentence?
- develop one—and only one—main idea?
- employ one or more kinds of development appropriate to the main idea?
- contain clear and effective transitions to signal the relationship between sentences? Between paragraphs?

SENTENCES

Sentence Structure

1. Is each sentence clear and complete?
   - Are there any fragments or run-ons?
   - Are there any misplaced or dangling modifiers?
   - Are all lists (whether words, phrases, or clauses) expressed in parallel form?
2. Are your sentences varied in length? Could some be combined to improve the clarity and impact of your message?

Grammar

1. Have you used verbs correctly?
   - Are all verbs in the correct form?
   - Do all verbs agree with their subjects?
   - Are all verbs in the correct tense?
   - Are there any confusing shifts in verb tense within a paragraph?
2. Have you used pronouns correctly?
   - Are all pronouns in the correct form?
   - Do all pronouns agree with their antecedents?
   - Have any vague pronoun references been eliminated?

When you're sure you've answered these questions satisfactorily, go to the third and last stage of the revision process.

Exercise 10.2*

Here is the first draft of the essay on e-mail. Revise it to correct errors in paragraph structure, sentence structure, and grammar. Then compare your answer with our suggestion on pages 519–20.

1   As the recipient of approximately 1,000 business-related e-mail messages every month, I am something of an expert on what is effective and what is not in e-mail correspondence. The three areas that need attention in most e-mail messages are the subject line, the content, and format of the message and the use of attachments.

2   Some people leave the subject line blank, this is a mistake. I want to know what the message is about before I open it so I can decide if it needs my immediate attention. Or can wait until later. A message with no subject line or with a line that didn't tell me nothing about the content of the e-mail get sent to the bottom of my "to-do" list. There are lots of readers like me busy people who receive tons of e-mail, much of it unsolicited advertising that clutter up their in-boxes. For this reason the subject line should always clearly state the subject of the message and should never be vague or cute like "hello" or "message" or "are you there?"

3   As for the message itself, it's function should be to tell the reader what action one wants, you need to be clear about this and be as brief as possible. What is it that you want the recipient to do. Who else needs to be involved. By when does the action need to take place. Communicate your message in plain English, not in "cyberspeak" Not everyone knows Net lingo, and even some who are famliar with it find it irritating not charming. Use an appropriate level of language (general level Standard English will always be appropriate) to convey you're message. Use the same level of language in you're salutation and closing or "signature." One should definitely not sign off a message to you're client or you're boss with "love and kisses." Format you're message so that the recipient will be able to read it quickly and understanding it easily. Use bullets to identify points you want to emphasize, separate the bullets with white space so they can be read at a glance and

reviewed individually if necessary. There are some important points of e-mail etiquette that you should observe. Don't type you're message in upper case letters, that's considered "shouting." Do avoid "smilies" and other "cute" computer shorthand symbols. Some of you're readers won't understand them others will have seen them so often they will be turned off.

4   Attachments should be included only if they are really necessary, for one thing, they may carry virruses and some people won't open them. Another disadvantage is that they take time to send download and open. Unless I am sure that an attachment is both urgent and vitally important— the agenda of tomorrow's meeting, for example—I don't bother to open it, for all I know, it might contain not only a virus but also footage of the sender's toddler doing her latest photogenic trick. As a general rule attach only what you must and attach text-only files. Try to include everything you need to say in the message itself and use attachments only as a last resort. Think of them as equivalent to footnotes supplementary to the message not an essential part of it.

5   If you follow my recommendations on these three points whenever you write an e-mail, you will make the recipient of your message very happy, especially if you're writing to me.

Step 3
Edit and Proofread

By now you're probably so tired of refining your paper that you may be tempted to skip **editing**—correcting errors in word choice, spelling, and punctuation—and **proofreading**—correcting errors in typing or writing that appear in the final draft. But these final tasks are essential if you want your paper to make a positive impression.

Misspellings, faulty punctuation, and messiness don't always create misunderstandings, but they do cause the reader to form a lower opinion of you and your work. Careful editing and proofreading are necessary if you want your writing to be favourably received.

Most word-processing programs include a grammar checker and a spell checker. The newer programs have some useful features. For example, they will question (but not correct) your use of apostrophes; they will sometimes catch errors in subject–verb agreement; and they will catch obvious misspellings and typos. But don't make the mistake of assuming these programs will do all your editing for you. Many errors slip past them. Only you or a knowledgeable and patient friend can find and correct all errors.

If spelling is a particular problem for you, you should first run your paper through a spell checker. After that, you're on your own. Read your paper backward word by word, from the end to the beginning. Reading backward forces you to look at each word by itself and helps you to spot those that look suspicious. Whenever you're in doubt about the spelling of a word, look it up! If you find this task too tedious to bear, ask a good speller to read through your paper for you and identify any errors.

Here are the questions to ask yourself when you are editing.

EDITING CHECKLIST
WORDS

Usage
Have you used words to "mean" rather than to "impress"?
- Have you eliminated any slang, pretentious language, or offensive language?
- Have you cut out any unnecessary words?
- Have you corrected any "abusages"?

Tone
- Is your tone consistent, reasonable, courteous, and confident throughout your essay?

Spelling
Are all words spelled correctly?
- Have you double-checked any homonyms?
- Have you used capital letters where they are needed?
- Have you used apostrophes correctly for possessives and omitted them from plurals?

PUNCTUATION

Within Sentences
- Have you eliminated any unnecessary commas and included commas where needed? (Refer to the comma rules on pages 417–22 as you consider this question.)
- Have you used colons and semicolons where appropriate?
- Are all quotations appropriately marked?

Beginnings and Endings
- Does each sentence begin with a capital letter?
- Do all questions—and only questions—end with a question mark?
- Are all quotation marks correctly placed?

Exercise 10.3*

Read the following sentences carefully and edit them to correct any errors in usage, spelling, and punctuation. Then compare your answers to our suggestions on pages 520–21. (Our thanks to *Fortune* magazine for collecting these howlers from real résumés and cover letters.)

1. I demand a salary commiserate with my qualifications and extensive experience.

2. I have lurnt Microsoft Word and Excel computor and spreasheet progroms.

3. I received a plague for being salesperson of the year.

4. Reason for leaving last job; maturity leave.

5. You will want me to be Head Honcho in no time.

6. I am a perfectionist and rarely if if ever forget details.

7. Marital status: single. Unmarried. Unengaged. Uninvolved. No commitments.

8. In my previous job I became completely paranoid, trusting completely no one and absolutely nothing.

9. As indicted, I have over five years of analyzing investments.

10. I was responsible for ruining the entire operation for a Western chain store.

TIPS FOR EFFECTIVE PROOFREADING

By the time you have finished editing, you will have gone over your paper so many times you may have practically memorized it. When you are very familiar with a piece of writing, it's hard to spot the small mistakes that may have crept in as you produced your final copy. Here are some tips to help you find those tiny, elusive errors:

1. Read through your essay line by line, using a ruler to guide you.
2. If you've been keeping a list of your most frequent errors in this course, scan your essay for the mistakes you are most likely to make.
3. Use the "Quick Revision Guide" on the inside front cover of this book to make a final check of all aspects of your paper.
4. Use the list of correction marks on the inside back cover to check for errors your instructor has identified in your writing.

Your "last" draft may need further revision after your proofreading review. If so, take the time to rewrite the paper so that the version you hand in is clean and easy to read. If a word processor is available to you, use it. Computers make editing and proofreading almost painless, since errors are so easy to correct.

At long last, you're ready to submit your paper. If you've followed the three steps to revision conscientiously, you can hand it in with confidence that it says what you want it to say. One last word of advice:

DON'T FORGET TO KEEP A COPY FOR YOUR FILES!

Exercise 10.4*

Now go through the revised first draft of the e-mail essay that you produced in Exercise 10.2. This is your last chance to make this essay error-free. Use the Editing Checklist and the Tips for Effective Proofreading to guide you as you make your final pass through this document. Then compare your answer with our suggestion on pages 521–22.

GO TO WEB

EXERCISE 10.1

Is the following essay ready for submission? Go over it carefully, correcting any errors. Then get together with another student and compare your proofreading skills. (There are 20 errors in this exercise.)

According to a recent survey in Maclean's magazine, only 43 percent of Canadians are satisfied with their jobs. What can you do to ensure that you will not be one of the 57 percent who are unhappy with the work they do. There are three questions to consider when seeking employment that will provide satisfaction as well as a paycheque.

First are you suited to the kind of work you are applying for. If you enjoy the outdoors, for example, and like to be active, your not going to be happy with a nine to five office job, no matter how much it pays.

Second is the job based in a location compatible with your prefered lifestyle. No matter how much you like your work, if you go home every night to an enviorment you are miserable in, it will not be long before you start transfering your disatisfaction to your job. If you like the amenities and conviences of the city, you probably will not enjoy working in a small town. If, on the other hand, you prefer the quiet and security of small town life, you may find the city a stressful place in which to live.

Finally, is it one that you want to work for. Do you need the security of generous benifits, a good pension plan, and incentives to stay and grow with one company? Or are you an ambitous person who is looking for variety, quick advancement, and a high salary. If so, you may have to forego security in favour of commissions or cash incentives and be willing to move as quickly and as often as opportunities occur. Some carful self-analysis now, before you start out on your career path, will help you chose a direction that will put you in the 43 percent minority of satisfied Canadian workers.

Exercise 10.6

This exercise will serve as a review of the three stages of the revision process. Below is a first draft of an essay. Applying all the principles you have learned in Chapter 10, revise this essay to make it a model of good communication: complete, correct, concise, and courteous. When you have finished, exchange papers with another student and compare your results. What errors did you miss? If this assignment were worth 20 percent of your final grade, would you hand it in now, or would you revise it again?

We are having a garbage crisis. There is so much waste being produced in North America, we no longer have any idea of were to put it. Toronto's garbage problem is so great that they are trucking thousands of tonnes of it to Michigan every year. But how long will that last? We must act now, and we must act as individuals. We cannot wait for the Government to save us from this crisis. We produce the garbage; we must solve the problem. In very practical, down to earth, concrete terms, here are some things we can do to reduce, recycle, and reuse.

First we must reduce the amount of garbage we produce. We can do this be refusing to buy products that are over packaged, like fast food that comes in styrafoam containers and chocolates that have a paper wrapping, a box, lining paper, a plastic tray for the candies, and foil wrap around each chocolate. By not purchasing such wasteful items, we say to the manufacturer, Either reduce the packaging in your product or lose business to your competition. We can also be less wastful in our own habits by carpooling, for example, or by using cloth diapers or biodegradable disposables.

We must recycle everything we can instead of sending it to the dump. Old cloths can be sent to the Salvation Army, the Scott mission, or other charitable organizations. As can furniture, appliances, books, and most other household items. There are dozens of ways to make useful items from packaging that would otherwise be thrown away, such as bird feeders from plastic jugs, braided rugs from old rags, and fire logs from newspapers. We don't need to consume as much as we do, and it won't hurt us to use things longer instead of buying new items before the old ones are completely worn out. Many companies now manufacture products from recycled goods, and we should be on the lookout for their products to support their efforts and to reduce the waste that is dumped into landfills.

Third, we can reuse most things. Composting vegetable garbage is a good way to put waste to valuable use. Or we can offer the things we no longer want to others through lawn sales and flea markets.

This is an absolute necessity. If we do not stop producing so much waste, we will inevitibly destroy our own enviornment. Unlike most efforts to improve things, the move to recycle, reuse, and reduce has one other advantage: it doesn't cost any money. In fact, it can save every household that practices it hundreds of dollars a year.

PART 5

The Research Paper

Introduction

A **research paper** is an essay that presents the results of a writer's investigation of a topic in print, electronic, or multimedia formats. The skills involved—finding, evaluating, and assimilating the ideas of other writers—are essential in any field of study. They will also be useful to you in your career. Much of the writing you do on the job, especially if you are in management, requires you to express in your own words the facts, opinions, and ideas of others.

Writing a research paper follows the same process as other kinds of writing, from planning through drafting to revising. The difference is that instead of relying exclusively on what you already know about a topic, you include source material—facts, data, knowledge, or opinions of other writers—to support your thesis. Chapter 18 explains the different kinds of source material you can choose from and tells you the strengths and weaknesses of each. Chapter 19 shows you how to integrate the information you have found into your paper.

A research paper is not simply a collection of what other people have said about a subject. It is your responsibility to shape and control the discussion, to make sure that what you include from your sources is interesting and relevant to your thesis, and to comment on its validity or significance. It is *your* paper, *your* subject, *your* main points; ideas from other writers should be included as support for *your* topic sentences.

One of the challenges of writing a research paper is differentiating between your ideas and those you took from sources. Readers cannot hear the different "speakers," so you have to indicate who said what. To separate your sources from your own ideas, research papers require **documentation**—a system of acknowledging source materials. Chapter 20 shows you how to provide your readers with a guide to the information contained in your paper—a play-by-play of who is "speaking."

Research papers are usually longer than essays, and the planning process is more complex. For these reasons, the time you are given to complete a research assignment is usually longer than the time allowed for an essay. Don't fool yourself into thinking you can put the assignment off for a few weeks. You will need all the time you've been given to find the sources you need, decide what you want to say, and then draft, revise, and polish your paper. Instructors assign research papers so that they can assess not only your research skills but also your writing skills.

Tips on Writing a Research Paper

1. Even though your instructor may be your only reader, think of your potential audience as your fellow students—those taking the course with you, those who took it in recent years, and those who will take it in the near future. This way, you can count on a certain amount of shared knowledge. For a course in economics, for example, you can assume your audience knows what the Phillips Curve relationship is; a definition would be superfluous. For a course in literature, you won't need to inform your readers that Jonathan Swift was an 18th-century satirist. Think of your readers as colleagues who want to see what conclusions you have reached and what evidence you have used to support them.

2. Manage your time carefully. Divide the work into a number of tasks, develop a schedule that leaves lots of time for revision, and stick to your schedule.

3. Choose a subject that interests you. Define it as precisely as you can before beginning your research, but be prepared to modify, adapt, and revise it as you research and write your paper.

4. If you cannot find appropriate sources, ask a reference librarian for help.

5. When making notes, *always* record the author, title, publication data, and page numbers of the source. For electronic sources, note also the URL and the date you accessed the site.

6. Use your source material to support your own ideas, not the other way around.

7. Document your sources according to whatever style your instructor prefers.

8. Revise, edit, and proofread carefully. If you omit this step, the hours and weeks you have spent on your assignment will be wasted, not rewarded.

18

Researching Your Subject

Your first step in writing a research paper is the same as your first step in any writing task: select a suitable subject, preferably one you are curious about. Whether you are assigned a topic or choose your own, don't rush off to the library or log onto the Internet right away. A little preparation up front will save you a lot of time and possibly much grief later on.

First of all, if you're not sure what your instructor expects, clarify what is required of you. Next, even if your subject is tentative, check it with the 4-S test: is it significant, single, specific, and supportable (researchable)? If not, refine it by using the techniques discussed in Chapter 3. Finally, consider what approach you might take in presenting your subject. Does it lend itself to a comparison? Process? Cause or effect? If the topic is assigned, often the wording of the assignment will suggest how your instructor wants you to develop it. Deciding up front what kind of paper you are going to write will save you hours of time, both in the library and at your desk.

Exercise 18.1

In the workplace, people rarely have the opportunity to select a research topic without consultation. In some cases, the subject is assigned or approved by a board of directors; in others, a committee is responsible for ensuring that a research project meets the company's needs.

Before you start your own research project, take some time to ensure that your proposed subject is appropriate for the time and space you have been given. The class should be divided into "committees" of four or five people. Each committee should be given four or five pieces of coloured paper, a different colour for each group.

- Each committee identifies a chairperson and a note-taker. At the direction of the chair, each member of the committee presents an idea for a research paper. After each presentation, discuss the subject in terms of its significance to the target audience (the whole class, including the instructor). If the committee feels a subject requires revision to be significant, make these revisions as a group. It is important that the committee come to a consensus regarding any revisions.
- Once each subject is agreed upon as significant, record it on a slip of the coloured paper assigned to your committee.
- Repeat this procedure until your committee has identified at least one significant subject for each of its members.
- Toss your committee's subjects into the company's think tank (a container), along with the subjects submitted by the other committees in the class.
- The chair of each committee draws out of the think tank four or five proposed research subjects. Be sure to draw a representative sampling of colours from other committees.
- As a committee, discuss each subject that has been drawn from the think tank. Since each has already been approved as significant by another committee, your task is to determine whether each proposed subject is single and specific.
- For each subject, record any revisions that the committee deems necessary and briefly explain why.
- Return the revised subjects to their appropriate committees according to the corresponding coloured paper.
- When every committee has received its original proposed research subjects, each group discusses the suggested revisions until everyone understands them.
- Next, as a committee, discuss whether each proposed subject is supportable. What sorts of research materials would you look for to help you explain and defend each subject?
- Record the final version of the proposed research subjects on a flip chart, ready to present to a board of directors. (You should have one subject for each member of the committee.)
- Present your committee's proposed research subjects before the board of directors (the whole class). Discuss the revisions and decide whether each proposal now meets the criteria of the 4-S test.

When you're sure your subject is appropriate and you've decided, at least tentatively, on the approach you're going to take, you are ready to focus on the kind of information you need to look for in your research. For example, if you've been asked to apply four theories of conflict to a case study, you won't waste time discussing the major schools of conflict theory or their development over the last few decades. You can restrict your investigation to sources that contain information relevant to your specific subject.

Once you have an idea of the kind of information you need in order to develop your topic, it's time to find the best sources you can. But how will you know if what you've found is "good" information?

Selecting Your Sources

Not all sources are created equal. There's no point in wasting time making notes on a source unless the information is relevant, current, and reliable. Evaluating the quality of source material before you use it is a key step in the research process.

To evaluate a print source, first check it over closely. Scan the table of contents, the headings, and chapters or articles to ensure the book or periodical contains information relevant to your topic. ("Periodicals" are publications that are produced at regular "periods," such as daily newspapers or monthly magazines.) Then check to see where the information comes from: its author, the date it was published, and the organization or company that published it. Most traditional print sources—newspapers, magazines, and scholarly journals—have fact-checkers and editorial boards to ensure that the information they publish is reliable.

Print sources are easier to assess for reliability than electronic sources. Yet the Internet and the World Wide Web have vastly increased the amount of potential research material, and it is essential to learn how to evaluate it. For example, if you are doing a report on a recent business venture or medical breakthrough, the most current information will be online. How do you decide, given the millions of pieces of information out there in cyberspace, what is useful for your specific purpose? Of course, when you use online editions of traditional print sources (e.g., electronic versions of newspapers, magazines, and books), you can assume the same standards of credibility and reliability. The CD-ROM full-text versions of *The Globe and Mail* or the *Financial Times* are no less (and no more) accurate than the printed versions.

With electronic sources that have no hard-copy equivalent, the domain name is one place to begin your evaluation. Does the source's URL end with .com (commercial), .gov (government), or .edu (educational institution)? Sites from these different sources will present data on a topic in different ways. A commercial site will probably attempt to influence consumers as well as to inform them. A .edu suffix suggests the credibility of a recognized college or university, but offbeat student web pages or the informal musings of faculty members at the institution may share the suffix as well.

Another difference between print and electronic sources is authorship. There is seldom any doubt about who wrote a particular book or article. In online material, however, often no author (or date) is identified. Sometimes the person who compiles ("comp") or maintains ("maint") the website is the only one named. For academic research, it's wise to be cautious of "no-name" sources. If you wish to use information from one of these sources, be sure the organization or institution where it originated is reliable. You wouldn't want to be researching the history of discrimination in Canada, for example, and find yourself quoting from the disguised website of a hate organization.

Recognizing that much online work is collaborative and that several writers may have contributed to a potential source, it is a good idea to check out the people who are involved in producing it. Powerful online search engines such as Google make checking the author's reliability easier for electronic sources than it is for print sources. Simply key the author's name into the search engine and then evaluate the results to see if he or she is a credible person in the field. Often you'll be able to check the author's biography, credentials, other publications, and business or academic affiliation. If no author's name is given, you can check out the company, organization, or institution in the same way. Cyber-sleuthing is a useful skill to learn!

In the end, however, with both print and electronic sources, you must apply your own critical intelligence. Is the information timely, accurate, and reliable? Is there evidence of any inherent bias? How can you best make use of the findings to support and enhance your own ideas? The answers to these questions are critical to producing a good research paper.

Taking Good Research Notes

Once you've found a useful source, record the information you need. You'll save time and money by taking notes directly from your sources rather than photocopying everything. Most often, you will need a summary of the information. Follow the instructions on summarizing given on pages 272–75. Alternatively, you can paraphrase (see pages 277–79). Sometimes a quotation is appropriate; when this is the case, it's wise to make a copy of your source. Whenever you take notes—in any form—from a source, be sure to record the information you will need about the source itself. For each published source that you use in your paper, you should write down the following information.

For Books

1. Author(s)' or editor(s)' full name
2. Full title and edition number (if any)
3. City of publication
4. Name of publisher
5. Year of publication
(You will find all this information on the front and back of the title page.)
6. Page(s) from which you took notes

For Journal Articles

1. Author(s)' full name
2. Title of the article
3. Name of the journal
4. Volume number of the journal
5. Year of publication
6. Inclusive page numbers of the article
7. Page(s) from which you took notes

For Internet Sources

1. Author(s)' full name
2. Title of the document
3. Title of the database, periodical, or site
4. Name of the editor (if any)
5. Date of publication or last update
6. Name of the institution or organization sponsoring the site (if any)
7. Network address, or URL
8. Date you accessed the source

For Newspaper or Magazine Articles

1. Author(s)' full name
2. Title of the article
3. Title of the newspaper or magazine
4. Date of publication
5. Inclusive page numbers of the article
6. Page(s) from which you took notes

Some researchers record each piece of information on a separate index card. Others write their notes on sheets of paper, being careful to keep their own ideas separate from the ideas and words taken from sources. (Using a highlighter or a different colour of ink will help you to tell at a glance which ideas you have taken from a source.) Use the technology available to help you record, sort, and file your notes. You can record and file information by creating a database, and you can use a photocopier (usually available in the library) to copy relevant pages of sources for later use. Whatever system you use, be sure to keep a separate record for each source and to include the documentation information. If you don't, you'll easily get your sources confused. The result of this confusion could be inaccurate documentation, which could lead your reader to suspect you of plagiarizing.

Avoiding Plagiarism

Plagiarism is presenting someone else's ideas as your own. It's a form of stealing (the word comes from the Latin word *plagiarius*, which means "kidnapper"). There have been famous cases of respected journalists and academics who have been accused of plagiarizing the articles or books they have written. Suspected plagiarists who are found guilty often lose their jobs. Sometimes the accusation alone is enough to compromise an author's reputation and thus prevent him or her from continuing to work as a scholar or writer.

Students who copy essays or parts of essays from source material, download them from the Internet, or pay someone else to write them are cheating. And, in so doing, they commit a serious academic offence. Sometimes, however, academic plagiarism is accidental. It can result from careless note-taking or an incomplete understanding of the conventions of documentation. It is not necessary to identify the sources of common knowledge (e.g., *The solstice occurs twice a year; B.C. is Canada's westernmost province*) or proverbial sayings (e.g., *Love is blind*), but when you are not sure whether to cite a source, it's wise to err on the side of caution and provide documentation. Statistics should always be cited because the meaning of numbers tends to change, depending on who is using them and for what purpose.

If, after you have finished your first draft, you are not sure which ideas need documenting and which don't, take your research notes and your outline to your instructor and ask. It's better to ask before submitting a paper than to try to explain a problem afterward. Asking saves you potential embarrassment as well as time.

Using the Library

The electronic age has transformed the library—traditionally a warehouse of information contained within print sources—into a Learning Resource Centre: a portal to sources of information such as databases, e-books, e-journals, and the Internet, together with the traditional print and audiovisual resources. With new technology, information retrieval is faster, easier, and more efficient than ever before. However, this fact does not make the library any less intimidating to inexperienced users. Many students are overwhelmed by what at first appears to be a vast and confusing array of collections. Using the library becomes a less daunting prospect when you realize that all of its contents are organized and classified in such a way as to make finding information easy, if not simple. First, you need to know the organizational system used by your library. In this section, we will describe the collections found in most academic libraries, give you tips on how to access them, and summarize their strengths and weaknesses as sources. We will also decode some of the terminology used by library staff to describe and arrange collections.

THE ONLINE CATALOGUE (OPAC)

All but the smallest libraries today use automated catalogue systems to access collections. These online catalogues are commonly called OPACs (Online Public Access Catalogues). They may be stand-alone computer terminals within the library or accessible via the library's website. OPAC search options usually include title, author, subject, or keyword. How you search the catalogue will depend on what you are looking for and on what you already know.

Along with books, the OPAC may list other resources available in the library, such as periodical titles. If a periodical title is available in full-text format from one of the library's subscription databases, there may be a link to the title and, possibly, the text from the OPAC. Many of today's OPACs allow the library to link to several useful online sources of information. Your library's OPAC should be the first place you check for resources when beginning your research paper.

BOOKS

Book collections are represented in the online catalogue and may be searched in a variety of ways: by author, title, subject, keyword, and sometimes call number.

If you know of a particular book by title, choose that option and enter the **title**—*English Online*, for example. If your search is successful, write down the call number of the book. Alternatively, if you know that Eric Crump wrote a book on using the Internet, but you aren't sure of the title, do an **author** search, using the last name first: Crump, Eric. If you don't know of any books or authors in your field of research, begin by doing a **subject** or **subject keyword** search, such as "online English composition instruction." Most systems will respond by identifying relevant holdings and listing instructions to follow at the bottom of the computer screen. One of the biggest advantages of automated systems is that they identify the **status** of the book, letting you know if the book is in or when it is due back. Many systems allow you to place a **hold** on a book that is out. This means that when the book is returned to the library, it will be set aside for a period of time to allow you to go in and pick it up.

In order to find a book on the shelves, you must match the **call number** as it appears on the screen or catalogue card with the number taped on the spine of the book. Every book has a unique call number, and books are arranged on the shelves according to their call numbers. Guide signs are usually posted on the ends of shelving units (sometimes called **stacks**). Most colleges and universities use the **Library of Congress** (LC) system of classification, which uses a letter or combination of letters to begin the call number. The LC system is generally more suitable to academic collections than the Dewey decimal system used by public and smaller libraries.

A title keyword search is often the fastest way of retrieving books on your topic. If the library carries a book on your subject of research, chances are the topic will appear somewhere in the title.

Strengths	Weaknesses
• Author may be an authority on the subject • Information is usually reliable (if published by a respected publisher) • Several aspects of the topic may be covered in the book	• Information cannot be as current as other sources

PERIODICALS

Your library's collection of **periodicals**—publications that are issued at regular intervals, such as magazines, newspapers, and scholarly or technical journals—may contain useful articles on the subject you are researching.

To locate specific articles, you need to use one or more of the databases and periodical indexes available from your library. Before you begin, read the description of the database to determine if it includes periodicals on your topic. Each database has specific strengths and will allow you to search a subject in a wide variety of periodicals. From the selection offered in your library, you may be able to search databases such as EBSCOhost, ProQuest, LexisNexis, or InfoTrac.[1] These databases are delivered using the Internet, but are paid for by the library; their use is limited by licence agreements to students and staff of the institution that pays for them. It may be possible to access them from home, but you will need a log-in or other means of identifying yourself as a student. Check with the library staff at your institution to find out more about access from your Internet service provider.

Databases have been created with users in mind; they have search interfaces that make finding information relatively simple. Once you have found the database you wish to use, you will be presented with a search box similar to those found on Internet search engines. Here you type in a word or phrase that relates to your research topic. For example, if you were researching the art movement known as Impressionism, you would enter this word in the text box. The search mechanism of the database would look for this term, and all articles containing the word "Impressionism"

---

[1]Your purchase of *Essay Essentials,* Fourth Edition, entitles you to free access to InfoTrac.

would be displayed on the screen. From the list, you would select those you think may be useful to you.

Most databases allow you to e-mail the results of your search. If you are pressed for time, do a quick search, e-mail the results to yourself, and check them later for relevancy. You can always delete them and start over.

Increasingly, full-text articles are included with each new release of these databases. This means you can print or download the text of an article without having to retrieve the actual magazine or journal. If you find a reference to a magazine article for which the full text is not available, be sure to note the title and date of the periodical in which it appeared; then check to see if your library subscribes to this periodical.

Strengths	Weaknesses
• Contain current information	• Some articles may be opinion
• Articles in databases are easy to retrieve	pieces but presented as factual
• Databases are accessible 24/7	

ENCYCLOPEDIAS

A useful source of general information on a topic is an encyclopedia; it is often a good place to begin your research. There are many types of encyclopedias, and several are now available online or on CD-ROM. Information is easy to find, usually through a user-friendly search screen, and CD versions of encyclopedias often include sound or video clips to enhance the text. You might begin your search with a general encyclopedia such as *Britannica*, *Colliers*, or the *World Book* and then move on to a specialized encyclopedia related to your subject. Look in the reference collection for a call number area that matches the one in which you found books on your topic (for example, medical encyclopedias are in the R section), or ask the reference librarian if a specialized encyclopedia exists on your subject.

Strengths	Weaknesses
• Provide a good overview of a subject	• Information in print versions
• Often list titles of major books on the subject	may be dated
• Online editions are convenient, easy to use, and updated regularly	

THE INTERNET

Most students today have grown up with the Internet and are accustomed to using it to meet their information needs. They turn to the Net for news reports, weather updates, and maps to destinations near and far; to find phone numbers and addresses, purchase theatre tickets, shop online, and plan vacations. They use search engines to locate information about topics ranging from medical disorders to building a deck. Canada is one of the world's leaders in per capita Internet use.

When you are gathering material to write a research paper, however, you should keep in mind that the Internet is not necessarily a reliable source of information. (Some instructors will not accept websites as legitimate resources for research papers, so be sure you have permission to use them before you spend hours on Google or Yahoo.) Evaluating Internet information for reliability is not a simple matter. We've already mentioned checking the domain name as one place to begin. A good guide to evaluating websites can be found at http://www.lib.berkeley.edu/TeachingLib/Guides/Internet/Evaluate.html.

The number of results called up by a keyword search can be overwhelming. All search engines offer advice on effective searching from the home page. Here are four ways you can limit and focus the results of an initial query:

- Use one or more of the shortcuts available on most search engines.
- Use an Advanced Search screen that allows you to combine concepts. For example, the Advanced Search screen at Google allows you to search for an exact phrase such as "breast cancer" and include the word "treatment" without the word "chemotherapy." You can also limit the type of domain you'd like returned (.edu) as an example, choose the language you'd like for your results, and decide where you'd like the search engine to look for your terms (in the title only, for example).
- Put quotation marks around your search term(s). Doing so turns your keyword search into a search for a phrase ("breast cancer treatment," for example).
- Use the tilde sign (~) or plus and minus signs to add or eliminate concepts. Plus and minus signs add or subtract words from your search word or phrase ("breast cancer" + treatment – chemotherapy). Google interprets the tilde as a signal to search for variations of a word. For example, "~treatment" would include the plural, "treatments," in your results list.

Get in the habit of using more than one search engine to vary results. A subject directory search engine, such as Yahoo, may be a better starting point for your topic than a general keyword search.

Librarians regularly scour the Internet for exceptional websites as good sources of information. Look for these recommendations on your library's website, or look for links to government websites or sources such as the Internet Public Library (http://www.ipl.org) from your library's OPAC.

Strengths

- Fast and convenient
- Excellent resource for directory-type information
- Websites of leading experts are sometimes available
- Increasingly, authoritative information sources are posted on the Net (e.g., government documents, databases of scholarly journals)

Weaknesses

- Number of results can be daunting
- Reliability and authority can be difficult to determine
- Amount of information is staggering (most users will not browse past the first two or three pages of results, so valuable information may be missed)
- Questionable content may appear to be valid

OTHER SOURCES

Most libraries contain other collections that may help you in your research. Don't overlook the possibility of finding useful information in the **audiovisual collection**, which normally includes videotapes, films, audiotapes, DVDs, and slide presentations. **Government publications** are another good source of information. The government, as one of the country's largest publishers, may have produced documents related to your topic. Many of these documents are available on the Internet.

Finally, the library is not the only source of information you can use. Interviews with people familiar with your subject are excellent sources because they provide a personal view, and they ensure that your paper will contain information not found in any other paper the instructor will read. It is perfectly acceptable to e-mail a question or set of questions to an expert in a field of study. **Original research**, such as surveys or questionnaires that you design, distribute, and analyze can also enhance your paper. Doing your own research is time-consuming and requires some knowledge of survey design and interpretation, but it has the advantage of being original and current.

A good research paper will contain references to material from a variety of sources. Some instructors require a minimum number of references from several types of sources: books, periodicals, encyclopedias, interviews, etc. Most, but not all, institutions will allow you to use Internet sources, but use them with caution. Be mindful that anyone can place information, reliable or not, on any subject at a website. For this reason, it is best to use research gathered from reliable sources such as books, encyclopedias, scholarly journals, and reputable magazines.

As you conduct your research and think about your paper, keep your reader in mind. Every teacher faced with a pile of papers hopes to find some that are not simply a rehash of known facts. Before anything else, teachers are learners; they like nothing better than discovering something new. If you cannot find new information about your subject, be sure to provide an original interpretation of the evidence you find.

Exercise 18.2

This exercise will quickly familiarize you with your school's library: the variety and extent of its holdings; the different ways you and your library can communicate with each other; and basic library policies you should know about.

1. Does your library provide handouts or other documents on how to conduct research? On how to format electronic source citations?
2. Check your library's OPAC (online catalogue) for a video that deals with study skills. Make a note of the title and call number.
3. How many newspapers does the library subscribe to? Name two and note how long the library keeps them.
4. What is the URL for the library's website? Find two unique resources or services listed there.
5. Is it possible to contact the library staff by e-mail? If yes, note the e-mail address.
6. What is the loan period for books? What is the fine charged for an overdue video?
7. What does it mean when a book is "on reserve"?
8. Using one of your library's subscription databases, search for an article on smoking-cessation programs. Give the title of the article, the author's name, and the name and date of the publication in which it appeared.
9. Using a different database from the one you searched in question 8, find a Canadian newspaper article that deals with genetically modified (GM) foods. Provide the article title and the name of the newspaper it appeared in.
10. Can you access your library's databases from your home Internet service provider? If so, what procedure do you follow?

19

Summarizing, Paraphrasing, and Quoting

Once you have identified and evaluated your research sources, you must make accurate notes of the information you think you might use in your paper. There are many ways to take notes, ranging from jotting down single words or phrases to photocopying entire articles. You will save time if you remember that there are three ways of incorporating source information into your own writing: **summary**, **paraphrase**, and **direct quotation**. When you summarize or paraphrase, you restate in your own words the idea(s) of another speaker or writer. When you quote, you reproduce the exact words of another speaker or writer. Before we examine those three techniques, it is worthwhile to review what plagiarism is and how to avoid it.

PREVENTING PLAGIARISM

You can avoid plagiarism—the single biggest problem faced by students writing research papers and the instructors who mark them—by acknowledging (citing) all information you found in the sources you used for your paper. Cite your sources in an approved documentation style (usually MLA or APA).

Here are some guidelines to follow:

- Facts or sayings that are common knowledge do not have to be attributed; that is, you need not give sources for them. Examples: "Quebec City is the capital of Quebec"; "Sir John A. Macdonald was Canada's first prime minister"; "Beauty is in the eye of the beholder."

- Any passage, long or short, taken word for word from a source must be marked as a quotation, and you must cite its source. (See below, pages 280–86, and Chapter 20.)
- Facts, opinions, or ideas that you discovered on the Internet, found in a book or article, or learned from any other source—even if you express the information in your own words—must be acknowledged. (See below, pages 280–86, and Chapter 20.)
- Facts, opinions, or ideas that you remember reading or hearing somewhere cannot be presented as your own. If you cannot find and acknowledge the source, you should not use the information.
- If you are not sure whether a fact, opinion, or idea should be acknowledged, err on the side of caution and cite it. It's better to be safe than sorry.

Summarizing

When you summarize information, you find the main ideas in an article, essay, report, or other document, and rephrase them. You shorten (condense) the most important idea or ideas in the source material and express your understanding of them in your own words. The purpose of summarizing is to give the reader an overview of the article, report, or chapter. If the reader is interested in the details, he or she will read the original.

It's hard to overstate how valuable the ability to summarize is. Note-taking in college is one form of summarizing. Abstracts of articles, executive summaries of reports, market surveys, legal decisions, research findings, and records (called "minutes") of meetings, to name only a few kinds of formal documents, are all summaries. Thesis statements and topic sentences are essentially summaries; so, often, are conclusions. In committee, group, or teamwork, imagination and creativity are valuable, but the ability to summarize is even more so. There is no communication skill that you will need or use more than summarizing.

As a matter of fact, you summarize for yourself and others in every conversation you have. With friends, you may summarize the plot of a movie you've just seen or what happened in class this morning. When your mother calls, you'll summarize the events of the past week that you want her to know about. But most of us are not very good at summarizing effectively, especially in writing. It is a skill that doesn't come naturally. *You need to practise it*. You'll improve very quickly, however, if you think about what you're doing—that is, if you are conscious rather than unconscious of the times and the circumstances in which you call upon your summarizing skills. The following exercise will get you started.

Exercise 19.1

1. In groups of three or four, choose a movie you have all seen, a course you have all taken, a party or concert you have all attended, or a book you have all read. Then, without discussing your topic first, spend five minutes each writing a one-paragraph summary. After you have written your summary, use a highlighter to accent your main points.
2. Read and compare your summaries. What similarities and differences do you notice? Can you all agree that one summary is both complete and accurate? If not, spend another five or ten minutes discussing which are the main ideas and which are secondary to a discussion of your topic.
3. Now revise your one-paragraph summary to include all the main ideas and no secondary details.
4. Once again, read and compare each other's paragraphs. Which paragraph summarizes the topic best? What features does this paragraph have that the others lack?

HOW TO WRITE A SUMMARY

The work you summarize can be as short as a paragraph or as long as a book, as the following passage demonstrates:

> One of Edward de Bono's books is called *Six Thinking Hats*. [In it] he proposes that you adopt six different mind sets by mentally putting on six different coloured hats. Each hat stands for a certain way of thinking about a problem. By "putting on the hat" and adopting a certain role, we can think more clearly about the issues at hand. Because we're only "playing a role," there is little ego riding on what we say, so we are more free to say what we really want to say. De Bono likens the process of putting on the six hats one at a time to that of printing on a multicoloured map. Each colour is not a complete picture in itself. The map must go through the printing press six times, each time receiving a new colour, until we have the total picture.

Perrin, Timothy. "Positive Invention." *Better Writing for Lawyers*. Toronto: Law Society of Upper Canada, 1990. 51.

Notice that Perrin is careful to tell his readers the source of the ideas he is summarizing: both the author and the book are identified up front.

Before you can summarize anything, you need to *read* and *understand* it. The material you need to summarize is usually an article, essay, or chapter (or some portion of it). Depending on how much of the piece you need, your summary will range from a few sentences to one or two paragraphs.[1] Here's how to proceed:

1. Read through the piece carefully, looking up any words you don't understand. Write their meanings between the lines, above the words they apply to.

2. Now read the article or essay again. Keep rereading it until you have grasped the main ideas and formed a mental picture of their arrangement. Highlight the title, subtitle, and headings (if there are any). The title often identifies the subject of the piece, and a subtitle usually indicates its focus. If the article is long, the writer will often divide it into a number of smaller sections, each with its own heading. These headings usually identify the main points. If there are no headings, pay particular attention to the introduction—you should find an overview of the subject and a statement of the thesis—and the conclusion, which often summarizes the information and points to the significance of the topic.

3. In point form, and in your own words, write out a bare-bones outline of the piece. Your outline should consist of the controlling idea (thesis) of the article and the main ideas, in the order in which they appear. Do not include any supporting details (statistics, specific facts, examples, etc.).

4. Working from your outline, draft the summary. In the first sentence, identify the article or essay you are summarizing (by title, enclosed in quotation marks) and the author (by name, if known). Complete the sentence by stating the author's controlling idea. Here's an example:

In his essay "The Canadian Climate," D'Arcy McHale divides Canadians into two types: warm and cool.

Then state, in order, the author's main points. After each sentence in which you identify a main point, include any necessary explanation or clarification of that point. (The author, remember, developed each idea in the supporting details.) Try to resist going back to the article for your explanation. If you have truly understood the article, you should be

---

[1]This restriction applies only to the kind of research paper we are discussing in this part: one prepared for a college course. Other kinds of summary are longer. A précis, for example, is one-third the length of the source document. An abstract, which is a summary of a dissertation, academic paper, or public presentation, can be several paragraphs long.

able to explain each point from memory. If the author's conclusion contains any new information (i.e., is more than a summary and memorable statement), briefly state that information in your conclusion.

5. Revise your draft until it is coherent, concise, and makes sense to someone who is unfamiliar with the original work. It's a good idea to get someone to read through your summary to check it for clarity and completeness.

6. Don't forget to acknowledge your source. (Chapter 20 will show you how.)

The paragraph below summarizes the essay found on pages 204–05. Read it first, before you read the summary that follows.

In his essay "The Canadian Climate," D'Arcy McHale divides Canadians into two types: "warm" and "cool." The first category includes people who are enthusiastic about Canada's scenery, climate, and recreational activities, which they encourage newcomers to enjoy. Warm Canadians are also sincerely interested in learning about what life is like in the visitor's country of origin. In contrast, Cool Canadians are negative about their country and find it hard to believe that anyone from a warm climate would choose to endure the cold, bleak Canadian winters. Cool Canadians are not interested in detailed information about the visitor's country of origin, either; they are comfortable with their stereotypes. Finally, McHale acknowledges that the two types are mixed: each can at times behave like the other. Canadians, like the weather, are unpredictable, and newcomers are encouraged to accept them as they are and for themselves.

This seven-sentence paragraph (140 words) captures the gist of McHale's 600-word essay. Admittedly, it isn't very interesting. It lacks the flavour of the original. Summaries are useful for conveying an outline or a brief overview of someone else's ideas, but by themselves they are not very memorable. Details and specifics are what stick in a reader's mind; these are what your own writing should provide.

A summary should be entirely in your own words. Your ability to identify and interpret the author's meaning is evidence of your understanding of the article or essay. If you must include a short phrase from the source because there is no other way to word it, enclose the quoted material in quotation marks.

When writing a summary, do not

- introduce any ideas not found in the original
- change the proportion or emphasis of the original
- introduce your own opinion of the material

Exercise 19.2

Following the first five steps of the process outlined above, summarize "Ready, Willing . . . and Employable," which appears on pages 74–75. When you have completed your work, exchange papers with a partner. Use the following checklist to critique each other's summary.

	Good	Adequate	Try Again
1. The first sentence gives the title and the author's name.			
2. The essay's thesis is clearly and concisely reworded.			
3. Each main point (topic sentence) is restated in a single sentence.			
4. Each main point is briefly explained.			
5. The summary includes no secondary details that could be eliminated without diminishing the reader's understanding.			
6. The summary is balanced and objective.			
7. The paragraph flows smoothly; there are no obvious errors in sentence structure, grammar, spelling, or punctuation.			

Exercise 19.3

Select an article from a professional journal in your field. Summarize it by following the six steps given on pages 274–75. Assume your reader is a professional in the field.

Exercise 19.4

Choose an article that interests you from one of the regular sections (e.g., business, medicine, education, music, art) of a general news magazine such as *Maclean's, Time, Newsweek,* or the *Economist*. Summarize the article for a friend who is not an expert in the field and who has not read it. Do not evaluate the article or give your opinion about it. In a paragraph of approximately 150 to 200 words, simply inform your friend of its contents. Don't forget to cite your source!

Paraphrasing

When you paraphrase, you restate someone else's ideas in your own words. Unlike a summary, a paraphrase includes both the main and supporting ideas of your source. The usual purpose of a paraphrase is to express someone else's ideas more clearly and more simply—to translate what may be complex in the original into easily understandable prose. A paraphrase may be longer than the original, it may be about the same length, or it may be shorter. Whatever its length, a good paraphrase satisfies three criteria:

1. It is clear, concise, and easy to understand.
2. It communicates the idea(s) of the original passage.
3. It doesn't contain any idea(s) not found in the original passage.

Occasionally, you may need to clarify technical language or explain an aphorism, a proverb, or other saying that states a principle, offers an insight, or teaches a point. Statements that pack a lot of meaning into few words can be explained only at greater length. For example, one of the principal tenets of modern biology is "ontogeny recapitulates phylogeny." It simply isn't possible to paraphrase this principle in three words. (It means that as an embryo grows, it follows the same pattern of development that the animal did in the evolutionary process.)

Exercise 19.5

Working with a partner or a small group, discuss the meaning of the following expressions. When you are sure you understand them, write a paraphrase of each one.

1. A picture is worth a thousand words.
2. Money talks.
3. More haste, less speed.
4. Birds of a feather flock together.
5. Too many cooks spoil the broth.

To paraphrase a passage, you need to dig down through your source's words to the underlying ideas and then reword those ideas as clearly and simply as you can. Like summarizing, the ability to paraphrase is not an inborn talent; it takes patience and much practice to perfect it. But the rewards are worth your time and effort. First, paraphrasing improves your reading skill as well as your writing skill. Second, it improves your memory. In order to paraphrase accurately, you must thoroughly understand what you've read—and once you understand something, you're not likely to forget it.

First, let's look at how *not* to paraphrase. Assume we are writing an essay on designing an energy-efficient home, and we want to use the information given in the following paragraph.

The site and how the building relates to it is a critical determinant in the calculation of energy consumption. The most profound effects, and the ones the individual has least control over, are the macro-climatic (regional) factors of degree days, design temperature, wind, hours of bright sunshine, and the total solar insolation. Other factors which can have an enormous effect on the energy consumption of a house are micro-climatic. These include the topography of a site, the sun path, specific wind regime, vegetation, soil, and the placement of other buildings.

Argue, Robert. *The Well-Tempered House: Energy-Efficient Building for Cold Climates.* Toronto: Renewable Energy, 1980. 14.

There are two pieces of information in this paragraph that we want to include in our essay:

1. Some of the factors influencing energy consumption relate to the climate and weather patterns of the region (macro-climatic factors).
2. Some of the factors influencing energy consumption relate to the specific characteristics of the building site (micro-climatic factors).

If we are not careful, or if we don't have much experience with paraphrasing, our paragraph might look something like this:

In *The Well-Tempered House*, Robert Argue explains that a designer must consider two critical determinants in building an energy-efficient home. The most important factors, and the ones the individual has least control over, are the macro-climatic (regional) factors of degree days, design temperature, wind, hours of sunshine, and the total solar insolation. The other significant factors are the micro-climatic ones, which include the topography of the site, the sun path, wind regime, vegetation, soil, and the location of other buildings on or near the site.

This is plagiarism. Although we have indicated the source of the information, we have not indicated that the wording is almost identical to that of the original. Of the total 90 words, 50 come from the source. There are no visual or verbal cues to alert the reader that these are Argue's words, not ours. Let's try again.

In *The Well-Tempered House*, Robert Argue identifies two significant influences the cost-conscious home builder must consider in designing an energy-efficient house. The first and strongest influence is the typical weather of the region. The designer must be familiar with such "macro-climatic factors" as "degree days" (the difference between the indoor comfort temperature and the average daily outdoor temperature), "design temperature" (the lowest temperature to be expected during the heating season), wind, and the total effect of the sun. The other influences are called "micro-climatic factors" and include the site's topography (elevation and slope of the land), sun path, prevailing wind pattern, and the presence or absence of vegetation and nearby buildings.

Although this draft is technically a paraphrase rather than plagiarism, it doesn't demonstrate very much work on our part. We have replaced the source's words with synonyms and added explanations where the original is too technical to be easily understood by a general reader, but our paragraph still follows the original too closely. A paraphrase should not be used to pass off someone else's ideas as your own by changing a few words and sentences. A good paraphrase goes further. It uses source information but rearranges it, rephrases it, and combines it with the writer's own ideas to create something new. Let's try once more:

The cost-conscious home builder must consider a number of factors that will affect the energy consumption of his or her new home. The exterior design of the house should take advantage of the natural slope of the land, the presence of sheltering vegetation, prevailing wind patterns, the path of the sun, and other characteristics of the building site (Argue 14). In addition to sufficient insulation, the interior should feature appropriate heating and cooling devices to keep the family comfortable during the coldest winter days and the hottest summer days. To keep costs down, these devices should take advantage of the natural energy sources available: wind, sun, and seasonal fluctuations in temperature can all be used to harness and conserve energy. With careful planning, a new home can be designed to maximize the advantages of even an apparently unlikely site, minimize the negative effects of temperature and weather, and cost surprisingly little to maintain at a comfortable temperature year-round.

Here we have used paraphrase to incorporate information from a published source into a paragraph whose topic and structure are our own. This is how paraphrase can be used both responsibly and effectively. If you want to take ideas more directly from a source, retaining the original arrangement and some of the wording, you should use quotations.

Quoting

Of the three ways to introduce ideas from a source into your research paper, direct quotation is the one you should use least. (The exception is the literary essay, in which quotations from the original work are the evidence in your argument; see, for example, Jess Friedland's essay on pages 320–24.) If you use too many quotations, your paper will be a patchwork of the ideas of others, in their words, and very little of your own thinking will be communicated to the reader. Remember that the main reason teachers assign research papers is to test your ability to find, digest, and make sense of specific information about a topic. If what you hand in consists of a string of quotations, your paper will demonstrate only one of these three capabilities.

In most research papers, the ideas, facts, and statistics are the important things, not the wording of an idea or the explanation of facts or statistics. Occasionally, however, you will find that someone else—an expert in a particular field, a well-known author, or a respected public figure—has said what you want to say eloquently, vividly, more memorably than you could ever hope to say it. In such cases, quotations, *as long as they are short and not used too frequently*, are useful in developing your topic. Carefully woven into your paragraphs, they help convince the reader of the validity of what you have to say. Use quotations in writing the way you use salt in cooking: sparingly.

You can quote from two kinds of sources—

- people you know, or have heard speak, or have interviewed
- print, electronic, or recorded materials (e.g., books, articles, CD-ROMs, websites, films, tapes)

—and your quotation may be long or short.

BLOCK AND SPOT QUOTATIONS

If the material you are quoting is more than 40 words or four typed lines, it is a long—or **block**—quotation. After you have introduced it, you begin the quoted passage on a new line and indent all lines of the quotation 10 spaces or 2.5 cm from the left margin. *Do not put quotation marks around a block quotation.* The ten-space indentation is the reader's visual cue that this portion of the paragraph is someone else's words, not yours. Here's an example:

> Committees put a lot of thought into the design of fast foods. As David Bodanis points out with such good humour in *The Secret House*, potato chips are

an example of total destruction foods. The wild attack on the plastic wrap, the slashing and tearing you have to go through is exactly what the manufacturers wish. For the thing about crisp foods is that they're louder than non-crisp ones. . . . Destructo-packaging sets a favourable mood. . . . Crisp foods have to be loud in the upper register. They have to produce a high-frequency shattering; foods which generate low-frequency rumblings are crunchy, or slurpy but not crisp. . . .

Companies design potato chips to be too large to fit into the mouth, because in order to hear the high-frequency crackling, you need to keep your mouth open. Chips are 80 percent air, and each time we bite one we break open the air-packed cells of the chip, making that noise we call "crispy." Bodanis asks:

How to get sufficiently rigid cell walls to twang at these squeaking harmonics? Starch them. The starch granules in potatoes are identical to the starch in stiff shirt collars. . . . [In addition to starch,] all chips are soaked in fat. . . . So it's a shrapnel of flying starch and fat that produces the conical air-pressure wave when our determined chip-muncher finally gets to finish her chomp.

Ackerman, Diane. *A Natural History of the Senses.* New York: Random House, 1990. 142–43.

Notice that Ackerman is careful to tell her readers the source of her quotations. To introduce the first one, she gives the author's full name and the title of his book. To introduce the second quotation, which is from the same book, she simply identifies the author by surname. Thus, she doesn't waste words by repeating information, nor does she leave readers wondering where the quotation came from. (The only information missing is the publication data—city, publisher, and date—which is provided in the list of sources. See Chapter 20 for information on how to document your sources.)

A **spot quotation** is a word, a phrase, or a short sentence that is incorporated into one of your own sentences. *Put quotation marks before and after a spot quotation.* The quotation marks are a signal to the reader that these aren't your words; a new voice is speaking. The following paragraph contains several spot quotations.

"You are what you quote," in the words of the American essayist Joseph Epstein, himself a heavy user of quotations and the writer who introduced "quotatious" into my vocabulary. Winston Churchill understood the value of a well-aimed quotation: as a young man he read a few pages of *Bartlett's Familiar Quotations* every day to spruce up his style and compensate for his lack of a university education. [Gradually,] he transformed himself from a quotatious writer into the most quoted politician of the western world. . . . Fowler's *Modern English Usage* warns against quoting simply to demonstrate knowledge: "the discerning reader detects it and is contemptuous," while the undiscerning reader finds it tedious. A few years ago Garry Trudeau made fun of George Will's compulsive quoting by inventing a researcher who served as "quote boy" in Will's office: "'Quote boy! Need something on the banality of contemporary society.' 'Right away, Dr. Will!'" . . . As for me, I say don't judge, because you might get judged, too. That's how the quotation goes, right?

Fulford, Robert. "The Use and Abuse of Quotations." *Globe and Mail* 11 Nov. 1992: C1.

HOW TO MODIFY A QUOTATION

In addition to illustrating how to introduce and format block quotations and how to punctuate spot quotations, the examples above also show how to modify a quotation to fit your space and suit your purpose. Although *you must quote exactly and never misrepresent or distort your source's intention*, you may, for reasons of conciseness or smoothness, omit or add a word or phrase or even a sentence or two.

- To leave out a word or words, indicate the omission by replacing the word(s) you've omitted with three spaced dots called **ellipses** (. . .). If the omission comes at the end of your sentence, add a fourth dot as the period.
- If you need to add or change a word or words to make the quoted passage more readable within your paragraph, use **square brackets** around your own words, as we did when we added "[In addition to starch,]" in Ackerman's second block quotation from Bodanis and "[Gradually,]" to Fulford's paragraph.

If you have omitted some words from a source, you may need to add a transitional phrase or change the first letter of a word to a capital: [T]hus. Another reason for changing words in a quoted passage is to keep the verb tenses consistent throughout your paragraph. If you are writing in the present tense and the passage you are quoting is in the past tense, you can change the verbs to present tense (so long as the change doesn't distort the meaning) and put square brackets around them so the reader knows you have made these changes.

Modifying short quotations to make them fit smoothly into your own sentences without altering the source's meaning takes practice. Reread the paragraph that we have quoted on pages 281–82. Notice that to make Fulford's original slightly shorter and easier to read, we made a couple of minor alterations to the original. The signals to the reader that something has been added or left out are the same as those used in a block quotation: square brackets and ellipses.

HOW TO INTEGRATE QUOTATIONS INTO YOUR WRITING

When you decide to quote source material, you should introduce it so that it will blend as seamlessly as possible into your writing. Don't simply park someone else's words in the middle of your paragraph; you'll disrupt the flow of thought. If Diane Ackerman were not so skillful a writer, she might have "dumped" quotations into her paragraph instead of integrating them. Contrast the readability of the paragraph below with that of Ackerman's second paragraph (on page 281).

Companies design potato chips to be too large to fit into the mouth because, in order to hear the high-frequency crackling, you need to keep your mouth open. Chips are 80 percent air, and each time we bite one, we break open the air-packed cells of the chip, making that crispy noise. "The starch granules in potatoes are identical to the starch in stiff shirt collars." Starch is just one of the ingredients that contribute to the crispiness of potato chips. "All chips are soaked in fat." "So it's a shrapnel of flying starch and fat that produces the conical air pressure wave when our determined chip-muncher finally gets to finish her chomp."

Without transitional phrases, the paragraph lacks coherence and doesn't make sense. Not convinced? Try reading the two paragraphs aloud.

Every quotation should be introduced and integrated into an essay in a way that makes clear the relationship between the quotation and your own argument. There are four ways to integrate a spot quotation.

1. You can introduce it with a phrase such as "According to X," or "Y states" (or *observes*, or *comments*, or *writes*), followed by a comma. Different verbs suggest different attitudes toward the quoted material. For example, "Fulford *suggests* that writers should not overuse quotations" is more tentative than "Fulford *warns* that writers should not overuse quotations." Other verbs you can use to introduce quotations are *asserts*, *notes*, *points out*, *maintains*, *shows*, *reports*, and *claims*. Choose your introductory verbs carefully, and be sure to use a variety of phrases. The repetitive "X says," "Y says," and "Z says," is a sure way to put your reader to sleep.

2. If your introductory words form a complete sentence, use a colon (:) to introduce the quotation.

   George Bernard Shaw's poor opinion of teachers is well known: "Those who can, do; those who can't, teach."

Oscar Wilde's opinion of teachers is less famous than Shaw's but even more cynical: "Everybody who is incapable of learning has taken to teaching."

3. If the passage you are quoting is a couple of words, a phrase, or anything less than a complete sentence, do not use any punctuation to introduce it.

Oscar Wilde defined fox hunters as "the unspeakable in full pursuit of the uneatable."

Wilde believed that people "take no interest in a work of art until they are told that the work in question is immoral."

4. If you insert your own words into the middle of a quotation, use commas to separate the source's words from yours.

"It is a truth universally acknowledged," writes Jane Austen at the beginning of *Pride and Prejudice*, "that a single man in possession of a good fortune must be in want of a wife."

In general, periods and commas are placed inside the quotation marks (see the examples above). Unless they are part of the quoted material, colons, semicolons, question marks, exclamation marks, and dashes are placed outside the quotation marks. Use single quotation marks to mark off a quotation within a quotation.

According to John Robert Colombo, "The most widely quoted Canadian aphorism of all time is Marshall McLuhan's 'The medium is the message.'"

Block quotations are normally introduced by a complete sentence followed by a colon (for example, "X writes as follows:"). Then you copy the quotation, beginning on a new line and indenting 10 spaces or 2.5 cm. If your introductory statement is not a complete sentence, use a comma or no punctuation, whichever is appropriate. The passage by Diane Ackerman on pages 280–81 contains examples of both ways to introduce block quotations. Turn to it now. Can you explain why Ackerman has used no punctuation to introduce the first block quotation and a colon to introduce the second one?

For each of the following quotations, make up three different sentences as follows:

a. Introduce the complete quotation with a phrase followed by a comma.
b. Introduce the complete quotation with an independent clause followed by a colon.
c. Introduce a portion of the quotation with a phrase or statement that requires no punctuation between it and the quotation. Use ellipses and square brackets, if necessary, to signal any changes you make in the original wording.

Example: Education is the ability to listen to almost anything without losing your temper or your self-confidence. (Robert Frost)

a. According to Robert Frost, "Education is the ability to listen to almost anything without losing your temper or your self-confidence." (complete quotation introduced by phrase + comma)
b. Robert Frost had a peculiar notion of higher learning: "Education is the ability to listen to almost anything without losing your temper or your self-confidence." (complete quotation introduced by independent clause + colon)
c. Robert Frost defined education as "the ability to listen to . . . anything without losing [one's] temper or [one's] self-confidence." (partial quotation introduced by phrase requiring no punctuation; changes indicated with ellipses and square brackets)

1. I find the three major administrative problems on a campus are sex for the students, athletics for the alumni, and parking for the faculty. (Clark Kerr, former president of the University of California)
2. Education is not a *product*: mark, diploma, job, money—in that order; it is a *process*, a never-ending one. (Bel Kaufman, author of *Up the Down Staircase*)
3. School days, I believe, are the unhappiest in the whole span of human existence. (H. L. Mencken, American humorist)
4. In the first place, God made idiots. This was for practice. Then he made school boards. (Mark Twain)
5. Education makes a people easy to lead, but difficult to drive; easy to govern, but impossible to enslave. (Lord Brougham, founder of the University of London, 1825)

TIPS ON USING QUOTATIONS IN YOUR WRITING

1. **Use quotations sparingly and for a specific purpose**, such as *for emphasis* or *to reinforce an important point.* Avoid the temptation to produce a patchwork paper—one that consists of bits and pieces of other people's writing stuck together to look like an original work. Far from impressing your readers, overuse of quotations will give them the impression you have nothing of your own to say.

2. **Be sure every quotation is an accurate reproduction of the original passage.** If you need to change or omit words, indicate those changes with square brackets or ellipses, as appropriate.

3. **Be sure every quotation is relevant.** No matter how interesting or well worded, a quotation that does not clearly and directly relate to your subject does not belong in your essay. An irrelevant quotation will either confuse readers or annoy them (they'll think it's padding), or both.

4. **Make clear the link between the quotation and your controlling idea.** Don't assume readers will automatically see the connection you see between the quotation and your topic sentence. Comment on the quotation so they will be sure to make the connection you intend. If you have used a block quotation, your explanatory comment can sometimes form the conclusion of your paragraph.

5. **Always identify the source of a quotation.** This can be done by mentioning in your paragraph the name of the author and, if appropriate, the title of the source of the quotation. Include the page number(s) in a parenthetical citation. See Chapter 20 for details, and follow the format your instructor prefers.

(**Exercise 19.7**)————————————————————

Read the passages below and then, with your partner, discuss and answer the questions that follow.

1.   Whenever college teachers get together informally, sooner or later the conversation turns to students' excuses. The stories students tell to justify absences or late assignments are a source of endless amusement among faculty. These stories tend to fall into three broad thematic categories.

     Accident, illness, and death are at the top of the list. If the stories were true, such incidents would be tragic, not funny. But how could any instructor be expected to keep a straight face at being told, "I can't take the test on Friday because my mother is having a vasectomy"? Or "I need a week's extension because my friend's aunt died"? Or—my personal favourite—"The reason I didn't show up for the final exam was because I have inverse testosterone"?

Problems with pets rank second in the catalogue of student excuses. Animals take precedence over tests: "I can't be at the exam because my cat is having kittens and I'm her coach"; and they are often responsible for a student's having to hand in an assignment late. The age-old excuse "My dog ate my homework" gets no more marks for humour than it does for originality, but occasionally a student puts a creative spin on this old chestnut. Would you believe "My paper is late because my parrot crapped in my computer"?

In third place on the list of students' tales of extenuating circumstances are social commitments of various sorts. "I was being arraigned in Chicago for arms dealing"; "I had to see my fence to pick out a ring for my fiancée"; and "I can't take the exam on Monday because my Mom is getting married on Sunday and I'll be too drunk to drive back to school" are just three examples collected by one college teacher in a single semester.

An enterprising computer programmer could easily compile an "excuse bank" that would allow students to type in the code number of a standard explanation and zap it to their professors. I suspect, however, that there would be little faculty support for such a project. Electronic excuses would lack the humour potential of live ones. Part of the fun comes from watching the student confront you, face to face, shamelessly telling a tale that would make Paul Bunyan blush.

1. Are all the quotations relevant to the subject of this brief essay? Are they sufficiently limited, or could the essay be improved by leaving any out?
2. Underline the specific connections the writer makes between her quotations and her controlling idea.
3. What purpose does the concluding sentence serve? Would the essay be equally effective without it? Why?

2.   U.S. federal drug policy, especially the mandatory minimum sentences for drug offenders enacted by Congress in 1987, has so distressed federal judges that approximately 10 percent of them will not hear drug trials. Judge Jack B. Weinstein of Brooklyn, N.Y., is a case in point. In an April 1993 memo to all the judges in his district, he announced that he would no longer preside over trials of defendants charged with drug crimes:

> One day last week I had to sentence a peasant woman from West Africa [with four dependent children] to forty-six months. . . . On the same day I sentenced a man to thirty years as a second drug offender—a heavy sentence mandated by the Guidelines and statute. These two cases confirm my sense of frustration about much of the cruelty I have been party to in connection with the "war on drugs" that is being fought by the military, police, and courts rather than by our medical and social institutions.

I myself am unsure how this drug problem should be handled, but I need a rest from the oppressive sense of futility that these cases leave. Accordingly, I have taken my name out of the wheel for drug cases. This resolution leaves me uncomfortable since it shifts the "dirty work" to other judges. At the moment, however, I simply cannot sentence another impoverished person whose destruction can have no discernible effect on the drug trade. I wish I were in a position to propose a solution, but I am not. I'm just a tired old judge who has temporarily filled his quota of remorse-lessness.

The sentencing guidelines that Congress requires judges to follow are so harsh they cause, in Weinstein's words, "overfilling [of] our jails and . . . unnecessary havoc to families, society, and prisons." As a senior judge, Weinstein can choose the cases he hears. But 90 percent of judges are not so fortunate. After they have imposed on a low-level smuggler or a poverty-stricken "mule" a sentence far harsher than those mandated for someone convicted of rape or manslaughter, one wonders how—or if—judges can sleep at night.

"The War on Drugs: A Judge Goes AWOL." *Harper's Magazine* Dec. 1993: 18.

1. This writer uses both block and spot quotations to develop her point. Where does she make clear the connection between the block quotation and her topic?
2. The original passage from which the writer extracted her spot quotation reads as follow: "Most judges today take it for granted, as I do, that the applicable guideline for the defendant before them will represent an excessive sentence. The sentencing guidelines result, in the main, in the cruel imposition of excessive sentences, overfilling our jails and causing unnecessary havoc to families, society, and prisons." Why did the writer modify the quotation the way she did?
3. In tip 4 (see page 286), we advise you not to introduce a quotation and just leave it hanging but to comment on it. Where does this writer comment on the quotations she has used?

Additional Suggestions for Writing

1. Interview someone two generations removed from you (e.g., a grandparent, an elderly neighbour) about his or her life as a young person. What were the sources of entertainment? Leisure activities? Work? Family responsibilities? Major challenge or concerns? Goals? Write an essay in which you tell this person's story, using summary, paraphrase, and quotation to develop your main points.

2. Interview a friend, classmate, or relative on one of the following topics. Then write an essay using summary, paraphrase, and quotation to help tell your reader how your interviewee answered the question.
   a. If you were to live your life over knowing what you know now, what would you do differently?
   b. Explain what being a Canadian (or a parent, or childless, or unemployed, or successful, or a member of a particular religious group) means to you.
   c. "Once I was _____; now I am _____."
3. Research a topic of particular interest to you and write an essay using summary, paraphrase, and quotation to develop your main points.
4. Select a news article or a group of articles dealing with a current issue in your career field. In a paragraph of approximately 200 to 300 words, summarize the issue for your instructor, who has just returned from spending six months in the wilderness without access to either print or electronic media.

20

Documenting
Your Sources

Documentation is the process of acknowledging source material. When you document a source, you provide information that

1. tells your readers that the ideas they are reading have been borrowed from another writer, and
2. enables your readers to find the source and read the material for themselves.

When acknowledging your sources in a research paper, you need to follow a system of documentation. There are many different systems, but one of the most widely used is that of the Modern Language Association (MLA). The instructions and examples in this chapter are a slightly simplified version of the principles outlined by Joseph Gibaldi in the *MLA Handbook for Writers of Research Papers*, 6th ed. (New York: MLA, 2003. http://www.mla.org). Most instructors in English and the humanities require students to use MLA style.

Instructors in the social sciences (psychology, sociology, political science, and economics) usually expect papers to conform to the principles of APA style, based on the *Publication Manual of the American Psychological Association*, 5th ed. (Washington, DC: APA, 2001. http://www.apa.org). You will find instruction and examples of APA style in Appendix B.

For research papers in the biological sciences, your instructor may require Council of Biology Editors (CBE) style, presented in *Scientific Style and Format: The CBE Manual for Authors, Editors, and Publishers* (http://www .councilscienceeditors.org).

Many academic institutions publish their own style guides, which are available in college and university libraries and bookstores. Be sure to ask your instructor which documentation style he or she prefers.

Introduction: The Two-Part Principle of Documentation

Documentation styles vary in their details, but all styles require authors to

- identify in a parenthetical reference any information taken from a source, and
- list all sources for the paper on a separate page at the end.

A **parenthetical reference** (called a **parenthetical reference citation** in APA style) tells the reader that the information preceding the parentheses[1] is borrowed from a source and provides a key to the full identification of that source. For the most part, footnotes are no longer used to document source material; they are used to give additional information that cannot be conveniently worked into the body of your paragraph. (Note the example in this paragraph.)

A **Works Cited** list (called **References** in APA style) is a list of all the sources from which you have borrowed words, ideas, data, or other material in your paper.[2] Preparing and presenting a Works Cited list requires paying close attention to the details of presenting the information required in each entry. The format—including the order of information, capitalization, and punctuation—prescribed by your style guide must be followed *exactly*. This requirement may sound picky, but there is a good reason to abide by it.

Every kind of source you use requires a particular format. If entries are formatted correctly, an experienced reader can tell by glancing at them what kinds of sources you have used: books, journal articles, newspaper articles, Web documents, etc. If you use the wrong style, or leave something out, or scramble the elements in a citation, you will mislead or confuse your reader. Fortunately, technology is available to help you make the task of documenting much less onerous than it once was. Before you begin taking notes, find a reference manager program such as EndNote or ProCite. (See http://www.isiresearchsoft.com for these and other managers.) Some programs offer a 30-day free trial. Different programs have different features, but most will help you keep track of the notes you've taken from various sources, and all will format your Works Cited or References list for you.

---

[1]A punctuation note: *parentheses* means the pair of curvy punctuation marks: ( ). *Brackets* are the pair of square marks that surround altered words or phrases in a quotation: [ ].
[2]Formerly, this list was called a *Bibliography*.

How to Punctuate Titles in MLA Style

Depending on your instructor's preference, you may *italicize* or <u>underline</u> titles and subtitles of any work that is published as a whole—e.g., the names of books, plays, periodicals (newspapers, magazines, and journals), films, radio and television programs, compact discs—or underline them if you are using a pen. Put quotation marks around the titles of works published within larger works—e.g., the names of articles, essays, poems, songs, and individual episodes of television or radio programs. Also put quotation marks around the titles of unpublished works, such as lectures and speeches. Use capital letters for the first, the last, and all main words in a title and subtitle even if your source capitalizes only the first word in a title.

Parenthetical References in MLA Style

Every time you include in your paper a quotation, paraphrase, summary, fact, or idea you have borrowed from another writer, you must identify the source in parentheses immediately following the borrowed material. The parenthetical reference tells your reader that what he or she has just read comes from somewhere else, and it points your reader to the complete information about the source in your Works Cited list. Parenthetical references should be as short and simple as possible while still fulfilling these two purposes.

The standard practice in MLA style is to provide the surname of the author of the source material and the page number where the material was taken from. Once your reader has the author's name and page number, he or she can find complete bibliographic information about the source in your Works Cited list at the end of your paper. Of course, electronic sources present a challenge to this author-based citation method because they often lack an identifiable author, and they rarely include page numbers. More on this later.

You need to include a piece of source information only once; don't repeat information unnecessarily. For example, if you've already mentioned the author's name in your paragraph, you only need to give the page reference in the parentheses.

On page 293 is an excerpt from a research paper. The writer uses summary, paraphrase, and quotation, and gives the necessary source information in parentheses immediately following each borrowing. This excerpt also demonstrates how to omit a word or words from a source, using ellipses, and how to add or change a word or words, using square brackets.

The Works Cited list that follows the excerpt gives the reader full bibliographic information about each source.

The attractive young people who are portrayed in tobacco advertising make it easy for viewers to forget the terrible consequences of tobacco addiction. Cigarette advertisements routinely portray happy, energetic young people engaging in athletic activities under invariably sunny skies. The implication of these ads is that smoking is not a deterrent to an active lifestyle; in fact, it may even be a prerequisite (Cunningham 67).

Full parenthetical citation

It is difficult to overstate the impact of tobacco advertising on young people. As Cunningham points out,

> Few teenagers begin smoking for cigarettes' inherent physical qualities. Instead, teens are attracted to smoking for its image attributes, such as the five S's: sophistication, slimness, social acceptability, sexual attractiveness, and status. Marketing gives a cigarette a false "personality." (66)

Block quotation

Abbreviated parenthetical citation

Is it any wonder that young people continue to take up the habit?

In an effort to reverse the trend of teenage tobacco addiction, the federal government sponsors awareness campaigns to demonstrate how the tobacco industry dupes and manipulates young people. According to Robert Sheppard, the industry plays on teenagers' "need [for] something to rebel against . . . [which] is exactly how cigarette manufacturers market their wares" (20). To counteract the image of smoking as a symbol of rebellion, government anti-tobacco campaigns present smoking as a symbol of conformity.

Short quotation with
• word changed
• words left out
• parenthetical citation

Yielding to pressure from the government and the community, the tobacco industry has begun to sponsor programs aimed at restricting youth access to tobacco products. In a comprehensive review, however, the Ontario Medical Association (OMA) concludes that these programs are ineffective and makes several recommendations to strengthen youth reduction initiatives (OMA).

Parenthetical citation of paraphrase

The OMA recommends that all parties interested in reducing tobacco use endorse a comprehensive tobacco control program. The Association offers to work with the Canadian Medical Association and other interested parties to ensure that its position statement is published as widely as possible. And finally, the OMA recommends that all tobacco industry-sponsored programs be carefully monitored in the future (OMA).

Parenthetical citation of summary

Works Cited

Cunningham, Rob. *Smoke and Mirrors: The Canadian Tobacco War*. Ottawa: IDRC, 1996.

Ontario Medical Association. "More Smoke and Mirrors: Tobacco Industry-Sponsored Youth Prevention Programs in the Context of Comprehensive Tobacco Control Programs in Canada." A Position Statement. Feb. 2002. 3 Feb. 2005 <http://www.oma.org/phealth/ smokeandmirrors.htm>.

Sheppard, Robert. "Ottawa Butts Up against Big Tobacco." *Maclean's* 6 Dec. 1999: 20–24.

Study the way the excerpt on page 293 uses parenthetical references to identify information sources. The introductory paragraph ends with a paraphrase, which is immediately followed by a full parenthetical reference. Because the author's name is not mentioned in the writer's paragraph, it is given in parentheses, together with the number of the page on which the information was found. For more details, the reader would turn to the Works Cited list, reproduced at the bottom of page 293.

The second paragraph includes a block quotation from the same source. The author's name is given in the statement that introduces the quotation, so the parentheses contain only the page number on which the quotation can be found.

The third paragraph includes a short quotation integrated into the writer's own sentence. The introductory phrase gives the author's name, so the parenthetical reference provides only the page number of the article on which this partial quotation is found. Complete bibliographic information for this source appears in the Works Cited list.

In the fourth paragraph, the writer includes both a paraphrase and a summary of information found in an unsigned article posted on the website of the Ontario Medical Association. The source document is not paginated, so no page number is given. Complete information about this source appears in the alphabetical list of Works Cited under Ontario Medical Association, the sponsor of the site.

EXAMPLES OF PARENTHETICAL REFERENCES: TRADITIONAL PRINT SOURCES

1. If you name the source author in your paragraph, give just the page number in parentheses.

   Isajiw asserts that the twentieth century "has produced more refugees and exiles than any other preceding period since the fall of the Roman Empire"(66).

   The Works Cited entry for this book is on page 298.

2. If you do not name the source author in your paragraph, give the author's surname and the page number.

   The effect of "status drop" on the psychological well-being of immigrants can be substantial: "Especially among those more highly educated, this experience can cause feelings of bitterness or hostility. . . ." (Isajiw 97).

3. If no author is named in the source, give the first few words of the Works Cited entry.

Legislation to reduce the amount of pollution generated by large-scale vehicles has been on the federal agenda for some time: "Canada has said it will toughen pollution-emission rules for all new vehicles, ending a loophole that allowed less stringent standards for popular sport-utility vehicles and minivans" ("Canada to Toughen" A6).

The Works Cited entry for this source is on page 300.

4. If your source was published in more than one volume, give the volume number before the page reference.

Only once in his two-volume work does Erickson suggest conspiracy (2: 184).

The Works Cited entry for this source is on page 298.

5. If you are quoting from a literary classic or the Bible, use Arabic numerals separated by periods to identify act, scene, and lines from a play or a biblical chapter and verse.

In Shakespeare's play, the duke's threat to give "measure for measure" (5.1.414) echoes the familiar passage in the Bible (Matthew 7.1–2).

EXAMPLES OF PARENTHETICAL REFERENCES: ELECTRONIC SOURCES

Parenthetical references for print sources in MLA style usually include the author's surname and the page number of the source. This principle is problematic for electronic sources since many of them lack one or both of these elements. Give enough information to guide your reader to the source listed in your Works Cited list.

1. If the electronic source lists an author, give the surname in your parenthetical reference.

Planespotting is a popular hobby, even an obsession, for growing numbers of people who are fascinated with aviation: "Some spotters take photographs. Others make videotapes. But the majority flock to airports around the world, equipped with scanners and notepads, with one goal in mind--recording the registration numbers painted on airplane tails" (Bourette).

This quotation comes from *Shift*, an online magazine. The Works Cited entry for this quotation is on page 302.

2. If the electronic source does not list an author, give the document title (or a shortened version of the title) in italics or quotation marks as appropriate, instead of the author's name.

New websites are available to help students navigate their way through the challenging works of William Shakespeare:

> There are some people who don't even attempt to learn Shakespeare because they think that Shakespeare is . . . only for English scholars. But that's not true! Shakespeare can be FUN. That's right—Shakespeare can actually be something you want to learn about. ("William Shakespeare")

This quotation comes from a website called *Shakespeare: Chill with Will*. The Works Cited entry for this quotation is on page 303.

3. You do not usually find page numbers or other navigation devices in an electronic source. If there are page, paragraph, or section numbers that could guide your reader to the specific material being quoted, include them. If the author's name is included in the parenthetical reference, put a comma after it and include the section or paragraph numbers. Use the abbreviations *sec.* and *par.*

Even Margaret Atwood must endure the editing process before her books are published:

> Being edited is like falling face down into a threshing machine. Every page gets fought over, back and forth, like WWI. Unless the editor and the writer both have in mind the greater glory of the work, . . . blood will flow and the work will suffer. Every comma, every page break, may be a ground for slaughter. (sec. 6)

This quotation comes from an article posted on Atwood's website. The Works Cited entry is found on page 303.

If there are no page, paragraph, or section numbers to identify the quotation, simply give the author's name or the title in parentheses. If your reader wants to locate the information, web browser search engines can often find it through a keyword search.

The Works Cited List

The Works Cited list appears at the end of your essay. It includes detailed bibliographical information for all the sources you have summarized, paraphrased, or quoted in your paper. The information listed in the Works Cited list enables your reader to assess the extent of your research and to find and check every source you used.

Begin the list on a new page and number each page, continuing the page numbers of your paper. (The page number appears in the upper right-hand corner, 1.25 cm from the top and lined up with the right margin.) Centre the heading, Works Cited, an inch from the top of the page. Double-space the entire list, including the title and the first entry. Begin each entry at the left margin. If an entry runs more than one line (and most do), indent the subsequent line or lines five spaces or 1.25 cm. This format is called a "hanging indent"[3] and can be found in most word-processing packages.

Arrange the entries alphabetically, beginning with the first word of the entry, which is often the author's surname. If no author is identified in your source, alphabetize by the first word in the title, ignoring *A*, *An*, and *The*. For example, *The Canadian Encyclopedia* would be listed under *C*, for *Canadian*. Separate the main parts of each entry with periods. Do not number your entries.

Below you will find instruction and examples for four different kinds of Works Cited entries: books, periodical articles, audiovisual sources, and electronic sources.

BOOKS, ENCYCLOPEDIAS, AND GOVERNMENT PUBLICATIONS

Here is the basic model for a book entry in a Works Cited list.

Last name of author, First name. *Title of Book.* City of publication:
    Publisher, year of publication.

Note the spacing, capitalization, and punctuation as well as the order of the information. If several cities are listed, use the first one. Shorten the publisher's name. For example, McGraw-Hill, Inc. is abbreviated to McGraw. If the publisher is a well-known university press, use the abbreviation UP: e.g., Oxford UP, U of Toronto P. The year the book was published is usually found on the back of the title page; if it is not given, use the latest copyright date.

---

[3]Hanging indents help readers locate authors' names in the alphabetical listing. If you have only one source to acknowledge, you do not need to indent the second line. For example, see the source citation for Robert Argue's book on page 278.

- **Book by one author or editor**

  Isajiw, Wsevolod W. *Understanding Diversity: Ethnicity and Race in the Canadian Context.* Toronto: Thompson, 1999.

  Barnes, Wendy, ed. *Taking Responsibility: Citizen Involvement in the Criminal Justice System.* Toronto: Centre of Criminology, University of Toronto, 1995.

- **Book by two or three authors or editors**

  Strange, Carolyn, and Tina Loo. *True Crime, True North: The Golden Age of Canadian Pulp Magazines.* Vancouver: Raincoast Books, 2004.

  France, Honoré, Maria del Carmen Rodriguez, and Geoffrey Hett, eds. *Diversity, Culture and Counselling: A Canadian Perspective.* Calgary: Detselig, 2004.

- **Book by more than three authors or editors**

  Beebe, Steven A., et al. *Interpersonal Communication: Relating to Others.* Scarborough: Allyn and Bacon, 1997.

- **Edition other than the first**

  Cooperman, Susan H. *Professional Office Procedures.* 3rd ed. Upper Saddle River, NJ: Prentice, 2002.

- **Recent edition of a classic text**

  Shakespeare, William. *The Tempest.* Ed. S. Orgel. Oxford: Oxford UP, 1994.

- **Multivolume work**

  Erickson, Edward W., and Leonard Waverman, eds. *The Energy Question: An International Failure of Policy.* 2 vols. Toronto: U of Toronto P, 1974.

- **Article, essay, story, or poem in a collection**

  Kliewer, Gregory. "Faking My Way through School." *Canadian Content.* Ed. Nell Waldman and Sarah Norton. 4th ed. Toronto: Harcourt, 2000. 311–12.

- **Encyclopedia reference**

  Driedger, Leo. "Ethnic Identity." *Canadian Encyclopedia.* 2000 ed.

- **Book published by a corporation (company, commission, or agency)**

  International Joint Commission. *Protection of the Waters of the Great
  Lakes: Final Report to the Governments of Canada and the United
  States.* Ottawa: The Commission, 2000.

- **Government publication**
  If the author is not named, identify the government first, then the
  agency, then the title, city of publication, publisher, and date.

  Canada. Canadian Heritage. *Canadian Content in the 21st Century: A
  Discussion Paper about Canadian Content in Film and Television
  Productions.* Hull, QC: Canadian Heritage, 2002.

  Ontario. Ministry of Training, Colleges and Universities. *Employment
  Profile: A Summary of the Employment Experience of 1999–2000
  College Graduates Six Months after Graduation.* Toronto: Ministry of
  Training, Colleges and Universities, 2001.

ARTICLES IN JOURNALS, MAGAZINES, AND NEWSPAPERS

As with a book, information for an article begins with the author's name,
if available, includes the title of the article, and ends with the details of
publication, including the date, and the complete pages of the article. For
a periodical that is published weekly or every two weeks, provide the day,
month, and year, in that order. Abbreviate all months except for May, June,
and July (Jan., Feb., Mar., Apr., Aug., Sept., Oct., Nov., Dec.). If the periodical is published monthly, provide month and year.

Works Cited entries for newspapers include the name as it appears on the
masthead (top front page of the paper) but omit *The* (e.g., *Globe and Mail*). If
the name of the city is not included in a locally published paper, add the city
in square brackets—not underlined—after the name so that readers will know
where it was published; for instance, *Comox Valley Record* [Campbell River].

Give the complete page span for each article in your Works Cited list. For
example, if an article begins on page 148 and concludes on page 164, put
a colon and the pages after the date: 5 June 2006: 148–64. If the article

begins on page 36, then skips to page 40 and concludes on page 41, give only the first page and a plus sign: 36+. In a newspaper, the sections are usually numbered separately, so include the section number as well as the page number: *Calgary Herald* 16 Aug. 2005: S1+.

Note the order, punctuation, and capitalization of the information in the model below.

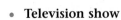

> Author's last name, First name. "Title of Article." *Title of Periodical*
> Volume no. [if any] Issue no. [if any] Date: pages.

- **Article in a scholarly journal**

  Lemire, Judith A. "Preparing Nurse Leaders: A Leadership Model."
  Nursing Leadership Forum 6.3 (2001): 39–44.

Some scholarly journals publish a number of issues each year; together, these issues make up an annual volume. Give the volume number (in this example, 6) right after the periodical title, add a period, and then give the issue number (here, 3) immediately before the date, which is given in parentheses in this type of entry, but not in those that follow.

- **Article in a monthly magazine**

  Reece, Erik. "Death of a Mountain: Radical Strip Mining and the
  Leveling of Appalachia." *Harper's* Apr. 2005: 41–60.

- **Signed article in a newspaper**

  Edwards, Steven. "Teenagers Told to Turn Off the Sun." *National Post* 18
  Mar. 2005: A19.

- **Unsigned newspaper article**

  "Canada to Toughen Auto-Emissions Rules." *Wall Street Journal* 5 Apr.
  2002: A6.

- **Review**

  Houpt, Simon. "Spamalot a Spoof to End All Spoofs." Rev. of *Monty
  Python's Spamalot*, by Eric Idle. Dir. Mike Nichols. Shubert Theatre,
  New York. *Globe and Mail* 19 Mar. 2005: R7.

AUDIOVISUAL SOURCES

- **Television show**

  Remembering Peter Gzowski. Host Mark Kelley. CBC Newsworld.
  30 Jan. 2002.

- **Radio show**

  "Hallway Confidential." *Outfront*. CBC Radio One, Toronto. 23 Mar.
  2005.

- **Recording**

  Chiarelli, Rita. *Breakfast at Midnight*. NorthernBlues, 2001.

- **Film, videocassette, laser disc, or DVD**

  Bowling for Columbine. Dir. Michael Moore. 2002. DVD. United
  Artists/Alliance Atlantis. 2002.

  If you wish to give credit to the contribution of a particular individual
  to a film or recording, begin with that person's name.

  Hitchcock, Alfred, dir. *Rear Window*. Perf. Jimmy Stewart, Grace Kelly,
  and Raymond Burr. 1954. DVD. Universal, 2001.

ELECTRONIC SOURCES

Documentation guidelines for electronic publications are now fairly standardized. Check with your Resource Centre to see if it provides handouts to help you cite these sources accurately. Works Cited entries should identify the source and provide enough information to enable a reader to locate it—author, title, publication information, and date. However, providing all this information is not always possible for online materials. Include as much information as you can, and remember that the key element in citing an electronic source is its electronic address or URL (uniform resource locator).

Do not use a hyphen to divide a URL over two lines; otherwise, you will make it invalid. Record the URL on a single line, or break it after a slash (/), and enclose it within angle brackets (<...>). Because the symbols, letters, and numbers that make up a URL are complex and must be recorded accurately, some recent guidelines suggest that angle brackets be omitted. Be sure to use the format your instructor prefers.

Along with the URL, other essential information includes the date of publication (if it is available) and the date that you, as the researcher, accessed the information. The access date is important because online documents can be altered at any time. (Use the abbreviation conventions provided in the guidelines for periodicals: e.g., Mar. for March.)

Download and print online material so that you can verify it if, at a later date, it is revised, unavailable, or inaccessible.

Follow this basic model for online source entries in a Works Cited list:

Author's last name, First name [if known]. "Title of Document or File." *Title of Complete Work or Site*. Date of document or of last revision. Date of access <URL, including protocol[4]>.

Several of your sources should come from the subscription databases available at your library. These databases provide access to full-text articles in reputable journals, magazines, newspapers, and other reliable research resources. When you use an online subscription service to retrieve articles, MLA style requires that you include the name of the library in the reference citation:

Author's last name, First name (if known). "Title of Article." *Title of Journal/Newspaper/Magazine*. Date of publication. Name of database. Name of library, City in which library is located. Date of access <URL of the subscription database>.

Many subscription databases will keep track of your citations and format them in various documentation styles (MLA, APA, Turabian, etc.). Look for this feature on the results page of the database, or ask a librarian if the database you are using offers this service. Databases, like humans, can make mistakes. Be sure to consult the style handbook or website to confirm that the citations generated by a database are correctly formatted.

- **Magazine article from an online (library subscription) database**

  Wahl, Andrew. "Emission Impossible." *Canadian Business* 28 Feb. 2005: 24. *eLibrary Canada*. Niagara College Library, Welland, ON. 21 Mar. 2005 <http://elibrary.bigchalk.com>.

- **Newspaper article from an online (library subscription) database**

  Claudia H. Deutsch. "Are Women Responsible for Their Own Low Pay?" *New York Times* 27 Feb. 2005, Late Edition (East Coast): 3.7. *National Newspaper Abstracts* (3). ProQuest. Niagara College Library. Welland, ON. 22 Mar. 2005 <http://www.proquest.com/>.

- **Article in an online periodical**

  Bourette, Susan. "Planespotting." *Shift* Mar. 2002: 20–24. 8 June 2005 <http://www.shift.com/content/10.1/53/1.html>.

---

[4]"Protocol" refers to a particular set of rules for performing tasks on the Internet, such as http (hypertext transfer protocol), nntp (network news transfer protocol), ftp (file transfer protocol), and so on.

- **Government publication**

  Canada. Health Canada. Health Products and Food Branch. *Natural Health Products in Canada—A History.* June 2003. 4 April 2005 <http://www.hc-sc.gc.ca/hpfb-dgpsa/nhpd-dpsn/ history_e.html#top>.

- **Online encyclopedia**

  "Art Deco." *Encyclopedia Britannica Online.* Encyclopaedia Britannica. 27 May 2005 <http://search.eb.com/eb/article?eu=9778>.

- **Online news service**

  MSNBC News Services. "Images Show Wide Rifts in Tsunami Seabed." MSN.Com 10 Feb. 2005. 1 Mar. 2005 <http:// www.msnbc.msn.com/id/6946276/>.

- **Personal or professional website**

  Atwood, Margaret. "The Rocky Road to Paper Heaven." *Margaret Atwood Reference Site.* N.d. 10 June 2005 <http:// www.owtoad.com/>.

  "William Shakespeare." *Shakespeare: Chill with Will.* N.d. 8 June 2005 <http://library.thinkquest.org/19539/front/htm>.

- **Personal e-mail communication**
  Follow this format:

  Author's surname, First name [or alias]. "Title of Message [from subject line]." E-mail to First name and Last name of recipient. Date of message.

  Note: Never give the writer's e-mail address.

  Zacharatos, Phil. "The Forest or the Trees?" E-mail to Caroline Bouffard. 1 Apr. 2005.

- **Online posting, listserv, or discussion group**

  Ballard, Rex. "Re: Windows vs. Linux." Online posting. 22 Apr. 2005. 2 May 2005 <news:comp.os.linux.advocacy>.

  Wincapaw, Celeste. "Cyber-Fem: New Perspectives on Midwifery." Online posting. 27 Mar. 2005. 5 June 2005. <http:// www.hsph.harvard.edu/rt21/talk/frame1.html>.

- **CD-ROMs**
  Follow this basic model, including as many elements as are given in the source:

Author's surname, First name. "Title of Article, Song, or Poem [if relevant]." *Title of the Publication.* CD-ROM. Edition, release, or version [if relevant]. Place of publication: Name of publisher, date.

Delmar's Community Health Nursing: A Case Study. CD-ROM. Clifton Park, NY: Delmar, 2003.

Ward, Al. *Photoshop for Right-Brainers: The Art of Photo Manipulation.* CD-ROM. San Francisco: Sybex, 2004.

Below, you will find a sample Works Cited list to show you what the final page of your paper should look like.

Author Name 15

Works Cited

Newspaper article from library database

Chang, Kenneth. "Nanoparticles." *Edmonton Journal.* 6 Mar. 2005. *eLibrary Canada.* Mohawk College Library. Hamilton, ON. 14 Apr. 2005 <http://elibrary.bigchalk.com>.

Online encyclopedia

Drexler, Eric. "Nanotechnology." *AccessScience.* 10 Apr. 2003. McGraw-Hill Encyclopedia of Science and Technology Online. Niagara College Library, Welland, ON. 15 May 2005 <http://www.accessscience.com>.

Posting to online forum

Fox, Fiona. "Nanotech—The Next Controversy alike GM?" Online posting. Mar. 2004. EuroScience.Net. 22 Mar. 2005 <http://www.euroscience.net/article6.html>.

Book

Hall, J. Storrs. *Nanofuture: What's Next for Nanotechnology.* New York: Prometheus, 2005.

Print interview from internet

Harris, Charles E. Interview. Nanotechnology Now. Mar. 2002. 14 Apr. 2005 <http://nanotech-now.com/charles-harris-interview-032002.htm>.

Magazine article

"Nanotech." *Technology Review* Dec. 2004: 31.

Website

National Institute for Nanotechnology. 2002. National Research Council Canada. 30 Mar. 2005 <http://nint-innt.nrc-cnrc.gc.ca/home/index_e.html>.

For each of the following quotations, write a short paragraph in which you use all or a portion of the quotation and credit it in a parenthetical citation. Be sure to punctuate titles correctly.

1. From a book entitled Getting it done: the transforming power of self-discipline by Andrew J. Dubrin, published by Pacesetter Books in Princeton in 1995. This sentence appears on page 182: "Stress usually stems from your interpretation and perception of an event, not from the event itself."

2. From a journal article by Linda A. White that appeared on pages 385 to 405 of Canadian Public Policy, a journal with continuous paging: "If a clear connection exists between the presence of child care and high levels of women's labour market participation, that would provide good reasons for governments and employers to regard child care as part of an active labour market policy." White's article is entitled Child Care, Women's Labour Market Participation and Labour Market Policy Effectiveness in Canada. The quotation appears on page 389 of the fourth issue of the 27th volume, published in 2001.

3. From the American Institute of Stress website, found on May 2, 2005, at http://www.stress.org: "Increased stress results in increased productivity—up to a point."

4. From a newspaper article that appeared on page A2 in the March 30, 2005 issue of The Vancouver Sun by Nancy Cleeland and found on the elibrary Canada database at your college library. The article is entitled As jobs heat up, workers' hearts take a beating. "For years, occupational health researchers have struggled to come up with formulas for measuring job stress and determining its effect on health."

5. From an interview with Hans Selye, conducted on Jan 1, 1982, shortly before his death, on the topic of his pioneering work on stress and illness: "Stress is the non-specific response of a human body to any demand made upon it."

6. From an e-mail message on the subject of time management from your friend, Janet Ford, on March 5, 2005: "Using a daily planner and checking e-mail only once a day are two ways I've found to manage my stress during the school year."

Prepare a Works Cited list in MLA style for the sources in Exercise 20.1 above.

21

Formatting a Research Paper

The appearance of your paper makes an impression on your reader. A correctly formatted paper reflects the care and attention to detail that instructors value in students' work.

Ask your instructor if he or she has any special requirements for the format of your research assignment. If so, follow them carefully. Otherwise, follow the guidelines in this chapter to prepare your paper for submission. These guidelines are based on MLA style. (You will find instruction on formatting in APA style on our website at http://www.essayessentials4e.nelson.com.) After the guidelines, you will find two model research papers, both formatted according to the MLA principles of documentation. The first, "Uncertain Future: Potential Dangers of Genetically Modified Crops," is an essay on a topic of general interest. The second, "The Evolution of Moral Balance in Charlotte Brontë's *Jane Eyre*," is an essay on a literary topic. Together, they provide examples of most of the possibilities you are likely to encounter when writing and formatting your own research paper.

Paper

Compose your final draft on 22 × 28 cm (8.5 × 11 inch) white bond paper. Be sure to use a fresh cartridge in your printer. If your instructor will accept a handwritten document, make sure it adheres to all of the guidelines that follow, including those regarding ink colour, margins, spacing, etc. Print out or write your research paper on *one side* of the paper only.

Fasten your paper together with a paper clip or a single staple in the upper left-hand corner. Unless your instructor specifically requests, don't bother with plastic or paper covers; most teachers find it annoying to disentangle your essay for marking.

Printing/Typing

Choose a standard, easily readable typeface, such as Times New Roman, in a 12-point font. Use black ink (or dark blue, if you are writing by hand).

Spacing and Margins

Unless you are instructed otherwise, double-space throughout your essay, including quotations and the Works Cited list. In a handwritten paper, write on every other line of a ruled sheet of white paper.

Adequate white space on your pages makes your paper more attractive and easier to read. It also allows room for instructors' comments. Leave margins of 2.5 cm at the top, bottom, and both sides of your paper. If you are using a word processor, click on the "justify left" formatting command.

Indent the first line of every paragraph five spaces or 1.25 cm; use the tab default setting in your word-processing program. Indent all lines of a block quotation ten spaces or 2.5 cm from the left margin.

Title Page

Do not prepare a separate title page unless your instructor requires it. Instead, at the top of the left margin of the first page of your essay, on separate lines, type your name, your instructor's name, the course number, and the date. Leave a double space and centre the title of your essay. Capitalize main words (see Chapter 40, page 478), but do not underline, italicize, or put quotation marks around your title (unless it contains the title of another author's work, which you should punctuate in the usual way).

Header and Page Numbers

Number your pages consecutively throughout the paper, including the Works Cited list, in the upper right-hand corner, 1.25 cm from the top and 2.5 cm from the right edge of the page. Type your last name before the page number. Use a word processor to create a running head consisting of your last name, a single space, and the page number—no punctuation or *p*. See the student papers at the end of this chapter for examples.

Copy

Always keep a copy of your paper for your files!

Projecting an Image

As well as presenting your understanding of the topic, a research paper demonstrates your writing skills and your ability to follow specific requirements of documentation and format. Meeting your instructor's submission requirements is as important as any other aspect of the preparation of your paper. This may be the last stage of your writing task, but it is the first impression your reader will have of your work.

The paper that follows is an example of a properly formatted, documented essay. Before writing her paper, Soraya prepared an outline. Notice that she included in her outline the sources she wanted to refer to in each section. This technique saves hours of paper shuffling when you sit down to write.

Uncertain Future: Potential Dangers
of Genetically Modified Crops

Attention-Getter: Most people eat genetically modified foods every day, but few of stop to consider their potential dangers.

Thesis Statement: Genetically modified crops may have disastrous health, environmental, and sociopolitical effects.

I.   GM foods pose incalculable risks to human health.

  A. GM foods may contain toxic proteins. (Commoner; Mellon)

  B. Despite the testing that goes on during the genetic engineering process, allergic reactions to GM foods are likely. (Hopkin; Humphrys)

  C. The spread of antibiotic resistant bacteria is also a possibility. (Hopkin)

II.   GM crops may have a catastrophic and unpredictable impact on the environment.

  A. Built-in pesticides have benefits, but they kill creatures other than agricultural pests, destroying the balance of ecosystems. (Brown; Suzuki)

  B. Pests develop tolerance to built-in pesticides. (Brown)

     C. The transfer of pollen from genetically modified plants to weeds creates superweeds. (Randerson)

III.   The social, economic, and political effects of GM crops may be harmful or even disastrous.

     A. Biotechnology corporations use patents and "terminator technology" to control GM seeds; people become dependent on these companies. (Kneen)

     B. GM crops won't feed the world. (Suzuki; Mellon)

Summary: The health, environmental, and sociopolitical effects of GM crops may be dreadful.

Memorable Statement: More research needs to be done before we can evaluate the impact of GM technology. Right now, the risks are largely unknown and unpredictable.

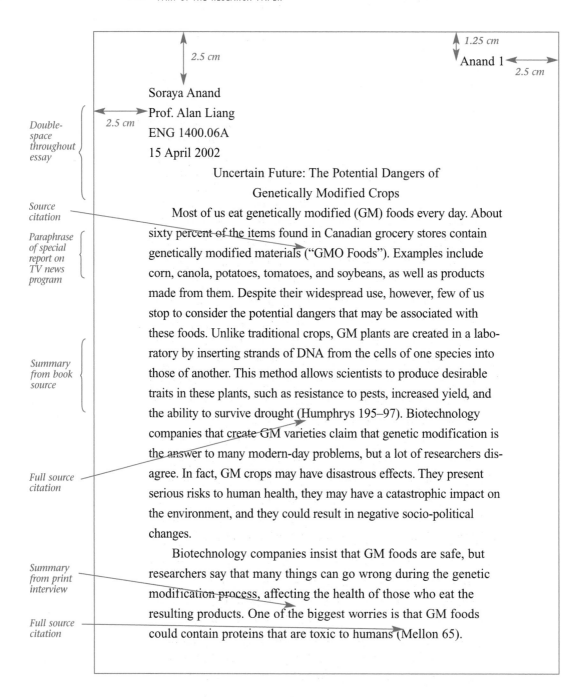

Double-space throughout essay

Source citation

Paraphrase of special report on TV news program

Summary from book source

Full source citation

Summary from print interview

Full source citation

2.5 cm

1.25 cm

2.5 cm

2.5 cm

2.5 cm

Anand 1

Soraya Anand

Prof. Alan Liang

ENG 1400.06A

15 April 2002

Uncertain Future: The Potential Dangers of
Genetically Modified Crops

Most of us eat genetically modified (GM) foods every day. About sixty percent of the items found in Canadian grocery stores contain genetically modified materials ("GMO Foods"). Examples include corn, canola, potatoes, tomatoes, and soybeans, as well as products made from them. Despite their widespread use, however, few of us stop to consider the potential dangers that may be associated with these foods. Unlike traditional crops, GM plants are created in a laboratory by inserting strands of DNA from the cells of one species into those of another. This method allows scientists to produce desirable traits in these plants, such as resistance to pests, increased yield, and the ability to survive drought (Humphrys 195–97). Biotechnology companies that create GM varieties claim that genetic modification is the answer to many modern-day problems, but a lot of researchers disagree. In fact, GM crops may have disastrous effects. They present serious risks to human health, they may have a catastrophic impact on the environment, and they could result in negative socio-political changes.

Biotechnology companies insist that GM foods are safe, but researchers say that many things can go wrong during the genetic modification process, affecting the health of those who eat the resulting products. One of the biggest worries is that GM foods could contain proteins that are toxic to humans (Mellon 65).

Anand 2

Barry Commoner, a senior scientist at City University of New York, points out that recent discoveries prove that the results of DNA transfer are unpredictable. Transferring genes from one organism to another, he says, "might give rise to multiple variants of the intended protein--or even to proteins bearing little structural relationship to the original one" (45). Margaret Mellon notes that "as scientists manipulate systems that they don't completely understand, one of the unexpected effects could be turning on genes for toxins" (65).

Allergic reactions are also a concern (Hopkin 60). In the mid-1990s, scientists tried to genetically improve soybeans with a gene from brazil nuts. The beans caused allergic reactions in people allergic to brazil nuts, so development was stopped (Humphrys 219–20). Supporters of GM technology cite this case as an example of the effectiveness of the testing process, but John Humphrys, the author of *The Great Food Gamble,* says that we may not be so lucky in the future:

> *10 sp* The brazil nut allergen was well known and could be specifically tested for . . . . In other cases, of course, the allergen might not be known. It is entirely possible that its effects might appear only over a period of time. It might produce a form of allergy of which we have no experience. It might simply not be identified. Far from exonerating the industry, what this little tale tells is that the risks exist. (220–21)

The spread of antibiotic resistant bacteria--bacteria that cannot be killed by known antibiotics--is another potential problem. Food engineers often use antibiotic resistant genes when designing GM crops (Greenpeace). The possibility that "resistance genes might

Quotation from magazine article

Abbreviated citation

Summary from article, with full citation

Author and title of book source

Block quotation from book

Paraphrase from website

Abbreviated book citation

Full citation for website

Anand 3

somehow jump from GM foods to bacteria in a consumer's gut" is small, but it cannot be ignored (Hopkin 61). If such a jump occurs, antibiotic resistant bacteria could quickly spread, adding to the already serious medical problem of antibiotic resistance.

Paragraph topic developed by paraphrase and block quotation

Genetically modified crops may also harm the environment. Most GM plant varieties are engineered to be resistant to pests such as insects. Supporters of GM crops point out that the farmers who plant them do not have to spray chemical pesticides on their fields, which is good for the environment (Brown 52). Yet there are other consequences as well. Studies indicate that insect-resistant GM crops may kill not only agricultural pests but also other creatures that happen to be exposed to them, such as monarch butterflies and green lacewing caterpillars (Brown 53–54). Long-term effects could be unpredictable but significant enough to affect whole ecosystems. David Suzuki warns readers:

Block quotation from article on website (no page, paragraph, or section numbers given)

> If we grow fields of crops that are toxic to all organisms except humans, what will that do to beneficial insects, or to the important microorganisms that live in our soils? This could have serious repercussions because depletion of insect numbers, for example, would lead to fewer birds and small mammals, and could have other implications up and down the food chain.

Paraphrase of idea found in two sources

In addition, even the defenders of GM crops are realizing that insect pests will develop a tolerance to built-in insecticides (Brown 54; McHughen 108). When this occurs, entire crops may suddenly fail, causing enormous losses. To prevent this disaster, farmers in the United States and elsewhere are now required to set aside a part of their farmland for crops that have not been genetically modified. In

Anand 4

these areas, "insects that have acquired some resistance . . . breed with those that have not, diluting the resistance trait" (Brown 57). Many environmentalists question the effectiveness of this strategy. They claim that the areas set aside "are either too small or too poorly designed to keep insect resistance at bay for long" (57). As resistance develops, another form of chemical control will have to be used or food engineers will have to develop new GM crop varieties, causing more environmental devastation.

Short quotation integrated into sentence

The transfer of pollen from a genetically modified species to other plants nearby can also lead to environmental damage. The main reason is that many GM crops are designed to be resistant to herbicides--chemical substances that kill plants. As a result, farmers can spray their fields with herbicides to eliminate weeds without damaging their own crops ("Herbicide"). The problem starts when pollen from one of these GM plants is carried to another plant species, such as a weed. The weed obtains the herbicide-resistant gene and can then grow unchecked, since it can no longer be killed by herbicides. It becomes a so-called superweed (Brown 55). According to a study commissioned by English Nature, the advisory body on conservation for the government of the United Kingdom, many superweeds already exist in Canada. Consequently, farmers are often forced to use older, stronger herbicides to kill them (Randerson).

Summary of encyclopedia article

Summary of online magazine article

The social, economic, and political implications of GM crops are also worrying. One problem often cited by critics is that a few large corporations control the industry. Because GM seeds can be patented, these companies not only dictate the price of seeds but also hold "intellectual property" rights for their products

Anand 5

(Humphrys 197–98). Brewster Kneen, the author of *Farmageddon: Food and the Culture of Biotechnology*, explains the results:

Words left out

> To say the seed is sold . . . is misleading, because in a sense the owners of the technology, the seed companies, do not sell it at all; they rent it out to the farmer for a season. The farmer is not allowed to keep any of the crop for replanting or to share it with a neighbor because the technology [is] owned and patented by one or another major transnational corporation. (107)

Word changed

To protect its interests, one company uses what has been called "terminator technology," which makes plants sterile (Robbins). As a result, farmers cannot save seeds from their plants to produce another harvest; they must buy new seeds instead. Kneen argues that as GM crops become more popular, control of the global food supply shifts dangerously. Eventually, he says, corporate ownership of seeds "will end the ability of the majority of the world's people to feed themselves and will make them dependent on corporate seed suppliers" (61).

In light of such practices, many people question what Bill Lambrecht, the author of *Dinner at the New Gene Café*, calls "the grand promise by some of the companies . . . that they will be able to more capably feed the world" with GM crops. Increased productivity will not solve the problem of starvation in developing countries because, as David Suzuki says, "most food shortages are caused by political and social issues, not an overall lack of food production capacity." There is more than enough food in the world, but it doesn't get to those in need (Mellon 64). Drought-tolerant GM crops could potentially benefit people in many countries, but

Paragraph topic developed by quotations and paraphrase

Anand 6

chances are that these people will not be able to afford them (Mellon 64).

The jury is out on GM foods. Scientists, corporations, governments, and the public continue to debate their pros and cons. In the meantime, most of us unknowingly eat products containing genetically modified ingredients every day. As we reach for the corn chips, we should realize that GM crops may have dreadful and unexpected health, environmental, and socio-political consequences. More research and testing need to be done before we can evaluate this technology and its impact on our lives and on the world. Right now, the risks are still largely unknown and unpredictable.

Anand 7

Works Cited

Brown, Kathryn. "Seeds of Concern." *Scientific American*
Apr. 2001: 52–57.

Commoner, Barry. "Unravelling the DNA Myth: The Spurious
Foundation of Genetic Engineering." *Harper's* Feb. 2002:
39–47.

"GMO Foods." *The National*. CBC-TV. Toronto. 23 Aug. 2001.
Transcript.

Greenpeace. "The Secret Ingredient." 10 Apr. 2002
<http://www.greenpeace.ca/e/resource/publications/gmo/
secret_ingredient.pdf>.

"Herbicide." *The Columbia Encyclopedia*. 2001 ed. 10 Apr. 2002
<http:// www.bartleby.com/65/he/herbicid.html>.

Hopkin, Karen. "The Risks on the Table." *Scientific American*
Apr. 2001: 60–61.

Humphrys, John. *The Great Food Gamble*. London: Hodder and
Stoughton, 2001.

Kneen, Brewster. *Farmageddon: Food and the Culture of
Biotechnology*. Gabriola Island: New Society Publishers, 1999.

Lambrecht, Bill. Interview. Canada AM. CTV. 1 Oct. 2001.
Transcript.

McHughen, Alan. *Pandora's Picnic Basket: The Potential and
Hazards of Genetically Modified Foods*. New York: Oxford
UP, 2000.

Mellon, Margaret. Interview. *Scientific American* Apr. 2001: 64–65.

Randerson, James. "Genetically-modified Superweeds 'Not
Uncommon.'" *New Scientist* 5 Feb. 2002. 10 Apr. 2002
<http://www.newscientist.com/news/news.jsp?id=ns99991882>.

Anand 8

Robbins, John. Interview. *Times-Herald 13* Jan. 2002: 3.

Suzuki, David. "Genetically Modifying Our Food." Science Matters series. 3 Nov. 1999; 10 Nov. 1999. 10 Apr. 2002 <http://www .davidsuzuki.org/Dr_David_Suzuki/Article_Archives/>.

Reprinted by permission of the author.

The following essay won the Sydney Singh Memorial Award at Grant MacEwan College in 2000. This award is given annually to the student who has written the best essay analyzing a work of literature in an English 101 class.

The Evolution of Moral Balance
in Charlotte Brontë's *Jane Eyre*

Introduction: Brontë's use of balancing elements contributes to the impact of *Jane Eyre*.

Thesis statement: Jane is pulled in opposing directions: between the values of Helen Burns and those of Bertha Mason; between the spirituality of St John Rivers and the sensuality of Rochester. Through her struggles with these opposing elements, Jane eventually finds a position on the moral continuum that satisfies her.

I.   Helen Burns and Bertha Mason represent the externalization of "the division of the Victorian female psyche into its extreme components of mind and body." (Showalter 68)

   A. Helen is an asexual child, focused on her spirituality to the point of physical self-denial.

   B. Bertha is a highly sexual woman, whose excessive indulgence has caused her to lose her reason.

   C. Brontë destroys the two "polar personalities" to make way for the integration of Jane's physical and spiritual beings. (Showalter 68)

   D. The values represented by Helen and Bertha influence Jane's moral development.

   E. The lessons she has learned are most clearly evident when she rejects Rochester's proposition.

II.   One of Rochester's arguments for an affair is that nobody will be harmed by it because Jane has no family to offend.

   A. Jane initially seems to accept his reasoning. (356)

   B. Helen's indoctrination about the value of one's good conscience (81) prevents her from acquiescing.

   C. She cannot live without self-respect. (356)

   D. Bertha's story shows her that if she were to become Rochester's mistress, she would share that fate: madness and estrangement from Rochester.

   E. Jane's moral position between the two extremes offered by Bertha and Helen is tested both by Rochester's proposition and by St John's proposal.

III. St John Rivers and Rochester are two characters who balance each other on many levels, from looks to lifestyle. The extremes they represent push her toward middle ground.

    A. Description of Rochester: 129–30.

    B. Description of St John: 386.

    C. Rochester's past: 355.

    D. St John's past: 393.

    E. Jane is offered contrasting choices: a passionate, illicit affair vs. a pious marriage of convenience.

    F. On the surface, the proposals are in contrast, but both would force her to suppress a part of her nature.

    G. Both proposals threaten the fulfillment Brontë has in mind for Jane. (Eagleton 33)

    H. Jane resists temptation; Brontë saves her for a transformed Rochester.

IV. *Jane Eyre* ends with Jane no longer having to compromise herself in order to be with Rochester.

    A. The humbled Rochester is no longer asking Jane to abandon her conscience to live in sin.

    B. Rochester and Jane are now a perfect match because he has moved away from his earlier extremes.

    C. Rochester's physical mutilation is a "symbolic castration" (Chase, qtd. in Gilbert and Gubar 368), but more than his masculinity, his spirit has been transformed.

    D. Humility has taught him wisdom. (495)

    E. Their "perfect concord" (500) is made possible by Rochester's movement away from his earlier extreme to become Jane's ideal mate.

    F. Their blissful marriage is contrasted with the life and death of St John in India.

    G. Brontë pays tribute to St John (417), while still validating Jane's choice.

    H. Jane has achieved an ideal moral balance; she can live a full life on earth and still earn the reward of heaven.

Summary: Jane's refusal to reject the demands of either her mind or her body is the essence of the novel. She is alternately taught and tested by Helen Burns and Bertha Mason, by St John Rivers and Rochester, and ultimately comes to reconcile the two extremes.

Memorable statement: Jane's journey to her own satisfying moral code and a life that celebrates it are intensified by Brontë's use of balancing elements.

Friedland 1

Jess Friedland
Professor MacDonald
EN101-354X
1 December 2000

The Evolution of Moral Balance in
Charlotte Brontë's *Jane Eyre*

A profusion of balancing elements contribute to the impact of
Charlotte Brontë's novel, *Jane Eyre*. Brontë uses these balances to
convey the maturation of Jane's value system. The diametrically
opposed characters of Helen Burns and Bertha Mason represent the
duality of Jane's nature, and ultimately influence her moral choices.
The proposals of Rochester and St John Rivers seem antithetical,
but display an underlying similarity. Jane is pulled in opposite
directions throughout the novel, but her final address to the reader
shows that she has found a position on the moral continuum that
satisfies her. The balances utilized to demonstrate her journey
enhance both our view of Jane's internal struggle and our understanding of her choices.

According to Elaine Showalter, Helen Burns and Bertha
Mason represent the externalization of "the division of the
Victorian female psyche into its extreme components of mind and
body" (68). Brontë's characterizations support this observation.
Helen is an unequivocally asexual child, focused solely on her spirituality to the point of physical self-denial. Bertha is an unequivocally sexual woman, who has seemingly lost her mind through
excessive indulgence in bodily pleasure. Showalter goes on to say:

> Brontë gives us not one but three faces of Jane, and she
> resolves her heroine's psychic dilemma by literally and
> metaphorically destroying the two polar personalities to make

Friedland 2

way for the full strength and development of the central consciousness, for the integration of the spirit and the body. (68)
Jane's rejection of either extreme validates this statement on a
metaphorical level. In the literal sense, however, both Bertha and
Helen influence Jane's morality in more relevant ways than merely
dying. Jane is neither an angel nor a demon, but she certainly ends
up closer to Helen's end of the spectrum than to Bertha's. Their lessons are most apparent during Jane's rejection of Rochester's
proposition.

One of Rochester's main arguments for an affair is that nobody
will be harmed by it as Jane has no family to offend. Jane pleads
with herself to "tell him you love him and will be his. Who in the
world cares for you? or who will be injured by what you do?"
(Brontë 356; ch. 27). Helen's indoctrination of the intrinsic value of
one's own good conscience prevents her from acquiescing. "If all the
world hated you, and believed you wicked, while your own conscience approved you, and absolved you from guilt, you would not
be without friends" (Brontë 81; ch. 8). The opposite must also hold
true: if Jane's conscience does not approve her, Rochester's love will
not matter. Jane will be without her own self-respect. Therefore, she
cannot stifle the "indomitable [. . .] reply--'I care for myself'"
(Brontë 356; ch. 27). Bertha's lesson is more subtle, but equally
effective. Her sexual nature has led her to madness and estrangement
from Rochester. Once her story is told to Jane, the implications are
clear. She must reject a life as Rochester's mistress or potentially
face similar consequences. Jane's moral position between the two
extremes offered by Bertha and Helen is more a function of their
lives than of their deaths. This moral position is tested most notably
by the aforementioned proposition and by the proposal of her cousin.

Friedland 3

St John Rivers and Rochester balance each other on many levels, from looks to lifestyle. Again, these extreme options, which are more literally presented to Jane, push her toward middle ground. Jane's first description of Rochester is of "a dark face, with stern features and a heavy brow"; she implies that he is far from being "a handsome, heroic-looking young gentleman" (Brontë 129–30; ch. 12). St John, on the other hand, is "young [. . .] tall, slender," with "a Greek face, very pure in outline: quite a straight, classic nose; quite an Athenian mouth and chin" (Brontë 386; ch. 29). Rochester's past is riddled with "lust for a passion--vice for an occupation" (Brontë 355; ch. 27), whereas St John is called "blameless in his life and habits [. . .] pure-lived, conscientious" (Brontë 393–94; ch. 30). Jane is offered a passionate, illicit affair by one, and a pious marriage of convenience by the other. These proposals are superficially contrary, but if Jane accepted either one, she would be forced to suppress part of her nature.

As Terry Eagleton states in his study of the novel, "Jane [. . .] must refuse Rivers as she has refused Rochester: loveless conventionalism and illicit passion both threaten the kind of fulfilment the novel seeks for her" (33). Fulfillment involves being accepted and loved without moral modification. Jane is sorely tempted, first to turn her back on her conscience for Rochester, and later to turn her back on her heart for St John. Brontë does not allow her to give in to either man at these crucial points, saving her instead for a revised Rochester.

The conclusion of *Jane Eyre* has Jane and Rochester married at last. Jane no longer needs to compromise herself in order to be with him, and his first wife is not the only obstacle that has been removed. The man who insisted that she abandon her conscience to live in sin has changed significantly. Rochester now complements

Friedland 4

Jane as never before. His mutilation has been referred to as a "symbolic castration" by Richard Chase (qtd. in Gilbert and Gubar 368), but it is his spirit rather than his masculinity that seems to have been honed. Rochester has been humbled, and the taste of humility has taught him wisdom. He is able to admit to Jane, "I did wrong: I would have sullied my innocent flower--breathed guilt on its purity" (Brontë 495; ch. 37). During their first engagement, Jane was unsure and often uncomfortable about her place in Rochester's life. In her description of their marriage however, she says that "we are precisely suited in character--perfect concord is the result" (Brontë 500; ch. 38). Such a perfect fit is only made possible by Rochester's movement away from his earlier extreme. He has become a close match for Jane on every level, and therefore becomes her ideal mate.

The final three paragraphs of the novel throw this blissful marriage into sharp contrast with the life and imminent death of St John in India. He is greeting his death at the end of ten years of martyrdom with eagerness, while Jane and Rochester are living life to its fullest. Brontë is giving respectful tribute to St John, but there remains a sense of validation for Jane's choices. St John's reason for clinging solely to his spirituality and rejecting his body is that he will not relinquish his "foundation laid on earth for a mansion in heaven" (Brontë 417; ch. 32). There can be no doubt, however, that Jane will be worthy of heaven upon her death. Jane's moral balance is thus portrayed as ideal; she can live a happy, full life on earth and yet not fear eternal damnation.

Jane's refusal to discount entirely either her mind or her body is the essence of the story. The course by which she comes to reconcile the two is compellingly wrought. She is alternately taught and tested by Helen Burns and Bertha Mason, by St John Rivers and Rochester. Jane's journey to her own satisfying moral code, and a life that celebrates it, are intensified by Brontë's use of balancing elements.

Friedland 5

Works Cited

Brontë, Charlotte. *Jane Eyre*. Harmondsworth, England: Penguin, 1996.

Eagleton, Terry. "*Jane Eyre*: A Marxist Study." *Charlotte Brontë's* Jane Eyre: *Modern Critical Interpretations*. Ed. Harold Bloom. New York: Chelsea House Publishers, 1987. 29–45.

Gilbert, Sandra M., and Susan Gubar. *The Madwoman in the Attic*. New Haven: Yale UP, 1984.

Showalter, Elaine. "Charlotte Brontë: Feminine Heroine." Jane Eyre: *Contemporary Critical Essays*. New Casebooks. Ed. Heather Glen. New York: St. Martin's Press, 1997. 68–77.

23

Solving Sentence-Fragment Problems

Every complete sentence has two characteristics. It contains a subject and a verb, and it expresses a complete thought. Any group of words that is punctuated as a sentence but lacks one of these characteristics is a **sentence fragment**. Fragments are appropriate in conversation and in some kinds of writing, but normally they are unacceptable in college, technical, and business writing.

There are two kinds of fragments you should watch out for: the "missing piece" fragment and the dependent clause fragments.

"Missing Piece" Fragments

Sometimes a group of words is punctuated as a sentence but is missing one or more of the essential parts of a sentence: a subject and a verb. Consider these examples.

1. Found it under the pile of clothes on your floor.

   Who or what <u>found</u> it? The sentence doesn't tell you. The subject is missing.

2. Their arguments about housework.

   The sentence doesn't tell you what the arguments <u>were</u> or <u>did</u>. The verb is missing.

3. During my favourite TV show.

Who or what was or did something? Both subject and verb are missing.

4. The programmers working around the clock to trace the hacker.

Part of the verb is missing. Remember that a verb ending in -*ing* needs a helping verb to be complete.

Finding fragments like these in your work when you are revising is the hard part. Fixing them is easy. There are two ways to correct sentence fragments. Here's the first one.

> To change a "missing piece" fragment into a complete sentence, add whatever is missing: a subject, a verb, or both.

1. You may need to add a subject:

Your sister found it under the pile of clothes on your floor.

2. You may need to add a verb:

Their arguments were about housework. (linking verb)
Their arguments about housework eventually destroyed their relationship. (action verb)

3. You may need to add both a subject and a verb:

My mother always calls during my favourite TV show.

4. Or you may need to add a helping verb:

The programmers have been working around the clock to trace the hacker.

Don't let the length of a fragment fool you. Students sometimes think that if a string of words is long, it must be a sentence. Not so. No matter how long the string of words, if it doesn't contain both a subject and a verb, it is not a sentence. For example, here's a description of children going from door to door for treats on Halloween:

In twos and threes, dressed in the fashionable Disney costumes of the year, as their parents tarried behind, grownups following after, grownups

Sentence Structure

bantering about the schools, or about movies, about local sports, about their marriages, about the difficulties of long marriages, kids sprinting up the next driveway, kids decked out as demons or superheroes or dinosaurs . . . beating back the restless souls of the dead, in search of sweets.

Moody, Rick. *Demonology*. New York: Little, Brown, 2001. 291.

At 68 words, this "sentence" is long, but it is a fragment. It lacks both a subject and a verb. If you add "The <u>children</u> <u>came</u>" at the beginning of the fragment, you would have a complete sentence.

In the following exercises, decide whether each group of words is a complete sentence or a "missing piece" fragment. Put *S* before each complete sentence and *F* before each fragment. Make each fragment into a complete sentence by adding whatever is missing: the subject, the verb, or both. Then compare your answers with our suggestions. Answers for exercises in this chapter begin on page 524.

Exercise 23.1*

1. _____ About historical events.

2. _____ To decide on the basis of rumour, not facts.

3. _____ Trying to be helpful, I offered to check the files.

4. _____ Cooking my famous tuna casserole.

5. _____ The party members gathering in the campaign office.

6. _____ We won.

7. _____ Hands over your head.

8. _____ To go anywhere without my iPod.

9. _____ Having worked hard all her life.

10. _____ Wanting to please them, she had coffee ready on their arrival.

GO TO WEB

EXERCISES 23.1, 23.2, 23.3, 23.4

Exercise 23.2*

_____ Professional athletes making millions of dollars a year. _____ At the same time, owners of sports franchises growing fantastically rich from the efforts of their employees, the players. _____ The fans being the forgotten people in the struggle for control over major league sports. _____ The people who pay the money that makes both owners and players rich. _____ I have an idea that would protect everyone's interests. _____ Cap the owners' profits. _____ Cap the players' salaries. _____ And, most important, the ticket prices. _____ A fair deal for everyone. _____ Fans should be able to see their teams play for the price of a movie ticket, not the price of a television set.

Dependent Clause Fragments

Any group of words containing a subject and a verb is a **clause**. There are two kinds of clauses. An **independent clause** is one that makes complete sense on its own. It can stand alone, as a sentence. A **dependent clause**, as its name suggests, cannot stand alone as a sentence; it depends on another clause to make complete sense.

Dependent (also known as **subordinate clauses**) begin with **dependent-clause cues** (subordinating conjunctions).

Dependent-Clause Cues

after	if	until
although	in order that	what, whatever
as, as if	provided that	when, whenever
as long as	since	where, wherever, whereas
as soon as	so that	whether
because	that	which, whichever
before	though	while
even if, even though	unless	who, whom, whose

Whenever a clause begins with one of these words or phrases, it is dependent.

A dependent clause must be attached to an independent clause. If it stands alone, it is a sentence fragment.

Here is an independent clause:

I am a poor speller.

If we put one of the dependent-clause cues in front of it, it can no longer stand alone:

Because I am a poor speller.

We can correct this kind of fragment by attaching it to an independent clause:

Because I am a poor speller, I have a spell checker in my PDA.

Exercise 23.3*

Put an *S* before each clause that is independent and therefore a sentence. Put an *F* before each clause that is dependent and therefore a sentence fragment. Circle the dependent-clause cue in each sentence fragment.

1. _____ Although she practised it constantly.

2. _____ Since the horse stepped on her.

3. _____ As soon as the troops arrived, the fighting stopped.

4. _____ Whichever route the bikers choose.

5. _____ Before Biff bought his bike.

GO TO WEB

EXERCISES 23.5, 23.6, 23.7, 23.8

Exercise 23.4*

Identify the sentence fragments in the paragraph below by highlighting the dependent-clause cue in each fragment you find.

Although many companies are experiencing growth, thanks to a healthy economy. Middle managers are not breathing easy. As long as there is a surplus of junior executives. Middle managers will continue to look over their shoulders, never sure when the axe will fall. Whether through early retirement, buyout, or termination. Their positions are being eliminated by cost-conscious firms whose eyes are focused on the bottom line. Because the executive branch of many businesses expanded rapidly during the years of high growth. Now there is a large block of managers who have no prospects of advancement. As one analyst observed, when he examined this block of largely superfluous executives and their chances of rising in the company hierarchy, "You cannot push a rectangle up a triangle."

Most sentence fragments are dependent clauses punctuated as sentences. Fortunately, this is the easiest kind of fragment to recognize and fix. All you need to do is join the dependent clause either to the sentence that comes before it or to the one that comes after it—whichever linkage makes better sense.

Read the following example to yourself; then read it aloud (remember, last sentence first).

Montreal is a sequence of ghettos. Although I was born and brought up there. My experience of French was a pathetically limited and distorted one.

The second "sentence" sounds incomplete, and the dependent-clause cue at the beginning of it is the clue you need to identify it as a sentence fragment. You could join the fragment to the sentence before it, but then you would get "Montreal is a sequence of ghettos, although I was born and brought up there," which doesn't make sense. The fragment should be linked to the sentence that follows it, like this:

Montreal is a sequence of ghettos. Although I was born and brought up there, my experience of French was a pathetically limited and distorted one. (Mordecai Richler)

If, as in the example above, your revised sentence *begins* with the dependent clause, you need to put a comma after it. If, however, your revised sentence *ends* with the dependent clause, you don't need a comma between it and the independent clause that precedes it.

My experience of French was pathetically limited although I was born and brought up [in Montreal].

See Chapter 31, Rule 3 (page 419).

Exercise 23.5*

Turn back to Exercise 23.4 and revise it by joining each dependent clause fragment to an independent clause that precedes or follows it, whichever makes better sense.

GO TO WEB

EXERCISE 23.9

Exercise 23.6*

The following paragraph contains both independent and dependent clauses (fragments), all punctuated as if they were complete sentences. Letting meaning be your guide, join each dependent clause fragment to the independent clause that comes before or after it—whichever makes better sense. Be careful to punctuate correctly between clauses.

In spite of what everyone says about the weak economy and the scarcity of jobs, especially for young people. I have financed my college career with a variety of part-time and seasonal jobs. Right now, for instance, while completing my third year at college. I have not one, or two, but three part-time jobs. I am a short-order cook three nights a week for a local bar and diner. And a telemarketer for a cable company after school. Or whenever I have free time. I'm also a server at a specialty coffee store on weekends. To maintain any kind of social life. While juggling three jobs and the requirements of my third-year program is not exactly easy, but I find it hard to turn down the opportunity for experience. Not to mention cash. I'm willing to put my social life on hold. For a while.

Exercise 23.7

As a final test of your skill in finding and correcting sentence fragments, try this exercise. Make each fragment into a complete sentence.

1. I had never eaten curry. But the first time I tasted it. I decided I liked it.
2. In France, they say that an explosion in the kitchen could have disastrous results. Such as linoleum blown apart.
3. Our family thinks my sister is too young to get married. Since she and her boyfriend want to be registered at Toys "R" Us.
4. It may surprise you to know that Canadians have made significant contributions to world cuisine. Two of the best known being baby pabulum and frozen peas.
5. Bathing the family cat. It's an activity that carries the same risks as tap dancing in a minefield. Or juggling with razor blades.
6. After working for three nights in a row trying to make my essay perfect so that I would get a high grade in my course. I lost my entire project when my brother crashed the computer while playing Grand Theft Auto.
7. I decided to take swimming lessons for two reasons. The first is fitness. Second, water safety.
8. There is good news. The man who was caught in an upholstery machine has fully recovered.
9. All of us are more aware of the effects of pollution now than we were 10 years ago. Because we are continually bombarded with information about the environment and our impact on it. In school, on television, and in newspapers.
10. My second favourite household chore is ironing. The first being hitting my head on the top bunk bed until I faint. (Erma Bombeck)

24

Solving Run-On Problems

Some sentences lack certain elements and thus are fragments. Other sentences contain two or more independent clauses that are incorrectly linked together. A sentence with inadequate punctuation between clauses is a **run-on**. Run-ons tend to occur when you write in a hurry, without first organizing your thoughts. If you think about what you want to say and punctuate carefully, you shouldn't have any problems with them.

There are two kinds of run-on sentences to watch out for: comma splices and fused sentences.

Comma Splices and Fused Sentences

As its name suggests, the **comma splice** occurs when two complete sentences (independent clauses) are joined together with only a comma between them. Here's an example:

I stayed up all night, I am exhausted.

Tea may be good for you, coffee is not.

A **fused sentence** occurs when two complete sentences are joined together with no punctuation at all:

I stayed up all night I am exhausted.

Tea may be good for you coffee is not.

There are four ways to fix run-on sentences.

1. Make the independent clauses into separate sentences.

I stayed up all night. I am exhausted.
Tea may be good for you. Coffee is not.

2. Separate the independent clauses with a comma followed by one of these words: *and, but, or, nor, for, so,* or *yet.*[1]

I stayed up all night, and I am exhausted.

You can insert one of the dependent-clause cues listed in Chapter 23, on page 342.

Because I stayed up all night, I am exhausted.

3. Make one clause dependent on the other by adding one of the dependent-clause cues listed on page 342.

Because I stayed up all night, I am exhausted.
I am exhausted because I stayed up all night.
Tea may be good for you although coffee is not.

4. Use a semicolon, either by itself or with a transitional word or phrase, to separate the independent clauses. (See Chapter 32.)

I stayed up all night; I am exhausted.
Tea may be good for you; on the other hand, coffee is not.

Note: All four solutions to comma splices and fused sentences require you to use a word or punctuation mark strong enough to come between two independent clauses. A comma by itself is too weak, and so is a dash.

The sentences in the following exercises will give you practice in fixing comma splices and fused sentences. Correct the sentences where necessary and then check your answers, beginning on page 525. Since there are four ways to fix

---

[1] These words are called **coordinating conjunctions** because they are used to join equal (or coordinating) clauses. If you are not sure how to punctuate sentences with coordinating conjunctions, see Chapter 31, Rule 2 (page 418).

each sentence, your answers may differ from our suggestions. If you find that you're confused about when to use a semicolon and when to use a period, be sure to read pages 427–31 before going on.

Exercise 24.1*

1. This is strong coffee, it has dissolved my spoon!
2. Just let me do the talking, we're sure to get a ticket if you open your mouth.
3. I keep buying lottery tickets, but I have won only free tickets.
4. If you have never tried it, hitting a golf ball may look easy, it's not.
5. As long as you smile when you speak, you can get away with saying almost anything.
6. Montreal used to be known as Ville St. Marie, before that it was known as Hochelaga.
7. Students today really need summer jobs and part-time employment, their tuition and living costs are too high for most families to subsidize.
8. Because I'm not very good at calculating odds, I'm afraid to play poker with you.
9. It's very windy, a ball hit deep to centre field will likely go into the stands.
10. "I was married by a judge, I should have asked for a jury." (Groucho Marx)

GO TO WEB

EXERCISES 24.1, 24.2

Exercise 24.2*

1. I use a keyboard all the time and my handwriting has become illegible.
2. Despite my parents' objections, I enjoy having long hair, it makes me feel attractive.
3. Casual meetings are fine for small groups, more formal settings are appropriate for larger groups.
4. I'd be happy to help you, just call when you need me, I'll be here all day.
5. In Canada, winter is more than a season it's a bad joke.
6. Perfection is probably impossible to achieve, but that doesn't mean you should stop trying your best.
7. For students in most technology programs, the future looks bright, however a diploma does not guarantee job security.

8. A Canadian who speaks three languages is called multilingual, one who speaks two languages is called bilingual, one who speaks only one language is called an English Canadian.
9. Skilled people are needed in specialized fields, currently, the top three are geriatrics, hospitality, and environmental technology.
10. I believe in a unified Canada, I believe that in 1867 the Fathers of Confederation were right, a federation of provinces can make a strong nation.

Exercise 24.3

As a final test of your ability to identify and correct run-on sentences, find and correct the 10 errors in the following paragraphs.

According to a news report, a private girls' school in Victoria was recently faced with an unusual problem, they solved it in a way that can only be described as creative, it is also a good example of effective teaching. Some of the grade 10 girls, forbidden by their parents to wear lipstick at home, began to apply it at school, in the second-floor washroom. That was the first problem, the second was that after applying the lipstick, they would press their lips to the mirror, leaving dozens of perfect lip prints. Every night, the maintenance crew would remove the prints, the next day the girls would reapply them and finally the principal decided that something had to be done.

She called the girls into the washroom where she met them with one of the maintenance men and he stood by while the principal addressed the girls. She explained that the lip prints on the mirrors were causing a problem for the maintenance crew, they had to clean the mirrors every night instead of doing other work. To demonstrate how difficult the cleaning job was and how much time was wasted on this needless chore, the principal asked the maintenance man to clean one of the mirrors, the girls watched with interest he took out a long-handled squeegee and began scrubbing at the lipstick prints. When he had scrubbed for a while, he turned, dipped his squeegee into one of the toilets, and continued to work on the mirrors and since then, there has not been another set of lip prints on the washroom mirror.

Sentence Structure

25

Solving Modifier Problems

Felix was complimented on a great game and a fine job of goaltending *by his mother.*

Snarling furiously and baring his teeth, Maurice crawled through a basement window only to confront an angry watchdog.

When she was a first-year student, the English professor told Mara she would *almost* write all her assignments in class.

These sentences show what can happen to your writing if you aren't sure how to use modifiers. A **modifier** is a word or phrase that adds information about another word in a sentence. In the examples above, the italicized words are modifiers. Used correctly, modifiers describe, explain, or limit another word, making its meaning more precise. Used carelessly, however, modifiers can cause confusion or, even worse, amusement.

You need to be able to recognize and solve two kinds of modifier problems: **misplaced modifiers** and **dangling modifiers**.

Misplaced Modifiers

Modifiers must be as close as possible to the words they apply to. Usually, readers will assume that a modifier modifies whatever it's next to. It's important to remember this, because, as the following examples show, changing the position of a modifier can change the meaning of your sentence.

Jason walked (only) as far as the corner store. (He didn't walk any farther.)

Jason (only) walked as far as the corner store. (He didn't jog or run.)

(Only) Jason walked as far as the corner store. (No one else went.)

Jason walked as far as the (only) corner store. (There were no other corner stores.)

> To make sure a modifier is in the right place, ask yourself "What does it apply to?" and put it beside that word or word group.

When a modifier is not close enough to the word it refers to, it is said to be misplaced. A misplaced modifier can be a single word in the wrong place.

The supervisor told me they needed someone who could use both Word and WordPerfect (badly.)

Is some company really hiring people to do poor work? Or does the company urgently need someone familiar with word processing programs? Obviously, the modifier *badly* belongs next to *needed*.

The supervisor told me they (badly) needed someone who could use both Word and WordPerfect.

> Be especially careful with these words: *almost, nearly, just, only, even, hardly, merely, scarcely*. Put them right before the words they modify.

Misplaced: She (nearly) answered every question.

Correctly placed: She answered (nearly) every question.

Misplaced: After driving all night, we (almost) arrived at 7:00 a.m.

Correctly placed: After driving all night, we arrived at (almost) 7:00 a.m.

A misplaced modifier can also be a group of words in the wrong place.

Bundled up in down clothing to keep warm, the dog team waited for the driver.

The modifier, *bundled up in down clothing to keep warm*, is too far away from the word it is supposed to modify, *driver*. In fact, it seems to modify *dog team*, making the sentence ridiculous. We need to rewrite the sentence.

The dog team waited for the driver, bundled up in down clothing to keep warm.

Look at this one:

I drove my mother to Saskatoon, where my aunt lives in a rental car.

In a rental car applies to *drove* and should be closer to it.

I drove my mother in a rental car to Saskatoon, where my aunt lives.

Notice that a modifier need not always go right next to what it modifies; it should, however, be as close as possible to it.

Occasionally, as in the examples above, the modifier is obviously out of place. The writer's intention is clear, and the sentences are easy to correct. But sometimes modifiers are misplaced in such a way that the meaning is not clear, as in the following example:

Raj said after the game he wanted to talk to the press.

Did Raj *say* it after the game? Or does he want to *talk to the press* after the game? To avoid confusion, we must move the modifier and, depending on which meaning we want, write either

After the game, Raj said he wanted to talk to the press.

or

Raj said he wanted to talk to the press after the game.

In Exercises 25.1 and 25.2, rewrite the sentences that contain misplaced modifiers, positioning them closely as possible to the words they modify. Check your answers to the first set before continuing. Answers for this chapter begin on page 526.

Exercise 25.1*

1. Trevor left the can of Pet Grrmet out for the dog that he had opened.

2. Our supervisor told us on the first day that no one takes coffee breaks.

3. I enthusiastically recommend this candidate with no experience whatever.

4. Professor Green told us in September he thought our class was a hopeless case.

5. We almost enjoyed the whole movie; only the ending was a disappointment.

6. Leo and Annie found an apartment in a highrise within walking distance of the campus with two bedrooms and a sunken living room.

7. There just are enough pieces to go around.

8. It almost seems there is a game every day during baseball season.

9. A charming, intelligent companion is sought by a vertically challenged but wealthy gentleman who looks good in evening gowns and diamonds.

10. One of us could only go because there was enough money just to buy one ticket.

Exercise 25.2*

1. One finds the best Chinese food in those restaurants where the Chinese eat usually.

2. He caught sight of a canary and several finches using his new binoculars.

3. Using my new camera, I can take professional-quality pictures with automatic functions.

4. The football practices have been organized for players who are not with a team in the summertime as a keep-fit measure.

5. Vancouver is a wonderful city for anyone who likes rain and fog to live in.

6. Some games are less demanding in terms of time and equipment, such as tiddlywinks.

7. The Human Rights Code prohibits discrimination against anyone who is applying for a job on the basis of race, religion, sex, or age.

8. We looked for a birthday present for our boss in a golf store.

9. Each year, 500,000 Canadian men almost have a vasectomy.

10. We hope to improve our students' performance using cash as a motivator.

Dangling Modifiers

A dangling modifier occurs when there is no appropriate word in the sentence for the modifier to apply to. That is, the sentence does not contain a specific word or idea to which the modifier could sensibly refer. With no appropriate word to modify, the modifier seems to apply to whatever it's next to, often with ridiculous results.

After a good night's sleep, my teachers were impressed with my unusual alertness.

This sentence seems to say that the teachers had a good night's sleep.

Trying desperately to finish an essay, my roommate's stereo made it impossible to concentrate.

The *stereo* was writing an essay?

Dangling modifiers are harder to correct than misplaced ones; you can't simply move danglers to another spot in the sentence. There are, however, two ways in which you can fix them. One way requires that you remember the following rule.

When a modifier comes at the beginning of a sentence, it modifies the subject of the sentence.[1]

This rule means that you can avoid dangling modifiers by choosing the subjects of your sentences carefully.

---

[1]The rule has exceptions, called adverbial modifiers, but they won't give you any trouble. Example: Quickly she did as she was told.

1. Ensure the subject is an appropriate one for the modifier to apply to.

Using this method, we can rewrite our two examples by changing the subjects.

(After a good night's sleep,) I impressed my teachers with my unusual alertness.

(Trying desperately to finish an essay,) I found it impossible to concentrate because of my roommate's stereo.

2. Another way to correct a dangling modifier is by changing it into a dependent clause.

After I had had a good night's sleep, my teachers were impressed with my unusual alertness.

When I was trying desperately to finish an essay, my roommate's stereo made it impossible to concentrate.

Sometimes a dangling modifier comes at the end of a sentence:

A Smart is the car to buy when looking for efficiency and affordability.

Can you correct this sentence? Try it; then look at the suggestions at the foot of the page.

Here is a summary of the steps to follow in solving modifier problems.

Summary

1. Ask "What does the modifier apply to?"
2. Be sure there is a word or group of words *in the sentence* for the modifier to apply to.
3. Put the modifier as close as possible to the word or word group it applies to.

Here are two suggestions.
1. Add a subject: Looking for efficiency and affordability, I decided a Smart was the car to buy.
2. Change the dangler to a dependent clause: A Smart is the car to buy since I am looking for efficiency and affordability.

Exercise 25.3*

Most of the following sentences contain dangling modifiers. Correct each sentence by using whichever solution given on page 357 best suits your purpose. There is no one right way to correct these sentences; our answers are only suggestions.

1. Driving recklessly and without lights, the police stopped Gina at a road block.

2. My supervisor gave me a lecture about punctuality after being late twice in one week.

3. After criticizing both my work and my attitude, I was fired.

4. With enough memory to store her favourite movies and more than 10,000 songs, Hannah knew that the iBook was the computer she needed.

5. After spending two weeks quarrelling over money, their relationship was over.

6. As a dedicated fan of Alice Munro, her last book is her best.

7. In less than a minute after applying the ointment, the pain began to ease.

8. Making her first formal presentation to her colleagues and her supervisor, Jake was probably more nervous than Allison was.

9. When handling hazardous waste, the safety manual clearly outlines the procedures to follow.

10. After spending the day in the kitchen preparing a gourmet meal, the guests drank too much wine to appreciate Kendra's effort.

Exercise 25.4*

In the following sentences, correct the misplaced and dangling modifiers in any way you choose. Our answers are only suggestions.

1. Only she was the baker's daughter, but she could loaf all day.

2. Being horribly hung over, the only problem with a free bar is knowing when to quit.

3. Rearing and kicking, Sam finally got the terrified horse under control.

4. In a hurry to get to the interview on time, my résumé was left lying on my desk at home.

5. As a college student constantly faced with new assignments, the pressure is sometimes intolerable.

6. Listening to the rumours, the newlyweds are already on the road to separation.

7. As a nondrinker, the display of liquor in the duty-free outlet held no interest.

8. Quartetto Gelato receives enthusiastic acclaim for its original arrangements and witty presentations from Vancouver to St. John's.

9. Rolling on her back, eager to have her tummy scratched, Queen Elizabeth couldn't resist the little Corgi puppy.

10. Wearing a small Canadian flag on a backpack or lapel, your reception abroad will be warm and enthusiastic.

GO TO WEB

EXERCISES 25.1, 25.2, 25.3, 25.4

Exercise 25.5

As a final test of your ability to use modifiers, correct the misplaced and dangling modifiers in the sentences below, using any solution you choose.

1. Obviously having drunk too much, I drove poor Tanya to her apartment, made her a pot of coffee, and called her mother.

2. When trying for your Red Cross bronze medal, your examiner will evaluate your speed, endurance, and resuscitation techniques.

3. The Riel Rebellion this month will be featured in *Canadian History* magazine.

4. Sinking like a ball of fire below the horizon, our sailboat was the perfect vantage point from which to watch the setting sun.

5. Not being reliable about arriving on time, I can't hire her to supervise others who are expected to be punctual.

6. While they were in my pocket, my children managed to break my glasses by leaping on me from behind.

7. Combining comfortable accommodation and economical travel, my wife and I find a camper van ideal for travelling both here and abroad.

8. The only used motorcycles we could find had been ridden by bikers that were in pretty bad shape.

9. After submitting the lowest bid that met all the developer's criteria, not being awarded the contract was bitterly disappointing.

10. "This bus has a seating capacity of 56 passengers with a maximum height of four metres." (Sign on a double-decker bus in Charlottetown)

26

The Parallelism Principle

Brevity, clarity, and force: these are three characteristics of good writing style. **Parallelism** will reinforce these characteristics in everything you write.

When your sentence contains a series of two or more items, they must be grammatically parallel. That is, they must be written in the same grammatical form. Consider this example:

Sophie likes *swimming, surfing,* and *to sail.*

The three items in this series are not parallel. Two are nouns ending in *-ing,* but the third, *to sail,* is the infinitive form of the verb. To correct the sentence, you must put all the items in the same grammatical form. You have two choices. You can write

Sophie likes *swimming, surfing,* and *sailing.* (all nouns)

Or you can write

Sophie likes *to swim, to surf,* and *to sail.* (all infinitives)

Now look at this example with two nonparallel elements:

Most people seek happiness in *long-term relationships* and *work that provides them with satisfaction.*

Again, you could correct this sentence in two ways. You could write "Most people seek happiness *in relationships that are long-term* and *in work that provides them with satisfaction,*" but that solution produces a long and clumsy sentence. The shorter version works better: "Most people seek happiness in *long-term relationships* and *satisfying work.*" This version is concise, clear, and forceful.

> Correct faulty parallelism by writing all items in a series in the same grammatical form; that is, all words, or all phrases, or all clauses.

One way to tell whether the items in a series are parallel is to write them out in list form, one below the other. That way, you can see at a glance if all the elements are in the same grammatical form.

Not Parallel	Parallel

My brother is *messy,*
    rude, and
    an obnoxious
    person.
	My brother is *messy,*
	    rude, and
	    obnoxious.

(This list has two adjectives and a noun phrase.)	(This list has three adjectives.)

I support myself by *delivering pizza,*
    poker, and
    shooting pool.
	I support myself by *delivering pizza,*
	    playing poker, and
	    shooting pool.

(This list has two phrases and one single word as objects of the preposition *by*.)	(This list has three phrases as objects of the preposition *by*.)

Jules wants a job that *will interest him,*
    will challenge him,
    and *pays well.*
	Jules wants a job that *will interest him,*
	    (will) challenge him,
	    and *(will) pay him well.*

(This series of clauses contains two future tense verbs and one present tense verb.)	(All three subordinate clauses contain future tense verbs.)

As you can see, achieving parallelism is partly a matter of developing an ear for the sound of a correct list. A parallel sentence has a smooth, unbroken rhythm. Practice and the exercises in this chapter will help. Once you have mastered parallelism in your sentences, you will be ready to develop ideas in parallel sequence—in thesis statements, for example—and thus to write clear, well-organized prose. Far from being a frill, parallelism is a fundamental characteristic of good writing.

Correct the sentences where necessary in the following exercises. As you work through these sentences, try to spot parallelism errors from the change in rhythm that the faulty element produces. Then revise the sentence to bring the faulty element into line with the other elements in the series. Check your answers to each set of 10 before going on. Answers for this chapter begin on page 528.

Exercise 26.1*

1. This program is easy to understand and using it is not difficult, either.

2. We were told that we would have to leave and to take nothing with us.

3. We organized our findings, wrote the report, and finally our PowerPoint presentation was prepared.

4. Both applicants were unskilled, unprepared, and lacked motivation.

5. Elmer's doctor advised that he should be careful with his back and not to strain his mind.

6. The company is looking for an employee who has a car and knowledge of the city would be a help.

7. If consumers really cared, they could influence the fast-food industry to produce healthy, delicious food that didn't cost very much.

8. When I want to get away from it all, there are three solitary pleasures I enjoy: a walk in the country, reading a good book, and fine music.

9. A recent survey of female executives claims that family responsibilities, being excluded from informal networks, and lacking management experience are the major factors keeping them from advancement.

10. If it is to be useful, your report must be organized clearly, written well, and your research should be thorough.

GO TO WEB

EXERCISES 26.1, 26.2

Exercise 26.2*

1. For my birthday, I requested either a Roots jacket or a scarf from Dior.

2. In my community, two related crimes are rapidly increasing: drug abuse and stealing things.

3. Bodybuilding has made me what I am today: physically perfect, very prosperous financially, and practically friendless.

4. After reading all the explanations and all the exercises have been completed, you'll be a better writer.

5. Bruce claimed that, through repetition and giving rewards, he had trained his centipede to be loyal and demonstrate obedience.

6. During their vacation in New Brunswick, Tracy and Jane visited many beautiful locations and wonderful seafood was eaten.

7. I'm an average tennis player; I have a good forehand, my backhand is average, but a weak serve.

8. The problem with being immortalized as a statue is that you will be a target for pigeon droppings and artists who write graffiti.

9. Never disturb a sleeping dog, a baby that is happy, or a silent politician.

10. I'd like to help, but I'm too tired, and my time is already taken up with other things.

GO TO WEB

EXERCISES 26.3, 26.4, 26.5, 26.6

Exercise 26.3*

Make the following lists parallel. In each case, you can make your items parallel with any item in the list, so your answers may differ from ours.

Example:	Wrong:	report writing	program a computer
	Right:	report writing	computer programming
	Also right:	write a report	program a computer

1. Wrong: wine   women   singing
   Right:

2. Wrong: doing your best   don't give up
   Right:

3. Wrong: lying about all   to do whatever I
                 morning   please
   Right:

4. Wrong: information   education   entertaining
   Right:

5. Wrong: individually   as a group
   Right:

6. Wrong: privately   in public
   Right:

7. Wrong: happiness   healthy   wisdom
   Right:

8. Wrong: employers   people working   workers on
                             full-time for an employer   contract
   Right:

9. Wrong: insufficient time   too little money   not enough
                                              staff
   Right:

10. Wrong: French is the   English is used   profanity
                   language of love   in business   sounds best
                                                       in German
    Right:

Exercise 26.4*

Correct the faulty parallelism in these sentences.

1. Not being able to speak the language causes confusion, is frustrating, and it's embarrassing.

2. Trying your best and success are not always the same thing.

3. The first candidate we interviewed seemed frightened and to be shy, but the second was a composed person and showed confidence.

4. To lick one's fingers and picking one's teeth in a restaurant are one way to get attention.

5. Our CEO claims his most valuable business assets are hitting a good backhand and membership at an exclusive golf club.

6. In order to succeed in this economy, small businesses must be creative and show innovation and flexibility.

7. Lowering our profit margin, raising prices, and two management lay-offs will enable us to meet our budget.

8. After an enjoyable dinner, I like to drink a cappuccino, a dark chocolate mint, and, occasionally, a good cigar.

9. Lying in the sun, consumption of high-fat foods, and cigarette smoking are three dangerous activities that were once thought to be healthy.

10. Business travellers complain of long delays at airports, they are paying higher costs for services, and tighter restrictions on their freedom of movement.

Exercise 26.5

As a test of your mastery of parallel structure, correct the six errors in the following paragraph.

The dictionary can be both a useful resource and an educational entertainment. Everyone knows that its three chief functions are to check spelling, for finding out the meanings of words, and what the correct pronunciation is. Few people, however, use the dictionary for discovery as well as learning. There are several methods of using the dictionary as an aid to discovery. One is randomly looking at words, another is to read a page or two thoroughly, and still another is by skimming through words until you find an unfamiliar one. It is by this last method that I discovered the word *steatopygous*, a term I now try to use at least once a day. You can increase your vocabulary significantly by using the dictionary, and of course a large and varied vocabulary can be used to baffle your colleagues, employers will be impressed, and your English teacher will be surprised.

7. In his essay "A Modest Proposal for a Divorce Ceremony," Pierre Berton proposed that Canada institute a formal divorce ceremony.
The divorce ceremony would be like a formal wedding ceremony.
All the symbolism would be reversed.

8. The bride, for example, would wear black.
Immediately after the ceremony, the newly divorced couple would go into the vestry.
They would scratch their names off the marriage register.

9. Twenty percent of adults in Canada are illiterate.
Fifty percent of the adults who can read say they never read books.
This is an astonishing fact.

10. Canada is a relatively rich country.
Most of us brush up against hunger and homelessness almost daily.
We encounter men, and less often, women begging.
They are on downtown street corners.

After you have combined a number of sentences, you can evaluate your work. Read your sentences out loud. How they *sound* is important. Test your work against these six characteristics of successful sentences:

Summary

1. **Meaning:** Have you said what you mean?
2. **Clarity:** Is your sentence clear? Can it be understood on the first reading?
3. **Coherence:** Do the parts of your sentence fit together logically and smoothly?
4. **Emphasis:** Are the most important ideas either at the end or at the beginning of the sentence?
5. **Conciseness:** Is the sentence direct and to the point? Have you cut out all redundant or repetitious words?
6. **Rhythm:** Does the sentence flow smoothly? Are there any interruptions in the development of the key idea(s)? Do the interruptions help to emphasize important points, or do they distract the reader?

If your sentences pass all six tests of successful sentence style, you may be confident that they are both technically correct and pleasing to the ear. No reader could ask for more.

28

Mastering Subject–Verb Agreement

Singular and Plural

One of the most common writing errors is lack of agreement between subject and verb. Both must be singular, or both must be plural. If one is singular and the other plural, you have an agreement problem. You have another kind of agreement problem if your subject and verb are not both in the same "person" (see Chapter 30, pages 396–415).

Let's clarify some terms. First, it's important to distinguish between **singular** and **plural**.

- "Singular" means one person or thing.
- "Plural" means more than one person or thing.

Second, it's important to know what we mean when we refer to the concept of **person**:

- "First person" is the person(s) speaking or writing: *I, me; we, us*
- "Second person" is the person(s) being addressed: *you*
- "Third person" is the person(s) being spoken or written about: *he, she, it; they, them*

Here's an example of the singular and plural forms of a regular verb in the present tense.

	Singular	Plural
first person	I win	we win
second person	you win	you win
third person	she wins (*or* he, it, the horse wins)	they win (*or* the horses win)

The form that most often causes trouble is the third person because the verb endings do not match the subject endings. Third-person singular present-tense verbs end in -s, but their singular subjects do not. Third-person plural verbs never end in -s, while their subjects normally do. Look at these examples.

> A <u>fire</u> <u>burns</u>.
> The <u>car</u> <u>skids</u>.
> The <u>father</u> <u>cares</u> for the children.

The three singular verbs, all of which end in -s (*burns*, *skids*, *cares*), agree with their singular subjects (*fire, car, woman*), none of which ends in -s. When the subjects become plural, the verbs change form, too.

> Four <u>fires</u> <u>burn</u>.
> The <u>cars</u> <u>skid</u>.
> The <u>fathers</u> <u>care</u> for the children.

Now all of the subjects end in -s, and none of the verbs does.

To ensure **subject–verb agreement**, follow this basic rule:

Subjects and verbs must both be either singular or plural.

This rule causes difficulty only when the writer doesn't know which word in the sentence is the subject and so makes the verb agree with the wrong word. As long as you decode the sentence correctly (see Chapter 22), you'll have no problem making every subject agree with its verb.

If you have not already done so, now is the time to memorize this next rule:

The subject of a sentence is NEVER in a prepositional phrase.

Here's an example of how errors occur.

> Only one of the 2,000 ticket buyers are going to win.

What is the subject of this sentence? It's not *buyers*, but *one*. The verb must agree with *one*, which is clearly singular. The verb *are* does not agree with *one*, so the sentence is incorrect. It should read

Only <u>one</u> ~~of the 2,000 ticket buyers~~ <u>is</u> going to win.

Pay special attention to words that end in *-one, -thing,* or *-body.* They cause problems for nearly every writer.

Words ending in *-one, -thing,* or *-body* are always singular.

When used as subjects, these pronouns require singular verbs.

anyone	anything	anybody
everyone	everything	everybody
no one	nothing	nobody
someone	something	somebody

The last part of the pronoun subject is the tip-off here: every*one,* any*thing,* no*body.* If you focus on this last part, you'll remember to use a singular verb with these subjects. Usually, these words cause trouble only when modifiers crop up between them and their verbs. For example, you would never write "Everyone are here." The trouble starts when you insert a group of words in between the subject and the verb. You might, if you weren't careful, write this: "Everyone involved in implementing the company's new policies and procedures are here." The meaning is plural: several people are present. But the subject (*everyone*) is singular, so the verb must be *is.*

More subject–verb agreement errors are caused by violations of this rule than any other. Be sure you understand it. Memorize it, and then test your understanding by doing the following exercise before you go any further.

Exercise 28.1*

Rewrite each of the following sentences, using the alternative beginning shown. Answers for this chapter begin on page 530.

    Example: <u>She</u> <u>wants</u> to make a short documentary.
            <u>They</u> <u>want</u> to make a short documentary.

1. He sells used essays to other students.
   They

2. That new guideline affects all the office procedures.
   Those

3. Everyone who shops at Pimrock's receives a free can of tuna.
   All those

4. The woman maintains that her boss has been harassing her.
   The women

5. That girl's father is looking for a rich husband for her.
   Those

So far, so good. You can match up singular subjects with singular verbs and plural subjects with plural verbs. Now let's take a look at a few of the complications that make subject–verb agreement such a disagreeable problem.

Five Special Cases

Some subjects are tricky. They look singular but are actually plural, or they look plural when they're really singular. There are six kinds of these slippery subjects, all of them common, and all of them likely to trip up the unwary writer.

> 1. Compound subjects joined by *or; either . . . or; neither . . . nor;* or *not . . . but*

Most of the compound subjects we've dealt with so far have been joined by *and* and have required plural verbs, so agreement hasn't been a problem. But watch out when the two or more elements of a compound subject are joined by *or; either . . . or; neither . . . nor;* or *not . . . but*. In these cases, the verb agrees in number with the nearest subject. That is, if the subject closest to the verb is singular, the verb will be singular; if the subject closest to the verb is plural, the verb must be plural too.

Neither <u>the coach</u> nor <u>the players</u> <u>are</u> ready to give up.

Neither <u>the players</u> nor <u>the coach</u> <u>is</u> ready to give up.

Exercise 28.2*

Circle the correct verb in each of the following sentences.

1. Not your physical charms but your honesty (is are) what I find attractive.

2. Either your job performance or your school assignments (is are) going to suffer if you continue your frantic lifestyle.

3. The college has decided that neither final marks nor a diploma (is are) to be issued to students who owe library fines.

4. Not unemployment but the rising cost of medical care (is are) Canadians' chief concern.

5. Neither the compensation nor the benefits (tempt tempts) me to accept your offer.

2. Subjects that look like compound subjects but really aren't

Don't be fooled by phrases beginning with words such as *with, like, together with, in addition to,* or *including*. These prepositional phrases are NOT part of the subject of the sentence. Since they do not affect the verb, you can mentally cross them out.

Mario's <u>brother</u>, ~~together with three of his buddies,~~ <u>is going</u> to the Yukon to look for work.

Obviously four people are looking for work. Nevertheless, the subject (<u>brother</u>) is singular, and so the verb must be singular (<u>is going</u>).

All my <u>courses</u>, ~~except economics,~~ <u>are</u> easier this term.

If you mentally cross out the phrase *except economics*, you can easily see that the verb (<u>are</u>) must be plural to agree with the plural subject (<u>courses</u>).

Exercise 28.3*

Circle the correct verb in each of the following sentences.

1. Some meals, like tagine, (is are) best enjoyed in a large group.

2. Our city, along with many other North American urban centres, (register registers) a dangerous level of carbon monoxide pollution in the summer months.

3. The Tour de France, like the Olympic Games, (is are) a world-class athletic competition.

4. Lori's mother, along with her current boyfriends, (wonder wonders) when she'll decide to settle down.

5. My English instructor, in addition to my math, biology, and even my learning skills instructor, (put, puts) a lot of pressure on me.

3. *Each (of), either (of), neither (of)*

Used as subjects, these words (or phrases) take singular verbs.

<u>Either</u> <u>is</u> acceptable to me.

<u>Each</u> <u>wants</u> desperately to win.

<u>Neither</u> of the stores <u>is</u> open after six o'clock. (Remember, the subject is never in a prepositional phrase.)

___

Exercise 28.4*

Circle the correct verb in each of the following sentences.

1. Unless we hear from the coach, neither of us (is are) playing this evening.
2. Each of these courses (involve involves) field placement.
3. When my girlfriend asks if she has lost weight, I know that either of my answers (is are) bound to be wrong.
4. Each of the women (want wants) desperately to win the Ms. Nanaimo bodybuilding competition.
5. Strict discipline is what each of our teachers (believe believes) in.

___

4. Collective nouns

A **collective noun** is a word that names a group. Some examples are *company, class, committee, team, crowd, band, family, audience, public,* and *jury.* When you are referring to the group acting as a *unit,* use a *singular* verb. When you are referring to the *members* of the group acting *individually,* use a *plural* verb.

The <u>team</u> <u>is</u> sure to win tomorrow's game. (Here *team* refers to the group acting as a whole.)

The <u>team</u> <u>are</u> getting into their uniforms now. (The members of the team are acting individually.)

___

Exercise 28.5*

Circle the correct verb in each of the following sentences.

1. The whole gang (plan plans) to attend the bikers' rally.

Grammar

2. The wolf pack (has have) been almost wiped out by local ranchers.
3. By noon on Friday, the whole dorm (has have) left their rooms and headed for the local pubs and coffeehouses.
4. After only two hours' discussion, the committee (was were) able to reach consensus.
5. The majority of Canadians, according to a recent survey, (is are) not so conservative about sex and morality as we had assumed.

5. Units of money, time, mass, length, and distance

When used as subjects, they all require singular verbs.

Four kilometres <u>is</u> too far to walk in this weather.

Remember that <u>2.2 pounds</u> <u>equals</u> a kilogram.

<u>Three weeks</u> <u>is</u> a long time to wait to get your paper back.

Exercise 28.6*

Circle the correct verb in each of the following sentences.

1. No wonder you are suspicious if $70 (was were) what you paid for last night's pizza.
2. Tim told his girlfriend that nine years (seem seems) like a long time to wait.
3. Forty hours of classes (is are) too much in one week.
4. When you are anxiously looking for a gas station, 30 km (is are) a long distance.
5. Ninety cents (seems seem) very little to tip, even for poor service.

In Exercises 28.7 and 28.8, correct the errors in subject–verb agreement. (Some rephrasing may be required.) Check your answers to each exercise before going on.

Exercise 28.7*

1. Neither of the following two sentences are correct.

2. The teachers, with the full support of the college administration, treats plagiarism as a serious offence.

3. Either good looks or intelligence run in our family, but never at the same time.

4. None of these computer programs are able to streamline our billing procedures.

5. The enjoyment of puns and jokes involving plays on words are the result of having too little else on your mind.

6. Anyone who jumps from one of Paris's many bridges are in Seine.

7. It is amazing how much better the orchestra play now that the conductor is sober.

8. The number of layoffs reported in the headlines seem to be rising again.

9. Her supervisors all agree that Emily need further training to be effective.

10. Canada's First Nations population are thought to have come to this continent from Asia thousands of years before the Europeans arrived in North America.

Exercise 28.8*

Quebec City, along with Montreal, Toronto, and Vancouver, are among Canada's great gourmet centres. Whereas Toronto is a relative latecomer to this list, neither Quebec City nor Montreal are strangers to those who seeks fine dining. Indeed, travel and food magazines have long affirmed that the inclusion of these two cities in a Quebec vacation are a "must." Montreal is perhaps more international in its offerings, but Quebec City provides exquisite proof that French-Canadian cuisine and hospitality is second to none in the world. Amid the Old World charm of the lower city is to be found some of the quaintest and most enjoyable traditional restaurants; the newer sections of town boasts equally fine dining in more contemporary surroundings. The combination of the wonderful food and the city's fascinating charms are sure to make any visitor return frequently. Either the summer, when the city blooms and outdoor cafés abound, or the winter, when Carnaval turns the streets into hundreds of connecting parties, are wonderful times to visit one of Canada's oldest and most interesting cities.

GO TO WEB

EXERCISES 28.1, 28.2, 28.3, 28.4

Summary

- Subjects and verbs must agree: both must be singular, or both must be plural.
- The subject of a sentence is never in a prepositional phrase.
- Pronouns ending in *-one, -thing,* or *-body* are singular and require singular verbs.
- Subjects joined by *and* are always plural.
- When subjects are joined by *or; either . . . or; neither . . . nor;* or *not . . . but,* the verb agrees with the subject that is closest to it.
- When looking for the subject in a sentence, ignore phrases beginning with *as well as, including, in addition to, like, together with,* etc. They are prepositional phrases.
- When *each, either,* and *neither* are used as subjects, they require singular verbs.
- Collective nouns are usually singular.
- Units of money, time, mass, length, and distance are always singular.

Exercise 28.9

As a final check of your mastery of subject–verb agreement, correct the following sentences as necessary.

1. Each of the options you outlined in your concluding remarks are worth examining further.

2. My opinion of the college's accounting programs are that neither of them are what I need.

3. Every one of the dozen people we interviewed qualify for the position.

4. My whole family, with the exception of the cat, dislike anchovies on pizza.

5. The applause from a thousand enthusiastic fans were like music to the skaters' ears.

6. Neither of your decisions are likely to improve sales, let alone morale.

7. Three thousand dollars per term, the students agree, are too much to pay for their education.

8. Neither age nor illness prevents Uncle Alf from leering at the nurses.

9. The birth of triplets, after six other children in eight years, were too much for the parents to cope with.

10. Everything you have accomplished in the last three years are wasted if you fail this assignment.

Using Verbs Effectively

Good writers pay especially careful attention to verbs. A verb is to a sentence what an engine is to a car: it's the source of power—but it can also be a source of trouble. Now that you've conquered subject–verb agreement, it's time to turn to the three remaining essentials of correct verb use: **form**, **consistency**, and **voice**.

Choosing the Correct Verb Form

Every verb has four forms, called its **principal parts**:

1. The **infinitive** form: used with *to* and with *can, may, might, shall, will, could, should, would, must*
2. The **simple past** (also called the **past tense**)
3. The **present participle** (the **-ing**) form
4. The **past participle** form: used with *has* or *have*

Here are some examples:

Infinitive	Simple Past	Present Participle	Past Participle
dance	danced	dancing	danced
learn	learned	learning	learned
play	played	playing	played
seem	seemed	seeming	seemed

weather was fine. Another mumble from the barber. This time, Glenn thought he'd been asked which college he planned to attend in the fall, and he answered politely. At this point, the conversation was stopped, and the barber got on with his work.

Half an hour later, the sheet was swept away, and the chair was spun so that Glenn could see his image in the mirror. To his horror, it was discovered that he was practically bald, except for an 8 cm high strip of hair running from his forehead to the nape of his neck. Glenn's scream was heard through the entire mall. After the excitement died down, it was learned by the crowds of curious shoppers that when Glenn had been asked what kind of haircut he wanted, Glenn had replied, "Mohawk."

So the prom was attended by Glenn in a tux, a startling haircut, and with a very unsympathetic date. The following week, Glenn left for Hamilton and Mohawk College. His high-school sweetheart was never seen by him again.

Solving
Pronoun Problems

Look at the following sentences. Can you tell what's wrong with them?

"Dev must choose between you and I," Miranda said.

When you are on a diet, it is a good idea for one to avoid Bagel World.

We had invited everybody to come with their partner, so we were a little surprised when Marcel showed up with his Doberman.

Everyone is expected to do their duty.

Mohammed's nose was badly sunburned, but it has now completely disappeared.

Most of the students that were protesting tuition increases were ones which had been elected to council.

These sentences all contain pronoun errors. After verbs, pronouns are the class of words most likely to cause problems for writers. In this chapter, we will look at the three aspects of pronoun usage that can trip you up if you're not careful: pronoun form, agreement, and consistency. We'll also look at the special problems of usage that can lead to sexist language.

Choosing the Correct Pronoun Form

First you need to be sure you are using the "right" pronouns—that is, the correct pronoun forms—in your sentences. Here are some examples of incorrect pronoun usage:

Her and me can't agree on anything.

The reason for the quarrel is a personal matter between he and I.

How do you know which form of a pronoun to use? The answer depends on the pronoun's place and function in your sentence.

SUBJECT AND OBJECT PRONOUNS

There are two forms of personal pronouns: one is used for subjects, and the other is used for objects. Pronoun errors occur when you confuse the two. In Chapter 22, you learned to identify the subject of a sentence. Keep that information in mind as you learn the following basic rule.

When a subject or a complement is a pronoun, the pronoun must be in **subject form**. Otherwise, use the **object form**.

Subject Pronouns

Singular	Plural
I	we
you	you
he, she, it, one	they

She and *I* tied for first place. (The pronouns are the subject of the sentence.)

The lucky winners of the all-expenses-paid weekend in Paris are *they*. (The pronoun is the complement and refers to the subject of the sentence, *winners*.)

The student who regularly asks for extra help is *he*. (The pronoun is the complement and refers to the subject of the sentence, *student*.)

Object Pronouns

Singular	Plural
me	us
you	you
him, her, it, one	them

Between you and *me*, I think he's cute. (*Me* is not the subject of the sentence; it is one of the objects of the preposition *between*.)

Omar asked *him* and *me* for help. (*Him* and *me* are not the subject of the verb *asked*; *Omar* is, so the pronouns need to be in the object form.)

Be especially careful when using pronouns in compound subjects or after prepositions. If you can remember the following two rules, you'll be able to eliminate most potential errors.

1. A pronoun that is part of a compound subject is *always* in subject form.
2. A pronoun that follows a preposition is *always* in object form.

Examples:

She and *I* had tickets to U2. (The pronouns are used as a compound subject.)

It is up to *you* and *her* to pay for the damage. (The pronouns follow the preposition *to*.)

When you're dealing with a pair of pronouns and can't decide which form to use, try this test.[1] Mentally cross out one pronoun at a time, then read aloud the sentence you've created. Applying this technique to the first example above, you get "*She* has tickets" and "*I* have tickets." Both sound right and are correct. In the second sentence, if you try the pronouns separately, you get "It is up to *you*" and "It is up to *her*." Again, you know by the sound that these are the correct forms. (You would never say "*Her* had tickets," or "*Me* had tickets," or "It is up to *she*.") If you deal with paired pronouns one at a time, you are unlikely to choose the wrong form.

Note, too, that when a pair of pronouns includes "I" or "me," that pronoun comes last. For example, we write "between *you* and *me*" (not

---

[1] This test is reliable only for those who are fluent in English. ESL students must rely on memorizing the rules.

"between *me* and *you*"); we write "*she* and *I*" (not "*I* and *she*"). There is no grammatical reason for this rule. It's based on courtesy. Good manners require that you speak of others first and yourself last.

Exercise 30.1*

Correct the pronouns in these sentences as necessary. Answers for the exercises in this chapter begin on page 534.

1. No one except you and I would go camping in this weather.
2. Him and I can't figure out this problem set any better than you and her could.
3. George and him fell asleep in class, as usual.
4. Do you want to work with Emma and she?
5. We can use the film passes all week, and you and her can use them on the weekend, when Biff and me are going skiing.
6. Thanks to the recommendations provided by your math instructor and I, you and her got the tutorial jobs.
7. As we were going to class, Karl and me heard that there had been an explosion in the lab.
8. If it hadn't been for Hassan and he, the only ones to show up would have been you and I.
9. Quentin and him agreed to split the price of a case with Stan and I.
10. Only two students passed the midterm: Nadia and me.

GO TO WEB

EXERCISES 30.1, 30.2

Using Pronouns in Contrast Constructions

Choosing the correct pronoun form is more than just a matter of not wanting to appear ignorant or careless. Sometimes the form you use determines the meaning of your sentence. Consider these two sentences:

Stefan is more interested in his new car than *I*.

Stefan is more interested in his new car than *me*.

There's a world of difference between the meaning of the subject form ("Stefan is more interested in his new car than *I* [am]") and the object form ("Stefan is more interested in his new car than [in] *me*").

When using a pronoun after *than, as well as,* or *as,* decide whether you mean to contrast the pronoun with the subject of the sentence. If you do, use the subject form of the pronoun. If not, use the object form.

Jay would rather watch television than I. (*I* is contrasted with the subject, *Jay.*)

Jay would rather watch television than me. (*Me* is contrasted with the object, *television.*)

To test your sentence, try putting a verb after the pronoun. If the sentence makes sense, then the subject form is the form you want.

Jay would rather watch television than I [would].

Some writers prefer to leave the added verb in place, a practice that eliminates any possibility of confusion.

Exercise 30.2*

Correct the following sentences where necessary.

1. At 14, my younger brother is already taller than me.

2. No one likes partying more than him and Anne.

3. Would you like to join Daniel and I for dinner and a movie?

4. Only one person in this firm could manage the department as well as him.

5. At last I have met someone who enjoys grilled liver as much as me!

6. We can skate as well as them, but they are much better at shooting and defending than us.

7. More than me, Serge uses the computer to draft and revise his papers.

Revise the following paragraph to correct the errors in pronoun form.

(1) My boyfriend and me have different opinions when it comes to food. (2) I like fast food better than him. (3) He likes vegetables better than me. (4) In fact, between you and I, he is a vegetarian, though he would deny it. (5) When we go out with friends, it is difficult for they to know where to take him and I because our tastes are so different. (6) The only type of restaurant where us and them can all have what we like is Italian. (7) There, him and his friends can sample pasta primavera and eggplant parmigiana while my friends and I tuck into spaghetti and meatballs and pepperoni pizza. (8) We are probably not as healthy as they, but they don't seem to enjoy their food as much as us.

Now that you know how to choose the correct form of pronouns within a sentence, let's turn to the problems of using pronouns consistently throughout a sentence and a paragraph.

Pronoun–Antecedent Agreement

The name of this pronoun problem may sound difficult, but the idea is simple. Pronouns are words that substitute for or refer to the name of a person, place, or thing mentioned elsewhere in your sentence or your paragraph. The word(s) that a pronoun substitutes for or refers to is called the **antecedent**.

Hannibal had his own way of doing things. (The pronoun *his* refers to the antecedent *Hannibal*.)

Chantal respects her boss. (The pronoun *her* refers to the antecedent *Chantal*.)

The computer is processing as fast as it can. (The pronoun *It* substitutes for the antecedent *computer*.)

Usually, as in these three examples, the antecedent comes before the pronoun that refers to it. Here is the rule to remember.

A pronoun must agree with its antecedent in
- number (singular or plural)
- person (first, second, or third)
- gender (masculine, feminine, or neuter)

Most of the time, you follow this rule without even realizing that you know it. For example, you would never write

Hannibal had *your* own way of doing things.

Chantal respects *its* boss.

The computer is processing as fast as *she* can.

You know these sentences are incorrect even if you may not know precisely why they are wrong.

There are three kinds of pronoun–antecedent agreement that you do need to learn about. They lead to errors that, unlike the examples above, are not obvious, and you need to know them so you can watch out for them. The rules you need to learn involve **indefinite pronouns ending in -*one*, -*body*, or -*thing;* vague references; and relative pronouns.**

1. INDEFINITE PRONOUNS: PRONOUNS ENDING IN -*ONE*, -*BODY*, OR -*THING*

The most common pronoun–antecedent agreement problem involves **indefinite pronouns:**

anyone	anybody	anything
everyone	everybody	everything

no one	nobody	nothing
someone	somebody	something
each (one)		

In Chapter 28, you learned that when these words are used as subjects they are singular and take singular verbs. So it makes sense that the pronouns that stand for or refer to them must also be singular.

> Antecedents ending in *-one*, *-body*, or *-thing* are singular and must be referred to by singular pronouns: *he, she, it; his, her, its*.

Please put everything back in *its* place.

Anybody can retire comfortably if *he* or *she* begins planning now.

Everyone is expected to do *his* share.

No one in *his* right mind would claim *he* enjoys living in this climate.

Now take another look at the last two sentences. Until about 30 years ago, the pronouns *he*, *him*, and *his* were used with singular antecedents to refer to both men and women. In order to appeal to the broadest possible audience, most writers today are careful to avoid this usage and other examples of what may be seen as sexist language.

In informal speech, it has become acceptable to use plural pronouns with *-one*, *-body*, or *-thing* antecedents. Although these antecedents are grammatically singular and take singular verbs, they are often plural in meaning, and in conversation we find ourselves saying

Everyone is expected to do *their* share.

No one has to stay if *they* don't want to.

This usage is acceptable in speech, but it is not acceptable in academic or professional writing.

Writers sometimes make errors in pronoun–antecedent agreement because they are trying to write without indicating whether the person referred to is male or female. A sentence such as "Everyone is required to do *their* oral presentation" is incorrect, as we have seen, but it does avoid making "everyone" male. It also avoids the awkwardness of "Everyone is required to do *his* or *her* oral presentation." There are two better ways to solve this problem.

1. Revise the sentence to leave the pronoun out.

Everyone is required to deliver an oral presentation in the last week of class.

or

An oral presentation is required of everyone in the last week of class.

Such creative avoidance of gender-specific or incorrect constructions can be an interesting challenge. The results often sound a little artificial, however. The second method is easier to accomplish.

2. Revise the sentence to make both the antecedent and the pronoun plural.

You are all required to deliver an oral presentation in the last week of class.

or

All students are required to deliver an oral presentation in the last week of class.

Here are two more examples for you to study.

Problem: Everybody has been given his or her assignment.
Revision 1:   Everybody has been given an assignment.
Revision 2:   All of the students have been given their assignments.

Problem: No one wants his copy edited.
Revision 1:   No one wants copy editing.
Revision 2:   Most writers object to having their copy edited.

Exercise 30.4*

In the following sentences, identify the most appropriate word(s) from the choices given in parentheses. (Note: the options may not be the best choices stylistically; just select the one that is grammatically correct in each case.) Check your answers on page 534 before continuing.

1. Everyone who enjoys a thrilling match will reserve (his their) seat for today's chess club meeting.

2. Despite the inconvenience, everyone climbed to the fourth floor to hand in (her their) course evaluation.
3. Each of her sons has successfully completed (his their) diploma.
4. Someone with a lot of cash left (her their) purse in the women's washroom.
5. Every reporter must decide for (himself themselves) how far (he they) will go in pursuit of a story.

Exercise 30.5*

Rewrite the sentences in Exercise 30.4 to eliminate sexist language.

Exercise 30.6*

Correct the following sentences where necessary, being careful to avoid awkward repetition and sexist language.

1. Virginia claims that every one of her male friends has a room of their own.
2. Almost everyone I know is concerned about finding a job that will be suitable for him or her.
3. Anybody who applies for a job with this institution can expect to spend a lot of their time in selection committee interviews.
4. Taking a picture of someone when they are not looking can produce interesting results.
5. Nearly every man who can cook will tell you that they enjoy preparing food.

2. VAGUE REFERENCE

Avoiding the second potential difficulty with pronoun–antecedent agreement requires common sense and the ability to think like your readers. If you look at your writing from your readers' point of view, it is unlikely that you will break the following rule.

Every pronoun must have a clearly identifiable antecedent.

The mistake that occurs when you fail to follow this rule is called **vague reference.**

Chris told his brother that he was losing his hair.

Who is going bald? Chris or his brother?

Here's another example:

The faculty are demanding higher salaries and fewer teaching hours, but the administration does not support them.

What does the administration not favour: higher salaries, fewer classes, or the faculty themselves?

In sentences like these, you can only guess the meaning because you don't know who or what is being referred to by the pronouns. You can make such sentences less confusing by using either more names or other nouns and by using fewer pronouns. For example:

Chris told his brother Sam that Sam was losing his hair.

The faculty are demanding higher salaries and fewer teaching hours, but the administration does not support their demands.

Another type of vague reference occurs when there is no antecedent at all in the sentence for the pronoun to refer to.

I sold my skis last year and can't even remember how to do it anymore. (Do what?)

Reading is Sophia's passion, but she says she doesn't have a favourite. (A favourite what?)

My roommate smokes constantly, *which* I hate. (There is no noun or pronoun for *which* to refer to.)

I hate homework; this is my downfall. (*This* refers to homework, but homework is not my downfall. My hatred of doing it is.)

How would you revise these sentences? Try it, then see our suggestions in the footnote below.[2]

Be sure that every pronoun has a clear antecedent with which it agrees in number, person, and gender. Once you have mastered this principle, you'll have no further trouble with pronoun–antecedent agreement.

---

[2]I sold my skis last year and can't even remember how to *slalom* anymore.

Reading is Sophie's passion, but she says she doesn't have a favourite *writer*.

My roommate is constantly smoking, *which* I hate.

She hates doing homework; *this* is her downfall.

Exercise 30.7*

Correct the following sentences where necessary. There are several ways to fix these sentences. In some cases, the antecedent is missing, and you need to supply one. In other cases, the antecedent is so vague that the meaning of the sentence can be interpreted in more than one way. You need to rewrite these sentences to make the meaning clear.

1. I know that smoking is bad for me and everyone else, but I can't give them up.

2. If your pet rat won't eat its food, feed it to the kitty.

3. Our cat is a picky eater, which is inconvenient and expensive.

4. Whenever Stefan and Matt played poker, he stacked the deck.

5. The gorilla was mean and hungry because he had finished it all in the morning.

6. Madonna has transformed herself at least four times in her career, which makes her unique.

7. Dani backed her car into a garbage truck and dented it.

8. Rocco was suspicious of handgun control because he thought everyone should have one for late-night subway rides.

9. Get your ears pierced during this week's special and take home an extra pair free.

10. Our car is in the shop, but this won't keep us from going to the party.

Exercise 30.8

To test your understanding of the pronoun problems we have covered so far, try this exercise, which contains all three kinds of pronoun–antecedent agreement errors. Correct the following sentences where necessary.

1. Each of her suitors had their faults, but Denise decided to overlook the shortcomings of the one that had the most money.

2. Embezzling is what he does best, but he hasn't been able to pull one off lately.

3. Everyone may pick up their exams in my office on Tuesday after 9:00 a.m.

4. None of the candidates came with their résumé, so we had to reject them all.

5. Every applicant must submit their portfolio of work, their essay on why they want to enter the program, and a neatly folded $50 bill.

6. When I go fishing, I expect to catch at least a few.

7. Every secretary knows that their boss is someone that could not survive for 15 minutes without competent secretarial assistance.

8. All the women in this beauty pageant are treated like a sister even though the competition is fierce.

9. Everybody that joins the tour will receive their own souvenir hat.

10. Before a Canadian votes, it is their responsibility to make themselves familiar with the candidates and the issues.

---

3. RELATIVE PRONOUNS

The third potential difficulty with pronoun–antecedent agreement is how to use relative pronouns—*who/whoever, whom/whomever, which,* and *that*—correctly. Relative pronouns refer to someone or something already mentioned in the sentence or paragraph. Here is the guideline to follow.

> Use *who/whom* and *whoever/whomever* refer to people.
> Use *that* and *which* to refer to everything else.

The student *who* won the Governor General's Academic Medal decided to go to Dalhousie.

For *whom* are you voting: the Liberals or the New Democrats?

The moose *that* I met looked hostile.

Her car, *which* is imported, is smaller than cars *that* are built here.

Tips:

1. Whether you need *who* or *whom, whoever* or *whomever,* depends on the pronoun's place and function in your sentence. Apply the basic rule of pronoun usage: if the pronoun is acting as, or refers to, the subject or the complement, use *who/whoever.* Otherwise, use *whom/whomever.*

My husband was the idiot *who* entered a contest to win a trip to Moose Factory. (The pronoun refers to the subject of the sentence, *husband.*)

The trip's promoters were willing to settle for *whomever* they could get. (The pronoun does not refer to the sentence's subject, *promoters*; it is the object of the preposition *for.*)

An even simpler solution to this problem is to rewrite the sentence so you don't need either *who* or *whom.*

My husband entered a contest to win a trip to Moose Factory.

The trip's promoters were willing to settle for anyone they could get.

2. *That* is required more often than *which.* You should use *which* only in a clause that is separated from the rest of the sentence by commas. (See Comma Rule 4 on page 420.)

The moose *that* I met looked hostile.

The moose, *which* was standing right in front of my car, looked hostile.

Exercise 30.9*

Correct the following sentences where necessary.

1. The actress that saw her first grey hair thought she'd dye.

2. I am a longtime fan of David Cronenberg, a director that began his career in Canada.

3. I wonder why we are so often attracted to people which are completely opposite to us.

4. I'm one of those people that should stay out of the sun.

5. People that take afternoon naps often suffer from insomnia as a result.

6. The vacuum-cleaner salesperson which came to our door was the sort of person that won't take no for an answer.

7. This is the brilliant teacher that helped me achieve the grades which I had thought were beyond me.

8. Marathon runners that wear cheap shoes often suffer the agony of defeat.

9. The math problems which we worked on last night would have baffled anyone that hadn't done all the problem sets.

10. We took the ancient Jeep, that we had bought from a friend that had lost his licence, to a scrapyard who paid us $200 for it.

GO TO WEB

EXERCISES 30.3, 30.4, 30.5, 30.6

Person Agreement

So far, we have focused on using pronouns correctly and clearly within a sentence. Now let's turn to the problem of **person agreement**, which means using pronouns consistently throughout a sentence or a paragraph. There are three categories of person that we use when we write or speak:

	Singular	Plural
First person	I; me	we; us
Second person	you	you
Third person	she, he, it, one; her, him *and all pronouns ending in* -one, -thing, -body	they; them

Here is the rule for person agreement.

Do not mix "persons" unless meaning requires it.

In other words, be consistent. If you begin a sentence using a second-person pronoun, you must use second person all the way through. Look at this sentence:

If *you* wish to succeed, *one* must work hard.

This is the most common error—mixing second-person *you* with third-person *one*.

Here's another example:

One can live happily in Vancouver if *you* have a sturdy umbrella.

1. We can correct this error by using the second person throughout:

You can live happily in Vancouver if *you* have a sturdy umbrella.

2. We can also correct it by using the third person throughout:

a. *One* can live happily in Vancouver if *one* has a sturdy umbrella.

or

b. *One* can live happily in Vancouver if *he* or *she* has a sturdy umbrella.

These examples raise two points of style that you should consider.

1. Don't overuse *one*.

All three revised sentences are grammatically correct, but they make different impressions on the reader, and impressions are an important part of communication.

- The first sentence, in the second person, sounds the most informal—like something you would say. It's a bit casual for general writing purposes.
- The second sentence, which uses *one* twice, sounds the most formal—even a little pretentious.
- The third sentence falls between the other two in formality. It is the one you'd be most likely to use in writing for school or business.

Although it is grammatically correct and nonsexist, this third sentence raises another problem. Frequent use of *he or she* in a continuous prose passage, whether that passage is as short as a paragraph or as long as a paper, is guaranteed to irritate your reader.

2. Don't overuse *he or she*.

He or she is inclusive, but it is a wordy construction. If used too frequently, the reader cannot help shifting focus from what you're saying to how you're saying it. The best writing is transparent—that is, it doesn't call attention to itself. If your reader becomes distracted by your style, your meaning gets lost. Consider this sentence:

> A student can easily pass this course if he or she applies himself or herself to his or her studies.

Readers deserve better. A paper—or even a single paragraph—filled with this clumsy construction will annoy even the most patient reader. There are two better solutions to the problem of sexist language, and they are already familiar to you because they are the same as those for making pronouns ending in -*one*, -*body*, or -*thing* agree with their antecedents.

- You can change the whole sentence to the plural.

> Students can easily pass this course if they apply themselves to their studies.

- You can rewrite the sentence without using pronouns.

> A student can easily pass this course by applying good study habits.

Exercise 30.10*

In each of the following sentences, select the correct word from the choices given in parentheses. Check your answers before continuing.

1. If you want to make good egg rolls, I advise (them her you) to buy the ready-made wrappings.

2. If you win tonight's lottery, will (one he you) tell (one's his your) friends?

3. Anyone who wants to swim should bring (their your his her a) bathing suit and towel.

4. Every person working in this office should know that (they she) helped to finish an important project.

5. When we toured the House of Commons, (you we he one) didn't see a single MP.

Exercise 30.11*

Correct the following sentences where necessary.

1. When a person lives in a glass house, they shouldn't throw stones.

2. Experience is something one acquires just after you need it.

3. Anyone who enjoys snowboarding can have your best holiday ever in western Alberta.

4. When she asked if Peter Tchaikovsky played for the Canucks, you knew she wasn't the woman for me.

5. From time to time, most of us think about the opportunities we've missed even if you are happy with what you have.

6. Managers who are concerned about employee morale should think about ending your policy of threats and intimidation and consider other means to improve your efficiency.

7. If you are afraid of vampires, one should wear garlic around one's neck and carry a silver bullet.

8. Any woman who wears a garlic necklace probably won't have to worry about men harassing them, either.

9. Can you really know another person if you have never been to their home?

10. A sure way to lose one's friends is to eat all the ice cream yourself.

Exercise 30.12*

Revise the following passage to make the nouns and pronouns agree in person (first, second, or third) and number (singular or plural). Use the italicized word in the first sentence of each paragraph as your marker.

When *people* see a dreadful occurrence on television, such as a bombing, an earthquake, or a mass slaughter, it does not always affect one. It is one thing for people to see the ravages of war oneself and another thing to see a three-minute newscast of the same battle, neatly edited by the CBC. Even the horrible effects of natural catastrophes that wipe out whole populations are somehow minimized or trivialized when I see them on TV. And though viewers may be horrified by the gaunt faces of starving children on the screen, you can easily escape into your familiar world of Egg McMuffins, Shake'n Bake, and Labatt Blue that is portrayed in commercial messages.

Thus, the impact of television on *us* is a mixed one. It is true that one is shown terrible, sometimes shocking, events that you could not possibly have seen before television. In this way, one's world is drawn together more closely. However, the risk in creating this immediacy is that one may become desensitized and cease to feel or care about one's fellow human beings.

GO TO WEB

EXERCISES 30.7, 30.8

Exercise 30.13

Revise the following paragraph, which contains 15 errors representing the three different kinds of pronoun–antecedent agreement error. If you change a subject from singular to plural, don't forget to change the verb to agree. Some of your answers may differ from our suggestions and still be correct. Check with your instructor.

Everyone that has been to Newfoundland knows that an outport is a small fishing community along the coast of that vast island province. Ladle Cove, for example, is a tiny outport with fewer than 200 residents that live there all year. Despite its small population, Ladle Cove is a village which enjoyed a nation-wide moment of fame when a man that lives there met the Queen. Fred had left Ladle Cove, as just about every man does when they need to find work, and gone to St. John's. Fred wanted to work, but he had few marketable skills to help him get one. Fortunately, he had relatives in St. John's that helped him find a place to stay and eventually found him a job at Purity Foods, a company famous for their baked goods—and for Newfoundland's favourite treat, Jam Jam cookies.

During Queen Elizabeth's visit to St. John's, the officials that organized her tour decided it would be a good idea for her to visit a local industry which had a national reputation. Purity Foods was the logical choice. While touring the plant, the Queen stopped to talk to a few of the men and women that were on the production line. Near the end of the tour, that was being filmed by the national media, the Queen stopped by one of the workers that were making the famous Jam Jams: Fred. As the television lights glared and each reporter held their pencil poised over their notebook, the Queen leaned toward Fred and asked, "And what are we making here?" With a courteous bow in Her Majesty's direction, Fred replied, "Ten-fifty an hour, Ma'am. Ten-fifty an hour."

Grammar

31

The Comma

Many writers-in-training tend to sprinkle punctuation like pepper over their pages. Do not use punctuation to spice up your writing. Punctuation marks are functional: they indicate to the reader how the various parts of a sentence relate to one another. By changing the punctuation, you can change the meaning of a sentence. Here are two examples to prove the point.

1. An instructor wrote the following sentence on the board and asked the class to punctuate it: "Woman without her man is nothing."

   The men wrote, "Woman, without her man, is nothing."
   The women wrote, "Woman! Without her, man is nothing."

2. Now it's your turn. Punctuate this sentence: "I think there is only one person to blame myself."
   If you wrote, "I think there is only one person to blame, myself," the reader will understand that you believe only one person—who may or may not be known to you—is to blame.
   If you wrote, "I think there is only one person to blame: myself," the reader will understand that you are personally accepting responsibility for the blame.

The comma is the most frequently used—and misused—punctuation mark in English. One sure sign of a competent writer is the correct use of commas, so it is very important that you master them. This chapter presents five comma rules that cover most instances in which you need to use commas. If you apply these five rules faithfully, your reader will never be confused by missing or misplaced commas in your writing. And if, as occasionally happens, the sentence you are writing is not covered by one of our five rules, remember the first commandment of comma usage: WHEN IN DOUBT, LEAVE IT OUT.

Five Comma Rules

1. Use commas to separate three or more items in a series. The items may be expressed as words, phrases, or clauses.

Words   The required subjects in this program are *math, physics,* and *English.*

Phrases   Punctuation marks are the traffic signals of prose. They tell us *to slow down, notice this, take a detour,* and *stop.* (Lynne Truss)

Clauses   *Karin went to the movies, Jan and Yasmin went to play pool,* and *I went to bed.*

The comma before the *and* at the end of the list is optional, but we advise you to use it. Occasionally, misunderstandings can occur if it is left out.

Exercise 31.1*

Insert commas where necessary in the following sentences. Answers for exercises in this chapter begin on page 536.

1. Holly held two aces a King a Queen and a Jack in her hand.

2. The food at the Thai Palace is colourful spicy delicious and inexpensive.

3. Life would be complete if I had a Blackberry a Porsche a Sea-Doo and a job.

4. The gear list for the Winter Wilderness course includes woollen underwear snowshoes Arctic boots and a toque.

5. In the summer, a cup of coffee a croissant and a glass of juice are all I want for breakfast.

6. Don't forget to bring the videos maps and souvenirs of your trip to Australia.

7. In Ontario, the four seasons are summer winter winter and winter.

Punctuation

8. My doctor and my nutritionist agree that I should eat better exercise more and take vitamins.

9. Sleeping through my alarm dozing during sociology class napping in the library after lunch and snoozing in front of the TV after supper are symptoms of my overactive nightlife.

10. Welcome home! Once you have finished your homework taken out the garbage and done the dishes, you can feed the cat clean your room and do your laundry.

---

2. Put a comma between independent clauses when they are joined by these connecting words:

for	but	so
and	or	
nor	yet	

(You can remember these words easily if you notice that their first letters spell FANBOYS.)

I hope I do well in the interview, for I really want this job.

I like Norah Jones, but I prefer Diana Krall.

We shape our tools, and our tools shape us. (Marshall McLuhan)

I knew I was going to be late, so I went back to sleep.

Be sure that the sentence you are punctuating contains two independent clauses rather than one clause with a single subject and a multiple verb.

We loved the book but hated the movie.
(We is the subject, and there are two verbs, loved and hated. Do not put a comma between two or more verbs that share a single subject.)

We both loved the book, but Kim hated the movie.
(This sentence contains two independent clauses—We loved and Kim hated—joined by but. The comma is required here.)

Exercise 31.2*

Insert commas where they are needed in the following sentences, then check your answers.

1. Either it is very foggy this morning or I am going blind.

2. We have an approved business plan and budget but we're still looking for qualified and experienced staff.

3. Talk shows haven't said anything new in years nor have they solved a single one of the problems they endlessly discuss.

4. We discovered that we both had an interest in fine art so we made a date to go to an exhibition at the art gallery next week.

5. Canadians are proud of their country but they don't approve of too much flag-waving.

6. Take good notes for I'll need them in order to study for the exam.

7. I'll rent a tux but I will not get a haircut or my shoes shined.

8. I chose a quiet seat on the train and two women with bawling babies boarded at the next station.

9. I have travelled all over the world yet my luggage has visited at least twice the number of countries that I have.

10. Jet lag makes me look haggard and ill but at least I resemble my passport photo.

3. Put a comma after an introductory word, phrase, or dependent clause that comes before an independent clause.

Lucas, you aren't paying attention. (word)

After staying up all night, I staggered into class 15 minutes late. (phrase)

If that's their idea of a large pizza, we'd better order two. (clause)

Until she got her promotion, she was quite friendly. (clause)

Punctuation

> **4.** Use commas to set off any word, phrase, or dependent clause that is NOT ESSENTIAL to the main idea of the sentence.

Following this rule can make the difference between your reader's understanding and misunderstanding what you write. For example, the following two sentences are identical, except for a pair of commas. But notice what a difference those two tiny marks make to meaning:

> The children who were dressed in clown costumes had ice cream. (Only the children wearing clown costumes ate ice cream.)

> The children, who were dressed in clown costumes, had ice cream. (All the children wore costumes and had ice cream.)

To test whether a word, phrase, or clause is essential to the meaning of your sentence, mentally put parentheses around it. If the sentence still makes complete sense (i.e., the main idea is unchanged; the sentence just delivers less information), the material in parentheses is *not essential* and should be set off from the rest of the sentence by a comma or commas.

Nonessential information can appear at the beginning of a sentence,[1] in the middle, or at the end of a sentence. Study the following examples.

> Alice Munro (one of Canada's best-known novelists) spends summer in Clinton and winter in Comox.

Most readers would be puzzled the first time they read this sentence because all the information is presented without punctuation, so the reader assumes it is all equally important. In fact, the material in broken parentheses is extra information, a supplementary detail. It can be deleted without changing the sentence's meaning, and so it should be separated from the rest of the sentence by commas:

> Alice Munro, one of Canada's best-known novelists, spends summer in Clinton and winter in Comox.

Here's another example to consider:

> The Queen (who has twice as many birthdays as anyone else) officially celebrates her birthday on May 24.

---

[1] Comma Rule 3 covers nonessential information at the beginning of a sentence.

Again, the sentence is hard to read. You can't count on your readers to go back and reread every sentence they don't understand at first glance. As a writer, your responsibility is to give readers the clues they need as to what is crucial information and what isn't. In the example above, the information in broken parentheses is not essential to the meaning of the sentence, so it should be set off by commas:

> The Queen, who has twice as many birthdays as anyone else, officially celebrates her birthday on May 24.

In this next sentence, the nonessential information comes at the end.

> Writing a good letter of application isn't difficult ⦃ if you're careful ⦄ .

The phrase "if you're careful" is not essential to the main idea, so it should be separated from the rest of the sentence by a comma:

> Writing a good letter of application isn't difficult, if you're careful.

And finally, consider this sentence:

> Writing a letter of application ⦃ that is clear, complete, and concise ⦄ is a challenge.

If you take out "that is clear, complete, and concise," you change the meaning of the sentence. Not all letters of application are a challenge to write. Writing vague and wordy letters is easy; anyone can do it. The words "that is clear, complete, and concise" are essential to the meaning of the sentence, and so they are not set off by commas.

> Writing a letter of application that is clear, complete, and concise is a challenge.

Exercise 31.3*

Insert commas where they are missing in the following sentences, then check your answers.

1. A good day in my opinion always starts with a few cuts of high-volume heavy metal.
2. This photograph which was taken when I was four embarrasses me whenever my parents display it.
3. Mira's boyfriend who looks like an ape is living proof that love is blind.

Punctuation

4. Isn't it strange that the poor who often are bitterly critical of the rich keep buying lottery tickets?
5. A nagging headache the result of last night's great party made me miserable all morning.
6. Our ancient car made it all the way to Saskatoon without anything falling off or breaking down a piece of good luck that astonished everyone.
7. Professor Repke a popular mathematics teacher won the Distinguished Teaching Award this year.
8. We're going to spend the afternoon at the mall a weekly event that has become a ritual.
9. No one who ever saw Patrick Roy play doubts that he was a superstar.
10. Classical music which I call Prozac for the ears can be very soothing in times of stress.

Exercise 31.4*

Insert commas where they are needed in the following sentences. Check your answers on page 538 before continuing.

1. Unfortunately we'll have to begin all over again.
2. Mr. Dillinger the bank would like a word with you.
3. In college the quality of your work is more important than the effort you put into it.
4. Hopelessly lost my father still refused to stop and ask for directions.
5. Finally understanding what she was trying to say I apologized for being so slow.
6. After an evening of watching television I have accomplished as much as if I had been unconscious.
7. Since the doctor ordered me to walk to work every morning I have seen three accidents involving people walking to work.
8. Having munched our way through a large bag of peanuts while watching the game we weren't interested in supper.
9. Whenever an optimist is pulled over by a police officer the optimist assumes it's to ask for directions.
10. That same year Stephen Leacock bought his summer home in Orillia, Ontario.

5. Use commas between coordinate adjectives but not between cumulative adjectives.

Coordinate adjectives are those whose order can be changed, and the word *and* can be inserted between them without changing the meaning of the sentence.

Our company is looking for energetic, courteous salespeople.

The adjectives *energetic* and *courteous* could appear in reverse order, and you could put *and* between them: "Our company is looking for courteous and energetic salespeople."

In a series of **cumulative adjectives**, however, each adjective modifies the word that follows it. You cannot change their order, nor can you insert *and* between them.

The bride wore a pale pink silk dress, and the groom wore a navy wool suit.

You cannot say "The bride wore a silk pink pale dress" or "The groom wore a navy and wool suit," so no commas are used with these adjectives.

One final note about commas before you try the review exercises: never place a SINGLE comma between a subject and its verb.

Wrong: Those who intend to register for hockey, must be at the arena by 8:00 a.m.

Right: Those who intend to register for hockey must be at the arena by 8:00 a.m.

Two commas, however, between a subject and its verb are correct if the commas set off nonessential material.

Saied and Mohamed, who intend to register for hockey, have never played before.

Exercise 31.5

Insert commas where they are needed in the following sentences. Check your answers before continuing.

1. The desk was made of dark brown carved oak.
2. Do you want your portrait in a glossy finish or a matte finish?
3. Bright yellow fabric that repels stains is ideal for rain gear.
4. Toronto in the summer is hot smoggy and humid.

Punctuation

5. Today's paper has an article about a new car made of lightweight durable aluminum.
6. Dietitians recommend that we eat at least two servings daily of green leafy vegetables.
7. This ergonomic efficient full-function keyboard comes in a variety of pastel shades.
8. We ordered a large nutritious salad for lunch, then indulged ourselves with a redcurrant cheesecake for dessert.
9. Danny bought a cute cuddly purebred puppy.
10. Ten months later that cute puppy turned into a vicious man-eating monster.

The rest of the exercises in this chapter require you to apply all five comma rules. Before you start, write out the five rules and keep them in front of you as you work through the exercises. Refer to the rules frequently as you punctuate the sentences. After you've finished each exercise, check your answers and make sure you understand any mistakes you've made.

Exercise 31.6 *

1. Pinot noir which is a type of grape grown in California Oregon British Columbia and Ontario produces a delicious red wine.
2. There are I am told people who don't like garlic but you won't find any of them eating at Freddy's.
3. I use e-mail to communicate with my colleagues a fax machine to keep in touch with clients and Canada Post to send greetings to my relatives.
4. Your dogs Mr. Pavlov seem hungry for some reason.
5. According to G. K. Chesterton "If a thing is worth doing it is worth doing badly."
6. Looking for a competent computer technologist we interviewed tested investigated and rejected 30 applicants.
7. How you choose to phrase your resignation is up to you but I expect to have it on my desk by morning.
8. Your superstitious dread of March 13 Senator Caesar is irrational and silly.
9. The lenses of my new high-fashion sunglasses are impact-resistant yellow UV-reflective optical plastic.
10. Canada a country known internationally for beautiful scenery peaceful intentions and violent hockey always places near the top of the United Nations' list of desirable places to live.

Exercise 31.7*

1. Whereas the Super Bowl tradition goes back about four decades the Grey Cup has a history that stretches back to the 19th century.
2. Otherwise Mrs. Lincoln said she had very much enjoyed the play.
3. Our guard dog a Rottweiler caught an intruder and maimed him for life.
4. Unfortunately my Uncle Ladislaw was the intruder and he intends to sue us for every penny we have.
5. The year 1945 marked the end of World War II and the beginning of assistance to war-torn nations.
6. We bought a lovely old mahogany dining table at auction for $300.
7. If there were more people like Gladys global warming would be the least of our worries.
8. We are pleased with your résumé and are offering you an interview this week.
9. Deciding on the midnight blue velvet pants was easy but paying for them was not.
10. Igor asked "May I show you to your quarters or would you prefer to spend the night in the dungeon?"

GO TO WEB

EXERCISES 31.1, 31.2, 31.3

Exercise 31.8

To test your mastery of commas, provide the necessary punctuation for the following paragraph. There are 15 errors.

When my brother and I were growing up my mother used to summon us home from playing by ringing a solid brass bell that could be heard for miles. All of the other kids to our great embarrassment, knew when our mother was calling us and they would tease us by making ringing noises. We begged her to yell like all the other moms but she knew she had a foolproof system and wouldn't change. One day while we were playing with our friends in the fields behind our homes the bell rang in the middle of

Punctuation

an important game. The other kids began their usual taunts that our mother was calling but this time we bravely ignored the bell. When it rang the second time we ignored it again. By the third ring, however we knew that we were in big trouble so we dashed for home. We agreed on the way that we would tell our mother that we just didn't hear the bell. We arrived hot sweaty and panting from our run. Before Mom could say a word my brother blurted out, "We didn't hear the bell until the third ring!" Fortunately for us our mother couldn't stop laughing and we escaped the punishment we deserved.

Summary

The Five Comma Rules

1. Use commas to separate items in a series of three or more. The items may be expressed as words, phrases, or clauses.
2. Put a comma between independent clauses when they are joined by *for, and, nor, but, or, yet,* or *so.*
3. Put a comma after an introductory word, phrase, or dependent clause that comes before an independent clause.
4. Use commas to set off a word, phrase, or dependent clause that is NOT ESSENTIAL to the main idea of the sentence.
5. Use commas between coordinate adjectives but not between cumulative adjectives.

32

The Semicolon

The semicolon and the colon are often confused and used as if they were interchangeable. They have distinct purposes, however, and their correct use can dramatically improve a reader's understanding of your writing. The semicolon has three functions.

1. A semicolon can replace a period; in other words, it can appear between two independent clauses.

You should use a semicolon when the two clauses (sentences) you are joining are closely connected in meaning, or when there is a cause-and-effect relationship between them.

I'm too tired; I can't stay awake any longer.

Montreal is not the city's original name; it was once called Ville Marie.

A period could have been used instead of a semicolon in either of these sentences, but the close connection between the clauses makes a semicolon more effective in communicating the writer's meaning.

2. Certain transitional words or phrases can be put between independent clauses to show a cause-and-effect relationship or the continuation of an idea.

Words or phrases used in this way are usually preceded by a semicolon and followed by a comma:

; also,	; furthermore,	; nevertheless,
; as a result,	; however,	; on the other hand,
; besides,	; in addition,	; otherwise,
; consequently,	; in fact,	; then,
; finally,	; instead,	; therefore,
; for example,	; moreover,	; thus,

The forecast called for sun; instead, we got snow.

My monitor went blank; nevertheless, I kept on typing.

"I'm not offended by dumb blonde jokes because I know I'm not dumb; besides, I also know I'm not blonde." (Dolly Parton)

In other words, *a semicolon + a transitional word/phrase + a comma* = a link strong enough to come between two related independent clauses.

Note, however, that, when these transitional words and phrases are used as nonessential expressions rather than as connecting words, they are separated from the rest of the sentence by commas (Chapter 31, Rule 4, page 420).

I just can't seem to master particle physics, however hard I try.

The emissions test, moreover, will ensure that your car is running well.

3. To make a COMPLEX LIST easier to read and understand, put semicolons between the items instead of commas.

A complex list is one in which at least one component part already contains commas. Here are two examples:

I grew up in a series of small towns: Cumberland, B.C.; Red Deer, Alberta; and Timmins, Ontario.

When we opened the refrigerator, we found a limp, brown head of lettuce; two small containers of yogurt, whose "best before" dates had long since passed; and a hard, dried-up piece of cheddar cheese.

Exercise 32.1*

Put a check mark next to the sentences that are correctly punctuated. Check your answers before continuing. Answers for this chapter begin on page 539.

1. _____We've eaten all the food, it's time to go home.
2. _____Many doctors claim weather affects our health; in fact, barometric pressure has a direct effect on arthritis.
3. _____ Your instructor would like to see you pass, however, there may be a small fee involved.
4. _____ Molly is going to Chicago, she wants to appear on *Oprah*.
5. _____ Many people dislike hockey; because some of the players act like goons rather than athletes.
6. _____ Orville tried and tried; but he couldn't get the teacher's attention.
7. _____ She presented her report using coloured charts and diagrams; these visual aids woke up even the accountants.
8. _____ Tomorrow is another day, unfortunately it will probably be just like today.
9. _____ Rumours of a merger had begun to circulate by five o'clock; so it's no wonder many employees looked nervous on their way home.
10. _____ We knew the party had been a success when Uncle Morty, drunk as usual, tap-danced across the top of the piano, Aunt Madeline, who must weigh at least 80 kg, did her Cirque du Soleil routine, and Stan punched out two of his cousins.

Exercise 32.2*

Correct the faulty punctuation in Exercise 32.1.

GO TO WEB

EXERCISES 32.1, 32.2

Punctuation

Exercise 32.3*

Insert semicolons where necessary in these sentences. Then check your answers.

1. The rain has to stop soon otherwise, we'll have to start building an ark.
2. Our finances are a mess the only way we can repay our debts would be to stop paying for rent and food.
3. We need you at the meeting, however, since you have another engagement, we will have to reschedule.
4. A day without puns is like a day without sunshine, it leaves gloom for improvement.
5. I work on an assembly line, all of us workers believe that if a job is worth doing; it's worth doing 11,000 times a day.
6. It is not impossible to become wealthy, if you're under 20, all you need to do is put the price of a pack of cigarettes into an RRSP every day, and you'll be a millionaire by the age of 50.
7. If, on the other hand, you continue to spend your money on smokes, the government will make the millions that could have been yours, you'll die early and broke.
8. As a dog lover and the owner of an Afghan, I suffer a great deal of abuse, for example, for my birthday, my wife gave me a book rating the intelligence of Afghans as 79th out of 79 breeds tested.
9. A plateau, according to the *Dictionary of Puns*, is a high form of flattery, this may be low humour, but it's a clever remark.
10. According to a *Gourmet Magazine* poll, four of the top ten restaurants in the world are in Paris, three—those ranking eighth, ninth, and tenth—are in the United States, two are in Tokyo and the other is in Thailand.

GO TO WEB

EXERCISE 32.3

Exercise 32.4

Test your mastery of semicolons and commas by correcting the punctuation in these sentences.

1. Growing old has never really bothered me in fact I consider aging a huge improvement over the alternative.
2. I visit a chiropractor twice a month, if I miss a treatment I have to crawl into work.

3. Our marketing campaign is based on sound principles, for example if we are sufficiently annoying people will buy our product just to make us go away.

4. The construction was so far behind schedule that we couldn't make up the time, consequently we lost our performance bonus our chance to bid on the next contract and an important client.

5. Among the many products being standardized by the European Community is the condom however a number of nations have officially complained that the standard size is too small.

6. Failing to stop at the light turned out to be the least of his offences the police were much more interested in his expired driving licence.

7. In her fridge we found a pound of butter dating from last August a mouldy piece of cake three containers of unidentifiable fur-bearing substances and an open can of beer.

8. A practice that works well in one country may not work in another for example every man in Switzerland is required to own a rifle. Such a policy might find acceptance in the United States however anyone who proposed it in Canada would be thought insane.

9. While some people find bird watching an exciting hobby and others are drawn to rock climbing or heli-skiing my own preference is for less strenuous pastimes such as those involving food.

10. To use or not to use the semicolon is sometimes a matter of the writer's choice, on the other hand, a few syntactical constructions require a semicolon, no other punctuation mark will do.

Punctuation

33

The Colon

The **colon** functions as an introducer. When a statement is followed by a list, one or more examples, or a quotation, the colon alerts the reader that some sort of explanatory detail is coming up.

When I travel, I am never without three things: sturdy shoes, a money belt, and my journal.

There is only one enemy we cannot defeat: time.

We have two choices: to study or to fail.

Early in his career, Robert Fulford did not think very highly of intellectual life in Canada: "My generation of Canadians grew up believing that, if we were very good or very smart, or both, we would someday *graduate* from Canada."

The statement that precedes the colon must be a complete sentence (independent clause).

A colon should never come immediately after *is* or *are*. Here's an example of what *not* to write.

The only things I am violently allergic to are: cats, ragweed, and country music.

This is incorrect because the statement before the colon is not a complete sentence.

10. Canadian sports broadcaster, Foster Hewitt, created a sports catch phrase "He shoots! He scores!" during an overtime game between the Rangers and the Leafs on April 4, 1933. The Rangers won.

Exercise 36.4

Correct the following paragraph, which contains 20 errors (each set of dashes and parentheses counts as two errors).

As a final review of punctuation here's a paragraph that should contain all the punctuation marks we have discussed in this section of the book however 20 pieces of punctuation are missing. Your job is to provide the missing punctuation. Let's quickly deal with punctuation marks one by one. The comma probably the hardest-working of them all is used to separate items in a series to set off nonessential material to join with a conjunction to separate independent clauses and to set off material that comes before a main clause. Whew. The semicolon can replace a period it often separates two independent clauses that are closely connected in meaning. The colon has a different function it follows an independent clause and introduces a list a clarification or a quotation. Did you remember that a colon should never follow "is" or "are". A question mark must be used at the end of all interrogative sentences. We all know this but sometimes we forget. Exclamation marks are used at the end of sentences for one purpose only to supply dramatic effect. But remember that they are seldom used in academic writing. Finally dashes and parentheses allow a writer to interrupt a train of thought and insert an "aside" into a sentence. That's it. If you have correctly inserted all the punctuation in this paragraph then you are ready to tackle Hazardous Homonyms.

Punctuation

37

Hazardous Homonyms

This chapter focuses on homonyms—words that sound alike or look alike and are easily confused: *accept* and *except*; *weather* and *whether*; *whose* and *who's*; *affect* and *effect*. A spell checker will not help you find spelling mistakes in these words because the "correct" spelling depends on the sentence in which you use the word. For example, if you write, "Meat me hear inn halve an our," no spell checker will find fault with your sentence—and no reader will understand what you're talking about.

Careful pronunciation can sometimes help you tell the difference between words that are often confused. For example, if you pronounce the words *accept* and *except* differently, you'll be less likely to use the wrong one when you write. You can also make up memory aids to help you remember the difference in meaning between words that sound or look alike.

Below is a list of the most common homonym hazards. Only some of the words on this list will cause you trouble. Make your own list of problem pairs and tape it on the inside cover of your dictionary or post it close to your computer. Get into the habit of checking your document against your list every time you write.

accept except	*Accept* means "take" or "receive." It is always a verb. *Except* means "**ex**cluding."
	I *accepted* the spelling award, and no one *except* my mother knew I cheated.
advice advise	The difference in pronunciation makes the difference in meaning clear. *Advise* (rhymes with *wise*) is a verb. *Advice* (rhymes with *nice*) is a noun.
	I *advise* you not to listen to free *advice*.

affect
effect

Affect as a verb means "change." Try substituting *change* for the word you've chosen in your sentence. If it makes sense, then *affect* is the word you want. As a noun, *áffect* means "a strong feeling." *Effect* is a noun meaning "result." If you can substitute *result,* then *effect* is the word you need. Occasionally, *effect* is used as a verb meaning "to bring about."

> Learning about the *effects* (results) of caffeine *affected* (changed) my coffee-drinking habits.
> Depressed people often display inappropriate *affect* (feelings).
> Antidepressant medications can *effect* (bring about) profound changes in mood.

a lot
allot

A lot (often misspelled *alot*) should be avoided in formal writing. Use *many* or *much* instead. *Allot* means "distribute" or "assign."

>   *many*   *much*
> He still has a ~~lot of~~ problems, but he is coping a ~~lot~~ better.
> The teacher will *allot* the marks according to the difficulty of the questions.

aloud
allowed

Aloud means out loud, not a whisper. *Allowed* means permitted.

> We were not *allowed* to speak *aloud* during the performance.

amount
number

Amount is used with uncountable things; *number* is used with countable things.

> You may have a large *number* of jelly beans in a jar but a small *amount* of candy.
> (Jelly beans are countable; candy is not.)

are
our

Are is a verb. *Our* shows ownership.

> Marie-Claire Blais and Margaret Atwood *are* two of Canada's best-known writers.
>
> Canada is *our* home and native land.

assure
ensure
insure

Assure means "state with confidence; pledge or promise."

> She *assured* him she would keep his letters always.
>
> The prime minister *assured* the Inuit their concerns would be addressed in the near future.

Spelling

Ensure means "make certain of something."

> The extra $20 will *ensure* that you get a good seat.

> No number of promises can *ensure* that love will last.

Insure means "guarantee against financial loss." We *insure* lives and property.

> Kevin *insured* the book before he sent it airmail.

> We have *insured* both our home and our car against fire and theft.

choose
chose

Pronunciation gives the clue here. *Choose* rhymes with *booze* and means "select." *Chose* rhymes with *rose* and means "selected."

> Please *choose* a topic.

> I *chose* filmmaking.

cite
sight
site

To *cite* is to quote or mention. A lawyer *cites* precedents. Writers *cite* their sources in research papers. You might *cite* a comedian for her wit or a politician for his honesty. A *site* is a place.

> You have included only Internet sources in your Works *Cited* list.

> The Plains of Abraham is the *site* of a famous battle.

> Tiananmen Square is the *site* of the massacre.

> Pape and Mortimer is the *site* of our new industrial design centre.

A *sight* is something you see.

> With his tattooed forehead and three nose rings, he was a *sight* to behold.

coarse
course

Coarse means "rough, unrefined." (Remember: the word *arse* is co*arse*.) For all other meanings, use *course*.

> That sandpaper is too *coarse*.
> You'll enjoy the photography *course*.
> Of *course* you'll do well.

complement compliment	A *complement* completes something. A *compliment* is a gift of praise.

> A glass of wine would be the perfect *complement* to the meal.
>
> Some people are embarrassed by *compliments*.

conscience conscious	Your *conscience* is your sense of right and wrong. *Conscious* means "aware" or "awake"—able to feel and think.

> After Katy cheated on the test, her *conscience* bothered her.
>
> Katy was *conscious* of having done wrong.
>
> The injured man was *unconscious* for an hour.

consul council counsel	A *consul* is a government official stationed in another country. A *council* is an assembly or official group. (Members of a council are *councillors*.) *Counsel* can be used to mean both "advice" and "to advise." (Those who give advice are *counsellors*.)

> The Canadian *consul* in Mexico was very helpful.
>
> The Women's Advisory *Council* meets next month.
>
> Maria gave me good *counsel*.
>
> She *counselled* me to hire a lawyer.

continual continuous	*Continual* refers to an action that goes on regularly but with interruptions. *Continuous* refers to an action that goes on without interruption.

> The student *continually* tried to interrupt the lecturer, who droned on *continuously*.
>
> There is a *continuous* flow of traffic during rush hour.

credible credulous creditable	*Credible* means "believable"; *credulous* describes the person who believes an incredible story.

> Nell was fortunate that the police officer found her story *credible*.
>
> My brother is so *credulous* that we call him Gullible Gus.

Creditable means "worthy of reward or praise."

Spelling

After two semesters, Eva has finally begun to produce *creditable* work.

desert
dessert

A *désert* is a dry, barren place. As a verb, *desért* means "leave behind." *Dessért* is the part of the meal you'd probably like a double serving of, so give it a double *s*.

The tundra is Canada's only *desert* region.

My neighbour *deserted* her husband and children.

Dessert is my favourite part of the meal.

dining
dinning

You'll spell *dining* correctly if you remember the phrase "wining and dining." You'll probably never use *dinning*. It means "making a loud noise."

The children are in the *dining* room.

We are *dining* out tonight.

The noise from the bar was *dinning* in our ears.

disburse
disperse

Disburse means "to pay out money," which is what **burs**ars do. *Disperse* means "to break up"; crowds are sometimes *dispersed* by the police.

The college's financial-aid officer will *disburse* the students' loans at the end of this week.

The protesters were *dispersed* by the police.

does
dose

Pronunciation provides the clue. *Does* rhymes with *buzz* and is a verb. *Dose* rhymes with *gross* and refers to a quantity of medicine.

John *does* drive quickly, doesn't he?

My grandmother gave me a *dose* of cod liver oil.

farther
further

You'll have no trouble distinguishing between these two if you associate *farther* with *distance* and *further* with *time*.

Dana wanted me to walk a little *farther* so we could discuss our relationship *further*.

faze
phase

Fazed usually has a *not* before it; to be *not fazed* means to be not disturbed, or concerned, or taken aback. *Phase* means "stage of development or process."

Unfortunately, Theo was not the least bit *fazed* by his disastrous grade report.

Since Mei Ling works full-time, she has decided to complete her degree in *phases*.

fewer
less

Fewer is used with countable things, *less* with uncountable things.

In May, there are *fewer* students in the college, so there is *less* work for the faculty to do.

The *fewer* attempts you make, the *less* your chance of success.

With units of money or measurement, however, use *less*:

I have *less* than $20 in my wallet.

Our house is on a lot that is *less* than four metres wide.

forth
fourth

Forth means "**for**ward" or "onward." *Fourth* contains the number *four*, which gives it its meaning.

Please stop pacing back and *forth*.

The B.C. Lions lost their *fourth* game in a row.

hear
here

Hear is what you do with your **ear**s. *Here* is used for all other meanings.

Now *hear* this!

Ray isn't *here*.

Here is your assignment.

imply
infer

A speaker or writer *implies*; a listener or reader *infers*. To *imply* is to hint or say something indirectly. To *infer* is to draw a conclusion from what is stated or hinted at.

I *inferred* from his sarcastic remarks that he was not very fond of Sheila.

In her introduction of the speaker, Sheila *implied* that she greatly admired him.

it's
its

It's is a shortened form of *it is*. The apostrophe takes the place of the *i* in *is*. If you can substitute *it is*, then *it's* is the form you need. If you can't substitute *it is*, then *its* is the correct word.

Spelling

It's really not difficult. (*It is* really not difficult.)

The book has lost *its* cover. ("The book has lost *it is* cover" makes no sense, so you need *its*.)

It's is also commonly used as the shortened form of *it has*. In this case, the apostrophe replaces the *ha* in *has*.

It's been a good year for us.

later latter	*Later* refers to time and has the word **late** in it. *Latter* means "the second of two" and has two *t*s. It is the opposite of *former*.

It is *later* than you think.

You take the former, and I'll take the *latter*.

loose lose	Pronunciation is the key to these words. *Loose* rhymes with *goose* and means "not tight." *Lose* rhymes with *ooze* and means "misplace" or "be defeated."

A *loose* electrical connection is dangerous.

Some are born to win, some to *lose*.

martial marshal	*Martial* refers to warfare or military affairs. *Marshal* has two meanings. As a noun, it refers to a person who has high office, either in the army or (especially in the United States) the police. As a verb, it means to arrange or assemble in order.

She is a *martial* arts enthusiast.

When the troops were *marshalled* on the parade grounds, they were reviewed by the army *marshal*.

miner minor	A **miner** works in a **mine**. *Minor* means "lesser" or "not important." For example, a *minor* is a person of less than legal age.

Liquor can be served to *miners*, but not if they are *minors*.

For me, spelling is a *minor* problem.

moral morale	Again, pronunciation provides the clue you need. *Móral* refers to the understanding of what is right and wrong. *Moréle* refers to the spirit or mental condition of a person or group.

> People often have to make *moral* decisions.
> The low *morale* of the workers prompted the strike.

peace piece	*Peace* is what we want on *Earth*. *Piece* means "a part or portion of something," as in "a **piece** of **pie**."

> Everyone hopes for *peace* in the Middle East.
> A *piece* of the puzzle is missing.

personal personnel	*Personal* means "private." *Personnel* refers to the group of people working for a particular employer or to the office responsible for maintaining employees' records.

> The letter was marked "*Personal* and Confidential."
> We are fortunate in having qualified *personnel*.
> Fatima works in the *Personnel* Office.

principal principle	*Principal* means "main." A *princip**le*** is a rule.

> A *principal* is the main administrator of a school.
> Oil is Alberta's *principal* industry.
> I make it a *principle* to submit my essays on time.

quiet quite	If you pronounce these words carefully, you won't confuse them. *Quiet* has two syllables; *quite* has only one.

> The librarian asked us to be *quiet*.
> We had not *quite* finished our homework.

roll role	Turning over and over like a wheel is to *roll*; a bun is also a *roll*. An actor playing a part is said to have a *role*.

> His *role* called for him to fall to the ground and *roll* into
> a ditch, all the while munching on a bread *roll*.

Spelling

simple simplistic	*Simple* means uncomplicated, easily understood. Something described as *simplistic* is too simple to be acceptable; essential details or complexities have been overlooked.

This problem is far from *simple*. Your solution to it is *simplistic*.

stationary stationery	*Stationary* means "fixed in place." *Stationery* is writing paper.

Sarah Ferguson works out on a *stationary* bicycle.

Please order a new supply of *stationery*.

than then	*Than* is used in comparisons. Pronounce it to rhyme with *can*. *Then* refers to time and rhymes with *when*.

Rudi is a better speller *than* I.

He made his decision *then*.

Eva withdrew from the competition; *then* she realized the consequences.

their there they're	*Their* indicates ownership. *There* points out something or indicates place. It includes the word *here*, which also indicates place. *They're* is a shortened form of *they are*. (The apostrophe replaces the *a* in *are*.)

It was *their* fault.

There are two weeks left in the term.

You should look over *there*.

They're late, as usual.

too two to	The *too* with an extra *o* in it means "more than enough" or "also." *Two* is the number after one. For all other meanings, use *to*.

He thinks he's been working *too* hard. She thinks so *too*.

There are *two* sides *to* every argument.

The *two* women knew *too* much about each other *to* be friends.

weather whether wether	*Whether* means "which of the two" and is used in all cases when you aren't referring to the climatic conditions outside (*weather*). A *wether* is a castrated ram, so that word's uses are limited.

Whether you're ready or not, it's time to go.

No one immigrates to Canada for its *weather*.

were
where
we're

If you pronounce these three carefully, you won't confuse them. *Were* rhymes with *fur* and is a verb. *Where* is pronounced "hwear," includes the word **here**, and indicates place. *We're* is a shortened form of *we are* and is pronounced "weer."

You were joking, *weren't* you?

Where did you want to meet?

We're on our way.

who's
whose

Who's is a shortened form of *who is* or *who has*. If you can substitute *who is* or *who has* for the *who's* in your sentence, then you are using the right spelling. Otherwise, use *whose*.

Who's coming to dinner? (*Who is* coming to dinner?)

Who's been sleeping in my bed? (*Who has* been sleeping in my bed?)

Whose calculator is this? ("*Who is* calculator" makes no sense, so you need *whose*.)

woman
women

Confusing these two is guaranteed to irritate your female readers. *Woman* is the singular form; compare **man**. *Women* is the plural form; compare **men**.

A *woman's* place is wherever she chooses to be.

The *women's* movement promotes equality between women and men.

you're
your

You're is a shortened form of *you are*. If you can substitute *you are* for the *you're* in your sentence, then you're using the correct form. If you can't substitute *you are*, use *your*.

You're welcome. (*You are* welcome.)

Unfortunately, *your* hamburger got burned. ("*You are* hamburger" makes no sense, so *your* is the word you want.)

Spelling

In Exercises 37.1 and 37.2, choose the correct word from those in parentheses. If you don't know an answer, go back and reread the explanation. Check your answers after each set. Answers for this chapter begin on page 543.

Exercise 37.1*

1. The limited (coarse course) selection will (affect effect) our academic development and subsequent job opportunities.
2. (Are Our) you going to (accept except) the offer?
3. Eat your vegetables; (than then) you can have your (desert dessert).
4. If (your you're) overweight by 20 kg, (loosing losing) the excess will be a long-term proposition.
5. It's (quiet quite) true that they did not get (hear here) until 2:00 a.m.
6. It is usually the saint, not the sinner, (who's whose) (conscience conscious) is troubled.
7. He (assured ensured insured) me he would keep the (amount number) of changes to a minimum.
8. (Its It's) hard to tell the dog from (its it's) owner.
9. To (choose chose) a (coarse course) of action against your lawyer's (advice advise) would be foolish.
10. (Continual Continuous) (dining dinning) out becomes boring after a while.

Exercise 37.2*

1. It is (simple simplistic) to claim that our society's (morals morales) have declined drastically over the last 20 years; to do so (infers implies) that morality is an absolute value.
2. After the accident, the (moral morale) of the (miners minors) did not recover for many months, but the owners appeared not to be (fazed phased) by the disaster.
3. The chief librarian did not mean to (imply infer) that (farther further) cuts to services are being considered by the board, which, in the circumstances, has done a very (credible credulous creditable) job.
4. The (affect effect) of trying to (disperse disburse) the mob of (less fewer) than 20 people was to cause a riot involving hundreds.
5. (Who's Whose) (principals principles) are so firm that they wouldn't pay (fewer less) tax if they could get away with it?
6. By reading between the lines, we can (infer imply) (wether weather whether) the author intends his (forth fourth) chapter to be taken seriously.

7. It's (your you're) fault that we are (continually continuously) harassed by salespeople because your welcoming smile (assures insures ensures) that they will return again and again.

8. Are you (conscious conscience) of the fact that (choosing chosing) this (site cite sight) for your business will take you (farther further) away from your client base?

9. Gloria could not (accept except) the fact that the (councillors counsellors) rejected her plan to (phase faze) out parking in the downtown core.

10. The (amount number) of people (aloud allowed) to participate depends on (fewer less) (then than) a dozen (woman women) who are entrusted with making the decision.

Exercise 37.3*

Each of the items below is followed by two statements. Identify the one that makes sense as a follow-up to the introductory sentence.

1. All former students will be welcomed back to class.
   a. We will except all former students.
   b. We will accept all former students.

2. The lawn mower next door has been running nonstop for over an hour.
   a. The continual noise is driving me crazy.
   b. The continuous noise is driving me crazy.

3. This author only hints at how the story ends.
   a. She implies that they live happily ever after.
   b. She infers that they live happily ever after.

4. Your proposal is not worth our consideration
   a. It's simple.
   b. It's simplistic.

5. We're looking for a female role model.
   a. The women must lead by example.
   b. The woman must lead by example.

6. How many assistants will be required?
   a. The amount of help we will need is hard to estimate.
   b. The number of helpers we will need is hard to estimate.

7. While their skill sets are very different, together, the two make a good team.
   a. She compliments his weaknesses.
   b. She complements his weaknesses.

8. Are you permitted to talk during the lectures?
   a. It is not allowed.
   b. It is not aloud.

9. When did she wake up?
   a. She regained her conscience during the prayers.
   b. She regained her consciousness during the prayers.
10. How many kilometres are left in your journey?
    a. We have only a little farther to go.
    b. We have only a little further to go.

GO TO WEB

EXERCISES 37.1, 37.2, 37.3, 37.4

Exercise 37.4

Now test your mastery of homonyms by correcting the 10 errors in the following paragraph.

I would advice anyone who's schedule seems to be full to try the solution I came up with less then three months ago. I pulled the plug on my TV. Overwhelmed with assignments and unable to chose among priorities, I realized I was making the problem worse by sitting for three or four hours a night in front of the tube. I decided I should spend more time on my coarses and less on watching television. To avoid temptation, I put the TV set in the closet. The results have been more dramatic then I thought possible. My apartment is now a haven of piece and quiet, and some of my assignments are actually handed in before their due. Occasionally there is a twinge of regret that I no longer know whose doing what to whom in the latest reality contest, but overall, I'm much happier for choosing to loose the tube.

38

The Apostrophe

Most punctuation marks indicate the relationship among parts of a sentence. Apostrophes and hyphens, on the other hand, indicate the relationship between the elements of a word. That's why we've chosen to discuss them in this section, along with other spelling issues.

Misused apostrophes display a writer's ignorance or carelessness. They can also confuse, amuse, and sometimes annoy readers.

- Sometimes you need an apostrophe so that your reader can understand what you mean. For example, there's a world of difference between these two sentences:

  The instructor began class by calling the students' names.

  The instructor began class by calling the students names.

- In most cases, however, misused apostrophes just amuse or irritate an alert reader:

  The movie had it's moments.

  He does a days work for every weeks salary.

  The Lion's thank you for your contribution.

It isn't difficult to avoid such mistakes. Correctly used, the apostrophe indicates either **contraction** or **possession**. It never makes a singular word plural. Learn the simple rules that govern these uses and you'll have no further trouble with apostrophes.

Spelling

Contraction

Contraction is the combining of two words into one, as in *they're* or *can't*. Contractions are common in conversation and in informal written English. Unless you are quoting someone else's words, however, you should avoid them in the writing you do for college or work.

The rule about where to put an apostrophe in a contraction is one of those rare rules that has no exception. It *always* holds.

> When two words are combined into one, and one or more letters are left out, the apostrophe goes in the place of the missing letter(s).

Here are some examples.

I am	→ I'm	they are	→ they're
we will	→ we'll	it is	→ it's
she is	→ she's	it has	→ it's
do not	→ don't	who has	→ who's

Exercise 38.1*

Correct these sentences by placing apostrophes where needed. Answers for this chapter begin on page 544.

1. Yes, its a long way from Halifax to Vancouver, but weve been in training for three months.
2. Were taking the train to Antigonish, and were biking to Halifax; then well begin the big trip west.
3. There wasnt a dry eye in the theatre when Spielbergs film reached its climax.
4. Whos discovered whats wrong with this sentence?
5. Wasnt it Mark Twain who said, "Its easy to stop smoking; Ive done it dozens of times"?

GO TO WEB

EXERCISES 38.1, 38.2

Exercise 38.2*

In some formal kinds of writing—academic, legal, and technical, for example—contractions are not acceptable. A good writer is able not only to contract two words into one, but also to expand any contraction into its original form: a two-word phrase. In the following paragraph, find and expand the contractions into their original form.

I'm writing to apply for the position of webmaster for BrilloVision.com that you've advertised in the *Daily News*. I've got the talent and background you're looking for. Currently, I work as a Web designer for an online publication, Vexed.com, where they're very pleased with my work. If you click on their website, I think you'll like what you see. There's little in the way of Web design and application that I haven't been involved in during the past two years. But it's time for me to move on to a new challenge, and BrilloVision.com promises the kind of opportunity I'm looking for. I guarantee you won't be disappointed if I join your team!

Possession

The apostrophe is also used to show ownership or possession. Here's the rule that applies in most cases.

Add *'s* to the word that indicates the *owner*.
If the resulting word ends in a double or triple *s*, delete the last *s*, leaving the apostrophe in place.[1]

---

[1]Many writers today prefer to keep the final *s* when it represents a sound that is pronounced, as it is in one-syllable words such as *boss* and *class*, and in some names such as *Harris* and *Brutus*.

Spelling

Here are some examples that illustrate the rule.

singer + 's = singer's voice   women + 's = women's voices
band + 's = band's instruments   student + 's = student's transcript
players + 's = players'~~s~~ uniforms   students + 's = students'~~s~~ transcripts

To form a possessive correctly, you must first identify the word in the sentence that indicates possession and determine whether it is singular or plural. For example, "the managers duties" can have two meanings, depending on where you put the apostrophe:

the manager's duties (the duties belong to one *manager*)
the managers' duties (the duties belong to two or more *managers*)

To solve an apostrophe problem, follow this two-step process:
1. Find the owner word.
2. Apply the possession rule.

Problem: Carmens hair is a mess.
Solution: 1. The word that indicates possession is *Carmen* (singular).
                 2. Add *'s* to *Carmen*.

Carmen's hair is a mess.

Problem: The technicians strike halted the production.
Solution: 1. The word that indicates possession is *technicians* (plural).
                 2. Add *'s* to *technicians*, then delete the second *s*, leaving the apostrophe.

The *technicians'* strike halted the production.

Sometimes the meaning of your sentence is determined by where you put the apostrophe.

Problem: I was delighted by the critics response to my book.

Now you have two possibilities to choose from, depending on your meaning.

Solution A: 1. The owner word is *critic* (singular).
                   2. Add *'s* to *critic*.

I was delighted by the *critic's* response to my book.

Solution B: 1. The owner word is *critics* (plural).

2. Add *'s* to *critics*, then drop the second *s*, leaving the apostrophe.

I was delighted by the *critics'* response to my book.

Both solutions are correct, depending on whether the book was reviewed by one critic (A) or by more than one critic (B).

Possession does not have to be literal. It can be used to express the notion of "belonging to" or "associated with." That is, the owner word need not refer to a person or group of people. Ideas or concepts (abstract nouns) can be "owners" too.

a month's vacation = a vacation of one month
a year's salary = the salary of one year
"A Hard Day's Night" = the night that follows a hard day

Note that a few words, called **possessive pronouns**, are already possessive in form, so they don't have apostrophes.[2]

yours	ours	whose
hers, his, its	theirs	

His music is not like *yours.*

Whose lyrics do you prefer, *theirs* or *ours*?

The dog lost *its* bone.

Four of these possessive pronouns are often confused with the contractions that sound like them. It's worth taking a moment to learn how to avoid this confusion. When you are trying to decide which spelling to use,

1. Expand the contraction into its original two words.
2. Then substitute those words for the contraction in your sentence.
3. If the sentence still makes sense, use the contraction. If it doesn't, use the possessive spelling.

---

[2]If you add an apostrophe to any of these words, you create an error. There are no such words as *your's, her's, their's,* or *our's.*

Spelling

Possessive	**Contraction**
its = *It* owns something	it's = it is/it has
their = *They* own something	they're = they are
whose = *Who* owns something	who's = who is/who has
your = *You* own something	you're = you are

Error: They're (they are) going to sing they're (they are) latest song.
Revision: They're going to sing *their* latest song.

Exercises 38.3 and 38.4 will test and reinforce your understanding of both contraction and possession.

Exercise 38.3*

Correct the following sentences by adding apostrophes where necessary.

1. The cars brakes are worn and its tires are nearly bald.
2. Diplomatic ambassadors wives or husbands are often as important to a missions success as the ambassadors themselves.
3. Near Chicoutimi is one of the countrys most beautiful parks, where the skills of canoeists, fishermen, and wildlife photographers can be put to the test on a summers day.
4. Janis career got its start when she sang seafarers songs in the yacht clubs dining lounge.
5. A countrys history is the main determinant of its national character.

Exercise 38.4*

In each of the sentences below, choose the correct word from those in parentheses. Check your answers before going on.

1. Where (your you're) going, (your you're) biggest problem will be maintaining (your you're) health.
2. (Someones Someone's) got to take responsibility for the large numbers of domestic animals (whose who's) owners have abandoned them.
3. The (ships ship's ships') captain agreed to donate a (weeks week's weeks') salary to the Scott Mission.
4. Contrary to some (people's peoples) opinions, postal (workers worker's workers') contracts are most often settled by both (sides side's sides') willingness to bend long before a strike is necessary.
5. My (turtles turtle's) legs are shorter than your (turtles turtle's), but I bet (its it's) going to run (its it's) laps faster than (yours your's).

EXERCISES 38.3, 38.4

Plurals

The third apostrophe rule is very simple. Memorize it, apply it, and you will instantly correct many of your apostrophe errors.

Never use an apostrophe to make a word plural.

The plural of most English words is formed by adding *s* to the root word (not *'s*). The *s* alone tells the reader that the word is plural: e.g., *memos, letters, files, broadcasts, newspapers, journalists*. If you add an apostrophe + *s*, you are telling your reader that the word is either a contraction or a possessive.

Incorrect: Never use apostrophe's to make word's plural.
Correct: Never use apostrophes to make words plural.

Exercise 38.5*

Correct the misused and missing apostrophes in the following sentences. There are 10 errors in this exercise.

1. When you feel like a snack, you can choose between apples and Timbit's.

2. Annas career took off when she discovered its easy to sell childrens toys.

3. Golfing requires the use of different club's: woods for long shots, irons for short ones.

4. Poker's an easy game to play if you are dealt ace's more often than your opponent's are.

5. Good writing skill's dont guarantee success in you're career, but they help.

Spelling

Exercise 38.6

Before you try the final exercise in this chapter, carefully review the information in the Summary box below. Then test your mastery of apostrophes by correcting the 15 errors in the passage below.

The following advisory for American's heading to Canada was compiled from information provided by the U.S. State Department and the CIA. It is intended as a guide for American traveller's:

Canada is a large foreign country, even bigger than Texas. It has 10 states (called provinces) and it's only neighbour is America. Canadas contributions to Western civilization include bacon, hockey players, geese, doughnut's, and the Mountie's red uniform's.

Canadians stand in line without complaining, seldom raise they're voices, and cheer politely when the home or visiting teams players do something worthwhile. Canada has two language's: French and American. Other linguistic oddities include "eh," which can turn any statement into a question, and the pronunciation of *ou* as *uoo*, as in *huoose* or *abuoot*.

The bright color's and funny picture's of Canadian currency may make the unwary tourist think of it as play money, but each blue Canadian five-dollar bill is worth about two real dollars. The one- and two-dollar coins, called loonies and toonies, make good souvenir's.

The Canadian government is somewhat left-leaning, providing health care for all and refusing to execute criminal's. Tourists are advised to avoid all political discussion and to remember that politician's in Canada are like politician's anywhere: popular with some people, unpopular with others.

Summary

- When contracting two words into one, put an apostrophe in the place of the missing letters.
- Watch for owner words: they need apostrophes.
- To indicate possession, add *'s* to the owner word. (If the owner word already ends in *s*, just add the apostrophe.)
- Possessive pronouns (e.g., *yours, its, ours*) do not take apostrophes.
- Never use an apostrophe to form the plural of a word.

Title of Paper 29

References

Bourette, S. (2002, March). Planespotting. *Shift*. Retrieved March 14, 2005, from http://www.shift.com/content/10.1/53/1.html

1.

Canada to toughen auto-emissions rules. (2002, April 5). *The Wall Street Journal*, p. A6.

2.

France, H., Rodriguez, M., & Hett, G. (2004). *Diversity, culture and counselling: A Canadian perspective.* Calgary: Detselig.

3.

Helson, R., & Pals, J. (2000). Creative potential, creative achievement, and personal growth. *Journal of Personality*, *68*(2), 39–44.

4.

Mistry, R. (2001). Journey to Dharmsala. In C. Meyer & B. Meyer (Eds.), *The reader: Contemporary essays and writing strategies.* (pp. 38–51). Toronto: Prentice.

5.

Moore, M. (Writer, Producer, Director). (2002). *Bowling for Columbine* [Motion picture]. Canada: Alliance Atlantis.

6.

Patterson, K. (2000). *The water in between: A journey at sea.* Toronto: Vintage Canada.

7.

Sreenivasan, A. (2002, February). Keeping up with the cones. *Natural History*, 40–46.

8.

Statistics Canada. (2002, October 11). Infant mortality rates. Retrieved October 12, 2005, from http://www.statcan.ca/english/Pgdb/ health21.htm

9.

Vassanji, M. G. (1997, August 8). *Canadian literature research service.* Retrieved April 28, 2005, from http://collection.nlc-bnc.ca/100/201/ 301/lecture/vassanji.htm

10.

Wahl, A. (2005, February 28). Emission impossible. *Canadian Business*, 24. Retrieved March 21, 2005, from eLibrary Canada database.

11.

Answers for
Selected Exercises

Answers for Chapter 1: Your Audience and You (pages 9–23)

Exercise 1.1

1. Audience: Literate readers who are interested in exploring a serious analysis of what is usually treated as a trivial topic.

   Writer's role: To provide information.

   Language: Formal. Sentences vary in length; one is quite long and complex. While there are no technical terms, the writer assumes the reader has a broad general vocabulary and good reading ability. Use of third-person point of view contributes to the impersonal tone.

2. Audience: Experts in woodworking.

   Writer's role: To provide information in an accessible way. The writer is not instructing the reader, but outlining the function of the tool and some of its possible applications.

   Language: General level, combining technical vocabulary with an informal tone. Sentences vary in length. Writer addresses reader as "you."

3. Audience: Educated business owners or high-level managers who are interested in doing business in China.

   Writer's role: To inform Canadian entrepreneurs who have little experience with Chinese business culture that it is very different from the Canadian culture, and that considerable preparation is needed if one is to be successful in that market.

   Language: Formal. Sentences are long and complex; vocabulary is highly sophisticated and includes a few examples of business jargon: e.g., "principals," "power brokers." Tone is serious.

4. Audience: General readers, probably not just parents of young children as might be suggested by the content.

   Writer's role: To make a point in an amusing, friendly way.

   Language: Informal. Includes contractions and colloquialisms ("kids," "slick operator") and slang ("junkies"), but also a couple of challenging phrases and words (e.g., "disdainfully"). Writer addresses readers as "you," as if speaking directly to them.

5. Audience: English professor.

   Writer's role: To demonstrate that she can write a good research paper.

   Language: Formal. Student assumes reader is familiar with Brontë's novel and presents her findings in sentences of varying lengths. Each conclusion is supported with an appropriate quotation from the text. Paragraph is fairly long (11 sentences), and tone is impersonal.

Answers for Chapter 2: Choosing the Right Words (pages 24–38)

Exercise 2.1 (suggested answers)

1. I do not think there is any basis for believing in UFOs.
2. I prefer contemporary furniture to antiques.
3. I think Alison is pretending to be sick so she won't have to go to work.
4. Our competitor's products, although inferior to ours, are selling better than ours.
5. My essay is as good as Jill's and deserves an equivalent mark, but the professor hates me.
6. I doubt that this innovation will succeed.
7. A course in English basics is a prerequisite to success in college, business, and the community.
8. "As a new teacher," we told our English instructor, "you should understand that you can't gain our respect if you insist on grammar rules that inhibit our creativity."
9. This trend can probably be reversed if we go back to our design fundamentals and introduce a few manufacturing innovations.
10. We have deleted any unlawful descriptors, such as race, age, gender, religion, and marital status, and now all our personnel documents are practically identical.

Exercise 2.4 (suggested answers)

1. When the rain began, we turned on the windshield wipers.
2. Young people often have difficulty communicating with parents and others in authority.
3. The witness lied when she claimed that the accused had confessed in a meeting with her.
4. The results of our study demonstrate that our survey instrument is as valid as any other.
5. Cancelling IMF loans to Pacific Rim countries could affect the relationship between developed and developing nations.

Exercise 2.6 (suggested answers)

1. The well-known producer Elaine May often regrets that she cannot go out in public without attracting the attention of fans and photographers.
2. Amy King first joined the company as a salesperson; only 10 years later, she was promoted to president.

3. An executive sitting in the first-class cabin rang for the flight attendant, a friendly woman who quickly arrived to assist him.
4. The list of ingredients on food packages contains information that may be important to consumers, especially if they are the parents of young children.
5. The typical family is often hard-pressed to find time for family recreation.

Exercise 2.7 (suggested answers)

1. Regardless of what you think, the problem between her and me has nothing to do with you.
2. If you want to be in the office pool, I need $5.00 from you today because there will be no spots left by tomorrow.
3. Because they didn't finish the job themselves the way they should have, we have to work late to get it done.
4. I didn't feel like seeing anybody, so I went home, turned on the TV, and did nothing for the rest of the night.
5. This used to be a good place to work, but now we're supposed to work a full shift every day, or a penalty is deducted from our pay.
6. Many young people today are trying to fight prejudice not only in society but also within themselves.
7. I'm supposed to ask you if the reason for the delay is that it's raining. (*Better*: . . . ask you if the rain is the reason for the delay.)
8. It's irresponsible of us to blame television or any other medium for causing violence.
9. Television is responsible, however, for the fact that many ungrammatical expressions sound all right to us.
10. Between you and me, the reason I didn't speak to anyone about Elmo's cheating on the test is that he would have broken my arm.

Answers for Chapter 3: Selecting a Subject (pages 39–43)

Exercise 3.1

1. significant
2. significant
3. revise
4. significant
5. revise
6. significant
7. revise

Exercise 3.2

1. revise
2. revise
3. revise
4. single (the subject is *the accuracy of reporting*, not the two media)
5. single
6. revise
7. revise

Exercise 3.3

1. specific
2. revise
3. specific
4. revise
5. revise
6. revise
7. specific

Exercise 3.4

1. supportable
2. supportable
3. supportable
4. revise
5. revise
6. revise
7. supportable

Exercise 3.5

1. not specific
2. not single
3. not supportable
4. satisfactory
5. not specific

Answers for Chapter 4: Managing the Main Points (pages 44–60)

Exercise 4.6

1. cell (not distinct, overlaps with *telephone*)
2. distance from suppliers and markets (not related)
3. repetitive (not related: repetition is a programming problem, not a characteristic of commercials)
4. procrastination (not distinct, overlaps with *poor study habits*)
5. *find a reliable real-estate agent* overlaps with *seek expert advice*; also not necessarily relevant—not all people need an agent
6. *competitors offer better pay* overlaps with *salary lower than industry standard*

Exercise 4.7

1. chronological (5, 1, 4, 3, 2)
2. climactic (2, 1, 3, 4)
3. random
4. climactic (3, 1, 2. This order reflects the amount of time it takes for a smoker to quit using each method and also the amount of agony the smoker will suffer in the process.)
5. random

Answers for Chapter 5: Writing the Thesis Statement (pages 61–70)

Exercise 5.1
1. <u>Students who try to combine a full-time job with a full-time program face problems</u> <u>at school</u>, <u>at work</u>, and <u>at home</u>.
2. <u>To be successful in a broadcasting career</u>, you must be <u>talented</u>, <u>motivated</u>, and <u>hardworking</u>.
3. <u>The ideal notebook computer for business applications</u> is <u>reliable</u>, <u>lightweight</u>, <u>powerful</u>, and <u>flexible</u>.
4. <u>Establishing a local area network</u> would increase <u>efficiency</u> and <u>flexibility</u> in the office.
5. <u>The chairperson's job calls for a responsible and sensitive person</u>, someone who is <u>knowledgeable about company policy</u>, <u>sensitive to personnel issues</u>, and <u>a creative problem solver</u>. It wouldn't hurt if he or she could also walk on water.
6. <u>The business traveller can learn much from the turtle</u>. <u>Carry everything you need with you</u>. <u>Move slowly but with purpose and consistency</u>. <u>Keep your head down until you are sure you know exactly what is going on</u>.
7. Large energy producers and some provincial governments say we cannot afford to live up to the terms of the Kyoto Accord, which seeks to reduce the production of greenhouse gases. <u>But can we afford not to comply with this international agreement</u>? <u>Can we afford to compromise the health of Canadians</u> by continuing to pollute? <u>Can we afford to risk the effects of global warming</u> on our environment? <u>Can we afford to fall behind the rest of the world in research and development leading</u> to a solution to the problem of greenhouse gases?

Exercise 5.6 (suggested answers)
1. When choosing between two fast-food restaurants, consider food, atmosphere, service, and price.
2. Urban overcrowding results in traffic jams, air pollution, homelessness, and violence.
3. Successful small businesses are usually those with adequate capital, a marketable product, dedicated personnel, and a workable business plan.

Answers for Chapter 7: Understanding Paragraph Form and Function (pages 81–97)

Exercise 7.3
1. Canada makes no economic sense.
2. All sports can be made ridiculous because the essence of sport is rules.
3. In reality, taste buds are exceedingly small.
4. Scholarly explanations of humor fall into three major categories.
5. With the huge variety of computers now on the market, the determining factor in a purchase should be the job the machine will be expected to do.

Answers for Chapter 8: Keeping Your Readers with You
(pages 98–109)

Exercise 8.1
1. sentence 6
2. sentence 4
3. sentence 5
4. sentence 5
5. sentence 6

Exercise 8.2
1. Therefore, ...
2. Finally, . . . but . . . .
3. Unfortunately, however, ...
4. On the other hand, ...
5. For example, ... In addition, ...

Exercise 8.4
The transitions in this exercise are identified by category. See the numbered list of coherence strategies on page 102.

1. Finally (5), developing the proper attitude is the key to winning tennis. I define winning tennis (1) as playing the game to the best of your ability, hitting the ball as well as you can, and enjoying the feeling of practised expertise (4). Winning tennis (1) has little to do with defeating an opponent. Naturally (5), if you learn the basics, practise sufficiently, and concentrate (4), you will win many matches, but that is the reward of playing well, not the reason for playing well (4). People who swear and throw their racquets when they lose are very useful: they (3) are the most satisfying players to trounce. But I do not understand why they (3) play a game (2) that causes them such pain. Tennis players who enjoy the feel of a well hit ball and the satisfaction of a long, skillfully played rally are winners, regardless of the score.

2. Travel abroad offers you the best education you can get. For one thing (5), travel (1) is a course in communication skills. In order to function in a foreign language, you must practise every aspect of the communication process (1, 2) from body language to pronunciation. In fact (5), just making yourself understood is a lesson in creativity, a seminar in sign language, and a lab in communication theory (2, 4). Another educational aspect of travel (5) is the history, geography, and culture (4) that you learn about almost unconsciously. Everywhere you go, you encounter memorable evidence of historic events (2) you may dimly recall from school, and you are continually confronted by the practical realities of geography (1) as you try to find your way around. As for culture (1, 5), no book or course of study could provide you with the understanding and appreciation of another society that living in it (3) can. A third way (5) in which travel (1) educates is through teaching you about yourself. Your ability—

or inability—to cope with unfamiliar customs, with language difficulties, and with the inevitable problems of finding transportation and accommodation (4) will tell you more than you might want to know about yourself (2). Without the safety net of family and friends, perhaps without even the security of knowing where you'll spend the night, you develop self-reliance or you go home. Either way (5), you learn valuable lessons. While you may not get a diploma from Travel U., you'll learn more about the world, about people, and about yourself (1, 4) than you will in any classroom.

Exercise 8.6
(We've italicized the words and phrases that require revision to change the tone of this paragraph from tactless to tactful. We've given some revision suggestions in square brackets following the offensive phrases.)

I'm from the city, so I may not know much about the subject, but it seems to me that we urban-dwellers have lost touch with the food we eat. By this I mean, *obviously,* [delete] that we no longer appreciate the farmers and farm workers who supply the food that we enjoy every day. *Anyone with half a brain should realize that* [delete] Most of the food we buy is prepackaged in Styrofoam, wrapped in plastic, or precooked and frozen by huge corporations *whose goal is to make humongous profits by selling us the packaging, not the contents.* [that put at least as much effort into designing attractive packaging as they do into preparing food.] *Do any urban consumers understand that* [How many urban consumers think about the fact that] their ketchup is made from farm-grown tomatoes? Do *any advertising-driven* [delete] supermarket shoppers *really think about the fact* [stop to consider] that those *over-* [delete] packaged frozen pork chops, so irresistible with their sprig of parsley, were once a pig, raised by a farmer? *Not only are we ignorant, but also we could care less* [Let's face the facts: Do many of us know or even care] about the journey our food makes from farm to fridge[?] My guess is that if you asked most *city kids* [urban children] where their food comes from, they'd say, "the food factory."

Here is how a final draft of this revision might read. (Note that we've added a conclusion to the paragraph.)

It seems to me that we urbanites have lost touch with the food we eat. By this I mean that we no longer appreciate the farmers and farm workers who supply the food that we enjoy every day. Most of the food we buy is prepackaged in Styrofoam, wrapped in plastic, or precooked and frozen by huge corporations that put at least as much effort into designing attractive packaging as they do into preparing food. How many urban consumers think about the fact that ketchup is made from farm-grown tomatoes? Do supermarket shoppers stop to consider that those packaged frozen pork chops, so irresistible with their sprig of parsley, were once a pig, raised by a farmer? Let's face facts: how many of us know or even care about the journey our food makes from farm to fridge? My guess is that if you asked most urban children where their food comes from, they'd say, "the food factory." But the correct answer is, "Canadian farmers." They deserve our attention and support.

Answers for Chapter 10: The Three Steps to Revision (pages 125–39)
Exercise 10.1
Attention-getter: As the recipient of approximately 1,000 business-related e-mail messages every month, I am something of an expert on what is effective and what is not in e-mail correspondence.

Thesis statement: The three areas that need attention in most e-mail messages are the subject line, the content and format of the message, and the use of attachments.

Main points:

I. Subject line
   A. Never leave the subject line blank (*or* Always include a subject line)
   B. Make sure the subject line states clearly what the message is about

II. Message
   A. Content
      1. Be concise and to the point
      2. Tell the reader what action is needed, by whom, and when
      3. Use plain English, not "cyberspeak"
      4. Use an appropriate level of language in your message as well as in your salutation and signature
   B. Format
      1. Use bullets to identify points you want to emphasize
      2. Leave white space between points
      3. Avoid sending your message in uppercase letters (shouting)
      4. Avoid smilies and other "cute" computer shorthand symbols

III. Attachments
   A. Use only if necessary
      1. may carry viruses
      2. take time to transfer and to open
   B. Attach text-only files, unless a graphic is absolutely necessary

Summary: If you follow my recommendations on these three points whenever you write an e-mail, you will make the recipient of your message very happy.

Memorable statement: Especially if you're writing to me.

Exercise 10.2 (suggested answer)
In the following answer, we have corrected only the errors in paragraph structure, sentence structure, and grammar. The passage still contains errors in spelling, punctuation, and usage. We will correct those errors at Step 3.

1   As the recipient of almost 1,000 business-related e-mail messages every month, I am something of an expert on what is effective and what is not in e-mail correspondence. The three areas that need attention in most e-mail messages are the subject line, the **content and format** of the message, and the use of attachments.

2   Some people leave the subject line blank. **This** is a mistake. I want to know what the message is about before I open it, so I can decide if it needs my immediate attention **or** can wait until later. A message with no subject line, or with a line that **doesn't** tell me **anything** about the content of the e-mail, **gets** sent to the bottom of my "to-do" list. There are lots of readers like me: busy people who receive tons of e-mail, much of it unsolicited advertising that **clutters** up **our** in-boxes. For this reason the subject line should always clearly state the subject of the message and should never be vague or cute, like "hello," or "message," or "are you there?"

3   As for the message itself, it's function should be to tell the reader what action **you want.** You need to be clear about this and be as brief as possible. What is it that you want the recipient to do. Who else needs to be involved. By when does the action need to take place. Communicate your message in plain English, not in "cyberspeak." Not everyone knows Net lingo, and even some who are famliar with it find it irritating, not charming. Use an appropriate level of language (general level Standard English **is** always appropriate) to convey you're message. Use the same level of language in you're salutation and closing or "signature." **Never** sign off a message to you're client or you're boss with "love and kisses."

4   Format you're message so that the recipient **can read it quickly and understand** it easily. Use bullets to identify points you want to emphasize **and** separate the bullets with white space so **that your points** can be read at a glance and reviewed individually if neccessary.

5   There are some important points of e-mail etiquette that you should observe. Don't type you're message in upper case letters. **This is** considered "shouting." Do avoid "smilies" and other "cute" computer shorthand symbols. Some of you're readers won't understand them. **O**thers will have seen them so often they will be turned off.

6   Attachments should be included only if they are really necessary. **One reason is that** they may carry virruses and some people won't open them. Another disadvantage is that **attachments** take time to send download and open. Unless I am sure that an attachment is both urgent and vitally important—the agenda of tomorrow's meeting, for example—I don't bother to open it. **F**or all I know, it might contain not only a virus but also footage of the sender's toddler doing her latest photogenic trick. As a general rule **you should** attach only what you must and attach text-only files. Try to include everything you need to say in the message itself; use attachments only as a last resort. Think of them as equivalent to footnotes: supplementary to the message, not an essential part of it.

7   If you follow my recommendations on these three points whenever you write an e-mail, you will make the recipient of your message very happy, especially if you're writing to me.

Exercise 10.3 (suggested answers)
1. I **expect** a salary **commensurate** with my qualifications and experience.
2. I have **learned** the Microsoft Word and **Excel spreadsheet programs**.
3. I received a **plaque** for being salesperson of the year.
4. Reason for leaving last job: **maternity** leave.
5. You will want me to be a **manager** in no time.
6. I am a perfectionist and rarely **if ever** forget details.

7. Marital status: **single.**

8. In my previous job, I **learned to trust no one.**

9. As **indicated**, I have **more than** five years **experience in** analyzing investments.

10. I was responsible for **running** a Western chain store. (*Better:* I was responsible for managing a Western chain store.)

Exercise 10.4 (suggested answer)

(Words that have been omitted are indicated by ***.)

1   As the recipient of approximately 1,000 business-related e-mail messages every month, I am something of an expert on what is effective and what is not in e-mail correspondence. The three areas that need attention in most e-mail messages are the subject line, the content *** and format of the message, and the use of attachments.

2   Some people leave the subject line blank. This is a mistake. I want to know what the message is about before I open it, so I can decide if it needs my immediate attention or can wait until later. A message with no subject line, or with a line that doesn't tell me anything about the content of the e-mail, gets sent to the bottom of my "to-do" list. There are lots of readers like me: busy people who receive tons of e-mail, much of which is unsolicited advertising that clutters up our in-boxes. For this reason, the subject line should always clearly state the subject of the message and should never be vague or cute. **Some examples of inappropriate subject lines include** "Hello," *** "Message," **and** "Are you there?"

3   As for the message itself, **its** function should be to tell the reader what action you want **taken.** *** Be clear about this**,** and be as brief as possible. What is it that you want the recipient to do**?** Who else needs to be involved**?** By when does the action need to **be completed?** Communicate your message in plain English, not in "cyberspeak." Not everyone knows Net lingo, and even some who are **familiar** with it find it irritating, not charming. Use an appropriate level of language (general level Standard English is always appropriate) to convey **your** message. Use the same level of language in **your** salutation and closing or "signature." Never sign off a message to **your** client or **your** boss with "love and kisses."

4   Format **your** message so that the recipient can read it quickly and understand it easily. Use bullets to identify points you want to emphasize, and separate the bullets with white space so that your points can be read at a glance and reviewed individually**,** if **necessary**.

5   There are some important points of e-mail etiquette that you should observe. Don't type **your** message in uppercase letters. This is considered "shouting." Do avoid "smilies" and other "cute" computer shorthand symbols. Some of **your** readers won't understand them. Others will have seen them so often **that** they will be turned off.

6   Attachments should be included only if they are really necessary. One reason is that they may carry **viruses,** and some people won't open them. Another disadvantage is that attachments take time to send**,** download**,** and open. Unless I am sure that an attachment is both urgent and vitally important—the agenda of tomorrow's meeting, for example—I don't bother to open it. For all I know, it might contain not only a virus but also footage of the sender's toddler doing her latest photogenic trick. As a general rule, you should attach only what you must, and

attach text-only files. Try to include everything you need to say in the message itself; use attachments only as a last resort. Think of them as equivalent to foot-notes: supplementary to the message, not an essential part of it.

7   If you follow my recommendations on these three points whenever you write an e-mail, you will make the recipient of your message very happy, especially if you're writing to me.

Exercise 10.5

According to a recent survey in **Maclean's** magazine, only 43 percent of Canadians are satisfied with their jobs. What can you do to ensure that you will not be one of the 57 percent who are unhappy with the work they do**?** There are three questions to consider when seeing employment that will provide satisfaction as well as a paycheque.

First**,** are you suited to the kind of work you are applying for**?** If you enjoy the out-doors, for example, and like to be active, **you are** not going to be happy with a nine-to-five office job, no matter how much it pays.

Second**,** is the job based in a location compatible with your **preferred** lifestyle**?** No matter how much you like your work, if you go home every night to an **environment** you are miserable in, it will not be long before you start **transferring** your **dissatis-faction** to your job. If you like the amenities and **conveniences** of the city, you prob-ably will not enjoy working in a small town. If, on the other hand, you prefer the quiet and security of small town life, you may find the city a stressful place in which to live.

Finally, is **the company you are applying to** one that you want to work for**?** Do you need the security of generous **benefits**, a good pension plan, and incentives to stay and grow with one company? Or are you an **ambitious** person who is looking for variety, quick advancement, and a high salary**?** If so, you may have to forego secu-rity in favour of commissions or cash incentives and be willing to move as quickly and as often as opportunities occur. Some **careful** self-analysis now, before you start out on your career path, will help you **choose** a direction that will put you in the 43 percent minority of satisfied Canadian workers.

Answers for Chapter 20: Documenting Your Sources (pages 290–305)

Exercise 20.2

Works Cited

American Institute of Stress. 2 May 2005 <http://www.stress.org>.

Cleeland, Nancy. "As Jobs Heat Up, Workers' Hearts Take a Beating." *Vancouver Sun*
    Mar. 2005: A2.

Dubrin, Andrew. *Getting It Done: The Transforming Power of Self-Discipline.*
    Princeton, NJ: Pacesetter, 1995.

Ford, Janet. "Time Management." E-mail to Sarah Norton. 5 June 2005.

Selye, Hans. Interview. 1 Jan. 1982.

White, Linda A. "Child Care, Women's Labour Market Participation and Labour
    Market Policy Effectiveness in Canada." *Canadian Public Policy* 27.4 (2001):
    385–405.

Answers for Chapter 22: Cracking the Sentence Code (pages 327–38)

Exercise 22.1
1. I <u>bought</u> a used car.
2. The used <u>car</u> <u>was</u> cheap.
3. <u>It</u> <u>needed</u> some repairs.
4. Unfortunately, the <u>repairs</u> <u>were</u> expensive.
5. <u>Insurance</u> for the car <u>was</u> expensive, too.
6. <u>Buying</u> a car <u>is</u> costly.
7. According to the salesman, the <u>car</u> <u>was</u> not <u>overpriced</u>.
8. [<u>You</u>] Always <u>get</u> a second opinion.
9. After 10 years, <u>cars</u> sometimes <u>develop</u> serious problems.
10. <u>Paying</u> for repairs <u>compensates</u> for the cheap price.

Exercise 22.2
1. Here <u>is</u> an <u>idea</u> to consider.
2. <u>William Lyon Mackenzie</u> <u>led</u> a rebellion against the Government of Canada.
3. <u>He</u> later <u>became</u> the mayor of Toronto.
4. <u>Who</u> <u>wants</u> the last piece?
5. <u>You</u> (understood) <u>Eat</u> slowly.
6. There, beyond the swimming pool, <u>is</u> the <u>gym</u>.
7. A moving <u>chicken</u> <u>is</u> poultry in motion.
8. Far behind the leaders <u>trailed</u> the main <u>group</u> of cyclists.
9. Here <u>are</u> the <u>results</u> of your examination.
10. Irish <u>coffee</u> <u>contains</u> ingredients from all four of the essential food groups: caffeine, fat, sugar, and alcohol.

Exercise 22.3
1. <u>He</u> <u>has talked</u> nonstop for three hours.
2. <u>I</u> <u>am</u> not <u>going</u> to drive.
3. <u>Could</u> <u>they</u> <u>return</u> the goods tomorrow?
4. <u>You</u> <u>cannot</u> <u>eat</u> your birthday cake before dinner.
5. <u>Carla</u> <u>should have been filing</u> the letters and memos.
6. <u>I</u> <u>will be</u> the first member of my family to graduate from college.
7. Paula's <u>lawsuit</u> <u>should</u> never <u>have been allowed</u> to proceed this far.
8. <u>Have</u> <u>you</u> ever <u>been</u> to the Zanzibar tavern?
9. There <u>has</u> never <u>been</u> a better <u>time</u> to travel to Greece.
10. How <u>are</u> the club <u>members</u> <u>identified</u>?

Exercise 22.4
1. ~~Among English teachers,~~ Santa's <u>helpers</u> <u>are known</u> as subordinate clauses.
2. ~~After his death,~~ <u>Terry Fox</u> <u>became</u> a national symbol ~~of heroic courage~~.
3. ~~In the state of Florida,~~ <u>it</u> <u>is</u> illegal ~~for single, divorced, or widowed women~~ to parachute ~~on Sunday afternoons~~.
4. ~~In Kentucky,~~ no <u>woman</u> <u>may appear</u> ~~in a bathing suit on any highway in the state~~ unless escorted ~~by two officers~~ or armed ~~with a club~~.
5. ~~In my wildest imaginings,~~ <u>I</u> <u>cannot</u> <u>understand</u> ~~these laws~~.
6. ~~During a break in the conversation,~~ Darryl's embarrassing <u>comment</u> <u>could be heard</u> ~~in every corner of the room~~.

7. ~~In my lawyer's dictionary~~, a <u>will</u> <u>is defined</u> as a dead giveaway.
8. ~~To the staff and managers of the project~~, I <u>extend</u> my congratulations ~~for an excellent job~~.
9. ~~Against all odds~~, and ~~despite their shortcomings~~, the St. John <u>Miners</u> <u>made</u> it ~~into the playoffs of the Southern New Brunswick Little League~~.
10. [You] <u>Walk</u> a mile ~~in my shoes at high noon with your head held high in order to avoid clichés like the plague~~.

Exercise 22.5

1. <u>Management</u> and <u>union</u> <u>met</u> ~~for a two-hour bargaining session~~.
2. <u>They</u> <u>debated</u> and <u>drafted</u> a tentative agreement ~~for a new contract~~.
3. The <u>anesthetist</u> and the <u>surgeon</u> <u>scrubbed</u> ~~for surgery~~ and <u>hurried</u> ~~to the operating room~~.
4. <u>Frederick Banting</u> and <u>Norman Bethune</u> <u>are known</u> ~~around the world~~ as medical heroes.
5. <u>Kevin</u> and <u>Sandra</u> <u>hiked</u> and <u>cycled</u> ~~across most of Newfoundland~~.
6. My <u>son</u> or my <u>daughter</u> <u>will meet</u> me and <u>drive</u> me home.
7. [You] <u>Knock</u> three times and <u>ask</u> for Stan.
8. ~~In the 17th and 18th centuries~~, the <u>French</u> and the <u>English</u> <u>fought</u> ~~for control of Canada~~.
9. [You] <u>Buy</u> the base model and <u>don't</u> <u>waste</u> your money ~~on luxury options~~.
10. <u>Ragweed</u>, <u>golden rod</u>, and <u>twitch grass</u> <u>formed</u> the essential elements ~~in the bouquet for his English teacher~~.

Answers for Chapter 23: Solving Sentence-Fragment Problems (pages 339–46)

Exercise 23.1 (suggested answers)

We have made the sentence fragments into complete sentences to give you an idea of how the sentences might be formed. Different sentences can be made out of the fragments in this exercise; just be sure each sentence has a subject and a verb.

1. F My favourite <u>movies</u> <u>are</u> about historical events.
2. F <u>It</u> <u>is</u> silly to decide on the basis of rumour, not facts.
3. S
4. F After cooking my famous tuna casserole, my <u>guests</u> politely <u>declined</u> to eat it.
5. F The party <u>members</u> gathering in the campaign office <u>called</u> for a recount.
6. S
7. F [You] <u>Put</u> your hands over your head.
8. F I <u>don't</u> <u>want</u> to go anywhere without my iPod.
9. F Having worked hard all her life, <u>she</u> <u>was</u> happy to retire.
10. S

Exercise 23.2 (suggested answers)

___F___ Professional athletes <u>make</u> millions of dollars a year. ___F___ At the same time, owners of sports franchises <u>grow</u> fantastically rich from the efforts of their employees, the players. ___F___ The fans <u>are</u> the forgotten people in the struggle for control over major league sports. ___F___ <u>They</u> <u>are</u> the people who pay the money that makes both owners and players rich. __S__ I have an idea that would protect everyone's interests. __S__ Cap the owners' profits. __S__ Cap the players' salaries. __F__ And, most important, [you] cap the ticket prices. __F__ This <u>plan</u> <u>would ensure</u> a fair deal for everyone. __S__ Fans should be able to see their teams play for the price of a movie ticket, not the price of a television set.

Exercise 23.3

1. F   Although
2. F   Since
3. S
4. F   Whichever
5. F   Before

Exercise 23.4

1. Although
2. As long as
3. Whether
4. Because
5. As

Exercise 23.5

Although many companies are experiencing growth, thanks to a healthy economy, **m**iddle managers are not breathing easily. As long as there is surplus of junior executives, **m**iddle managers will continue to look over their shoulders, never sure when the axe will fall. Whether through early retirement, buyout, or termination, **t**heir positions are being eliminated by cost-conscious firms whose eyes are focused on the bottom line. Because the executive branch of many businesses expanded rapidly during the years of high growth, **n**ow there is a large block of managers who have no prospects of advancement. As one analyst observed, when he examined this block of largely superfluous executives and their chances of rising in the company hierarchy, "You cannot push a rectangle up a triangle."

Exercise 23.6

In spite of what everyone says about the weak economy and the scarcity of jobs, especially for young people, I have financed my college career with a variety of part-time and seasonal jobs. Right now, for instance, while completing my third year at college, I have not one, or two, but three part-time jobs. I am a short-order cook three nights a week for a local bar and diner, **a**nd a telemarketer for a cable company after school **o**r whenever I have free time. I'm also a server at a specialty coffee store on weekends. To maintain any kind of social life **w**hile juggling three jobs and the requirements of my third-year program is not exactly easy, but I find it hard to turn down the opportunity for experience, **n**ot to mention cash. I'm willing to put my social life on hold **f**or a while.

Answers for Chapter 24: Solving Run-On Problems (pages 347–51)

Exercise 24.1

1. This is strong coffee. It has dissolved my spoon!
2. Just let me do the talking. We're sure to get a ticket if you open your mouth.

3. Correct
4. If you have never tried it, hitting a golf ball may look easy, **but** it's not.
5. Correct
6. Montreal used to be known as Ville St. Marie. **B**efore that it was known as Hochelaga.
7. Students today really need summer jobs and part-time employment **because** their tuition and living costs are too high for most families to subsidize.
8. Correct
9. It's very windy, **so** a ball hit deep to centre field will likely go into the stands.
10. "I was married by a judge; I should have asked for a jury." (Groucho Marx)

Exercise 24.2

1. I use a keyboard all the time**, and** my handwriting has become illegible.
2. Despite my parents' objections, I enjoy having long hair **because** it makes me feel attractive.
3. Casual meetings are fine for small groups, **but** more formal settings are appropriate for larger groups.
4. I'd be happy to help you. Just call when you need me; I'll be here all day.
5. In Canada, winter is more than a season. It's a bad joke.
6. Correct
7. For students in most technology programs, the future looks bright**;** however, a diploma does not guarantee job security.
8. A Canadian who speaks three languages is called multilingual**;** one who speaks two languages is called bilingual**; and** one who speaks only one language is called an English Canadian.
9. Skilled people are needed in specialized fields**;** currently, the top three are geriatrics, hospitality, and environmental technology.
10. I believe in a unified Canada**. I** believe that in 1867 the Fathers of Confederation were right**:** a federation of provinces can make a strong nation.

Answers for Chapter 25: Solving Modifier Problems (pages 352–60)

Exercise 25.1

1. Trevor left out the can of Pet Grrmet he had opened for the dog.
2. On the first day, our supervisor told us no one takes coffee breaks. (*Or:* Our supervisor told us no one takes coffee breaks on the first day.)
3. With no experience whatever, I enthusiastically recommend this candidate.
4. In September, Professor Green told us he thought our class was a hopeless case. (*Or:* Professor Green told us he thought our class was a hopeless case in September.)
5. We enjoyed almost the whole movie; only the ending was a disappointment.
6. In a highrise within walking distance of the campus, Leo and Annie found an apartment with two bedrooms and a sunken living room.
7. There are just enough pieces to go around.
8. It seems there is a game almost every day during baseball season.

9. A charming, intelligent companion who looks good in evening gowns and diamonds is sought by a vertically challenged but wealthy gentleman.
10. Only one of us could go because there was just enough money to buy one ticket.

Exercise 25.2

1. One usually finds the best Chinese food in those restaurants where the Chinese eat.
2. Using his new binoculars, he caught sight of a canary and several finches.
3. Using my camera with automatic functions, I can take professional-quality pictures.
4. The football practices have been organized as a keep-fit measure for players who are not with a team in the summertime.
5. Vancouver is a wonderful city to live in for anyone who likes rain and fog.
6. Some games, such as tiddlywinks, are less demanding in terms of time and equipment.
7. The Human Rights Code prohibits discrimination on the basis of race, religion, sex, or age against anyone who is applying for a job.
8. We looked in a golf store for a birthday present for our boss.
9. Each year, almost 500,000 Canadian men have a vasectomy.
10. Using cash as a motivator, we hope to improve our students' performances.

Exercise 25.3

1. Because she was driving recklessly and without lights, the police stopped Gina at a roadblock.
2. After I had been late twice in one week, my supervisor gave me a lecture about punctuality.
3. After criticizing both my work and my attitude, she fired me.
4. With enough memory to store her favourite movies and more than 10,000 songs, the iBook was the computer Hannah knew she needed.
5. After they spent two weeks quarrelling over money, their relationship was over.
6. As a dedicated fan of Alice Munro, I believe her last book was her best.
7. In less than a minute after applying the ointment, I felt the pain begin to ease.
8. Jake was probably more nervous than Allison, who was making her first formal presentation to her colleagues and her supervisor.
9. When you are handling hazardous waste, the safety manual clearly outlines the procedures to follow.
10. After spending the day in the kitchen preparing a gourmet meal, Kendra felt her efforts weren't appreciated because the guests drank too much wine.

Exercise 25.4

1. She was the baker's only daughter, but she could loaf all day. (*Or:* She was only the baker's daughter, but she could loaf all day.)
2. Being horribly hung over, I came to the realization that the only problem with a free bar is knowing when to quit.
3. Sam finally got the terrified horse, which was rearing and kicking, under control.

4. In a hurry to get to the interview on time, I left my résumé lying on my desk at home.

5. As a college student constantly faced with new assignments, I find the pressure is sometimes intolerable.

6. Listening to the rumours, I'll bet the newlyweds are already on the road to separation.

7. The display of liquor in the duty-free outlet held no interest for me because I am a nondrinker.

8. Quartetto Gelato receives enthusiastic acclaim from Vancouver to St. John's for its original arrangements and witty presentations.

9. Queen Elizabeth couldn't resist the little Corgi puppy, which was rolling on her back, eager to have her tummy scratched.

10. If you wear a small Canadian flag on your backpack or lapel, your reception abroad will be warm and enthusiastic.

Answers for Chapter 26: The Parallelism Principle (pages 361–66)

Exercise 26.1

1. This program is easy to understand and to use.
2. We were told that we would have to leave and that we could take nothing with us.
3. We organized our findings, wrote the report, and finally prepared our PowerPoint presentation.
4. Both applicants were unskilled, unprepared, and unmotivated.
5. Elmer's doctor advised him not to strain his back or his mind.
6. The company is looking for an employee who has a car and who knows the city.
7. If consumers really cared, they could influence the fast-food industry to produce healthy, delicious, inexpensive food.
8. When I want to get away from it all, there are three solitary pleasures that I enjoy: walking quietly in the country, reading a good book, and listening to fine music. (*Or:* . . . a walk in the country, a good book, and fine music.)
9. A recent survey of female executives claims that responsibility for their families, exclusion from informal networks, and lack of management experience are the major factors keeping them from advancement.
10. If it is to be useful, your report must be clearly organized, well written, and thoroughly researched.

Exercise 26.2

1. For my birthday, I requested either a Roots jacket or a Dior scarf.
2. In my community, two related crimes are rapidly increasing: drug abuse and theft.
3. Bodybuilding has made me what I am today: physically perfect, financially prosperous, and practically friendless.
4. After reading all the explanations and completing all the exercises, you'll be a better writer.
5. Bruce claimed that, through repetition and reward, he had trained his centipede to be loyal and obedient.
6. During their vacation in New Brunswick, Tracy and Jane visited many beautiful locations and ate wonderful seafood.

7. I'm an average tennis player; I have a good forehand, an average backhand, but a weak serve.
8. The problem with being immortalized as a statue is that you will be a target for pigeon droppings and graffiti artists.
9. Never disturb a sleeping dog, a happy baby, or a silent politician.
10. I'd like to help, but I'm too tired and too busy.

Exercise 26.3

1. wine	women	song
2. do your best	don't give up	
3. lying about all morning	doing whatever I please	
4. information	education	entertainment
5. as individuals	as a group	
6. privately	publicly	
7. happy	healthy	wise
8. employers	full-time employees	contract workers
9. lack of time	[lack of] money	[lack of] staff
10. French is the language of love	English is the language of business	German is the language of profanity

Exercise 26.4

1. Not being able to speak the language is confusing, frustrating, and embarrassing.
2. Trying your best and succeeding are not always the same thing.
3. The first candidate we interviewed seemed frightened and shy, but the second was composed and confident.
4. Licking one's fingers and picking one's teeth in a restaurant are one way to get attention.
5. Our CEO claims his most valuable business assets are a good backhand and membership at an exclusive golf club.
6. In order to succeed in this economy, small businesses must be creative, innovative, and flexible.
7. Lowering our profit margin, raising our prices, and laying off two managers will enable us to meet our budget.
8. After an enjoyable dinner, I like to drink a cappuccino, eat a dark chocolate mint, and, occasionally, smoke a good cigar.
9. Lying in the sun, consuming high-fat foods, and smoking cigarettes are three dangerous activities that were once thought to be healthy.
10. Business travellers complain of long delays at airports, higher costs for services, and tighter restrictions on their freedom of movement.

Answers for Chapter 27: Refining by Combining (pages 367–71)

Exercise 27.1

1. We cannot sell our cottage, **so** we will live there instead.
2. There are three solutions given for this problem, **and** all of them are correct.
3. The people in our firm work very hard, **but** they wouldn't want it any other way.
4. We could spend our day off shopping at the mall, **or** we could spend the day fishing.

5. Great leaders do not bully their people, **nor** do they deceive them.
6. I will not be able to finish my report, **for** there are only two hours before the deadline.
7. Jennifer knows that she likely will not get the vice-president's job, **yet** (*or* **but**) she wants the experience of applying for it.
8. Finish the estimate, **but** do not begin work until it has been approved.
9. Today has been the worst day of my life, **so** my horoscope was right.
10. The government did not offer me a job, **nor** did it even reply to my letter.

Exercise 27.2 (suggested answers)

1. Leonardo da Vinci was a great artist and inventor **who** invented scissors, among other things.
2. Cats can produce over 100 vocal sounds, **whereas** dogs can make only 10.
3. **Although** it is said that men don't cry, they do while assembling furniture.
4. The name Wendy was made up for a book **that** was called *Peter Pan*.
5. **Although** 10 percent of Canadians are heavy drinkers, 35 percent abstain from alcohol.
6. Travel broadens the mind **even though** it flattens the bank account.
7. We are seeking an experienced and innovative director **who** is fluent in French.
8. One hundred thousand Vietnam veterans have taken their own lives, **which** is twice the number who were killed in action.
9. **After** my cooking class went on a field trip to gather greens for a salad, we discovered that what we thought was watercress was, in fact, poison ivy.
10. Eight of the ten classmates who ate the salad were hospitalized, **although** no one was seriously affected.

Answers for Chapter 28: Mastering Subject–Verb Agreement (pages 372–81)

Exercise 28.1

1. They sell used essays to other students.
2. Those new guidelines affect all the office procedures.
3. All those who shop at Pimrock's receive free cans of tuna.
4. The women maintain that their boss has been harassing them.
5. Those girls' fathers are looking for rich husbands for them.

Exercise 28.2

1. is
2. are
3. is
4. is
5. tempt

Exercise 28.3

1. are
2. registers
3. is

4. wonders

5. puts

Exercise 28.4

1. is

2. involves

3. is

4. wants

5. believes

Exercise 28.5

1. plans

2. has

3. have

4. was

5. are

Exercise 28.6

1. was

2. seems

3. is

4. is

5. seems

Exercise 28.7

1. Neither of the following two sentences **is** correct.
2. The teachers, with the full support of the college administration, **treat** plagiarism as a serious offence.
3. Either good looks or intelligence **runs** in our family, but never at the same time.
4. None of these computer programs **is** able to streamline our billing procedures.
5. The enjoyment of puns and jokes involving plays on words **is** the result of having too little else on your mind.
6. Anyone who jumps from one of Paris's many bridges **is** in Seine.
7. It is amazing how much better the orchestra **plays** now that the conductor is sober.
8. The number of layoffs reported in the headlines **seems** to be rising again.
9. Her supervisors all agree that Emily **needs** further training to be effective.
10. Canada's First Nations population **is** thought to have come to this continent from Asia thousands of years before the Europeans arrived in North America.

Exercise 28.8

Quebec City, along with Montreal, Toronto, and Vancouver, **is** among Canada's great gourmet centres. Whereas Toronto is a relative latecomer to this list, neither Quebec City nor Montreal **is a stranger** to those who **seek** fine dining. Indeed, travel and food magazines have long affirmed that the inclusion of these two cities in a Quebec vacation **is** a "must." Montreal is perhaps more international in its offerings, but Quebec City provides exquisite proof that French-Canadian cuisine and hospitality **are** second to none in the world. Amid the Old World charm of the lower city

are to be found some of the quaintest and most enjoyable traditional restaurants; the newer sections of town **boast** equally fine dining in more contemporary surroundings. The combination of the wonderful food and the city's fascinating charms **is** sure to make any visitor return frequently. Either the summer, when the city blooms and outdoor cafés abound, or the winter, when Carnaval turns the streets into hundreds of connecting parties, **is a** wonderful **time** to visit one of Canada's oldest and most interesting cities.

Answers for Chapter 29: Using Verbs Effectively (pages 382–95)

Exercise 29.1

1. lay	6. chosen
2. eaten	7. printed
3. ridden	8. lent
4. sat	9. worn
5. lie	10. known

Exercise 29.3

1. After he accused me, I **called** him a liar.
2. Hank Aaron broke Babe Ruth's record of 714 home runs in a lifetime when he **hit** number 715 in 1974.
3. Children are quite perceptive and **know** when you are lying to them.
4. She went up to the counter and **asked** for a refund.
5. When Brad Pitt walked into the room, the girls **went** crazy.
6. correct
7. Tim walked into the room, took one look at Leroy, and **smashed** him right through the wall.
8. First you will greet the guests; then you **will show** them to their rooms.
9. The largest cheese ever produced took 43 hours to make and **weighed** a whopping 15,723 kg.
10. He watches television until he finally **goes** to sleep.

Exercise 29.4

For some reason, when mistakes or accidents happen in radio or television, they **are** often hilariously funny. If, in the course of a conversation, someone said, "Here come the Duck and Doochess of Kent," listeners would probably be mildly amused. But many years ago, when an announcer **made** that slip on a live radio broadcast, it **became** one of the most famous blunders in radio history. Tapes of the slip **were** filed in "bloopers" libraries all over the world. This heightened sense of hilarity is the reason that so many people who work in radio **dedicate** their creativity to making the on-air announcer laugh while reading the news. To take one example, Lorne Greene's **was** the deeply serious voice that **was** heard on the CBC news during World War II. He **was** the victim of all kinds of pranks aimed at getting him to break up while reading the dark, often tragic, news of the combat overseas. The pages of his news script **were** set on fire while he **read**. He **was** even stripped naked as he **read**, calmly, and apparently without strain. Lorne Greene **was** a true professional. Many other newscasters, however, **have been** highly susceptible to falling apart on air at the slightest provocation. And there **are** always people around a radio station who cannot resist giving them that little push.

Exercise 29.6

1. The department head called a meeting.
2. The server will make expresso in a few minutes.
3. When it gets cold, we plug in the block heater overnight.
4. For many years, professional athletes have used steroids to improve speed and endurance.
5. You must not knead the dough, or your pastry will be tough.
6. My parents wrote this postcard while they were hiking through Nepal.
7. A crew of students made this movie for less than $900,000.
8. Thieves broke into our neighbours' house while they were vacationing in the Caribbean.
9. You made an error in the code you wrote for this program.
10. The Mighty Ducks have replaced the Red Sox and the White Sox as the team with the stupidest name in sports.

Exercise 29.7

1. Another Juno was won by Sarah McLachlan. (Active is more effective.)
2. The ball was spiked by Carl, after scoring the winning points. (Active is more effective.)
3. A bylaw forbidding smoking in bars and restaurants has been passed by city council. (Passive is more effective, because it focuses the readers' attention on the law rather than on who brought the law into being.)
4. Forty-eight hours later, the technician added 2 mL of sterile water to the culture in the petri dish. (Passive is more effective; it puts the focus on the procedure rather than on the person.)
5. Four tickets for the concert were got by Courtenay after standing in line all night. (Active is more effective.)
6. The truth behind the famous Doobie Brothers scandal was revealed on the 10 p.m. news. (Passive is more effective; what was revealed is of more interest than who revealed it.)
7. The judge finally announced her judgment today, almost a year after the environmental hearings were concluded. (Passive is more effective, for the same reason as in sentence 6.)
8. After a long debate, Yasmin's fundraising proposal was finally endorsed by the committee. (Passive is more effective, because it focuses attention on the individual proposal rather than on the anonymous committee.)
9. Dr. Hans Steiner, a psychologist at Stanford University, has developed a computer program that analyzes speech patterns. (Passive is more effective, for the same reason as in sentence 6.)
10. After years of research among college students, Dr. Steiner has concluded that people who frequently use passive-voice constructions tend to be maladjusted. (Active is more effective.)

Answers for Chapter 30: Solving Pronoun Problems (pages 396–415)

Exercise 30.1

1. No one except you and **me** . . .
2. **He** and I can't figure out this problem set any better than you and **she** could.
3. George and **he** fell asleep . . .
4. Do you want to work with Emma and **her**?
5. We can use the film passes all week, and you and **she** can use them on the weekend when Biff and **I** are going skiing.
6. Thanks to the recommendations provided by your math instructor and **me**, you and **she** got the tutorial jobs.
7. As we were going to class, Karl and **I** heard . . .
8. If it hadn't been for Hassan and **him** . . .
9. Quentin and **he** agreed to split the price of a case with Stan and **me**.
10. Only two students passed the midterm: Nadia and **I**.

Exercise 30.2

1. At 14, my younger brother is already taller than **I** [am].
2. No one likes partying more than **he** and Anne.
3. Would you like to join Daniel and **me** . . . ?
4. Only one person in this firm could manage the department as well as **he** [could].
5. At last I have met someone who enjoys grilled liver as much as **I** [do].
6. We can skate as well as **they**, but they are much better at shooting and defending than **we** [are].
7. More than **I** [do], Serge uses the computer . . . .

Exercise 30.3

1. My boyfriend and **I** . . . .
2. I like fast food better than **he** [does].
3. He likes vegetables better than **I** [do].
4. In fact, between you and **me** . . . .
5. . . . it is difficult for **them** to know where to take him and **me** . . . .
6. The only type of restaurant where **we** and **they** can all have what we like is Italian.
7. There, **he** and his friends . . . .
8. We are probably not as healthy as **they**, but they don't seem to enjoy their food as much as **we** [do].

Exercise 30.4

1. his
2. her
3. his
4. her
5. himself, he

Exercise 30.5

1. Everyone who enjoys a thrilling match will reserve a seat . . . .
2. . . . everyone climbed to the fourth floor to hand in the course evaluation.

3. Each of her sons successfully completed his diploma.
4. Someone with lots of money left a purse in the women's washroom.
5. All reporters must decide for themselves how far they will go . . . .

Exercise 30.6

1. Virginia claims that every one of her male friends has a room of his own.
2. Almost everyone I know is concerned about finding a suitable job.
3. Anybody who applies for a job with this institution can expect to spend a lot of time in selection committee interviews.
4. Taking pictures of people when they are not looking can produce interesting results.
5. Nearly every man who can cook will tell you that he enjoys preparing food.

Exercise 30.7

1. I know that smoking is bad for me and everyone else, but I can't give up cigarettes.
2. If your pet rat won't eat its food, feed the pellets to the kitty.
3. Our cat is a picky eater; her food preferences are inconvenient and expensive.
4. Whenever Stefan and Matt played poker, Stefan stacked the deck.
5. The gorilla was mean and hungry because he had finished all his food in the morning.
6. Madonna has transformed herself at least four times in her career, an accomplishment that makes her unique.
7. Dani backed her car into a garbage truck and dented her fender.
8. Rocco was suspicious of handgun control because he thought everyone should have a gun for late-night subway rides.
9. Get your ears pierced during this week's special and take home an extra pair of earrings free.
10. Our car is in the shop, but we're still going to the party.

Exercise 30.9

1. The actress **who** saw her first grey hair thought she'd dye.
2. I am a longtime fan of David Cronenberg, a director **who** began his career in Canada.
3. I wonder why we are so often attracted to people **who** are completely opposite to us.
4. I'm one of those people **who** should stay out of the sun.
5. People **who** take afternoon naps often suffer from insomnia as a result.
6. The vacuum-cleaner salesperson **who** came to our door was the sort of person **who** won't take no for an answer.
7. This is the brilliant teacher **who** helped me achieve the grades **that** I had thought were beyond me.
8. Marathon runners **who** wear cheap shoes often suffer the agony of defeat.
9. The math problems **that** we worked on last night would have baffled anyone **who** hadn't done all the problem sets.
10. We took the ancient Jeep, **which** we had bought from a friend **who** had lost his licence, to a scrapyard **that** paid us $200 for it.

Exercise 30.10
1. you
2. you, your
3. a
4. she
5. we

Exercise 30.11
1. People who live in glass houses shouldn't throw stones.
2. Experience is something **you acquire** just after you need it.
3. Anyone who enjoys snowboarding can have **her** (*or* **his** *or* **the**) best holiday ever in western Alberta.
4. When she asked if Peter Tchaikovsky played for the Canucks, **I** knew she wasn't the woman for me.
5. From time to time, most of us think about the opportunities we've missed even if **we're** happy with what **we** have.
6. Managers who are concerned about employee morale should think about ending **their** policy of threats and intimidation and consider other means to improve efficiency.
7. If you are afraid of vampires, **you** should wear garlic around **your** neck and carry a silver bullet.
8. Any woman who wears a garlic necklace probably won't have to worry about men harassing **her**, either.
9. Can you really know another person if you have never been to **his** (*or* **her**) home?
10. A sure way to lose **your** friends is to eat all the ice cream yourself.

Exercise 30.12
When people see a dreadful occurrence on television, such as a bombing, an earthquake, or a mass slaughter, it does not always affect **them**. It is one thing for people to see the ravages of war **themselves** and another thing to see a three-minute newscast of the same battle, neatly edited by the CBC. Even the horrible effects of natural catastrophes that wipe out whole populations are somehow minimized or trivialized when **people** see them on TV. And though viewers may be horrified by the gaunt faces of starving children on the screen, **they** can easily escape into **their** familiar world of Egg McMuffins, Shake'n Bake, and Labatt Blue that is portrayed in commercial messages.

Thus, the impact of television on us is a mixed one. It is true that **we are** shown terrible, sometimes shocking events that **we** could not possibly have seen before television. In this way, **our** world is drawn together more closely. However, the risk in creating this immediacy is that **we** may become desensitized and cease to feel or care about **our** fellow human beings.

Answers for Chapter 31: The Comma (pages 416–26)

Exercise 31.1
1. Holly held two aces, a King, a Queen**,** and a Jack in her hand.
2. The food at the Thai Palace is colourful, spicy, delicious**,** and inexpensive.
3. Life would be complete if I had a Blackberry, a Porsche, a Sea-Doo**,** and a job.

4. The gear list for the Winter Wilderness course includes woollen underwear, snowshoes, Arctic boots, and a toque.
5. In the summer, a cup of coffee, a croissant, and a glass of juice are all I want for breakfast.
6. Don't forget to bring the videos, maps, and souvenirs of your trip to Australia.
7. In Ontario, the four seasons are summer, winter, winter, and winter.
8. My doctor and my nutritionist agree that I should eat better, exercise more, and take vitamins.
9. Sleeping through my alarm, dozing during sociology class, napping in the library after lunch, and snoozing in front of the TV after supper are symptoms of my overactive nightlife.
10. Welcome home! Once you have finished your homework, taken out the garbage, and done the dishes, you can feed the cat, clean your room, and do your laundry.

Exercise 31.2

1. Either it is very foggy this morning, or I am going blind.
2. We have an approved business plan and budget, but we're still looking for qualified and experienced staff.
3. Talk shows haven't said anything new in years, nor have they solved a single one of the problems they endlessly discuss.
4. We discovered that we both had an interest in fine art, so we made a date to go to an exhibition at the art gallery next week.
5. Canadians are proud of their country, but they don't approve of too much flag-waving.
6. Take good notes, for I'll need them in order to study for the exam.
7. I'll rent a tux, but I will not get a haircut or my shoes shined.
8. I chose a quiet seat on the train, and two women with bawling babies boarded at the next station.
9. I have travelled all over the world, yet my luggage has visited at least twice the number of countries that I have.
10. Jet lag makes me look haggard and ill, but at least I resemble my passport photo.

Exercise 31.3

1. A good day, in my opinion, always starts with a few cuts of high-volume heavy metal.
2. This photograph, which was taken when I was four, embarrasses me whenever my parents display it.
3. Mira's boyfriend, who looks like an ape, is living proof that love is blind.
4. Isn't it strange that the poor, who often are bitterly critical of the rich, keep buying lottery tickets?
5. A nagging headache, the result of last night's great party, made me miserable all morning.
6. Our ancient car made it all the way to Saskatoon without anything falling off or breaking down, a piece of good luck that astonished everyone.
7. Professor Repke, a popular mathematics teacher, won the Distinguished Teaching Award this year.

8. We're going to spend the afternoon at the mall, a weekly event that has become a ritual.
9. correct
10. Classical music, which I call Prozac for the ears, can be very soothing in times of stress.

Exercise 31.4
1. Unfortunately, we'll have to begin all over again.
2. Mr. Dillinger, the bank would like a word with you.
3. In college, the quality of your work is more important than the effort you put into it.
4. Hopelessly lost, my father still refused to stop and ask for directions.
5. Finally understanding what she was trying to say, I apologized for being so slow.
6. After an evening of watching television, I have accomplished as much as if I had been unconscious.
7. Since the doctor ordered me to walk to work every morning, I have seen three accidents involving people walking to work.
8. Having munched our way through a large bag of peanuts while watching the game, we weren't interested in supper.
9. Whenever an optimist is pulled over by a police officer, the optimist assumes it's to ask for directions.
10. That same year, Stephen Leacock bought his summer home in Orillia, Ontario.

Exercise 31.5
1. correct
2. correct
3. correct
4. Toronto in the summer is hot, smoggy, and humid.
5. Today's paper has an article about a new car made of lightweight, durable aluminum.
6. Dietitians recommend that we eat at least two servings daily of green, leafy vegetables.
7. This ergonomic, efficient, full-function keyboard comes in a variety of pastel shades.
8. We ordered a large, nutritious salad for lunch, then indulged ourselves with a redcurrant cheesecake for dessert.
9. Danny bought a cute, cuddly, pure-bred puppy.
10. Ten months later that cute puppy turned into a vicious, man-eating monster.

Exercise 31.6
1. Pinot noir, which is a type of grape grown in California, Oregon, British Columbia(,) and Ontario, produces a delicious red wine.
2. There are, I am told, people who don't like garlic, but you won't find any of them eating at Freddy's.
3. I use e-mail to communicate with my colleagues, a fax machine to keep in touch with clients(,) and Canada Post to send greetings to my relatives.
4. Your dogs, Mr. Pavlov, seem hungry for some reason.

5. According to G. K. Chesterton, "If a thing is worth doing, it is worth doing badly."
6. Looking for a competent computer technologist, we interviewed, tested, investigated(,) and rejected 30 applicants.
7. How you choose to phrase your resignation is up to you, but I expect to have it on my desk by morning.
8. Your superstitious dread of March 13, Senator Caesar, is irrational and silly.
9. The lenses of my new high-function sunglasses are impact-resistant, yellow, UV-reflective optical plastic.
10. Canada, a country known internationally for beautiful scenery, peaceful intentions(,) and violent hockey, always places near the top of the United Nations' list of desirable places to live.

Exercise 31.7

1. Whereas the Super Bowl tradition goes back about four decades, the Grey Cup has a history that stretches back to the 19th century.
2. Otherwise, Mrs. Lincoln said, she had very much enjoyed the play.
3. Our guard dog, a Rottweiler, caught an intruder and maimed him for life.
4. Unfortunately, my Uncle Ladislaw was the intruder, and he intends to sue us for every penny we have.
5. correct
6. We bought a lovely, old, mahogany dining table at auction for $300.
7. If there were more people like Gladys, global warming would be the least of our worries.
8. correct
9. Deciding on the midnight blue velvet pants was easy, but paying for them was not.
10. Igor asked, "May I show you to your quarters, or would you prefer to spend the night in the dungeon?"

Answers for Chapter 32: The Semicolon (pages 427–31)

Exercise 32.1

1. incorrect	6. incorrect
2. correct	7. correct
3. incorrect	8. incorrect
4. incorrect	9. incorrect
5. incorrect	10. incorrect

Exercise 32.2

1. We've eaten all the food; it's time to go home.
2. correct
3. Your instructor would like to see you pass; however, there may be a small fee involved.
4. Molly is going to Chicago; she wants to appear on *Oprah*.
5. Many people dislike hockey because some of the players act like goons rather than athletes.
6. Orville tried and tried; but he couldn't get the teacher's attention.

7. correct
8. Tomorrow is another day; unfortunately, it will probably be just like today.
9. Rumours of a merger had begun to circulate by five o'clock, so it's no wonder many employees looked nervous on their way home.
10. We knew the party had been a success when Uncle Morty, drunk as usual, tap-danced across the top of the piano; Aunt Madeline, who must weigh at least 80 kg, did her Cirque du Soleil routine; and Stan punched out two of his cousins.

Exercise 32.3

1. The rain has to stop soon; otherwise, we'll have to start building an ark.
2. Our finances are a mess; the only way we can repay our debts would be to stop paying for rent and food.
3. We need you at the meeting; however, since you have another engagement, we will have to reschedule.
4. A day without puns is like a day without sunshine; it leaves gloom for improvement.
5. I work on an assembly line; all of us workers believe that if a job is worth doing, it's worth doing 11,000 times a day.
6. It is not impossible to become wealthy; if you're under 20, all you need to do is put the price of a pack of cigarettes into an RRSP every day, and you'll be a millionaire by the age of 50.
7. If, on the other hand, you continue to spend your money on smokes, the government will make the millions that could have been yours; you'll die early and broke.
8. As a dog lover and the owner of an Afghan, I suffer a great deal of abuse; for example, for my birthday, my wife gave me a book rating the intelligence of Afghans as 79th out of 79 breeds tested.
9. A plateau, according to the *Dictionary of Puns*, is a high form of flattery; this may be low humour, but it's a clever remark.
10. According to a *Gourmet Magazine* poll, four of the top ten restaurants in the world are in Paris; three—those ranking eighth, ninth, and tenth—are in the United States; two are in Tokyo; and the other is in Thailand.

Answers for Chapter 33: The Colon (pages 432–36)

Exercise 33.1

1. incorrect
2. correct
3. correct
4. incorrect
5. incorrect
6. correct
7. correct
8. incorrect
9. incorrect
10. incorrect

Exercise 33.2

1. I have set myself three goals this year: to achieve an 80 percent average, to get a good summer job, and to buy a car.
2. Right after we moved in, we discovered we had a problem: termites.

Exercise 36.2

1. Five of the students (I was asked not to name them) have volunteered to be peer tutors.
2. The apostrophe is explained in the unit on spelling (pages 463–70).
3. Jason complained that being a manager (he became one in March) was like being a cop.
4. I have enclosed a cheque for one hundred and fifty dollars ($150).
5. More members of the Canadian Armed Forces died in World War I (1914–18) than in any war before or since.
6. Although Mozart lived a relatively short time (he died when he was 36), he composed hundreds of musical masterpieces.
7. As news of her "miracle cures" spread (patients began to come to her from all over the province), the country doctor had to move her clinic to a more central location.
8. The new contract provided improved working conditions, a raise in salary (3 percent), and a new dental plan.
9. Ontario and British Columbia now produce world-class wines from three small estate wineries (Inniskillin, Hillebrand, Quail's Gate) that compete and win internationally.
10. "One of the most important tools for making paper speak in your own voice is punctuation; it plays the role of body language; it helps readers hear you the way you want to be heard" (Baker 48–49).

Answers for Chapter 37: Hazardous Homonyms (pages 450–62)

Exercise 37.1

1. course, affect
2. Are, accept
3. then, dessert
4. you're, losing
5. quite, here
6. whose, conscience
7. assured, number
8. It's, its
9. choose, course, advice
10. continual, dining

Exercise 37.2

1. simplistic, morals, implies
2. morale, miners, fazed
3. imply, further, creditable
4. effect, disperse, fewer
5. whose, principles, less
6. infer, whether, fourth
7. your, continually, ensures
8. conscious, choosing, site, farther
9. accept, counsellors, phase
10. number, allowed, fewer, than, women

Exercise 37.3

1. b
2. b

3. a
4. b
5. b
6. b
7. b
8. a
9. b
10. a

Answers for Chapter 38: The Apostrophe (pages 463–70)

Exercise 38.1

1. Yes, **it's** a long way from Halifax to Vancouver, but **we've** been in training for three months.
2. **We're** taking the train to Antigonish, and **we're** biking to Halifax; then **we'll** begin the big trip west.
3. There **wasn't** a dry eye in the theatre when **Spielberg's** film reached its climax.
4. **Who's** discovered **what's** wrong with this sentence?
5. Wasn't it Mark Twain who said, "**It's** easy to stop smoking; **I've** done it dozens of times"?

Exercise 38.2

I am writing to apply for the position of webmaster for BrilloVision.com that **you have** advertised in the *Daily News*. **I have** the talent and background **you are** looking for. Currently, I work as a Web designer for an online publication, Vexed.com, where **they are** very pleased with my work. If you click on their website, I think **you will** like what you see. **There is** little in the way of Web design and application that I **have not** been involved in during the past two years. But **it is** time for me to move on to a new challenge, and BrilloVision.com promises the kind of opportunity **I am** looking for. I guarantee you **will not** be disappointed if I join your team!

Exercise 38.3

1. The **car's** brakes are worn and its tires are nearly bald.
2. Diplomatic **ambassadors'** wives or husbands are often as important to a **mission's** success as the ambassadors themselves.
3. Near Chicoutimi is one of the **country's** most beautiful parks, where the skills of canoeists, fishermen, and wildlife photographers can be put to the test on a **summer's** day.
4. **Janis'(s)** career got its start when she sang **seafarers'** songs in the yacht **club's** dining lounge.
5. A **country's** history is the main determinant of its national character.

Exercise 38.4

1. you're, your, your
2. Someone's, whose
3. ship's, weeks'

4. people's, workers', sides'
5. turtle's, turtle's, it's, its, yours

Exercise 38.5

1. When you feel like a snack, you can choose between apples and **Timbits.**
2. **Anna's** career took off when she discovered **it's** easy to sell **children's** toys.
3. Golfing requires the use of different **clubs:** woods for long shots, irons for short ones.
4. Poker's an easy game to play if you are dealt **aces** more often than your **opponents** are.
5. Good writing **skills don't** guarantee success in **your** career, but they help.

Answers for Chapter 39: The Hyphen (pages 471–74)

Exercise 39.1

1. Jill decided to sublet her **fifth-floor** apartment.
2. Fraser claims he is allergic to classical music but addicted to **hip-hop** music.
3. Just before the critical play, the **hard-fought** game was **pre-empted** by the movie *Heidi*!
4. **Hand-knit** sweaters are usually more expensive than **factory-produced** ones.
5. In 1950, at the age of **forty-seven**, George Orwell died of tuberculosis.

Exercise 39.2

1. For months after Saddam Hussein was **overthrown**, the world was shocked by revelations of the repression suffered by the Iraqi people.
2. Would you **relay** this message to Mr. Chan: the masons would like to **re-lay** the bricks this evening.
3. Our **next-door** neighbour teaches in a **high school**, but she does not like to be introduced as a **high-school** teacher.
4. A **face-to-face** meeting with an **anti-intellectual** always gets my adrenalin going.
5. Because Angela was an **attorney-at-law** and had once been an **all-Canadian** athlete, her former coach was not surprised when she became **Minister of Recreation.**

Answers for Chapter 40: Capital Letters (pages 475–81)

Exercise 40.1

1. **T**ime is nature's way of keeping everything from happening at once.
2. Brad whispered, "**T**here's a light in the Frankenstein house."
3. Learning Standard **E**nglish is, for many people, like learning another **l**anguage.
4. Richard Harkness, writing in *The New York Times*, said "**A** committee is a group of the unwilling, picked from the unfit, to do the unnecessary."
5. **I**n conclusion, I want you to consider the words of Wendell Johnson: "*Always* and *never* are two words you should always remember never to use."

Exercise 40.2

1. After a brief stay in the **Maritimes**, **Captain Tallman** and his crew sailed west up the **St. Lawrence**.
2. The **Broadcast Department** of **Niagara College** has ordered six **Sony** cameras for their studios in **Welland**, **Ontario**.
3. Do you find that **Visa** is more popular than **American Express** when you travel to faraway places such as **Mexico**, **France**, or **Jupiter**?
4. Our stay at the **Seaview Hotel** overlooking the **Pacific Ocean** certainly beat our last vacation at the **Bates Motel**, where we faced west, overlooking the city dump.
5. As the fundraiser for our alumni association, I am targeting companies like **Disney**, **Canadian Tire**, the **Bank of Montreal**, and the **CBC**, all of which employ our graduates.

Exercise 40.3

1. The **Crusades**, which were religious wars between **Muslims** and **Christians**, raged through the **Middle Ages**.
2. The **Hindu** religion recognizes and honours many gods; **Islam** recognizes one god, **Allah**; **Buddhism** recognizes none.
3. The **Koran**, the **Bible**, and the **Torah** agree on many principles.
4. The **Jewish** festival of **Hanukkah** often occurs near the same time that **Christians** are celebrating **Christmas**.
5. After **World War** I, many **Jews** began to emigrate to Palestine, where they and the **Muslim** population soon came into conflict.

Exercise 40.4

1. My favourite months are **January** and **February** because I love all **w**inter sports.
2. This **Monday** is **Valentine's Day**, when messages of love are exchanged.
3. In the summer, big meals seem too much trouble; however, after **Thanksgiving**, we need lots of food to survive the winter cold.
4. A **n**ational **h**oliday named **Flag Day** was once proposed, but it was never officially approved.
5. By **Thursday**, I'll have finished my **St. Patrick's Day** costume.

Exercise 40.5

1. The review of my book, ***The Life and Times of a Chocoholic***, published in ***The Globe and Mail***, was not favourable.
2. Clint **Eastwood** fans will be delighted that the two early movies that made him internationally famous, ***A Fistful of Dollars*** and ***For a Few Dollars More***, are now available on DVD.
3. Joseph **Conrad's** short novel ***Heart of Darkness*** became the blockbuster movie ***Apocalypse Now***.
4. Her poem, "**A Bright and Silent Place**," was published in the **April** issue of ***Landscapes*** magazine.
5. **Botticelli's** famous painting, ***Birth of Venus***, inspired my poem "**W**oman on the **Half Shell**."

Exercise 40.6

1. After studying geography for two years, I began taking courses in ancient **Greek** and modern history.

STUDENT EXEMPLARS

TREATMENT FOR

ALCOHOLISM IN PETERBOROUGH:

A LOOK AT TWO RECOVERY OPTIONS

COMM79

RESEARCH PAPER

Treatment for Alcoholism in Peterborough: A Look at Two Recovery Options.

Are you ready to stop abusing? If you live in Peterborough and suffer from alcohol addiction, help is not far away. There are two options for treatment available in Peterborough: Four Counties Addiction Services Team (FourCAST), and Alcoholics Anonymous (A.A.). There are several similarities between FourCAST and A.A. Both of these services are free, and they have helped a great many people overcome issues with alcohol addiction. Neither FourCAST nor A.A. offer residential treatment or medically supervised detoxification. Both services seek to help and support individuals to live free from the negative effects of alcohol abuse. However, FourCAST and A.A. differ greatly in the model of treatment, the immediacy of access and the on-going support that they offer.

Once people choose to seek treatment for alcohol abuse they need to make contact with a service. If the service they choose is A.A. they will have a great many meetings to choose from. These meetings are held at a many locations, and at many times of the day (A.A. 2007). Krista (A.A. members do not divulge their last names), a member and recovering alcoholic, explains that A.A. is an exclusively volunteer run organization which is self supporting through completely voluntary donations made by the members themselves (Personal communication. March 12, 2007). Ken, a volunteer and a twenty years sober alcoholic himself, says that alcoholics who wish to begin recovery may simply show up for a meeting or phone the main office. Help is offered immediately, and to whatever degree the alcoholic desires. Ken also points out that since this help offered is by individuals who are recovering alcoholics themselves, there is great motivation to assist recovery as quickly as possible (Personal communication. March 16, 2007). This urgency ensures that help from A.A. is swift and immediate.

FourCAST is funded by the Ministry of Health and employs counselors who are trained in the art of helping people recover from addiction to alcohol. Leeann Cormier, a counselor at FourCAST for many years, says that when alcoholics seeking treatment first make contact, they are immediately screened for intake. Intake screening looks at the severity of the problem, levels of mental and physical health, as well as abuse and suicide issues. The alcoholic may be referred to additional services for treatment of any physical and mental health problems. Following this, the alcoholic is given an appointment to see a counselor so that treatment may begin. She then adds that the alcoholic is also invited to participate in daily group meetings while waiting for their first appointment. The wait for this appointment may be as long as four weeks (Personal communication. March 16, 2007). Such a long wait time is in sharp contrast to the immediacy of help available through A.A. Some addicts simply can not wait that long and may need to seek help elsewhere (Peterborough Examiner. Jan 24, 2007). Counselors at FourCAST are frustrated by this, but their hands are tied by the lack of additional funding by the Ministry of Health (Cormier. Personal communication. March 16, 2007). The unlimited resources of A.A. volunteers cannot be matched by The paid employees of FourCAST. However, the screening and support for additional health problems included at FourCAST, ensures that the alcoholic gets total care.

In the treatment of substance abuse (including alcoholism), the 'model' is the core view, or belief system that serves as the foundation of the treatment method. FourCAST, as with all government agencies, uses the Cognitive-Behavioural model (www.dart.on.ca), while A.A. follow the Moral and Disease models (Johnson. Fundamentals of substance abuse practice. The success, in part, of either organization will depend on the client's compatibility, or willingness to engage with either model. Each model has a distinctly different approach which could make a fundamental difference to the recovery process of the alcoholic.

The Moral model takes the approach that the alcoholic is... "different -in a negative way –from the majority of... citizens", ...and that alcoholism is caused by... "poor personal decision making and bad moral judgement" (Johnson. Fundamentals of substance abuse practice. pg.62 & 64). The Disease model promotes the idea that alcoholism is an inherited disease. Alcoholics have some sort of chemical imbalance, or physical processing defect, which causes them to become addicted to alcohol (Cormier. Personal communication. March 16, 2007). Alcoholics are viewed as having a sickness, as being morally defective, and that they are powerless to control their use (Johnson. Fundamentals of substance abuse practice. p 79, 80). These models see the alcoholic as a victim. The 12 Steps of A.A.'s recovery process are heavily based on these models and, for some, this presents an insurmountable barrier. Ken (Personal communication. March 12, 2007) admits that the idea of there being "too much God", coupled with resistance to the idea of being "powerless against alcohol", makes A.A. a choice some alcoholics are unwilling to make.

The Cognitive-Behavioural model considers people's thoughts and actions. This model believes that badly adapted coping mechanisms and poor self concepts are what rest at the heart of alcoholism. Perceptions, ideas, thoughts, and beliefs are all learned and can therefore be changed (Johnson. Fundamentals of substance abuse practice. p 74).

Counselors working with the Cognitive-Behavioural model, assist alcoholics to recognize destructive thought processes and beliefs so that they may begin to change by choice and learned technique. Alcoholics are supported as they learn to take control of their lives, and to make better choices (Cormier. Personal communication. March 16, 2007). This model sees the alcoholic as having the power to change.

Depending on an alcoholic's own way of thinking, one model may be more helpful than the other. While both services offer a program of steps and changes for recovery, each core view, or approach is very different. If alcoholics can see themselves, with the guidance and support of the counselor, as capable of creating positive change in their lives, then they will benefit well from the program of recovery offered by FourCAST. If alcoholics believe that surrender to a higher power is the only way to achieve sobriety, then they will benefit from participation with A.A. The alcoholic's core beliefs and relationship with religion or spirituality will play a big part in the choice of treatment.

When alcoholics successfully negotiate all the steps and changes on the road to recovery, there remains the issue of maintenance. Achieving sobriety or learning to manage alcohol is, for many, a whole new way of being. On-going support and the knowledge of this support is an important part of the recovery process. A.A. believes that a person remains an alcoholic in recovery forever. A.A. is a community of recovering alcoholics who give and receive on-going support. In fact, A.A. believes service and support are an essential part of the recovery process (Krista. Personal communication. March 12, 2007). Members can and often do participate for the rest of their lives. In this way, A.A. becomes a way of life.

Agencies such as FourCAST, on the other hand, unfortunately have neither the mandate nor the resources to provide such permanent on-going support. Treatment may only last six or eight sessions before alcoholics are more or less on their own. Recovering and recovered alcoholics may, however, periodically return to FourCAST for "tune-up" appointments with the idea of "keeping on track" (Cormier. Personal communication. March 16, 2007). Also, it is common for the counselors at FourCAST to suggest that their clients seek out on-going support from participation with an A.A. group (Cormier. Personal communicaton. March 16, 2007). In this way, recovering alcoholics may even be considered to get the best of both worlds. They can have confidence in themselves and their own ability to remain sober, as well as confidence in the support of a community and a higher power.

There are differing opinions on the effectiveness of Ministry of Health programs offered by agencies like FourCAST , versus community programs such as offered by A.A. Some people feel that the on-going support and lifestyle of A.A. is the only way full recovery is possible. The core belief in this case is that only other alcoholics can understand the alcohol recovery process because of their own personal experience. It is only through this sympathetic understanding that meaningful help is possible. Others feel that it is only by working with a competent addictions counselor such as those employed by FourCAST, that genuine recovery is possible. The core belief here is that alcoholics must be assisted to work through the underlying personal issues that cause their self destructive behaviours. Also, that medical support agencies are integrated into the program is seen as essential. There is no argument that the two approaches are very different, but if taken from the perspective that help is help, no matter what form it comes in, the differences do not matter. Ultimately it will come down to the individual

alcoholic. What works for one will not always work for the other. Or what works at first

may not continue to work. All that matters is that people suffering from alcoholism can

be helped by one, the other, or both of these programs. Fortunately both are currently

available, at this moment, right here in Peterborough. If you are ready to stop, call them.

References

Addictions carry a cost of $40B each year. (2007, January 24). *The Peterborough Examiner,* p A2.

Alcoholics Anonymous World Services Inc. *The story of how many thousands of men and women have recovered from alcoholism.* New York City, 2001.

Alcoholics Anonymous. *Who! Me? (Brochure, Feb. 2007)*

Johnson, J. L. (2004). *Fundamentals of substance abuse practice.* Brooks/Cole-Thomson Learning. Belmont, CA.

DARTwebpage:http:www.dart.on.ca?DART?owlive?dart_program_info_v2.show_program?p_orgsiteprogram=102441427

Your Baby, Your Touch

Claire Bradley

COMM 79 S06

Nancy Rishor

Friday, March 23, 2007

Your Baby, Your Touch

Imagine your baby is crying. You have tried everything to calm him or her down. Feeding, burping, and diaper changing have all failed, so what do you do next? Have you ever thought about giving your baby a massage? The simple stroking action can have amazing effects on your baby, "just as music hath charms to soothe the savage beast, massage hath charms to soothe the sobbing – and soggy – baby" (Nesteruk, 1989, p.147). Infant massage has been practiced by mothers in Asia and Europe for centuries, with the knowledge being passed down through the generations (Bagshaw & Fox, 2005). But despite all its benefits, infant massage has only become popular in North America in the last 30 years (Zissu, 2005). Recently, more and more parents are realizing that infant massage has the ability to help ease common problems, decrease stress, facilitate growth and development, and to create a strong bond between parent and baby.

Many common problems that infants experience, such as colic, constipation, and teething, can be treated with infant massage. By using a rhythmical stroking motion over the baby's abdomen, along the base of the spine, and even by bending the baby's knees toward the chest, parents can help the baby expel gas, relieving him or her of the pain caused by colic (Heath & Bainbridge, 2000). By following the flow of the small intestine, in clockwise motions from the navel out, the caregivers can ease a baby's constipation by moving the contents of the bowel along the Gastrointestinal Tract (Heath & Bainbridge, 2000). Even teething, the most common of problems babies have to endure, can be soothed with massage. By simply massaging the baby's upper and lower gums, the care giver can ease pain and help the baby to relax, distracting him or her from the pain and discomfort (Heath & Bainbridge, 2000). In addition, if a full body massage is given, often the endorphins released in the body during the massage will help to alleviate the pain of teething (Heath & Bainbridge, 2000). No parents want to see their babies suffer from pain and discomfort, so with a little knowledge of infant massage, parents can make a significant difference in the comfort level of their infant.

Most people probably do not realize that infants suffer from stress. Consider that babies "experience new feelings and situations every day – many of which create excitement, joy, and wonder, but others of which aren't quite so pleasant" (Bagshaw & Fox, 2005, p.23). Babies can develop stress, much like adults do, and believe it or not, stress can have the same effect on babies as it has on adults. Often stress can cause an increase in illness by causing the immune system to become weak, as well as leading to emotional difficulties (Bagshaw & Fox, 2005). By using specific strokes, parents can help their babies to learn to relax. As infants become more familiar with massage, they can then use their memories of the techniques to relax on their own in between sessions (Bagshaw & Fox, 2005). Relaxation triggers a decrease in stress hormones, allowing the infant's immune system to become more efficient. When the immune system is working well, the infant is better equipped fight off illness. In addition, babies can suffer from emotional distress, such as depression, just like adults do. By teaching the baby how to relax naturally, emotional difficulties can be alleviated, as secretion of stress hormones causing depression is inhibited or decreased (Bagshaw & Fox, 2005). This can be done by massaging the baby, as well as the use of simple touch therapy, known as static contact. The feeling of the hands, as well as the heat that radiates from them can help to soothe over-stimulated babies, giving them the feeling of security and love.

It sounds impossible, but in fact, massage can also help to promote growth and development in infants. Regular massage promotes circulation, which in turn increases weight gain, aids in neurological development, and causes an increase in sensory awareness (Bagshaw & Fox, 2005). Babies who receive 5 to 15 minutes of massage per day have a weight gain which is considerably higher than babies who do not receive regular massage (Bagshaw & Fox, 2005). This is caused by enhanced digestion, which allows for better absorption of nutrients in the bowel (Bagshaw & Fox, 2005). Additionally, touch stimulates the human growth hormone, which leads to accelerated growth (Bagshaw & Fox, 2005). Many people wonder why female dogs lick their young so often. The reason why dogs do this is because touch stimulates growth, by licking their young, female dogs help to promote growth (Bagshaw & Fox, 2005). On another note, massage can speed up the process of myelinization of neurons in the brain and spinal cord. Myelinization improves communication between the brain and the body, enhancing the speed at which nerve impulses travel, thus enhancing the neurological development (Infant Massage Information Service, 2006). Lastly, by bringing attention to different parts of their bodies, babies discover what their bodies can do, and how they can experience pleasure (Bagshaw & Fox, 2005). For loving parents, nothing makes them more proud than to see that their babies are thriving, and experiencing the beginning of their lives in the healthiest way possible.

Finally, massage can create a wonderful bond between parent and child. By focusing all their attention on the baby during the massage, parents have the ability to learn about their baby's emotional queues as well as the baby's needs. The ability to trust is very important for babies, so it is important that when parents touch their babies, they do it with all of their attention. Massage can encourage incredible amounts of trust in a baby if done with care (Bagshaw & Fox, 2005). Trust is an important part of personality development, because "babies who are massaged tend to develop strong feelings of trust for their caregivers, and as a result they tend to have experiences with other people that are warm, nurturing, and loving" (Bagshaw & Fox, 2005, p.21). By helping the infant to trust others at such a young age, these feelings of trust can carry on into childhood and adolescence. Additionally, infant massage can also help new or unsure parents to gain more confidence in themselves as caregivers (Bagshaw & Fox, 2005). Many parents feel as though they are failing their children if they can not successfully comfort them. Massage can greatly increase the confidence of the parent, which will reflect on the baby's ability to trust (Bagshaw & Fox, 2005). If the baby feels secure with the parent, he or she will reap all the benefits of a loving and trusting relationship. Bagshaw and Fox (2005) claim that "these early moments truly lay the foundation for [the] relationship" (p.21).

So next time when your baby is in the middle of a crying fit, remember to give your baby a massage. With the numerous benefits that infant massage has to offer from helping to relieve common problems, aiding in growth and development, reducing infant stress, and creating strong bonds between parent and baby, it is nothing but beneficial for you and for your baby. Imagine how much easier it would have been for your parents and grandparents if they had known how beneficial infant massage can be. With nothing but the gentlest touch, you can make a world of difference to your baby.

References

Bagshaw, J., & Fox, I. (2005). *Baby massage for dummies*. Hoboken, NJ: Wiley.

Heath, A., & Bainbridge, N. (2000). *Baby massage: the calming power of touch*. New York: Dorling Kindersley Publishing.

Infant Massage Information Service. (n.d.). *Benefits of infant and childhood massage*. Retrieved March 1, 2007, from http://www.infantmassageimis.com/au/benefits/index.html

Nesteruk, C., Barone, D., Capwell, M., Grandinetti, D., Holman, M., Jacobs, L., LeGro, W., et al. (1989). *Prevention magazine's hands-on healing: massage remedies for hundreds of health problems*. Avenel, NJ: Rodale Press.

Zissu, A. (2005, May 15). For baby, all you knead is love. *The New York Times*. Retrieved from http://www.nytimes.com.

Needle Exchange Programs: a Benefit to Society

Communications for Community Development and Health

Comm79- Section 03

Friday, March 23, 2007

In 2001, The Centres for Disease Control and Prevention (CDC) released a shocking piece of information, alarming the American public and evidating a need for change. An estimated one million individuals within the United States had tested positive for HIV. 36% of these infections were affiliated with contaminated syringes and injection drug use. The Substance Abuse and Mental Health Services Administration suggest that 2.4 million Americans have used injection drugs as of 2001 (Aids Action, 2001). Although Needle Exchange Programs (NEPs) are often misperceived as a form of encouragement or validation for drug use, many benefits have been demonstrated. NEPs improve the lives of injection drug users as well as the community in which they live. Although controversy exists surrounding the idea, Needle Exchange Programs help drug users battle their addiction, prevent the transmission of HIV and decrease the cost of long term medical care.

Exchange Programs bring forth change beginning with the drug users themselves. One of the most important messages that NEPs deliver is that the well-being of the user is still valued although their addiction exists. Fuller (1998) counsels individuals struggling with addictions. He asked his patients who have contracted HIV, for their views on Exchange Programs. Amongst the patience responses, "most wished that someone had cared enough for their welfare to make such an option available when they were in the throes of addiction, possibly preventing the life-threatening condition with which they now struggle" (p.5).

Methadone clinics are another resource offered through NEPs to assist individuals with addictions. The implementation of methadone clinics evolved from the recognition of the body's physical dependence on injections drugs. Many NEPs make referrals to local methadone clinics; however some NEPs have incorporated an on-site clinic

(Addictions Foundation, 2005). Methadone clinics first assess clients for regularity of

drug use, number and duration of unsuccessful attempts to discontinue using and to

which degree the drug use overcomes other important life activities. This is the first step

to determining the individuals requirements of the program and prescribed levels of

methadone. This customized program reduces the occurrence of set-backs. Within one

year of methadone supplementation, clients have "increased coping skills, better

relationships, improved finances and physical health" (para.12). The final step is to

discontinue methadone use; this decision is made by both the client and the physician.

Clients are informed and prepared for the effects of the tapering process and strongly

supported by staff.

A recent addition to many NEPs is a unique venture, the peer education program.

Previous workshops were facilitated by highly educated counsellors who had little to no

personal experience. This lessened the ability to connect to the group and the group's

common goals. "You hire a person who uses drugs- that's an expectation" stated Mason

(2006, p.10). Peer education programs hire a previous user who may have no formal

education or experience in group facilitation, however are provided with training. In turn,

the addiction experience facilitator relies on group input regarding the participant's goals,

expectations and experience to create a program to suite the needs of the group. This

heightens the likeliness of success and improvements of the participants drug usage.

Selecting the peer facilitator is an important part of the process. As stated by Mason

(2006), "for peers who's 'lived experience' is recent, some of the issues and

circumstances they will be dealing with may still be very painful, or even traumatic" (p.11). Though peer education programs can be difficult to initially establish, once in working order. The effectiveness in assisting those through addictions is priceless and life saving.

The transmission of HIV and other blood borne infections have been drastically decreased amongst the general public (Aids Action, 2001). Through NEPs, the safe disposal of used syringes lowers the number of used needles discarded in public areas. It is important to note that users are supplied only one needle in the exchange of a used syringe, and are not simply distributed (Shields, 2005). This method lessens the number of contaminated needles in circulation. In addition, educational programs and reading materials are offered to injection drugs users, raising awareness of how the careless disposal of used syringes in public areas heighten the chances of further transmission of disease. Education is a vital component in the prevention of continued transmission.

For drug users who have contracted HIV, lifestyle management programs are offered as well as referrals to financial assistance in covering costs of medical needs (Aids Action, 2001). The psychological effects and discrimination associated with an individual who has contracted HIV, often leads to low self-esteem and self-worth. Those who have not learned to manage or finance their disease often become resentful towards others and careless about disease prevention. The Canadian Aids Society (2003) states,

> Another study illustrated the connection between poverty and health among people living with HIV, indicating that *low-income* people living with HIV are more likely than high-income people living with HIV to experience depression and helplessness, HIV related discrimination, family tension because of HIV, rejection by family and friends, and alcohol and drug use (p.3).

HIV lifestyle management programs through NEPs educate individuals of the importance in self-care and build on self-worth. In turn, people living with HIV show greater respect for their community and the people around them, lowering instances of the careless transmission of HIV.

In terms of dollars and funding, Exchange programs are economically important. On average, a person who has contracted HIV is expected to live 10.6 years as of 1991. Following this date it should be considered that improvements in medications and medical care have lengthened this time. Over 10.6 years, costs of "inpatient, outpatient costs, physician services and medical costs..." for one individual is estimated at $100,167 "...not including community based services or the increase cost of medications" (Gold, Gafni, Nelligan, Millson, 1997, p.258). The Van Needle Exchange Program in Hamilton, had all costs were monitored in a study over one year. The methods of organization and services offered are generalizable in comparison with many Exchange Programs through out Ontario. The cost of needle exchange services and other services were $76,775 over the year of 1995. Although difficult to monitor for ethical reasons, an estimated 24 cases of injection related HIV transmission would be prevented over 5 years of services through the Hamilton Exchange Program according to Gold et.al. (1997). The previous figures calculate an ultimate saving of $1.3 million after program costs, equalling a 4:1 ratio.

An important note in economical evaluation as stated by Gold et.al. (1997), is that 40% of drug users who tested HIV positive admitted to intimate relationships with non-drug users who did not have HIV. In 1995, of all HIV positive heterosexual men and woman, 80% contracted the disease through intimate relations.

In conclusion, it is evident that NEPs are beneficial to individual drug users, the communities in which they live and are economical to medical institutions and support services. Although controversial at first glance, once all aspects surrounding Exchange Programs are accounted for, it is obvious that support is deserved to all NEPs across the globe.

References

Addictions Foundation of Manitoba. (2005). Services rehabilitation. Retrieved on March

    18, 2007 from www.afm.mb.ca/Services/methadone.htm

Aids Action. (2001, June). *Policy Facts.* Retrieved March 13, 2007 from

    www.aidsaction.org

Canadian Aids Society. (2003, August). HIV and disability policy: evaluating the

    disability tax credit and medical expense tax credit. *Technical Advisory*

    Committee on Tax Measures for Persons with Disabilities. Retrieved on March

    18, 2007 from www.disabilitytax.ca/subs/cas.e.pdf

Fuller, J. (1998, July 18). Needle exchange: saving lives. *The National Catholic Weekly.*

    Retrieved on March 13, 2007 from

    www.americamagazine.org/articles/needleexchangesethics.cfm

Gold, M., Gafni, A., Nelligan, P., Millson, P. (1997, August 1). Needle exchange

    programs: an economical evaluation of a local experience. *Canadian Medical*

    Association. Retrieved on March 18, 2007 from

    www.cmaj.ca/cgi/reprint/157/3/225.pdf

Mason, K. (2006, April). Best practices in harm reduction peer projects. Retrieved on

    March 18, 2007 from www.streethealth.ca

Shields, L. (2005, September). Pharmacy participation in needle exchanges and disposal

    programs for the reduction of the transmission of HIV/AIDS. *Canadian*

    Pharmacists Journal, 138 (7) 5.

Annotated Bibliography

Bernhardt, J., Bernhardt, F. (2007, Feb). *ADHD requires a medical diagnosis what does that mean?*. Retrieved March 5, 2007 from the ADRN website: www.adrn.org

This website explains how Attention Deficit Hyperactivity Disorder must be medically diagnosed. The symptoms must be observable in all settings and last longer than six months. First arrange for a psycho-educational assessment, then medical examination and finally meet with the school. If the child is diagnosed ADHD than the school will implement an Individual Education Plan (IEP) and monitor the child's progress. All documentation of medical history, report cards, family history and surveys completed by the parents and teacher must be provided in order for the diagnosis. There is no blood test to diagnosis ADHD.

This source is useful because it provides a breakdown on how a child's is actually diagnosed with ADHD. The language is very common and easy to understand. This website provides a phone number and a link to contact them with any questions. This makes me believe that it is a creditable source. It was last updated only one month ago so the information is current.

Rubin, R. (2007). FDA orders warning "guides" for ADHD drugs. *USA Today*, 734 (7456), 06d.

The makers of 15 drugs related to the treatment of ADHD have 30 days to finalize warning labels for 7% of school age and 4% of adults taking the drugs. There were many reports of unexpected death, psychosis, manic behavior, heart and psychiatric risks. Other drugs related to asthma have been issued a "black box" warning, which is the strongest warning of all. Some of the drugs included in the warnings are, Adderal (XR), Concerta, Daytrana, Desoxyn, Ritalin and many more drugs associated with ADHD.

This article is useful because it proves what an epidemic it is with all these children taking harmful drugs to alter their behavior. The language is easy to understand and I found no grammatical errors. The source if from the FDA which should be creditable although, there are no names or credentials provided from that source. It was only published one month ago, so the information is current and accurate with the times.

Debate over warnings for ADHD stimulants. (2006). *Child Health Alert*, 24, 1.

An advisory committee recommended a warning used on stimulant drugs used to treat ADHD because of reports of sudden death and cardiovascular problems. Cardiovascular problems are unlikely in children and FDA officials are worried that warning patients may scare them away from a drug that they need. The FDA comments that the committee's have not been careful enough in the past and it is predicted that they now will be overly cautious.

This article is not useful because it only provides speculation and no actual facts. The language is easy to understand however, it is only left to assume what FDA stands for. The grammar is very well put together and professional. There are no credentials or author so the creditability is not backed up. This article was from the year 2006, so the information is out dated. I know from other research that the warnings have already been put into place.

Grant, J.D. (2006, Oct 18). Rethinking ADHD: pills may not be the solution. *The Chronicle Herald*, p.A11.

In Canada, drugs associated with ADHD are in the top six of most prescribed medication, although, not long term studies have shown these drugs to be very beneficial and provide little evidence that they reduce "core" features of ADHD. There are many side effects of the drugs from chest pain to as severe as sudden death. Perhaps it is time to rethink the current strategy of drug treatment and explore other measures.

I found this article to be very useful, with lots of facts and statistics, only I am unsure where the statistics came from. I found the language easy to read. The author has a Masters Degree in Pediatrics and it even offers the town in which he lives. This shows me that he is willing to back up his work and it is accurate.

JOURNAL/ NEWSPAPER ARTICLES

Love, Language, and Emergent Literacy

Debby Zambo and Cory Cooper Hansen

Kelsey heard her first stories while still in her mother's womb. Her dad would curl up close and tell her about the family anxiously waiting for her and the love they already felt for her. Oral stories continued after Kelsey was born, and they became an important part of her life, along with other forms of language and literacy: floppy fabric books, chunky board books, quiet lullabies, favorite nursery rhymes, and a vinyl sleeve of family photos.

Kelsey experienced language and literacy with all her consistent care-givers—her parents, a sibling, relatives, a neighbor, and child care providers. She began to associate language and literacy experiences with her growing feelings of love and happiness. When tired and irritable, she signaled her need to be wrapped up with language and literacy, pressing a favorite book against the leg of the person caring for her. To Kelsey, books became a way to communicate her need to be held, soothed with a familiar voice, and comforted with love and a story or lullaby.

Pathways to Emotional Development of the Very Young

HOW CAN LANGUAGE AND LITERACY enhance emotional development in the very young (birth to three years)? Although all children begin to understand their world through language and social interaction, literacy differs from culture to culture. It can range from oral stories of personal and cultural relevance to songs of ethnic pride and includes a variety of ways to record language and experiences.

Our purpose in this article is to explain the language/literacy connection to emotional development and to focus particularly on young children's experiences with various forms of picture books. Emotional competence, however, can develop through virtually any form of literacy, whether it is a magazine, a cereal box, or an electronic story on a computer.

Developing emotional competence, or the ability to control one's emotions in an age-appropriate way, hinges on the quality of children's attachment established in the first three years of life. Attachment is the strong emotional bond developed between young children and their caregivers (Honig 2002). Children use the attachments they form as a secure base from which they explore the world (Siegel 1999). A part of the important development of attachment happens in read-aloud times, as storybook sharing becomes an occasion through which children learn language, play with ideas, and build trust and understanding.

Emotions: The foundation of learning

Babies who do not develop strong attachments often fail to learn how to control their emotions and organize their world. Language can be difficult to master, and children may feel emotionally distraught (Greenspan & Shanker

Debby Zambo, PhD, is an assistant professor at Arizona State University in Phoenix. Before coming to the university, Debby worked as a special education teacher of primary age children. She can be reached at debby.zambo@asu.edu. Debby and Cory collaborate to explore children's literature within child development issues.

Cory Cooper Hansen, PhD, is an assistant professor in the Early Childhood Department at the west campus of Arizona State University. Cory is an early childhood reading specialist and currently teaches language and literacy methods.

Illustrations © Sylvie Wickstrom.

2004). If this happens repeatedly, they come to judge the world as a place without caring and develop feelings of mistrust and doubt (Erikson [1950] 1993).

Emotions are the feelings, both psychological and physiological, that people have in response to events that are personally meaningful to their needs and wants (Goleman 1995; Saarni 1998). A century ago, however, when William James ([1890] 1950) published *The Principles of Psychology,* he believed the minds and hearts of young children possessed few emotions. His notion held for a very long time. Infants were thought to be simple-minded creatures able to express only primitive emotions like anger, happiness, and sadness. In the time since 1890, scientists have used new methodologies to discover a much different picture of young children, one that shows how innately emotional babies are (Greenspan & Shanker 2004). Now we know that newborns begin life with basic emotions (fear, anger, and joy) and begin to experience complex feelings (jealousy, frustration, empathy) early on in their development.

Learning through sensory experiences: Birth through 18 months

The very young feel sensations, respond with emotions, and look to caregivers to help them understand and interpret the things they feel. They draw on these caregiving experiences to cope with intense feelings or emotions that are uncomfortable sometimes. Through experiences of loving care, infants begin to regulate and modulate the new emotions they feel.

Voice. Hearing is one of the early senses through which infants create a bond with their mothers, and this happens even before birth. DeCasper and Fifer (1980) had pregnant women read a Dr. Seuss book to their babies. After they were born, the babies sucked harder on special pacifiers when listening to the same familiar voice and soothing rhythm. Other researchers note that comfort also can come from the voices of fathers, siblings, relatives, and child care providers (Howes 1998). This universal occurrence explains why caregivers from all cultures use songs and lullabies to soothe infants (Honig 2005).

Sight. At one month, infants tend to gaze longer at faces than at objects (Ludeman 1991). By four months, they recognize emotions in facial expressions, and this ability becomes a key to social development (Nelson & Collins 1991). By six months, babies are imitating facial

expressions associated with emotions, and they react to the emotional state viewed (Montague & Walker-Andrews 2001).

Games such as Peekaboo and I'm Gonna Get You help infants see emotions on our faces, feel intense emotions themselves, and regulate their feelings. Playing games with facial expressions becomes instructive as well as fun, helping infants learn how to react to situations that may be out of the ordinary or confusing (Walden & Baxter 1989). This ability, called social referencing, is one of the most important learning experiences young children encounter in their bridging an understanding between the self, others, and the world (Greenspan & Shanker 2004).

Touch and taste. Infants' mouths and hands are highly sensitive areas (Owens 2002). All over the world, babies explore new objects by reaching for and putting them in their mouths. Sensations arising from skin-to-skin or skin-to-fabric contact become coded with emotional responses, like happiness, comfort, and love (Greenspan & Shanker 2004). The soothing from a gentle massage promotes bonding and security between caregiver and child. Cuddling with a soft, snuggly blanket or with one's caregiver can make any child feel loved. Multisensory exploration of the environment, with loving support from those who care, helps children experience the sensory integration they need to get ready to learn.

Babies who have had responsive, consistent experiences with caregivers develop self-soothing behaviors like thumb sucking or touching a favorite blanket or toys (McDevitt & Ormrod 2004). These behaviors help them regulate or cope with stressful emotions in age-appropriate ways or when caregivers cannot respond immediately.

Read-alouds with infants

Most infants find out about books the same way they discover the rest of the world—tasting the pages, smelling the book, rubbing the cover, banging it against a surface, and imitating what the important people in their lives do with books. From birth to three months, read-alouds are purely an emotional connection between infant and caregiver. Being held, feeling good, and hearing a familiar, comforting voice are more important than the kind of book or the content of the story. Lullabies, singsong stories, and other repetitive, rhythmic experiences bring joy and comfort to infants and establish a special time together for child and caregiver.

> **Brightly colored illustrations and a single object on a page invite babies to reach for the picture.**

The way a book is made becomes more important when reading to four- to six-month-olds. Cloth and vinyl books are appropriate because they are easy to grasp and will not hurt babies when they try to explore them with their mouths. These first books are often washable and will not disintegrate when being gummed. Brightly colored illustrations and a single object on a page invite babies to reach for the picture. Combined with a familiar voice and simple text, babies can begin the important act of interacting with books.

By seven to nine months, the developed pincer grip allows infants to handle board books, which are made to fit little hands and sturdy enough to withstand repeated readings. Books with stiff pages are easily turned by chubby fingers and attractive enough to briefly capture a baby's fleeting attention. Bright, colorful illustrations encourage the reader to name objects and invite babies to point to the pictures, further promoting interaction with the book and developing emerging language skills (Green, Lilly, & Barrett 2002).

> **Well-chosen picture books can open up conversations about fears and allow caregivers and toddlers both to address the issue.**

Babies approaching one year show strong involvement when being read to. They babble along in tones that sound like reading and take turns in turning the pages (Schickedanz 1999). The reader's exaggerated facial expressions capture babies' attention and help them develop social referencing skills (Greenspan & Shanker 2004). Voice tone and rhythm too continue to be important stimulation. Infants further associate the contact, comfort, and security that reading brings with their growing feelings of attachment.

Stories begin to capture the one-year-old's attention and interest, and more give-and-take occurs in the reading experience. Traditional favorites, like *Pat the Bunny*, by Dorothy Kunhardt, have interactive pages that allow for sensory stimulation. For example, the child can stroke a page with soft fur like that of a bunny or touch scratchy sandpaper that feels like daddy's beard.

Learning through social experiences: 18 months to three years

Children have developed a range of emotions by toddlerhood, along with a sense of self, language skill, and physical independence.

Sense of self. By two years of age most children recognize themselves in a mirror, and with this recognition they develop a new self-consciousness and emotions like guilt, envy, embarrassment, and pride. They feel proud when they accomplish a task that once seemed insurmountable and embarrassed when they violate a social norm (Kagan & Snidman 2004). As children begin to know themselves, they begin to understand how other people feel. Toddlers can show empathy and caring, especially toward others who are hurt or in distress (Wardle 2003).

Not all emotions are positive, and fear also emerges in toddlerhood. In a toddler's mind, fear is often connected to unknown situations. Many are afraid of the dark and of imaginary creatures. Such worries are common but of little continuing concern for most children (Wardle 2003). Readalouds with a sensitive caregiver help address these stressful emotions. Well-chosen picture books can open up conversations about fears and allow caregivers and toddlers both to address the issue (see examples in "Appropriate Books for Infants and Toddlers," p. 37).

Language. With growing language skills, toddlers begin to talk about their emotions and develop a vocabulary of emotional words, such as *mad*, *happy*, and *yucky*. As early as two to three years of age, children can talk about emotions they and others feel, and they realize that emotions connect with desires and needs (Wellman et al. 1995).

Read-alouds are one way to promote the use of vocabulary to describe emotions and to encourage empathy and caring. Talking about a character's feelings can allow toddlers to vicariously experience emotions and consider how others might feel.

Physical development. Toddlers begin to assert a growing independence that is now possible because of their developing physical and motor skills. Asserting themselves often involves the word *no* and their refusal to do things they once did happily. Emotions correlated with their growing independence can sometimes get the best of toddlers, such as when they do not get their own way.

Caregivers need to model appropriate ways to handle strong emotions and can lower the frustration levels of toddlers by being attuned and responsive to their needs. Many read-aloud books are available to help toddlers and their caregivers explore appropriate emotional responses.

Read-alouds with toddlers

In settings where story reading is connected with feelings of comfort, safety, and love, toddlers come to associate the language and social interaction as being as much a part of the experience as the book itself (Barrera & Bauer 2003). For many toddlers, the read-aloud is an active experience. For example, Kelsey's mother (introduced in this article's opening vignette) often found herself reading aloud while her two-year-old played in the bathtub or in her high chair. Most toddlers who have grown up with the established routine of read-alouds will themselves initiate times for reading together. They will choose storybooks and plead to hear their favorites repeatedly.

By age 18 months children begin to recognize story characters and enjoy books about familiar, beloved friends. Most toddlers love books containing animal characters and books about children who look like them and experience everyday events, like taking a bath, eating, getting dressed, and learning to use the potty (Schickedanz 1999).

Books for toddlers are typically organized by child development topics, such as learning the ABCs, 123s, colors, and shapes, along with categories such as touch-and-feel books or topics like toilet training or dealing with new expe-

riences. Some of today's publishers offer well-illustrated infant and toddler books featuring a wide diversity of cultures and ethnicities.

Toddlers who are encouraged to play with books and listen to stories develop book-handling skills (where to open a book, how to hold it, and where to look for pictures and the story), and they have an easier time learning to read (Morrow 2004). Pointing to pictures, asking questions, and gesturing to key elements promote children's vocabulary development, sense of gaining mastery over the environment and their emotions, and development of important emergent literacy skills (Schickedanz 1999).

Most 18-month-olds become interested in words and picture books because of their usefulness. Playing the name game has caregivers asking, "What's that?" with toddlers looking closely before announcing the names of objects. Before long, children who have had this experience ask, "Wa dat?" and the conversation goes back and forth. An adult's enthusiastic responses can contribute to toddlers' language development, their play with ideas, and a growing confidence as they learn about their families and life outside their homes.

Phonemic awareness (of the sounds that make up words) is an important emergent literacy skill developed by children as they talk with caregivers and respond to books. This auditory skill developed through play with language is a powerful predictor for early reading success (Adams 1990). For example, after hearing a favorite Dr. Seuss book many times, Nick (27 months old) chanted "lalla la lee lo" while he played (Green, Lilly, & Barrett 2002).

Books with songlike features, repetitive parts, and rhymes invite children to join in the play with language and to experiment with the sounds of words. Increasingly, board book publishers have recognized authors skilled at providing these kinds of literary experiences and are publishing books that promote language skills and emotional development. As a result, caregivers and their toddlers can have fun with language, use it in play experiences, and together create shared literacy experiences.

Conclusion

Babies come into the world as emotional beings, but still they have much emotional growth to accomplish. The real work in infancy is establishing a strong emotional attachment between the child and at least one person who returns a comparable depth of emotion. Two identified characteristics of parenting that

> **Reading to babies is a sensory experience; reading with toddlers is an active, joyous challenge contributing to cognitive growth.**

lead to secure attachment are responsiveness and warm physical contact (Greenspan & Shanker 2004). Engaging in read-alouds with infants addresses both characteristics. The comforting sound of the caregiver's voice, touch, and emotional attunement to a baby's needs demonstrates responsiveness. Being held, feeling safe, gazing into a caregiver's face, and experiencing love exemplify warm physical contact.

Reading to babies is a sensory experience; reading with toddlers is an active, joyous challenge contributing to cognitive growth. Regular read-alouds establish times for toddlers and caregivers to connect socially, emotionally, cognitively, and physically. New experiences, scary thoughts, everyday events, and the whole world outside can all be explored through the pages of a book and the reassurances of a caregiver.

References

Adams, M. 1990. *Beginning to read: Thinking and learning about print.* Cambridge, MA: MIT Press.

Barrera, R.B., & E.B. Bauer. 2003. Storybook reading and young bilingual children: A review of the literature. In *On reading books to children: Parents and teachers,* eds. A. van Kleeck, S.A. Stahl, & E.B. Bauer, 253–70. Mahwah, NJ: Lawrence Erlbaum.

DeCasper, A.J., & W.P. Fifer. 1980. Of human bonding: Newborns prefer their mother's voice. *Science* 208: 1174–76.

Erikson, E.H. [1950] 1993. *Childhood and society.* New York: Norton.

Goleman, D. 1995. *Emotional intelligence.* New York: Bantam.

Green, C.R., E. Lilly, & T.M. Barrett. 2002. Families reading together: Connecting literature and life. *Journal of Research in Childhood Education* 16 (2): 248–61.

Greenspan, S.G., & S. Shanker. 2004. *The first idea: How symbols, language and intelligence evolved from our primate ancestors to modern humans.* Cambridge, MA: DaCapo.

Honig, A.S. 2002. *Secure relationships: Nurturing infant/toddler attachment in early care settings.* Washington, DC: NAEYC.

Honig, A.S. 2005. The language of lullabies. *Young Children* 60 (5): 30–36.

Howes, C. 1998. The earliest friendships. In *The company they keep: Friendships in childhood and adolescence,* eds. W.M. Bukowski, A.F. Newcomb, & W.W. Hartup, 66–86. New York: Cambridge University Press.

James, W. [1890] 1950. *The principles of psychology.* New York: Dover.

Kagan, J., & N. Snidman. 2004. *The long arm of temperament.* Cambridge, MA: Belknap of Harvard University Press.

Appropriate Books for Infants and Toddlers

The following are books that can help foster conversations with children and promote emotional development. To build an engaging library, search out book publishers and authors who understand the needs and interests of babies and toddlers.

Fears and new situations

Albee, S. 2003. *Blue's checkup*. New York: Simon and Schuster.
Frankel, A. 1979. *Once upon a potty*. New York: Harper Festival.

Gomi, T. 1997. *Everyone poops*. La Jolla, CA: Kane/Miller.
Johnson, M. 1987. *Caillou: What's that noise?* Montreal, Quebec, Canada: Chouette Publishing.

Emotional understandings and expression

Agassi, M. 2002. *Hands are not for hitting*. Minneapolis, MN: Free Spirit Publishing.
Parr, T. 2000. *The feelings book*. New York: Little, Brown.
Shannon, D. 2005. *David smells!* New York: Blue Sky.

Play with language, repetitive or predictable parts, and rhythm

Books by Sandra Boynton, Margaret Wise Brown, Eric Carle, Bill Martin Jr., Dr. Seuss, and Peter Sis.

Cloth, bathtub, and touch-and-feel book series

Innovative Kids. 2005. *My giant 123 bath book*. Norwalk, CT.
Priddy Books. 2004. *Touch colors*. New York: St. Martin's Press.
Taggies. 2004. *Sweet dreams*. New York: Scholastic.

Concept and vocabulary development

Baby Einstein Series. New York: Hyperion Books for Children.

Dorling Kindersley Board Book Series. London, England.
Katz, K. 2000. *Where is baby's belly button?* New York: Little Simon.

Diverse illustrations and experiences

Acredolo, L., & S. Goodwyn. 2002. *My first baby signs*. New York: Harper Festival.
Bauer, M.D. 2003. *Toes, ear, and nose*. New York: Little Simon.
Newcome, Z. 2002. *Head, shoulders, knees, and toes*. Cambridge, MA: Candlewick Press.

Interaction with book features and the reader

Aigner-Clark, J. 2005. *Baby da Vinci: My body*. New York: Hyperion. (Mirrors focus attention.)
Kunhardt, D. 1940. *Pat the bunny*. New York: Golden Books Publishing. (Touching and playing peekaboo.)
My happy baby. 2004. New York: Scholastic. (Cloth books attach to crib, stroller, or car seat.)

Ludeman, P.M. 1991. Generalized discrimination of positive facial expressions by 7- and 10-month-old infants. *Child Development* 62: 55–67.
McDevitt, T.M., & J.E. Ormrod. 2004. *Child development: Educating and working with children and adolescents*. 2nd ed. Upper Saddle River, NJ: Merrill Prentice Hall.
Montague, D.P.F., & A.S. Walker-Andrews. 2001. Peekaboo: A new look at infants' perceptions of emotion expression. *Developmental Psychology* 37: 826–38.
Morrow, L. 2004. *Literacy development in the early years: Helping children read and write*. 5th ed. Boston: Allyn & Bacon.
Nelson, C.A., & P.E. Collins. 1991. Event-related potential and looking-time analysis of infants' responses to familiar and novel events: Implications for visual recognition memory. *Developmental Psychology* 27: 50–58.
Owens, K.B. 2002. *Child and adolescent development: An integrated approach*. Belmont, CA: Wadsworth/Thompson Learning.

Saarni, C. 1998. *The development of emotional competence*. New York: Guilford.
Schickedanz, J.A. 1999. *Much more than the ABCs: The early stages of reading and writing*. 2nd ed. Washington, DC: NAEYC.
Siegel, D.J. 1999. *The developing mind*. New York: Guilford.
Walden, T.A., & A. Baxter. 1989. The effect of context and age on social referencing. *Child Development* 60: 1511–18.
Wardle, F. 2003. *Introduction to early childhood education: A multidimensional approach to child-centered care and learning*. New York: Allyn & Bacon.
Wellman, H.M., P.L. Harris, M. Banerjee, & A. Sinclair. 1995. Early understanding of emotion: Evidence from natural language. *Cognition and Emotion* 9: 117–49.

Using Time-Out Effectively in the Classroom

Joseph B. Ryan

Sharon Sanders

Antonis Katsiyannis

Mitchell L. Yell

Teachers of students with disabilities frequently use time-out as a behavior management strategy. When implemented properly, time-out procedures can be effective in reducing maladaptive behaviors across a wide range of student populations. Time-outs, however, are subject to abuse when educators fail to understand and apply the behavioral principles that make the procedures effective in reducing problem behaviors. Some teachers continue to use time-outs even when they are not effective in reducing a student's inappropriate behavior. Moreover, the inappropriate use of time-out may lead to legal problems; recent court cases have ruled that extreme use of time-out procedures may violate students' individual rights (Yell, 2006).

What does "time-out" mean, in practice? What are the major types of time-outs, and what is their efficacy in schools? What common practices lead to the ineffective use of time-out? In this article, we examine these questions, and provide recommendations for using time-out in an appropriate and effective manner.

Educators who work with students with emotional and behavioral disorders (E/BD) frequently face the challenge of striving to increase desirable behaviors of their students while simultaneously decreasing antisocial behaviors. Research has demonstrated that consistently and systematically reinforcing a desirable behavior maintains or increases it (Alberto & Troutman, 2006; Wolery, Bailey, & Sugai, 1988). However, when teachers encounter student problem behaviors that need to be decreased, they may need to use behavior reduction procedures such as time-out. Time-out has been used by teachers to address a broad range of maladaptive behaviors across a variety of educational placements (Costenbader & Reading-Brown, 1995). A survey of teachers of students with E/BD in the Midwest found that nearly three quarters (70%) used time-out in their classrooms at some time (Zabel, 1986).

What Is "Time-Out"?

To identify articles related to time-out, we searched the Educational Resources Information Center database, LEGALTRAC, psychINFO and FindArticles using relevant keywords (*time-out, seclusion, exclusion, inclusion, think time, contingent observation,* and *cool down*). Second, we completed a hand search of studies published between 1970 to 2005 in peer-reviewed journals (*Journal of Special Education, American Journal of Orthopsychiatry, Journal of Emotional and Behavioral Disorders, Behavioral Disorders,* and *Exceptional Children*). Finally, we conducted an ancestral search by checking the citations from relevant studies to determine if any of the articles cited would qualify for inclusion in this review. We did not review literature related to time-out if it pertained to procedures conducted outside the educational environment (e.g., home settings, parent training).

From a behaviorist perspective, time-out is defined as a behavior reduction procedure or form of punishment in which students are denied access to all opportunities for reinforcement, contingent upon their displaying inappropriate behavior (Alberto & Troutman, 2006). Thus, a behavior is reduced by withdrawing the opportunity for reinforcement for a period of time following the occurrence of the behavior (Nelson & Rutherford, 1983). However, teachers often think of time-out as a procedure to allow a student to calm down, typically by being quiet and disengaging from current stressors (Ryan, Peterson, Tetreault & van der Hagen, in press a). Regardless of these popular definitions, a wide range of variations of this procedure is currently implemented in schools across the United States.

Types of Time-Out

"Time-out" is not a single strategy, but rather refers to a number of related procedures designed to reduce inappropriate student behavior by removing a student from a reinforcing environment.

There are four primary types of time-out, which range from the least intrusive to the most restrictive: inclusion time-out, exclusion time-out, seclusion time-out, and restrained time-out. In each of these procedures, when a student exhibits the target behavior, the student's teacher reduces the student's access to reinforcement for a period of time.

Inclusion Time-Out

Inclusion time-out (sometimes called nonexclusionary time-out) is the least intrusive form of time-out; it generally involves removing reinforcement from a student rather than removing the student from the reinforcing environment (Cooper, Heron, & Heward, 1987; Harris, 1985; Wolery et al., 1988). The student continues to observe classroom instruction, but is denied an opportunity to participate in activities or receive reinforcement from either peers or the teacher (Ryan, Peterson, Tetreault & van der Hagen, in press b). A number of variations of inclusion time-out have been defined in the literature, including: (a) planned ignoring, (b) withdrawal of materials, (c) contingent observation, and (d) time-out ribbon.

Planned Ignoring. This procedure involves the "systematic withdrawal of social attention for a predetermined time period upon the onset of mild levels of problem behavior" (Knoster, Wells, & McDowell, 2003, p. 12). Nelson and Rutherford (1983) described planned ignoring as in-seat time-out. In planned ignoring time-out a teacher—contingent on the occurrence of inappropriate behavior—removes his or her attention from a student for a brief period of time (Wolery et al., 1988). At the end of the time-out interval, the teacher returns attention to the student.

When using planned ignoring time-out, it is important to focus on praising a student's appropriate behaviors while ignoring those that are inappropriate. Research conducted on planned ignoring has shown mixed results regarding its efficacy. For example, although the procedure was shown to be effective in increasing a preschool student's prosocial behaviors in general education (Allen, Hart, Buell, Harris, & Wolf,

1964), it was unsuccessful in reducing the inappropriate behaviors of a preschool student with E/BD (Plummer, Baer, & LeBlanc, 1977).

Withdrawal of Materials. As the name implies, this time-out procedure involves removing reinforcing materials from a student for a specified period of time when the student exhibits inappropriate behavior. For example, if a student throws a crayon at a peer during class, the teacher would remove the student's crayons for a predetermined time frame. Usually, the withdrawal of materials is accompanied by the removal of adult attention (Wolery et al., 1988). In earlier studies, withdrawal of materials (i.e., loss of tokens) was shown to be as effective at reducing noncompliance as using an inclusion time-out procedure (Contingent Observation) with students with mental retardation (MR; Burchard & Barerra, 1972; Gresham, 1979).

"Time-out" is not a single strategy, but rather refers to a number of related procedures designed to reduce inappropriate student behavior by removing a student from a reinforcing environment.

Contingent Observation. In contingent observation time-out, a student (contingent on an inappropriate behavior) is required to move to another location in the classroom and is instructed to observe the class without participating or interacting in any way for a predetermined period of time. "Sit and watch," "cool down," and "penalty box on the playground" are all variations of contingent observation. Wolery and colleagues (1988) stated that although instructional activities are interrupted when contingent observation is used, students may learn appropriate ways of behaving through imitation because they can still observe classroom activities. Hence, this is often considered to be the least restrictive form of time-out a teacher can implement. There is also some research that supports the concept

that contingent observation is as effective, if not more so, than more restrictive forms of time-out. Mace and Heller (1990) demonstrated that contingent observation was as effective as the more restrictive exclusion time-out in reducing disruptive behavior in a 7-year-old boy with E/BD. Similarly, Gallagher, Mittelstadt, & Slater (1988) showed that contingent observation time-out could be as effective in reducing undesirable behaviors as the more restrictive seclusion time-out for a student with E/BD in a special day school.

Time-Out Ribbon. The time-out ribbon is another example of inclusion time-out; the student wears a ribbon or other object as long as he or she behaves appropriately. When a student exhibits inappropriate behavior, the ribbon is removed for a brief period of time. When the ribbon is removed, so is access to reinforcement (Salend & Gordon, 1987). There are four primary advantages to using the time-out ribbon procedure: (a) a teacher does not have to remove a student from instruction; (b) when in time-out, students can observe other students behaving appropriately; (c) the teacher and other adults in a classroom can clearly see who is eligible for reinforcement; and (d) the ribbon clearly signals students when reinforcement is available and when they are in time-out.

Earlier research has shown the use of the time-out ribbon to be effective in reducing talking out of turn and out of seat behavior in four general education elementary school classrooms (Fee, Matson, & Manikam, 1990); elementary special education classrooms (Salend & Gordon, 1987; Salend & Maragulia, 1983); and for students with MR (Foxx & Shapiro, 1978; Huguenin & Mulick, 1981; Solnick, Rincover, & Peterson, 1977; Spitalnik & Drabman, 1976).

Exclusion Time-Out

Often when teachers use time-out, they remove the student who exhibited the inappropriate behavior from the reinforcing setting. This is referred to as exclusion time-out. In exclusion time-out, a student is excluded from the reinforcing area, usually repositioned away from his or her peers. Wolery and colleagues (1988) defined exclusion time-out as any procedure that (a) requires that a student be removed from instructional activities, (b) does not require the student to watch others (as in contingent observation or sit-and-watch), and (c) does not require a student to sit in a specifically designated time-out room (seclusion time-out). Some examples of exclusion time-out include placing a student (a) in the corner of a classroom facing the wall, (b) behind a partition in the classroom, or (c) in another teacher's classroom (e.g., "think time"). The efficacy of exclusion time-out has not been researched as thoroughly as inclusion time-out. In one of the first studies exploring exclusion time-out, it was shown to be effective in reducing disruptive behaviors in a general education elementary school classroom (Nau, Van Houten, & O'Neil, 1981). A decade later, exclusion time-out proved to be more effective at reducing noncompliance than a guided compliance technique in which the teacher helped preschool children complete a requested task using guided hand-over-hand movement (Handen, Parrish, McClung, Kerwin, & Evans, 1992).

Seclusion Time-Out

Seclusion time-out, sometimes called isolation time-out, is a very restrictive form of time-out. In seclusion time-out a student is removed from the classroom and placed in a room or area in which s/he is prohibited from leaving until the time-out period is served (Busch & Shore, 2000). The procedure typically involves placing a student in a (a) comfort room, (b) quiet room, (c) cool-down room, or (d) time-out room. The efficacy of seclusion time-out has only been investigated twice in an educational setting, with mixed results. The first study (Webster, 1976) was conducted with only a single student with E/BD, and demonstrated a significant decrease in aggressive behaviors. However, the second study (Smith, 1981) showed seclusion time-outs had no effect on maladaptive behaviors for students with E/BD or MR. We do not recommend that seclusion time-out be used by staff without specific training and established policy guidelines due to

the inherent risk of injury and potential abuses commonly associated with its use.

Restrained Time-Out

Restrained time-out, sometimes referred to as physical time-out or movement suppression, is the most restrictive form of time-out. This procedure combines both a restraint and time-out procedure. Its use is typically limited to younger children (e.g., preschool) who refuse to comply with a teacher-directed time-out. The adult places the student into a time-out position and maintains the student in time-out through the use of physical (ambulatory) restraint. This restraint is typically accomplished by the teacher using a basket-hold technique. Restrained time-out, also called movement suppression, was effective in reducing aggressive behaviors for a student with E/BD (Noll & Simpson, 1979), and another with MR (Luiselli, Suskin, & Slocumb, 1984). It was also effective in reducing self-injurious behaviors for a student with E/BD (Rolider & Van Houten, 1985). Again, we do not recommend that seclusion time-out be used by staff without specific training and established policy guidelines due to the inherent risk of injury and potential abuses commonly associated with its use.

Common Problems That Make Time-Out Ineffective

Many educators successfully incorporate some form of time-out procedures into their approaches to reducing a student's inappropriate behavior. Unfortunately, the effectiveness of this procedure may be compromised if any of several common mistakes are made by teachers when using time-out. Typical pitfalls include classroom environments that are insufficiently reinforcing to the students, and time-out procedures that lose their punishing qualities and take on reinforcing qualities for both the student and teacher.

Insufficiently Reinforcing Classrooms

Perhaps the most important concept for teachers to recognize is that for time-out to be effective, students must want to

participate in ongoing classroom activities. The term "time-out" implies that the "time-in" environment (i.e., the classroom) is reinforcing, and that a student would prefer to remain in that setting. Therefore, there must be a meaningful difference between the level of reinforcement during time-in and time-out (Harris, 1985); too often, however, the "time-in" environment is not sufficiently reinforcing to make time-out a punishment, thereby effectively reducing the level of inappropriate behaviors. In fact, in classrooms that are not sufficiently reinforcing, students may find the time-in environment to be more aversive than rewarding (Plummer et al., 1977).

Perhaps the most important concept for teachers to recognize is that for time-out to be effective, students must want to participate in ongoing classroom activities.

Reinforcing Aspects of Time-Out

A second reason time-out may be ineffective in reducing maladaptive behavior is that both the teacher and student are often inadvertently being reinforced by the implementation of time-outs within the classroom. For example, most teachers have experienced a student whose levels of misbehavior escalate whenever s/he is assigned a difficult task. As a result of the student's disturbance, the teacher responds by using a time-out procedure such as exclusion, sending the student outside the classroom to sit in the hallway. In such cases, the time-out serves as an opportunity for the student to escape (at least temporarily) from performing an assignment. In effect, this time-out has inadvertently reinforced the student for misbehaving, by removing an aversive task. As a result, the child is more likely to repeat the inappropriate behavior the next time a similar task is assigned.

To make matters worse, teachers might also find themselves being reinforced because the student's absence from the classroom eliminates the student's disruption, thus allowing the teacher to escape the aversive behavior. The teacher is also allowed to continue teaching unimpeded by the student's maladaptive behavior. As a result, the teacher often has little or no incentive to call the student back into the classroom. This inadvertent negative reinforcement or removal of aversive stimuli for both the teacher and student alike may result in time-out procedures losing their punishing qualities in reducing inappropriate behaviors. In such cases, research has shown the frequency and duration of time-out may even increase with each recurring incidence as the procedure itself becomes a reinforcer for maladaptive behavior (Nelson & Rutherford, 1983). How can a teacher ensure time-outs are effective in reducing maladaptive behaviors without violating a student's inherent rights to safety and his or her access to the educational environment?

Recommendations

Make the Classroom Reinforcing

Time-out procedures are only effective in reducing maladaptive behaviors when the student is removed from an environment that s/he finds reinforcing. If the student does not have a desire to be included or to participate in the classroom or activity, it is unlikely that implementing a time-out will have the desired effect. For example, when a child is removed from a recess activity (e.g., playing tag) due to unsportsmanlike conduct, s/he will typically comply with a teacher's request to sit quietly on the sidelines for a few minutes to gather composure and think about their transgressions. The child willingly complies with the teacher directed time-out because of a desire to participate in the recess activity. The likelihood of compliance decreases, however, when students are placed in an unrewarding environment in which they do not perceive they are receiving sufficient positive reinforcement. In this instance, the time-out does not serve as a time-out from reinforcement, but rather as a

means of escape from or avoidance of an unpleasant task or activity.

To ensure time-out procedures are an effective behavior management strategy, teachers can make their classrooms more reinforcing for their students, by increasing the ratio of positive to negative comments, and use effective teaching strategies.

Strive for a 5-to-1 Ratio of Positive to Negative Comments. Although teacher praise has been supported as an empirically sound practice (Maag & Katsiyannis, 1999; see also Lewis, Hudson, Richter, & Johnson, 2004), in actuality negative comments or reprimands for inappropriate behavior exceed by far positive reinforcing comments (Sutherland, 2000). In fact, research indicates that classes in which the teacher has a strongly positive reinforcement ratio often have fewer behavior problems (Sugai & Horner, 2002). When teachers use a 5-to-1 ratio of positive to negative comments, the classroom will have a more reinforcing atmosphere—an atmosphere from which students will not want to be removed. For example, when a student enters the room in an appropriate manner or completes an assignment, the teacher should reinforce these behaviors by thanking the student for each specific behavior. Such focus on positive attributes helps the student better understand what behaviors are expected, increases on-task behaviors, and creates a more positive atmosphere in the classroom (see Sutherland, Wehby, & Copeland, 2000).

Use Effective Teaching Strategies. An essential ingredient for effective classroom management is the overall strength of instruction. This includes good time management procedures, such as quick pace and well-planned transitions; good instructional implementation, such as guided practice and planned review; and effective academic monitoring. Engaging students in interesting instructional activities minimizes the likelihood of behavioral disturbances. When students experience downtime and teachers are distracted from instruction, however, misbehavior is more likely to occur.

Additionally, there is a substantial body of literature supporting the importance of high levels of correct on-level academic responding by students (see Gunter & Denny, 1998). When students have more opportunities to respond and accuracy of responses is increased, it is likely that on-task behavior will improve and inappropriate behavior will decrease (Sutherland & Wehby, 2001).

Develop a Hierarchical Behavior Management Plan

The Individuals With Disabilities Education Act (IDEA) Amendments of 1997 and 2004 require that if students with disabilities exhibit behaviors that interfere with their learning or the learning of peers, that their IEP team must consider the use of positive behavioral interventions and supports and other strategies to address that behavior (IDEA, 20 U.S.C. § 614(d)(3)(B)). This, however, assumes that all teachers are trained in implementing effective behavioral interventions. Unfortunately, in the absence of training and awareness, teachers may tend to rely on punishing inappropriate behaviors rather than reinforcing positive behaviors. One difficulty with behavior management plans that merely focus on punishment is that every behavioral infraction, regardless of how minor or severe, is managed in a similar manner. Without an appropriate behavior plan that strategically handles minor offenses with less intensive behavior strategies, any intervention is a response or reaction instead of a preventive measure. Moreover, the use of behavior reduction procedures does not teach or strengthen appropriate behaviors.

Teachers sometimes use time-out exclusively; that is, they fail to use other behavioral interventions. This may result in time-out being used for mild undesirable behaviors such as talking out (Nelson & Rutherford, 1983), and a failure to use positive behavioral interventions as required by the law. Teachers should be trained in various methods of controlling behavior so that the more extreme strategies can be reserved for more extreme behaviors. Ryan and colleagues (in press a) suggest

Figure 1. Sample Time-Out Log

Student's Name	Date	Begin Time-Out	End Time-Out	Duration	Location/ Academic Subject	Behavior	Antecedent	Staff	Comments
Tim Smith	12/08/06	09:35	09:40	5 minutes	Math Class	Swearing	Verbal instigation by peer	Ms. Jones	Timmy continued to argue after being assigned time-out for one minute before complying.

a "gated" schoolwide behavior intervention plan requiring staff members to begin with less restrictive forms of interventions before moving to more restrictive procedures. Specifically, they recommend educators implement a hierarchal strategy that includes:

1. *Simple intervention techniques.* When a staff member notices inappropriate behavior. the first step is to talk to the student or redirect the student to another activity.

2. *Problem-solving strategies.* If simple intervention techniques prove ineffective, the next step entails problem solving in which the staff and student discuss the behavior, the consequence(s), and then evaluate the situation and develop an intervention plan as well as a follow up. This step teaches students coping skills and replacement behaviors.

3. *Reinforcement-based strategies and extinction of inappropriate behavior.* Early level behavioral strategies should focus on reinforcing appropriate behavior while working strategically toward extinguishing inappropriate behaviors. Rather than concentrating on an undesirable behavior, the teacher should look for a positive alternative that will result in reinforcement for the student. This involves identifying the specific activity the student is not presently doing, then teaching a replacement

behavior and reinforcing it (Alberto & Troutman, 2006).

4. *Inclusion time-out (3 minutes).* Inclusion time-out, the least restrictive time-out procedure, is the next step if the previous strategies do not work. The student can sit and watch without being involved in the classroom activities. This step can last approximately 3 minutes, but we recommend it last no longer than the age of the student.

5. *Exclusion time-out (5 minutes).* If the student continues the inappropriate behaviors, the staff can then implement exclusion for 5 to 15 minutes.

6. *Seclusion time-out (15 minutes).* If these strategies are still not effective, the student could be moved to a seclusion time-out, perhaps in a time-out room with the door left open. The student is always provided with the opportunity to return to class after processing with a staff member or demonstrating 5 minutes of compliance. While the procedures for processing can vary, they typically entail (a) helping the student identify the situational and internal cues of the event, (b) giving meaning to those cues that led up to the event, (c) selecting or clarifying a student goal, (d) generating possible student responses, (e) evaluating the outcomes of various responses and

selecting an appropriate response, and (f) agreement upon a specific behavioral enactment for future events (Crick & Dodge, 1994). Regardless of the behavior, the teacher should ask the student to rejoin the class after a 30-minute period. (Ryan et al., in press a).

Without an appropriate behavior plan that strategically handles minor offenses with less intensive behavior strategies, any intervention is a response or reaction instead of a preventive measure.

Make Data-Based Decisions

Since time-out is meant to be a behavior reducing strategy, a punishment, it is important that the staff collect and analyze data on the frequency of inappropriate behaviors that are followed by time-out to determine if it is accomplishing its intended goal of reducing the inappropriate behavior. If time-out is being used with a student and the inappropriate behavior is not decreasing, then time-out is not producing the desired outcome and another strategy should be implemented. However, it may not always be obvious to the staff that the procedure is not accomplishing its desired effect. This is where data collection contributes to effective decision-making.

Document the Use of Time-Out

Staff members can document time-outs in a time-out log (Figure 1) which includes information such as student name, date/time of the incident, location/academic subject, behavior, antecedent, and duration. This information can assist staff in determining if time-out is indeed effective in reducing the inappropriate behaviors, and also can help identify the underlying causes and/or triggers of the behavior. Due to the severity and restrictiveness of seclusion time-outs, the Wisconsin Department of Education developed a more extensive reporting sheet (see Figure 2).

Establish a Time-Out Policy

To ensure that student rights are protected and to safeguard districts from lawsuits, many states and schools have begun developing policies concerning the use of time-out procedures. Currently 23 states (Arkansas, Colorado, Connecticut, Florida, Idaho, Illinois, Iowa, Kentucky, Maine, Maryland, Massachusetts, Minnesota, Montana, New Mexico, New York, Ohio, Oregon, Rhode Island, Texas, Utah, Vermont, Virginia, and Wisconsin) have either established a policy or provide guidelines governing the use of time-out procedures. These policies or guidelines are critically important to ensure student safety, especially when schools incorporate seclusionary time-out practices. Ryan and Peterson's (2005) review of these procedures identified important attributes of effective time-out policies.

- *Purpose.* Time-out procedures should be used only to reduce student maladaptive behavior; students should not be subjected to unreasonable use of increasingly restrictive interventions. The time-out room should provide students an opportunity to regain control.
- *Time-out rooms for seclusion.* A school's time-out room(s) should be free of objects and fixtures which

Figure 2. Wisconsin Department of Education Seclusion Reporting Sheet

Student Name	Date
Teacher/class	Time in/time out
Staff person initiating seclusion; others present/involved:	
Describe the behavior that led to seclusion, including time, location, activity, others present, other contributing factors:	
Procedures used to attempt to de-escalate the student prior to using seclusion:	
Student behavior during seclusion: Was there any injury or damage? ❏ Yes ❏ No If yes, describe:	Student behavior after seclusion:
Follow-up with student after the seclusion	
Is other follow-up needed (e.g., IEP meeting, additional evaluation, discussion with others)? ❏ Yes ❏ No If yes, specify:	
Parent contact:	Administrative contact:

Source: Wisconsin Department of Education.

might harm the student; should have adequate light, ventilation, and heat; should provide the staff opportunity to observe the student at all times; and should not be locked or secured to prevent the student from leaving the room. The room should also be an adequate size; no smaller than 6' × 6' with normal ceiling height.

- *Training.* School personnel should be well trained in all the time-out procedures as well as other less restrictive yet effective behavioral strategies (such as functional behavioral assessment and behavior intervention planning). Knowledge of other, less restrictive behavior management strategies provides options to the staff, and they will be less likely to use time-out procedures for minor infractions.

- *Plan.* The staff should have a time-out plan, including the elements listed previously, and should be trained in its use.

- *Duration.* The time-out should be limited to the time necessary for the student to compose him/herself, but should not exceed 30 minutes, to help limit the impact on academic instruction time. An age appropriate guideline is 1 minute in time-out for every year of age of the student. Pendergrass (1971) found that time-out durations of 5 and 20 minutes were equally effective, although the effectiveness of short time-outs are diminished if a longer time-out has been previously used.

- *Documentation.* Each incident of seclusion and/or restraint time-out should be logged and should include information such as name, date, time, duration, setting, antecedent behavior, interventions attempted prior to seclusion, notification of parents, and so forth.

- *Analysis.* To determine if time-out procedures have been effective, the school should periodically analyze the time-out information log in order to identify patterns of behavior that could be used preventively (Ryan et al., in press a).

Final Thoughts

Time-out is an extremely common behavior reduction procedure used in schools across the United States. Unfortunately, time-out is sometimes used inappropriately and may even be used excessively with some students (Ryan, et al., in press a). In the two decades since nearly three quarters of E/BD teachers reported using time-out in their classrooms (Zabel, 1986), there has not been extensive research investigating its efficacy in classrooms (with the exception of inclusion time-outs). To help ensure time-outs are used effectively in reducing maladaptive behaviors without jeopardizing the individual rights of students, educators should (a) make their classrooms reinforcing, (b) develop a hierarchical behavior man-

agement plan, (c) make data-based decisions, and (d) establish a class or school policy for time-outs. The combination of effective training in the effective use of time-out procedures and an established policy on its use in classrooms will help ensure that time-outs are used safely and effectively in reducing inappropriate behaviors.

References

Alberto, P. A., & Troutman, A. C. (2006). *Applied behavior analysis for teachers.* Upper Saddle River, NJ: Merrill-Prentice Hall.

Allen, K. E., Hart, B., Buell, J. S., Harris, F. R., & Wolf, M. M. (1964). Effects of social reinforcement on isolate behavior of a nursery school child. *Child Development, 35*(2), 511–518.

Burchard, J. D., & Barrera, F. (1972). An analysis of timeout and response cost in a programmed environment. *Journal of Applied Behavior Analysis, 5*(3), 271–282.

Busch, A., & Shore, M. (2000). Seclusion and restraint: A review of recent literature. *Harvard Review, 8*(5), 261–270.

Cooper, J. O., Heron, T. E., & Heward, W. L. (1987). *Applied Behavior Analysis.* Upper Saddle River, NJ: Prentice-Hall.

Costenbader, V., & Reading-Brown, M. (1995). Isolation timeout used with students with emotional disturbance. *Exceptional Children, 61*, 353–362.

Crick, N. C., & Dodge, K. A. (1994). A review and reformulation of social information processing mechanisms in children's social adjustment. *Psychological Bulletin, 115*, 74–101.

Fee, V. E., Matson, J. L., & Manikam, R. (1990). A control group outcome study of a nonexclusionary time-out package to improve social skills with preschoolers. *Exceptionality, 1*(2), 107–121.

Foxx, R. M., & Shapiro, S. T. (1978). The timeout ribbon: A nonexclusionary procedure. *Journal of Applied Behavior Analysis, 11*(1), 125–136.

Gallagher, M. M., Mittelstadt, P. A., & Slater, B. R. (1988). Establishing time-out procedures in a day treatment facility for young children. *Residential Treatment for Children & Youth, 5*(4), 59–68.

Gresham, F. M. (1979). Comparison of response cost and timeout in a special education setting, *The Journal of Special Education, 13*(2), 199–206.

Gunter, P. L., & Denny, R. K. (1998). Trends and issues in research regarding academic instruction of students with emotional and behavioral issues. *Behavioral Disorders, 24*(1), 44–50.

Handen, B. L., Parrish, J. M., McClung, T. S., Kerwin, M. E., & Evans, L. D. (1992). Using guided compliance versus time-out to promote: A preliminary comparative

analysis in an analogue context. *Research in Developmental Disabilities, 13*(2), 157–170.

Harris, K. R. (1985). Definitional, parametric, and procedural considerations in timeout interventions and research. *Exceptional Children, 51*, 279–288.

Huguenin, N. H., & Mulick, J. A. (1981). Nonexclusionary timeout: Maintenance of appropriate behavior across settings. *Applied Research in Mental Retardation, 2*(1), 55–67.

Individuals With Disabilities Education Improvement Act of 2004, 118 Stat. 2647 et seq., §§ 601 et seq. (2004).

Knoster, T., Wells, T., & McDowell, K. C. (2003). *Using time-out in an effective and ethical manner.* Des Moines, IA: Iowa Department of Education.

Lewis, T. J., Hudson, S., Richter, M., & Johnson, N. (2004). Scientifically supported practices in emotional and behavioral disorders: A proposed approach and brief review of current practices. *Behavioral Disorders, 29*, 247–259.

Luiselli, J. K., Suskin, L., & Slocumb, P. R. (1984). Application of immobilization time-out in management programming with developmentally disabled children. *Child & Family Behavior Therapy, 6*(1), 1–15.

Maag, J. W., & Katsiyannis, A. (1999). Teacher preparation in E/BD: A national survey. *Behavioral Disorders, 24*(3), 189–196.

Mace, F. C., & Heller, M. (1990). A comparison of exclusion time-out and contingent observation for reducing severe disruptive behavior in a 7-year old boy. *Child & Family Behavior Therapy, 12*(1), 57–68.

Nau, P. A., Van Houten, R., & O'Neil, A. (1981). The effects of feedback and a principal mediated timeout procedure on the disruptive behavior of junior high school students. *Education and Treatment of Children, 4*(2), 101–113.

Nelson, C., & Rutherford, R. (1983). Timeout revisited: Guidelines for its use in special education. *Exceptional Education Quarterly, 3*(4), 56–67.

Noll, M. B., & Simpson, R. L. (1979). The effects of physical timeout on the aggressive behaviors of a severely emotionally disturbed child in a public school setting. *AAESPH Review, 4*(4), 399–406.

Pendergrass, V. E. (1971). Effects of length of time-out from positive reinforcement and schedule of application reinforcement and schedule of application in suppression of aggressive behavior. *The Psychological Record, 21*, 75–80.

Plummer, S., Baer, D. M., & LeBlanc, J. M. (1977). Functional considerations in the use of procedural timeout and an effective alternative. *Journal of Applied Behavior Analysis, 10*(4), 689–705.

Rolider, A., & Van Houten, R. (1985). Movement suppression time-out: An effective way to suppress undesirable behavior in psychotic and severe developmentally delayed children. *Journal of Applied Behavior Analysis, 18,* 275-288.

Ryan, J. B., & Peterson, R. L. (2005, September). *Current use of timeout procedures in educational settings.* Presentation session at the International Conference on Children and Youth With Behavior Disorders, Dallas, TX.

Ryan, J. B., Peterson, R. L., Tetreault, G., & van der Hagen, E. (in press a). Reducing the use of seclusion and restraint in a day school program. In M. A. Nunno, L. Bullard & D. M. Day (Eds.), *For our own good: Examining the safety of high-risk interventions for children and young people.* Washington, DC: Child Welfare League of America.

Ryan, J. B., Peterson, R. L., Tetreault, G., & van der Hagen, E. (in press b). Reducing seclusion timeout and restraint procedures with at-risk youth. *Journal of At-Risk Issues.*

Salend, S., & Gordon, B. D. (1987). A group oriented timeout ribbon procedure. *Behavioral Disorders, 12*(2), 131-136.

Salend, S., & Maragulia, D. (1983). The timeout ribbon: A procedure for the least restrictive environment. *The Journal of Special Educators, 20,* 9-15.

Smith, D. E. P. (1981). Is isolation room timeout a punisher? *Behavioral Disorders, 6*(4), 247-256.

Solnick, J. V., Rincover, A., & Peterson, C. R. (1977). Some determinants of the reinforcing and punishing effects of timeout. *Journal of Applied Behavior Analysis, 10*(3), 415-424.

Spitalnik, R., & Drabman, R. (1976). A classroom time-out procedure for retarded children. *Journal of Behavioral Therapy & Exceptional Psychiatry, 7,* 17-21.

Sugai, G., & Horner, R. H. (2002). The evolution of discipline practices: Schoolwide positive behavior supports. *Child and Family Behavior Therapy, 24*(1), 23-50.

Sutherland, K. S. (2000). Promoting positive interactions between teachers and students with emotional/behavioral disorders. *Preventing School Failure, 44,* 110-116.

Sutherland, K. S., & Wehby, J. H. (2001). Exploring the relationship between increased opportunities to respond to academic requests and the academic and behavioral outcomes of students with E/BD. *Remedial and Special Education, 22,* 113-121.

Sutherland, K. S., Wehby, J. H., & Copeland, S. R. (2000). Effects of varying rates of behavior-specific praise on the on-task behavior of students with E/BD. *Journal of Emotional & Behavioral Disorders, 8,* 2-9.

Webster, R. E. (1976). A time-out procedure in a public school setting. *Psychology in the Schools, 13*(1), 72-76.

Wolery, M. R., Bailey, D. B., Jr., & Sugai, G. M. (1988). *Effective teaching: Principles and procedures of applied behavior analysis with exceptional students.* Boston: Allyn & Bacon.

Yell, M. L. (2006). *The law and special education* (2nd ed.). Upper Saddle River, NJ: Merrill/Prentice Hall.

Zabel, M. (1986). Time-out use with behaviorally disordered students. *Behavioral Disorders, 12,* 15-21.

Joseph B. Ryan *(CEC SC Federation), Assistant Professor of Special Education;* **Sharon Sanders** *(CEC SC Federation), Research Project Coordinator; and* **Antonis Katsiyannis** *(CEC SC Federation), Professor of Special Education, Clemson University, South Carolina.* **Mitchell L. Yell** *(CEC SC Federation), Professor of Special Education, University of South Carolina, Columbia.*

Address correspondence to Joseph B. Ryan, Special Education Programs, 228 Holtzendorff Hall, Clemson University, Clemson, SC 29634 (e-mail: jbryan@clemson.edu).

TEACHING Exceptional Children, *Vol. 39, No. 4, pp. 60-67.*

Learn to identify boundaries between mental-health counseling and the kind of communication appropriate within the massage therapist-client relationship

Communication vs. Counseling

by Phyllis Nasta

Massage therapist Andrea Jones* had a client, Claire, a middle-aged woman who came regularly for massage for three years. They had a great rapport and often chatted about their families, work, and philosophies of life.

Then Claire's son was killed in Iraq. His wife and baby came to live with her, and her grief combined with the chaos of a newly configured household plunged Claire into an agitated state. Because she felt comfortable with Andrea, she continued to receive massage weekly and talk about her situation.

Andrea felt loyal to, and protective of, Claire, but also noticed that she started feeling overwhelmed by the enormity of Claire's problems. Claire was having panic attacks, sleeplessness, dark thoughts and disturbing dreams. She told

Andrea that massage was the only thing helping her, and at times she cried through the whole massage.

Andrea responded to this by being more supportive and spending more time with Claire after the massage, talking. Without realizing it, Andrea had unceremoniously moved into the role of counselor—but she didn't have the tools to recognize, evaluate and treat the symptoms of post-traumatic stress disorder, which was what Claire had. Andrea was hooked by her client's telling her that she was the only one who really helped, and she ignored her own feelings of being overwhelmed.

One day Andrea received a call from a family member, telling her that Claire had been hospitalized. It started as a medical admission due to an anxiety attack, but quickly became a psychiatric stay. Claire was exhausted, in shock and suicidal. Andrea felt awful about this, but she also learned valuable lessons. She learned that feeling overwhelmed is a red flag for her. (For others it may be a different feeling, such as annoyed or helpless.) She learned that a client in crisis might lean on her for more support than she is able to provide, and that it is safer for herself *and* the client if she recognizes this and directs him or her to mental-health intervention.

This example illustrates what might happen when a massage therapist migrates into a counseling role. Therapists should understand that when this migration occurs, they are exposing themselves to liability on the

> It is vital that you don't engage in activities that are outside your scope of practice as a massage professional.

pragmatic levels of licensing and malpractice insurance, and that they may be exposing the client to harm by inadvertently allowing a disturbing emotional state to come up, which might be difficult or impossible for the massage therapist to safely resolve with the client.

There are three general boundaries that need to remain in place between the fields of massage and counseling: pragmatic issues, approach and intention, and trust.

Pragmatic issues

First, on a pragmatic level, there are the licensing, certification and malpractice issues. There are separate licenses that are regulated by separate state boards, and separate malpractice-insurance policies for each profession.

It is vital for your own professional safety that you don't engage in activities that are outside your scope of practice as a massage professional.

Approach and intention

The second boundary between massage and counseling has to do with the roles that the two professions play, in terms of general approach and intention.

On a very simplistic level, when we massage someone we're intending that he feel better at the end of the session than he did when he arrived at our office. Even when we utilize techniques to help him work through a difficult spot, such as a knotted muscle, our goal is to make him feel better. We take his lead. If he says the pressure is too much, we back off. We don't force an issue if the client asks us to lighten up. We don't take the attitude that we know better than the client. We don't try to convince him to get a certain number of sessions, or present him with ultimatums.

If asked our opinion, we offer it, based on studies and professional experience, but we don't portray ourselves as experts in any category of the health field except for massage. We generally don't contradict clients. If a client says, "I have bad cramps today, so don't massage my stomach," we don't suggest that she might be in denial and should really let us dig in there.

Massage therapists don't intentionally raise anxiety in clients, nor do we encourage clients to dredge up old problems. And we don't confront clients, unless the client is being abusive.

While these examples—of confrontation, contradiction, raising anxiety, persuasion and taking charge of treatment—might sound ridiculous in the context of massage, they are all representative of techniques that are utilized in the field of mental health.

Counselors go through graduate school, supervised

---

3 STEPS TO REFERRING TO A MENTAL-HEALTH PROFESSIONAL

1 For counseling resources, Google "community information and referral (and your city name)." Most cities have a centralized resource, and they usually have a fully staffed crisis phone line. You can give the number to clients and use it for information if you encounter challenging issues, such as suicidal expression, child abuse or domestic violence.

2 If you have clients who are in counseling, discourage them from telling you about their sessions. Keep boundaries clear. Remember, if they talk about their sessions you are only hearing one side. If you sympathize with the client you might be sabotaging the treatment plan that the counselor developed.

3 If clients have health insurance, suggest that they call their insurance provider to find out the names of approved mental-health counselors, psychologists and psychiatrists in the area.

—*Phyllis Nasta*

practicum, and years of practice in order to become licensed. Along the way they learn about the easier stuff, such as helping people through normal, everyday anxieties and getting them to open up through reflective listening skills, and they also learn how to handle the tougher issues, including addictions, mental illness, recovery from abuse and torture, suicidal and homicidal thoughts, criminal behavior and eating disorders. They also learn to recognize the symptoms that may mask some of those problems.

Trust

The third area of boundaries between massage and counseling has to do with trust. Massage clients take off clothes, lie down on a table, and allow the therapist to touch them for an hour without anyone else in the room. There aren't too many other forms of therapy that have this much vulnerability built in. When a client comes back to the same therapist, it is because she trusts the therapist. Over several or many sessions, a bond develops.

Massage clients also develop trust in their therapists because of the power of positive, nurturing touch. Even though a client is a paying customer, the time frame is defined and the therapist obeys the rules of professional boundaries, we should not ignore or underestimate the potential power that touch has to generate strong trust between client and therapist.

This trust can make the client vulnerable to any communication the massage therapist puts forward. Because of the special power of touch to generate trust, a massage therapist should be aware that migrating into a counseling role can cause the client harm, either through things said or through things unsaid.

For example, I recall a workshop in which a massage therapist spoke about a client of his who had been sexually abused as a child. When she began receiving massage from him she was tense and withdrawn, but after several sessions she relaxed and started flirting with him. He thought this was great, a sign of success that she was opening up to a man and to her sexuality.

The teacher of the class didn't contradict him. I bit my tongue for a while and then couldn't contain myself, having worked in the field of child sexual abuse for 20 years. In essence, the client's flirting with the therapist was a sign that she was not healed from her molestation. She still saw her primary value as sexual, and that's how she related to him. Her flirting illustrated her poor boundaries and her desire to offer herself sexually, because that's where she saw her worth. It is easy for us to agree that a 5-year-old girl who flirts overtly with adult men is exhibiting unhealthy behavior. It's not so clear that flirting by an adult can also be unhealthy.

If that massage therapist had continued thinking that her flirting signified progress, he might have encouraged it and ultimately caused her harm by reinforcing the very behavior that she needs to heal from.

Stay safe

To keep yourself safe and within your scope of practice, here are some cues to attend to so that you can be empathetic but avoid taking on the role of a counselor:

• **Clients talking about their marriage or relationship problems.** Usually, when people talk about romantic or marriage problems without their partner present, it's because they

> The most important aspect of keeping good boundaries is to listen to your inner voice.

feel misunderstood or threatened by the potential break-up of the relationship. Without the partner there, you can't verify any of the accusations or information the person is putting forth.

Your client may assume you'll take her side because you are so nurturing to her. It's best in these situations to be empathetic, but avoid giving advice. You can use reflective listening and respond by saying, "It sounds like you and your partner are going through a rough time"—and leave it at that. If the client continues to bring it up, say something like, "You've been going through a lot lately and that can put stress on a relationship—it might be helpful to consider getting into counseling, either as a couple or by yourself, to have someone to talk it over with."

• **Suicidal expressions.** When people talk about suicide, it is important to remember a simple fact: Suicide is a crime. That is why police can take suicidal people into custody, and why psychiatric facilities can lock them up. What is not so simple, however, is the range and variety of suicidal expression.

If you believe a client is suicidal, it's important to protect the client *and* yourself. Before the situation even arises, get the phone number of the suicide hotline in your community and have it on hand for advice and to give to clients. Be clear in directing suicidal clients to get mental-health help. If they go to a counselor but continue to talk to you about suicide, tell them that you want to speak to the counselor or psychiatrist, and take direction from that professional on how to address the client.

If the client refuses to get mental-health help, is still suicidal, and continues to see you for massage, seriously consider discontinuing the sessions. Be clear with him that you've recommended he get help and have given him a suicide hotline number, and that it isn't safe to receive massage while he has a serious, untreated mental-health condition. If a client is in imminent danger, evidenced by stating something akin to, "I'm going to kill myself," call 911.

Listen to yourself first

Generally speaking, as massage therapists, we know that people are going to talk to us about their lives. Each of us has our own threshold of tolerance for listening to and talking with clients. But it's important to remember that when people bring up anxiety or depression that lasts for more than a few weeks or interferes with their functioning, when they have experienced significant abuse, or are experiencing breaks with reality from drug use or mental illness, they need more than a compassionate ear.

Clearly, the most important aspect of keeping good boundaries is to listen to your inner voice. You probably will have a feeling of being overwhelmed when a client is nudging you across the border between normal conversation and counseling. Listen to that feeling, and address it with yourself and the client.

I hope that my observations help you, as a massage therapist, to push yourself to grow, through the process of thinking about mental-health issues, and to reflect upon some concrete information about possibly dangerous situations you might encounter.

*Names have been changed

Phyllis Nasta has been a mental-health counselor for 30 years and a massage therapist for 20 years. She teaches a course, "Ethics and Personal Growth for Massage Therapists," in which she offers an opportunity for massage therapists to ponder their role, reflect upon their experiences, and glean practical information they can use with clients. Contact her at pfnasta@prodigy.net with "massage article" in the subject line.   M

THE Aging HEART

Prehospital cardiac assessment & care in the geriatric population

By Lindsey Simpson, BS, EMT-P,
& David Hostler, PhD, NREMT-P

You and your partner are dispatched for an ill person with a history of atrial fibrillation and pulmonary emboli. When you arrive on scene, you find an elderly female in a wheelchair in the living room, with her daughter and son-in-law present. According to her daughter, the woman's legs just "gave out from under her," and the patient reports that "everything went black, and then I was sitting here."

Family members state she didn't hit the ground. The patient denies any chest pain or discomfort. You find that, in addition to atrial fibrillation, she has a history of congestive heart failure, hypertension and emphysema. She reports her doctor recommended she get a pacemaker and that she is being evaluated for diabetes. She is compliant with her medications of digoxin, Zocor, furosemide, potassium chloride and Celebrex.

The patient tells you that she hasn't been too active lately because she finds herself getting dizzy when she stands up too quickly. As you provide reassurance and complete a physical assessment, your partner places her on oxygen, pulse oximetry and a cardiac monitor with 12-lead ECG capabilities, and checks her blood glucose while starting an IV.

The patient denies any allergies to medications. She's alert and oriented. Pulse is 96, irregular and strong at the radius, respirations 18 and regular, pulse oximetry 98% on room air, and blood pressure is 156/88. A 12-lead analysis reveals atrial fibrillation with possible left ventricular hypertrophy without active **infarction** or ischemia. Her blood glucose is 196 mg/dL. You run your IV TKO and continue to assess the patient during transport to the hospital for further evaluation.

The graying population

Another person turns 50 every seven seconds in the United States. America's baby boomer population started turning 50 in 1996, and the children of the 1940s and '50s are now entering their sixth and seventh decades of life. The field of gerontology (the scientific study of the effects of aging and age-related diseases on humans) has grown dramatically in response to the increasing number of older patients.

The 75 million people in the baby boomer generation represent 25% of all people in the United States. This fast-growing population, especially those 65 years of age and older, use 36% of total dollars spent on health care. This amount comprises all aspects of health care, including EMS response and transport.

Obviously, improved health care allows people to live longer. Although most would agree living longer is better, entering old age increases the opportunity for people to suffer such debilitating diseases as stroke, cancer and myocardial infarction (MI). Therefore, geriatric patients are more likely to use EMS and intensive care units than their younger counterparts and could require more extensive diagnostic testing and evaluation. They also require longer hospital stays and extended care services, such as rehabilitation and assisted living.

The aging process

The American College of Physicians in Geriatric Emergency Medicine defines the following five characteristics of aging:

1. Aging is universal; it affects all living organisms.
2. Aging is progressive; the aging process is continuous.
3. The changes associated with aging are detrimental.
4. Aging by itself is not a disease.
5. Aging makes the individual more vulnerable to disease.

Aging affects all individuals from the moment they're born. Initially, aging in humans is positive, allowing a child to develop the body and mind, realize potential, start careers and bear children. However, like every other machine, at some point the body begins to show signs of wear. Aches and pains increase, and the health and vigor of youth declines. At this point, aging is often associated with chronic disease and a failing body.

Every organ in the body suffers the effects of aging. Specifically, the cardiovascular system undergoes many progressive changes, which can lead to acute illness or predisease states, such as subclinical **atherosclerosis**. An older patient may appear healthy, but their heart is beginning to display changes associated with cardiovascular disease. This article describes some of the changes seen in the aging

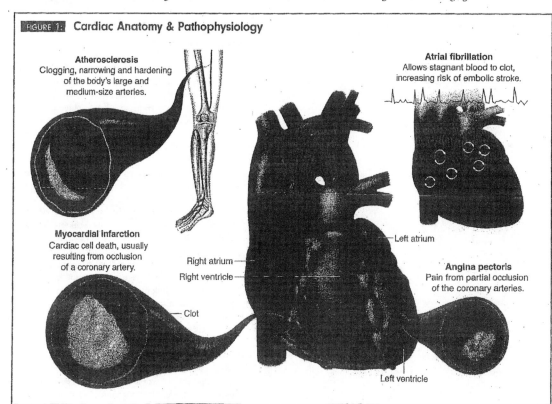

FIGURE 1: Cardiac Anatomy & Pathophysiology

Atherosclerosis
Clogging, narrowing and hardening of the body's large and medium-size arteries.

Atrial fibrillation
Allows stagnant blood to clot, increasing risk of embolic stroke.

Myocardial infarction
Cardiac cell death, usually resulting from occlusion of a coronary artery.

Left atrium

Right atrium

Right ventricle

Angina pectoris
Pain from partial occlusion of the coronary arteries.

Clot

Left ventricle

Objectives

* Describe the anatomy and physiology of the heart.
* Describe common pathophysiology of the aging heart.
* Apply the principles of cardiac care to EMS scenarios.

heart that will help prehospital providers better understand and treat their older cardiac patients.

Cardiac anatomy

About the size of a clenched fist, the heart weighs approximately 250–350 g and is located in the mediastinum (see Figure 1, p. 49). In a standing person, the heart extends from the second to the fifth ribs and rests on the diaphragm. The apex of the heart points anterior and slightly to the left, placing the right ventricle and atrium immediately posterior to the sternum.

The heart is surrounded by an inner (visceral) and an outer (parietal) pericardial membrane. A thin layer of fluid between these membranes minimizes friction, allowing the heart to expand and contract without resistance. Outside the parietal pericardium is a fibrous membrane made of connective tissue. This thickened membrane is resistant to stretching. This prevents overfilling and anchors the heart to the surrounding structures.

The four chambers of the heart are arranged to provide two parallel pumps. The right atrium and ventricle pump blood through the pulmonary vasculature, and the left atrium and ventricle pump blood to the rest of the body. The left and right heart each pump the same volume, but the resistance pressure is vastly different. The high-pressure systemic vasculature requires the left ventricle to pump forcefully, causing the walls to thicken and become more muscular than those of the right ventricle.

Valves prevent the reversal of blood flow during contraction. The tricuspid valve and bicuspid valves are located between the right and left atria and ventricles respectively, and are closed during ventricular contraction. The pulmonary and aortic semilunar valves are positioned at the exit of the right and left ventricles and are closed during ventricular relaxation. The bicuspid valve incurs considerable stress during a lifetime, causing it to become either fibrous or sclerotic. These thickened valve flaps do not close completely during contraction, allowing a small backflow of blood into the left atrium. This backflow can be heard as a heart murmur and is common in the elderly.

The closing of the heart valves produces the heart sounds that can be heard when auscultating the chest. The typical "lub-dub" sounds created by the closing of the atrioventricular and semilunar valves are called the S1 and S2 sounds.

Additional heart sounds, S3 and S4, sometimes can be heard during ventricular relaxation. When heard as a string of three or four consecutive sounds, it may remind you of a galloping horse. The S3 sound is related to ventricular filling and probably represents over-filling and stretching of the ventricular wall. Although difficult to detect, an S3 sound in the elderly may be an early sign of heart failure. The S4 heart sound is related to atrial contraction, providing the final ventricular filling. When an abnormal S4 is heard, it could indicate that the patient has a weak ventricle.

Cardiac physiology

A healthy heart is an amazing machine, able to respond instantly to changes in blood volume by pumping with more or less force, which describes the **Frank-Starling law of contraction**. In a resting adult, the left and right heart will each push 75 mL of blood into the arterial circulation with every contraction. This amount is known as the **stroke volume** (SV). Multiplying the stroke volume by the heart rate (SV x HR) calculates the patient's **cardiac output** (CO). When the blood returning to the heart changes, the SV adjusts proportionally.

The blood returning to, and filling, the heart after each contraction is called the **preload**. Preload can change in response to many factors, including blood volume, degree of vasoconstriction and heart rate. For example, when blood volume is low, as seen in profound dehydration, less blood returns to the heart with each beat, causing the preload to decrease.

In order to maintain a normal CO, the heart will beat faster to compensate for the falling SV. When the demands of the body are high in times of stress or strenuous exercise, the large veins of the body constrict, forcing more blood back to the heart and increasing stroke volume. Increased stroke volume combined with a higher heart rate raises cardiac out-

Glossary

Afterload: The pressure in the arterial system that the ventricle must overcome to move blood forward.

Anginal equivalent: Signs and symptoms associated with myocardial infarction other than chest pain (e.g. dyspnea, diaphoresis).

Angina pectoris: Thoracic pain caused by oxygen deprivation to the heart, often associated with atherosclerosis.

Atherosclerosis: Clogging, narrowing and hardening of the body's large and medium-size arteries.

Arteriosclerosis: Calcium deposits in the extremity vessel walls that cause hardening, reducing the compliance of the arteries.

Automaticity: Ability of cardiac cells to self-depolarize without nervous stimulation.

Cardiac output: The amount of blood pumped by the heart in one minute (stroke volume x heart rate).

Cardiac reserve: The difference between maximal and resting cardiac output.

Endothelium: The innermost lining of the blood vessel, providing a relatively frictionless environment for blood flow.

Frank-Starling law of contraction: The ability of the healthy heart to instantly adjust and pump all the blood it receives.

Infarction: Death of ischemic tissue.

Myocardial infarction: Cardiac cell death, usually resulting from coronary artery occlusion.

Preload: The volume of blood entering the ventricle during diastole.

Stroke volume: The amount of blood flowing into the arterial circulation with every contraction.

put to meet the body's need for oxygen and nutrients.

At rest, the cardiac output in a normal, non-athletic adult is approximately 5 L/min (i.e., normal SV of 75 mL/beat x resting HR of 75 bpm = 5,625 mL/min). The maximum CO in a healthy adult can be as high as 25 L/min. The difference between resting and maximal cardiac output is known as the **cardiac reserve**. This represents the capacity for the heart to increase blood flow in response to increasing physical demands by beating faster and more forcefully (i.e., increasing SV).

One of the unfortunate aspects of aging is the loss of cardiac reserve. Resting cardiac output changes little with age. However, as a person gets older, the normal changes in the cardiac conduction system and a loss of beta receptors causes the heart to become less responsive to natural catecholamines, and the maximum heart rate decreases.

You can estimate a healthy person's maximum heart rate by subtracting the age from 220. In a healthy 70 year old, the maximum heart rate will be 150. Maintaining a higher level of fitness will help counter the loss of maximum heart rate and cardiac reserve. Unfortunately, a sedentary lifestyle (often adopted by people as they age) makes this lost capacity an unavoidable consequence.

Cardiac conduction

Cardiac tissue has the unique property of **automaticity**, meaning that certain cells in the heart, called pacemaker cells, will depolarize without nervous stimulation. This effect allows the heart to maintain a normal resting heart rate that can be modified by the autonomic nervous system.

The pacemaker cells are connected together beginning in the right atrium with the sinoatrial (SA) node. Depolarization of the SA node signals the atrial cells to contract, forcing the last portion of the preload into the ventricle. The impulse generated at the SA node is conducted to the atrioventricular (AV) node and bundle, where it's held for a fraction of a second before traveling down the bundle branches to the apex of the heart and into the Purkinje fibers. From the Purkinje fibers, the impulse is then transmitted to the cardiac cells near the apex, causing the cells to contract.

A distinctive feature of cardiac muscle is the end-to-end connection of the cells, allowing all the ventricular cells to seamlessly communicate. This network of ventricular cells is called a *syncytium*. As the cells at the apex contract, the impulse travels to more superior cells, resulting in an organized wave of contraction from apex to base, forcing the blood into the aorta and pulmonary trunk.

Although the conduction system can fail at any age, atrial fibrillation is largely a disease related to aging. It has been estimated that 1% of the U.S. population (or about 3 million people) has atrial fibrillation, and with the growing elderly population, that number could double in the next 50 years.

Atrial fibrillation is a disease in which atrial contraction is chaotic and disorganized. Instead of one impulse from the SA node causing a uniform contraction of the atrial syncytium, multiple errant impulses cause random contractions. On the ECG, the P wave is replaced by random fibrillatory waves and an irregular ventricular response is present. These patients will have an irregular pulse and may be tachycardic, depending on how many waves pass through the AV node.

An unfortunate consequence of atrial fibrillation is the increased risk of embolic stroke. The lack of unified atrial contraction allows pockets of stagnant blood to persist in the atrial chambers, resulting in clots. When these clots are dislodged, they can travel to the brain and become lodged in the vasculature. The risk of stroke is two to seven times higher for people with atrial fibrillation compared with people in a normal sinus rhythm, and the total mortality is more than doubled.

Other age-related changes in the SA node are common, including fibrosis, atrophy, and a loss of nodal cells. These changes can result in a loss of SA node function, leading to lower resting heart rates. If these changes become symptomatic, a person may receive a pacemaker.

Although pacemaker failure is rare, the opportunity for EMS providers to treat patients with malfunctioning pacemakers increases with the expanding elderly population. If a pacemaker fails to sense the patient's bradycardia or fails to fire, you may need to administer the appropriate

PHOTO KEVIN LINK

Atypical symptoms of MI include nausea, gastric distress and dyspnea, and are often seen in the elderly, diabetics and females.

while the circumflex provides blood to the left lateral and posterior walls of the heart. When the ventricles relax (in diastole), blood in the aorta is forced back against the aortic semilunar valve and redirected into the coronary arteries, perfusing the cardiac cells with oxygenated blood. During cardiac contraction (i.e., systole) the pressure created by the contracting cells is so great that it temporarily occludes the coronary arteries.

The transient occlusion of the coronary arteries can lead to pain known as **angina pectoris**. The chest pain and discomfort associated with angina is often relieved with rest and nitroglycerin. Patients with chronic stable angina usually self-treat their disease at home and rarely access EMS. However, extensive or long-term disruption in coronary blood flow will cause the cardiac cells to become ischemic and may result in the signs and symptoms of a myocardial infarction. The disease progression leading to this state is called atherosclerosis and begins in the second or third decade of life.

Lipid plaques, called *atheroma*, grow in the walls of the coronary arteries between the middle and inner layers of the vessel. As the plaque enlarges with age, the **endothelium** stretches thin and becomes fibrous. The growing plaque intrudes into the lumen of the vessel, causing decreased blood flow. This condition is known as *subclinical atherosclerosis* and represents the period of time when a person is at risk for suffering angina or a heart attack but has not become symptomatic.

If the diseased endothelium is broken, the flowing blood is exposed to lipid, and a clot will form. The initial stage of clot formation is the aggregation of platelets onto the exposed lipid plaque. The positive feedback mechanism associated with platelet activation will attract more platelets to the site. Eventually, the final steps of the clotting cascade will result in the deposition of fibrin protein onto the platelet plug, resulting in a stable clot.

interventions for symptomatic bradycardia, including atropine, transcutaneous pacing or beta agonist drugs. (To learn more about caring for patients with pacemakers and to obtain CE credits, read "Decoding the Electrical Heart," September 2006 *JEMS*.)

Coronary artery disease

The heart is the first organ to receive blood as it's pumped from the left ventricle. The left and right coronary arteries branch off the ascending aorta just above the aortic semilunar valve. The right coronary artery (RCA) circles the heart between the right atrium and ventricle, feeding smaller vessels by providing blood supply to the right heart and the cardiac conduction system. After it reaches the inferior wall of the heart, the RCA is renamed the posterior interventricular artery and supplies blood to the portion of both right and left ventricles that rest on the diaphragm.

After branching from the aorta, the left coronary artery (LCA) splits into the anterior interventricular and circumflex arteries. The anterior interventricular artery (also known as the left anterior descending artery, or LAD) provides blood supply to the anterior portions of both ventricles,

v

AGING HEART

The increasing size of the platelet plug in the coronary vessel lumen can nearly or completely occlude blood flow, causing the tissue distal to the clot to become ischemic. If flow is not restored, the ischemic tissue may die (infarct), causing permanent damage to the myocardium, known as an MI. The severity of the MI and the quality of the recovery will depend on the location of the clot and the timeliness and effectiveness of the treatment.

Clots in the proximal portions of the LCA and RCA will affect larger areas of tissue and typically have devastating consequences. For example, an occlusion in the LCA before the split into circumflex and anterior interventricular arteries will deprive the entire anterior, left lateral and posterior walls of the heart of blood, resulting in an extensive infarction. This will potentially cause most of the left ventricle to infarct, thus leaving the person incapable of effectively pumping blood to the rest of the body. Cardiac cells have a limited capacity to heal and regenerate, and people who survive this type of MI suffer from severe heart failure after the event. In contrast, a clot in the distal coronary arteries or in a minor branch will cause smaller infarction, leaving the patient with a good quality of life after recovery and rehabilitation.

Patients suffering an MI may complain of classic symptoms, including chest pain and difficulty breathing. Often, the pain will be described as crushing and may radiate into the arm or jaw. This radiating, or referred, pain is the result of sensory nerves from the skin and heart entering the spinal cord in close proximity. It may trick the brain into believing the pain is located in multiple places.

However, for every patient with classic MI symptoms, you're just as likely to encounter a patient with atypical symptoms. The atypical symptoms are called **anginal equivalents** and include nausea, gastric distress and dyspnea. These atypical symptoms are often seen in the elderly, diabetics and females. It's important to identify those patients with atypical symptoms who are having a myocardial infarction and provide appropriate treatment.

Employing a 12-lead ECG on patients with chest pain may identify ischemic areas of the heart by revealing ST segment elevation. The ST segment starts when the QRS complex ends and extends to the beginning of the T wave. When this segment is elevated more than 2 mm above baseline, it's presumptive evidence of ischemia and myocardial infarction.

Omitting the 12-lead in favor of the simpler 3-lead ECG may mislead you. The lead II view typically used in the prehospital setting provides information about only the inferior wall and conduction system. It won't reveal ischemia in the anterior or lateral walls of the heart. Further, the 3-lead ECG is heavily filtered and may not show ST segment elevation on the inferior wall even when it's present.

Treatment: Definitive treatment for myocardial infarction is the reestablishment of coronary blood flow, preferably before significant amounts of cardiac tissue have infarcted. Although it's not usually possible in the prehospital setting, other early treatments provided by EMS are critical for preserving non-infarcted cardiac tissue and triaging patients to the appropriate medical facility.

Oxygen is a critical intervention for the patient with cardiac chest pain, because it helps ensure that the myocardium is maximally oxygenated. Nitroglycerin and a narcotic, such as fentanyl or morphine, work to relax the coronary arteries and the peripheral vasculature. This therapy reduces the preload, allowing the heart to beat less forcefully and lowering the oxygen requirement of the myocardium, and it may return some small amount of blood flow to the ischemic portion of the heart. Use caution before providing the first dose of nitroglycerin. It should not be given to patients who are hypotensive or to patients who have recently used Viagra or similar medications. The interaction between nitroglycerin and erectile dysfunction drugs can cause profound hypotension. The drop in blood pressure could be so extreme that it may cause unconsciousness or cardiac arrest.

Don't underestimate the benefit from the pain-relieving properties of the narcotic for cardiac chest pain. Relieving pain is not simply a "nice thing" to provide the patient. Pain relief decreases the catecholamines produced by the body during physiologic stress. These stress hormones make the heart beat faster and more forcefully and cause platelets to become stickier, potentially extending the size and severity of the infarction.

A critical prehospital therapy for cardiac chest pain is oral aspirin. It poisons the platelets, preventing them from aggregating and expanding the platelet plug. Interestingly, aspirin by itself is as effective as the clot-busting fibrinolytic drugs. For patients who ultimately receive fibrinolytic drugs in the hospital, providing aspirin in the prehospital setting will potentiate (or enhance) the drug effect. Therefore, it should be the goal of every EMS agency to have 100% compliance with the provision of aspirin to patients with chest pain of suspected cardiac origin.

Because cardiac events and coronary artery reperfusion are becoming more common, you're likely to encounter patients who have received stents or angioplasty to reopen blocked coronary arteries and those who have received bypass grafts. These patients are always at risk for vessel reocclusion and a second, third or even fourth MI. Early recognition and treatment of prehospital chest pain will minimize the size of the infarction and improve your patient's outcome.

Heart failure

With an aging population comes an increased incidence of heart failure. Heart failure can be a residual effect after myocardial infarction if a large enough portion of the ventricle has died and the heart is incapable of moving sufficient blood into the arteries. The result is a drop in cardiac output and congestion behind the failing ventricle.

In the case of left heart failure, fluid backs up into the lungs, causing pulmonary edema. In right heart failure, fluid collected in the peripheral tissues causes edema in the feet, ankles and lower legs.

A natural loss of ventricular compliance with aging results in a stiffening of the ventricle wall. This less-compliant chamber is more difficult to fill during diastole, resulting in high pressure at the end of diastole. The condition is worse in people with chronic hypertension; the increased **afterload** resulting from high arterial pressure forces the heart to work harder and increases the amount of blood left in the ventricle at the end of systole (i.e., end systolic volume).

In response to increased filling pressure and end systolic volume, the heart will compensate by contracting more forcefully. Over time, the cardiac cells will enlarge to maintain stroke volume, much like skeletal muscle responding to weight training. Although initially beneficial, the heart's ability to increase ventricular mass (or hypertrophy) is limited. The cells begin to fail and are replaced with connective tissue. This often results in a dilated ventricle with a diminished capacity to pump blood.

The falling cardiac output causes the body to secrete sympathetic hormones and the kidney to reclaim water from filtrate. Although this would benefit other conditions, the combination of vasoconstriction and increased blood volume delivers more preload to the failing heart, resulting in more dysfunction.

Although heart failure was once associated with rapid deterioration and death, drug therapy has allowed many patients to live longer and enjoy a better quality of life than in prior years. Many patients are now prescribed beta-blockers and angiotensin converting enzyme (ACE) inhibitors to reduce the cardiac workload. Beta-blocking drugs prevent catecholamines, such as epinephrine, from attaching to the beta receptors. This will reduce the heart rate and force of contraction, preventing a rise in blood pressure and reducing work stress for the heart.

ACE inhibitors are a class of diuretics. These drugs prevent the formation of the hormone angiotensin II. Keeping angiotensin II levels low prevents vasoconstriction and reduces the amount of water reclaimed by the kidneys. This combination of effects reduces blood pressure and volume, thereby reducing the cardiac workload.

Although it's not yet possible to regenerate damaged heart muscle, a number of surgical and mechanical options are available to people with heart failure. One surgical technique removes dead tissue from an enlarged ventricle, returning the heart wall to a normal dimension and improving function.

More commonly, people with severe heart failure can be fitted with a left ventricular assist device (LVAD). An LVAD is implanted in the abdomen and provides an alternate route from the left ventricle to the aorta. By taking a portion of the stroke volume from the left ventricle and moving it mechanically to the ascending aorta, the left heart is allowed to move a smaller portion of blood, thus reducing the demands on the myocardium.

This device is often used to "bridge" a person until a heart transplant is available or for those patients who aren't eligible for a transplant. Although survival after LVAD placement is higher than ever before, its weakness continues to be the infection that can form around the line passing through the skin to the external battery and the formation of clots that can become lodged in the lungs and the brain.

Aging vasculature

The cardiac consequences of aging are not limited to the heart. Remodeling of the blood vessels will affect cardiac function and the cardiovascular system. In addition to atherosclerosis of the coronary arteries, **arteriosclerosis** of the extremity vessels places additional strain on the heart. Calcium deposits in the vessel walls cause hardening of the walls, reducing the compliance of the arteries.

Lost compliance prevents sufficient expansion during ventricular contraction. With age, arteriosclerosis progresses until the vasculature becomes rigid and "pipe-like." This lack of extensibility forces the ventricle to contract with more force to ensure sufficient stroke volume is delivered with every beat. Seen as chronic hypertension, this increase in workload over a period of years can lead to left heart failure.

Although some degree of hypertension and vascular disease is inevitable as we age, the modern American lifestyle is probably more destructive than aging is. Cigarette smoking remains prevalent in the aging population. Having smoked throughout their adult lives, many people believe they can't stop or believe it's too late to stop and regain any measurable health. In addition to causing pulmonary disease, cigarette smoking produces oxidants and creates chronic low-level inflammation, which causes platelets to adhere to vessel walls and results in occlusion and peripheral artery disease. This prolonged state encourages the atherosclerosis disease process and forces the aging heart to work harder and fail earlier.

The modern lifestyle also includes a diet of high-fat, protein-rich, empty-calorie foods. Diets rich in these foods increase the levels of "bad" cholesterol and triglycerides and contribute to the rate and extent of atherosclerosis. People consuming this diet typically exercise the least, despite the fact that regular exercise lowers "bad" cholesterol, raises "good" cholesterol and maintains heart health.

Conclusion

The normal aging heart is affected by many different factors, including genetics, lifestyle and medication. Although the diseases described here continue to plague the aging population, new treatments have extended the number of years and the quality of life for these patients. Advances in pharmacology, reperfusion

The "graying of America" will continue to shape and change the health-care system. EMS crews will see an increasing number of geriatric patients in the future. As the geriatric population continues to rise, so will the incidence of injuries and illnesses associated with old age. Further, as long-term therapies improve, the number of people living with cardiovascular disease will rise and subsequently increase the number of patients accessing the EMS system with cardiac complaints.

The primary education on geriatric medicine provided by the National Standard Curriculum can be expanded and enhanced with new offerings, such as Geriatric Education for Emergency Medical Services (GEMS). EMS providers often will provide the entry into the health-care system, making it critical to understand the diseases encountered in this group. ᴊᴇᴍs

Lindsey Simpson, BS, EMT-P, is an instructor at Loma Linda University in the Emergency Medical Care Program and works for AMR in Ventura County as a field paramedic.

Dave Hostler, PhD, NREMT-P, is an assistant professor at the University of Pittsburgh and the director of the University of Pittsburgh Emergency Responder Human Performance Lab. He has 19 years' experience as a firefighter/paramedic. He's a member of Guyasuta Volunteer Fire Department and the Allegheny County HazMat Medical Response Team.

This continuing education activity is approved by the Center for Emergency Medicine of Western Pennsylvania Inc., an organization accredited by the Continuing Education Board for Emergency Medical Services (CECBEMS), for 1.5 hours credit for First Responder, Basic and Advanced providers. If you have any comments regarding the quality of this program and/or your satisfaction with it, please contact CECBEMS by mail at CECBEMS, 5111 Mill Run Road, Dallas, TX 75244; by phone at 972/387-2862; by fax at 972/716-2007; or by e-mail at lsibley@cecbems.org.

Resources

- Chop W, Robnett R (Eds.): *Gerontology for the healthcare provider.* F.A. Davis Company: Philadelphia, Pa., 1999.
- Meldon S, Ma OJ, Woolard R: *Geriatric Emergency Medicine.* McGraw Hill Professional: New York City, 2003.
- Lakatta EG: "Arterial and cardiac aging: Major shareholders in cardiovascular disease enterprises: Part III: Cellular and molecular clues to heart and arterial aging." *Circulation.* 107(3):490–497, 2003.
- Lakatta EG, Levy D: "Arterial and cardiac aging: Major shareholders in cardiovascular disease enterprises: Part II: The aging heart in health: Links to heart disease. *Circulation.* 107(2):346–354, 2003.
- Lilly SL: *Pathophysiology of Heart Disease: A Collaborative Project of Medical Students and Faculty,* 3rd ed. Lippincott, Williams and Wilkins: Philadelphia, Pa., 2003.
- Nikitin NP, Witte KK, Ingle L, et al: "Longitudinal myocardial dysfunction in healthy older subjects as a manifestation of cardiac ageing." *Age and Ageing.* 34(4):343–349, 2005.
- Marieb EN, Hoehn K: *Human Anatomy and Physiology,* 7th ed. Benjamin Cummings: San Francisco, 2006.
- Rosse C , Gaddum-Rosse P: *Hollinshead's Textbook of Anatomy,* 5th ed. Lippincott-Raven: Philadelphia, Pa., 1997.

Should families be present during resuscitation?

Weigh the pros and cons of family presence during a crisis, then tell us what you think.

BY LINDA LASKOWSKI-JONES, RN, APRN,BC, CCRN, CEN, MS

A 52-YEAR-OLD WOMAN pushes open the door of an emergency department (ED) room and walks straight into a nightmare—cardiopulmonary resuscitation (CPR) in progress on her husband. Having left the room for just a few minutes to make a phone call, she returns to find the situation gravely different from the one she'd left. Yes, he'd been in pain, but he'd assured her he'd be fine. He'd had chest pain in the past and waved it off, blaming indigestion. But what's happening now can't be ignored—not by her or by ED team members who now have to abruptly factor her unexpected presence into their code blue response.

Though this scenario is fictional, it's similar to an event that once caught me by surprise in my ED, when I suddenly found myself in just such a situation. It was a role I wasn't expecting or prepared to handle at that moment.

If you'd been in my place, how would you have responded? Would you have escorted the wife out of the room, or would you have made provisions for her to stay? Would your answer be different if the patient were her child instead of her husband?

These dilemmas occur daily in hospitals across the country. Coming to grips with your personal feelings and having unit-based or institutional guidelines to support you can help in all of these instances.

In this article I'll explore the issues surrounding family presence during resuscitation efforts, including the pros and cons and current trends. I'll also share my personal experience as both a veteran trauma nurse and a family member of a critically injured patient. I hope to stimulate you to form a personal perspective that will help guide you in your practice and your personal life.

Emotionally charged

Family presence during resuscitation is an emotionally charged and controversial issue. Current literature is replete with articles and research that present conflicting points of view and advice.[1-3] Most of the research data on this subject has been obtained by soliciting the health care professionals' opinions and interviewing family members and patients.

Nurses' and physicians' personal attitudes run the gamut from staunchly advocating for family presence to flatly refusing to consider it. Whether family presence helps or harms family members and patients is hotly debated.

Some clinicians firmly believe that allowing family members to be present during resuscitation efforts—very possibly the last moments of the patient's life—is the ethically correct thing to do. But others argue that witnessing a

DENNIS BALOGH

With *Issues in Nursing*, our purpose is to lay the groundwork for further discussion about current controversies in the nursing profession. To succeed, we need to hear from you. Please write to tell us your views; we'll publish a sampling of reader responses to this topic in an upcoming issue. E-mail us at Betsy.Lowe@wolterskluwer.com; place "Issues" in the subject line. Be sure to include your full name, credentials, city, state, and daytime phone number.

futile resuscitation attempt can be psychologically damaging for relatives and may increase liability risks for caregivers.

Professional groups weigh in

Despite varying opinions among individual providers, many professional organizations including the American Heart Association, the Emergency Nurses Association, and the American Association of Critical-Care Nurses support family presence in their publications, resuscitation guidelines, and position statements.[4-6] Because these organizations exert significant influence on facility standards for patient management, acceptance of family presence appears to be growing.

Even so, some important generalizations still apply: More nurses than physicians support family presence, and barriers to family presence have been overcome to a greater degree in pediatrics than in adult resuscitation settings.[1-3]

Let's look at the pros and cons of family presence in more detail.

Advantages to family presence

Those in favor of family presence during resuscitation efforts cite these reasons:
• The patient's family can give their love, care, and support to the patient in the most critical situations. This preserves the family's sense of connectedness with their loved one, instead of making them feel they've abandoned him in his time of need. Family members can tell the patient what's on their minds and in their hearts—perhaps for the last time. Knowing that those words were said can comfort them after the crisis.
• The presence of family members may stimulate the patient's will to live or provide comfort as he dies.[7]
• Depending on the circumstances,

family members may gain a sense of peace from witnessing intense resuscitation efforts. This reassures them that everything possible was done to save the patient's life.
• Being present during resuscitation efforts helps confirm the reality of the patient's illness or death and may help them cope.
• Family members may be able to help the health care team by answering questions about the patient's medical or medication history.

Arguments against family presence

Health care providers who don't endorse family presence during resuscitation point to these potential pitfalls:
• The presence of family may distract the health care team from patient-care decisions and tasks, possibly impairing the resuscitation attempt.
• If a family member witnesses an error (or misunderstands an action or intervention), she may lose confidence in the health care team's competence.
• Family members who witness errors or misunderstand what they see or hear may be more likely to sue, especially if the patient dies. The team must be aware of this risk and strictly avoid saying or doing anything that could be misconstrued. This awareness could create another distraction from their work.
• Some health care workers worry that family members who observe resuscitation will be traumatized by the unfamiliar sights, sounds, and odors. This is especially relevant if family members aren't properly prepared for what they'll experience ahead of time or don't have the benefit of a support person to interpret lifesaving interventions for them.

• An overwrought family member might faint and hurt herself. Having to attend to the injured family member further diverts resources from the patient. The observer could also be accidentally exposed to blood or body fluids or contaminate equipment.
• Some people cope with anxiety, fear, or grief with anger or violence. In the emotionally charged atmosphere of a resuscitation attempt, a family member who becomes aggressive jeopardizes staff and compromises patient care. In my career, I've seen people punch holes in walls, throw furniture, and even tip over a stretcher when confronted with bad news. This danger is particularly acute when the patient and family are involved in gang violence. Family presence isn't an option if a family member's behavior endangers hospital personnel, patients, or visitors.

Creating a protocol

Don't wait for a crisis to formulate a policy or approach on the issue of family presence. Ideally, personal biases should be explored and consensus achieved beforehand, so vulnerable family members aren't subjected to staff conflict during a crisis.

Start by assessing the attitudes and beliefs of staff nurses and physicians to find out under what circumstances they support—or don't support—family presence. Strategies to begin a consensus-building dialogue include conducting a comprehensive literature search on the topic and setting aside time for frank discussion of the issues with unit leaders and the multidisciplinary health care team. If possible, consult with experts in the field who've successfully implemented a family presence policy or protocol. Consider distributing an informal survey or questionnaire about family presence to the staff.

If the general consensus is in favor of trying a family presence approach, define the conditions in which the option will be offered to families. For example, will the option be offered to family members of children who are being resuscitated? If yes, will both parents be allowed to stay in the room or only one? How will the rules change, if at all, for adults receiving lifesaving interventions? Should the number of family members be limited? Who will be empowered to make the final decision if the advisability of family presence is in question?

Here are some other issues to settle as you develop a protocol.
• Spell out circumstances that might preclude family presence. The option must be denied in any circumstance that would jeopardize the patient or staff; for example, when family members may become violent. Take into account whether hospital security should be notified and under what conditions.
• Define a protocol for facilitating family presence, including assigning staff member roles and responsibilities. For example, who'll meet the family member, explain the situation, accompany her into the room, and stay by her side as her support person? Besides unit nurses, consider other staff members—psychiatric nurses, social workers, chaplains, and even trained volunteers. Also make sure you have backup personnel for this role if the designated support person isn't available; for example, the charge nurse or perhaps a properly prepared nurse from another unit. Also decide who'll be called to provide continued family support if the patient is transported to another area, such as the operating room.

• Consider writing scripted responses to common questions, using everyday language. For example, if a family member asks, "What are they doing to him?" a support nurse might reply as follows: "The doctors and nurses are providing CPR by compressing his chest and breathing for him through a tube. They're also giving him drugs in an effort to restart his heart."
• Think about infection control precautions. Should the family member be asked to don gloves, a gown, or eye protection to prevent exposure to blood or body fluids? Where in the room should the family member stand, and when should she be given the opportunity to touch and communicate with the patient?
• Be prepared for a family member's unexpected reactions. Keep a chair close at hand if she feels faint and needs to sit down. Decide on factors that indicate she needs to be escorted from the room; for example, if she becomes distraught, dizzy, or nauseated.

After you draft a family presence protocol, send it for review by multidisciplinary team leaders, the risk manager, and the hospital's attorney, who can identify potential areas of liability. The protocol should also include provisions to facilitate prompt review and intervention by the risk manager if a legal issue arises during a resuscitation attempt.

When the protocol is finalized, multidisciplinary staff education is essential to promote a consistent approach to family presence. Disseminate the protocol to staff via the facility's communication media and conduct staff-development sessions to spell out standards, expectations, and situations that preclude family presence. Also address options for staff members

who are uncomfortable with family presence.

Debriefing after the event

A topic that receives little attention in the literature regarding family presence is the need for family members to debrief with selected members of the health care team after the crisis, especially when the outcome isn't good. Debriefing offers a forum for families to express their perceptions, questions, and fears about their loved one's illness or injury and lifesaving attempts they observed.

Not all families want to sort out these issues with health care professionals, but making provisions for those who do is important. Perhaps your unit could organize a bereavement team to make follow-up phone calls or send condolence cards that include an offer for a family conference if desired. In my experience, most families don't seek debriefing immediately after the event, but some family members have initiated discussions weeks or even months afterward.

I had the opportunity to be present with my father after he was critically injured in a motor vehicle crash (see *Family presence: A personal perspective*). Because I worked in the hospital where he was cared for, I had the luxury of speaking with the trauma surgeon anytime I felt the need to ask questions. In the case of my mother, who died at the scene of the crash, I also felt a strong need to debrief with the medical examiner who performed her autopsy. That conversation gave me the assurance and subsequent peace of mind that she didn't suffer at any point after impact—a concern that had haunted me.

Family presence: A personal perspective

On May 17, 2003, the world I knew was shattered when my parents were involved in a devastating car crash. The broadside impact killed my mother instantly and critically injured my father. By the time I got to the ED—*my* ED, where I was the director of trauma, emergency, and aeromedical services—my father was already undergoing a computed tomography scan. The studies confirmed extensive intra-abdominal injuries, and he was rushed to the OR.

I found myself in the family room, where I'd been so many times before as a nurse giving news to anxious family members. Now I was quite unexpectedly on the other side of the fence. My staff—clearly sharing my pain—gently told me of my mother's death. While I was still reeling from that news, the trauma surgeon—a friend and colleague of 11 years—asked me if I wanted to go to the OR to see my dad before he went under anesthesia. I did.

The invitation included my husband, an emergency medical technician. After rapidly donning gowns, shoe covers, hats, and masks, we were led into the OR. My dad was still awake. I touched his arm and told him I loved him. He told me how much pain he was in. I assured him the team would take good care of him. We didn't speak of my mother, although I suspected he knew from the look on his face. With a nod, I indicated to the anesthesiologist that he should proceed with intubation. My husband and I then left the room. The OR staff, although certainly not used to family presence, was incredibly supportive.

Over the past 4 years, I've often thought of that single moment because it was the last time I ever heard my dad's voice. Although he survived the surgery, he remained intubated and on mechanical ventilation for the next 5 weeks. Ultimately, he died. Though he had moments of awareness before his death, I had to read his lips and was never certain how much he understood. So I'm comforted by the memory of the brief time we had to speak to each other in the OR.

I'm sure both my position in the hospital and my education as a trauma nurse allowed me and my husband a rare privilege that isn't typically offered to families and might not be feasible in most OR settings. The experience gave me insight into the needs of family members confronting the potential loss of a loved one and made me an even stronger advocate for family presence.

—*Linda Laskowski-Jones, RN, APRN,BC, CCRN, CEN, MS*

Taking a stand

Since gaining my own perspective on this issue in a way I'd never wish on anyone, I firmly believe that family presence during resuscitation efforts should be offered as the rule, not the exception, as long as it doesn't pose significant risks to the staff or patient. It conveys to the family a sense of caring and investment in the patient as a unique person and shows respect for the family bond. And it needn't be disruptive if staff is prepared ahead of time and has clear procedures and protocols to guide them. ‹›

REFERENCES
1. Moreland P. Family presence during invasive procedures and resuscitation in the emergency department: A review of the literature. *Journal of Emergency Nursing.* 31(1):58-72, February 2005.

2. Nibert L, Ondrejka D. Family presence during pediatric resuscitation: An integrative review for evidence-based practice. *Journal of Pediatric Nursing.* 20(2):145-147, April 2005.

3. Helmer SD, et al. Family presence during trauma resuscitation: A survey of AAST and ENA members. *Journal of Trauma Injury, Infection, and Critical Care.* 48(6):1015-1024, June 2000.

4. American Heart Association. Part 2: Ethical issues. *Supplement to Circulation.* 112(24):IV-6–IV-11, December 2005.

5. Emergency Nurses Association. Position statement: Family presence at the bedside during invasive procedures and resuscitation. **http://www.ena.org/about/position/PDFs/4E6C256B26994E319F66C65748BFBDBF.pdf.** Accessed August 13, 2006.

6. American Association of Critical-Care Nurses. Practice alert: Family presence during CPR and invasive procedures. *AACN News.* November 2004.

7. Simpson SM. Near-death experience: A concept analysis as applied to nursing. *Journal of Advanced Nursing.* 36(4):520-526, November 2001.

RESOURCES
Eichhorn DJ, et al. Family presence during invasive procedures and resuscitation: Hearing the voice of the patient. *American Journal of Nursing.* 101(5):48-55, May 2001.

Henderson DP, Knapp JF. Report of the National Consensus Conference on Family Presence during Pediatric Cardiopulmonary Resuscitation and Procedures. *Pediatric Emergency Care.* 21(11):787-791, November 2005.

York NL. Implementing a family presence protocol option. *Dimensions of Critical Care Nursing.* 23(2):84-88, March/April 2004.

Linda Laskowski-Jones is vice-president of emergency trauma and aeromedical services for Christiana Care Health System, Wilmington, Del., and a member of the *Nursing2007* editorial advisory board.

After all was said and done, I came to understand the value of frank dialogue to help order chaotic thoughts. This was something I'd never fully realized before, even though I'd been involved in many similar family meetings over the years as a nurse.

I've found that a team composed of a physician and nurse with excellent interpersonal skills who were involved in the event can help family members explore their feelings. These clinicians can help validate family members' concerns and dispel misunderstandings, which may help them cope with their loss.

As a nurse, I've been personally involved in many discussions with family members after a loved one's death. Debriefing offers a constructive forum for them to express their perceptions, questions, and fears about their loved one's illness or injury and lifesaving attempts they observed. When conducted with sensitivity and empathy, debriefing sessions are nearly always well received by family members and professionally gratifying to staff.

 Research Databases

Basic Search   Advanced Search   Visual Search   Choose Databases   Select another EBSCO service   **SIR SANDFORI**

New Search   Keyword

   Result List | Refine Search   🖶 Print ✉ E-mail 💾 Save ⊞ Export 🗁 Add to folder

View: 🖼 Citation 📄 HTML Full Text 📄 PDF Full Text

Title:	**Why Focus on the Whole *Child*?**
Authors:	Scherer, Marge
Source:	Educational Leadership; May2007, Vol. 64 Issue 8, p7-7, 1p
Document Type:	Article
Subject Terms:	PREFACES EDUCATIONAL ideologies
Abstract:	The author discusses the Association for Supervision and Curriculum *Development child* campaign and introduces various articles on that topic in this issue, including F "Assessment Through the Student's Eyes."
Full Text Word Count:	805
ISSN:	0013-1784
Accession Number:	25102086
Persistent link to this record:	http://search.ebscohost.com/login.aspx?direct=true&db=fth&AN=25102086&site=eh
Database:	MasterFILE Elite
Full Text Database:	Academic Search Premier
Notes:	This title is not held locally

Why Focus on the Whole Child?

Section: PERSPECTIVES

The best way to achieve academic achievement is to focus on academic achievement." "You don't need to 1 child. You need to teach him how to read."

"Is there another way to measure success besides test scores? I'm sure it is something squishy and subjective.

These hostile words from the blogosphere echo as I begin to write about why ASCD embraces a campaign c; the whole child." A topic that speaks to many educators' hearts because they see it as the reason they ente education for the whole child can be misunderstood by school critics as anti-accountability, anti-testing, and e reading. It's none of those things. This issue of Educational Leadership urges educators to reclaim the idea skills and subjects, but, above all, children.

First reclaim the curriculum. Back when Thomas Jefferson's library shelves held the world's core knowledge, th educate the young elite did not list reading and basic math as the only subjects worth learning. They set challenging goals for public education. Among them, as Richard Rothstein and colleagues (p. 8) write, were to enable them to know their rights, and to teach them to conduct their social relations with intelligence and hear no matter their economic class--want a lot more than the basic skills for their children, too. They want a chal critical thinking, social skills, citizenship, health, the arts, and preparation for skilled employment.

At a recent symposium, participants noted that schools are stealing time from history, the arts, and rece instructional time to tested subjects. Diane Ravitch, who espouses a core curriculum, spoke eloquently:

Education must aim for far more than mastery of the basics, far more than the possession of tools for econom Certainly it should aim for enough (content) for an examined life, enough for civic virtue, and enough for those incline one to think, to read, to listen, to discuss, to feel just a bit uncertain about one's opinions, and to love l Week, Jan. 30, 2007)

Marion Brady, an opponent of traditional curriculum, interestingly expresses a similar idea. He writes:

We've created a way of life that makes specialized studies indispensable. But assuming that the core fields a whole story has also cost much, and the costs are escalating. School finally isn't about disciplines and subje they were originally meant to do-help the young make more sense of life, more sense of experience, more sens future. (Education Week, Aug. 30, 2006)

Next, reclaim instruction. Emily Dickinson wrote, "Tell all the truth, but tell it slant. Success in circuit lies." An taught knows that "telling it doesn't mean teaching it." To engage students in learning, a master teacher n Tomlinson and Amy Germundson write (p. 27), do something like create jazz: One must borrow from many tra the melody line, blend surprise and improvisation, and, most important, connect with those for whom one i virtually impossible to make things relevant for or expect personal excellence from a student you don't know teacher must find some way to move the student with the music."

Reclaim assessment. Historically, a major role of assessment has been to rank students. Today despite cla student to proficiency, tests still create winners and losers. How to reclaim assessment as an educative proces focus. (p. 22). He writes:

When we use assessment for learning, assessment becomes far more than merely a onetime event stuck instruction unit. It becomes a series of interlaced experiences that enhance the learning process by keeping stu focused on their progress, even in the face of occasional setbacks.... Even the most valid and reliable asse regarded as high quality if it causes a student to give up.

Reclaim kids. The teenagers in the study The Silent Epidemic told researchers that the main reason they dro was boredom with classes. Other reasons were that they missed too many days and could not catch up, that th interested in school, and that they were failing. Seventy-one percent indicated that they started becoming d school as early as 9th and 10th grade.

ASCD's whole child campaign is a way of stopping the waste of too much talent and the loss of too many potential is the hard reality against which educators do battle every day. Squishy? Subjective? Far from it.

~~~~~~~~~~

By Marge Scherer

View: Citation HTML Full Text PDF Full Text

SECOND OPINION

Who will endure as nursing's leading light?

ANDRÉ PICARD
MAY 10, 2007

International Nurses Day is celebrated each year on May 12, Florence Nightingale's birthday.

The "lady with the lamp" who selflessly ministered to the sick remains the enduring symbol of nursing.

But is that an appropriate image for the modern nurse, or is it time to say "Goodnight, Florence," and retire Ms. Nightingale as the icon for the largest health-care profession, as was suggested by a British nursing union?

If not the lamp alit, what is the appropriate contemporary symbol of nursing? And what of the legacy of the founder of modern nursing?

Print Edition - Section Front

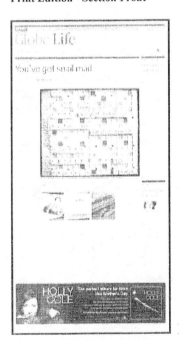

life of privilege to pursue her "calling," tending to British soldiers during the Crimean War.

Ms. Nightingale's most celebrated achievement, however, was not hers alone. Her floor-scrubbing and laundering is credited for the drop in the death rate at a British barracks hospital to 2 per cent from 40 per cent.

In reality, that dramatic turnabout did not come about when nurses arrived, but only after the sewers at the barracks were cleaned out.

Regardless, Ms. Nightingale was a crusader and reformer. While she didn't shovel out the sewers herself, she nonetheless revolutionized battlefield medicine. She greatly advanced public health and hygiene, made nursing a respectable profession, did pioneering work on the link between poverty and health, campaigned for the rights of prostitutes and property rights for women, and made groundbreaking use of health statistics.

Modern nurses have a similarly diverse range of interests and achievements. They toil not only in hospitals and nursing homes, but on inner-city streets, battlefields in Afghanistan, refugee camps in Sudan, and in schools, public health units, northern nursing stations and myriad other locales.

When Ms. Nightingale began nursing in 1851, as the superintendent of the Institution for Gentlewomen in London, hospitals were squalid places with horrid working conditions. Nursing was a lowly, menial task.

In relative terms, today's health-care institutions are not much better, and the work environment of nurses continues to be disgracefully bad. Nurses' pay is not paltry, but it is not commensurate with the skills and training required, and nursing is one of the few professions where the hiring of people on a casual, rather than permanent, basis is rampant.

(None of which is coincidental to the fact that 96 per cent of nurses are women.)

Nurses, paradoxically, are among Canada's sickest workers. They have epidemic rates of back injury, troubling levels of depression, astronomical rates of sick days. Early retirement due to burnout is becoming the norm.

As in Victorian times, the most persistent challenge for most nurses - the greatest impediment to caring for their patients - is pathogens, the bacteria, viruses and other bugs that stalk the halls.

So, if Ms. Nightingale were a nursing leader today, whatever would she do?

Without a doubt, she would promote professionalism and education. Thanks to her wealthy background, she was able to get a "man's education."

She recognized that nursing required more than soft hands and a warm heart (as the condescending saying goes). Rather, good care has a scientific basis.

A modern-day Florence Nightingale would, no doubt, embrace politically unpopular causes such as safe injection sites, decriminalization of prostitution, provision of affordable housing, the raising of the minimum wage and so on, because all have clear public health benefits.

She would rail against the nursing shortage - which is expected to hit 113,000 in Canada by the year 2011 - decry excessive workloads and the fact that nurses continue to be relegated to second-class status among health professionals.

Reborn, Ms. Nightingale would push for the expansion of practice guidelines, for a greater role for nurse practitioners, and for nurses as leaders of interdisciplinary health-care teams.

A leader of her ilk would, as she did 1½centuries ago, recognize the primordial importance of cleanliness and good hygiene in hospitals. She would be appalled by the rate of medical errors, and the routine spread of pathogens.

The 21st-Century incarnation of Florence Nightingale would also use all the tools at her disposal to fight the problem, including good research and new technology like personal digital assistants to track patient health records.

Today's nurse is not the romanticized docile, obedient lady with the lamp.

Today's nurse is the educated, headstrong, professional woman with a PDA. (And probably a backache, too.)

That is the legacy of Florence Nightingale, and the image that should be celebrated on International Nurses Day.

And, in that vein, the leaders of our health-care sector - hospital administrators, policy makers and politicians alike - should be marking May 12 with concrete proposals for improving the working conditions of nurses, not merely cake, balloons and feel-good speeches.

apicard@globeandmail.com

globeandmail.com and The Globe and Mail are divisions of CTVglobemedia Publishing Inc., 444 Front St. W., Toronto, ON Canada M5V 2S9
Phillip Crawley, Publisher

Personal Support Workers

Announcements

1st Annual PSW Conference 2007

March 14: 2007: OCSA is pleased to announce a launch of a new division, the **Personal Support Network of Ontario (PSNO)**.

Membership Information

Any personal support worker, community care worker, personal attendant or other frontline staff involved in personal care is eligible for a PSW Individual membership with the Ontario Community Support Association.

Benefits

- A subscription to OCSA's PSW newsletter which is published twice a year. The PSW Newsletter provides updates on what's new in community health affecting frontline staff, information on what is happening across the province, training information and job postings
- 10% discount off fees for all PSW Enhancement Training offered by Capacity Builders
- Certificate of membership
- Membership discount for the 1st Annual PSW Conference
- Free Prior Learning Assessments for those with training from outside the province
- Online job board
- Answers to your most frequently asked questions
- Access to Group Home and Auto Insurance Coverage (coming Jan 2007)
- Access to Professional Liability Insurance and Abuse Coverage (now available)
- Access to Short and Long Term Disability Coverage

What is a PSW?

PSW Training Background

PSW FAQs

Log into PSW Members Only

PSW Career Board

PSW Training Opportunities

PSW News

How to become a member

PSW Section Homepage

(coming Winter 2007)
- Networking via a PSW email Listserv and an online "members only" section

PSW membership: Discounts for Larger Groups

We have had several inquiries from members about the possibility of discounting the PSW membership for providers who would like to fund it for a group of personal support workers. **The following rates are available to providers and groups who wish to enroll 50 or more PSW's:**

50-100 PSW's:	15% discount
101-500 PSW's:	20% discount
501-1000 PSW's:	25% discount
1001+ PSW's:	30% discount

Other options to discount rates for larger groups of personal support workers include:

- splitting the cost between agency and staff
- organizing staff to all sign up at once and the group receives the discount (versus the agency)

For more information, contact Lori Payne at: 416-256-3010 x242, or email: lori.payne@ocsa.on.ca

A membership application form is available here.

Helping People Live at Home

COMMUNICATION AT WORK

PART ONE

INTRODUCTION TO COMMUNICATION

"Say what's on your mind, Harris—the language
of dance has always eluded me."

CHAPTER ONE

THE COMMUNICATION PROCESS

Chapter Objectives

Successful completion of this chapter will enable you to:

1 Identify the three parts of the communication process.

2 Identify your purpose for communicating in a given situation.

3 Identify the needs and relevant characteristics of your audience.

4 Select the medium best suited to your purpose and audience.

5 Use nonverbal communication to enhance the effectiveness of a verbal message.

6 Plan your oral or written message to overcome communication barriers.

1 INTRODUCTION: THREE PARTS OF THE COMMUNICATION PROCESS

Communication is a process. A process is a set of actions or changes that brings about a specific result. In the communication process, a message is conveyed from sender to receiver. Because a message is something you can see or hear, it is tempting to think that the message *is* communication. But communication involves an interaction among sender, message, and receiver; it is a process, not a product. This point is important to remember when you are planning communication or trying to improve it.

In the communication process, the **sender** formulates an idea or set of ideas that he or she wishes to communicate to a receiver. The sender selects the verbal and/or nonverbal means that will be used to convey the idea to the receiver. In this way an idea becomes a **message.** The message is then transmitted to its audience by a channel or medium such as speech, writing, or gesture. The **receiver** receives the message—that is, he or she sees or hears it. The receiver must also **decode** the message, so that he or she understands the idea that the sender was attempting to convey (see also Figure 1.1).

FIGURE 1.1 The Communication Process

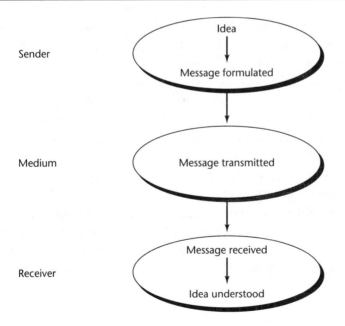

Planning Your Message

Getting all the elements of the communication process to interact successfully takes planning. Just as a well-run meeting has an agenda to make sure that important issues are discussed and decisions are made, a well-crafted message has a plan to ensure that the sender's ideas reach the receiver accurately and effectively. On page 13 you will see a sample **planning worksheet.** You wouldn't want to fill one out every time you had to write or speak, but you may find it a useful tool for planning your assignments in this course. By the end of the semester, the planning steps should have become internalized so that you automatically consider purpose, audience, medium, and message whenever you communicate.

2 IDENTIFYING YOUR PURPOSE

In our everyday social life, communication is often an end in itself. We enjoy sharing our ideas and feelings as a way of expressing ourselves and building relationships. At work, however, we are generally communicating to achieve a purpose related to the goals of the organization. When we say that the communication process has been a success, we mean that the sender's message has produced the desired impact on the audience. In your job, you may have little choice about messages that must be conveyed—your car is ready, you're overdrawn, your cheque is in the mail—but you are able to determine whether these messages are communicated effectively to your audience.

Try to express your purpose as something that can be seen or measured. This will help you evaluate the success of your message after you send it. For example, if you are sending an e-mail message to your supervisor about problems with your computer, think of your purpose as "getting a new computer" or "getting a visit from a technical support person" rather than as "letting my supervisor know I'm having problems." The more clearly you understand your purpose in communicating, the more effectively you can plan the format, the content, and the words that will help you achieve this purpose.

Remember that messages often have more than one purpose. If you are answering a customer's questions about your package tours, you are giving information, but you should also—if you're a good company representative—be trying to persuade the customer to choose your tour rather than someone else's. If you are turning down a request for a refund, you are conveying bad news, but you should also be trying to retain the goodwill of your audience toward your organization.

See if you can identify the purpose or purposes of the following messages:

(a)

BRING A FRIEND. BUY ONE, GET ONE FREE.

Present this card when you purchase a ticket for any of our shows and receive a second ticket with our compliments.

Lighthouse Theatres

_____

_____

(b) Covering letter enclosed with a résumé.

_____

_____

(c) Announcement of a special discount offer from a newly opened shop.

_____

_____

(d)

Emma's mom just stopped shopping for diapers.

Forever.

She joined The Bottom Line and now cloth diapers are delivered right to their door and picked up for washing too!

JOIN TODAY AND RECIEVE
your first week free when you sign up
for 3 months of service

The Bottom Line
1-866-555-9278
www.thebottomlinecompany.ca

© Royalty-free/Corbis

_____

_____

(e) Letter to the manager of a hotel describing the unsatisfactory service you received.

_____

_____

(f) Tips on preventing car theft that are enclosed with insurance renewal notice.

_____

_____

(g) Letter of thanks from a business to a printing company that rushed a special order.

_____

_____

(h) Store plaque with name and picture of the "Employee of the Month."

_____

_____

(i) Letter to an unsuccessful job applicant.

_____

_____

(j)

**AN URGENT MESSAGE TO OWNERS
OF COFFEE CADDY COFFEE MAKERS:
STOP USING THE COFFEE MAKER
FOR ANY PURPOSE**

- Some Coffee Caddy coffee makers can be dangerous to use.
- The complete plastic top may separate from the glass pot without warning.

If you have a Coffee Caddy coffee maker, please fill out and return the coupon below.

Do not return the coffee maker. Keep it until you hear from Coffee Caddy. We will send you further information and a special offer.

We regret any inconvenience; however, we are concerned for your safety. Thank you for your cooperation.

---

3 IDENTIFYING YOUR AUDIENCE

Once you have established your purpose in all its dimensions, your next consideration should be your **audience.** Who will be reading or listening to your message? In personal situations, you have already had extensive practice in shaping your message to your audience. For example, consider how you would tell a friend that you were behind on a project and how you would tell the same thing to a teacher from whom you were hoping to get an extension. A change of audience means a change of vocabulary, of tone, of content, and of length. The more you know, or can intuitively guess, about your audience, the better you can tailor your message to meet their needs.

Think about the experience and occupation of your audience. What general knowledge or special knowledge do they have about your subject? What is their attitude to your subject—friendly, hostile, neutral, or bored? What is your relationship to your audience? What direction will your message be travelling in? As you plan and/or write your message, imagine that you are getting feedback from your audience throughout the process. What are some of the questions your audience might ask you? Does your message answer typical questions like Why? How? and So what?

4 SELECTING THE APPROPRIATE MEDIUM

"The medium is the message." This statement by communications theorist Marshall McLuhan was a buzz phrase in the 1960s but is still relevant today. The means you use to transmit your message will contribute almost as much to its success in achieving its purpose as your choice of words will. Sometimes you will be told to "put it in writing." At other times, you will be asked to "say a few words" at a meeting or "get on the phone to head office." In these situations, you have no chance to decide which medium you would prefer. Sometimes, however, you will be able to choose whether to write, visit someone in person, phone, or use other technology. Your decision should be based on more than personal preference: the advantages of each medium should be carefully weighed.

Advantages of Oral Communication

1. **Speaking takes less time than writing.** The average person speaks at a rate of about 150 words a minute. Composing a 150-word message on paper, even a rough draft, would take much longer. Even the physical act of transcribing on a keyboard does not approach the speed of oral communication.

2. **There are fewer mechanical problems to worry about.** Grammar and punctuation are much more flexible in oral communication, and, of course, spelling doesn't exist in speech. Errors can be corrected immediately, and in any event they are less likely to be remembered, or even noticed, by the audience.

3. **The speaker's voice and body language add meaning and variety.** A speaker can communicate with gesture, tone, volume, eye contact, and physical appearance. These details not only expand and clarify the message but also hold the attention of the audience.

4. **Speaking allows feedback from the receiver.** Because the sender and receiver are together at the same time and often in the same place, it is easier for the sender to feel in control of the communication process and more confident that his or her message is being received. The more one-to-one feedback the situation permits, the more control the sender has, because an oral message can be easily revised to meet the needs of the receiver and thereby fulfill the sender's purpose.

5. **Speaking is more personal.** The audience generally feels closer to the sender and more involved in the communication process when a message is delivered orally. The speaker also generally feels closer to his or her audience. Speaking emphasizes the human element in communication.

Disadvantages of Oral Communication

Oral communication does, however, have its downside. Its special characteristics, so valuable in some situations, can pose a major barrier to communication in others.

1. **The speaker's voice, appearance, or body language can compete with the verbal message for the listener's attention.** Overlapping verbal and nonverbal messages often lead different listeners to come away from a meeting or a conversation with very different memories of what they "heard."

2. **Internal or external distractions can cause the listener to miss the message.** Your listeners may be more concerned with their personal problems or their plans for the weekend than they are with your message. Or they may be unable to hear or focus because of noise or activity going on at the same time.

3. **Speaking is more personal.** This factor becomes a disadvantage when conflict exists between speaker and listener. People often find it difficult to respond to the message rather than the messenger.

4. **Oral communication is most effective when speaker and listener are together at the same time.** It can be challenging to find a time when busy people are all available, especially if they are in different time zones.

Advantages of Written Communication

1. **The receiver must take an active role in the communication process.** Written communication places much more control in the hands of the receiver. Because a reader has so much control over the delivery of the message, a writer can cover more complex material than a speaker can and still be confident that the audience can take it all in.

2. **Reading is faster than listening.** You can read from three to five times more in an hour than you could hear delivered orally.

3. **Writing is less personal.** A written report makes it much easier to concentrate on the contents rather than on the author. Likewise, writers can distance themselves from negative feelings they may have about the intended audience. This distance also relieves the stress of anticipating some kind of immediate negative feedback.

4. **Writing provides a permanent record.** If you have ever forgotten someone's name five seconds after you were introduced, you will recognize the impossibility of retaining in your head even a tiny fraction of the information necessary to run a business. The economic and cultural structure of modern society depends on our ability to store and retrieve immense amounts of information.

Modern electronic media now make it possible to preserve oral records, but the expense, the trouble, and the difficulty of efficient access to oral records make written records better and more efficient.

5. **Writing can be revised.** It's the Big Meeting. You are scheduled to give a short report on your department's progress in employment equity. Just before your turn comes, the person beside you accidentally sets a jelly doughnut on your notes. You get to the podium, trying to be subtle as you wipe off your note cards. Unfortunately, the ink is coming off with the jelly. You're very nervous, so some of the connections you want to make get lost in the delivery. Things seem under control until you discover that your last two note cards are stuck together. You wind up as best you can and return to your seat. Only when you sit down do you notice the blob of jelly on your tie.

Well, you may console yourself that there will be other opportunities. But this one is gone for all time. Circumstances did not allow you to make the best of it. Writing, on the other hand, gives you an infinite number of second chances. If your first draft is a failure, there can be a second, third, fourth—until the final version represents the best effort you are capable of. Your audience will not be aware of the sweat and toil and the many inferior attempts; all they will see will be the polished final result.

Matching the Medium to Your Audience

Fortunately, modern technology can help you enjoy the advantages of speaking or writing in any given situation while overcoming the disadvantages. For example, e-mail has made it possible to send a message and receive feedback at high speed, while still allowing you to edit the message, send it to one person or many people, and keep a copy on file. Thus it combines some of the best features of the letter and the telephone call. Cell phones and voice mail have reduced the frustration of "telephone tag," where two people with conflicting office schedules could never reach one another by phone.

To select the medium that is best suited to your message, audience, and purpose, ask yourself how important each of the following criteria will be to you in this situation:

- **Speed.** How long can I wait for my message to be received?
- **Security.** Is privacy important? Is legal confidentiality an issue?
- **Visual impact.** Is it important for the message to look impressive?
- **Accessibility and permanence.** Do I expect my message to be referred to more than once?

- **Efficiency.** How important is it to me to reduce the cost or effort of sending this message?

Ask yourself about the needs of your audience as well. Generally everyone opens mail and answers the telephone. But many people will not open an e-mail message unless they know who sent it, and other people are slow to answer e-mails, or return phone messages, or do either. A letter, a phone call, or a phone message saying an e-mail is being sent are good ways to begin the communication process.

Generally it is best to respond to a message in the same medium in which it was sent. The person who left a voice-mail message will be expecting a call back; the person who e-mailed you will be checking his or her messages for your reply.

Suppose you wished to transmit some detailed tax calculations to your supervisor. Should you deliver them orally by phone, or in person? Spoken communication is faster, more interesting and personal, and allows feedback from the receiver. How relevant are these considerations to your task? Written communication allows the receiver to control communication, takes less time on the part of the receiver, and provides a permanent record. Clearly, these considerations far outweigh the advantages of oral communication in this case. Writing allows busy administrators to receive the information at their convenience. They can spend as much time as necessary to go through the complex data and then file the information for later reference. The transmission of written material within an organization is usually rapid.

In another situation, a client might have called with a problem. You need to negotiate a solution. Speaking gives you the immediate two-way communication you require. Or, imagine that you are soliciting donations to the Canadian Coalition Against Acne. Because the sender has greater control in speaking than in writing, you choose a phone campaign, knowing that it is harder to hang up on someone than it is to sling junk mail in the wastebasket. Or you go door to door, because personal contact makes it yet more difficult to refuse a request. Often a stressful situation, such as handling a complaint or firing someone, requires all the resources of face-to-face discussion.

Here are some examples of communication situations in which you might find yourself. Assume that you have access to all of the communication media on the list below. For each of the following situations, write the number of the medium you would use on the blank line. In case of a tie, put both numbers, joined by "or." If you would use more than one medium in a situation, put both numbers, joined by "and."

1. personal visit
2. phone call
3. voice mail
4. letter
5. fax
6. paper memo
7. e-mail

_____ 1. You need to confirm the location of a meeting taking place tomorrow.

_____ 2. A colleague who works at another office has sent you a draft of the proposal you are working on together. You find some errors when you are proofreading it. Your colleague has the disk.

_____ 3. A long-time client in another city has written an angry letter about a major foul-up.

_____ 4. You wish to request a leave of absence from your job.

_____ 5. You are coordinating a national conference. Since the time you sent out the information package to registrants, there have been important changes to the program. The conference begins in two weeks.

_____ 6. An employee has asked you for details about company life insurance benefits.

_____ 7. You want to introduce yourself to a new employee.

_____ 8. Your former supervisor, who transferred to head office six months ago, has been promoted to vice-president. You want to congratulate her.

_____ 9. Another employee has been helping herself to goodies you've stashed in the fridge.

_____ 10. A shipment of gazingus wires arrived from Vancouver minus 52 units. You must inform the supplier.

5 NONVERBAL MESSAGES

Nonverbal messages can compete with verbal messages and create distraction. In these situations, nonverbal messages create barriers to effective communication. Ideally, however, nonverbal messages such as appearance, gesture, expression, and tone of voice should support what you write or say and increase its positive effect on your audience. For example, a crisply printed report with a well-laid-out title page and an appropriate cover will suggest that the writer has put thought and effort into the content as well. The following sections discuss some basic ways to enhance communication nonverbally.

PLANNING WORKSHEET

Purpose

Why am I sending this message? What will be the measurable result if my message is successful?

_____

_____

_____

_____

_____

Audience

Who will be reading or listening? What do I know, or what can I predict about him/her/them?

_____

_____

_____

_____

Medium

How will I be sending this message? Why is this the best choice?

_____

_____

_____

_____

Message

What information does my audience want/need to achieve my purpose?

_____

_____

_____

_____

Appearance and Grooming

If you hope to be a supervisor some day, observe what people in senior jobs wear and how they look. It's more important to reflect the standards of your workplace than to make a fashion statement. If your job as a salesperson, for example, takes you to many different kinds of workplaces, a conservative, tailored look is a safe choice. Invest in a good briefcase, and clean it out and organize it regularly. Never root around in it in front of supervisors or clients. Buy an expensive, or at least expensive-looking, pen.

Gesture and Body Language

Whether you are speaking or listening, your body language should show that you are involved with the communication process. Lolling back in your chair, folding your arms, looking away or carrying out tasks like straightening your desk, all send the opposite message. Maintain eye contact during conversation and turn to face the speaker in a meeting. If you are sitting, avoid slumping, but don't sit too rigidly; it's normal to listen actively with your whole body. Keep your arms off the arms of the chair. When you are speaking, it is natural to emphasize your point with your hands; some people do this more than others. Just avoid gestures that can be seen as hostile, such as touching or finger-pointing. Negative body language, such as eye-rolling, pinching the lips, or heaving a sigh, is just as offensive as a negative comment.

Tone of Voice

The human voice is a very expressive instrument, and with a simple change of emphasis, anyone can turn a statement like "How great to see you!" from a friendly greeting to a crushing insult. Even a voice without expression communicates a nonverbal message; when a telemarketer says, "I'm sure you, like all Canadians, are very interested in receiving liposuction in the privacy of your home," in a complete monotone, we know that he or she is reading off a script. More and more people in service jobs, in both the public and private sectors, are also being trained to use a kind of script; for example, to greet every caller by saying "I'm X. How may I help you today?" In theory, this should get across the message that the agency or the business is here to help you, the client. In practice, depending on the way in which the greeting is spoken, the message is often, "Why are you bothering me?"

The fact is that if there is a choice between believing the words or the tone of voice, your listener will choose the tone of voice every time.

6 ELIMINATING COMMUNICATION BARRIERS

Earlier in this chapter you were encouraged to express the purpose of a message as something observable or measurable, so you would be able to judge whether or not you had communicated successfully. What happens if your purpose is not achieved? How can you do better next time? The planning worksheet is a useful tool for finding barriers to communication and creating a better message when the first attempt has been unsuccessful. Look at your original plan, or fill out the sheet if you did not fill it out before. Then ask yourself the following questions:

Purpose

Is my purpose clear to me? If I have more than one purpose, do they conflict in any way? Do I have a way of measuring the success of my message?

Audience

Do I know the needs of my audience? Have I tried to put myself in the reader's or listener's place in creating this message to make it clear, complete, and respectful?

Medium

Did I decide to send the message this way because it was convenient and familiar, or did I choose the best medium for my audience and message? Did unexpected events prevent delivery of my message? What backup plan do I need in case of technical failure or human mistakes?

Message

Is everything in my message relevant to my audience and purpose? Am I sending a nonverbal message that conflicts with my purpose?

CHAPTER REVIEW/SELF-TEST

1. "Communication" is
   (a) an oral or written message.
   (b) a three-part process.
   (c) a medium for transmitting ideas.
   (d) all of the above.

Chapter One: The Communication Process

2. The first step in communication planning is
   (a) choosing the appropriate format.
   (b) discovering and expressing your feelings on the subject.
   (c) building a relationship with the receiver.
   (d) identifying the measurable result if your message is successful.

3. Knowing the needs and characteristics of the intended receiver of your message will help you choose
   (a) the length of the message.
   (b) the vocabulary and sentence structure of the message.
   (c) the tone of the message.
   (d) all of the above.

4. If you have the choice of how to send your message, you should consider
   (a) what is fastest and most convenient for you.
   (b) which medium will be most likely to help you achieve your purpose.
   (c) which medium is the most commonly used.
   (d) your personal preferences.

5. Oral communication is a good choice if
   (a) you are delivering bad news to a coworker.
   (b) your message is long and detailed.
   (c) your relationship with the receiver has been negative.
   (d) your receiver is very busy.

6. Written communication is a good choice if
   (a) your message is urgent.
   (b) you haven't had a chance to think much about the subject.
   (c) your message has legal importance.
   (d) your receiver may consider your subject boring or unpleasant.

7. Written communication is particularly important in the workplace because
   (a) it can be revised for accuracy and good style.
   (b) it provides a permanent record.
   (c) it is easy to store and retrieve.
   (d) all of the above.

8. E-mail can be used in any situation where written communication is appropriate except
   (a) with elderly clients or customers.
   (b) when the contents are confidential.
   (c) when it is important that the message have no spelling or grammar errors.
   (d) when the message must be well laid out on the page.

9. Use electronic communication to
   (a) combine the advantages of oral and written communication.
   (b) impress clients and coworkers with your state-of-the-art equipment.
   (c) compensate for weaknesses in your message.
   (d) all of the above.

10. When your message does not achieve its intended purpose, you should
    (a) blame the receiver.
    (b) send it again.
    (c) use a planning worksheet to analyze your audience and identify possible problems with your purpose, medium, or message.
    (d) upgrade your technology.

Answers

1.B   2.D   3.D   4.B   5.A   6.C   7.D   8.B   9.A   10.C

EXERCISES

1. John Green had been running the marketing department at World Trek Tours for 12 years. Perhaps "running" wasn't quite the word; John's attitude was that since the employees all knew their jobs, he should just let them get on with it. As a result, the department was inefficient but friendly. The employees were genuinely shocked when John got the axe, apparently without warning, just before it was time to start planning the summer holiday promotions. No one knew anything about his replacement, Ed Harley. According to the grapevine, Ed was right out of a marketing program, with no experience in the travel industry. Someone had suggested that his primary purpose was to shake up the department and send some people out the door after John Green. So Dan wasn't exactly looking forward to his first meeting with Ed.

   As head of the advertising department for eight years and a personal friend of John Green, Dan was closely identified with the "old guard." Ed had scheduled the meeting for 9:30; by 9:50, sitting in the reception area, Dan had had plenty of time to become nervous. Through the door he could hear Ed's voice: "Well, I'm not talking about soya beans, sweetheart, so what are you telling me? See if you can get your rear in gear." The phone slammed down, and Ed's door burst open. "Dan—c'mon in and sit down." Dan was motioned to an armless swivel chair. Ed continued to stand, staring out the window, with his back to Dan. Suddenly he swung around. "Dan, can you answer one question for me? Why is the marketing department such a complete and utter disaster area?" Dan's eyes goggled as he took this in.

"Now, I know," Ed continued, "that John Green was a burnt-out incompetent who didn't know a marketing mix from a cake mix, and I know that this department has been a refuge for every loser and lead-swinger in the company, but I'm still mystified, genuinely mystified, at how *totally* inept the whole operation has become. Do you recognize this?" Ed whipped a sheet of paper off his desk and held it an inch from Dan's nose. "No, I'm … that is … " Dan tried to focus on the page. "It's a memo regarding planning the summer promotions," Ed answered his own question. "Oh, yeah—Tina James and Ted Burton put that out. It's … " "It's a hunk of crud," Ed snapped. "I wouldn't use these guidelines to plan a trip to the men's room, let alone a $1.3 million campaign! What's going on here?"

"Well, I'm … " Dan cleared his throat. "Well, I'm not in on that part of the process. They usually get that stuff from Brenda and Roy, and then the research team works on it. I'm not involved until … " "I don't care if they got it from Mickey and Goofy. It's not worth the paper to print it." Ed moved over behind Dan's chair. "Now, things here have just—bumbled along; everybody doing his own thing and all one big happy family. Well, let's get one thing straight." Ed swivelled the chair around and bent down until he and Dan were nose-to-nose. "The party's over." He straightened up. "That's all I have to say. You can go now." Dan made his way toward the door. Ed picked up the phone and started to dial. "Close the door behind you, would you."

Use the following questions to identify some barriers to communication in this situation:

(a) What communication barriers existed between Ed and Dan even before they met?
(b) What nonverbal messages were sent from Ed to Dan? How would these messages be likely to affect Dan?
(c) What statements by Ed would be likely to create communication barriers between him and Dan?
(d) What impression of Ed will Dan convey to his fellow workers? Will this help Ed communicate effectively in future interviews with other personnel?
(e) Ed seems to be using intimidation as a management strategy. How can this backfire?

2. Identify barriers to communication that could arise in the following situations:
(a) A caller begins a telephone conversation with the comment, "You're a hard person to get hold of."
(b) During a business meeting, your cell phone rings several times. Your ring tone is a version of "The Drugs Aren't Working."
(c) A job hunter uses her present employer's machine to fax résumés to other companies.
(d) A company produces a brochure to recruit college graduates. Pictures of a diverse workplace appear to have been created by Photoshop.

(e) A job hunter applies a generous splash of Olde Gymbagg aftershave before he leaves for an interview.

(f) A customer phones and is kept on hold for 17 minutes. Every 30 seconds she is told, "Your call is important to us."

(g) A fundraising auction for the Animal Welfare League includes a fur stole and a barbeque.

3. Select an example of any of the following: magazine advertisement, office memo, instruction manual or package insert, informational or promotional brochure, personal letter, short business report, "junk" mail. In a brief essay (250 words):

(a) describe why the message was delivered in writing rather than orally;

(b) state what changes would have to be made in the text of the message to adapt it to effective oral communication.

4. You are the owner/manager of Head-to-Toe Beauty Spa. Decide whether you would handle the following communication situations in person (P), in writing (W), or by telephone (T), or write in another technology, such as fax or e-mail:

(a) You want to contact the placement service of your local community college to recruit students for part-time jobs. _____

(b) You want to contact a European supplier about a product line that you recently read about. _____

(c) You want to let your regular customers know about upcoming specials. _____

(d) You discovered some items missing in a recent shipment of beauty supplies. _____

(e) Customers have complained that your massage therapist has cold hands; you want to let her know. _____

(f) You need information about municipal health regulations. _____

(g) You want to tell someone who recently sent you a résumé that you have no full-time openings. _____

(h) Because of a cancellation, an appointment is available tomorrow for a waiting customer. _____

(i) A cheque from a regular customer was recently returned NSF from the bank. _____

(j) You need some advice about expanding the floor area of your shop. _____

5. Prepare a **planning worksheet,** following the example on page 13, for one of the following situations:

(a) Your daughter's soccer team needs a sponsor. You wish to approach a local business for support.

(b) A friend is looking for a job. You want to get her an interview at your workplace.

(c) A client regularly sends you e-mail, which your workplace computer thinks is "spam." You would like him to use a different server to avoid this problem, which has been going on for several months.

(d) Your workplace currently rewards the "Employee of the Month" with a special parking spot near the front door. You would like to see an appropriate alternative offered to any "Employee of the Month" who doesn't drive to work.

(e) You have evidence that one of your employees is using his workplace computer to sell items on the Internet during working hours.

CHAPTER TWO

· ·

STYLE IN BUSINESS COMMUNICATION

Chapter Objectives

Successful completion of this chapter will enable you to:

1 Edit your written messages to eliminate wordiness and unclear phrasing.

2 Deliver a clear, concise oral message.

3 Edit your written communication to ensure a positive, reader-oriented, and non-discriminatory tone.

4 Use a positive, audience-oriented, and non-discriminatory tone in your oral communication.

INTRODUCTION

You may think at first that the word "style" is out of place in a book about communicating in the workplace. It may suggest to you a kind of literary decoration, a polished surface that has nothing to do with the real content of the message. It is true that on the job we are concerned with getting a task done, not impressing others with our artistic use of language. But while the style of a poem or novel might be inappropriate in the workplace, everything you say or write has a style. You want to find the style that is most effective in achieving the purpose of your message.

Some people still think that "business writing" requires special jargon—long words for simple ideas, phrases like "as per your request" or "with regard to the above." In fact, these are leftovers from a more formal era, no more appropriate in today's environment than green eyeshades or quill pens. Contemporary practice is simply to adapt good English to work situations by applying a few simple principles:

1. Make your message clear by being concise and using simple, concrete words.
2. Proofread to ensure standard spelling, grammar, and punctuation.
3. Emphasize the importance of your audience by using the words "you" and "your" as often as possible.
4. Create a positive impression by avoiding words with strong negative overtones, putting statements in positive form, and emphasizing positive characteristics.
5. Eliminate racist or sexist bias in speaking and writing.

1 WRITING FOR CLARITY

Unclear communication causes costly delays and mistakes. Your style must be clear to ensure that your audience receives your ideas quickly and accurately.

CASE 1

Brad had worked hard on his message for Mr. Santos. He knew that communication skills were really important in the department, and he wanted Mr. Santos to know that he could be counted on to carry some of the responsibility for report writing and correspondence. So this assignment had been a big challenge. Mr. Santos had just picked up Brad's draft from his mailbox. If he liked it, the whole department would soon be reading it. Of course, it would be under Mr. Santos's name, so Brad had tried to make it sound as businesslike and formal as he could. "Those of us who are on the management team have identified the personnel situation as an area of concern. Something that could be done about this is to implement regular opportunities for group discussion, which could take place on a scheduled basis without interfering with your normal work routines. If you are of the opinion that this could change things in a positive direction, please come prepared at a meeting which will be held in the boardroom next Wednesday morning at 10 AM."

About an hour later Brad found a message in his mailbox:

"Subject: Meeting, Wednesday 10 AM"

Brad started to read eagerly. But, wait a minute — almost every word had been changed. Mr. Santos didn't like his draft. What had gone wrong?

Why had Mr. Santos not used Brad's version of the message? Unfortunately for Brad, his writing lacked conciseness and clarity. His message was obscured by vague, wordy phrases, while Mr. Santos wanted something that could be read and understood quickly and precisely. Here is Mr. Santos's version:

Are you concerned about staff cutbacks? If you are, come to a meeting and share your views. Several meeting times will be offered to fit your work schedule. The first will be held this Wednesday at 10 AM in the boardroom.

Here are some suggestions to help you avoid Brad's mistakes and achieve a clear, concise, and readable style.

Conciseness

Planned repetition—for example, repeating an important deadline at the end of a memo—can help your audience understand and remember your message better. Unplanned repetition—redundancy—wastes reading and listening time and may confuse your audience. Eliminate redundant expressions like the following:

Redundant	Concise
have need of	need
for the purpose of	for
the amount of $38.50	$38.50
period of time	time
red in colour	red
the city of Edmonton	Edmonton
attractive in appearance	attractive
the month of December	December
I would like to take this occasion to ...	I would like to ...

Chapter Two: Style in Business Communication

past experience	experience
until such time as	until
he is engaged in researching	he is researching
refer back	refer
a matter of managing	managing
at a time when	when
on the subject of	on

Some expressions, while not redundant, contain more words than are needed to express the thought. While it may not seem worth your while to eliminate one or two words, think of it in percentage terms. Reducing a ten-word sentence to eight words is a 20 percent saving; it means reducing a five-page report to four pages, with the resulting saving in keyboarding, paper, photocopying, and so on. Here are some examples of wordy expressions. Write a concise version beside each.

Wordy   **Concise**

due to the fact that   _____

in the neighbourhood of   _____

in the event that   _____

it may be that   _____

at an early date   _____

in reference to   _____

at this point in time   _____

sometime in the future   _____

it would appear   _____

in view of the fact that   _____

Do not feel that business situations demand special long-winded phrases. Contemporary practice recognizes that the appropriate style for business is clear English. Expressions such as the following should be eliminated altogether, since they add nothing to the message:

it has come to my attention
this is to inform you
in closing

please be advised that
I am writing to tell you that

Examples

✗ POOR
It has come to my attention that not everyone is contributing to the coffee money.

✓ IMPROVED
Not everyone is contributing to the coffee money.

✗ POOR
I am writing to inform you that your application for our management trainee program has been received.

✓ IMPROVED
Thank you for applying to our management trainee program.

Some old-fashioned expressions do carry a message, although the vocabulary is so outdated that the meaning becomes obscured. You can express the same ideas in simple vocabulary that is part of your everyday speech.

Examples

✗ POOR
Enclosed herewith please find a map of Winnipeg as per your request.

✓ IMPROVED
Here is the map of Winnipeg you asked for.

✗ POOR
Kindly respond at your earliest convenience.

✓ IMPROVED
Please let us know as soon as possible.

Simple Vocabulary

As a general rule, choose the simplest, commonest words that express your meaning. When you use familiar words that are part of your everyday vocabulary, you will have more control over your message. You will avoid looking phony or pretentious, or saying something you didn't intend.

Furthermore, your message is less likely to be misinterpreted when you use simple, ordinary words, regardless of the educational or job status of the audience. Do not think that the workplace demands fancy, formal language. A clear, readable message will always sound professional. Though the jargon specific to your job can help make a message more concise and exact if your audience is familiar with the terms you are using, it is not appropriate for an audience unfamiliar with your job. Jargon borrowed from other disciplines quickly becomes stale and clichéd—for example: parameters, equation, reference or impact (used as verbs), bottom line, final analysis, touch base, materialize, and many others.

Find simpler, more familiar substitutes for the following words:

Unfamiliar	Simple
ascertain	_____
terminate	_____
endeavour	_____
commence	_____
indicate	_____
initiate	_____
remuneration	_____
pursuant	_____
subsequent	_____
facilitate	_____

ESL TIP

Communicating in a second or third language is particularly challenging in the workplace. It is not enough for your message to be understandable; it must also be "correct." And it is not even enough for your message to be correct; it must also be "idiomatic." That is, it must be expressed in a way that is typical of a native English speaker. A very formal style will sound strange and old-fashioned in today's workplace, even if your dictionary or writer's handbook tells you that it is grammatically correct. On the other hand, many expressions that native English speakers use in everyday speech are too casual for the office, especially written communication. Sentences such as "Our sales presentation bombed," "The auditors ratted us out," or "The legal department messed up big time," would never be acceptable in a report or an e-mail going to file. Dictionaries and grammar checks on your computer are not very helpful here as these expressions may be acceptable standard English when used in a different context. You need to train your own eye and ear by reading good examples of workplace writing. Remember that books, newspapers, and magazines are written to entertain as well as inform. Your goals in communication at work are much narrower. Try reading annual reports; customer information brochures given out at banks, cable and phone companies; product user's manuals. These are generally written by professionals in the corporate communication field and put into practice all the objectives of this course.

Concrete Words

A concrete word is one that denotes something that exists in the material world. The opposite, an abstract word, is one that denotes a concept or quality. "Many people are out of work" is a concrete sentence; "Unemployment is high" is an abstract one. Concrete words and sentences are appropriate in the workplace because they emphasize the fact that actions carried out by people cause things to happen. Abstract language often gives the impression that situations are unchanging and unchangeable because that's the way the world is. So we have:

The availability of funding is diminishing.

instead of:

Money is getting scarcer.

or:

Cessation of buying has set in.

rather than:

People have stopped buying.

Some writers like to use vague, abstract words to disguise the fact that they have only vague, unformed ideas about their subject. Unfortunately, these words tend to cloud their ideas even further. Avoid these abstractions:

situation
aspect
position
concept
basis
factor

Examples

✗ POOR
The development of the staffing situation is proceeding quite well.

✓ IMPROVED
Three qualified caseworkers have joined our staff.

✗ POOR
The position will soon be reached where all vacancies will have been filled.

✓ IMPROVED
Soon all vacancies will have been filled.

✗ POOR
This situation is the basis for our position on the concept of expansion.

✓ IMPROVED
Because of a steady increase in orders, we plan to expand.

Make an effort to eliminate sentences beginning with "There is/are ..." and "It is...."

Examples

✗ POOR
There are a number of reasons why people come in late.

✓ IMPROVED
People come in late for a number of reasons.

✗ POOR
It is a long drive from Winnipeg to Toronto.

✓ IMPROVED
Winnipeg is a long drive from Toronto.

Standard Spelling, Grammar, and Punctuation

A letter, e-mail, or report that contains mechanical errors will leave a poor impression of the writer's competence. It may also leave the wrong impression of the writer's message. Standard spelling, punctuation, and sentence structure are closely related to meaning and thus are a vital part of communication. Without punctuation, a sentence like "Alex loved Laura and Kathy and Vicki loved him" is very hard to decipher. Nonstandard punctuation puts up barriers to the reader's understanding. For example, "The first movie, made by David Cronenberg, was *Transfer*" implies that David Cronenberg invented the movie.

Likewise, faulty sentence structure leaves doubt in the mind of your reader. "Lying on a shelf, I spotted the book I was looking for" literally means that the speaker was lying on a shelf. Common sense and sentence structure are in conflict. The reader can never be completely certain what is meant. Spelling errors that change meaning usually involve proper names, but problems can also arise when similar-sounding or -looking words are confused. For example, "We didn't mean to except Larry" means "We didn't mean to leave Larry out," whereas "We didn't mean to accept Larry" means almost the opposite.

Here are some statements whose meanings are obscured by nonstandard grammar or punctuation. Rewrite each sentence to make its meaning clear.

1. Never give an apple to a baby that hasn't been peeled.

   _____

   _____

2. Having corrected the errors, the contract was ready to be signed by the agent.

_____

_____

3. My supervisor finally read the report I had written on the weekend.

_____

_____

4. Rowing lifting weights running all of these can improve cardiovascular fitness.

_____

_____

5. The Health and Safety Committee held a lunch-hour forum on safe sex in the employee lounge.

_____

_____

The handbook at the end of this text will help you with questions about punctuation and sentence structure in your own writing.

2 CLARITY IN ORAL COMMUNICATION

Conciseness

Although people listen more slowly than they read, their ability to absorb detailed information through listening is not very great. Consequently, oral communication needs much more repetition to ensure that the message gets across. The secret is knowing when enough turns into too much. Obvious repetition will bore and frustrate your audience. In addition, wordy phrases will slow down the pace at which real information is delivered and tempt your listeners to let their attention wander.

Word Choice

Whatever you have learned about choosing simple, concrete words in writing is even more important in speaking. No one is going to get up and consult a dictionary while you are talking. Your message cannot be examined once it's delivered, so your meaning must be immediately evident to your listeners.

Speaking offers many communication channels, such as words, gestures, and facial expressions. Give them all time to do their job; don't overwhelm your listeners with words.

Pronunciation

Standard pronunciation contributes to clarity in speaking in the same way that standard spelling contributes to clear writing. Standard pronunciation ensures that your audience correctly identifies the word you are trying to use. Here are some guidelines to help you avoid errors:

1. **Confirm the pronunciation of any proper names you plan to use.** For example, if you will be mentioning fellow workers in a meeting or presentation, it is easy to check the preferred pronunciation of their names with them ahead of time. Phone the office of a prospective employer or client with whom you will be meeting, to check with a secretary or receptionist. Many people are very sensitive about their names, so your effort will be appreciated.

2. **If you discover a new word in print, check it in a dictionary** or with a trustworthy colleague before you try it out in public. The English language is full of traps for the unwary; the pronunciation of words such as "epitome," "misled," and "rationale" is not obvious.

3. **Listen for lazy pronunciation habits.** Saying things like "akkrit" for "accurate," "could of" for "could have," or "innawinna" for "in the window" blurs meaning and detracts from your professional image.

3 **TONE**

Tone is the subjective element of style, the overall feeling or impression conveyed to the audience by the sender's choice of words.

To a computer, clarity is everything. If it can understand a command, it will carry it out. A computer never gets in a snit, changes its mind, or loses interest. But human beings are not computers. The command "Sit down and shut up" is admirably clear and concise, yet it could not be used to call a meeting to order without creating deep offence. Human beings respond as much or more to the tone of a message as to its content. Your experience as a communicator has taught you a lot about choosing words that will make the tone of your message appropriate to your audience, and of course you will continue to apply these skills when you are a full-time worker. There are, however, a few elements of tone that are particularly important on the job, although you may not have given them much thought in everyday life.

You-Centred Tone

First of all, communication on the job demonstrates the importance of the audience by using the words "you" and "your" as much as possible. For most of us, what we do at work involves the active cooperation of other people. They must approve a recommendation, or carry out instructions, or buy a product, or respond in some other way to what we say and do. Communication at work underlines this cooperative element by making the audience the subject of what is said or written as often as possible. The simplest application of this is replacing "we" and "I" with "you."

Examples

✘ POOR
We are attaching some pictures of our new conference facilities.

✓ IMPROVED
You will find attached some pictures of the new conference facilities available for your group.

✘ POOR
We are open Thursday and Friday nights until nine.

✓ IMPROVED
You can use the drop-in centre until 9 PM on Thursday and Friday nights.

The word "you" attracts the reader or listener and tells him or her that the message is relevant and requires a response. (This response may be simply paying attention.) On the other hand, "I" and "my," or "we" and "our," send the message that the speaker or writer is chiefly interested in himself or herself. An employee reading a memo in which every sentence begins with "we"—"We have planned ... ," "We have decided ... ," "We have introduced ... "—isn't likely to feel that his or her concerns or suggestions have much value. A potential employer listening to a candidate who spends the whole interview saying, "I'm looking for ... ," "I'm interested in ... ," "I want to ... ," will assume that this candidate sees the job as a mere stepping stone in his or her career path.

Rewrite the following passages to make them more you-centred:

(a) To: All Employees
   Starting January 15, all employees are asked to park in the north parking lot only.

   _____

   _____

(b) We offer a full line of accounting and tax services for small businesses.

   _____

   _____

(c) For the convenience of our customers, we are introducing our new phone order service.

   _____

   _____

(d) We would be pleased to have the opportunity to answer your questions about our new product.

   _____

   _____

(e) I hope you will be able to come to our meeting, as I am not very familiar with the issues and I'll need some support.

   _____

   _____

Of course, this can't be just a mechanical exercise in substituting "you" for "I" or "me," although it may start out that way. To sound genuinely "you-centred," put yourself in your audience's place and see things from their perspective. Doing this will improve not only the tone of your writing or speaking, but your content and message as well.

CASE 2

Maria looked at the pile of applications on her desk with a sinking heart. The personnel department staff had screened them all for the minimum qualifications, but there were still at least 50 qualified applicants to be considered. How could she get them down to a short list of ten in time for the first interview appointment? Reluctantly, she picked up the first covering letter. "Dear Ms. Palma:" it began, "I would like to apply for the job of General Accountant which I saw advertised in this morning's *Daily Times-Bugle*. I will be graduating from Pacific College this June with a diploma in Accounting and Finance, and a job with a moderate-sized firm like Mountain View Tours would give me the practical experience I need to choose a field for further specialization. I am enclosing a copy of my résumé with details of my education and experience. I hope I will be hearing from you soon, as it will make the semester a lot more relaxed if I know I have a job lined up. Sincerely, Lotta Ego." Maria watched the letter flutter gracefully into the wastebasket. A few more like this and she would be down to a short list in no time.

Every sentence in Lotta's letter began with the word "I." In fact, she used the word "I", "me," or "my" twelve times, and the word "you" only once. But this is only a symptom of her deeper lack of concern for the needs of her audience. Lotta described what this job had to offer her, not what she could offer Mountain View Tours. Telling her reader about her plans to "move on" was just another way of saying, "Invest time and money training me, and then watch me take my newly acquired skills elsewhere." In addition, she implied that she was destined for better things than Mountain View Tours—the company for which her reader worked.

Here is Lotta's letter rewritten in "you-centred" style:

Dear Ms. Palma:

I am applying for the job of General Accountant, which you advertised in the April 12 *Daily Times-Bugle*. As you can see from the attached résumé, I will be graduating from Pacific College this June with a diploma in Accounting and Finance. Your firm would benefit from my thorough grounding in accounting practice and previous experience in the travel industry. I would appreciate an opportunity to discuss this position with you personally.

This version uses the words "I" and "my" four times and the word "you" or "your" four times. More important, it stresses what Lotta has to offer Mountain View Tours, not what it has to offer her. Lotta's first letter said, "Do me a favour, give me a job." This one says, "Do *yourself* a favour."

Of course, the purpose of emphasizing "you" and "your" is to put the reader or listener in the picture. If your message implies blame or criticism, it would be more tactful to leave out "you" and "your," perhaps by using the passive voice as in the following examples:

✗ POOR
You must return both copies of the form next time.

✓ IMPROVED
Both copies of the form must be returned next time.

✗ POOR
You did not complete the paperwork for the GST refund.

✓ IMPROVED
The paperwork for the GST refund was not completed.

Positive Tone

Just as the repetition of "we" or "I" throughout a message creates an overall impression of self-centredness and lack of concern for the reader, the repetition of negative words and phrases can create a negative impression that goes beyond the content of the message. A positive tone extends the sense of cooperation that is created by you-centred communication. It emphasizes what you or your organization **can** do, not what you can't; what is possible, rather than what is impossible. This reinforces values like negotiation and problem-solving that are vital to a healthy working environment. Here are four ways to create a positive tone in your communication:

1. **Avoid words with strong negative overtones, such as**

deny	unacceptable
reject	incompetent
refuse	ignorant
regret	neglect
impossible	complaint
fail	fault

These are powerful words that convey feelings of judgment and even punishment, and they make most people uncomfortable. Attention will be focused on these feelings instead of on your message. These feelings are intensified if the word "you" is used—for example, "Your suggestion has been rejected," "Your question shows that you are ignorant of our return policy," or "You have failed to follow instructions." Do not risk clouding the issue by using these loaded words or similar expressions. Find more objective, emotionally neutral phrases.

Examples

✗ POOR
Your complaint has been forwarded to the payroll office.

✓ IMPROVED
Your concerns have been forwarded to the payroll office.

✗ POOR
You failed the aptitude test.

✓ IMPROVED
Your mark on the aptitude test was below 65.

Write improved versions of the following sentences. Compare your answers with the ones on page 46.

✗ POOR
(a) You have neglected to turn off the photocopier.

✓ IMPROVED

_____

✗ POOR
(b) It is impossible to fill your order as requested.

✓ IMPROVED

_____

✘ POOR
(c) The committee found your solution unacceptable.

✓ IMPROVED

_____

2. **Do not apologize for your message unless it is clearly negative.** Words and phrases like "unfortunately" and "I regret to inform you" tell your audience that anger or disappointment are appropriate responses to your message. Use them only if the circumstances are serious and an apology or expression of sympathy is appropriate—for example, "Unfortunately, the theft of these items is not covered by your insurance policy." Do not turn a neutral message into bad news by using negative expressions.

Examples

✘ POOR
Unfortunately, we'll be meeting in a different room next week.

✓ IMPROVED
We'll be meeting in a different room next week.

3. **Put statements in positive form.** Look at a sentence such as "Your interview cannot be scheduled before 3 o'clock." Regardless of when you would prefer to be interviewed, the tone of the sentence suggests that you are being deprived of something. Change the sentence to "Your interview can be scheduled any time after three o'clock," and that sense of deprivation disappears.

Examples

✘ POOR
Your account cannot be credited without a transaction number.

✓ IMPROVED
As soon as you give us the transaction number, your account can be credited.

✘ POOR
Local bus service to the site is only available during July and August. The rest of the year, you have to get there by car.

✓ IMPROVED
You can get to the site year-round by car, or by local bus service during July and August.

Chapter Two: Style in Business Communication

Edit the following sentences to emphasize the positive:

(a) The conference room will not be vacant until noon.

_____

_____

(b) We do not provide a pool insurance policy; however, your pool is already covered by your house insurance.

_____

_____

(c) Your stationery order cannot be filled until Thursday.

_____

_____

(d) Pre-authorized payment will ensure that your bills are never paid late, even when you're away.

_____

_____

(e) This item is available only in white, grey, or tan.

_____

_____

Compare your answers with those on page 46.

4. **Create a positive association for ideas or products you are promoting.** When promoting an idea or a product, tell your audience about the good features it has, not the bad ones it doesn't have. Look at this example: "Beautiglo won't make your hair look greasy and lifeless." What two words will stick in your mind when you think of Beautiglo? Or consider this sentence from a memo: "The new pension regulations are not designed to lower employer contributions at the employees' expense." Doesn't this raise suspicions in your mind? In a real situation, employees who had supported the changes might reconsider. Rewrite the following sentences to emphasize positive characteristics:

(a) WonderLawn offers all these added features, yet it doesn't cost more than franchised lawn service.

_____

_____

_____

(b) Community college instructors are not out of touch with recent developments in their fields.

_____

_____

_____

(c) Eden's Best silk plants will not wilt, turn yellow, or become diseased like real plants.

_____

_____

_____

(d) The new parking garage will not be more expensive or less convenient than the old lot.

_____

_____

_____

(e) You won't be bored and lonely at Club Paradiso.

_____

_____

_____

Compare your answers with those on page 46.

Changing words and phrases will help give your writing a positive rather than a negative tone. But just as the real source of a you-centred tone is genuine concern for and sympathy with the audience's point of view, so a really positive message must reflect the problem-solving approach of the writer or speaker. If you are trying to punish your audience and find excuses for not meeting their requests, or if you lack commitment to your job, it will be hard to sound positive. Good editing simply ensures that your communication reflects your positive orientation to your audience and message. This in turn reinforces a working environment that is open and committed to productivity.

Read the following memo. What do you think it says about Fred's attitude to his job?

To: Bill Smith
From: Fred Bloom FB
Re: Faulty Desk

Date: 07 06 30

Would it be too much trouble for the company to get around to doing something about my desk? Three weeks ago you told me to speak to Edna about it, and I'm still waiting. I'm tired of operating with one drawer and two square feet of work space. It's hard enough to do my job, without this kind of aggravation.

Rewrite this memo to convey a more positive, cooperative tone.

_____

_____

_____

_____

_____

_____

_____

_____

Non-Discriminatory Tone

Effective communication requires respect between speaker or writer and audience. Non-discriminatory language is one way of demonstrating and fostering respect. People cannot work together productively or work effectively with customers or clients if they do not feel mutually valued as individuals, regardless of age, sex, race, disability, or any other characteristic. Thoughtless language habits can jeopardize this necessary trust. Two potential pitfalls are racism and sexism.

Racism

1. **Do not allude to someone's racial or ethnic origin unless it is relevant to the matter at hand.** The following are examples of how unnecessary racial references should be eliminated.

   ### Examples

   ✘ POOR
   Nelson, who came here from Jamaica eight years ago, is joining us as junior sales manager.

   ✓ IMPROVED
   Nelson is joining us as junior sales manager.

   ✘ POOR
   A Chinese woman came into the store.

   ✓ IMPROVED
   A customer came into the store.

2. **Do not give the impression that all or most people from a similar racial or ethnic background share similar characteristics, even if they are positive ones.**

   ### Example

   ✘ POOR
   As an Asian, Julie has adapted quickly to the wireless environment.

   ✓ IMPROVED
   Julie has adapted quickly to the wireless environment.

When planning promotions, social events, or similar activities, remember that "ethnic" themes should be very carefully thought out. You may perceive your "Mexican Night" with its sombreros and serapes, donkeys and cacti as cute and harmless, but a person from Mexico might find it a demeaning stereotype. Don't assume it's all right just because no one says anything.

Sexism

1. **Try to treat men and women equally in writing and speaking.** Do not identify women by marital and family status or by appearance unless these are relevant considerations.

   Example

    POOR
   Vivian Tam, a mother of two, is currently head of quality control.
   Tom Rossi, a systems analyst, is joining our department.

    IMPROVED
   Vivian Tam, a graduate engineer, is currently head of quality control.
   Tom Rossi, a systems analyst, is joining our department.

2. **Use the correct form of address.**

   Example

    POOR
   Tom and Mrs. Tam

   ✓ IMPROVED
   Tom and Vivian

   or

   Mr. Rossi and Mrs. Tam

Do not assume that a married woman shares her husband's last name or uses the courtesy title "Mrs." Of course, many do, but those who don't may have strong views on the subject and find your assumption offensive. In any event, you should use a woman's full name if you have used the man's full name.

Example

✗ POOR
Bill Rivers and his wife Laura

✓ IMPROVED
Bill Rivers and his wife Laura Zawiski

or

Bill Rivers and his wife Laura Rivers

If you are unsure of the preferred form of address, use "Ms.," or omit it altogether:

Ms. Joan Solomon

or

Joan Solomon

3. **Watch for words ending in "-man."** Look for terms—such as "firefighter," in place of "fireman"—that do not make an assumption about the sex of the person holding that job.

Sexist	Non-discriminatory
workman	_____
repairman	_____
salesman	_____
businessman	_____
mailman	_____
policeman	_____
handyman	_____

Titles like "cleaning lady" and "saleslady" are also sexist. The word "lady" is generally regarded as demeaning in any context, except when it is paired with "gentleman."

4. Do not draw attention to a person's sex unless it is relevant.

Example

✘ POOR

Jackie Giannidis, our leading woman sales rep, will be taking over in Western Canada.

✓ IMPROVED

Jackie Giannidis, a leading sales rep, will be taking over in Western Canada.

4 TONE IN ORAL COMMUNICATION

In speaking, just as in writing, the words you choose will send a message about your attitude toward your subject and your audience. If you begin every sentence with the word "I" or "we," your audience will quickly come to feel that your first concern is yourself. If you speak to people in the third person—"Staff will please return to their desks"—you will create a sense of alienation rather than community. Likewise, if you begin every conversation with "I'm afraid that … ," "I can't … ," "We don't … ," "You're not allowed to … ," your listeners will soon learn to avoid you when something needs to be accomplished. The principles discussed under "You-Centred Tone" and "Positive Tone" on pages 32 and 35 are equally important in oral communication, as we will see from Gary's experience with Acme Computer.

CASE 3

Gary had recently been given a printer to hook up to his computer. It was an older model, the kind that used tracked paper, but it was clean and in working order except for the paper feeder, which had lost a few teeth on one side. Gary decided to phone the manufacturer for some help. Here is what happened:

Acme Computer (AC):	Good morning, Acme Computer.
Gary:	Hello, I have a question about a model …
AC:	You'll have to talk to Customer Service. Just a minute …
AC:	Customer Service, Andrea speaking.
Gary:	Hello, I have a question about a model LX-4 Jetwriter printer.

AC: I'm sorry, we don't make that model anymore. Did you say LX-4? We haven't made those since 1998.

Gary: Yes, I know, but I have one and it's in pretty good shape except for one of the sort of wheel things that pull the paper in …

AC: We call that the paper feeder.

Gary: Thank you. Yes, well one side has lost some teeth, and …

AC: You can't use the printer like that. The paper will get jammed.

Gary: Yes, I know, so I was wondering if this wheel part could be replaced.

AC: Well, we don't make that printer anymore. That's an old printer.

Gary: Well, perhaps there's another wheel that would fit.

AC: We build precision products here. You can't just put a part from one machine into another. Besides, that whole mechanism is obsolete.

Gary: Maybe the wheel could be repaired.

AC: This is a manufacturing company. We don't service computers.

Gary: Well, could you tell me who does repairs for Acme products?

AC: There are so many places, I couldn't give you all the names over the telephone.

Gary: Okay, well, I guess that's it.

AC: If you need any more help, give us a call.

When you write, you have an opportunity to revise your work. You can look for places where "I" can become "you" and where "This can't be done until …" can be changed to "This can be done when…." In speaking, you have only one chance. If you are delivering a prepared speech, of course you can edit it for you-centred, positive words. But most oral communication, even if it is planned, is not scripted word for word. Thus, your attitude comes across more obviously, without the benefit of editing. Fortunately, your writing practice will reinforce the you-centred, positive, non-discriminatory attitude you want to project.

Writing and speaking skills influence each other. In addition, you should include your goals for achieving an appropriate tone whenever you plan oral communication, whether it's a phone call or a major meeting. Try to be consciously aware of other people's choice of "I" or "you," "can" or "can't." Their example, good or bad, will also reinforce your decision to make your tone reflect a more cooperative, can-do attitude.

Tone of Voice

Tone in oral communication has the added dimension of tone of voice — the emotional quality of the sound of our speech. Tone of voice can reinforce our choice of words or totally contradict it. A warm, caring speech full of "you" and "your" will lose all credibility if it is delivered in a monotone, without eye contact. Because our earliest experiences are preverbal, we instinctively believe the messages that tone of voice and body language send us, rather than those of the words alone.

Answers to Chapter Questions

Page 36:
(a) The photocopier was not turned off.
(b) We cannot fill your order as requested.
(c) The committee did not accept the suggestion that was put forward.

Page 38:
(a) The conference room will be free at noon.
(b) Your pool is already covered by your house insurance.
(c) Your stationery order will be filled on Thursday.
(d) Pre-authorized payment will ensure that your bills are always paid on time, even when you're away.
(e) This item is available in white, grey, or tan.

Page 39:
(a) WonderLawn gives you all these added features for the same price as a franchised lawn service.
(b) Community college instructors keep up to date with recent developments in their fields.
(c) Eden's Best silk plants retain their natural beauty forever.

(d) The new parking garage will provide the convenience of the parking lot at the same price.

(e) You'll enjoy yourself and meet new friends at Club Paradiso.

CHAPTER REVIEW/SELF-TEST

1. Good business writing style means
   (a) expanding your ideas with impressively long words and phrases.
   (b) using special formal phrasing found only in business writing.
   (c) entertaining people with your literary brilliance.
   (d) all of the above.
   (e) none of the above.

2. A message is clear if your intended audience
   (a) agrees with everything you say.
   (b) receives your ideas quickly and accurately.
   (c) is impressed by your expertise and large vocabulary.
   (d) enjoys reading or listening to it.

3. Make your message clear to your intended audience by
   (a) repeating each point for emphasis.
   (b) writing exactly as you speak.
   (c) being concise and using simple, concrete words.
   (d) searching for new words in a thesaurus.

4. Grammar errors can make your message unclear by
   (a) distracting the reader or listener.
   (b) allowing it to be interpreted two different ways.
   (c) creating a conflict between common sense and what the message actually says.
   (d) all of the above.

5. The tone of a message refers to
   (a) its emotional impact on the audience.
   (b) the educational level of the speaker or writer.
   (c) whether it is formal and correct.
   (d) whether it is good news or bad news.

6. Under which circumstances would you avoid using the word "you"?
   (a) You want your audience to follow instructions or procedures.
   (b) You want your audience to approve an idea or decision.

(c) Your message draws attention to a problem or mistake.

(d) You are selling a product.

7. Which of the following is **not** a reason why negative messages are less effective than positive messages?

(a) Negative messages are less clear.

(b) Negative messages can make the audience feel resentful and uncooperative.

(c) Negative messages turn people off.

(d) Negative messages raise people's suspicions.

8. Language is non-discriminatory when it

(a) says nice things about everybody.

(b) treats ladies, the elderly, and the disabled with special respect.

(c) points out positive characteristics of minorities.

(d) treats all equally without reference to membership in any group.

9. It is appropriate to mention someone's ethnic origin in the workplace if

(a) you are curious about what it is.

(b) you have had a positive experience with other people who share that background.

(c) it is clearly relevant to a work-related issue.

(d) you enjoy food from that country.

10. It is appropriate to mention someone's family status in the workplace if

(a) he or she is heterosexual.

(b) he or she is middle-aged.

(c) he or she is wearing a ring.

(d) it is clearly related to a work-related issue.

Answers

1.E 2.B 3.C 4.D 5.A 6.C 7.A 8.D 9.C 10.D

EXERCISES

1. Rewrite the following sentences to make them clear and concise:

(a) This paper is the kind of paper that looks more expensive than ordinary paper, yet doesn't cost more than ordinary paper costs.

(b) While the construction crew is refinishing the floorboards they will be inspected for termites.

(c) At this point in the year individuals are often experiencing difficulty in the cash flow area with reference to back-to-school expenses.

(d) After removing all the clutter the office looked more professional and efficient.

(e) Suits that are double-breasted do not look good on men who are short.

(f) There are several aspects of the salary situation which suggest an upward trend.

(g) A refund in the amount of $58.95 has been credited to your account, as per your request.

(h) It has come to my attention that the area of parking fees has experienced a falling-off in revenue.

(i) I would be prepared to buy a house from an independent contractor, if well-built.

(j) It is expensive to rent an apartment in the city of Vancouver.

2. Rewrite the following sentences to make them positive, reader-oriented, and non-discriminatory:

(a) Obviously, you failed to calculate the bank deposits accurately.

(b) These are not the cheap, mass-produced hairpieces that always look fake.

(c) We have a wide assortment of styles in stock.

(d) Workmen will be installing the carpet on Tuesday.

(e) Customers will please refrain from leaving valuables in their lockers.

(f) Get one of the ladies in the cash office to handle it.

(g) You won't be disappointed by the food and service at Antonio's.

(h) Our district manager, a girl with years of experience, handled your account personally.

(i) We were delighted to have the opportunity to answer your questions about Gemstone wall coverings.

(j) Emerald Weave outdoor carpeting won't rot or fade like other carpets.

3. You work for the head office of Dominion Suites, a hotel chain. Two weeks ago your supervisor asked you to prepare a report on "Dominion Plus Points," the reward program offered to guests who stay frequently at Dominion Suites hotels. Your job was to compare the benefits your program offers to its members with the benefits offered by your top three competitors. Here is the first draft of your opening paragraph:

> I am happy to report that Dominion Plus Points is still ahead of the competition. However, I have to point out that our rivals are doing everything they can to close the gap. The study I recently completed shows that many of the benefits we introduced last year have been imitated by other reward programs. Let me stress that most of our rewards have been items like free accommodation and room upgrades that appeal to business travellers. Although this is an important target market, I want to emphasize that more and more customers have

expressed an interest in consumer items like sports equipment and electronics. Because of this trend, I want to present some recommendations that Dominion Suites might pursue.

Rewrite this paragraph to make it more "you-centred."

4. Read the following dialogue. Identify statements that would be likely to alienate the listener. Be prepared to improve them in a role-play exercise.

Deborah has been walking around the "separates" section of a large department store for several minutes. Finally she approaches Lisa, a salesclerk.

Deborah: Excuse me, I wonder if you could help me ...

Lisa: Are you looking for something?

Deborah: Yes, I need a blouse to go with a grey tweed skirt—perhaps in a pale blue, or maybe yellow.

Lisa: Well, I don't think we have any blue blouses. If we do, they're over there.

Deborah: Perhaps you could show me.

Lisa: Well, there's what we have. What size are you looking for?

Deborah: Ten.

Lisa: Most of the tens are gone. Here's something. (She takes it off the rack.)

Deborah: Okay, I'll try that. And maybe this peach one.

Deborah: (returns from change room) I think the blue one fits a bit loosely.

Lisa: Well, that style of blouse doesn't really suit you; that collar doesn't look good if you don't have much up top. What about the peach?

Deborah: It's a bit too orange for me ...

Lisa: Yeah, if your skin has a greenish tint, that shade really brings it out.

Deborah: Does it come in another colour?

Lisa: Our colour selection is pretty limited. There's this raspberry shade ...

Deborah: That's nice.

Lisa: Yeah, a lot of older women like this because it sort of brightens up your face.

Deborah: I see. Would it go with grey tweed?

Lisa: Yeah, it wouldn't look too bad. Depends on your taste.

Deborah: Well, I think I'd like to take it home and try it on with the skirt. Can I bring it back if I don't like it?

Lisa: There are no exchanges unless you bring it back within ten days with your receipt.

Deborah: That shouldn't be a problem. If you ring it up, I'll write a cheque.

Lisa: We only accept cheques with a printed address and two pieces of ID.

Deborah: That's not a problem. *(She starts to write.)* What's the total?

Lisa: It's on the bill. $41.68.

Deborah: Well, thank you. Bye.

Lisa: Bye. I hope it doesn't clash with your skirt.

PART TWO

COMMUNICATION STYLES

© 2004 Ted Goff

"It wasn't my fault. Someone put the wrong information in my notes, memos and letters to the customers."

© 2004 Ted Goff www.newslettercartoons.com

CHAPTER THREE

PRESENTING WRITTEN MESSAGES

Chapter Objectives

Successful completion of this chapter will enable you to:

1 Produce an attractive, well-spaced letter using a standard letter format.

2 Present a memorandum using a standard format.

3 Prepare a message for e-mail transmission.

4 Lay out a written message for transmission by facsimile machine.

INTRODUCTION

First impressions are important in the working world. The layout and general appearance of a written message start to communicate even before the first word is read. This chapter shows you how to present letters, memos, and electronically transmitted written messages so that they make a positive first impression.

1 LETTER PRESENTATION

Before you begin to organize the content of a letter, you need to think about its layout and general appearance. With many options available for sending written messages, a letter sent through the postal system is still the usual choice for an important, formal message. A letter is also the best means for establishing written communication with a new or potential customer or business associate, before fax numbers or e-mail addresses are exchanged. Many people will not open e-mail messages from unknown senders. Thus it is particularly important that every element of your letter look its best.

Paper

1. Invest in top-quality white bond paper and matching envelopes. Ask a stationery store to help you find the right weight or thickness of paper, keeping in mind the requirements of your printer.
2. Never use letterhead paper or envelopes from your workplace for personal correspondence. This practice sends a very negative message about the writer's regard for other people's property. Use letterhead only when you are writing on behalf of that organization.
3. If you are starting your own business, get professional help in designing your letterhead. The expense per sheet will be low and, in any case, well worth it for the boost an expert design gives to your company's credibility.
4. Use letterhead paper only for the first page of a letter. Type or print the following pages on plain, matching bond.

Spacing

1. Plan your message to ensure that it is well placed on the page. Ideally, the left and right margins should be of equal width, and so should the top and bottom margins. No matter how short your letter, it should come below the midpoint of the page to look balanced.
2. Do not carry over to a second page unless you have at least two more lines of text before the closing.

3. A business letter should be divided into short paragraphs with lots of white space in between. This invites the reader into the page, instead of hitting him or her with a wall of text.

Typeface (Font)

1. Use a standard typeface such as Courier or Helvetica, 10 or 12 points. Aim for a conservative "typed" appearance. Save script and other fancy fonts for rock band flyers.
2. Never mix fonts in a letter. Do not "cut and paste" unless the font and size are consistent.

Elements of a Business Letter

A business letter consists of four parts: heading, opening, body, and closing. Certain rules, or, more accurately, conventions, dictate how each part of a business letter should be presented. These conventions change, just as conventions in business attire change—slowly. Careful attention to small details will make the difference between an attractive, functional, and professional-looking letter and one that reflects the writer's lack of knowledge and experience.

Heading

Letterhead stationery requires only the addition of the dateline to complete the heading. Type the date at least two lines below the letterhead and four lines above the receiver's address. Use either the traditional form:

February 28, 2007

or the newer all-numeric date:

2007 02 28

If you are using plain paper, put your return address at least 3 cm below the top of the page. **Do not put your name in the heading.** Type the date immediately under the return address.

Opening

The **receiver's name and address** direct the letter to its intended reader and provide you with a reference on your file copy. Include the receiver's courtesy title (Miss, Mrs., Ms., Mr., Dr., Prof.), if known; the receiver's name; job title, if known; organization name; and full mailing address. See Figures 3.1, 3.2, and 3.3 for the position of each item.

The **salutation** greets the reader personally. If your reader's name is, for example, Ms. Leslie Khan, you may begin "Dear Ms. Khan," or, if you are on friendly terms, "Dear Leslie."

If you are not using a courtesy title such as "Mr." or "Ms." in the receiver's address, omit it in the salutation: "Dear Leslie Khan," or "Dear Leslie," if you know your reader well. The practice of omitting courtesy titles is becoming more popular. It is particularly helpful if you do not know which of Miss, Mrs., or Ms. would be most acceptable, or whether Chris Suarez is a man or a woman.

The proper form of salutation is "Dear Courtesy Title Family Name," or if you are not using a courtesy title, "Dear Given Name Family Name." **Never use a courtesy title with both names.**

Example

✗ POOR
Ms. Rose Chu
38 Wynford Dr., Apt. 1302
North York ON M5P 1J3

Dear Ms. Rose Chu

✓ IMPROVED
Ms. Rose Chu
38 Wynford Dr., Apt. 1302
North York ON M5P 1J3

Dear Ms. Chu

or

Rose Chu
38 Wynford Dr., Apt. 1302
North York ON M5P 1J3

Dear Rose Chu

If you do not know your intended reader's name it is better to omit the salutation. "Dear Sir or Madam" sounds very old-fashioned. If the letter is short you could begin immediately with the first sentence of the body of the letter, as in Figure 3.2. Or, you could use an **attention line,** directing the message to a particular department or to someone with a particular job title.

Example

Best Buy
20 City Centre Drive
Brampton ON N5G 1E9

Attention: Customer Service Manager

Another alternative to a salutation is a **subject line.** The subject line summarizes the contents of your letter and helps a receptionist or mailroom employee direct it to the appropriate reader.

Example

Great Lakes Insurance Company
34 Confederation Way
Thunder Bay ON N4G 1H6

Subject: Liability Insurance Rates

Example

Box 423, Report on Business
444 Front St. W.
Toronto ON M5V 2S9

Subject: Job File 93-701

Do not use "To Whom It May Concern." How can your readers know if the message concerns them until they have read it? This phrase simply wastes everyone's time.

Body

A letter with a salutation may also have a subject line. This can be a useful way of focusing the attention of a busy person who receives and files a lot of correspondence.

Example

Dear Mr. Ackerman
<u>Subject: Applications for Youth Employment Grants</u>

Subject lines are not necessary for letters to private individuals.

Lay out the body of the message in short paragraphs. Follow the spacing guidelines on page 61.

Closing

If you have used a salutation, you should end your letter with a **complimentary closing.** Formal complimentary closings include "Yours truly," "Sincerely," and "Yours sincerely." Note that only the first word is capitalized. Informal closings include "Good luck," "Best wishes," and so on. Omit the complimentary closing if you began your letter with a subject or attention line instead of a salutation. After the complimentary closing, or immediately after the body of the letter, if you are omitting the salutation and closing, comes the **signature block.**

Leave at least three blank lines for your handwritten signature (more if your writing is large). Type your name, and include your job title beneath your name if you are writing on behalf of your organization. Normally, courtesy titles are omitted in the typed name. You may prefer to use your courtesy title if your name is one that could be either a man's or a woman's (Kim, Terry, Pat). A woman who has strong feelings about being addressed as "Miss" or "Mrs." may wish to include the title she prefers in her typed name. If there is no title, it is generally assumed that she prefers "Ms." Always omit your courtesy title in your handwritten signature.

Examples

Sincerely

Ravi Edwards-Singh
Manager, Accounts Receivable

Sincerely yours

Kim Greenough

Mr. Kim Greenough
President

Best wishes

Maureen Laird

Maureen Laird, Director
Food Services

ESL TIP

In English-speaking countries, people always introduce themselves and sign their names in the order Given Name Family Name. For example, three members of the Burgess family might introduce themselves as Tanya Burgess, James Burgess, and Matthew Burgess. This may not be the order you are accustomed to, but it is important to follow this convention when communicating in English. Otherwise, people will unintentionally address you by your family name when they are intending to establish a friendly "first name" relationship. They will be unable to find your name in a list alphabetized by family name, such as a telephone directory. Messages and files will be misplaced.

The form Family Name, Given Name or FAMILY NAME Given Name (e.g., Burgess, Tanya or BURGESS Tanya) might appear in a list or extract from a list. The comma or spacing tells the reader that normal English-language name order is not being used. This form is not appropriate for correspondence.

Letter Format

The format of a letter refers to the arrangement of the four elements on the page. The two letter formats most commonly used in business today are the Full Block and the Modified Block. In the **Full Block** format (Figure 3.1), every line begins at the left margin. This format is becoming the preferred choice in most businesses

FIGURE 3.1 Full Block Format: Plain Stationery

95 Glencairn Drive
Hamilton ON L4B 6M4
2006 11 23

Mr. Rene Laplace, President
Mohawk College of Applied
Arts and Technology
2951 Fennell Ave. W.
Hamilton ON L9C 5R2

Dear President Laplace

Thank you for participating in our class symposium on Management in the Public Sector. Your varied examples from your own wide range of experience were very helpful in illustrating the points we were hoping to explore.

With your permission we would like to post the text of your opening remarks on our website. In the meantime you might enjoy seeing some pictures from the event at www.collegebusnet.ca.

Thank you again for helping to make our symposium a highlight of the semester.

Sincerely

Michael Swoboda

Michael Swoboda, Convener
Symposium Organizing Committee

because it is the easiest to keyboard. You do not have to worry about lining up the return address with the signature block or indenting the first line of each paragraph. The Full Block format generally has **open punctuation,** which means that only the body of the letter is punctuated. There is no punctuation after the salutation or complimentary close. On a letterhead, the formatting rules are the same. The only difference, as Figure 3.3 shows, is that you need not type the return address.

The **Modified Block** (Figure 3.2) is somewhat more old-fashioned. The return address, date, complimentary close, and signature block are placed at the halfway point across the page. The first line of each paragraph is not indented. A letter in Modified Block format may use open punctuation or **mixed punctuation.** Mixed punctuation means that the salutation is followed by a colon ("Dear Mr. Healey:") and the complimentary close by a comma ("Sincerely,"). Unless your organization has a standard format, you can choose either the Full Block or Modified Block, open or mixed punctuation; just follow your preferred style consistently. Note the presentation of a modified block letter in Figure 3.4.

FIGURE 3.2   Modified Block Format: Plain Stationery

1281 Grand Blvd.
Oakville ON L6N 2F6
2007 06 19

Optima Corporation
28 Taylor Road
Toronto ON M2A 3T4

Please send me a copy of your latest catalogue. I am enclosing a cheque for $4.00 and a stamped, self-addressed envelope.

Winsome Lincoln

Winsome Lincoln

FIGURE 3.3 Full Block Format: Letterhead Stationery

Insulate Inc.

22 Sussex Drive Ottawa Canada   K1S 1A5

2006 01 06

Mr. Albert Fleury
82 Waterloo Ave.
St. John's NL A1P 6Y2

Dear Mr. Fleury

Here are the brochures you requested on home insulation. On the back cover of "Conserving Home Heat," you will find a list of installers who can provide you with information about specific products. Good luck with your renovation plans.

Sincerely

Susan Giordano
Consumer Information Officer

Use the lines provided on the next page to show the placement in the Full Block format of the following elements:

1. return address (use your home address)
2. date (today's date)
3. receiver's name and address (president of your college)
4. complimentary close
5. signature block

Compare your letter with the one in Figure 3.1.

_____

_____

_____

_____

_____

_____

_____

_____

_____

_____

_____

_____

_____

_____

_____

_____

_____

Correct the errors in the following according to the guidelines given in this chapter. Circle the errors and write the correct version beside each example.

Heading

1. Michael Bowden, Manager

   Aug. 23rd, 2008

1. _____

   _____

2. 2006 15 01

   Teresa Perez

   16 Wellesley Crt.

   Guelph, ON N2R 8A9

2. _____

   _____

   _____

   _____

Opening

3. Western Metallurgical Industries

   Calgary, Alberta

   Dear Sir:

   Subject: Request for Survey Results

3. _____

   _____

   _____

   _____

4. Sales Manager, Monte Carlo Sportswear

   218 Spadina Ave.

   Toronto, ON M6G 2W4

   Attention: Ms. Barbara Dimopoulos

   Dear Barbara Dimopoulos

4. _____

   _____

   _____

   _____

   _____

Closing

5. Sincerely:

   Mr. Chris Yeung

   Mr. Chris Yeung, Assistant Account Director

5. _____

   _____

   _____

6. Yours Sincerely—

   Betty

6. _____

   _____

FIGURE 3.4 Modified Block Format: Letterhead Stationery

SUPREME WIRE & CABLE

298 B.C. Place Drive   Vancouver BC   V2A 3B3   (604) 218-5252

November 15, 2007

Mr. Norman Cheung
Senior Sales Representative
Niagara Industrial Cleansers
234 Lake St.
St. Catharines ON L6R 4S3

Dear Mr. Cheung:

After testing the solvent samples you sent us last week, we have some questions:

1. Is there any difference in flammability among the three samples?

2. Are all the solvents compatible with your K-900 grease foam?

3. Can you supply the Cascade-30 solvent in 60-litre drums?

Your early reply will enable us to complete our December order.

Sincerely,

Neil Hall, Director
Purchasing

FIGURE 3.5 Addressing an Envelope

Example of the proper address format.

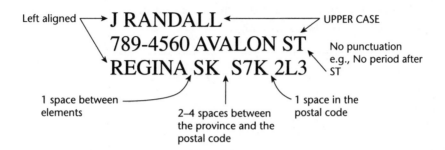

TABLE 3.1 Canadian Provinces and Territories

English Name	Symbol	French Name
Alberta	AB	Alberta
British Columbia	BC	Colombie-Britannique
Manitoba	MB	Manitoba
New Brunswick	NB	Nouveau-Brunswick
Newfoundland and Labrador	NL	Terre-Neuve-et-Labrador
Northwest Territories	NT	Territoires du Nord-Ouest
Nova Scotia	NS	Nouvelle-Écosse
Nunavut	NU	Nunavut
Ontario	ON	Ontario
Prince Edward Island	PE	Île-du-Prince-Édouard
Quebec	QC	Québec
Saskatchewan	SK	Saskatchewan
Yukon	YT	Yukon

Source (Figure 3.5 and Table 3.1): © Canada Post Corporation, 2005. Reproduced with the permission of Canada Post Corporation. Parties interested in obtaining current information for mailing purposes should consult Canada Post Corporation's website www.canadapost.ca.

2 MEMORANDUM PRESENTATION

When a written message is sent within an organization it is called a memorandum, memo for short, rather than a letter. Most organizations use standard memo forms or computer macros. These may be mass-produced for use by any company, like the following memo,

---

INTER-OFFICE MEMO

TO: DATE:
FROM:
SUBJECT:

---

or they may be specially produced for one organization. In any case, a standard form ensures that anyone reading or filing a memo in that organization will know where to look for information about the contents of the memo, who sent it, and for whom it was intended. This saves reading, filing, and access time. Regardless of the order in which the headings are placed, each line has an important function.

To:

This line corresponds to the envelope address, the inside reader's address, and the salutation of a letter. Routine paper memos are not put in an envelope, other than perhaps a reusable mailer. The **To** line should thus have all the necessary identifying information, for example:

To: All Employees
To: All Warehouse Staff
To: All Part-time Cashiers
To: Tina Bandi, Director, Staff Development

Using your reader's title makes your memo more formal. This is appropriate if you are writing to someone you haven't met, or rarely meet, or someone senior to you in the company. Always use your reader's title if the memo is going to file, in case the original reader leaves or changes jobs. Always use your reader's full name. These practices prevent mix-ups and are valuable for future reference.

From:

This line takes the place of the complimentary close and signature block. Some writers like to sign their memos, but expressions like "Sincerely" are always omitted. The preferred method of giving personal authorization to a paper memo is to write your initials beside your typed name, like this:

From: Toby Rich, Supervisor—Accounts Receivable

Subject: *or* **Re:**

This line is an important part of your message and requires some thought. The subject line motivates your readers to read the memo, focuses their attention for better reading comprehension, and helps them find the message for later reference. In order to do this the subject line must be specific, clearly identifying the contents of the memo.

 POOR
Subject: Meeting

 IMPROVED
Subject: Budget Meeting May 8

Date:

You may use the traditional month/day/year form:

October 7, 2007

or the newer all-numeric form:

2007 10 07

3 E-MAIL PRESENTATION

E-mail offers you the speed of the telephone and the permanence and convenient access of a written message. You can use it for internal correspondence, in place of a paper memo, and to communicate with outside organizations, customers, or clients. At the moment, e-mails are regarded as less formal than letters. E-mail messages are certainly less secure and should never be used to transmit information you wish to keep confidential. Employers and fellow employees may be able to legally access messages, even deleted ones, sent to or from your workplace computer.

When you send or reply directly to an e-mail you do not have much control over the appearance of your message, as it may change in transmission. If the layout of the contents is important, or if you expect that the message will be printed and circulated or kept for reference, you should send it as an attachment, assuming your receiver knows you and will be willing to open an attachment. An attachment will give you all the advantages your computer offers in creating a well-laid-out page. Letter format is not necessary, but be sure to include your name on the attachment so that it can stand alone without the transmitting e-mail.

If you are sending a brief message or carrying on an e-mail dialogue, an attachment is not necessary. It is always a good idea to use your receiver's name, if known, at the beginning of the message and to include your own at the end, even though this information appears on the frame. It adds a "you-centred" touch and is helpful if your receiver wishes to forward the message.

If you will be communicating with organizations from your home server—for example, applying for jobs or obtaining information—it is best to avoid Yahoo! and Hotmail addresses and screen names like lovrrgrrl and L'il_Buffy as many spam filters will screen out or quarantine your messages.

FIGURE 3.6 Sample E-Mail Screen Layout

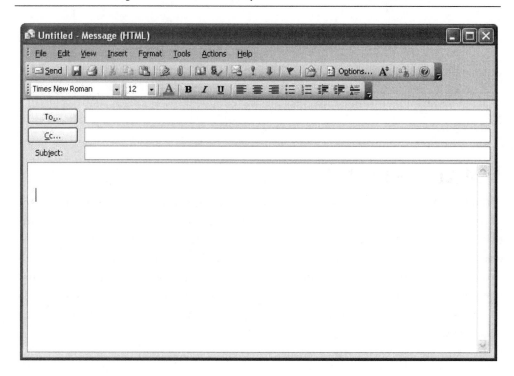

The subject line is the most important part of an e-mail. It should help your reader to open your message promptly, file or forward it appropriately, and find it again when it is needed. Make it clear and specific. Be particularly careful to avoid any phrases that could be mistaken for "spam"; for example, "Important New Offer," "Management Action," or "Latest Positions."

4 FACSIMILE MESSAGE PRESENTATION

The most efficient use of a fax machine is to send messages that already exist in print; for example, you might fax your accountant a copy of a letter you received from the Canada Revenue Agency, or fax a floor plan of your office to a supplier of office furniture. If you have to prepare a message from scratch for immediate transmission, it makes more sense to send it directly from your computer by e-mail. You may have to prepare a message specifically for facsimile transmission if you wish it to arrive as soon as possible and you are in one of the following situations:

(a) You or your intended receiver do not have access to a computer with e-mail capacity.

(b) You have the receiver's fax number, but no e-mail address.

(c) You are faxing other documents and need to attach a further message to the receiver.

(d) You have been told to communicate by fax.

(e) You have been told to communicate by letter, but must use a faster method to meet a deadline.

In these situations, or any time you expect your receiver to reply by letter mail, you can put your message in letter format and then fax it. If you expect a faxed reply, an e-mail reply, or no reply, you can simplify your layout by omitting information that is only relevant to the postal system. Most companies provide a fax cover sheet (see Figure 3.7), which can contain an informal message, or direct attachments or a more formal message to the right person. Brief answers to a faxed message can be handwritten on the bottom of the original message, if this is convenient. A handwritten message shows that you gave an urgent message your immediate personal attention.

When a fax is sent, the sender's fax number is automatically printed on the receiver's copy. A business fax usually prints the company name as well. Using your employer's fax machine for personal correspondence (like a job application) sends the same message as using your employer's stationery: "I am a thief."

FIGURE 3.7 Sample Facsimile Cover Sheet

Seneca College
FAX Transmission Cover

Transmit To: _A. E. NEWMAN, PRES._

Company: _ACCC_

FAX Number: _(416) 555-1212_

Pages (Incl. Cover) _6_

Message:

I am sending you a revised copy of my report. The changes you requested have been made. Give me a call if you have any further changes; otherwise I will send it to the Committee Tomorrow.

Originator: _L. BLOTZ_

Department: _PRESIDENT'S AREA_

Telephone (416) 491-5050 Extension _2000_

CHAPTER REVIEW/SELF-TEST

1. Under which circumstance would a letter **not** be a good choice for sending a written message?
   (a) The message is important and formal.
   (b) The message needs an immediate response.
   (c) You are communicating with someone for the first time.
   (d) All of the above.

2. A business letter has the following parts, in the following order:
   (a) opening, body, closing.
   (b) heading, body, closing.
   (c) heading, opening, body, closing.
   (d) opening, heading, body, closing.

3. Space your letter to ensure that
   (a) it is all on one page.
   (b) some part of it comes below the midpoint of the page.
   (c) the right margin is wider than the left margin.
   (d) you have at least two lines on which to write your signature.

4. Always use a salutation in a letter unless
   (a) you do not know the receiver's name.
   (b) you do not expect a reply.
   (c) the letter is friendly and informal.
   (d) you are writing on behalf of an organization.

5. Do not use a complimentary closing unless
   (a) you are on friendly terms with the receiver.
   (b) you have lots of room at the bottom of the page.
   (c) you are writing on behalf of an organization.
   (d) you opened with a salutation.

6. Sending a message within an organization in memo format ensures
   (a) that important information identifying the sender, receiver, and subject is included.
   (b) that the message looks authorized and work-related.
   (c) that important information about the sender, receiver, and subject is easy to find.
   (d) all of the above.

7. Under which circumstance would an e-mail **not** be a good choice for a written message?
   (a) It is important for the message to look clear and professional.
   (b) You have never met the receiver personally.
   (c) The contents of the message are confidential.
   (d) The message does not need an immediate response.

8. Use an attachment to control the appearance of your e-mail message on the page unless
   (a) your receiver might be unable or reluctant to open attachments.
   (b) your message is brief and informal.
   (c) you and your receiver are sending related messages back and forth.
   (d) all of the above.

9. The best way of avoiding spelling and grammar errors, which could spoil the impact of your e-mail messages, is by
   (a) proofreading on the screen before you send the message.
   (b) printing the message and proofreading the hard copy.
   (c) using the spelling and grammar tools on your computer.

10. The fax machine is a good choice if you wish to
    (a) forward a document that already exists in hard copy.
    (b) create a new message for immediate delivery.

(c) send a confidential message.

(d) ensure the professional appearance of your message.

Answers

1.B 2.C 3.B 4.A 5.D 6.D 7.C 8.D 9.B 10.A

EXERCISES

1. Number the items below in the order in which they appear in a business letter. In the space provided, write an example of each item.

_____ complimentary closing

_____ salutation

_____ receiver's address

_____ sender's address

_____ signature block

_____ date

2. Proofread the following letter, correcting all errors in presentation. Rewrite on plain stationery.

Lisa Crawford
418 Lynford Cres.
Toronto, M4Q 2P3

Oct. 28th/08

Mrs. Doreen Park
Park Floral Designs
Windsor, Ont.

Dear Mrs. Doreen Parks,

Thank you for the estimates you provided for our wedding flowers. Unfortunately the engagement has been called off and we will not be requiring your services. I will keep your brochure on hand for future reference.

Lisa Crawford

Student

---

3. (a) Reformat the following message for facsimile transmission.

Home Care Associates
4140 Main St. Ste. 307
Hamilton ON L2G 1H9
May 14, 2009

Mr. Lawrence Washburn
1289 Broadway Ave.
Hamilton ON L2G 1H9

Dear Mr. Washburn

Thank you for your interest in Home Care. Here are the answers to your questions:

1. The services of Home Care personnel are fully paid for by the Ministry of Health if they are considered medically necessary physical care. This recommendation can be made by any of the professionals listed on the attached application.

2. Other services are provided on a user-pay basis. Financial assistance may, however, be available from other agencies such as Veterans' Affairs or Regional Social Services.

3. An appointment can be made to assess your circumstances as soon as an intake worker has opened a file for you. To do this, we need your Health Card and SIN numbers.

We look forward to hearing from you soon. Home Care can usually be put in place within two weeks of your intake appointment.

Sincerely

Tracy Boateng

Tracy Boateng
Administrative Assistant

(b) Assume that you are the receiver of this message. Write a reply at the bottom that could be faxed back to the sender.

4. Proofread the following memo for errors in presentation. Create a suitable subject line.

TO: Imram   DATE: Tues.

FROM: Al

SUBJECT:

We need to get together to prepare an agenda for the March 4 meeting. If you could leave a copy of your timetable in my mailbox, I'll get back to you with some possible times.

Sincerely,

Al

---

5. Identify problems in presentation that might prevent the following messages from achieving their purpose:

(a)

SUBJECT: RE: Problems with my mark
FROM: Katy Rogers katy.rogers@collegenet.on.ca
DATE: Fri, 07 May 2006 11:38:25 -500
TO: Professor Larry Enfield lcenfield@collegenet.on.ca

hi Larry,

I thouhgt i did good on the exam. why I get F in the course?

(b)

SUBJECT: What was done in meeting today!!!
FROM: "shanellegreene greene" shanellegreene@hotmail.com
DATE: Wed, 12 Mar 2006 19:53:36 +0000
TO: anna.tang@scotiabank.com
Hi,
I was wondering if you can just
reply
tom me what was done in the staff meeting
today
because I could not make it due to not feeling
well :(...One more thing
when
are we suppose to file our RRSP journals ...I
will
appreciate it is you can send this message back
as
soon as possible.

(c)

SUBJECT: Let's get together
FROM: Diane Aloe dcaloe@admin.cora
DATE: Tue, 09 Sep 2008 14:32 -500
TO: Floor Managers floormanagers@admin.cora

IT'S TIME TO GET TOGETHER
A meeting to evaluate the summer sale period July 15-August 15 will take place
Friday afternoon in the Board Room.
MEETING SEPTEMBER 12, 2:30 PM BOARD ROOM 1408
Please call me at x3129 if you have any questions or concerns.

SEE YOU THERE!

CHAPTER FOUR

· ·

ROUTINE MESSAGES

Chapter Objectives

Successful completion of this chapter will enable you to:

1   Write a message requesting information.

2   Write a message placing an order.

3   Write a positive reply to an order or a routine request.

4   Request information, place an order, and take routine requests and orders in person or over the telephone.

INTRODUCTION

Most of the communicating you do on the job will involve asking for or giving information. Because the flow of information is vital to a successful organization, it is important to master the simple techniques that will help you handle inquiries and replies quickly and clearly. In this chapter, we concentrate on routine requests and affirmative responses. Special requests are dealt with in Chapter 7, "Persuasive Messages," and negative replies are discussed in Chapter 6, "Bad News: The Indirect Approach."

The contents of a routine request or reply follow the **direct order.** This means that the **main idea** is placed first, **supporting details** or necessary information follow the main idea, and a brief **goodwill close** ends the message.

1 MAKING A ROUTINE REQUEST

A request is most likely to be answered if the reader can easily discover what information you want. If your request is vague, incomplete, or confusing, your audience will have a difficult job. You may face delays while you clarify your request. Here are some suggestions for writing clear inquiries that get the answers.

1. **Identify the purpose of your message in the first line.** Be as specific as possible. This will ensure that your message is read by the appropriate person and that it will focus his or her attention on your request. Don't let your reader get lost in lengthy introductory formulas.

   ### Examples

   ✘ POOR

   I was looking at some old reports the other day and I happened to notice that you served on the United Way Committee at one point and it occurred to me that you might have some information I have been trying to locate.

   ✓ IMPROVED

   Do you have the name of the United Way coordinator in York Region?

   ✘ POOR

   I am currently shopping around for a monitor and I noticed in a back issue of a computer magazine that you have some equipment I might be interested in.

   ✓ IMPROVED

   I would like some technical specifications for your XC LCD monitor advertised in the November issue of *Hardware Central.*

2. **Add any details that will help your reader help you.** The more specific your request, the more likely you are to get the information you require.

Example

 POOR
I would like some information about Quebec City.

This request puts no limit on the potential contents of the reply. The sender could easily receive an armload of brochures by return mail, and perhaps none of them would contain answers to the writer's real questions.

 IMPROVED
Please send me some information on hotel packages during the Quebec Winter Carnival.

This focuses the request and saves time for the sender and receiver. Do not include details that will not enable your audience to give a better response—for example, your motivation for writing, or background details about yourself or your company. Test every statement by asking yourself, "Will this help my reader answer my question?"

3. **Use questions rather than statements.** Write "Is your restaurant accessible for people in wheelchairs?" rather than "I was wondering whether your restaurant is accessible for people in wheelchairs." The question mark acts as a prompt to your reader that a reply is required. Questions also help your reader to check back to make sure that he or she has told you everything you want to know. Number your questions if you have asked more than two.

Example

THIS MUD'S FOR YOU COFFEE SERVICE:
After reading your brochure, we still have some questions about your office coffee service:
1. Does your "per user" rate distinguish between full- and part-time employees?
2. Does your "per kit" rate require the purchase of a minimum number of kits per month?
3. Can items such as cups and filters be ordered separately, or only as part of a kit?

4. Use lists or a table to display complex information.

Example

 POOR

Recently we received an invoice from you, number G84669, for $120.00 for two and a half hours of photocopy repair service on our Clearox L-600 at $48.00 per hour. In addition, we later needed four hours of repair service, presumably at the same rate. This was invoiced on invoice number G90421. The first invoice was dated October 7, and the second November 2. But the second invoice was for $212.00. Since the rate presumably remained the same, we are enclosing a cheque for $312.00 as payment in full.

 IMPROVED

We have received two invoices for photocopier repair totalling $332.00. We believe the amount should be corrected to read $312.00. Here is the calculation we used.

Invoice Number and Date	Hours	Rate	Total	Amount of Invoice
G84669 October 7	2.5	$48/hr	$120.00	$120.00
G90421 November 2	4	$48/hr	$192.00	$212.00
			$312.00	$332.00

Some e-mail programs do not transmit tables and columns, even though they appear on your screen as you are creating the message. It is safer to use a series of parallel sentences separated by blank lines.

Example

Inv. # G84669   Date 10 07   Hrs. 2.5   Rate $48   Total $120   Inv. $120
Inv. # G90421   Date 11 02   Hrs. 4   Rate $48   Total $192   Inv. $212

5. Use an action close. An action close motivates your reader to reply promptly by setting a target date.

Examples

We would appreciate having this information in time for our December 16 meeting.

If a date is not appropriate, offer some other form of motivation.

I am looking forward to visiting my nearest Burger Barn as soon as I hear from you.

Please let me know as soon as possible so that I can complete my travel plans.

It is not necessary to thank your reader if supplying information is part of his or her routine job. If you are asking for some extra effort—for example, answers to many detailed questions, or information in situations where there is no apparent benefit to your reader (if, for instance, you are not a fellow worker or a potential customer)—you may want to add a sentence such as "Thank you for your help" or "I appreciate your assistance." Do not thank your reader for taking the time to read your letter; this is false humility of the "pardon me for living" variety, and it will make your message sound very unprofessional.

Read the advertisement in Figure 4.1. Using the Modified Block format, use the lines following it to write a routine request for at least three items of information about Sea Breeze Vacation Homes. Compare your letter with Figure 4.2.

FIGURE 4.1   Advertisement—Sea Breeze Vacation Homes

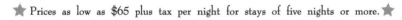

YOUR HOME AWAY FROM HOME ... IN SUNNY ORLANDO

Come to Sea Breeze and enjoy live-in convenience only 10 kilometres from Orlando's popular theme parks. Choose a three, four, or five bedroom home in a residential neighbourhood, all with

- Private outdoor pool
- Secure parking
- Satellite TV
- Internet access
- Full kitchen
- Multiple bathrooms
- Laundry facilities

Prices as low as $65 plus tax per night for stays of five nights or more.

FOR INFORMATION, WRITE

Sea Breeze Vacation Homes

235 Vista Blvd. N.
Orlando FL   34746
Or visit **www.seabreezeorlando.com**

FIGURE 4.2 Letter to Sea Breeze Vacation Homes

1233 63rd Avenue
Edmonton AB T6J 2E5
Canada
May 5, 2007

Sea Breeze Vacation Homes
235 Vista Blvd. N.
Orlando FL 34746
USA

I would like more information about your vacation homes advertised in the May issue of *TravelValue*. Specifically, please answer the following questions:

1. How many people can be accommodated in a three bedroom house?
2. Are the rates quoted on your website per person rates?
3. How much tax would be added to the daily rate?
4. Is the outdoor pool heated?

I would appreciate hearing from you soon, as I hope to have my vacation plans completed by June 1.

Christine D'Alfonso

Christine D'Alfonso

2 PLACING AN ORDER

An **order** resembles a routine request in several ways. Your reader is motivated to fill your order—that's what keeps the company in business. Your job is to make it as easy as possible for your reader to find out exactly what you want, when you want it, and how you plan to pay for it. Consequently, an order follows the same direct order as a routine request. Here are the steps:

1. **Identify your purpose in the first sentence.**

Examples

I would like to order a copy of *Microwave Mania* by Arlene McKean.

Please send me the following items from your spring catalogue:

If you are ordering something from an advertisement, it is helpful if you mention the name and date of the magazine or newspaper in the first sentence.

Example

I would like to order the Ultra Glide ski wax kit advertised in the October issue of *Canadian Skier.*

2. **Add information to identify exactly what you are ordering.** Study the catalogue, advertisement, or other source to find all the identifying information—for example, page number, catalogue or item number, and the name of the product exactly as it is written. Identify any choices you have to make about size, colour, and so on.

3. **Organize the details for easy reading.** Look at a catalogue order form for an example of how to organize information in a clear, easy-to-read format. A table format is a good choice, especially if you are ordering several items. If you are asking your reader to make a decision, make this very clear in the text—for example, "If the Tripmaster hiking boot is not available in half sizes, please send size 9, along with the Tripmaster innersole, catalogue 19 54806, size 9." Order fillers are expected to work quickly, so ensure that important information is noticed rather than skimmed over.

4. **Close with payment and delivery details.** State in your letter if a cheque or money order is enclosed. If you are paying by credit card or on an account, remember to include the account number and the expiry date and type of card (if applicable). Sign the letter with your signature as it appears on your card. You may also request payment on delivery (C.O.D.) if the catalogue or advertisement indicates that this is an option.

If you have an account with your reader, your goods will be delivered to the address stored in the computer unless you clearly request other arrangements. If you are a new customer, delivery will be to the return address on your letter—again, unless you request an alternative. If you must have your order by a certain date, mention this in your letter. Omit closing formulas like "Thank you in advance" and other tired clichés.

Read the advertisement in Figure 4.3. Using the Full Block format, use the lines following it to order two items. Compare your letter with the one in Figure 4.4.

FIGURE 4.3 Advertisement—Life's a Beach, Inc.

Born to Bronze
beach towel—thick, thirsty terry.
24" x 72"
White/bronze or bronze/white.
$18.99

No Ray Sunglasses
Eliminate harmful UVA and UVB, and blue light.
Finest polarized lenses. Brown or grey.
Frames in white, blue, red, black, or chrome.
$29.99

Authentic Panama Hat
Imported from Ecuador. Lightweight,
fashionable protection in natural fibre.
White, cream, or khaki.
Please specify hat size when ordering.
$48.00

Life's a Beach, Inc.
2365 Marine Drive North Vancouver BC V7J 4T2

We pay GST. We pay shipping. B.C. residents add 8% sales tax.
CanExpress next-day delivery $5.00 extra for each order.

FIGURE 4.4   Letter to Life's a Beach, Inc.

39 Woodlawn Circle
Sydney NS B2J 2E7
June 10, 2007

Life's a Beach, Inc.
2365 Marine Drive
North Vancouver BC V7J 4T2

Please send me the following items from your advertisement in the <u>Courier-Loyalist</u>, June 9, 2007:

1 pair of No-Ray sunglasses, brown lenses, chrome frames
1 panama hat, khaki, size 6 1/4

I enclose a money order for $77.99. Please send by parcel post.

Nadine Klein

Nadine Klein

3 ROUTINE REPLIES

A reply is considered "routine" if you can supply the information or product requested. Otherwise the reply is "bad news." These messages are discussed in Chapter 6. Replies are easier to write than requests because contact with your audience has already been established. The message you are answering should give you important clues about the person you are writing to. Study it carefully before you plan your letter. Try to establish the age, occupational status, and educational level of the writer. The paper, the quality of the typing or handwriting, and the spelling and sentence structure, as well as the message itself, provide clues. Next, identify what the writer wants and what questions, if any, you will have to answer. Follow these guidelines in writing your reply:

1. **Open with a reader-oriented statement.** You may wish to begin directly with the answer to the first question.

Examples

QUESTION

Does the Voyage Inn in Owen Sound ON have a discount rate for seniors?

OPENING SENTENCE

Yes, seniors' discounts are available at all Voyage Inn locations.

QUESTION

Does Lambkin Knitwear make natural fibre clothing?

OPENING SENTENCE

You will find a complete selection of natural fibre knitwear on our website.

QUESTION

Can you help us authenticate this certificate? We cannot find any contact information for the institution.

OPENING SENTENCE

The certificate you enclosed was issued by the Acme Training College, which was taken over by Zenith Institute in 1986.

If this seems too abrupt, you may prefer a brief introduction.

Example

QUESTION

Can you give me a detailed description of the fibre content of the items listed below? I do not wear clothing made with any animal or insect by-products.

OPENING SENTENCE

Thank you for your interest in Lambkin Knitwear.

Remember to use the words "you" and "your" in any introductory formula. Avoid statements like "We at the Athlete's Foot Foundation were happy to receive your letter." Your reader is not interested in your emotional state.

Do not repeat information from the letter you are replying to.

✗ POOR

Thank you for your inquiry about the biofeedback program for allergy sufferers which you heard about during the September 24 edition of "Radio Noon" when Les Ragweed was describing recent results with this technology.

✓ IMPROVED

Here is the information you requested about treating allergies with biofeedback.

2. **Respond to all of the questions in the original message.** Number your answers if the original questions were numbered. Even if you do not have the answers to some questions, or if the answer to one question makes an answer to the next one redundant, it is safer to acknowledge each question so that your reader knows that you have seen it. Answer questions in the order in which they were asked. Look at the message again to see if there are any questions that are implied without being asked directly.

Example

I was wondering if your store handled online or telephone orders, as I have two small children and I am not able to get out to shop very frequently.

A good answer to this question would mention your child-care and play area and other services for people with young children as well as provide information about shopping online and by phone.

3. **Do unto others as you would have them do unto you.** Do not draw attention to the failings of the message you are replying to. Do not feel that you can commit the same faults. In fact, if your correspondent is confused, you must be especially clear; if he or she is rude and abrupt, you must be especially polite and gracious.

4. **Use sales-oriented language** if you are writing about a product or service supplied by your organization. Compare these examples:

✗ POOR

The Belvedere Motel can accommodate your group from August 9 to 12.

✓ IMPROVED

Your group can enjoy the first-rate accommodation and conference facilities provided by the Belvedere from August 9 to 12.

5. Use a goodwill-building close. Here are some examples:

You can enjoy the luxury of Fleecetyme mattress covers at special prices during our upcoming January "White Sale" promotion. Watch for it at your local department store.

I hope this information assists you in planning your home security system. Please write again if you have more questions.

Avoid the formula "Please do not hesitate to contact me if you have any further questions." This has become an empty cliché.

Figure 4.5 shows an effective answer to the request on page 85.

ESL TIP

A computer template is a dummy document that serves as a pattern for the layout of a real document. You can create a kind of template routine reply to help you answer written questions more quickly. Begin with a very simple all-purpose opening sentence:

Here are the answers to your questions:

Then answer the questions. If you are answering routine questions from a coworker, you can end the message with the answer to the last question. If you are writing to someone outside your organization, use a simple closing such as

You can find more information on our website at www.—.

or

You can find more information in the attached brochure.

or

Please write again or call xxx-xxxx if you have more questions.

Keep this model in a file to help you compose routine replies quickly.

FIGURE 4.5 Letter from Sea Breeze Vacation Homes

Sea Breeze Vacation Homes

235 Vista Blvd. N.   Orlando FL   34746   (407) 555-2324

www.seabreezeorlando.com

May 11, 2007

Ms. Christine D'Alfonso
1233 63rd Ave.
Edmonton AB T6J 2E5
Canada

Dear Ms. D'Alfonso

Thank you for your interest in Sea Breeze Vacation Homes. Here are the answers to your questions:

1. A three bedroom house can sleep up to eight guests in two double-bedded rooms, one twin-bedded room, and a pull-out couch in the living room.

2. All rates quoted on the website are per night for up to eight guests in a three bedroom house.

3. Florida sales tax of 6%, county lodging tax of 3%, and tourist impact tax of 1% are added to the daily rate.

4. Pool heat is not included in the daily rate but is available for an additional fee. If you are planning to vacation in June, July, or August you will find the pool stays at approximately 72°F without additional heat.

You will find a brochure enclosed with more details of the attractive and convenient homes available for your Orlando vacation, as well as information on the many recreation possibilities in the area. If you would like to reserve a Sea

(continued)

Breeze Vacation Home, please call toll-free at 1-800-555-3838. You can also reserve securely on our website.

Sincerely

Frank O'Brien

Frank O'Brien, Manager

BUSINESS CORRESPONDENCE EVALUATION SHEET

A. Visual Appeal
1. Does the letter have a pleasing appearance (well centred, adequate margins, good paragraph length)?
2. Are there any sloppy corrections (obvious erasures, smudges, strikeovers)?

B. Form
1. Are all essential elements included and conventionally presented (letterhead or return address, date, inside address, salutation, complimentary closing, signature)?
2. Have abbreviations been avoided (except for those specified by Canada Post)?
3. Has the format been followed consistently?

C. Salutation and Complimentary Closing
1. Are they appropriate and compatible?
2. Are they correctly punctuated?

D. Opening
1. Does the opening clearly establish the purpose of the letter?
2. Does it establish a positive tone?

E. **Closing**

1. Is the closing positive and calculated to leave the reader with a good impression?

2. Is it action-oriented, if that is appropriate to the situation?

F. **Content**

1. Is the information that is given complete (are any essential details missing)?

2. Are there any irrelevant details?

3. Is the content presented in a logical order?

4. Are the paragraph divisions logical?

4 ORAL COMMUNICATION

Making Routine Requests in Person or by Telephone

If the information you need is lengthy, detailed, or complicated, a written message is your best choice. Writing saves you time and money, because the receiver gathers and verifies information on his or her time, not yours. But if your requests are simple—"When does the subway start running on Sunday?"—or you need the information right away—"How do you treat a rattlesnake bite?"—then you will probably want to speak to someone personally or over the phone. Here is a typical telephone inquiry.

CASE 1

Texmore Ltd.:	Good morning, Texmore.
Sandra:	Hello. I'd like to speak to someone who could give me some information about the sales representative's job that was advertised in this morning's *Sun*.
Texmore:	One moment please, I'll put you through to Personnel.
Personnel:	Good morning, Personnel.
Sandra:	Good morning, this is Sandra Irving. I'm calling to find out some information about the sales representative's job in this morning's *Sun*.
Personnel:	Certainly—how can I help you?

Sandra:	Will this position be based in Ottawa, or will it require travelling?
Personnel:	It will be primarily in the Ottawa area, but there will probably be some travelling required—about two or three days a month.
Sandra:	Do you provide a company car?
Personnel:	Yes, we do.
Sandra:	And is a training program provided by the company?
Personnel:	Yes, sales reps have a five-week program on full salary from the company.
Sandra:	I think those are all the questions I had. Thank you for your help. I'll be putting my résumé in the mail today.
Personnel:	Goodbye.
Sandra:	Goodbye.

Sandra followed a few simple guidelines to adapt good inquiry skills to the telephone.

1. **Make the purpose of your call clear immediately.** This will help your listener connect you to the person who can help you.
2. **Once you have reached the appropriate person, identify yourself.** This will reinforce the fact that communication is a process in which both of you are participating. In stores or offices, a name tag or sign on a desk or door may give you the name of the person with whom you are speaking. Try to use it.
3. **Ask concise, specific questions.** Open-ended, general questions put your audience on the spot, without much time to consider the best response. Breaking your request down into specific questions will ensure more reliable answers. Long, rambling questions will confuse your listener and tempt him or her to stop paying attention.
4. **Be courteous.** Personal contact requires considerate touches like "please" and "thank you," even for routine business.

Placing an Order

Placing an order over the telephone enables you to find out more about the product or service you're ordering and make appropriate decisions based on that information. On the other hand, the amount of information you must give an order taker is usually large. You will probably need to write a lot of it down and simply read it. Remember to have with you:

1. a copy of the catalogue, advertisement, or other document, open at the right page
2. the order number and name exactly as printed
3. a choice of colour, size, and anything else that must be decided on by the person ordering; make a second choice just in case
4. the shipping address, including postal code
5. a decision on the shipping method: post office, parcel service, and so on
6. the billing information, account number, expiry date, and so on

Taking Telephone Inquiries or Orders

Like a written inquiry or order, a telephone inquiry or order is an important opportunity to build goodwill with potential clients or customers. A successful organization handles every telephone call like a sales call. Look at the following case:

CASE 2

Bruce had just started working at Steel Master Office Supplies. There had been so much to do during the first few days that he hardly had time to sit at his new desk. Finally, he was enjoying a few peaceful minutes, when the phone rang.

Bruce:	Hello?
Pamela Reed:	Hello, is this Steel Master Office Supplies?
Bruce:	Yes, it is.
Pamela Reed:	Well, I'm Pamela Reed from Shamrock Insurance, and I'm calling about the office system that was featured in this month's *Canadian Business*.
Bruce:	Um, I'm afraid I don't know which system you mean, Mrs. Reed — would you have the name there?
Pamela Reed:	It's Ms. Reed, and I think it was called the Landmark II.
Bruce:	Oh yes, uh, that's a new line, I think. What did you want to know?
Pamela Reed:	We're expanding here, putting in some new offices for our senior people, and we're looking for some new ideas, something different.
Bruce:	That is our latest line, pretty up-to-date.
Pamela Reed:	Well, I wondered if you had some brochures or catalogues with the different components.
Bruce:	Oh yeah, I'm sure we can get one of those out to you.

Pamela Reed: Well, could you send it to me at Shamrock Insurance, 4430 38th Avenue N.W., Calgary T4N 6G8?

Bruce: Sure, just let me get a pen here. What was that again?

Pamela Reed: Shamrock Insurance, 4430 38th Avenue N.W., Calgary T4N 6G8.

Bruce: Well, we'll get that right out to you, Mrs. Reed. Bye now.

Shamrock Insurance subsequently had its entire office redone—by a rival firm. How did Bruce blow this opportunity? List eight things Bruce did, or didn't do, that cost Steel Master Office Supplies a chance for a big sale. Compare your list with the one on page 99.

1. _____

2. _____

3. _____

4. _____

5. _____

6. _____

7. _____

8. _____

The following guidelines will help you handle telephone requests and orders effectively:

1. Answer the telephone by identifying yourself and your business or organization.

2. Listen to the speaker's statement of his or her purpose in calling. Determine whether you are the appropriate person to take the call.

3. Ask questions to clarify exactly what the caller wants. Do not point out that he or she is confused, inaccurate, or unclear.

4. Be alert for sales or service opportunities. Listen for information about your caller's wants and needs. Suggest ways in which your organization could meet those needs.

5. Give the caller positive feedback about his or her choices and decisions. For example, a hotel reservations clerk might affirm a client's choice by saying, "The weekend package is really a great bargain," or, "You'll appreciate the extra space in your deluxe room." This is called "resale," and it is an important goodwill-builder.
6. Confirm all details if the caller is placing an order.
7. Suggest appropriate follow-up to an inquiry: sales call, visit by caller, information in the mail, call back. Take the initiative.
8. Thank the caller. Repeat your name and indicate that you will be happy to help him or her again.

Answers to Chapter Questions

Page 98:
1. Did not give proper identification when he answered the phone.
2. Was not familiar with current promotion or products.
3. Assumed caller wished to be called "Mrs."—repeated this error after he had been corrected.
4. Failed to use sales-oriented language when discussing company products.
5. Did not look for sales opportunity when caller described needs.
6. Did not volunteer to provide more information—the caller had to ask for brochures.
7. Was not prepared to take caller's name and address.
8. Ended call without determining if the caller needed anything more.

CHAPTER REVIEW/SELF-TEST

1. Use the **direct order** to make a request when
   (a) you have the power to make the receiver do what you tell them.
   (b) you are pressed for time.
   (c) the request is part of the receiver's normal job responsibilities.
   (d) the request is easy for the receiver to carry out.

2. Begin a routine request by
   (a) making friendly, ice-breaking statements.
   (b) stating the purpose of the message.
   (c) giving the receiver some background information about who you are.
   (d) explaining why you need information or help.

3. Include details that
   (a) give the reader a sense of you as a whole person.
   (b) explain why you are making this request to this particular person or organization.
   (c) keep the audience from losing interest.
   (d) will help you get a more useful response.

4. Close the message by
   (a) asking the receiver to respond to your message.
   (b) thanking the receiver for taking the time to read or listen to your message.
   (c) explaining why you need information or help.
   (d) saying, "Please do not hesitate to contact me if you require further assistance."

5. When placing an order, use
   (a) any format you like. The receiver is lucky to have your business.
   (b) the "special request" format to persuade the receiver to do you the favour of selling you something.
   (c) the direct order format to avoid mistakes and delays.

6. Use the **direct order** to send a reply when
   (a) you must say no to a request.
   (b) you can say yes to a routine request.
   (c) the receiver has no power to object.
   (d) the receiver is pressed for time.

7. Begin a reply by
   (a) expressing your pleasure at having the opportunity to give information or help.
   (b) telling the receiver something about your product or organization.
   (c) repeating the key points from the sender's message.
   (d) none of the above.

8. Help your audience by
   (a) answering all his or her questions in the order they were asked.
   (b) pointing out when he or she is mistaken or confused.
   (c) answering his or her questions in the order they should have been asked.
   (d) ignoring pointless or repetitive questions.

9. When you are answering questions about a product or service provided by your organization you should
   (a) point out that this information was already available elsewhere.
   (b) keep your answers brief and factual.
   (c) treat this as a sales opportunity.
   (d) all of the above.

10. End your reply with
    (a) a friendly expression and a suggestion for follow-up where appropriate.
    (b) a statement of how much you enjoyed the opportunity to give information or help.
    (c) the phrase "Please do not hesitate to contact me if I can be of further assistance."
    (d) none of the above.

Answers

1.C 2.B 3.D 4.A 5.C 6.B 7.D 8.A 9.C 10.A

EXERCISES

1. Find an ad for a product or service in which you are interested. Write a letter requesting at least four items of information not given in the ad. Use one of the formats illustrated in this textbook. Hand in **two** typed copies of your letter and a stamped envelope addressed to the company. Include the ad with your assignment.

2. Write a short (200-word) critique of the reply you receive to the letter of inquiry, above. Use the Business Correspondence Evaluation Sheet on page 94 to help you.

3. You wish to sell crests and pins with the emblem of your organization. Prepare a fax to be sent to Impact Manufacturing Ltd., 1-800-555-3784, outlining your requirements and requesting an estimate. Include a line drawing of your emblem.

4. You are opening your own business and want a distinctive letterhead. Find on the Internet the name of a company that designs stationery, and write a message outlining your requirements.

5. You are employed in the personnel department of a large retail business. In a trade journal you have seen an advertisement for *Go-to-Sell*, a training video for salespeople. The ad mentioned only one rate: "Rental as low as $39." If this video is appropriate, you would like to show it to your new salesclerks. Write a letter requesting all appropriate information, addressed to Western Media, 1948 29th St. N.W., Calgary, AB T4N 3R6.

6. Write a letter of inquiry based on the following: You have heard that the provincial government is starting a program awarding grants to companies that can provide jobs to unemployed people between the ages of 18 and 24. Write to the Ministry of Labour requesting more information. Specifically, you want to know what your company would have to do to qualify and how the program works. Consider giving some details about the nature of your company.

7. You have volunteered to organize a graduation banquet for your program. Design an e-mail message to be sent to hotels and banquet halls in your community, requesting information about their facilities. Outline your requirements, and ask at least four relevant questions.

8. Identify an organization for which you think you might like to work. Phone the organization to arrange a meeting to gather information about job opportunities for community college graduates. This is not a job interview. In your phone call, be sure to:
(a) explain the purpose of your proposed meeting;
(b) obtain the name of the appropriate person to meet with;
(c) arrange a mutually convenient date and time.
This meeting will form the basis for the research interview assignment described on page 245. The information you obtain would make a worthwhile class presentation.

9. Prepare a reply to the following e-mail message:

Subject: New account information
Date: Aug/23/2007 1:04:24 PM Eastern Daylight Time
From: carla.mycek@hotmail.com
To: municipalcreditu.ca

I will be moving to Windsor in September to attend college and I would like to open an account with you. Please answer the following questions:

1. Do I need to withdraw all the money from my existing bank account and bring it with me or can it be transferred some other way?
2. What identification will I need to open an account?
3. How soon after opening my account will I receive a chequebook?
4. Do you offer debit cards?

Please reply as soon as possible so I can open my account before school starts.

Carla Mycek

---

10. Write a reply to one of the following letters:

(a)

Leisure and Recreation Department
Bristol Local Council
Bristol, England
January 16, 2008

Centennial Community Centre
Arkona ON L9C 1E4

I am the director of the Leisure and Recreation Department of Bristol Local Council, Bristol, England. In late May, I and a group of my staff will be touring recreational sites in southern Ontario, and we are very interested in visiting your facility, which has been recommended to us as a model of its type. We are as yet uncommitted for the 21, 22, and 23 of May, 2008. Would it be possible to arrange a tour for seven people on one of these dates? If so, how long would it last? What areas of your operation would you recommend to our particular attention? We hope to have a firm agenda by February 8, so we would appreciate receiving your reply by the end of this month.

Leslie Henderson

Leslie Henderson

(b)

Business Division, Atlantic College
1790 Tacoma Drive
Dartmouth NS B2W 6E2
April 11, 2008

Canadian Magazine Association
401 Richmond Street West
Toronto ON M5V 3A8

The Business Division at Atlantic College has recently created a budget for magazine subscriptions. Your answers to the following questions would be appreciated:

1. What business periodicals are currently published in Canada?
2. Do any of these periodicals focus on Atlantic Canada?
3. Can you recommend three or four Canadian general-interest magazines that college students might enjoy?
4. Are there special subscription rates for institutions?

Your prompt reply will enable us to order magazines in time for the beginning of the fall semester.

Kelly Fraser

Kelly Fraser

(c)

82 Maple Gardens
Godfrey ON K0H 1L2
May 2, 2009

[Your city] Tourist Information Centre
683 King St.
[Your city]

Please send me some information about tourist attractions in your area. I will be taking a summer course there in July and I would like to take some additional vacation time with my husband and children ages 5 and 10. What do you recommend for family accommodation: hotels or short-term apartment rental? What attractions are particularly suited for families in the area? My husband and I enjoy going to the theatre so we would also like information about local shows. We plan to stay about three weeks. Please reply before May 12 so that we can complete our travel plans.

Rose Ruiz

Rose Ruiz

(d)

75 Church St.
Saskatoon SK S4K 1P2
2008 01 08

[Name and address of your college]

Attention: [Your program] Course Director

Please answer the following questions regarding your program:

1. What high school courses would be good preparation for this program?
2. How important are communication skills to success in this program?
3. What job opportunities are open to your graduates?
4. Approximately how much money would an out-of-town student require for tuition, books, and living expenses for one academic year?

I would appreciate your reply before February 1, as I am planning to apply to college for September.

Barat Savunth

Barat Savunth

CHAPTER FIVE

· ·

GOOD NEWS: THE DIRECT APPROACH

Chapter Objectives

Successful completion of this chapter will enable you to:

1 Deliver good news effectively, orally or in writing, using the direct approach: good news, explanation, goodwill closing.

2 Give a good news response to a problem or complaint.

3 Deliver good news orally, using the direct approach.

INTRODUCTION

A routine message is one which the receiver expects and predicts. When you have a pleasant surprise for your audience, or when you are able to turn a negative situation into a positive one, then your message is good news.

 # WRITING GOOD NEWS MESSAGES

CASE 1

Thank you for entering the "Why I Like Old Mexicali Taco Sauce" Jingle Contest. We were gratified that so many people responded to our contest—over 40 000 happy users of Old Mexicali, the taco sauce that fights back. We at Mescalito Mexican Foods have been making this sauce for over 70 years, using only the finest ingredients, including deluxe chilis grown specially to give Old Mexicali the taste that just won't quit. And the same high standards are followed in making all our fine products—El Paso Taco Chips, Rio Grande Refried Beans, and South of the Border Down Mexico Way Chili con Carne. So you can be proud to hear that your jingle has won the first prize of $50 000. Congratulations.

Everyone would like to win a contest with a $50 000 first prize. But the lucky winner of this jingle contest may have to read about it in the paper. This letter takes so long to deliver the good news that the reader might well give up before getting there.

A message brings good news when we can reasonably assume that the audience will be immediately pleased to read or hear it. The good news may be a reply to a request, such as a job application or a customer complaint, or it may be an announcement of some favourable event. In any case, you will want to capitalize on your audience's positive response to the good news by putting it right at the beginning. This **direct order** is similar to the order you used in routine messages in Chapter 4:

1. Good news
2. Explanation
3. Goodwill close

1. Putting the **good news** first accomplishes several things. It gets the audience's attention and ensures that they receive the important part of the message, even if they do not read it all the way through. Ideally, the positive impact of the good news will motivate your audience to keep on reading.

In a memo or e-mail message, put the good news in the subject line if you can. If you do not have space, at least indicate that good news is coming in the body of the message.

Example

Subject: Good news on contract talks

2. The **explanation** follows up the good news with details your audience will naturally want or need. For example, if you are telling an applicant that she has been selected for a job interview, she will need to know where and when it will take place. If you are announcing a pay raise, your reader will want to know when it takes effect. If your explanation is too long, it will detract from the impact of the good news. Ask yourself what purpose each part of the explanation will serve from the reader's point of view. Leave out anything that isn't important right now. You can always follow up with additional details in a further message.

Handling the explanation in response to customer complaints requires a special approach. Item 2 on page 111 will give you more details.

3. Close the good news message with a brief, you-centred **expression of good-will.**

Example

Date: 2009 06 04
To: Ingrid Forrest
From: Lance Binkley   L. B.
Re: Vacation request

Your vacation dates have been changed to August 7–18, as you requested. Greg King has agreed to cover the August 9 meeting for you. Please make sure that he has all the audit material by July 15. Good luck with your plans.

The text below is the body of a letter sent to a student who had applied to a college program that was in high demand:

Thank you for your interest in the Computer Animation Arts program at Metropolitan College. Over the last three months we have been reviewing the portfolios of over 200 highly qualified applicants to select only 35 students for the upcoming year. Your application for the Computer Animation Arts program has been approved. Canada is taking a leading role in this exciting combination of art and technology. After graduation you will have an opportunity to work in advertising, television, or the feature film industry, and lifelong learning opportunities at Metropolitan College will keep your skills current and in demand. Congratulations. We look forward to seeing you this fall. Registration will take place at the main campus on September 3, 2008, from 9 AM to 12 PM. An information package will be sent to you in early August.

Beside the right number below, copy: 1. the good news, 2. the explanation, 3. the goodwill close. Omit any unneeded information.

1. _____

   _____

2. _____

   _____

3. _____

   _____

Why is this message more effective than the original letter?

2 RESPONDING TO COMPLAINTS OR PROBLEMS

Handling customer complaints requires special attention. Your audience is angry or disappointed. Your organization, and perhaps you personally, are being criticized. Even if you are prepared to make the adjustment that the customer requests, this good news is tempered by the bad news that your company or your product failed in some way the first time around.

A good news message tells customers that their problem has been looked into and that their request has been granted. It may even tell customers that they will be receiving additional compensation for any loss or inconvenience. Whenever possible, a good news message also rebuilds customer confidence by explaining what steps you are taking to prevent problems from recurring. Following a few simple guidelines for modifying the **direct order** will ensure the most effective presentation of your message.

1. **Put the good news first.** The good news is your quickest means of restoring good feeling between you and your customer. The rest of your message will be bathed in its glow. Tell the reader right away that her refund is enclosed,

her deck is being repaired free of charge, her video-phone is being delivered by courier. Leave apologies or other negative statements for later. Avoid limp, ambiguous openings such as:

Thank you for your letter describing your experiences with our Gel Flite running shoes.

or

We were sorry to receive your letter regarding the cracks in your driveway.

The following openings give the audience an immediate, positive message:

Enclosed you will find a full refund for the shoes you recently returned.

A repair person will be coming to your house early next week to repair your driveway at no cost to you.

2. **Give the customer an explanation.** Restoring customer confidence usually requires more than simply offering compensation. The customer has been disappointed or inconvenienced in some way by your company. He or she wants to be sure that it won't happen again. A good explanation conveys honest concern and a commitment to quality.

Examples

✗ POOR
We process thousands of requests every day. Inevitably some get misplaced or misfiled.

This writer implies that the company is not really concerned with providing good service. The customer will probably feel that his problem was not taken very seriously.

✓ IMPROVED
Our aim is to fill every request as promptly and accurately as possible. Although no system can be 100 percent perfect, we are always working on ways to improve ours.

✗ POOR
Exposure to temperatures above 30 degrees Celsius causes cocoa butter to rise to the surface of the chocolate and crystallize, turning the chocolate pale brown or white. This does not affect taste or quality. Nevertheless, we are prepared to exchange the chocolates you bought, if you can provide proof of purchase.

This explanation is defensive and grudging. The customer will probably feel that she is being offered compensation just to spare the company further trouble, not because there is any merit in her request. This will not restore her goodwill toward the company.

✓ IMPROVED

Exposure to temperatures above 30 degrees Celsius causes cocoa butter to rise to the surface of the chocolate and crystallize, turning the chocolate pale brown or white. Although this does not affect taste or quality, we can understand that you want your Black Beauty chocolates to look as good as they taste. Please send your proof of purchase to the address above and you will receive your free replacement box.

✗ POOR

The clerk who handled your original order didn't take the time to confirm that the parts he was dispatching were compatible with your machine.

The writer is attempting to make the company as a whole look better by passing blame to a single individual. But customers justifiably assume that a company must take responsibility for the actions of people it has hired and trained.

✓ IMPROVED

Unfortunately, the parts dispatched to you had not been matched to the specifications of your machine.

✗ POOR

It appears that poor maintenance led to a breakdown in the machine that date-stamps our orders. Everything for the last month has been dated June 14, and consequently the boys in the warehouse have just been picking them at random instead of on a first-come, first-served basis.

This explanation puts the writer's company in an unflattering, unprofessional light. The customer's image of the company will probably be worse, not better, after reading this.

✓ IMPROVED

A malfunction in the machine that date-stamps orders led to a breakdown in our priority shipping system.

A good explanation, like the following, is tactful without being evasive. It creates a concerned, responsible image for the company:

Normally, Parti-Tyme Cakes are sprayed lightly with an edible vegetable gum after icing to preserve their fresh taste and eye appeal. A jammed timing mechanism permitted one batch of cakes to go through the spraying process several times, which produced the crusty texture you mentioned. As the appearance of the cakes was not affected, several passed visual inspection and were packaged before a spot check discovered the malfunction and corrected it.

At the end of the explanation you may wish to add an apology, especially if the customer had a particularly negative experience or seems very angry. **Keep it brief,** however; don't go into details that will revive the customer's sense of deep grievance.

✗ POOR
We are terribly sorry for all the inconvenience you suffered because of the complete collapse of your balcony.

✓ IMPROVED
We are sorry for the inconvenience this caused you.

3. **Close with a positive message.** The end of the good news message should sustain the positive note of the opening. Never apologize again at the end. Avoid "don't hate us" closings like:

We hope you will consider giving Tasti-Lite diet fudge another try.

"We hope you will ... but you probably won't" is the message this sends to the customer. Instead, look forward to the re-establishment of a good business relationship with your customer — to your benefit and the customer's. Here are some good examples that are you-centred and use resale tactfully:

With your shipment we have included ten litres of our new Pumpkin Ripple ice cream free of charge — just in time for Hallowe'en. We're sure your customers will enjoy it.

Your battery operated lint-picker is now ready to provide years of trouble-free service.

Enclosed is a brochure outlining many new courses and family activities offered this fall.

CASE 2

"Dear Jay-Mor Realty," the letter began, "On a number of occasions I have called the attention of your Clearwater Avenue parking lot attendant to the fact that the paving needs repair in several places, creating dangerous ridges and potholes. Last Tuesday evening, as I was picking my way across the lot, I slipped on a patch of slush and fell into a puddle which had collected in one of these potholes. If I had been carrying something, I might have been seriously injured; as it was, I merely tore the knee out of a pair of good pants and drenched my suede coat with muddy water. You will find enclosed a bill for $65.97 for replacing the former and $57.63 for cleaning the latter. I would appreciate reimbursement for these expenses incurred because of your inadequate maintenance."

Well, the guy had a point. Fred Morrone, the maintenance manager, had noticed how badly the pavement needed repair. The construction strike in the fall had set the regular maintenance schedule back at least six weeks, and now the temperatures were too low to consider any resurfacing. Maybe the worst hazards could be fenced off till the spring. In the meantime, he'd better do something about this claim. Fred started drafting a reply:

> Dear Ed Drenna
>
> We were very sorry to receive your complaint about our parking lot. Due to circumstances beyond our control, we were not able to bring the parking lot surface up to standard before the winter. Hopefully this situation will resolve itself by next spring. We are sending you a cheque for the damages you claimed were caused by a fall in the parking lot. Once again, please accept our apologies.

Fred's first draft is not an effective good news reply. List seven things that make this letter a failure.

1. _____

_____

2. _____

_____

3. _____

_____

4. _____

_____

5. _____

_____

6. _____

_____

7. _____

_____

Compare your list with the one on page 120.

Write an improved version of Fred's letter. Compare your version with the one in Figure 5.1.

The message in Figure 5.2 presents a problem that requires a different kind of solution. The writer does not want compensation; the person wants to know that the problem will not occur again. You will find the answer on page 118.

ESL TIP

When you give good news in response to a problem or complaint your main objective is to restore the goodwill of your client, customer, or employee. To achieve this objective you must ensure that the tone of your message is as positive as the good news you are giving. You can do this in several ways. First, emphasize the words "you" and "your." "Here is your refund," is a better choice than "I am going to give you a refund." You do not wish to call attention to your power as the decision-maker or your self-interest in making the customer happy. Do not use expressions like "You claim it was broken when you opened the package," or "You say you did not have this near anything magnetic." These forms imply that you do not necessarily believe the other person's statement. Avoid suggesting that fixing a problem is a chore for you. "I will send this back to the warehouse and then a new part can be attached for you," is a better choice than "I'm going to have to send this back to the warehouse and get a new part attached."

FIGURE 5.1   Good News Response to a Complaint

Jay-Mor Realty, Ltd.

948 Sherwood Ave. Winnipeg MB   R2M 6A5 (204) 555-7222

February 16, 2008

Ed Drenna
43 River St.
Winnipeg MB R3T 2P4

Dear Ed Drenna

Enclosed you will find a cheque for $123.60, as you requested in your letter of February 9.

Normally, our parking lots are resurfaced every other autumn. Unfortunately, a construction strike put our contractor seriously behind schedule, and we were unable to arrange a date for repairs to our Clearwater Avenue lot before low temperatures forced us to postpone the work until spring. We are sorry for the inconvenience this has caused you. Our maintenance staff will be systematically checking the parking lot surface next week and putting barriers around any potential hazards. Full resurfacing will take place as soon as warmer weather arrives.

Your safety and satisfaction are important to our parking lot staff. The enclosed card will entitle you to park free at any Jay-Mor lot for the next thirty days. Just have it validated by the attendant the next time you park at Jay-Mor.

Sincerely

Fred Morrone

Fred Morrone
Maintenance Manager

FIGURE 5.2 Message of Complaint

Subj: Washroom access for disabled patrons
Date: Oct/27/2009 1:04:24 PM Eastern Standard Time
From: Quoc Vinh Tran qvt@hotmail.com
To: www.harbour55.com

<u>Attention: Manager</u>

Last Friday night I visited your restaurant with some friends to celebrate a birthday. Because one of the group uses a wheelchair, I looked in the <u>Downtown Restaurant Guide</u> to find an appropriate place for our party.

The listing for Harbour 55 indicated that it was wheelchair accessible. I also looked on your website and saw a "disabled" icon, so I confidently made a reservation. But while we were happy to see that the entrance had a ramp and the restaurant had no interior steps, we were very unhappy to discover that the washrooms were in the basement.

It doesn't seem very realistic to call a restaurant accessible if it is not possible for someone in a wheelchair to visit the washroom. I think you should change your listing and the information on your website.

Quoc Vinh Tran

FIGURE 5.3   Good News Response to a Complaint

Subj: Re: Washroom access for disabled patrons
Date: Oct/27/2009 4:18:04 PM Eastern Standard Time
To: Quoc Vinh Tran qvt@hotmail.com
From: Alena Makavets, Manager, Harbour 55 www.harbour55.com

You are right to assume that "wheelchair accessible" should refer to all the facilities of our restaurant.

When the <u>Downtown Restaurant Guide</u> was published last January we had a main floor washroom in place for patrons who had difficulty with stairs. However, during an inspection in June we were told that the placement of the washroom was in violation of the fire code and could no longer be used. I am sorry that this caused a problem when you visited the restaurant.

We have drawn up a new floor plan and are waiting for approval by the building inspectors. We hope to have a new accessible washroom by the new year. In the meantime we will take the icon off our website and add a note explaining the current situation. Please accept our invitation to visit again when the renovations are complete. You will receive an announcement by e-mail.

Alena Makavets, Manager
Harbour 55

3 DELIVERING GOOD NEWS ORALLY

The techniques suggested for writing good news messages can easily be adapted to oral communications. Most of us enjoy the opportunity to deliver good news in person. The **direct order**—getting right to the point—comes easily when you anticipate that your audience will be happy to receive your message. Here is the direct order:

1. Good news
2. Explanation
3. Goodwill closing

1. **Give the good news as soon as possible.** Don't leave your audience in suspense with an "I suppose you're wondering why I called you in here" opening. Limit

yourself to the briefest formula: "I have some good news for you ...," or, "This is Dr. Freeman's office; I have some good news from your test results." Then deliver the good news.

2. **Add any necessary explanation.** Give your listener a chance to ask questions. Let the needs of your audience determine how long or short the explanation should be.
3. **Wind up the conversation with an expression of goodwill.**

CASE 3

Mark Dubois had recently written some exams that would upgrade his professional classification — if he passed. They were tough exams and he had been waiting almost a month to get the results. So when he was called to the Personnel Office, he was pretty nervous. Here's how it went:

Dave: Well, come in, Mark. The results of your exams are in, I have them right here. Why don't you sit down? I guess you've been kind of nervous about them. A lot of people write these but not too many pass the first time. I remember a couple of years ago someone sat them four times before he passed. But I guess it's worth it in the end. Anyway, you did fine; passed every one.

Mark: Well, that's a relief. Could I see ...

Dave: Now, of course, you'll want to make some decisions about following up, maybe going up another level. You might like to talk to Theresa Comisso — she's done that. Of course, you have to enroll within the next two years, but I guess that's not a problem unless you're planning to transfer to another branch. We're opening up a northern office, lots of good promotion opportunities, but a little isolated, you know. How'd you feel about that? Or, of course, this opens up some possibilities right here; I was reading in the last newsletter about Fred's retirement. Now, of course, this would qualify you for his area ...

Mark: I think I'd just like to look at my results for a while.

Dave: Well, sure. I just need you to fill out a receipt for your transcript and it's all yours. Why don't you give me a call next week and we can go over your options.

Mark: Okay, then ...

Dave: Well, you're lucky, you know. A lot of the people here haven't been able to keep up with their professional training. You know Al's mother's living with him now; she's had a lot of health problems. And then Christine's husband walked out; that was a real mess. And of course it takes time away from your family. But congratulations; I'll look forward to giving you any help I can with your plans.

Mark: Thanks, I'll be in touch.

Cross out everything in Dave's conversation that detracts from the impact of his good news message.

Answers to Chapter Questions

Page 114:
1. Doesn't begin with good news.
2. Uses negative word "complaint" in reference to reader.
3. First sentence implies that the company was sorry to get the letter, not sorry about the accident.
4. Explanation doesn't explain. Cliché phrase "due to circumstances beyond our control" is vague and meaningless.
5. Cliché phrase "hopefully this situation will resolve itself" implies that the company will not take any active steps to deal with the problem.
6. Phrase "damages you claimed were caused ..." suggests that reader may be lying.
7. Closes with a negative message.

CHAPTER REVIEW/SELF-TEST

1. A message should be presented as good news when
   (a) you have nothing negative to say.
   (b) you have a pleasant surprise for your receiver.
   (c) you are trying to sell something.
   (d) you can say yes to a routine request.

2. Begin a good news message with
   (a) the good news.
   (b) an expression of goodwill.
   (c) a brief introductory formula.
   (d) any of the above.

3. In a memo or e-mail message, try to put the good news
   (a) in the closing.
   (b) in a different font.
   (c) in the subject line, if you have space for it.
   (d) in an attachment.

4. The explanation section of a good news message explains
   (a) why the news is good.
   (b) how you reached your decision.
   (c) full details of all the results of the good news.
   (d) what your audience needs to know right now to take advantage of the good news.

5. The closing of the good news message
   (a) thanks the audience for taking the time to read or listen to the message.
   (b) repeats the explanation, for emphasis.
   (c) reinforces the good news with an expression of goodwill.
   (d) should do all of the above.

6. A good news response to a problem or complaint should begin with
   (a) an apology.
   (b) a statement about how you felt when you learned of the problem.
   (c) good news.
   (d) a summary of the problem or complaint as you understand it.

7. The purpose of the explanation in a good news response to a problem or complaint is to
   (a) restore faith in your product, service, or organization.
   (b) pass blame to someone who wasn't following the rules.
   (c) avoid a lawsuit.
   (d) tell the reader or listener exactly what happened.

8. An apology in a good news letter should
   (a) describe the problem in complete detail.
   (b) come at the end of the explanation.
   (c) be repeated at the end of the message.
   (d) all of the above.

9. Close the good news response to a problem with
   (a) a promise that no problems will ever happen again.
   (b) a statement of how you feel about the inconvenience your customer or client experienced.
   (c) a hope that the audience will give your product or service another try.
   (d) none of the above.

10. Re-establish goodwill at the end of your message by
    (a) offering additional compensation to your audience.
    (b) looking forward to a continued good business relationship with your audience.
    (c) a you-centred statement.
    (d) any of the above.

Answers

1.B 2.A 3.C 4.D 5.C 6.C 7.A 8.B 9.D 10.D

EXERCISES

1. Revise the following messages to improve their tone and organization:
    (a) Thank you for your letter regarding the explosion in your VCR. We have examined the machine in our lab, and it appears that a faulty connection allowed a spark to contact gases apparently generated by the head cleaner you were using. We are glad to hear that no one was seriously injured. We will be sending you a replacement machine shortly. I hope you will continue to rely on Lectron for all your electronics needs.
    (b) We were interested to hear of your experience with our Right Off stain remover. It appears from our analysis of the blouse you sent us that the spray has combined chemically with the dimethylcellulose protein in the fabric to produce those large orange blotches when heated in the dryer. We have received several similar complaints, and our product scientists are working on changing the formulation of Right Off. All existing stock will be relabelled in the meantime. We are enclosing a cheque for $38.42, as requested, to cover the cost of replacing the blouse, as well as some samples of our other fine cleaning products. Thank you for drawing this problem to our attention.
    (c) Thank you for applying for the job of assistant retail manager. Many fine candidates were interviewed for the job, and it was indeed a difficult decision to select one person from so many qualified applicants. Therefore, we at Marks and Sparks are happy to be able to offer you this position. Please phone 481-1111 for information regarding starting date, required documentation, etc.
    (d) Memo:
    Jim, it's always difficult to change vacation schedules once they're set. People have made plans around their dates, and naturally these have priority. In addition, our secretarial and other support requirements are fixed according to the staff who will be in the office at any given time. However, it seems that Louise had her reservations in Quebec City fall through, so she is willing to trade July 8–27 for August 2–22. So—bon voyage!

2. You are the manager of Trendway Catalogue Sales. Prepare the following good news messages:

    (a) To all customers: To benefit the environment, Trendway will be eliminating over-packaging and using lighter, less bulky mailers made from recycled materials.

    (b) To Preya Ramroop, a Trendway employee: Because of her leadership in developing these packaging changes, this employee will be receiving an Excellence Award from the company.

3. Kindly Fruits of the Earth Natural Market has been named Canadian Small Business of the Year by the *Canadian Business Post*. As president of Kindly Fruits of the Earth, write an e-mail to be sent to all employees, telling them of this honour.

4. Write a good news response to one of the following messages:

    (a)

5990 Kingston Rd. #238
Toronto ON M2N 5Y7
2006 04 06

Bloomsday Florists
3080 Yonge St.
Toronto ON M4N 3P3

Three months ago I ordered four table centre arrangements from you for a party I gave last Saturday. When the flowers were delivered Saturday morning they seemed droopy but I assumed some water would pick them up. Instead, by party time they were losing petals and looking faded. This was very disappointing, especially as I had planned to present the flower arrangements to the guests of honour after the party. I am enclosing the bill and I would appreciate a refund for the full purchase price.

Moira Cole

Moira Cole

(b)

194 Gleneagle Ave.
Toronto ON M4K 3P2
February 28, 2008

Underwear Underworld
595 Main St.
Flesherton ON N4G 1E6

When is two days the same as two weeks? When it's the two weeks spent waiting for your company's guaranteed two-day delivery. On February 11 I faxed an order to you for three pairs of red silk briefs as a Valentine's Day gift for my husband. As your order form promised two-day delivery anywhere in Canada I was confident that the gift would be here in good time. Instead I waited until February 25—long past the special day. I think it would be appropriate to refund the price of the briefs as well as the $15 I paid for express delivery. A copy of the packing slip is enclosed.

Jing-mei Li

(c)

Dept of Earth Studies
Sanford Dettweiler Memorial College
3250 Bonaventure Park Blvd. W.
Kapuskasing ON K2J 8V8
February 28, 2009

Acme Management Institute
40 Alta Vista Dr.
Ottawa ON K0K 1G3

Enclosed you will find my application for your Supervisory Skills Workshop to be held
May 1–4. I attempted to register online, as I note that you offer a $25 discount to
online registrants; however, after I spent quite a bit of time filling out the form it was
not accepted because my address was too long for the field. As this was not my
fault I think it would be fair to give me the $25 discount anyway.

Gayathri Sivalogonathan

Gayathri Sivalogonathan

(d)

Subj: Car rental ref. #618039967
Date: Oct/19/2008 1:04:24 PM Eastern Daylight Time
From: Lincoln Barnes linbarn@sympatico.ca
To: www.eeezed.ca

Two weeks ago I booked a car with you for the Thanksgiving Day weekend. I
specified a non-smoking vehicle, but the car I was given had no "No Smoking"
sticker and smelled distinctly of smoke. Later I found an EEE-ZED logo air freshener
in the glove compartment, as though someone had quickly taken it off the rear-view
mirror and hidden it. If no non-smoking car was available I think I should have been
told and given the choice of cancelling or receiving a discount or free upgrade.

Lincoln Barnes

CHAPTER SIX

BAD NEWS: THE INDIRECT APPROACH

Chapter Objectives

Successful completion of this chapter will enable you to:

1 Deliver bad news appropriately, in writing, using the indirect approach: neutral opening, explanation, bad news, and goodwill closing.

2 Deliver bad news in response to a complaint or problem.

3 Deliver bad news orally, using the indirect approach.

INTRODUCTION

If good news is a message that you expect will please your audience, bad news is anything you expect to have the opposite effect. It may be a negative answer to a request. It may be the announcement of some change for the worse—increased prices, layoffs, or reduced benefits or privileges. The biggest challenge is delivering bad news in response to a complaint or problem. In this situation, your audience is already in a negative frame of mind. The most important thing to remember is to keep your message clear and logical, avoiding anything that suggests that the news is bad because your reader or listener is a bad person. Bad news is unavoidable, but a well-organized message can help your audience deal with bad news in a productive way.

1 WRITING BAD NEWS MESSAGES

When your message is definitely "bad news," it requires tactful handling. The **indirect order** breaks it gently:

1. Neutral opening
2. Explanation
3. Bad news
4. Goodwill close

1. **A neutral opening avoids starting off on a negative note,** without going too far in the opposite direction and leading the audience to expect a positive message. A factual statement is a good way to open the subject without making it obvious that bad news is coming. Here are some examples:

   For the past three years, A Woman's Place has provided its meeting rooms free of charge to outside groups.

   I have been putting together the vacation schedule for June, July, and August.

   Revise the following subject lines to eliminate the negative tone:

   (a) To: All employees   Date: 2009 04 18
       From: Marie Turco, Human Resources MT
       Subject: Reduction in Employee Benefits

(b) To: Allan Singh   Date: July 31, 2007
     From: Don Snyder DS
     Subject: Loss of Entitlement to Company Car

(c) To: Carla Williams   Date: 2008 01 15
     From: Ray Lebeau RL
     Subject: Failure to Meet December Sales Quota

---

2. **The explanation prepares the audience for the bad news.** To do this effectively, it must be clear and logical.

Examples

POOR

Bottom-line considerations require us to do something about the continuing revenue deficit in our parking lot. Car owners have enjoyed a "free ride" long enough—it's time for you to pay your fair share.

IMPROVED

For the last two years, parking lot revenues have not covered the cost of maintenance, snow removal, and security. Covering the deficit from the general budget means that transit users, many of whom are in lower-paid job classifications, are in effect subsidizing car drivers.

Both explanations make it easy for the audience to predict that an announcement regarding higher parking fees is coming. But the first example does not give any specific reasons; "bottom-line considerations" sounds like management jargon for plain old greed. The second sentence passes judgment on car drivers, and its use of the word "you" makes the accusation of unfairness offensively personal. The result of this paragraph would probably be resentment and anger over increased parking fees.

The second explanation tells the audience specifically what the problem is. It appeals to a sense of fair play without accusing anyone of deliberately ripping off anyone else. The audience is now prepared to see the increased parking fees as necessary and reasonable.

3. **Now you're finally ready to deliver the bad news.** If your explanation is clear and complete, your audience should be expecting bad news as the logical outcome. You can emphasize this relationship between the explanation and the bad news with a phrase like "As a result ... " or "I think you can see from this...."

   Try to deliver the bad news in an impersonal way. This is not the place for an attitude that stresses the "you" in the message. Avoid words with strong negative overtones, such as "reject," "deny," or "refuse."

Examples

✗ POOR
For this reason, your request for extra vacation time has been denied.

✓ IMPROVED
For this reason, extra vacation time cannot be approved.

4. **Close on a note of goodwill.** Do not end with the bad news, or with an apology. It may be possible to point out a positive feature in the "bad" news. Perhaps you can offer a helpful suggestion. At the very least, offer to provide information to anyone who wants to ask questions or make comments.

Examples

✗ POOR
We're sorry that the ventilation system won't be fully operational until June.

✓ IMPROVED
By the time warm weather arrives in June, our all-new, state-of-the-art ventilation system will be fully operational.

✗ POOR
Consequently, you will be unable to purchase hot drinks from the cafeteria during the week of November 13–17.

✓ IMPROVED
During the week of November 13–17, you may wish to buy coffee or tea from Wilt's Variety next door, while the cafeteria equipment is being replaced.

The following is an example of a bad news message that uses the **indirect order** effectively:

> May 27, 2008
> To: All Employees
> From: Ralph Choy, Director RC
>   Physical Plant
> Re: Changes in Food Service
>
> Over the past four months we have been surveying the operation of our three food outlets. Lunch and coffee-break items are enjoying good sales, but the hot breakfast business has been losing customers. While the number of breakfasts sold has declined steadily, the cost of opening the grill has increased sharply. In order to maintain full breakfast service, prices would have to be increased by 48 percent, or a lesser increase would have to be subsidized by lunch and snack eaters. In preference to these alternatives, the cafeteria will be ending hot breakfast service as of June 1. A larger selection of self-serve items will be available for early morning eaters. The cafeteria staff welcomes suggestions for appropriate items. Please call me at X490 if you have any comments or concerns regarding food service.

2   RESPONDING TO COMPLAINTS OR PROBLEMS

Generally speaking, good news should be your first choice when dealing with problems and complaints. While it may cost time and money to make your customer, client, or employee satisfied, you will generally find it a worthwhile investment. But there will inevitably be times when you cannot respond positively to a complaint. The claim may not have a leg to stand on, no matter how generously it's interpreted. There may be some justification for complaint, but the compensation or change requested may be out of all proportion to the problem. Or the complaint may be valid, but you cannot make the adjustment requested—for example, when replacements are no longer available. So you can't always avoid delivering bad news.

1. **Begin with a neutral statement.** Just as the good news opening in a good news message sets a positive tone for the whole message, a bad news opening would negatively affect the reader's view of the entire contents—assuming he or she reads that far. **Never** begin with the bad news. Find something neutral and factual to say. Here are some examples:

The battery charger you recently returned to us has been thoroughly tested in our laboratory.

I have spoken to the claims representative who originally handled your accident report.

The personnel department has supplied me with a record of your sick leave and vacation days for the past eighteen months.

Referring to an area of agreement or empathy is another good way to open. For example, if a customer's message began "I booked my vacation through TraveLand Tours because your brochure promised first-rate professional service," you could begin by saying, "You are right to expect first-rate service from every TraveLand agent." These openings invite reader agreement and set a positive, reasonable tone without raising false hopes. Do not apologize in the first line — or anywhere else in a bad news message. An apology implies that your company is accepting **responsibility** for the problem.

Here are five possible opening sentences for a bad news message. Put a check mark beside the ones that achieve a neutral, factual tone. Rewrite any that are not appropriate.

(a) Your Timecraft watch has been carefully inspected by our repair department.

_____

_____

(b) We regret to inform you that your cosmetic dental work is not covered by your dental plan.

_____

_____

(c) Thank you for telling us about your problems in keeping up with the payments on your loan.

_____

_____

(d) Offices in the accounts receivable division are assigned on the basis of job classification and seniority.

_____

_____

(e) We were sorry to hear that you were not happy with the service you received at our parts department last Tuesday.

_____

_____

2. **Give an explanation.** The explanation is even more important in a bad news message than in a good news message. A successful explanation presents your side of the situation persuasively and prepares the reader to accept bad news as the logical consequence. The explanation should review the facts that are relevant to your decision, leading the reader clearly from step to step. Never attempt to intimidate the reader by resorting to emotional or moral judgment. This will only invite the reader to become emotional and judgmental, too. This is not a helpful climate for a professional relationship.

Examples

✗ POOR
Obviously, you failed to read the instructions.

✓ IMPROVED
In order to produce a smooth, bubble-free finish, each coat of Nu-Gleem must be allowed to dry thoroughly before another coat is applied. The package directions suggest a minimum drying time of eight hours. From the description in your letter, it appears that a second coat of Nu-Gleem was applied before the first was completely dry.

A fair decision has benefit for your audience as well as for you. You can point this out in a tactful way.

✗ POOR
Surely you don't expect to be able to return something you bought "As Is" at an end-of-season sale.

✓ IMPROVED
By shopping during our end-of-season "As Is" sale, you were able to buy your patio table for approximately half the regular price. We offer these markdowns in order to clear floor and warehouse space for the new season's merchandise. The savings in inventory and storage costs are passed on in special prices to you. These items are, however, generally one-of-a-kind and may have been on display for some time.

Do not become defensive.

✗ POOR

Our chicken pies are made from the finest government-inspected ingredients. No one has ever complained of a "funny taste" before.

✓ IMPROVED

The ingredients and seasonings used in Chicken Ranch Pot Pies are selected to appeal to the taste of typical Canadian consumers, as revealed in surveys, test groups, and comments from our customers.

3. **Deliver the bad news.** If your explanation has been clear and well planned, your reader should already be expecting bad news as a logical outcome of the facts. An introductory word or phrase like "consequently" or "for this reason" will underline the connection. The bad news should be stated in a neutral tone.

Keep it brief but unambiguous. Hope dies hard, so make sure your audience doesn't misinterpret your overly tactful refusal. Don't make the mistakes these writers made.

Examples

✗ POOR

The delicate colours of your Airloom blouse were achieved by using pure vegetable dyes. These dyes are unstable in water; consequently, the blouse is clearly labelled "Dry Clean Only" both on the package and on the fabric care label sewn into the blouse itself. The blouse you returned to us has apparently been machine washed, causing the dye to bleed and fade. We are sorry, but we cannot replace the blouse free of charge as you requested.

The writer's explanation is clear and logical. Then she destroys its impact by apologizing, as if the company's decision were something to be ashamed of.

✓ IMPROVED

As a result, the blouse cannot be replaced free of charge.

✗ POOR

Health Department regulations prohibit the resale or exchange of bathing suits. Consequently, we regret to inform you that we must reject your request for a refund.

Chapter Six: Bad News: The Indirect Approach

This reply is loaded with negative words: "regret to inform you" sounds like a death announcement, and "reject" is a very hostile word. It is the customer who will probably feel rejected.

✓ IMPROVED
Consequently, we cannot offer a refund or credit for a returned bathing suit.

✗ POOR
As the malfunction is not covered by our warranty, it does not appear that a refund is justified at this time.

The phrase "at this time" leaves the reader in doubt. Will a refund be justified if he tries again?

✓ IMPROVED
For this reason, the warranty on your air conditioner is no longer in force.

✗ POOR
Obviously you are not entitled to a reduction.

The word "obviously" labels the customer as either dishonest or stupid for even asking.

✓ IMPROVED
Consequently, the amount of $85.50 is still owing on your account.

4. **Close with a positive message.** Now that the painful part is over, use the closing of the message to help the reader find a positive solution to his or her problem. If possible, offer an alternative, as in the following example:

For this reason we cannot refund the purchase price of your Lawn Girl lawn mower. However, if you would like to come in and look at the full Lawn Girl line, I think you would find several models with the features you require. Should you wish to invest in one of these, you will receive a generous trade-in allowance on your used mower.

At least assure the customer that you will be glad to explain your decision in more detail or consider anything further he or she has to say. Underline your sincerity with a sentence like the following:

If you have any questions or you would like to discuss this further, please call me at 222-1234.

Do not apologize for your decision. Leave your customer with an impression of what you **can** do for him or her, not what you can't or won't.

CASE 1

When I joined The Thin-Is-In Gym, your employee told me that your exercise program could help me lose fifteen pounds in two months. Well, I've been working out for six weeks and I haven't lost a thing. Your skinny instructor stands up there twisting herself into a pretzel, I'm killing myself trying to follow along, and at the end of it all I'm not a pound lighter. So I sit downstairs with my coffee and butter tarts and feel depressed. Well, who needs it? I want my money back.

Write a bad news letter to Darlene Winter in the space provided below. Compare your answer with Figure 6.1.

_____

_____

_____

_____

_____

_____

_____

_____

_____

_____

_____

_____

_____

_____

_____

FIGURE 6.1   Bad News Response to a Complaint

THE THIN-IS-IN GYM
45 Maywood Drive Oakville ON   L6P 1N9

November 4, 2007

Ms. Darlene Winter
19 Brock Ave., Apt. 602
Oakville ON L9Z 6F5

Dear Ms. Winter

The Thin-Is-In Gym <u>can</u> help you lose fifteen pounds in two months.

To achieve this goal, you need to follow a routine of exercise and diet in accordance with the personal assessment you received when you became a member. Because every person's body is unique, we do not guarantee a specific weight loss in a specific time. But following your exercise and diet plan will enable you to meet your weight loss goal at a rate that is safe and healthy for your body. For this reason, we cannot offer a refund of membership fees.

However, we would like you to come in for a personal meeting with our dietician and fitness specialist. They will help you re-evaluate your program and get back on the road to your ideal weight. As an added incentive, your membership will be extended for an additional six weeks at no extra charge.

Sincerely

Gwen Nguyen

Gwen Nguyen, Manager

CASE 2

Mario Simard, manager of Maple Leaf Video, wasn't around on Thursday night when the fight broke out, but he heard all about it from Dave, the clerk on duty. While he was checking out a couple of DVDs for a customer, Dave noticed on the screen that the customer had one that was overdue; in fact, it had been out for almost two months. When he drew this to the customer's attention, the customer denied all knowledge of this item and demanded that Dave delete it from his file. Of course, Dave wasn't authorized to do this, and a loud and pointless argument took place while the line of impatient customers got longer and longer. Finally the customer threw his DVDs at Dave and stomped out of the store. Mario had been expecting some follow-up, and today he received a letter from the customer:

> Last Thursday, while I was attempting to take out some DVDs from your store, your clerk accused me of having an overdue DVD. Since I have never even heard of this item, let alone rented it, it is obvious that your store has made a mistake and entered someone else's DVD under my number. I tried to explain this to your dimwit clerk but, of course, he was covering up for someone else's incompetence and wouldn't listen to reason. Unless you sort this out quick, you won't be seeing me or any of my kids in your store again.

You can read Mario's reply in Figure 6.2.

ESL TIP

Before you start to compose a response to someone who has a problem or a complaint, ask yourself these questions:

- What is my most important objective in sending this message?
- Do I have any other objectives?
- What do I know about my audience?
- What is my plan for achieving my objectives with this audience?

Remember that building a good relationship with customers, clients, and employees is an objective whenever you communicate. If you must deliver a negative message, you will have to plan carefully to avoid creating bad will.

FIGURE 6.2   Bad News Response to a Complaint

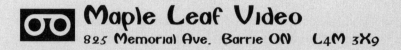

Maple Leaf Video
825 Memorial Ave. Barrie ON   L4M 3X9

September 20, 2008

Mr. Kevin Aucoin
33 Georgian Dr.
Barrie ON L4T 6D2

Dear Mr. Aucoin

Your membership file for the last three months has been carefully checked by our staff.

When you borrow an item from Maple Leaf Video, an automatic scanning device reads the bar code on your membership card and on the items you have selected. It is not possible for rentals to be wrongly charged to your account through clerical error, since no manual data entry takes place.

Our records show that <u>Night Call Nurses Behind Bars</u> was borrowed on your card on July 24, 2008, and has not been returned. If you cannot find this item, a $60.00 replacement fee is payable, as described in the cardholder agreement you signed when you joined Maple Leaf Video. This fee covers the purchase and cataloguing of a replacement. In addition, late fees of $3.50 a day are payable, which reflect the revenue lost while the DVD has been unavailable for rental to other customers. Normally fees stop accumulating when the replacement fee is paid, but in view of the concerns expressed in your letter I have put the late fees on hold as of September 18, provided that your account is settled by September 25.

Copies of your rental record and cardholder agreement are enclosed. If you have further questions, please call me at 555-2139.

Sincerely

Mario Simard

Mario Simard, Manager

3 DELIVERING BAD NEWS ORALLY

The techniques suggested for writing bad news messages can easily be adapted to oral communications.

Given a choice, most of us would prefer to deliver bad news in writing. The personal element in oral communication, and the potential for immediate feedback, make it an unattractive choice. But you will often have to deliver bad news in person or over the telephone. Someone may ask you a direct question: "Did I get the job?"; "Can I change the date of my flight?" Or your audience may need the support of a personal message. A bad news message with serious consequences for the receiver, such as job loss, demotion, or a poor performance review, should always be delivered orally, although you will probably follow up with a written message. An effective bad news message uses the **indirect order** to break it to them gently:

1. Neutral opening
2. Explanation
3. Bad news
4. Goodwill closing

1. **Don't blurt out the bad news right away,** even in response to a direct question. A **neutral opening** raises the subject while ensuring that you will have a chance to explain why the news has to be bad. Don't announce that you have bad news in store.

Examples

✗ POOR
Come in, Toni. I'm afraid I have some bad news about your application for reclassification.

✓ IMPROVED
Come in, Toni. I want to talk to you about your application for reclassification.

✗ POOR
No, Mr. Ang, your refund cheque hasn't been processed yet.

✓ IMPROVED
Well, Mr. Ang, we're processing about 500 refund requests a week here.

2. **Prepare your listener for bad news with a clear, logical explanation.** Keep your tone matter-of-fact. Don't sound as though you are apologizing or looking for approval from your listener.

3. **Deliver the bad news.** If your decision is final, be sure that your message makes this clear.

Examples

✗ POOR
I think, then, that we'll have to consider this a non-warranty repair.

✓ IMPROVED
The repairs to your transmission will not be covered by the warranty.

✗ POOR
I don't think that we can back-order sale items.

✓ IMPROVED
Sale items cannot be back-ordered.

4. **You may pause for a minute or two while your audience digests the news.** Be prepared to go through the explanation again or to answer any other questions. These questions are usually a way of coming to terms with the bad news, not a personal reflection on you. In any event, try not to take any reaction personally. Phrases like "I understand your disappointment" or "I can see your problem" express sympathy without undermining your decision. Once you sense that your audience has dealt with the news, close the conversation with a **goodwill closing.** This could be a helpful alternative or an offer to answer any more questions. Do not apologize for your decision.

CHAPTER REVIEW/SELF-TEST

1. Begin a bad news message with
   (a) the main point of the message: the bad news.
   (b) an apology.
   (c) a statement that introduces the subject in a neutral way.
   (d) a positive statement.

2. A good explanation
    (a) is clear and logical.
    (b) avoids blaming the reader or listener.
    (c) prepares the receiver for the bad news.
    (d) all of the above.

3. The bad news should come as
    (a) the logical conclusion of the explanation.
    (b) a surprise to the receiver.
    (c) a personal, "you-centred" message.
    (d) none of the above.

4. End a bad news message with
    (a) an apology.
    (b) a helpful suggestion.
    (c) the bad news.
    (d) an upbeat statement like "Have a nice day."

5. Respond to a problem or complaint by giving bad news when
    (a) the request is rude or poorly expressed.
    (b) you feel like it. You're the boss.
    (c) you can find any loophole or technicality that would justify saying "no."
    (d) the solution that has been requested is impossible or inappropriate.

6. You may open your response with
    (a) an apology.
    (b) a reference to something you and your audience both agree on.
    (c) a statement that suggests that good news is on the way.
    (d) the bad news.

7. A good explanation
    (a) points out that the problem was caused by your reader or listener, not by you.
    (b) questions the honesty of your reader or listener.
    (c) points out that no one else has complained about this problem.
    (d) does none of the above.

8. Deliver the bad news in a way that
    (a) shows you are sorry you have to say no.
    (b) makes it clear that you are saying no.
    (c) leaves the door open to either a positive or a negative interpretation.
    (d) is "you-centred."

9. End your bad news response to a problem by
   (a) offering an alternative solution, if available.
   (b) apologizing for having to say no.
   (c) closing with the phrase "We are sorry we were not able to help you."
   (d) thanking the receiver for bringing the problem to your attention.

10. It is a good idea to deliver a bad news message in person when
    (a) you are angry or upset.
    (b) you are afraid that putting it in writing might lead to a lawsuit.
    (c) the receiver is likely to be made angry or upset by the news.
    (d) all of the above.

Answers

1.C 2.D 3.A 4.B 5.D 6.B 7.D 8.B 9.A 10.C

EXERCISES

1. Revise the following messages to improve their tone and organization:
   (a) I can see by your letter that you know very little about car maintenance. The fact that you were not aware of any problems with your car before you brought it in for a spring tune-up is irrelevant. A good mechanic is trained to spot trouble *before* a major breakdown occurs. All the parts that were replaced were just about to give out. This is to be expected in a car as old as yours. Consequently, you are not entitled to a refund. We look forward to seeing you next fall.
   (b) We regret to inform you that we cannot replace your no-wax flooring free of charge. According to the sales representative who examined it at your house, you failed to follow instructions regarding proper cleaning and maintenance. We cannot guarantee a finish that has been abused with steel wool and cleaning solvent. Thank you for choosing Acme Beautifloor. If we can be of any further assistance, please let us know.
   (c) This will acknowledge receipt of your order dated February 1. Unfortunately, we cannot fill your order as requested. The Cheese 'n' Cracker Hostess Pack is a specially prepared hamper of delicious gourmet foods; you must realize that if we allowed customers to make substitutions we would not be able to sell it for $19.95 and still make a profit. We have sold hundreds of these gift hampers and our customers have always been delighted with the selection of cheeses— we are sure that you will enjoy the peppermint cheddar once you try it. We are sorry we are unable to help you.

(d) We regret to inform you that we must deny your request for a refund. If we allowed everyone to return merchandise just because it didn't match their decor, we'd go broke in short order. Deck furniture is seasonal merchandise, and if we don't sell it by June we'll be stuck with it all winter. Thank you for shopping at Waldorf's.

(e) Thank you for writing us about your unfortunate experience with Pearlite shoe dye. However, we cannot assume responsibility for your shoes when the directions are not followed properly. When used as directed, Pearlite will not harm leather or suede. We are enclosing a coupon good for a free package of Pearlite in a colour of your choice.

2. You are the manager of The Daily Grind Gourmet Coffee Shop. Prepare the following bad news messages:

(a) To all members of your "buy ten cups, get one free" coffee club: Because of changes in tax regulations, sales tax and GST are now payable on the "free" cup.

(b) To all employees: Because of a dramatic increase in claims, premiums for extended health benefits will be going up 14 percent on June 30.

3. Owing to lack of use and budget constraints, the Royal Bank will be removing its banking machine from the foyer of the Acme MicroChip building. As employee relations officer at Acme, write a memo to all employees.

4. Write a bad news response to one of the following messages:

(a)

> Subject: Swimming Lessons
> From: Kristine Vovtchok
> Date: Thurs, 28 Oct 2008 14:01-4000
> To: Ross Rebagliati Community Centre
>
> Yesterday when I dropped my daughter off in the beginner's class at 4 o'clock I stayed for a while to watch the lesson. I can't say I was impressed. To me, it looks as though the kids are just having a good time instead of learning anything. I'm not paying good money for playtime in the pool. I want to see some work out there.

Chapter Six: Bad News: The Indirect Approach

(b)

3250 Lakeshore Blvd. Apt 3110
Toronto ON M9D 1E6
2004 10 07

Gemstone Financial Services
20 Carlson Court
Toronto ON M9W 6V4

When I contacted you about investing my early retirement severance package, you
assured me that I would be receiving guidance from a trained professional. Yet
virtually all the stocks I invested in on the advice of your company's representative
have gone down. My portfolio is worth less now than it was a year ago. I think I'm
entitled to a full refund of the purchase price.

Al Fresco

Al Fresco

(c)

Subject: Your rip-off wing night
From: Chris Zamora
Date: Wed, 18 Nov 2007 14:01-400
To: Riverside Sports Bar <RSB.net>

Listen, creeps. What kind of joint are you running? You advertise Tuesday as "All You
Can Eat" Wing Night—eight bucks a head. So I show up yesterday to give them a
try. Not bad wings, but after five, maybe six trips to the buffet, the guy starts doling
them out by ones and twos. Pretty soon I'm burning more calories walking back and
forth to the buffet than I'm getting from the wings. Then he tries to stop me from
dipping into the dip. So is it All You Can Eat or what? Get rid of that guy or I'm calling
the paper or the Department of Health or something.

(d)

54 Myrtle Gardens
New Liskeard ON P0J 1J0
November 18, 2008

Sunseeker Tours
138 Ridpath Dr.
Toronto ON M4L 2K3

I recently purchased a holiday package to the Dominican Republic from you, transaction #58-622A. Since I made this booking I have been talking to some friends who were there last year and they recommended a hotel, the Sand Dollar, which they said was much better than the Hispaniola Princess where our tour is booked in. So I would like a refund for the hotel portion of the package so I can make my own arrangements at the Sand Dollar, or you could just change my reservation to the Sand Dollar, which would be even more convenient.

Karri Pasqualini

Karri Pasqualini

(e)

Subj: Removal of my name from mailing list
Date: Feb/06/2007 1:04:24 PM Central Standard Time
From: Elaine Littlemore
To: www.cufdl.org

When I made a donation to the Canadian Urban Fowl Defence League I did not expect to be bothered by an avalanche of requests from every pigeon, sea gull, and Canada goose organization in North America. Three attempts to have my name removed from your mailing list have failed; meanwhile the list has been circulated to an ever-growing army of fundraisers. When will this wasteful invasion of my mailbox and my privacy come to an end?

Elaine Littlemore

Chapter Six: Bad News: The Indirect Approach

CHAPTER EIGHT

ORAL COMMUNICATION
WITHIN THE ORGANIZATION

Chapter Objectives

Successful completion of this chapter will enable you to:

1 Describe the importance of oral communication on the job.

2 Deliver effective oral presentations.

3 Participate effectively in meetings and small groups.

4 Participate effectively in teleconferencing, videoconferencing, and Web conferencing.

1 INTRODUCTION: THE IMPORTANCE OF ORAL COMMUNICATION

Why do we need to study oral communication? Talking seems to come naturally, except perhaps for public speaking, something most people do not do very often. The truth is that oral communication is an integral part of most jobs. Personal interaction is the central focus for salespeople, health-care workers, educators, counsellors, and many managers, but wherever people work together or serve the public in some way, listening and talking are an essential part of the job.

Chapter 1 discussed some advantages and disadvantages of oral communication, the barriers to effective oral communication, and strategies for overcoming these barriers. This text has also discussed oral strategies in most of its chapters. In this chapter, we discuss specific guidelines for effective oral communication within the organization. Topics include oral presentations, working in groups, and participating in meetings, both the usual face-to-face meetings and newer forms like teleconferencing, videoconferencing, and Web conferencing.

2 DELIVERING EFFECTIVE ORAL PRESENTATIONS

Few people look forward to giving oral presentations. A number of surveys have shown that public speaking is one thing people fear most—ahead of death! However, whether or not you fear public speaking, learning to do it effectively is vital. Making an oral presentation allows you to highlight your expertise, demonstrate your ability to use oral skills to achieve corporate goals, and be an active participant in the corporate arena. In addition, oral communication skills are valued by employers (see The Conference Board of Canada's chart on "Employability Skills Profile" on page xiii).

Most people never have to give formal speeches or address large groups at work. Oral presentations usually occur in front of small groups, like committees, or in formal or informal meetings involving only a few people. Here are some guidelines for delivering effective oral presentations in any setting.

Preparation

1. **Prepare, prepare, prepare.** Preparation may be the most important aspect of delivering a successful presentation. Obviously, you cannot always be completely prepared for unexpected questions in a meeting. However, being "more than ready" not only ensures that your knowledge of the topic is ade-

quate, but it also helps to calm your nerves. Your comfort with the material and your organized mode of delivery create confidence, which is very important for effective communication. It is usually painfully obvious to an audience when a presentation has not been carefully thought through and rehearsed, or when the presenter is uncomfortable with the material or presentation technology.

2. **Find out how long your presentation is expected to take.** Normally, a speech is delivered at about 150 words a minute. Make sure your material is adequate for the time allotted. This does not mean that a ten-minute oral report should be as dense as a 1500-word written report. You will need to minimize details and use repetition to ensure that you are getting your point across. However, rehashing points you have already made in order to fill up your allotted time is a sure-fire way to annoy and frustrate your listeners. Leave time for questions and feedback. If the audience doesn't respond, don't fill the gap by answering questions nobody asked. This suggests that you are having second thoughts about the organization and planning of your presentation. **Never take more than your allotted time.** It is always counterproductive to run overtime.

3. **Learn as much as you can about your audience.** Find out what they already know and what they need to know about your topic. Avoid telling them things they already know or presenting information that is inappropriate for their level of expertise (either too abstract or simplistic), especially if you are presenting technical information. If you are trying to persuade your listeners, some prior research into their values, needs, and wants is worthwhile, particularly if you are selling a product or idea.

4. **Decide what method of delivery is appropriate.** Very few situations call for reading or memorizing a fully scripted speech. In fact, both of these methods require a very talented speaker who can bring the script to life. In place of scripted speeches, presentation software programs such as PowerPoint or Corel are now commonly used. However, there are still times when presentation software is not suitable. The technology can be overused, especially if an audience has seen too much of it. Speaking with only a few point-form notes can be a much better choice if you wish to create an informal atmosphere or you wish to appeal more directly to your audience's emotions. If you are very confident and you know your material well, you can make a powerful impression by speaking without any notes. In all cases, audiences respond best if you "speak from the heart."

5. **Plan an overall structure.** For instance, a common pattern is to introduce your topic, make three to five main points, draw a conclusion, make recommendations, and then summarize all of these sections. To leave a lasting impression, some repetition is desirable. In your introduction and conclusion, always relate the material to your listeners' needs and interests.

Presentation Software

Presentation software has become the technology of choice in the workplace. Programs such as Microsoft PowerPoint or Corel give you several advantages:

- Slides provide a colourful visual focus for your audience.
- Your audience will both see and hear your most important information.
- Slides double as your speaker notes.
- You can easily incorporate graphics.
- You can easily make handouts.
- Presentations may be shared electronically.

Using the software is relatively easy. Without instruction, most users can quickly learn how to create basic slides. However, some of the features, such as graph and diagram creation, are best learned with some help from an expert.

Guidelines for Creating Presentations

1. Create a strong opening, possibly using a photograph, quotation, question, or other dramatic device. Organize your information carefully for simplicity, logical flow, and visibility. The most common error is to place too much information on a single slide.
2. Use contrasting colours so that text stands out against the background. Keep the text size at 22+ font size.
3. Reduce your main points to short phrases and sentences that provide a clear meaning for both you and the audience. The general rule of thumb is five phrases of about five words each. To avoid a repetitive, list-like quality, cluster two or three minor points under a subheading where possible. As long as the font size doesn't end up being too small, it is good to add pictures to illustrate your themes.
4. Plan to expand on each point (know your material well). Consider using preset animation, which allows you to bring in one point at a time. Both you and your listeners can easily get lost when all points on a slide are seen together, so it pays to bring in each new point just as you are ready for it. However, some types of information are best viewed all at once, for example, a graph and text that interprets the graph (see the example presentation, Figure 8.1).

FIGURE 8.1   Example Presentation Created with Microsoft PowerPoint

YOUR LIFE

Employee Lifestyle Study Results

By Robbie Pinkney
Organizational Research

D+M Manufacturing

Why did we ask about your lifestyle?

- A balanced healthy lifestyle
  - Reduces stress
  - Reduces illness
  - Helps family well-being
- Employers can help

> Our Employee Health
> 1995-2005 sick days rose by 20%
> Employee assistance plan
> stress counselling rose by 30%

How we did the research

- Held staff focus group
- Designed survey based on focus group
- Sent survey to all 978 employees
- 70% were returned
  - 558 plant staff
  - 87 office staff

Findings: Exercise Habits

- We need 30 minutes, moderate to vigorous, minimum 4 times per week
- Most of us do not:
  - Vigorous 8%
  - Moderate 19%
  - Mild 40%
  - None 33%

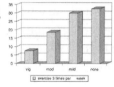

Findings: Eating Habits

- We need approximately 1200 mL (4 to 5 cups) of fruits and vegetables a day.
- Very few eat enough:
  - 5% eat 5 or more
  - 28% eat 3 to 4
  - 60% eat 1 to 2
  - 8% eat none

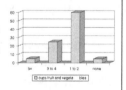

Findings: Family Time

- Family fun time (without TV or formal sport activity) is also very limited:
  - 4% had 6 hours or more
  - 32% had 3-5 hours
  - 40% had only 1-2 hours
  - 24% had none!

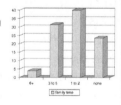

What does it all mean?

- A small number of employees are meeting their food and exercise needs.
- Family time is losing out for many.
- It is time to help!

Where do we go from here?

- Take two immediate actions:
  - evaluate cafeteria offerings
  - install a small gym
- Establish a lifestyle planning team
- Company will support by:
  - giving work time for meetings
  - helping to implement team's plans

5. Insert photos, clip art, graphs, and charts to enhance and replace text.

6. Use special effects, such as moving text, video, and sound, sparingly and judiciously. If you are using researched information to create graphs, or if you use graphs taken from websites such as Statistics Canada, give the source.

7. Prepare a strong ending. In most cases you will have a summary slide that pulls together the meaning of the entire presentation. In addition, you may choose to have a final slide that is designed to evoke discussion.

8. It is customary to provide handouts of your slides. Be sure to print off enough for everyone. You can save paper by printing more slides per page and making sheets two-sided. However, beware of reducing slides below a readable size. To decide when to distribute the handouts, think about whether your audience will want to take notes on them. Some people may need to remember details of your presentation. On the other hand, in some situations such as sales talks, you might prefer to discourage note-taking so that you can engage your audience with more eye contact. If you decide to hand out copies after the presentation, inform your audience that you will be doing so. Remember that your audience may also wish to have electronic copies of your presentation.

Guidelines for Delivering Presentations

1. Rehearse several times, with a friend if possible. Be sure of your timing. Arrive early and ensure the technology is working ahead of time. Be prepared with a backup in case of a technical problem, the ever-present disadvantage of this method. Don't make your audience wait while you open up the presentation. Have it ready to go.

2. Resist the temptation to look constantly at your screen, and beware of reading the points in a list-like manner. Reading is one of the most common errors. Never start with "OK" and end with "That's it." Be creative!

3. Take advantage of the technology's design, which allows you to face your audience at all times. To do so, look at your computer screen and not at the projection screen; and, of course, look up at your audience as much as possible. Do not make the common error of looking at the projection screen over your shoulder.

4. Always explain graphs and charts fully. Here you can approach the projection screen and use your hands, or use the on-screen pointers that can be created ahead of time.

5. If you have a discussion or question period, it may be important to leave your last slide in place. In addition, you may need to go back to some slides. Be prepared to do this quickly and graciously. Take care to exit from the presentation and bring closure.

Presentation Tips

1. **Use transition words to help your audience follow the presentation.** If you are making three main points, say so at the beginning of your presentation and then announce each point as you arrive at it. Let your listeners know when the end is coming. If they have drifted off or are watching the clock, announcing your conclusion brings them back to hear your summation.

2. **Use nonverbal communication to enhance your message.** Make sure your body language emphasizes what you are saying. Important nonverbal aspects of public speaking include the following:

   (a) **Posture.** Always stand up. Standing while others are sitting automatically confers authority and commands attention. It also helps you to project your voice to your listeners and to make eye contact with the whole group. Staying in your seat may make you feel secure, but this is a trap. A good presentation demands alertness and a bit of an edge. Good posture helps you breathe properly, which makes you feel and sound more relaxed. Do not pace or rock from foot to foot; your audience will find this distracting.

   (b) **Facial expression.** Your facial expression naturally provides a model for the audience's reaction to your presentation. You set the mood: audiences respond to your enjoyment and enthusiasm. Never appear apologetic for the nature or content of your report. Project involvement and conviction, but don't try to consciously arrange your face. Facial expression must come from within to be convincing.

   (c) **Eye contact.** Make brief contact with everyone in the group as you speak. Don't look at your computer screen any more than absolutely necessary; keep your eyes on the audience. Turn off equipment not in use; remove information from the screen that isn't relevant to the discussion.

3. **Use your voice effectively.** Several factors contribute to the impact of your speaking voice.

   (a) **Volume.** Speaking too loudly makes your message seem forced and impersonal, but this is not a common problem in public speaking. You are more likely to speak too softly or let your volume drop at the end of a sentence, especially if you are nervous. Eye contact with your audience will help you judge the volume that is both natural and clearly heard.

(b) **Pitch and emphasis.** When you are nervous, your voice rises in pitch. Some people have a habit of raising their pitch at the ends of sentences, projecting a sense of uncertainty. Make a conscious effort to lower your vocal pitch when you speak in public. Breathe deeply, and relax your shoulders whenever you pause.

(c) **Rate.** Nervousness, or even excitement and involvement, will cause you to speak more rapidly than usual. Some speakers deliberately speak quickly to convey the nonverbal message, "I know this isn't news to you/very interesting/very well thought through, so let's get it over with." Keep up an engaging pace, and slow down occasionally for emphasis or for clarity on difficult information.

4. **Project a positive attitude.** State your purpose without personal comment. Don't try to "lighten the atmosphere" by downgrading the importance or interest of your presentation. Others will accept your self-evaluation. Remember, too, that a casual attitude reflects negatively on the person or group that requested the presentation—often your supervisor or client.

5. **Adopt a "you-centred" attitude.** As pointed out in Chapter 2, think of your audience when you speak. Avoid using self-centred words like "I" or "we." If you are trying to persuade your audience, use the AIDA sequence discussed in Chapter 7.

6. **In a small-group setting, be prepared to move from the role of leader to group member once your presentation is over.** Some speakers find the transition from giving a presentation to participating in a meeting or discussion very difficult. Take your seat to indicate that you are leaving the "authority" role. If there is any negative feedback from the group, do not become defensive.

TIPS FOR RELAXED PRESENTING

Know that it is normal to feel nervous about presenting. The famous writer and speaker Mark Twain said, "There are two types of speakers: those that are nervous and those that are liars."

- Prepare your content thoroughly so that you are confident in your material.
- Try meditating beforehand: Close your eyes, breathe deeply, and visualize yourself speaking easily and happily. Wayne Dwyer, another famous writer and speaker, meditates before every presentation.
- Focus on your audience rather than yourself. Remember that your audience members are just people like you. Think about their needs. They will enjoy your presentation more if you are focused on their comfort and understanding rather than on being perfect yourself.
- Continue to breathe deeply and slowly before and throughout the presentation. If you are especially nervous, it would be worth your while to learn the technique of diaphragmatic breathing, which is taught in yoga classes and other venues.

Transparencies

If you do not have access to the equipment mentioned above, black-and-white overhead transparencies are easy to make. Create them on a word processor, making sure that the print is large enough for your audience to see, and print them. Place a blank transparency sheet in the paper feeder of a regular photocopier, and then proceed as if you were making a regular photocopy. With some machines, you can simply feed the blank transparency into a special slot so that making a monochrome transparency is even easier. To get colour transparencies, you may have to go to a professional copying firm, since many businesses do not have photocopying machines capable of producing colour copies.

Chapter 14 provides some examples of visuals that you can use to enhance your presentation. As well, Figure 8.1 provides an example of a simple and effective set of slides.

CONFESSIONS OF A SCARED SPEAKER

In my professional life, I speak publicly on a regular basis and people tell me that I seem confident and capable. Here is what they don't know. When I was a child, we had to give memorized speeches in school. I was so frightened that it seemed I became someone else at the front of the room, a person who could not see, hear, or think. I most certainly couldn't remember the words I had memorized so carefully!

Being a compliant student, I continued to give speeches as required over the years, and I always suffered extreme anxiety. When I had to speak once in front of 300 people, I found myself experiencing tunnel vision and nearly fainting on the way to the podium. Ironically, I was drawn to acting in high school and college plays. The glamour of the stage outweighed my stage fright. As a result, I had plenty of practice in overcoming my nerves.

Now, I have realized as an adult that other people are generally very anxious about public speaking. It seems most of us have a fear of looking "stupid" and I continue to experience this anxiety, although it has diminished to a large extent. I am so grateful for the brilliant invention of presentation software because it ensures that I remember my main points and it helps take the audience's eyes off me!

People will give you many suggestions about how to conquer your nerves, such as taking deep breaths or imagining your audience in their underwear. Some of these strategies will help you, but I can tell you that the only real way to gain confidence is to keep giving presentations. It is very helpful to take public speaking courses that give you weekly practice in front of other people. The instructor starts you with very short talks, and everyone supports you so that you gain self-assurance and skill. Eventually, you will feel more comfortable, so never give up!

3 MEETING AND WORKING IN SMALL GROUPS

Many jobs consist largely of attending meetings, sitting on committees, and working on group projects. Working efficiently with other people presents special challenges and requires well-developed social skills and an understanding of protocol for various situations.

Making Meetings Productive

Meetings involve productive exchanges of information and decision-making. They also are opportunities to demonstrate your professionalism and build working relationships. Since they are very expensive to companies, always consider whether a meeting is necessary. Could the goal be accomplished in another way, such as an e-mail exchange? If a meeting is needed, plan well to ensure it is productive. Routine business meetings should last no more than two hours.

Planning Meetings

Much of the responsibility for productive meetings rests with the chairperson. If you are chairing a meeting, your first task is to prepare an agenda. An example is shown in Figure 8.2. Think carefully about the most appropriate order for the topics to be discussed, because some discussions may logically follow others, and list each topic with an estimated amount of time to be spent on it. Consulting with others about the agenda helps to ensure that no important topic is forgotten; however, limiting the number of topics will keep the meeting focused and of reasonable length. Send the agenda to participants at least two days before the meeting, and include the minutes from the previous meeting, even if you distributed them earlier.

Choosing a Meeting Format

Meeting formats vary from informal chats to the very formal structure following *Robert's Rules of Order*. It is likely that you will choose a less formal procedure for meetings with colleagues. Whether formal or informal, a productive meeting is organized and leads to definite action. If you have attended formal meetings where Robert's Rules were in use, you will likely remember such terms as "seconding the motion" and "motion carried." Robert's formal rules are normally used when there are many people and there is a need for transparency. If you need to conduct meetings of this type, you can learn the rules by reading the book *Robert's Rules of Order.*

Conducting Meetings

As chairperson, you should start with a brief introduction, stating the goal and length of the meeting. Provide copies of the agenda for those who may not have one. If the group is not too large, make sure that everyone has been introduced. Since your job is to moderate the discussion, assign someone else to take minutes. A common practice is to appoint a time-keeper as well. Always start meetings on

FIGURE 8.2 Sample Meeting Agenda

Georgian College
Student Activities Council

Communications Subcommittee Meeting

Thursday, September 18, 2006
8 a.m. – 9:30 a.m.
Location: Room D304

Invited: Subcommittee members, Fast-go Printing representative
Facilitator: Cathy Volpe ext. 1342

Note: Please contact Cathy by September 12 if you cannot attend.

Introduction	Cathy	2 minutes
Minutes of the last meeting	Jarrett	3 minutes
Business arising from the minutes	Cathy	10 minutes
Updates on plan for outdoor clean-up day	Krishna, Tosha	20 minutes
Presentation of proposed student newspaper format	Fast-go rep	20 minutes
Discussion and vote on adoption of new student newspaper format	All	25 minutes
Other business		5 minutes

---

time. During discussions, your main tasks are to adhere to the agenda and ensure that everyone has a chance to speak—one person at a time. Never dominate the discussion or allow another person to do so. When a group decision is required, try to move the group toward consensus, once everyone has had an opportunity to express his or her views. It is your responsibility to bring the meeting to a close on time and arrange the way in which any unfinished business will be handled. Thank the group, and announce that the minutes will be sent out.

Participating in Meetings

If you are a participant in a meeting, you have a large role to play in making the meeting productive. Read the agenda ahead of time, finish any tasks assigned to you at the previous meeting, and gather relevant information wherever possible. During the meeting, listen carefully to other participants. When expressing your ideas, remain positive and courteous. Where there is disagreement, build on others' ideas rather than directly contradicting them. Always try to move the discussion forward and maintain a cooperative atmosphere. And remember, the chairperson requires your assistance in staying on topic and on time.

Recording and Sending Minutes

The term "minutes" may seem very old-fashioned, but the value of minutes never declines. A set of minutes is a record of what was said, what was decided, and what must be done after the meeting. Regardless of the procedural format you have chosen, a set of minutes should be taken at every meeting. Some groups require very detailed minutes while others want only decisions and action items to be recorded. Discuss with your group what is appropriate for your purposes. For easy recording and reading, it is best to use the same format at successive meetings. All minutes must include these items: the names of persons who attended or sent regrets, topics discussed, and actions to be taken with completion time lines, along with the names of the people who will take each action.

People will often have intentions of following through on tasks but forget in the rush of their work lives. Minutes sent out by e-mail soon after a meeting will remind everyone of tasks to be done. If there are no follow-up tasks to be done, minutes may be sent later with the next meeting's agenda so that people can save valuable meeting time by reviewing them beforehand. To lighten the burden of producing and sending out minutes, groups that meet regularly often rotate the responsibility. However, the meeting chair is ultimately responsible to ensure that the minutes are produced and distributed.

Working in Project Groups

Many occupations involve working together on projects. In developing a computer application, for example, a computer research lab might employ engineers, systems analysts, researchers, managers, support staff, and consultants. Students and visiting experts may round out the group.

FIGURE 8.3 Example of Meeting Minutes

Georgian College
Student Activities Council

Minutes

Communications Subcommittee Meeting
Thursday, September 18, 2006

Present: Krishna Dash, Dragos Ilas, Jarrett Smith, Cathy Volpe

Regrets: Tosha Vandenberg

Guest: Bill Nelson (Fast-go Printing representative)

Facilitator: Cathy Volpe, ext. 1342
Minutes recorded by Krishna Dash

Action	Member to take action	Completion date
Minutes from August 18 meeting were approved		
Council approved the plans for an outdoor clean-up day. A decision was made to write an article outlining the plan in the student newspaper.	Krishna will write an article and send to student newspaper editor	September 25
Council viewed the presentation by Bill Nelson, discussed the pros and cons of the new poster format and logo, and voted to adopt them. All voted in favour.	Dragos will follow up with Bill to arrange changeover of all print templates	Completion before next poster printing October 1

Next Communications Subcommittee Meeting:
  4 pm – 6 pm, October 17
  Student Council Meeting Room

Project groups are always in one of four stages:

1. **Inception:** A group accepts a project and sets its initial goal and strategies.
2. **Problem-Solving:** The group works out technical problems and procedures for attaining the goal.
3. **Conflict Resolution:** The group works through conflicts in points of view or interests and motives.
4. **Execution:** The group members carry out the technical tasks needed to reach the goal.

Stages 2 and 3 may be skipped if the tasks are very straightforward, but a group may have to return to earlier stages, perhaps repeatedly, if technical problems or conflicts arise.

A group must also pay attention to three main functions during all stages:

1. **Production:** A group needs to focus on the project goal, but not at the expense of the group well-being and member support.
2. **Group Well-being:** It is essential to make sure the group is working by establishing complementary roles and maintaining interaction.
3. **Member Support:** Each individual needs to feel included, valued, rewarded, and not unfairly burdened.

Here are some guidelines for getting along in a project group and making it productive:

1. Seek feedback from others regularly, listen to them carefully, and incorporate their suggestions whenever possible.
2. Always seek group approval before you proceed with a specific task on your own.
3. Always do what you said you would do, and do it on time.
4. Do not manipulate, dictate, show off, or slack off. Be an equal team member.
5. Avoid "group think," in which people feel they must always agree rather than propose alternative points of view.
6. When a problem arises, consider using the following problem-solving model with all group members:
   (a) Define and analyze the problem.
   (b) Brainstorm possible solutions, recording without criticism all that are proposed.
   (c) Agree on criteria for a solution.
   (d) Evaluate possible solutions using the agreed criteria.
   (e) Select a solution.

(f) Plan a course of action.

(g) When the action has been taken, evaluate its effect.

The following cases present typical problems that occur in meetings or project groups. Read each one, and suggest what has gone wrong. Compare your answers with those on page 193.

CASE 1

On Tuesday, Luda, director of programming at Newsoft Canada, received an e-mail from a client who wanted to speed up work on a new program. She called a meeting for the following day of programmers in the software development division. Since she was quite concerned about the fact that the project was not yet finished, she placed this item on the quickly drawn-up agenda: "Development delays." When she arrived at the meeting, she was met with coolness and averted eyes. She proceeded with the agenda in spite of her discomfort, but when it was time to discuss the delays no one spoke. Finally, the programmer responsible for liaison with clients broke the silence: "We will finish that program tomorrow. It took an extra week because the client called and asked for some changes about a month ago." What mistake did Luda make?

CASE 2

Robert works for a landscaping company. During a meeting about the design of lawns for a new public building, Robert said, "I think it might be important to create a windbreak with trees along the north boundary. I've gone into the building during construction, and the wind really rips across the main walkway." Ron said, "No, we haven't enough money in the budget for large trees." Robert felt a wave of resentment and said no more, but he wondered quietly why they couldn't plant young trees that would do the job after three or four years had passed. What mistake did Ron make?

CASE 3

Pierre was really excited about his proposal for a composting system outside the kitchen of the large restaurant where he worked as a sous-chef. He had done his homework and designed a system that would be inexpensive to build and easy to use. The finished compost would be used on the herb garden that was just outside the back entrance. He had been given a 20-minute slot in the monthly meeting to present his ideas and seek his coworkers' support in using the system. Pierre was so keen that he talked about the way composting works for 17 of his 20 minutes. He didn't notice the yawns, but he noticed the lack of enthusiasm the following week. What mistake did Pierre make?

CASE 4

Adina was invited to work with four other hospital staff on a project to brighten up the playroom in the pediatric wing. She was pleased because she felt she had a talent in interior decorating. At the first meeting, some ideas were brought up, but the group decided to think about possibilities for another week and meet again to make decisions. Adina couldn't keep her mind from picturing how it should be. She spent her two days off that week drawing up a plan for the room, including the colour of the paint, the type of furniture, and the selection of toys. At the next meeting, she handed out copies of her plan. The others glanced at the paper in their hands. After politely thanking her for her work, they carried on with discussing their ideas. She felt very angry that her efforts and talent were being ignored. What mistake did Adina make?

4 TECHNOLOGICAL COMMUNICATION

An organization may have offices, branches, staff, or clients in other parts of the country or the world. New technologies have brought about new meeting forms like teleconferencing, videoconferencing, and Web conferencing, which allow people to hold meetings without having to spend time and money on travelling. All the participants can now meet at the same time, wherever they are.

Teleconferencing

Teleconferencing enables more than two people to interact verbally via telephone lines. Meeting by teleconference has become commonplace because of the savings in travel time and costs. Like a face-to-face meeting, teleconferencing must be properly planned and conducted to be productive, and participants must be prepared to speak and listen effectively.

Planning and Conducting a Teleconference

The technical preparation for a teleconference varies depending on the system at your disposal. Always test the system before the actual meeting. Contact all the participants to make sure that everyone will be ready for the teleconference at the proposed time. Then, using the fax machine or e-mail, send participants copies of the agenda and other necessary documents so that they can be ready with useful questions and comments. During a teleconference with several participants, it is easy for them to get "lost" without visual contact, so you must work harder than in a face-to-face meeting to keep everyone involved.

Participating in a Teleconference

Effective performance in a teleconference demands listening skills that many people no longer possess. Most of us have learned to use the eye rather than the ear to take in new material. It requires a special effort to detect the feelings in a speaker's tone of voice and to concentrate on processing spoken information. When you contribute a comment, pay attention to the clarity and volume of your voice, and identify yourself so that everyone knows who is speaking.

Videoconferencing and Beyond

Videoconferencing allows a number of people to see and hear each other. Industrial projects can be so large that participants may live and work in different continents. Some companies are using this audio-visual technology to train geographically separate teams, such as sales teams, which earlier had to be brought together in one place — an expensive undertaking.

Videoconferencing

Videoconferencing equipment can cost more than $15 000 for a fully equipped conference room. If your company has chosen to purchase equipment, use it when face-to-face interaction is needed but travel costs are high. In organizing a videoconference, the same rules apply as with any other technology: know how it works, test it thoroughly, and prepare people by confirming their attendance and sending all the information they need ahead of time. Videoconferencing systems work in different ways, so the facilitator must be prepared to explain to participants what they must do, such as positioning themselves for the camera, pushing the right buttons before they speak, and using the mute feature when not speaking.

Web Conferencing

A variety of conferencing software has been invented for the purpose of group interaction. You may use these relatively inexpensive systems to write, talk, and work on the same documents in real time, all without leaving your computer. Some allow you to see each other as well. These systems are known by several names, such as groupware, Web conferencing software, and electronic meeting software. Recently, the line between technologies has been blurring as video and online conferencing technologies blend. However, a useful distinction is made by the terms "asynchronous" and "synchronous." Asynchronous technologies, sometimes called forums or bulletin boards, allow people to leave messages and documents that all members can access at a later time. Synchronous technologies, sometimes called chats or video-chats, allow real-time interaction. Each type has its own advantages and limitations and should be chosen with care.

Asynchronous interaction is generally good for in-depth discussions but poor for decision-making. Many work teams use a combination of both types, holding real-time meetings for decisions and asynchronous forums for ongoing communication and document sharing. Sometimes, these technologies are part of a company's intranet, a system that connects all employees electronically. It is important to make yourself aware of the capabilities of your organization's communication system.

Answers to Chapter Questions

Page 190:

1. Luda made the mistake of not consulting anyone in the department before setting the agenda. If she had, she would have discovered that there was no need for a meeting at all, and she could have avoided alienating her programmers.
2. Ron directly contradicted Robert rather than building on his idea. By doing so, he annoyed his fellow worker and missed a potentially good idea.
3. Pierre monopolized the time he had been given. When seeking the support of coworkers, it is essential to allow them time to ask questions and express their doubts or objections.
4. Adina proceeded with a task before seeking approval from the group. Some preparation for a meeting is desirable, but all members of a project group need to feel valued and included. If one person goes too far ahead on her own, she is bypassing the necessary group process as well as missing the ideas the group can generate.

CHAPTER REVIEW/SELF-TEST

1. Giving an oral presentation at work is a good way to
   (a) demonstrate your oral skills.
   (b) demonstrate your expertise.
   (c) control decision-making in a meeting.
   (d) a and b.
   (e) a, b, and c.

2. In order to ensure you have your listeners' attention
   (a) start your presentation by saying "OK."
   (b) use a dramatic device such as asking them a question or giving a startling fact.
   (c) take your time opening up the presentation so they will feel suspense.

3. Common problems with presentations are
   (a) too much text per slide.
   (b) not using preset animation to bring in one point at a time.
   (c) clustering of details.
   (d) a and b.
   (e) a, b, and c.

4. Special effects such as sound and moving text should be used
   (a) on most slides to entertain listeners.
   (b) on controversial slides to put listeners in a good mood so they won't challenge your ideas.
   (c) very sparingly to emphasize the most important aspects of your presentation.

5. Graphs and charts can
   (a) illustrate your ideas to make a stronger impact.
   (b) increase your listeners' understanding of difficult information.
   (c) confuse your audience if not fully explained.
   (d) all of the above.

6. When presenting orally, you should
   (a) face your audience and look at them over the computer screen.
   (b) keep your eyes on the computer screen so you won't be nervous.
   (c) read each point quickly and move on.
   (d) b and c.

7. Common voice problems are
   (a) trailing off in volume at the ends of sentences.
   (b) raising voice pitch at the ends of sentences, giving the impression of uncertainty.
   (c) speaking too quickly.
   (d) all of the above.

8. Meeting minutes should contain at least the following items:
   (a) names of persons who attended and who sent regrets.
   (b) topics discussed.
   (c) actions to be taken.
   (d) name of the person who will take each action.
   (e) all of the above.

9. Teleconferencing provides the chairperson with these advantages:
   (a) you can get other work done while attending the meeting and no one will notice.
   (b) you can save time and travel costs.
   (c) you can avoid preparing an agenda, consulting with other people on needed agenda items, or sending out minutes after the meeting.
   (d) a and b.

10. As chairperson of a videoconference, you must do the following:
    (a) know the technology well so that you can instruct participants in its use.
    (b) talk at least 50 percent of the time so that there is no lost air-time while people are thinking.
    (c) take time to ensure that everyone is positioned correctly for the camera.
    (d) a and c.
    (e) all of the above.

Answers

1.D 2.B 3.D 4.C 5.D 6.A 7.D 8.E 9.B 10.D

EXERCISES

1. In groups of three to five, choose a current decision that someone in the group is facing—for example, whether to complete the requirements for a diploma or take a job. Follow the problem-solving model on page 189 to help this person make a decision. You will need someone to write down the ideas generated during brainstorming. Every idea is recorded without judgment at this stage. Then proceed with the remaining steps.

2. Describe the characteristics of a team in which you have participated and that worked very well. Compare your list with that of a classmate, and present your combined list to the class.

3. Attend a meeting at your college or city council. Write a critique of the interaction you see. Submit it in memo format to your instructor.

4. This exercise will help you gain confidence. Give a one-minute speech describing your favourite music or musician. Follow the pattern of:
   (a) introduction, with an attention-grabber and your main point;
   (b) three characteristics of the music that you appreciate; and
   (c) a memorable closing about what the music means to you. Preparation may be done in class.

5. In pairs, select a product or service and develop a five-minute presentation to sell the product or service to your class. Keep their wants and needs foremost in your mind. Use the most up-to-date audio-visual equipment available to you to make a strong visual impact.

6. The following is a two-part assignment that gives you knowledge of Web conferencing systems, as well as skill development with Web research, evaluation, report writing, and meetings.

   (a) Work in pairs for this assignment. You both work for a company that has offices in Canada, Europe, and Asia. Your director has asked you to research Web conferencing systems that would allow international teams to function better at a lower cost. According to your career interests, decide what kinds of projects these teams would carry out, listing details of the tasks involved, such as planning meetings and working on technical drawings together. Find three different systems that offer a variety of features and compare them for their usefulness in accomplishing these tasks. Write a 700–800 word report evaluating the three systems and recommending one of them. (Refer to Chapters 12 and 13 for help with research and reporting.)

   (b) Continuing with your partner, prepare to hold a meeting to decide which of the above conferencing systems would be most appropriate for your company. Create an agenda and assign one person to be the meeting facilitator and the other to take minutes. In your next class, hold 20-minute meetings in groups of four. One pair will lead using their agenda and evaluation report, and then the other pair will lead. In the meetings, share the evaluation reports you have prepared and base your discussion on them. In the following class, submit two items to your instructor: your pair's evaluation report (working with it may show how it could be improved) and your meeting minutes. Your instructor may also ask you to evaluate each individual's participation in the meetings.

7. This exercise gives you practice in interacting positively with your colleagues and awareness of several errors often made by presenters. Change the following negative comments into constructive feedback, suggesting what to do in order to correct the problem. Eliminate all negative words such as "don't" and "couldn't." Your instructor may ask you to use constructive comments to evaluate other students' presentation.

   (a) Don't read your slides in a list-like manner.
   Example of constructive version: *Strive for varied pace and pitch. Talk about each point fully before moving to the next point on your slide.*

   (b) Don't start with "OK."
   Example of constructive version: *Plan a strong opening line to focus people's attention, avoiding expressions such as "OK."*

   (c) Don't talk through your nose. The tone is very unpleasant.

(d) Don't raise your pitch at the ends of your sentences as if you were asking a question. It makes you seem unsure of yourself.

(e) Don't rock from side to side.

(f) Don't wander aimlessly.

(g) Your slides are too crowded.

(h) We couldn't hear you from the back of the room.

(i) I couldn't read your chart. The text was too small.

(j) I couldn't follow your talk because what you were saying didn't match the slides I was seeing.

8. Develop an evaluation sheet for oral presentations that will be delivered in your class. List ten performance items based on the guidelines given in this chapter. Use the sheet to evaluate your own and your classmates' presentations.

CHAPTER NINE

RÉSUMÉS

Chapter Objectives

Successful completion of this chapter will enable you to:

1 Analyze your experience, aptitudes, and goals in preparation for writing a résumé.

2 Prepare an attractive résumé using a format appropriate to your experience and employment goals.

3 Prepare an electronic résumé suitable for scanning.

INTRODUCTION

Finding the right job will make a significant contribution to your happiness in life. The right job for you is one that uses your talents and expresses your values. It follows that in order to find the right job, you need to know what your talents and values are. You may have given them a lot of thought already, or you may have thought about them very little. This unit will help you analyze your experience to clarify your ideas about your future. Then you will want to match your goals to current job opportunities and, finally, present yourself to potential employers. This process is demanding, but the reward will be a job that offers satisfaction and achievement, rather than "the daily grind."

1 PRE-RÉSUMÉ ANALYSIS

The first step in finding a job is to spend some time thinking about yourself. This serves two purposes: first, it puts you in touch with your personal goals and helps you identify what you want out of life—what gives you satisfaction and a sense of achievement. Knowing these things will help you identify the kind of job you want and the kind of organization you would like to work for. Second, it helps you work out a strategy—in your résumé, application letters, and interviews—for presenting your skills and knowledge in an effective way to a prospective employer.

Several exercises may stimulate your thinking. You might like to try telling your "story" in an autobiography. In four or five pages, try describing your significant family experiences, activities you enjoyed and didn't enjoy, subjects you did well in at school and ones you had difficulty with, jobs you've had, and values and/or experiences that led you into your present course of study. When you are finished, look for patterns. Have you had consistent success or satisfaction with one kind of activity? Do you enjoy doing only the things you're good at? Are you conservative, or do you crave new experiences? Do you value external recognition, or is your own evaluation more important than that of other people?

Many psychologists who study life-span development believe that personal characteristics like these do not change significantly over time. You will probably be happier if you accept your strengths and limitations and look for jobs that are suited to them, rather than trying to change yourself in some radical way.

In addition to, or instead of, this narrative approach, you may like some more structured analytical activities. Here are some you might like to try:

Exercise 1

Activities Checklist

Circle any of the activities in the following list that you think you are good at. Add more activities at the bottom if anything important is missing. Then, using a different-coloured pen or pencil, circle the ones you enjoy doing.

fixing	thinking
teaching	designing
communicating	evaluating
writing	learning
analyzing	organizing
listening	motivating
coordinating	managing
cooperating	selling
counselling	decision-making
supervising	decorating
negotiating	leading
creating	performing
helping	planning
understanding	persuading
explaining	researching
reading	scheduling
observing	maintaining
problem-solving	speaking
coping	budgeting
investigating	building
directing	inventing

Exercise 2

From the previous list, identify the activities that you have circled as ones that you both enjoy and are good at. List them in the left-hand column of the following chart. In the right-hand column, write down situations that demonstrate you have the skills you listed.

Example

SKILL	EVIDENCE
leading	investment club president, successful minor hockey coach
scheduling	able to maintain B+ average while working part-time and participating in varsity sports

SKILL	EVIDENCE

Exercise 3

Think about activities that you enjoy. List five of your favourites in the left-hand column of the chart below. Opposite each one, try to identify what it is you enjoy about each activity.

Example

ACTIVITY	WHAT I ENJOY
Going to parties	Being with a large group of people, meeting new people, relaxed unstructured activity, eating and drinking, music

ACTIVITY	WHAT I ENJOY

Exercise 4

Personal Qualities

Rate each of the following qualities as they apply to you, using the following scale:

1. That's me
2. Describes me to some degree
3. Not me

_____ neat	_____ punctual
_____ accurate	_____ organized
_____ responsible	_____ outgoing
_____ cooperative	_____ helpful
_____ dependable	_____ tactful
_____ aggressive	_____ thorough
_____ conscientious	_____ efficient
_____ ambitious	_____ innovative
_____ hard-working	_____ decisive
_____ competitive	_____ self-disciplined
_____ enthusiastic	_____ adaptable
_____ imaginative	_____ assertive
_____ positive	_____ self-starting
_____ patient	_____ easygoing
_____ flexible	_____ quiet
_____ energetic	_____ relaxed
_____ supportive	_____ self-motivated
_____ sociable	_____ creative

Exercise 5

List the personal qualities that you ranked number 1 from the previous list. Write a paragraph justifying your choices.

Example

aggressive   assertive
ambitious   energetic
hard-working   competitive
decisive   self-starting

Whatever I do, I do to win. In sports, I practise by myself as well as with the team so that I can be the best on the field. I am working part-time and saving my money so that I can open my own business. I like to set concrete goals and work toward them. I enjoy my job as a commissioned salesperson because I like to know that how much I earn is directly related to how hard I work.

Exercise 6

Preferred Coworker Exercise

I prefer coworkers who are (check as many as apply)

_____ male   _____ in their thirties and forties

_____ female   _____ middle-aged

_____ both sexes   _____ a variety of ages

_____ in their twenties

_____ from a cultural background similar to mine

_____ from an educational background similar to mine

_____ from a variety of backgrounds

I prefer to work with people who

_____ like to work with objects or machines

_____ like to observe and investigate

_____ like to work with numbers or data

_____ like to use their imagination and creativity

_____ like to help or train people

_____ like to persuade or lead people

Exercise 7

Working Conditions Exercise

Use a blank sheet of paper to make a larger version of the table below:

Column 1	Column 2	Column 3
Jobs I have had	Things I disliked about job	Opposites
		Other positive things

In the first column, list all your jobs. In column 2 write down anything you disliked about the jobs in column 1, for example, low pay, unfair boss, or boring job. Don't worry about keeping these negative factors next to the right job. In column 3, write the opposite of the negative factor; for example, if you wrote "low pay" in column 2, put "high pay" in column 3. If you put "boring work" in column 2, put "interesting, challenging work" in column 3. When you finish, add any *positive* factors about your previous jobs that haven't appeared in the list in column 3. Then number your list of positive factors. Write the numbers down again on a separate piece of paper. Now go through the list, making a *forced choice* between each pair of factors. For example, if you listed

1. high pay
2. interesting, challenging work
3. regular hours
4. travel opportunities

you would decide which was more important to you in a job: high pay or interesting work. Then you would decide between high pay and regular hours, and then high pay and travel opportunities. Next compare "interesting, challenging work" with regular hours, and then with travel opportunities. Each time you choose one item over another, put a tick under that number on your separate piece of paper. For this list, you would have eleven tick marks distributed over four numbers. Count up the tick marks for each item, and rank the positive factors; for example, if "interesting, challenging work" received four ticks, "high pay" received three, and "regular hours" and "travel opportunities" two each, your "prioritized" list would look like this:

1. interesting, challenging work
2. high pay
3. regular hours ⎫
4. travel opportunities ⎬ tie

Exercise 8

Work Values Exercise

The following list describes a wide variety of rewards that people obtain from their jobs. Look at the definition of each satisfaction and rate the degree of importance that you would assign to it for yourself, using the scale below.

1. Very important
2. Somewhat important
3. Not very important

_____ Helping Others: Involved in helping other people in a direct way, either individually or in small groups.

_____ Public Contact: Frequent public contact with people.

_____ Making Decisions: Power to decide the courses of action, policies, and so on.

_____ Influencing People: Change attitudes or opinions or alter people's behaviour.

_____ Working Alone: Do projects by myself.

_____ Knowledge: Pursue knowledge, truth, and understanding.

_____ Creativity: Create new ideas, programs, systems; not following a format previously adopted by others.

_____ Change and Variety: Work responsibilities that frequently change in their content and setting.

_____ Precision Work: Work in situations that require dexterity or attention to detail.

_____ Stability: Job duties that are largely predictable and not likely to change over a long period of time.

_____ Security: Assurance of keeping my job and a reasonable financial reward.

_____ Excitement: Experiencing a high (or frequent) degree of stimulation in my work.

_____ Recognition: Visible or public recognition for the quality of my work, so that people are aware of my accomplishments.

_____ Profit, Gain: A strong likelihood of accumulating large amounts of money or possessions.

_____ Independence: Being able to work without much intervention or direction from others.

_____ Physical Challenge: Physical demands; speed, strength, stamina.

_____ Time-Freedom: Work responsibilities that I can do according to my own schedule; no specific working hours required.

If you find this kind of analytic activity helpful, you will benefit from Richard Nelson Bolles's *What Color Is Your Parachute? A Practical Manual for Job-hunters and Career-changers* (Ten Speed Press, revised annually). This book has been described as "the bible of the job-search field."

2 PREPARING A RÉSUMÉ

Once you have increased your awareness of your areas of interest and competence, you will be ready to begin to put this information into a form that will be easily accessible to a potential employer. A **résumé** is a summary of relevant data about your qualifications and accomplishments. An appropriate format presents information in a concise, easy-to-read fashion. It shows that you are a person with excellent writing and presentation skills. A résumé must also reflect high ethical standards. Never "pad" your résumé by changing dates or job titles, exaggerating accomplishments, or adding nonexistent qualifications. Your résumé will stay in your file when you are hired. If any deliberate inaccuracies ever came to light they could be grounds for dismissal.

Choosing a Format

The **chronological** format is the résumé format you are probably most familiar with. The two examples in Figures 9.1 and 9.2 illustrate a typical chronological résumé. This format has separate sections for education, job experience, and other activities. Within the first two categories, the writer presents a year-by-year summary of his or her educational achievements and job responsibilities. Even if you decide not to use a chronological résumé for your job search, you might wish to prepare one for your own reference, as an organized record of your education and employment experience. The chronological format highlights **dates** and **job titles.** It is a good choice if you want to emphasize:

(a) the length of time you have spent in a particular job area,
(b) a consistent work history,
(c) a work history that shows progressive responsibility,
(d) your age.

For example, if you have a diploma in marketing and sales and have spent several years in a firm, starting as a salesperson and progressing to sales manager, and you now wish to move to a larger firm as a sales manager, a chronological résumé would be a good choice. It would be a poor choice if any of the following apply to you:

1. **You are looking for your first responsible job.** The emphasis on job titles will not be appropriate if the job titles are not obviously related to your career goal or if they are low-level titles like "salesclerk," "server," or "pizza delivery person." The description of duties performed will be pointless for many of these jobs; if this description is omitted, however, there won't be much to put in the résumé. Many important achievements—for example, as an athlete or student leader—will be relegated to the last part of the résumé.

2. **You are changing career goals.** If you are graduating in early childhood education but have learned that you hate kids and actually want to sell real estate, you don't want the title of your diploma to be the first thing a potential employer reads. Likewise, a consistent work history may not be an asset if you are trying to get into a new field. The reader's attention will be drawn to the job title, not the transferable skills.

3. **You have gaps in your academic or work history.** Because the chronological format emphasizes dates, gaps in the sequence will be very noticeable. If you made a few tries at your high-school or college diploma, have been unemployed, have worked in the home, or have changed jobs a lot, the chronological format is probably not for you.

If you fit any of these categories, a better choice would be the **functional,** or **skills,** format. This format, illustrated in Figures 9.3 and 9.4, emphasizes what you can do rather than when or where you learned how to do it. It integrates skills acquired through education, work, and other activities, so that achievements outside paid work get more recognition. Identifying your major skills leaves less work for your reader. Remember that during the initial screening a potential employer spends less than ten seconds on your résumé.

Preparing a Chronological Résumé

If you choose the chronological résumé, here are some pointers. The four headings correspond to the parts of the résumés illustrated in Figures 9.1 and 9.2.

Identification

Give your name, postal address, e-mail address, and phone number. If you have two addresses—for example, if you will be returning home at the end of the school year—include both with appropriate dates. The phone number should be a daytime number. Identify a pager or voice-mail number as such. If you are regularly out during the day and cannot receive calls or messages, add "after 6 PM" or whatever other information is relevant. Employers take a dim view of applicants who appear to be unreachable. Do **not** include your date of birth, sex, marital status, health, height, or similar data unless these factors are bona fide job requirements, which is very rare. Otherwise you are inviting employers to break the law by discriminating on the basis of age, sex, marital status, or disability. Do not put your social insurance number on your résumé. This number is confidential and should be used only on official personnel documents when you are hired.

Employment

Education or employment should be the next section; lead with the category that is likely to be the stronger factor in obtaining a job. List job titles and employers in reverse chronological order. Use years, not names of months. Put "part-time" or "summer employment," if applicable, beneath the job title, not in the column of dates.

Do not list job responsibilities if they are obvious—everyone knows a server takes food and beverage orders, brings food, takes payment, wipes off tables, and so forth. Note responsibilities only if the job title is vague (clerk) or if you performed additional duties (for example, if you were a salesclerk but acted as manager two days a week, regularly closing the store and making bank deposits). If you have held a number of similar jobs, do not list the responsibilities of each one. The repetition will make your résumé very long and very boring, without adding anything significant. Do not lock yourself into an elaborate structure that is not appropriate to someone at your career stage.

Education

List diplomas or degrees obtained in reverse chronological order; that is, start with the most recent. Put dates in years, omitting the names of months. Distinguish the name of the diploma obtained from the name of the institution

FIGURE 9.1 Sample Chronological Résumé

Allison Ghorbani
63 Pacific Wind Cres
Brampton ON L6R 2B1
(905) 555-1802 (cell phone)
aghorb@aol.com

EMPLOYMENT OBJECTIVE   A supervisory position in payroll management

SUMMARY   After completing an accounting diploma with a 3.5 GPA,
I worked in a variety of business settings and discovered
an aptitude for payroll management. In three years I
earned two professional certificates and was promoted
three times. Improvements I made to my current
employer's payroll system have eliminated the need for
costly seasonal outsourcing.

EXPERIENCE

2003–present   Chinguacousy Resource and Administration
Brampton ON
Senior Payroll Specialist (2005–present)
Payroll Specialist (2003–5)

2002–2003   NEBS
Cambridge ON
Payroll Clerk

2002   OfficeSolutions Temporary Placements
Cambridge ON
Clerical Worker

EDUCATION
2005   Canadian Payroll Association
Toronto ON
Payroll Supervisor Certificate

2003   Canadian Payroll Association
Toronto ON
Payroll Administrator Certificate

(continued)

FIGURE 9.1   Sample Chronological Résumé *(continued)*

1999–2002   Conestoga College
Cambridge ON
Business Administration–Accounting Diploma

ACTIVITIES AND INTERESTS

Posting indie music blog
Coaching girls' soccer team
Travel

REFERENCES

Supplied on request

---

by using underlining, shading, capitals, or some other visual device. Go back only as far as high-school graduation; omit even that, if it was more than ten years ago, unless you see it as a definite asset.

Do not list all the courses you took. The titles will mean little to your reader and take up a lot of space. Academic distinctions such as graduating with high honours or being on the Dean's Honour List can be noted on your résumé.

Other Activities

This is the place to list participation in sports, student government, volunteer organizations, and clubs. You can include interests and hobbies, if you wish. Remember that interviewers often use this information to get an interview started. Interests like "sports" or "music," shared by 90 percent of the population, don't give him or her much to go on. Use specific entries, such as "amateur weightlifting, coaching girls' soccer, cheering for the Blue Jays."

FIGURE 9.2 Sample Chronological Résumé

George H. Vandermeer
Apt 12 - 1233 Academy Dr
Windsor ON N9A 7G9
(519) 555-8938 (cell)
geevan@sympatico.ca

EMPLOYMENT OBJECTIVE
A management position in retail electronics or telecommunications

WORK EXPERIENCE

Sunset Radio	**Store Manager** (2004–present)	2002–present
Windsor ON	**Management Trainee** (2003)	
	Sales Associate (2002)	

Recommended for management training after two months with my current employer. Completed course with "outstanding" rating. Under my management, store has increased sales volume almost 35% and cut employee turnover in half.

All Geek to Me	**Service Technician**	2000–2002
Toronto ON		

Contributed to my employer's rating as "Best Computer Store" by *Now* magazine. Developed a significant customer base through referrals by satisfied clients.

The Phone Store	**Sales Associate (part time and**	1999–2000
Toronto ON	**summer employment)**	

Time spent helping first-time cell phone buyers get the right phone and plan earned me two Employee Achievement Awards.

EDUCATION

Centennial College	**Computer Electronic Engineering**	1999–2000
Toronto ON	**Technician Diploma**	

President's Honour List

ACTIVITIES AND INTERESTS
Keyboard player in band
Maintain web page for local youth volunteer agency
Enjoy sailing, camping, travel

REFERENCES
Available on request

Preparing the Functional Résumé

The headings in a **functional résumé** reflect the areas of skill you have to offer to a potential employer. These can be skills acquired in school, on the job, or through outside activities. A good pre-résumé analysis as described on page 201 is a prerequisite for a good functional résumé. Look over the exercises or other pre-résumé writing you have done. Think about the skills you have that would benefit a potential employer and that you would like to employ in your job. If you have a particular career in mind, try to identify the major skills required for success in that job. Some examples of skill areas are:

supervisory	creative
sales	management
computer	personnel
mechanical	problem-solving
clerical	accounting
child care	counselling

Depending on your education and career goal, you may choose fairly specific headings, like accounting or technical skills, or more general ones like flexibility, initiative, or people skills. Select the two or three headings that would be most important to a potential employer. The résumé in Figure 9.3 illustrates how to organize your education and experience under each heading. Practise creating your first entry in the space provided on page 215. Try to begin each line after the heading with a verb (for example, "successfully **completed** course in personal sales," "**supervised** four employees as head of work crew," "**organized** Student Awards Banquet for 200 guests as student council social convener"). Figure 9.4 presents another example of a functional résumé, which, though shorter than the one shown in Figure 9.3, is still effectively written.

If you will be applying for jobs in several fields, you may wish to change or reorganize parts of your functional résumé to include or emphasize different skills. Do not create a new résumé every time you apply for a job, however. A résumé that presents the skills you have to offer in an honest and appealing way should be appropriate for most jobs you are likely to be applying for.

Identification

The identification section of a functional résumé is the same as that of the chronological résumé.

Skill Heading

Education

Put in the year you completed your degree(s) and/or diploma(s). Give the name and subject area of the diploma or whatever you received, and the name of the institution. Do not include any other information because all relevant information should be somewhere under the skill headings.

Work Experience

List the years you worked at each job. Give the name and address of the company. Omit job titles, unless they are impressive. Do not list your duties because relevant information will be included under the appropriate skill headings.

Employment Objective

Two sections have not been discussed because they are optional features of either résumé format. The first is the **employment objective.** You may wish to prepare an employment objective statement **if you will accept only a specific type of job.**

FIGURE 9.3 Sample Functional Résumé

Madeleine Miranda
1053 Rushton Drive
Mississauga ON L5C 2E3
mmiranda@aareas.ca
(416) 555-9977

Employment Objective

A responsible position in industrial or retail promotions.

Skills and Abilities

Marketing and Sales Skills
— successfully completed courses in marketing, marketing research, and retailing
— received grade of "A with Distinction" in personal sales course
— "Employee of the Month" eight times in three years of part-time retail sales
— participated in marketing and advertising decisions
— responsible for merchandising and display in a variety of retail settings
— attended customer service programs offered to SportLine employees
— designed and implemented recruitment campaign that doubled
  membership of college racquetball club in two months

Management Skills
— successfully completed courses in management, organizational behaviour, and
  administrative communication
— prepared work schedules for eight employees
— trained and supervised employees
— president of college racquetball club
— vice-president of college student council, responsible for planning and implementing college-wide entertainment programs

Office and Computer Skills
— successfully completed courses in business communication
— type 55 wpm
— applied knowledge of Word and computerized inventory to school and work
  assignments

FIGURE 9.3 Sample Functional Résumé *(continued)*

Education

Sheridan College of Applied Arts and Technology   2007
Oakville, Ontario

Diploma: Marketing Administration

Work Experience

Pizza Buona Restaurant and Take-Out Inc.   2005–present
Whitby, Ontario

Night Manager

MaxiStores SportLine Division   2005
Weston, Ontario

SportLine Dufferin Mall   2003–2005
Toronto, Ontario

Night Manager/Salesperson (part-time)

Starr & Dean Sales   2003
North York, Ontario

Telemarketing Group Leader (summer employment)

Interests

Racquetball, field hockey, collecting Mickey Mouse memorabilia

FIGURE 9.4 Sample Functional Résumé

Sarah Yan Feng Chen
3432 Broadway W apt 4011
Vancouver BC V6R 2B3
(614) 555-2345
syfc1@aol.ca

OBJECTIVE
A career in the hospitality industry

QUALIFICATIONS
Diploma in General Business Studies
Successful work experience in a hotel
Ability to communicate effectively in writing, in person, and over the telephone
People orientation and commitment to service

EDUCATION
Diploma   Kwantlen Community College
           Surrey BC
           General Business Studies 2006

EXPERIENCE
Travel and Hospitality
- Completed one-semester field placement at the Coast Plaza Hotel, Vancouver
- Successfully applied knowledge of computerized reservation system, customer service, general office skills
- Travelled widely in North America and Asia

Communication
- Speak fluent English, Cantonese, and Mandarin
- Maintain personal web page
- Successfully completed courses in business communication and public speaking

People and Service
- Volunteer campus guide and tour leader for international students at Kwantlen College
- President, Surrey/Zuhai Sister City Friendship Committee
- Active in volunteer fundraising for United Way, Terry Fox Run, WaterCan, and other local causes

Examples

Employment Objective: A sales position with potential supervisory responsibility.

Employment Objective: A position in personnel or labour relations with opportunity for advancement.

If your mind is made up, this type of statement will save you from wasting time in interviews discussing jobs outside your field of interest. It is also useful if you are sending unsolicited applications to large companies with many employment areas (for example, a retail operation that has sales, marketing, accounting, personnel, and other departments). If, however, you are undecided about your career goals, an employment objective statement would be inappropriate. A vague, open-ended phrase like "a responsible position that uses my education and skills" is worse than useless, since it applies to virtually everyone in the world. Remember that you will want to have a résumé that can be sent out to many prospective employers. If your objective is too specific ("Mediterranean cruise director") you will get very little use out of your résumé. **Never** mention that your long-term objective is self-employment. You are telling the reader that you wish to learn the business from his or her company and then become part of the competition. This information will not get you an interview.

References

The other section you may wish to include is a list of **references.** Since references take up a lot of space, you may want to use just the phrase "References supplied on request." Have a typed sheet of references prepared to take to interviews. Always ask permission to use someone's name as a reference. If he or she does not agree immediately, find someone else. You want someone who will be unqualifiedly positive about you.

ESL TIP

If you plan to use a functional résumé, begin by creating a list of your educational qualifications and the jobs you have held. Add other significant experiences like volunteer positions or sports. Then make a list of three, four, or five skills that would be important to a potential employer in your field. Look at job postings online or in the newspaper if you need help identifying relevant skills. Look through your first list to find items that would show that you had these skills, and put them under the appropriate headings. Try to begin each item with a verb, in the present tense if you are doing something now, in a current job, or in the past tense if you did something in a previous job. Remember that communication skills are needed in every job. If you can communicate in more than one language be sure to mention this important asset.

Spelling or grammar errors on your résumé will give the impression that you do not know enough, or you do not care enough, to make it perfect. Check all proper names yourself, and then ask someone with excellent English skills to proofread what you have written.

Presenting the Résumé

The appearance and accuracy of your résumé are extremely important. During the initial screening of applications, an employer will spend approximately ten seconds on each résumé. What comes across in ten seconds?

1. **Paper.** This should be good quality, in a conservative shade. White is always a safe choice.
2. **Typeface.** Clear type in an easy-to-read style will be appreciated by your reader. Print from your disk on a letter-quality printer. Photocopy on a high-quality machine, or have copies made for you by a printer. Choose a conservative font. Italics and other fancy fonts are hard on the eyes.
3. **Layout.** A one-page résumé is ideal, but only if it fits easily on the page without overloading it. Lots of white space invites the reader into the page. A dense, crowded page discourages the potential reader. Leave generous left and right margins. Ensure that your spacing and margins are consistent. If you need two pages, try to make the amount on each page fairly equal. The layout is particularly significant to someone glancing at the résumé for an overall impression.

4. **Emphasis.** Quick reading will be easier if key information stands out. Add emphasis and variety by underlining, capitalization, shading, and other devices.

If your résumé passes this first test and is read more closely, other factors will determine whether you are called for an interview. Mechanical errors in spelling and grammar will almost always be fatal. Proofread rigorously, and then ask someone with good English skills to go over it again. Don't forget your name, address, and other proper names. Personnel officers report that this is where mistakes are most often made, because proofreaders assume these words are easy and therefore will be error-free. Your résumé will represent you to your potential employer. Everything about it should reflect your best effort.

3 ELECTRONIC RÉSUMÉS

Of course, your résumé does not have to exist only as a piece of paper. Putting your résumé online will enable you to apply immediately to a job posting. Some employers may ask you to submit your résumé on a form, somewhat like the older paper application form. You can see an example of an application form on page 240. In the future, it may be common to link your résumé to other documents that support your application, like a portfolio or newspaper article, or even to multimedia displays. If you have the expertise to create such a résumé now, it could put you on the cutting edge in fields where innovative thinking is valued. Do not attempt this unless you can create a high-quality, professional-looking presentation that accurately reflects what you have to offer to a potential employer. Avoid pictures of yourself. Employers do not want to be open to accusations of selecting applicants on the basis of race or physical appearance.

Whether your résumé is online or in print, an employer may choose to scan it electronically before deciding whether to give your application further consideration. Electronic scanning is frequently used by large organizations that receive many unsolicited résumés and that wish to develop a pool or database of candidates for openings as they arise. Any organization that receives large numbers of applications might choose electronic scanning as a labour-saving and objective way of identifying the most qualified applicants. Of course, a computer cannot "read" a résumé with the same judgment as a human being. All it can do is search for preprogrammed keywords, and identify résumés that contain a certain quota of them. Keywords are usually nouns, so unlike the typical résumé, particularly the functional résumé, a scannable résumé avoids phrases like "performed reception duties" or "organized activities for 40-member youth group" because these phrases get their punch from verbs—action words. To adapt your résumé for computer scanning, you can keep your existing skill headings and change the entries from verb phrases to nouns.

Example

CONVENTIONAL RÉSUMÉ

Communication Skills

— edited college newspaper
— created website for Student Council
— successfully completed course in workplace communication
— type 80 wpm
— speak fluent English and Cantonese

SCANNABLE RÉSUMÉ

Communication Skills

college newspaper editor

website development for Student Council

report writing course

typist: 80 wpm

English speaker; Cantonese speaker

You may add a "Keyword Summary" at the beginning of the résumé. This is a list of all the likely keywords from your résumé, separated by commas or periods. It should contain synonyms and other forms and tenses; for example, manager, management, managing, managed. Use both abbreviations and full words; for example, A/R, Accounts Receivable. Even if you correctly identify the important keywords in the job area you are applying for, it is impossible to know the exact form chosen by the human programmer.

Scanners get confused by fancy fonts or unusual punctuation such as bullets, slashes, or dashes. Since they read horizontally across the page, avoid a layout with parallel columns or strong vertical emphasis. Many features that work well in the typical résumé for human readers are not very effective for scanners. It is better to prepare a conventional résumé first and then create a separate scannable version if you think that a particular employer will be using this technology. If you are delivering a paper résumé that may be scanned, do not fold it. Use an envelope the same size as the paper.

CHAPTER REVIEW/SELF-TEST

1. Before you start writing your résumé you should
   (a) download a résumé template.
   (b) spend time thinking about your talents, values, and goals.
   (c) invest in a colour printer.
   (d) choose a standard format and stick to it.

2. The purpose of a résumé
   (a) is to convince an employer that you have the skills and qualities needed for success in the job you are applying for.
   (b) is to give a sample of your high standard of presentation.
   (c) is to provide a summary for your personnel file if you are hired.
   (d) includes all of the above.

3. The chronological résumé format is a good choice if
   (a) you have a consistent work history that is obviously relevant to the job(s) you are applying for.
   (b) you don't know what skills or experience an employer might be looking for.
   (c) you have only had one or two paying jobs.
   (d) all of the above.

4. The functional résumé is a good choice if
   (a) you wish to focus on what you have achieved in the past.
   (b) you are changing careers.
   (c) you wish to emphasize job titles and dates.
   (d) your most important qualifications come from paid employment.

5. The functional format
   (a) never includes dates or employment history.
   (b) always begins with a summary of qualifications.
   (c) must include skill headings clearly relevant to the job(s) you are applying for.
   (d) should include a list of your jobs and the duties you performed.

6. The Identification section of a résumé
   (a) should include the word "Résumé" in large letters.
   (b) should be no more than three lines long.
   (c) should have all the information the employer needs to get in touch with you immediately for a job interview.
   (d) is optional.

7. The Employment Objective section of a résumé
   (a) gives you an opportunity to describe your long-term career aspirations.
   (b) should be general enough to ensure that you will be considered for any available job.
   (c) should use the exact title of the job you are applying for.
   (d) limits the type of job you wish to be considered for.

8. The visual presentation of a résumé
   (a) should invite the audience to start reading.
   (b) is just as important as the contents.
   (c) must be flawless.
   (d) all of the above.

9. An e-mail résumé
   (a) should be as visually exciting as a paper résumé.
   (b) makes having a paper résumé unnecessary.
   (c) may include a keyword summary if you expect it to be scanned electronically.
   (d) all of the above.

10. Deliberate errors of fact on your résumé
    (a) are grounds for dismissal if they are discovered, even if you have been doing a good job.
    (b) are expected from people who are trying to show initiative and aggressiveness in looking for a job.
    (c) will not matter once you have proven yourself as an employee.
    (d) are not likely to be discovered.

Answers

1.B 2.D 3.A 4.B 5.C 6.C 7.D 8.D 9.C 10.A

EXERCISES

1. Select a partner in the class (try to find someone you do not know very well). Tell your partner about your top three achievements—things you have done that you are proud of. Ask your partner to write down the skills and personal qualities that each achievement demonstrates, in his or her opinion. When you have finished, change roles.

2. Select a partner in the class. Take turns interviewing one another about your personal histories. Here are some sample questions:

(a) Where were you born?

(b) How does coming from _____ benefit you?

(c) What is the most important value you learned from your family?

(d) Can you give an example of how this value applies to your future?

(e) What did you enjoy most about your experiences in school?

(f) What did you enjoy least?

(g) Why did you choose your present course of study?

(h) How has your college education changed your ideas about your future?

(i) Do you have a job? (*If yes:*) What is it?

(j) If the money was right, would you do this job full-time? Why or why not?

3. Prepare a list of keywords related to the kind of job you will be looking for when you have graduated. Include job titles, skills, education, computer applications, and any special terms related to your field.

4. If you have a paper résumé, go through it with a highlighter to identify the keywords currently there. Create a keyword summary using the words in your résumé and variations on them.

CHAPTER TEN

LOCATING AND APPLYING FOR JOBS

Chapter Objectives

Successful completion of this chapter will enable you to:

1 Research the job market and locate potential employers and job postings in newspapers, at placement centres, and through the World Wide Web.

2 Write an unsolicited letter of application.

3 Respond to a job posting effectively in writing.

4 Fill in application forms.

5 Respond to a job posting effectively by telephone.

INTRODUCTION

The process of preparing a résumé, if you have taken it seriously, will have given you a good insight into your goals in life and the skills and abilities you possess that will help you meet them. Now you have to consider what kind of employer needs those skills and can help you meet those goals. You need to identify what type of work you want to do and what kind of workplace you want to do it in. Finally, you have to identify specific employers who have this kind of job available. In the past, newspaper advertisements and personal contacts were the main source of information about job openings. New technology has made it possible to identify many more job possibilities. Regardless of how you learn about a job opening, you will need to approach the potential employer with an effective message asking him or her to review your résumé and give you the chance to be interviewed.

1 RESEARCHING THE JOB MARKET

Your résumé is now complete. The next question is, "Where do I send it?" Of course, you know about "help wanted" ads, but only about 20 percent of the jobs available are advertised in this way. If you are free to relocate, you can use the World Wide Web to search the help wanted ads in newspapers across Canada and in other countries. Other websites list jobs that may not have appeared in print. The Internet is a good recruitment tool for large organizations that often have many locations, experience high turnover, and are constantly hiring at the entry level.

You will also want to enhance your chances of finding the right job by tapping the 80 percent of jobs that are not advertised. This research can take two forms, depending on how firm your ideas are about what you want to do. You may have fairly fixed ideas by now, especially if you are graduating from a well-defined course such as cosmetics retailing, early childhood education, or marketing. If so, you will be interested in discovering potential employers. Ideally, this is a long-term project.

Newspapers, especially their business section, and community newspapers are a good source of information about new companies, expansions, new branch offices, and other changes that will open up jobs. Visit your college library regularly to look at professional journals and newsletters in your field, especially Canadian ones. These not only report new job opportunities but often give you an inside look at a potential workplace. Visit the websites of organizations in your field. If you do not know anyone personally who is employed in your field, consider making an appointment for an information-gathering interview as described in Exercise 2 at the end of this chapter. A company that has hired graduates from your program in the past would be a good place to look for someone to interview. Go to large events where you will have an opportunity to meet many people in your field. Visit local trade shows related to your future employment area. Watch for relevant conventions or professional meetings, especially ones that encourage students to attend by offering special rates.

Another way of obtaining an inside look is to talk to as many people as possible who are working in your field. The information gathered in either of these two ways will always be useful—if not in choosing an employer, then certainly in a job interview. An applicant who is knowledgeable and curious about the field will have a strong advantage.

When it is time to begin sending out unsolicited application letters, gather names and addresses from the Internet, trade directories (in your library), your college placement office, your personal contacts, and the Yellow Pages. Tell everyone—literally, everyone—you know or meet that you are looking for a job in a particular area, and follow up any leads. It has been estimated that 60 percent of all jobs are filled through personal contacts. If you have prepared yourself by keeping up-to-date on the job market in your career area, you will be able to be more selective about the employers' names you take from directories and personal contacts. You will also be able to write a more effective letter of application.

If you are graduating from a general program, such as business administration, or if you are contemplating a career change, you will want to research the job market in a broader way. You should be reading the newspaper and a variety of professional journals to learn not only about employers but also about occupations. Your college placement office should have reference books describing typical duties of various job titles. The National Occupation Classification, available on the Department of Human Resources and Skills Development website, describes over thirty thousand job titles organized by occupational groups, and is a valuable resource for understanding the Canadian labour market. A first-rate way of getting up-to-date information is to visit a company, social agency, or whatever interests you and talk to a supervisor who works there. This will not only give you an idea of the duties performed but also tell you about the personality factors that are important in that workplace. The exercises at the end of this chapter give more information about how to arrange an information-gathering interview.

Talk to employed friends and relatives about their jobs and employers. As you begin to focus on job areas that would be appropriate to your skills and values, you can start to use the research techniques suggested for job hunters who have defined their career goals. It is generally a mistake to choose a career simply because there are lots of jobs available in it, if it doesn't otherwise appeal to you very much. Job markets will change a lot in the 30 or 40 years you'll be working. You may already have observed radical changes in a brief time; one day employers are desperate for ticker-tape tossers, the next month ticker-tape tossers are being laid off in droves. If you are in a career because your personality and skills are suited to it, you will survive the ups and downs. If not, you won't; it's as simple as that.

ESL TIP

While an obvious form letter is not a good choice when you are applying for a job, it will be helpful if you create a simple template for your solicited and unsolicited letters of application, using the AIDA format. Then it will be easy to fill in the name of the job you are applying for or the area of employment you are seeking, and the skills, experience, or qualities that this employer is looking for. Do not copy letters from websites; some of them are good, but many are self-promoting in an exaggerated way. Create your own letter, and then have someone with excellent English skills help you proofread it. Because a covering letter typically refers to the past, the present, and the future, it will inevitably use many different tenses. Pay particular attention to the verbs in your letter when you are proofreading a final copy.

2 WRITING AN UNSOLICITED LETTER OF APPLICATION

An unsolicited letter of application is one that is not written in response to a job posting. It is a persuasive message, so it follows the AIDA sequence.

Attention

The best way to get **attention** is to use the name and title of the appropriate reader. Phone the organizations you wish to apply to, and get the name (with the right spelling) and title of the person who normally hires people for the type of position you are seeking. Focus your reader's attention by stating your employment objective in the first line of your letter.

Examples

POOR

Dear Sir:

I will be graduating from Amor De Cosmos Community College in June of this year and I have done a lot of research into employment opportunities in my chosen field.

IMPROVED

Mr. Gerald P. Slater

Pacific Micro Industries

Burnaby BC V1C 2E3

Dear Mr. Slater

I will be graduating in Business Administration from Amor De Cosmos Community College this June, and I am writing to inquire about employment opportunities at Pacific Micro Industries.

If you have a personal contact in the organization who has suggested that you send an application, mention this in the opening of the letter.

Example

A fellow Lakeview College graduate, Kelly Baxter, now working as a resource quality technician in your division, suggested that I write to you to inquire about potential job openings at Metro Works.

Interest

Like any persuasive message, an application letter creates **interest** by appealing to a need. In this case, the need is not a personal one like belonging or esteem, but a corporate one. For example, a manufacturing company needs salespeople, a social agency needs people with interpersonal skills and experience, and a film production company needs people with technical skills. The more you have learned about a particular organization, the more specific your analysis of their needs can be and the more persuasively written your interest section can be. Naturally, you will want to emphasize reader benefit and reinforce it by using "you" and "your."

Examples

✗ POOR
I will be graduating with a diploma in fashion design and I am looking for an opportunity to gain experience in the fashion industry.

✓ IMPROVED
Your reputation as an industry leader is built on well-trained, dedicated staff; I believe my education and commitment would make me an asset to your team.

Desire

Create a **desire** in your audience to learn more about you by describing your particular qualifications. Do not repeat what is on your résumé. Draw your reader's attention to your résumé with a sentence like this one:

As you can see from the attached résumé, I have a diploma in retail floristry and three years' part-time experience as a floral assistant.

Use the rest of the paragraph to tell some things about yourself that do not find a place on a résumé, such as personal qualities. Do not be afraid to say that you are hard-working, flexible, outgoing, self-starting—if you are. It won't sound arrogant, just confident. If you give some evidence supporting your statement, as occurs in the following example, it will be even more effective.

During the past three years I have demonstrated my capacity for hard work and organization by maintaining a high grade-point average while holding down two part-time jobs.

Knowledge of the organization you are applying to should be demonstrated in a way that emphasizes reader benefit.

Since Chunky Chicken is expanding into Quebec, my language skills would be an asset to your firm.

If you have a particular interest in the organization or job you are applying for, it is a good idea to mention this, as long as you state it in a reader-centred way. After all, employers want motivated, enthusiastic employees.

Examples

 POOR
Working at Rad would really be a thrill for me.

IMPROVED
As a lifelong Rad wearer, I would bring a sincere dedication to maintaining your image of quality and value to any job with your firm.

A well-written desire section should add a personal, more subjective dimension to the skills and achievements listed on your résumé. The flavour of your personality should come through.

Action

The purpose of a letter of application is to get you an interview. Always make a specific request at the end of the letter.

Example

I believe my education and skills could contribute to the success of Leisuretyme Health Spa. I would appreciate the opportunity to discuss this with you in person at your convenience.

If your schedule is not completely flexible, suggest a time, or a number of times, when you will be available. You may want to put your phone number here, even though it is on your résumé.

The letter in Figure 10.1 is an example of an effective unsolicited letter of application.

Several days after you have sent the letter, follow up by calling the person to whom you sent it. Identify yourself as the sender of the letter, ask if it has been read, and if so, whether you could come in for a discussion. This request serves several purposes. It will motivate your audience to read the letter, if they haven't already. If they are undecided about interviewing you, it may tip the balance, because it is harder to say no over the phone. If you are turned down, ask why. This may be painful, but you may learn something about the present situation of the organization and its hiring plans, about how your qualifications fit or don't fit the needs of that workplace, or even about the contents of your résumé and covering letter. Even if you don't get an interview, you will be gathering valuable information.

FIGURE 10.1   Sample Unsolicited Letter of Application

95 Borden Gate
North York ON M5Q 2G7
May 12, 2009

Mr. Jerome Doucette
Director, Sales Division
IBM Microelectronics Canada Ltd.
3900 St. Hilaire Ave. E.
Montreal QC H1C 2T9

Dear Mr. Doucette

I am writing to inquire about employment opportunities in the sales division of
IBM Canada. As a graduate of the Business Computer Studies program at
Seneca College and an IBM-PC owner, I can offer your company a thorough
knowledge of IBM products and their business applications. In addition, I have
completed courses in marketing and personal sales.

As you can see from the enclosed résumé, I have financed my college
education by working part-time at Gentlemen's Tailors. While this experience
gave me the chance to apply knowledge acquired through college courses, the
most important thing I learned at Gentlemen's Tailors is I CAN SELL.

I believe that my education and sales ability would be an asset to your
company, and I would appreciate an opportunity to discuss this
personally with you in an interview. I am available any weekday before 2 PM.

Sincerely

James Gatti

James Gatti

3 ANSWERING A JOB ADVERTISEMENT

While you are researching potential employers through directories and personal contacts, you will, of course, be participating in the other job-seeking ritual: reading job postings in newspapers, college placement offices, Human Resource Centres of Canada, and on the Internet. While you will want to adapt good ideas from your unsolicited letters, the solicited letter of application has some different features. Begin by reading the advertisement or job posting several times, very carefully. A typical newspaper advertisement appears at the top of page 235.

Underline or highlight the words and phrases that would be particularly relevant if you were answering this ad. Remember that it costs money to run an advertisement. If an employer pays for space to include more information than the job title and the place to apply for it, it would be a fatal mistake to ignore this additional information. This may include both objective and subjective requirements. Objective requirements are measurable, for example, **previous sales experience, type 55 wpm, college diploma, CGA, speak Italian.** Subjective requirements are personal qualities such as **motivated, outgoing, self-starting, able to work without supervision, detail-oriented.** Pay particular attention to these subjective qualities; they give you valuable insight into how the employer perceives the job and the work environment. Compare the second and third advertisements on page 235. The objective requirements are the same, but the wording of the advertisements, particularly the personal qualities considered appropriate by each firm, reveals the different styles of the two workplaces. Perhaps you can see immediately that you would enjoy working at one place but not the other. In this case you need to write only one letter, showing that you are compatible with this job. If you feel that you could work in either environment, you could apply for both jobs, but you would need two very different letters of application.

Do not be tempted to falsify your personality. You may be flexible, but if you are a quiet, steady worker who prefers doing things on your own, with your own system, you would be very frustrated in a free-wheeling, team-oriented environment that required everyone to achieve consensus and then abide by the decisions of the group. On the other hand, if you like to socialize at work and be in a lively environment, you will soon grow depressed in a two-person office where you spend long periods of time staring at the screen. You may get a job by misrepresenting your personal qualities, but you won't keep it (or want to keep it) if you have to be someone you're not for 40 hours a week.

SHIPPING / RECEIVING / CUSTOMER SERVICE
$28 500

Nansen Laboratories, a leading manufacturer of veterinary drugs, requires a mature, self-motivated individual to fill the Assistant Manager position at our Regina location.

Experience incorporating shipping/receiving, customer service, computer entry is preferred.

Company benefits package available.

Résumé to Nansen Laboratories.

CASH AUDIT / ACCOUNTING CLERK

We are a ladieswear chain looking for a responsible individual who has an aptitude for figures and enjoys problem-solving. This person must be detail-oriented and capable of meeting deadlines. Familiarity with Microsoft Great Plains and Word required. Please send your résumé to ...

ACCOUNTING ASSISTANT

We are an expanding retail chain with an aggressive young management team. You possess the accounting, interpersonal, and organizational skills necessary to provide support for our busy operations. If you have Microsoft Great Plains and Word experience and are interested in career advancement, call ...

Assuming that the employee profile identified by the advertisement matches your attributes and qualifications and that you have marked in the ad the information you will need to write your letter, you can begin. The solicited letter of application is a persuasive message and follows the AIDA sequence.

Attention

Bring your letter to the **attention** of the appropriate reader by using his or her name and title. This may be stated in the advertisement. If not, or if the information is not complete, phone the company to get it. This is an important step; it demonstrates that you can take initiative and gives your letter a professional-looking opening. If it is absolutely impossible to get the name and title—for example, if you are replying to a box number or you can't afford to phone across the country to get a name—use a subject line instead of a salutation.

Example

Alberta Government Employment Office
10011–109 Street
Edmonton AB T5J 3S8

Subject: <u>Application for position as Director of Market Standards, competition no.</u>
<u>CCM942-3GM</u>

Interest

By advertising a job opening, your potential employer has already identified his or her need. Begin by stating the position applied for, using the job title exactly as posted, and state where and when you heard of it. This will ensure that your application reaches the appropriate person. An organization may have advertised various job openings.

Example

I am applying for the position of Special Events Assistant Coordinator advertised in the April 21 <u>Globe and Mail</u>.

Remember to underline the title of a newspaper, magazine, or website.

Desire

Since you have prepared a résumé to summarize most of the exact details normally included in the **desire** section, make sure your reader takes a look at it. If specific qualifications are called for in the advertisement (for example, recreation graduate, previous experience working with the disabled), mention briefly that you meet these requirements.

Example

As you can see from the enclosed résumé, I have a diploma in Office Administration from Mountainview College. In addition, I have worked part-time for four years as a receptionist.

If you do **not** have a particular qualification, say nothing about it. Avoid negative sentences like, "Although I do not have any work experience in this field...."

If relevant experience for this particular job is not on your résumé, add a sentence describing it.

Begin a new paragraph to describe your personal qualities. If some are called for in the ad, make sure that you talk about them. Support your statements with evidence.

Example

As a sales assistant in a small sporting goods store, I was frequently left in sole charge. This required responsibility, self-direction, and lots of problem-solving skills.

If no qualities are specifically mentioned, you should still describe your strong personal attributes. Look at the section on creating desire in the unsolicited letter (see page 231) for some suggestions.

Action

Ask for an interview, following the suggestions on page 232 under **action** in the unsolicited letter. See Figure 10.2 for a reply to the first advertisement on page 235.

Faxing an Application

Often a job posting will ask you to fax your résumé. Should you send just the résumé, or should you include a letter of application? On the one hand, asking for a fax suggests that the employer is pressed for time and wishes to make a decision quickly. A lengthy letter may well be ignored. On the other hand, unless the job requirements are completely objective—which is usual only in low-level, mechanical jobs—your résumé alone cannot supply all the relevant information. You might like to compromise by sending a fax cover sheet with a brief message pointing out the relevance of your skills and experience to the job you are applying for. If you send a longer message, avoid laying it out like a letter to be sent through the mail. Give it a more open format like the message on page 160.

Applying for Jobs Online

You can use the Internet to apply for jobs in two ways. The first is to use it as a kind of electronic bulletin board by posting your résumé where you hope it will be seen by a prospective employer. Current statistics for this method of finding a

FIGURE 10.2   Sample Solicited Letter of Application

23 Applewood Rd.
Saskatoon SK S7B 1E9
May 10, 2009

Ms. Lorna Harris
Manager, Nansen Laboratories
2230 Millgate Pkwy.
Regina SK S4G 3K2

Dear Ms. Harris

I am applying for the position of Assistant Manager advertised in the May 9
<u>Regina Leader Post</u>. As you can see from the enclosed résumé, I will be
graduating from the General Business program at Prairie College this June.
Before returning to school, I had three years' experience as a shipper/receiver.
College courses in data entry and computer applications, as well as customer
service training as night manager at Cooperative Cable, have given me the
experience you require.

As a returning student, I maintained a high B average while working at a
demanding part-time job and doing volunteer work with the People's Food Bank.
Your firm would benefit from my motivation, attention to detail, and excellent
communication skills. I would welcome the opportunity to discuss this position
with you further in an interview at your convenience.

Sincerely

George Kourakos

George Kourakos

job are not very encouraging. For example, workopolis.ca encourages employers to pay to search its database by pointing out that they have over one million résumés on file. The website jobhuntersbible.com estimates your chances of finding a job in this way as less than one-half of 1 percent.

A far better way to use the Internet is to look for job postings and apply to them electronically. Many company and government websites have a field where you can fill out or download an application form. Sites like monster.ca and workopolis.ca post job advertisements and allow you to reply to them by creating or attaching your résumé and forwarding it to the employer, with a covering letter if you wish. Remember that most employers posting jobs here will be screening for keywords.

4 APPLICATION FORMS

Application forms perform two functions for an employer. First, they assemble information about every employee's education, skills, and work history in a standard format. For this reason, you may be asked to fill out an application form **after** you have been offered a job, so that the employer can have this information officially on file. This application form will be part of your permanent record. If you have misrepresented any details on your application form, and this is discovered even years later, it could be grounds for firing you.

The second function of the application form is to create a streamlined résumé that can be quickly scanned by the person making the hiring decision. This saves time for someone looking for applicants with specific experience and education, usually for low-level jobs that do not require a wide variety of skills. Postings for these jobs often ask you to reply by telephone. If you pass the first screening, you will be asked to come in and fill out an application form. The employer may review your application on the spot and then interview you, or you may be asked to leave your application and wait to be contacted for an interview later. A hiring decision will be based mainly on whether your qualifications meet the requirements of the job, but of course, neat, accurate presentation will help your application make the best possible impression. Bring your chronological résumé with you to help you get the details complete and avoid having to cross out or add anything. Figure 10.3 shows you a typical application form filled out.

FIGURE 10.3   Sample Application Form

APPLICATION FOR EMPLOYMENT
(PLEASE PRINT)

08/06/06 Date
(Day, Month, Year)

Name Birdella Matthews

Address 15 Muriel Ave.   City Toronto   Prov ON   Apt No.

Postal Code M4K 3C3   Telephone No. (416) 555-1212

PLEASE INDICATE DATES AVAILABLE: Immediately

EDUCATION	Name of School	Course	DATE Started Mth\Yr	Left Mth\Yr	Grade Completed
High School	Eastern Commerce		Sept. 03	June 04	12
Vocational School					
College\University	Seneca College	Gen. Business	Sept. 04	June 06	Diploma

Details of other courses completed Computer Design, George Brown Continuing Education, 2005

Employment History: (Show most recent position first)

Employer & Address	Supervisor	Type of Work	Reason for Leaving	Date Started	Left
1. Black's Camera Gerrard Square	T. Lam	Ass. Manager Retail	Currently Employed	Dec. 04	
2. Tim Horton's 328 Pape Ave.	R. Richie	Food Service	Better Employment Opportunity	Sept. 03	Dec. 04
3. Pape Recreation Centre 821 Pape Ave.	J. Ross	Recreation Leader	Summer Contract	June 03	Sept. 03
4. Acme Marketing 231 Bathurst Ave.	E. Chau	Telemarketer	Return to School	June 02	Sept. 02

If applying for clerical\secretarial position:

List computer skills: Lotus ☐   W.P. ☐   Keyboarding Speed(wpm) [   ]
Other (list)

If applying for warehouse position, indicate experience.

Receiving ☐   Order filling ☐   Packing ☐   Shipping ☐   Lift Truck ☐   Pallett Truck ☐

General Information:

Have you any outside business activities or part-time jobs?   No   Describe

PERSON TO BE NOTIFIED IN CASE OF ACCIDENT OR EMERGENCY(Only if Hired)

Verna Matthews   (416) 555-1212
NAME   HOME TELEPHONE NUMBER
Mother   (416) 555-3800
RELATIONSHIP   BUS TELEPHONE NUMBER

It is understood and agreed that my employment is subject to receipt of satisfactory references.
The Company is authorized to make inquiries concerning the information given hereon and I agree to release any person or
organization from the consequences of answers to such inquiries. I understand that any deliberate misrepresentation by me on
this application will be sufficient cause for dismissal should I be employed by the company.

SIGNATURE Birdella Matthews

5 ORAL COMMUNICATION: REPLYING TO A JOB POSTING BY TELEPHONE

Sometimes organizations prefer to screen applicants by phone. If so, the advertisement will invite you to call a number and ask for a particular person. The person taking the calls will probably ask you a few questions, describe the job, and then take your name or ask you to come in with your résumé for an interview, or to fill out an application. Since a phone conversation can't be revised like a letter if you make mistakes, and since phoning can be naturally stressful anyway, you will need to prepare yourself if you want to make a good impression. Here are some general hints:

1. Read the ad thoroughly, and look over your résumé just before you call.
2. Have the advertisement and your résumé in front of you for reference. Have pen and paper handy to note directions and write in your calendar or date book.
3. When you are connected, identify yourself and the purpose of your call.
4. Listen carefully. Ask questions if you are confused or need to know something important. The location of the job, whether it is full-time or part-time, and the type of business are important questions, but don't get into details about the dental plan.
5. Listen carefully to the questions you are asked. Answer as briefly as possible; this is a screening call, not an interview. Put yourself in a positive light; sound confident. Don't apologize or put yourself down, even as a joke.
6. If you are asked to come in, be prepared to suggest a time and date (that's why you need your calendar or date book handy). Get directions and write them down.
7. If you are not asked, but you think you might like working there, take the initiative and ask if you can bring or mail a copy of your résumé.
8. Thank your listener and hang up.

Here is a sample telephone application:

Reception:	Hello, Acme Associates.
Kris Chong:	Hello. May I please speak to Donna Ross?
Reception:	May I ask who's calling?
Kris Chong:	My name is Kris Chong. I'm calling about the advertisement for a Junior Programmer in this morning's *Toronto Star*.

Reception:	One moment, please.
Donna Ross:	Donna Ross speaking.
Kris Chong:	Hello. My name is Kris Chong, and I'm calling about the Junior Programmer position advertised in the *Star* this morning.
Donna Ross:	Yes, Mr. Chong. Could you tell me something about your educational background?
Kris Chong:	I'm graduating this month in computer programming and operating from Maple Leaf College.
Donna Ross:	Have you had any work experience with computers?
Kris Chong:	I've used a computerized inventory system at my part-time job at National Tire, and I demonstrated software at the computer show this spring.
Donna Ross:	Well, we're looking for someone who's familiar with Lotus and is prepared to do some shiftwork. We're located in an industrial plaza, so you would need your own transportation.
Kris Chong:	Would this shiftwork involve weekends?
Donna Ross:	Saturdays, but no Sundays. Would you be available for an interview later today or tomorrow?
Kris Chong:	I could come in after 11:00 tomorrow.
Donna Ross:	Fine, if you could come in at 11:15 tomorrow and ask for me. Please bring a copy of your résumé. I'll just put you back to reception and you can get the directions.
Kris Chong:	Thank you very much. I look forward to meeting you.
Donna Ross:	Yes, I'll see you tomorrow, then. Goodbye.

CHAPTER REVIEW/SELF-TEST

1. A majority of people find a job through
   (a) posting a résumé on the Internet.
   (b) personal contacts.
   (c) answering an ad in the newspaper.
   (d) applying online.

2. If you have already chosen your preferred employment area you should be
   (a) relying on job advertisements to find openings.
   (b) posting your résumé and waiting for employers to contact you.
   (c) reading and networking to make contacts and find openings in your field.
   (d) postponing your job search until graduation.

3. You can explore possible areas of employment by
   (a) informally interviewing people who are currently working in jobs that might interest you.
   (b) researching job descriptions on the Human Resources and Skills Development Canada website.
   (c) finding tests and career advice on the Internet.
   (d) doing all of the above.

4. Researching the job market
   (a) is important only if you do not know what kind of job you are interested in.
   (b) will help you appear more knowledgeable in an interview.
   (c) can be left until you need to apply for a job.
   (d) is not important when the economy is booming.

5. A covering letter accompanying your résumé
   (a) is a waste of your reader's time and should be omitted.
   (b) helps your reader see how your qualifications would meet his or her needs.
   (c) is only useful when you are applying for a job by mail.
   (d) explains why this job is important to your career plans.

6. An **unsolicited** letter of application
   (a) uses the AIDA format.
   (b) begins by explaining why you need a job.
   (c) is written in response to a job posting.
   (d) all of the above.

7. A letter applying for a job that has been advertised
   (a) should focus only on objective job requirements.
   (b) should repeat all relevant information from your résumé.
   (c) is called a solicited letter of application.
   (d) should point out any qualifications mentioned in the advertisement that you don't have, along with the ones you do.

8. A **solicited** letter of application begins
   (a) by explaining why you want this job.
   (b) by identifying the job you are applying for.
   (c) with an attention-getting gimmick.
   (d) with a brief overview of your qualifications.

9. Which of the following sentences would be appropriate in the Desire section of a letter of application?
   (a) "I have always been a loyal customer of Club Casino fashions and it would be great to get an employee discount."
   (b) "Although I have only worked part-time in an electronics store up to now, I think I can handle the responsibilities of a management trainee in retail fashion."
   (c) "Please look over my résumé and see if you have any jobs I'm qualified for."
   (d) "Your business would benefit from my retail experience and knowledge of your product line."

10. Which of the following sentences would be appropriate in the Action section of a letter of application?
    (a) "I would appreciate the opportunity to discuss this position with you personally in an interview at your convenience."
    (b) "Thank you for taking the time to read this letter."
    (c) "I hope I will be hearing from you soon as I am anxious to start working for your wonderful firm."
    (d) all of the above.

Answers

1.B 2.C 3.D 4.B 5.B 6.A 7.C 8.B 9.D 10.A

EXERCISES

1. Select a company or organization you might like to work for. Using the resources of your library, collect a nucleus of ten to fifteen newspaper or magazine articles about your company. Throughout the semester, check current periodicals to select at least five more articles. On the basis of your material, give a five-minute class presentation on the positive features of working there.

2. Select a company or organization you might like to work for. Phone the company and request an appointment for an information-gathering interview with an appropriate person. The purpose of the interview is to obtain information about employment opportunities for college graduates. Here are some sample questions:
   (a) Does your company hire community college graduates?
   (b) What kinds of jobs are currently held by college graduates?
   (c) What college programs prepare students for employment at this company?
   (d) What further training, if any, is offered?
   (e) What strengths do community college graduates bring to employment with this company?
   (f) Has this employer identified any consistent weaknesses in the preparation of college graduates?
   (g) What additional skills or education would enhance a college graduate's chances of promotion?
   Share the information you have gathered with your classmates in the form of a handout or informal oral presentation.

3. Using your clipping file and/or interview as a resource, write an unsolicited letter of application to a company or organization that interests you.

4. Take a page from the employment section of a newspaper that contains jobs for which you will be qualified after graduation. Make a list of all the personal qualities asked for. Identify those that are requested most frequently. Select five qualities that you think you possess. For each one, write a sentence beginning, "My _____ is demonstrated by _____."

5. Choose an employment advertisement from a newspaper, college placement service, or other source. Write a letter applying for the job, using your own qualifications.

6. Visit one of the following:
   (a) Human Resource Centre of Canada
   (b) college placement office

(c) employment agency

(d) company that offers a trainee program (e.g., for management or sales jobs)

In a five-minute oral presentation, tell your class what kinds of jobs were available and what the advantages and disadvantages are of using this method of finding a job.

7. From the newspaper files in your college library, select an employment advertisement for a job in your field that appeared about a month ago. Call or visit the company, and ask the following questions:

(a) Why did you choose a newspaper advertisement to fill this job?

(b) Did you use additional methods?

(c) How many applicants responded to the advertisement?

(d) Were most of them qualified for the job?

(e) Did the successful applicant learn about the job from the newspaper?

(f) Did the successful applicant have all the qualifications you asked for?

Report your findings to the class.

CHAPTER THIRTEEN

· ·

PLANNING THE INFORMAL REPORT

Chapter Objectives

Successful completion of this chapter will enable you to:

1 Define "informational report," "analytical report," and "persuasive report."

2 Understand the basic principles of organizing the introduction, body, and closing of an informal report.

3 Plan and write an informal informational report, such as an incident report, a progress report, a trip report, or a periodic report.

4 Understand the purpose of printed report forms.

5 Plan and write the first draft of an analytical report.

6 Plan and write the first draft of a persuasive report.

1 INTRODUCTION: WHAT IS A REPORT?

A report is an account of what has been learned by any combination of study, observation, experimentation, measurement, experience, and analysis. It organizes the information gained from these activities in a way that is relevant to its purpose and clear and meaningful to the intended audience. In other words, there is no single "correct" report form. This chapter will give you some models to use when selecting and organizing information for any kind of purpose or audience.

Reports generally fall into three main categories: informational, analytical, and persuasive.

- **Informational reports** are written to present information clearly and concisely. Four types of informational reports are discussed in this chapter: incident reports, progress reports, trip reports, and periodic reports.
- **Analytical reports** are written to solve problems. The writer not only presents information but analyzes that information, draws conclusions, and recommends a solution or course of action.
- **Persuasive reports** are similar to analytical reports but are written to convince supervisors, colleagues, or other decision-makers to approve a new idea or practice. Proposals are the most common type of persuasive report.

2 REPORT FORMATS

Short reports (fewer than three pages) are usually written as **informal** reports, that is, as letters or memos. You would use a memo when writing to someone inside your organization, and a letter when reporting to someone outside your organization. In this chapter, all of the sample reports are informal.

A longer and more complex report usually requires a **formal** report format. In Chapter 14, you will find an example of a formal report and a discussion of the sections required in formal reports.

Introducing the Informal Report

The opening section of your report should help your audience interpret the information you are presenting. A good introduction contains at least the following four items: authorization, purpose, methodology/sources, and plan of presentation. The **authorization** tells the reader who requested the preparation of the report, and the **purpose** explains why. The **methodology/sources** section explains how you went about gathering the information in the report and where you found it. This section establishes the credibility of the contents of the report. The **plan of presentation** outlines the contents of the report in order.

Two other items may be appropriate in your introduction: background and recommendations. Give **background** information if your audience will need it to interpret the contents of the report. Make **recommendations** in the introduction of the report if you are using **direct order,** that is, if you have been asked to make recommendations and you do not expect any resistance to them on the part of your audience. If you are using **indirect order** because you think that your audience will regard your recommendations as bad news, or if you are adding recommendations on your own initiative, simply state that recommendations will be found at the end of the report. Figure 13.1 illustrates an appropriate introduction to the report discussed in exercise 1 on page 326.

Organizing the Body of the Report

The body of a report contains findings and supporting details. This is where you will present the information you have gathered relevant to the purpose of your report. Some **objective** models for organizing the body of a report include:

- **Geographic or Spatial.** A report on company hiring could be organized by store location.

FIGURE 13.1   Sample Introduction to an Informal Report

To: Maple Leaf College Student Council
From: Julie Yan Ping Chen, Fashion Retailing Student Representative *JC*
Date: 2008 11 26
Subject: Report on Fashion Boutique

At the request of Travis Ali, President of the Student Council, I have prepared a report on the Fashion Boutique at Maple Leaf College, with particular attention to problems raised by the Fashion Retailing students. Information was gathered from interviews with FRM students, the FRM Course Director, and the College Financial Officer. College policy on laboratory requirements was also researched. The following report presents information on the place of the boutique in the FRM program, the effectiveness of the current boutique as a teaching lab, and the feasibility of expanding the boutique. As a result of my investigation I recommend that the Student Council support the Fashion Retailing Students Association's petition to expand the boutique to be presented to the Board of Governors at their next meeting.

- **Functional.** A performance review of the president of your college might include sections on Government Liaison, Financial Management, Community Outreach, and other functions of the position.
- **Chronological.** A security guard would report an incident that required intervention by describing the events in the order they happened.

These models are objective, or natural, because the order is based on observable or measurable criteria such as location, function, or time. An objective model is often the best choice for a report that presents facts with few opinions or inferences and no recommendations.

Some **subjective** models include:

- **Comparison or Contrast.** The similarities and differences of two software programs could be examined to see which one was better suited to your company's needs.
- **Problem-Solution.** A report on campus traffic congestion would first identify the problem and the factors involved in finding and evaluating a solution, and then analyze the advantages and disadvantages of possible solutions.
- **Priority.** A progress report on IT upgrades on campus would begin with the most urgent requirements and end with "nice-to-have" items.

These models are subjective, or logical, because they depend on the writer's judgment. They are generally appropriate to analytical, persuasive, and problem-solving reports.

Closing the Report

A short informal report can end with the last item of the body. Do not waste your time summarizing what your audience took only a few moments to read in the first place. If you decided to put recommendations at the end of your report, use the heading **Recommendations** and then give a numbered list. If you are sending your report as a letter or memo, you may wish to add a brief action close mentioning appropriate follow-up.

3 PLANNING AND WRITING INFORMAL INFORMATIONAL REPORTS

Incident Reports

Many companies provide printed forms for incident reports (see Figure 13.6). However, if a form is not available, the following organization, also illustrated in Figure 13.2, is appropriate for a memo:

1. **Subject Line:** Clearly tell the reader what event the report describes.
2. **Introduction/Summary:** State briefly what happened, who was involved, when and where the incident took place, and what the significant outcomes were.
3. **Description of the Incident:** Detail exactly what happened, in chronological order, in objective language, and possibly under appropriate subtitles.
4. **Possible Causes:** You may offer your own opinion about possible causes and preventive measures.
5. **Action Taken:** State what you've done to follow up or correct the incident.
6. **Action Required:** List any further steps that need to be taken.

Progress Reports

Progress reports are usually written in memo format to inform management of the progress of a project. However, they are also required for other reasons, as is shown in the sample progress report in letter format in Figure 13.3. In this case a physiotherapist is reporting to the lawyer on the progress of a motor vehicle accident victim. When writing a progress report, describe the work completed, the work in progress, and the work still to be done. In some cases recommendations for adjustments to the project plan may be in order. The following sections are appropriate for a progress report, although variations, such as those illustrated in Figure 13.3, may be used, depending on the type of work being done.

1. **Subject Line:** Identify the document as a progress report, and name the project and dates covered by the report.
2. **Opening/Summary:** Fully identify the project and the people involved. Cover very briefly what has been done, what remains to be done, and whether the work is on time and on budget if applicable.
3. **Work Completed:** Describe what you've accomplished, perhaps including an overall schedule. If you're behind schedule, give the reasons.
4. **Work Underway or Problems Encountered:** Include this section only if needed. It is essential to be objective. Never place blame for a problem on an individual.
5. **Work to Be Completed:** Describe what needs to be done and how long it will take. If you are behind schedule, include a revised version. If you are over budget, request added funding, and justify the costs. Suggest how to solve problems if possible.

FIGURE 13.2 Sample Incident Report

To: Garret Johns, Director
From: Marilyn Solicki, Receptionist   *MS*
Date: February 12, 2007
Subject: Customer Injury at the Front Entrance

At 4:15 PM on February 12, a customer fell on a patch of ice that had accumulated at the front entrance. The customer, whose name is Hema Nalla, was able to walk but went directly by taxi to the emergency department at Queen's Hospital.

Description of Incident
When Ms. Nalla slipped on the ice just outside the front door, she fell on her left elbow. From my desk in the reception area, I was able to reach her quickly and help her to her feet. However, she was in pain and expressed concern as to whether she might have fractured a bone. I offered to call a taxi, which arrived ten minutes later. I waited inside the front doors with her until the taxi arrived. During this time, I took her phone number.

Possible Causes of Ice Accumulation
Since I am stationed near the front door, I am able to see a constant drip of water from the roof onto the concrete when it rains. My assessment is that the accumulation of water from this drip creates a dangerous situation when it has rained and the temperature then drops below the freezing point.

Action Taken
To avoid another accident, I retrieved some salt from the storeroom and spread it on the concrete.

Action Required
I will call Ms. Nalla tomorrow morning to inquire about her condition. The best solution to the problem of ice accumulation, although it occurs rarely, would be to repair the eavestrough over the front entrance.

FIGURE 13.3   Sample Progress Report

GRAAF PHYSIOTHERAPY CLINIC
199 Colborne Street Sarnia ON   N7T 6B2

February 3, 2009

Mr. William Nelson
Nelson, Johnson, and Associates
34 Dunlop Street
Barrie ON L4M 3X7

Dear Mr. Nelson

Re: Paul Goldstein's Progress, September 22, 2008 to present

Paul Goldstein has been receiving physiotherapy since September 22, 2008, to rehabilitate injuries sustained in a motor vehicle accident on September 18, 2008. A report of the initial assessment was sent to you on September 26, 2008. Paul has been making satisfactory progress, except for his right shoulder, which appears to need orthopedic intervention. He is now ready to attempt work in a volunteer position similar to his former employment.

<u>Treatment and progress to date</u>
Treatment consisted of education regarding posture, self-mobilization exercises, home stretching, strengthening routines, stabilization, and functional retraining of the trunk, upper extremities, and neck. Paul was shown progressively more home exercises with the use of weights, latex tubing, and "physio ball." I occasionally applied manual techniques to the cervical and thoracic areas to promote flexibility, as well as stimulation to the right shoulder to reduce irritability of the glenohumeral joint.

Paul has shown good motivation and compliance throughout and expressed good insight into his situation. The pain is still a daily presence but much less of a limitation on Paul's functioning. The right shoulder seems to be at a static level, despite regular stretching, and seems to need orthopedic intervention. I wrote a report on November 21, 2008, to his physician, Dr. Angela Harris, regarding my concern about the shoulder. In this report I requested the services of Dr. Carolina Avendano, an orthopedic specialist and well known as an expert on shoulder and knee evaluation and arthroscopy.

Treatment dates
September 25, 27, 29
October 2, 4, 6, 10, 13, 20, 23, 25, 27, 31
November 1, 7, 13, 15, 20, 22, 24, 27, 29
December 1, 4, 6, 8, 15, 16, 20, 27, 29
January 5, 9, 12, 16, 19, 23, 26, 30

Plans
Paul is starting a volunteer assistant position at the Salvation Army shop in
February, 2009 for a few hours three times weekly. This will allow him to slowly
test the functioning of his upper body and extremities on the job. I will continue
to adjust his exercise for at home and at the clinic until we have a thorough
impression of his functioning in the shop. Then I will start to plan his discharge,
unless the orthopedic intervention necessitates further physiotherapy.

Prognosis
The prognosis for Paul's neck is reasonably good, providing the nerve
regeneration progresses as expected. The neck function will never be
100 percent but should allow him to function within his chosen trade. The
prognosis for his right shoulder depends on the intervention of a specialist. At
the moment, the shoulder has limited function and will not allow Paul to reach a
normal level of capacity in his trade.

If you require more information, please call me at 728-1992.

Sincerely

Sebastian Graaf

Sebastian Graaf
M.C.P.A., M.A.A.O.M., C.A.F.C.
Registered Physiotherapist

Chapter Thirteen: Planning the Informal Report

Trip Reports

A trip report is usually required when an employee is sent on a business trip or to a conference. Even if a report is not required, managers appreciate receiving an account of information or accomplishments that could be helpful to the company. The report should focus on the most important gains made on the trip. An itinerary (chronological account of activities) may be appropriate in some situations and can be included as an attachment. A sample trip report is provided in Figure 13.4.

1. **Subject Line:** Give the name of the conference or destination.
2. **Opening/Summary:** Give the destination, purpose, and the dates of the trip, as well as an overview of the contents of the report. Name the colleagues who went with you.
3. **Background:** It may be appropriate to give background information to establish the context within which the trip occurred, or to elaborate on the purpose of the trip.
4. **Discussion:** Describe the main gains you have made and the benefits to the company. Use appropriate headings.
5. **Closing:** Using an appropriate heading, suggest action to be taken or explain the value of the experience.

Periodic Reports

Periodic reports are those that are produced regularly to keep people informed of some aspect of operations. Some reports, such as accounts of weekly sales, can be produced with very little effort by software designed for keeping track of daily activities. If a company uses point-of-sale software to record inventory, sales, customer profiles, appointment schedules, or other valuable information, reports summarizing any of this information can be produced with a few keystrokes. If you are submitting a report of this kind to a manager, place it in a memo with an appropriate explanation. It is helpful to you and your readers to develop a standard format for such reports. Figure 13.5 is an example of a periodic report.

FIGURE 13.4   Sample Trip Report

MEMORANDUM

To: Marsha Lipman, Sales Manager   Date: September 18, 2007
From: Peter Wood, Sales Representative   PW
Subject: Western Region Sales Conference

On September 14, I attended the Acme Cleaning Products Ltd. regional conference in Hamilton, Ontario. Don Hammond, Ann Cheung, and I arranged a car pool to keep expenses down. The most interesting and practical parts of the conference were the keynote speech and the packaging display.

President's Message on Environmental Issues
The keynote speech, by Alan Drucker, president, outlined the efforts of the research division to develop more environmentally friendly products. Mr. Drucker cited market research showing that future sales will depend more and more on a reputation for environmental consciousness. He stressed the importance of sales representatives' efforts to make sure retailers understand the company's strength in this area. To increase our product knowledge, he is planning a monthly newsletter that will go to all sales personnel, describing the advances made by our research division.

Packaging Issues
Proposed packaging designs were displayed at lunch with the intention of garnering feedback from sales representatives on their effectiveness. I was pleased to see this move toward more communication between the two departments because our contact with retailers gives us insight into the effects of package designs once the products are on the shelves.

Action Planned
To follow up on the president's keynote speech, I think it would be a good idea to devote ten minutes to discussing the contents of the newsletters at our monthly meetings. If you agree, I would be happy to provide a quick summary of the information and lead the discussion. In addition, I have begun to write down my thoughts on packaging improvements and will submit a memo detailing my suggestions to the director of packaging, with a copy to you.

FIGURE 13.5 Sample Periodic Report

MEMORANDUM

To: Marianne Lightfoot Date: November 1, 2007
cc. Jan Welby
From: Joan Desrosiers, Atlantic Foundations Program (ext. 1631) JD
Subject: Mid-term count for Fundamentals of Mathematics

Here is the mid-term count of the number of students in Fundamentals of Math. We have 363 active students (students who have appeared for at least one test) out of the 407 students enrolled in the course. The 44 students who are not active are all shown on the registrar's list. We can expect that, as usual, many of the inactive students have dropped out of college entirely, but these figures will not be known until next semester. As a matter of interest, I have found at least eight students who were exempted by the College Placement Test but are attending classes.

<u>Figures by Program Area</u>

Program Area	Active	Inactive	Total
Business	162	19	181
Hotel Management	23	4	27
Technology	<u>178</u>	<u>21</u>	<u>199</u>
Total	363	44	407

Please call me if you have any questions.

---

4 PRINTED REPORT FORMS

Many organizations provide **printed forms** for frequently written reports. For instance, incident report forms are standard in hospitals. Although filling out forms may seem an unpleasant chore, they have been designed to save work. The writer does not have to plan a report from scratch, and the people who make use of the reports can quickly locate specific information on the form. Figure 13.6 shows a typical report form.

FIGURE 13.6 Sample Report Form

Incident Report Form

Date: _____ Time of incident: _____

Type of incident: _____

_____

Patient/other involved: _____

Staff involved/witness: _____

Other witness(es): _____

Description of incident: _____

_____

_____

Action taken: Ambulance _____ First aid _____ CPR _____ Other _____

Equipment involved (if any): _____

Signed: _____   _____
            (patient/other)   (staff/witness)

5 PLANNING AND WRITING AN ANALYTICAL REPORT

Analytical reports are written to solve problems. The writer must define a problem clearly, present researched information about its causes and possible solutions, analyze the information, draw conclusions, and often make recommendations.

The first step in planning your report is to review your research notes and ensure that all your material is relevant to your **main question.** Focus on the **purpose** of your report, not the **subject** of your report, when deciding what information you will present to your audience. Then prepare an outline, beginning with the main headings you will use in your report. A major difference between a report and an essay or a piece of correspondence is that a report has **conspicuous** organization. Your audience will be guided through your report by headings and perhaps subheadings, which provide an outline of the report's contents. Once you have selected appropriate headings you will want to put them in order. An analytical report generally uses a subjective order such as order of importance or problem-solution. It should be clear to your audience that you have a reason for presenting the information in the order you have chosen; no jumping from minor items to major ones and then back to minor items, for example.

If any section is longer than 150–200 words you may wish to make it easier to read by using subheadings to divide the information into smaller units.

The ways in which information can be divided and combined depend on your audience and purpose, so they are infinitely varied. There are, however, rules for testing the logic and consistency of the divisions you have chosen. Here are some important ones:

1. **Keep all divisions equal in their respective orders.** For example, if you are discussing forest conservation, using New Brunswick, Quebec, and British Columbia as major headings, Northern Ontario cannot be added to this list without violating this rule. You would have to use "Ontario" as the major heading, with Northern and Southern Ontario as subheadings, if required.

2. **Apply a consistent principle of division.** The headings New Brunswick, Quebec, British Columbia, and Ontario indicate a geographical or political principle of division. A major heading like "History of Forest Conservation" would be inconsistent with this principle. It could, however, be used as a subheading under each major heading.

3. **Create subheadings only when discussing more than one topic under a heading.**

✗ POOR
   1.0 Opponents of Free Trade Deal
   1.1 Labour unions

   2.0 Impact on Selected Industries

✓ IMPROVED
   1.0 Opponents of Free Trade Deal
   1.1 Labour unions
   1.2 Arts community

   2.0 Impact on Selected Industries

or

✓ IMPROVED

1.0 Opposition by Labour Unions to Free Trade Deal

2.0 Impact on Selected Industries

4. **Keep all headings and subheadings grammatically parallel.** Do not mix noun phrases with verb phrases, or sentences with sentence fragments.

✗ POOR

1.0 Beginning the process

2.0 To monitor the final product

3.0 The location of markets

✓ IMPROVED

1.0 Beginning the process

2.0 Monitoring the final product

3.0 Locating markets

In the proposal report on page 321, the four rules of division are effectively integrated.

Once you have created your outline you can write your introduction, which will include a brief overview of your plan of presentation. If you are using the **direct order,** your introduction will also include your recommendations for appropriate action. If you are offering recommendations without having been asked to, or if you feel that your recommendations will be more effective after the audience has read the rest of the report, you should use **indirect order,** placing them at the end in a separate section.

Review your completed report for an objective tone. Remember that a primary purpose of every report is to present information. Support your analysis with facts, which your audience can use to evaluate your conclusions and recommendations.

A sample analytical report is shown in Figure 13.7.

FIGURE 13.7   Sample Analytical Report

To: Members of the Management Committee
From: Filipa Chen, Assistant Building Manager   *FC*
Date: 2008 06 06
Subject: Report on Reducing Parking Costs

At the last Management Committee meeting, Building Manager John Soriano
reported that providing parking for an estimated 38 new employees would cost
the company approximately $12 000 annually. As requested by the committee,
the building manager's office has explored ways of reducing this potential
expense. Information has been obtained from the Victoria Transport Policy
Institute (www.vtpi.org) and the Canadian Urban Transportation Association
(www.cutaactu.ca) as well as the General Accounting Manager. This report
explains how savings can be realized from reduced parking demand and
recommends financial incentives to encourage more efficient commute modes.

Parking Costs
Financial
Currently Acme Systems' building lease includes the use of 153 parking
spaces on the surrounding land. On a typical day the lot is filled close to
capacity. Additional parking spaces currently cost $438 each per year. Local
tax increases and zoning restrictions may cause this price to rise faster than
inflation.

Indirect
Acme has no free parking available for visitors, which may discourage some
potential clients. Land previously leased for equipment storage was converted
to parking space in 2001, requiring the leasing of storage space off-site
costing $8300 per year.

Strategies for Reducing Employee Parking Demand
Pay Parking
Ninety-five percent of employees in this community park free at their
workplace. Charging Acme employees for the use of a parking space could
create problems with recruitment and retention.

Transit Benefits
In the United States, where transit benefits are not taxable, offering free or
subsidized transit passes as an employee benefit has been shown to reduce
car commute trips by an average of 20%. In Canada, transit benefits are

currently taxable, reducing their potential value to our employees. Efforts are underway to change this policy, so far without success.

<u>Parking Cash Out</u>
This plan offers employees the cash equivalent of the value of a parking space if they use an alternative method of getting to work. Employees can agree to use this method all the time, or a certain number of days per week or month for a smaller percentage of the benefit. This plan has been shown to reduce car commute trips by 20% to 39% in a large number of studies available at the websites mentioned above. Administration typically requires two minutes per employee per month.

Recommendations
Acme Financial Systems should implement a Parking Cash Out plan to encourage employees to use transit, carpools, and other alternatives to single occupant vehicles for getting to work.

To realize the greatest financial benefit from this plan, Acme should request that parking space be shown as a separate line item in its building lease. If the plan succeeds, the need for parking space may drop below the current 153 spaces.

6 PERSUASIVE REPORTS

Although problem-solving reports often have a persuasive element, proposals are written expressly to convince someone to approve or take some kind of action. The greatest challenge to the writer is to anticipate all the questions the reader might ask in order to make a "yes" or "no" decision. The typical headings in a proposal are found in Table 13.1. The headings are matched with questions the reader is expected to ask. They may be varied to suit the content of the report. Figure 13.8 is an example of an effective proposal.

TABLE 13.1   Comparison of Proposed Headings and Reader Questions

Typical Heading	Reader Questions
Proposal	What do you want to do?
Problem Statement	What's the problem and its background?
	Why do we need to act at all?
Benefits	How will your proposal solve the problem?
	What's in it for me? For the company?
Project Details	What are the details of your proposal?
(Implementation)	What are the main tasks for implementing your proposal? What specifically has to be done?
	How will it all work (the nitty-gritty details)?
Schedule/Deadlines	What's your schedule?
	What are the details of that schedule?
Evaluation	How will you know if your proposal is successful?
	How do you plan to evaluate your results?
Other	What are the potential problems with your proposal?
Considerations	But what if ...?
	How do you plan to overcome these difficulties?
Personnel	Who will be involved in this project?
Qualifications	What are their qualifications?
	Why should I believe you can do the job?
Cost/Budget	How much will all this cost?
	Where exactly will the money be spent?
Alternatives	What else did you consider to arrive at your solution?
Considered	Why did you rule out those solutions?
	Using what criteria?

Source: From *Business Communication Strategies and Skills*, 4/E by HUSEMAN. © 1996. Reprinted with permission of Nelson, a division of Thomson Learning: www.thomsonrights.com. Fax 800-730-2215.

FIGURE 13.8   Sample Proposal

To: Leona Hutchison, Coordinator, Student Summer Project Fund,
          Seneca College
From: Tony Bastien, Student, Centre for Individualized Learning   *TB*
Date: March 19, 2007
Subject: Request to Student Summer Project Fund for an interest-free loan as
          starting capital for a catering service.

Proposal
A survey of job sites in York Region has shown the need for a catering service during the busy construction period from May 15 to August 15. This proposal asks for $2478.38 in a 120-day, non-interest loan to enable three students to set up a business to meet this need.

Problem Statement
During the summer, many seasonal projects—short- and long-term, government and private—are planned for areas not served by established catering companies. Since January 2007, I have been in touch with 37 construction and contracting firms intending to do business in York Region this summer. My survey has identified 18 sites starting up from May 15 that are still without catering contracts, and they are interested in having students supply this need. Each site employs an average of 23 workers. The total workforce is 415. More sites may become available.

Area of Operation
The area of York Region surveyed is bounded by Steeles Avenue in the south, Hwy. 404 in the west, Hwy. 48 in the east, and the Stouffville Side Road in the north.

Employees
There will be three employees: one driver/salesman and two cooks. I have delivered food products in the past and have an extensive background in retail sales.

Gerry Big Canoe is a student in George Brown College's chef program. He has worked several summers at the Royal York Hotel.

John McBeak is a business management student at the University of Toronto. Last summer he worked for a catering company.

(continued)

Operating Procedures

Cooks:

Sunday to Thursday, food will be prepared during the day and refrigerated overnight. (We live together, so we will cook on our own stove and use our spare refrigerator.)

Monday to Friday, at 8:00 AM, one cook will pick up fresh produce and supplies at the wholesaler. At 10:00 AM, the other employee will make the bank deposit.

Driver:

8:00 AM Heat up food in microwave and place everything in coolers in the van.

10:00 AM Leave for first call.

10:45 AM Make first call on route designed to cover 18 sites in 3 1/2 hours (about average for a caterer).

2:15 PM Finish lunch route and begin return calls to larger sites.

4:00 PM Fuel van and return home.

Supplies and Equipment Needed

—Van (Econo-Van leased for $340.00 per month)

—Coffee urn (100-cup; works on 12 volt auto system $299.39)

—Coolers (two for hot food, one for cold food, one for cold drinks $213.79)

—Stove

—Microwave oven—at home

—Refrigerator

—Food supplies: A friend in the catering business told me that with 415 potential customers, I'd have to prepare 50 hot lunches, 150 hot sandwiches, 100 cold sandwiches, 200 cups of coffee, and 200 cold drinks per day, not including snacks.

Table A

Operating Costs and Income

Breakdown of Food Costs:

	Cost	Retail	Cost	Retail	Gross Profit
Hot lunch (50)	$1.95	$2.75	$ 97.50	$137.50	$ 40.00
Hot sandwich (150)	1.30	1.80	195.00	270.00	75.00
Cold sandwich (100)	1.00	1.40	100.00	140.00	40.00
Coffee (200)	.20	.40	40.00	80.00	40.00
Cold drinks (200)	.45	.55	90.00	110.00	20.00
			$522.50	$737.50	$215.00

Table B
Detailed Budget

Start-up Costs

Fixed Costs:
—Coolers 4 at $49.95 + tax = $199.80 + $13.99 $ 213.79
—Van @ $340/pm × 3 mo. = $1020.00: Deposit on van   340.00
—Coffee urn $279.99 + 19.60 tax   299.59
—Insurance for 3 months   162.50
                                                    $1015.88 $1015.88

Operating Costs (First Week):
—Gasoline $30.00/day × 5 $150.00
—Salaries $120.00/day ($5.00/h × 8h/d × 3) × 5   600.00
                                                     $750.00   750.00

Food Preparation Cost (First Week):
—See Table A $522.50 × 5 $2612.50   2612.50
                                                                    4378.38
Less own start-up capital   1900.00
Total amount requested $2478.38

Table C

Total Projected Costs and Income (12 weeks or 60 days):
—Fixed costs from Table B $ 1 015.88
—Van for two remaining months   680.00
—Operating costs (Table B) $750.00 × 12   9 000.00
—Food costs (Table B) $2612.50 × 12   31 350.00
                                                     42 045.88

—Retail income (Table A) $737.50/d × 60   44 250.00
—Net profit $ 2 204.12

Conclusion
Table A shows that the daily gross profit will be about $215.00.

(continued)

Table B outlines the fixed start-up costs plus the first week's costs for operating and food preparation. These figures form the basis for the funds requested under the student assistance program.

Table C indicates that when all is said and done at the end of the summer, there should be a healthy net profit for the three partners to divide.

As you can see, this gives us considerable leeway if the profits are not as good as anticipated. On the other hand, we may do better.

The fact that we are putting up 43.4 percent of the start-up capital indicates that we are serious in our planning. We are considering a partnership in this area after we graduate, with hopes of hiring students to fill future summer needs.

I would be glad to discuss this proposal with you at any time. I would also appreciate any suggestions.

CHAPTER REVIEW/SELF-TEST

1. A report is considered **informal** if
   (a) you don't worry too much about planning or presentation.
   (b) it has no more than three pages and is presented as a letter or memo.
   (c) it provides information but does not draw conclusions or make recommendations.
   (d) its contents have not yet been completely researched or verified.

2. The **introduction** to an informal report should contain at least
   (a) the authorization, purpose, methodology, and plan of presentation of the report.
   (b) a summary of the report and any recommendations you wish to make.
   (c) a brief statement of your personal views on the subject of the report.
   (d) three important things that the reader will learn by reading the report.

3. The most important factor in deciding where to place any recommendations you will be making in your report is
   (a) visual impact on the page.
   (b) the length of your report.
   (c) maintaining the reader's interest in reading the entire report.
   (d) whether you expect your audience to respond positively or negatively to your recommendation(s).

4. The **body** of an informal report
   (a) follows an invariable format.
   (b) contains five sections: who? what? where? when? why?
   (c) presents findings and important details in a meaningful order.
   (d) does all of the above.

5. The **conclusion** of an informal report should not require
   (a) a summary.
   (b) recommendations.
   (c) any suggestions regarding appropriate follow-up.
   (d) any of the above.

6. Incident reports, progress reports, trip reports, and periodic reports
   (a) are examples of informal informational reports.
   (b) are usually organized in an objective or natural order.
   (c) can often be done on a printed form or computer template.
   (d) all of the above.

7. Analytical reports
   (a) present opinions and logical conclusions rather than facts.
   (b) can often be done on a printed form or computer template.
   (c) use facts and logic to define a problem and present possible solutions.
   (d) always use the direct order.

8. Headings for the sections of your report
   (a) are optional.
   (b) should give the reader an outline of the contents of the report.
   (c) can be limited to three: Introduction, Body, Conclusion.
   (d) should be general so as not to give away too much information.

9. Which of the following is **not** a rule for dividing your report under appropriate headings?
   (a) Apply a consistent principle of division.
   (b) Keep all headings and subheadings grammatically parallel.
   (c) Keep all divisions in order.
   (d) Create a subheading only when discussing at least two items under a main heading.

10. Unlike an analytical report, a proposal
    (a) is explicitly committed to persuading the audience to make a specific decision.
    (b) uses facts and logic to support its conclusions.
    (c) makes a recommendation.
    (d) can be presented as a memo or a letter.

Answers

1.B 2.A 3.D 4.C 5.A 6.D 7.C 8.B 9.C 10.A

EXERCISES

1. Your college operates a fashion boutique on the ground floor of the main college building. It is used as a teaching lab by the fashion program. All fashion students are required to work in the boutique as part of their course requirements. Students have complained for a number of years that the boutique is too small. You have been asked to investigate problems with the boutique and to prepare a report for the student council. Here are the notes, in no particular order, that you gathered from students, faculty, and the college's Financial Officer.

   - The boutique stocks women's clothing and accessories.
   - The boutique has an area of 22 m².
   - All students in the fashion program must work in the boutique.
   - Boutique receipts are given for all purchases.
   - There is no storage area in the boutique.
   - College policy allows 1 m² of lab space for each student.
   - Forty-seven percent of the college's students are women.
   - If more space were available, the boutique manager would like to involve marketing and accounting students in running the boutique.
   - There are 237 fashion students.
   - Students consistently give working at the boutique high marks in their course evaluation.
   - The main customers of the boutique are members of the college support staff.
   - There are two change rooms in the boutique.
   - Sixteen fashion students are men.
   - Taking over the lounge next door would double the area of the boutique.
   - Customer traffic is highest between noon and 2 PM.
   - Expanding the boutique would cost $113 000.
   - The lounge is now a lunch spot and make-out zone.
   - Spending per student in the fashion program is the third-lowest in the college.
   - With increasing enrollment, leisure space for students is declining in absolute terms.
   - Everything in the boutique is sold at reduced prices at the end of the school year.

Create an outline for your report, grouping your information in a logical order. Eliminate any irrelevant material. Write a 150-word introduction containing your principal recommendation(s).

2. You are the Assistant Director of Building Services at your college. Currently the college spends $473 000 per year to have its garbage collected. You have been asked by your supervisor, Fatima Khan, to think about ways this expense could be reduced. After looking at information about composting on Internet sites, checking with local government sources, and talking to a manager at another college, which has a composting program in place, you believe that composting could be part of the solution at your college.

   (a) Create an outline of appropriate headings and subheadings for a two-page report on establishing a composting program at your college.

   (b) Write the introduction to your report. Include at least two recommendations.

3. Write a periodic report covering your school-related activities for the past week.

4. You have received the following e-mail from your supervisor at Helping Hands Placement Service.

Subject: Search for new marketing ideas
From: Robert Cirillo, Director
Date: Wed, 31 May 2006 14:01-0400
To: emailuser <emailuser@helphands.ca>

According to the front page of today's business section, 47% of employed Canadians work in businesses with fewer than 100 employees. Is there some way Helping Hands could do a better job finding clients in this sector? Currently our agency places almost all its temporary workers in medium and large firms. E-mail me with your thoughts on this before our meeting on Friday.

Robert Cirillo, Director

Which of the following short reports would be a better response to this message? Explain your choice.

(a)

I was very happy to get your request as I have been thinking about this issue myself. I decided to talk to some of the small businesses which do use our services and ask them to tell me what attracted them to Helping Hands. Typically a business uses a temp agency when they foresee that workers will only be needed for a short-term project or when an absent worker needs to be replaced until he or she returns. Companies do not want to make a long-term commitment in these circumstances. Because large companies experience these situations all the time, it is natural for them to deal regularly with a placement agency. A small business may have this situation arise very rarely. I think that in these situations they are more likely to try to make do by double-tasking workers who are already there.

But hiring a temporary worker is really a more efficient and cost-saving choice. Of course, if we say this it looks as though we are just trying to get more business. I think we should ask some of the small businesses who do use Helping Hands to offer testimonials in an advertising campaign. In my opinion a small business owner would be more likely to take the word of another small business owner.

(b)

In response to your message I looked in the company database to find the names of two small businesses which have used Helping Hands in the last year, and contacted the managers to ask why they used our service. Both Sherene Hariprasad at Fitness Basics and Tim Chan at Acme Systems explained that they had previously worked at larger companies which had hired workers from Helping Hands. They knew from that experience that hiring a temporary worker is more efficient and cost-saving than trying to get regular workers to take on extra tasks. If we could get this word out to more small businesses we could build our client base. An advertising campaign using the experiences of real small business owners could help us do this. Both Hariprasad and Chan were willing to be involved. Let me know if you would like me to follow up on this for Friday's meeting.

5. You are the Assistant Director of Communications for the Canadian Olympic Hall of Fame. To publicize the Hall of Fame, the director wants to place an advertising supplement celebrating the centennial of Canada's first Olympic gold medal in *Maclean's*. The magazine publisher is interested in the concept, and you have been asked to prepare a proposal for her. Which of the following would be a better outline? Explain your choice.

(a) I. The history of the Canadian Olympic movement
    A. The founding of the modern Olympic Games
    B. Canada participates for the first time
    C. Olympic Games in Canada
    D. Who are Canada's Olympic medalists?
  II. The Hall of Fame magazine insert
    A. Historic events to be included
    B. Athletes to be featured
    C. Interviews and pictures
    D. Production schedule
  III. Pros and Cons of magazine insert

(b) I. Introduction: Why is this insert a good idea?
    A. Insert would make money for magazine
    B. Insert would raise Olympic profile
    C. Insert would attract visitors to Hall of Fame
  II. Insert Description
    A. High points of Canada's Olympic history
    B. Interviews with Olympic medalists
    C. Pictures of Hall of Fame exhibits
    D. Advertisements
  III. Production Plan
    A. Organizational overview
    B. Timeline
    C. Magazine's responsibilities
  IV. Next Steps

6. Create an outline suitable for a report on the factors that influenced your choice of college program.

7. Indicate which report plan would be most effective for the following situations: indirect order (recommendations at the end) or direct order (recommendations within the introduction).
   (a) The audience reading report has no power to implement or change recommendations—report simply keeps the audience informed. _____
   (b) The report's conclusions are good news. _____
   (c) The report's recommendations are very technical and complex. _____
   (d) The supporting data are very technical and complex. _____
   (e) The audience has a strong bias. _____
   (f) The audience is pressed for time. _____
   (g) The recommendations are significantly different from what was originally suggested. _____
   (h) The conclusions of the report are bad news. _____

HANDLE WITH CARE

Chapter 9

Marketing in the Human Services: Creating Brochures and Flyers

Overview: This chapter discusses marketing in human services agencies, explaining the uses of marketing and methods of reaching the public.

Why Market My Service?

An American manufacturer of baby food used to advertise its products with the slogan "Babies are our business—our only business." Community service agencies might rephrase that old slogan as "People are our business—our only business." Without clients, the agency cannot perform its function, which is, after all, helping clients. That's why agencies need to market—they need to reach people to be effective. An agency or centre that no one is aware of is failing to live up to its mandate as a community service organization.

Who Is My Audience?

Your target audience depends on your purpose. Do you want to be sure that other professionals are aware of your agency, so that they can make referrals? Do you want potential clients to be aware of your existence, so that they can self-refer?

Do you want companies and civic organizations to realize that your agency would be a worthy recipient of their charitable contributions? Do you want to reach potential individual donors?

If part of your mandate is education, is there a group you wish to reach, either with information or with an invitation to a specific function, such as a demonstration, lecture, or workshop?

How Do I Market?

This is the tough part, at first. However, the process of marketing the community service agency can be learned, and it can be enjoyable. It is important to remember that you are advertising your agency, and *advertising* is primarily a *visual medium*. It is essential that whatever brochures or flyers you produce be attractive visually. The steps below outline the details more fully, but be aware at the outset that whatever you produce must be pleasing to the eye.

Marketing Step One: Selecting a Medium

You are the director of a youth outreach service, called Freedom, which deals with drug and alcohol addiction in youths aged 8 to 16. You do not do counselling; your mandate is to provide education and referral. Your catchment area is Sydney, Nova Scotia. The service has just opened, and your profile is so low as to be nonexistent. How do you make people aware of your agency?

First of all, whom do you want to be aware of your services (who is your target audience)?

- adolescents
- their parents
- their teachers
- other professionals

Different groups can be reached through different media. What are the options?

- *Newspapers:* Local or community newspapers are ideal for reaching a specific audience. Newspaper staff are always looking for human-interest or newsworthy material, so a call to the paper might lead to an article being written on your service. Many newspapers also have a community page, where nonprofit groups can advertise free of charge. You could also place a classified ad in the personals section, but the first two options would be more likely to reach people.

- *Television:* Cable TV provides community channels where nonprofit groups can often advertise free of charge.
- *Letters:* Letters to community leaders, such as school principals, presidents of school PTAs, and religious leaders (notices can sometimes be placed free of charge in church bulletins)—all of these things can serve to introduce your service. You also need to introduce your agency to other professionals.
- *Presentations:* An open house, a presentation at a PTA meeting, or a talk at a lodge meeting are good ways to directly contact your audience.
- *Brochures and flyers:* These can be effective methods of marketing, but how will you distribute them? Direct mailing on a wide scale is prohibitively expensive. An alternative, especially when dealing with a geographically defined area, is contracting for house-to-house delivery. You could also make use of community groups again, such as by delivering brochures to schools to be given to each student. Public libraries are also useful distribution points.

Let's say you decided to explore all these possibilities. You contacted the community paper, and a reporter will be interviewing you next week. You contacted the cable company, and they'll be running the following ad for you:

TEENS
Problems or questions about
alcohol or other drugs?

FREEDOM
can help. We're confidential.
Call us anytime.
622-5465

You also have written a semipersonalized letter to the school principals in the area (by semipersonalized I mean that each principal gets the same form letter, but with appropriate names and addresses changed so that it doesn't look like a form letter). The letter looks like this:

Semipersonalized Letter

```
FREEDOM
Youth Outreach Service
54 Mimico Avenue
Sydney, Nova Scotia

Dear          :

FREEDOM is a community-based youth outreach ser-
vice, dealing with drug and alcohol addiction in
Sydney youths aged 8 to 16. We do not do counselling
but, rather, concentrate on education and referrals
to other agencies. We focus on drug and alcohol edu-
cation and are available to speak to students and
to community, parent, or religous groups. We are
ready to talk to groups of any size. Our presenta-
tions are, of course, free of charge.

We also refer youths or families with addiction-
related problems to appropriate agencies. Our ser-
vice is confidential.

Please feel free to call on us at any time, either
to book a presentation or to ask any questions you
may have about our agency or about youth drug/alco-
hol use in Sydney. We have enclosed a brochure
describing our agency. We would be happy to forward
extra copies if you would like to distribute our
brochures to your students.

Children in trouble need our help. Please introduce
your students to FREEDOM.

Sincerely,

Jean Paul Gauthier
Director
```

You're sending the same letter to the schools' PTA presidents, and a slightly different letter to the religious leaders in the area, requesting that they mention the new service in a bulletin or in front of their congregation.

You're working on the letter announcing your agency to the professional community, and you are planning to ask some community groups if they would consider you as a guest speaker. What you need to work on immediately, though, is a brochure and a flyer to send out with all these letters.

Brochures and Flyers

What's the difference between a brochure and a flyer? A flyer, as I'm using the term, is a single sheet of paper, often meant to be posted, and always meant to attract attention and to convey a message almost instantaneously. A brochure might also be just one sheet of paper, but it is folded, contains more information, and takes a bit longer to read. Brochures for community service agencies are sometimes produced professionally, but agency staff can also create brochures themselves. The following are not the only styles of brochure, but they are probably the easiest:

- 8 1/2" x 11" sheet folded in half
- 8 1/2" x 14" sheet folded in three, two ends meeting in the middle
- 8 1/2" x 11" sheet folded in even thirds, the first third folded to the right, and the last third folded to the middle, under the first

To see how each might look (imagine them folded), take a look at Figure 9.1.

Marketing Step Two: Writing Copy

You have chosen the third type of brochure style. Now you need to write your copy (compose the text of the brochure). Actually, you would never really think of the text separately; you must always consider, at the same time, how your ad will

Figure 9.1

STYLES OF BROCHURES

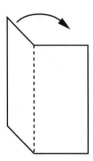 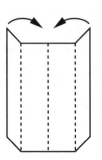 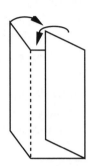

look. However, for the sake of simplicity let's talk just about text, or copy, for now.

You can't say everything. A good ad is an economical one—economical not just in terms of getting the most for your money, but also in getting the most for your words. Choose what is most important. What do you most want to tell people about your agency?

With a brochure, you must capture readers' attention, tell them a few significant things, and then let them go. In selecting what to put in the brochure, consider it from the reader's point of view: Does the reader really want or need to know this particular information? If yes, fine; otherwise, leave it out.

As you write, keep in mind the literacy level of your target audience. Don't be patronizing in your language, but remember that some of your readers may be functionally illiterate. Write clearly, simply, and concisely.

Let's assume you have decided on the information you want to convey in the brochure:

- the agency's name
- the agency's philosophy and mandate
- agency services
- agency hours
- agency location

Now you need to put that information into words—appealing words. Here's where you begin to think visually at the same time.

Marketing Step Three: Designing a Brochure

With the style of brochure you have chosen, you have six usable surfaces:

- page 1, actually, the last third of the back of the sheet
- pages 2 through 4, each a third of the front of the sheet
- pages 5 and 6, the other two-thirds of the back of the sheet

Confused? Get out a sheet of paper, turn it 90 degrees, fold the last third to the left, then the first third to the right. Number the pages as indicated above.

On page 1 you want the *headline*, something to catch the reader's attention. Pages 2 through 4 could describe the agency's philosophy, mandate, and services. Page 5 could give the hours and phone number, and page 6 could contain a map giving your location in relation to a major intersection.

Figure 9.2 on page 112 shows how the brochure might look.

Figure 9.2

EXAMPLE OF A BROCHURE

How to Reach Us

We are located at
54 Mimico Avenue in
Sydney. You can drop in
any day between
9:00 a.m. and 9:00 p.m.
You can call us anytime,
day or night,
at **622-5465**.

Queens Avenue

Mimico Avenue X 54 X

Centre Blvd. W.

River Road

FREEDOM

YOUTH OUTREACH SERVICE

Who We Are

FREEDOM is a
community–based
youth outreach
service that deals
with drug and
alcohol addiction in
Sydney youths aged
8 to 16.

What We Do

FREEDOM focuses on
drug and alcohol
education. We are
available to speak to
school, community,
parent, and religious
groups of any size.
Our presentations are
free of charge.

We also refer youths
or families with
addiction related
problems to
appropriate agencies.
Our service is
confidential.

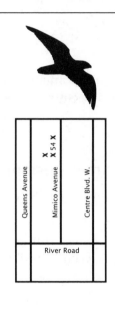

Designing a Flyer

As I mentioned, a flyer is designed for quick visual impact. Like the brochure, it consists of both headline and copy, but the copy is very brief.

When designing both the brochure and flyer, it is useful to do a thumbnail sketch of the finished project. A thumbnail sketch of the flyer might look like the one shown in Figure 9.3 on page 114.

You work with the thumbnail sketch, moving things around, changing things until you like the look of the ad. Then you perfect each separate item by following these steps:

- write the headline
- write the copy
- prepare the illustrations
- do a "paste-up" of the finished ad, taping each item in place
- duplicate the ad, using a photocopier or professional printer, or create the flyer using a word-processing or a presentation software program. These programs are easy to learn and manipulate.

Figure 9.4 on page 115 shows an example of a completed flyer, created using a common word-processing software program and its "Insert picture" function. However you complete it, here are a few hints for designing a flyer:

- For visual interest, use *contrast*—different type sizes, different lines (diagonals, horizontals, verticals). Compose your ad as you would a painting.
- Remember that English-speakers read from left to right, and from top to bottom; ensure that the order of the text or illustrations works with our natural reading tendencies.
- Be sure to leave plenty of white space (space where there is neither text nor illustration); the eye becomes fatigued if a page is too "busy" and if there is no white space for the eye to rest. But watch out for too much white space—it will look as though you have nothing to say!

Figure 9.3

THUMBNAIL SKETCH

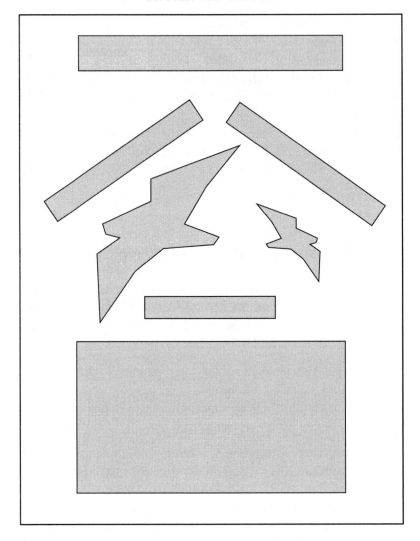

Figure 9.4

EXAMPLE OF A FLYER

ARE YOU BETWEEN 8 AND 16?

DO YOU HAVE QUESTIONS ABOUT ALCOHOL OR DRUGS?

DO YOU HAVE DRUG OR ALCOHOL-RELATED PROBLEMS?

FREEDOM CAN HELP

We're a youth outreach service

Teaching about addictions
Making referrals
Listening when you need a friend

We're confidential

Give us a call, anytime, day or night

622-5465

EXPLORATIONS

9.1 Analyze three to five actual brochures or flyers for their effectiveness. Discuss their strong and weak points. Offer suggestions for improvement, if needed.

9.2 Advertise your daycare centre to the surrounding area. Prepare a brochure, a flyer, and a distribution plan for your advertising materials.

9.3 Prepare a parent handbook for your daycare centre.

9.4 If you have been assigned the funding-proposal project, prepare an advertising campaign to create awareness of your new agency or service. Prepare a letter to relevant community services or to other professionals who should be aware of your agency, as well as a brochure and, if appropriate, a flyer.

9.5 Advertise the following workshops, and prepare a booklet to be distributed at each workshop:

   a. a parenting workshop, covering discipline
   b. an in-service workshop for elementary schoolteachers on mainstreaming students who are developmentally delayed
   c. a workshop on kids and drugs for an elementary school or high school PTA
   d. a workshop for an advocacy group for persons with disabilities on providing travel opportunities for clients
   e. a workshop for the community on home care of aging parents
   f. a workshop for low-income pregnant mothers on nutrition during pregnancy
   g. a workshop on the benefits of child life (recreational therapy) activities in a hospital setting for the hospital's Parent Committee
   h. a workshop for travel agents on wilderness treks
   i. a workshop for parents of children with learning disabilities on how summer camping can help their children's self-esteem
   j. a workshop for workers in your field on stress management and avoiding burnout

9.6 Prepare a booklet for your group home/community-living residence entitled "Rules for Residents."

9.7 Prepare a brochure and/or letter to solicit funds for your organization.

9.8 Prepare a flyer for a fundraising yard sale.

9.9 Prepare a flyer for a fundraising bake sale.

9.10 Create a flyer advertising a lunch-and-learn series for staff.

9.11 Create a flyer advertising the reward and recognition program from Exploration 2.13 and a brochure explaining the program's procedures.

9.12 Create a flyer and handouts for a workshop on any of the topics in the Explorations in Chapter 5.

CREDITS

1. Love, Language and Emergent Literacy
CREDIT: Zambo, D., & C.C. Hansen. 2007. Love, language, and emergent literacy: Pathways to emotional development of the very young. Young Children 62 (3): 32-37 Reprinted with permission from the National Association for the Education of Young Children. Copyright (c) 2007 NAEYC.

2. Why Focus on the Whole Child?
CREDIT: From the May 2007 issue of Educational Leadership 64(8), p. 7. "Why Focus on the Whole Child?" by Marge Scherer. Used with permission. The Association for Supervision and Curriculum Development is a worldwide community of educators advocating sound policies and sharing best practices to achieve the success of each learner. To learn more, visit ASCD at www.ascd.org

3. Using time-out effectively in the classroom
CREDIT: From "Using time-out effectively in the classroom" by Joseph B. Ryan, Sharon Sanders, Antonis Katsiyannis, Mitchell L. Yell, Teaching Exceptional Children, Mar/Apr 2007, Volume 39, Number 4, pp. 60-67 (c) 2007 by The Council for Exceptional Children. Reprinted with permission.

4. Who will endure as nursing's leading light?
CREDIT: © Copyright 2006 Bell Globemedia Publishing Inc. All Rights Reserved.

5. CREDIT: Linda Laskowski-Jone, "Should families be present during resuscitation?" Nursing 2007, Vol 37, No 5, pp 44-47.

6. CREDIT: Lindsey Simpson and David Hostler, "The Aging Heart", JEMS, December 2006, Vol 31, No 12, pp 48-57.

7. Communication vs. Counselling (text only; no photos in this article)
CREDIT: (C) Phyllis Nasta; Phyllis Nasta can be contacted at pfnasta@prodigy.net with "massage article" in the subject line.

8. Personal Support Workers Announcements CREDIT: Ontario Community Support Association http://www.ocsa.on.ca